DUMBARTON OAKS
MEDIEVAL LIBRARY

Jan M. Ziolkowski, General Editor

THE VULGATE BIBLE

VOLUME III

DOML 8

The Vulgate Bible

VOLUME III

THE POETICAL BOOKS

DOUAY-RHEIMS TRANSLATION

Edited by

SWIFT EDGAR

with ANGELA M. KINNEY

DUMBARTON OAKS
MEDIEVAL LIBRARY

HARVARD UNIVERSITY PRESS
CAMBRIDGE, MASSACHUSETTS
LONDON, ENGLAND
2011

Library of Congress Cataloging-in-Publication Data
Bible. English. Douai. 2011
   The Vulgate Bible : Douay-Rheims translation / edited by Swift Edgar
   with Angela M. Kinney.
      v. cm. — (Dumbarton Oaks medieval library ; DOML 8)
   English and Latin text on facing pages.
   Includes bibliographical references.
   Contents: v. 1. The Pentateuch. v. 2a. The Historical Books, part a. v. 2b.
   The Historical Books, part b. v. 3. The Poetical Books
   ISBN 978-0-674-05534-6 (v. 1 : alk. paper)
   ISBN 978-0-674-99667-0 (v. 2a : alk. paper)
   ISBN 978-0-674-06077-7 (v. 2b : alk. paper)
   ISBN 978-0-674-99668-7 (v. 3 : alk. paper)
   I. Edgar, Swift, 1985–   II. Dumbarton Oaks.   III. Title.
   BS180 2010
   222'.1047—dc22   2010015238

Contents

Introduction   *vii*
Abbreviations   *xxxiii*

JOB   1

PSALMS   149

PROVERBS   559

ECCLESIASTES   685

CANTICLE OF CANTICLES   731

WISDOM   755

ECCLESIASTICUS   839

Note on the Text   *1071*
Notes to the Text   *1075*
Alternate Spellings   *1177*
Bibliography   *1185*

Introduction

The Vulgate Bible is a collection of Latin texts compiled and translated in large part by Saint Jerome (ca. 345–420) in the late fourth and early fifth centuries CE. Roughly speaking, Jerome translated the Old Testament—except for the books of Wisdom, Ecclesiasticus, Baruch and 1 and 2 Maccabees— and he revised existing Latin versions of the Psalms and the Gospels. Jerome's Bible was used widely in the Western European Christian (and later, specifically Catholic) tradition from the early Middle Ages through the twentieth century.

The adjective "Vulgate" (from the Latin verb *vulgare*, meaning "to disseminate") lacks the connotation of coarseness often inherent in its relative "vulgar," but both words imply commonness. Indeed, the Vulgate Bible was so widespread that its significance can hardly be overstated. It made critical contributions to literature, visual art, music and education during the Middle Ages and the Renaissance, and it informed much of the Western theological, intellectual, artistic and even political history of that period. Students of almost any aspect of European civilization from the seventh century (when the Latin Bible existed more or less in the form we know today) through the sixteenth century (when translations of scripture into various European vernaculars

became widely available to the public and acceptable to religious authorities) must refer frequently to the Vulgate Bible and have a thorough knowledge of it.

In this edition, the Latin is presented opposite the first English version of the Bible sanctioned by the Roman Catholic Church. This English Bible is typically referred to as the Douay-Rheims Version, after the present-day names of its places of publication. The New Testament was published in 1582 by the English College at Rheims, and the Old Testament (to call it the Hebrew Bible would be inaccurate, since it includes nine books that have never belonged to the Hebrew canon) was published in 1609 and 1610, in two volumes, by the English College at Douay. The entire Douay-Rheims Bible was revised several times, notably by Bishop Dr. Richard Challoner (1691–1781) in 1749 and 1750.

In this introduction, I use the terms "Catholic" and "Protestant" in their current senses. Adherents to the Church of England in the sixteenth century at times referred to themselves as Catholics and to those who followed the religious authorities in Rome as Popish or Papists. The members of the Roman Church called their Anglican rivals various names, such as heretics, Protestants, Lutherans and Calvinists, but they would not have called them Catholics.

Douay and Rheims were major centers of learning for English-speaking Catholics, who faced hostility in Protestant England. The English College, a prominent Catholic institution, was exiled from Douay to Rheims in 1578, near the beginning of the Eighty Years' War between the Netherlands (to which Douay at the time belonged) and Philip II of Spain, who had founded the college.[1] The exile lasted until 1593. The college undertook these translations of the Bi-

ble primarily in response to the English versions produced under the Church of England that did not treat Jerome's text as the ultimate authority. Protestant English translators did use the Vulgate, but they also consulted the German rendering by Martin Luther (1482–1546), the Greek Septuagint and New Testament, testimonia in Hebrew and other sources. In contrast, the Douay-Rheims Version was directly translated from the Latin Bible as it was known to the professors at the English College in 1582.

While the English College was working on its translations at Douay and Rheims, Pope Sixtus V (r. 1585–1590) called for the preparation of an authoritative Latin text. This Latin Bible was published in 1590, just prior to his death, but it contained errors and was soon suppressed for fear that Protestants would use them to attack the Catholic Church.[2] Three corrected printings followed, in 1592, 1593 and 1598, during the papacy of Clement VIII (r. 1592–1605). These four editions, substantially the same, are referred to collectively as the Sixto-Clementine Version. While it strongly resembles the Latin Bible that evidently served as the basis for the Douay-Rheims translation, the two are not identical. The Dumbarton Oaks Medieval Library (DOML) here presents a reconstructed Latin text of the lost Bible used by the professors at Douay and Rheims, and Challoner's revision of the English translation faces the Latin. Challoner's text, discussed in detail below ("The English Text of This Edition"), sometimes reflects the Sixto-Clementine Bible more closely than did the English College translations of 1582, 1609 and 1610, but many of the revision's features are not at all related to the Sixto-Clementine Bible, and some lead the translation even further from the Latin.

Although the Douay Old Testament was not published until 1609–1610, most of the work on the translation seems to have been completed much earlier, before any Sixto-Clementine edition. Despite its publication date, therefore, this section of the English translation still provides a valuable witness to a Latin text that predated the Sixto-Clementine Version. Most scholars accept the conclusion by Charles Dodd that "the work may be entirely ascribed to Mr. [Gregory] Martin [who died a decade before publication of the Sixto-Clementine edition] . . . He translated the whole Bible; tho' it was not publish'd all at one time."[3] There is good reason to believe that Dodd was right: an entry in the "Douay Diaries,"[4] records of the activities at the young English College, attests that Martin began translating the Bible in October 1578 and that he translated two chapters a day, which were revised by two other professors. Since there are 1,353 chapters in the Bible—including the Books of Tobit, Judith, Wisdom, Ecclesiasticus, Baruch, 1 and 2 Maccabees and 3 and 4 Ezra, and counting the Prayer of Manasseh as one chapter—the task would have taken Martin and his team slightly more than 676 days, far less time than the thirty years that elapsed between the project's commencement and the complete publication of the Bible. Indeed, this calculation is confirmed in the address "To the right vvelbeloved English reader" in the first volume of the Old Testament (1609), which states that the Bible was translated "about thirtie yeares since" (fifth page of the section). The translation thus almost certainly preceded the Sixto-Clementine text, which immediately became the standard edition upon its printing in 1592. The lag between translation and publication is explained on the first page of the

same section: "As for the impediments, which hitherto haue hindered this worke, they al proceded (as manie do know) of one general cause, our poore estate in banishment"—that is, the exile of the English College to Rheims.

The Douay-Rheims translation used here mostly follows the version printed in 1899, a slight revision of Challoner's editions, incorporating elements from the 1749, 1750 and 1752 printings. Challoner's principal contribution was to make the original Douay-Rheims easier to read by updating obscure phraseology and obsolete words. This volume modifies the 1899 version to bring the punctuation and the transliteration of proper nouns and adjectives into line with modern practice (see Alternate Spellings in the endmatter for this edition's policies regarding transliterations) and to restore some readings from Challoner's 1750 and 1752 editions that had been changed (mostly due to printers' errors) in the 1899 version. In addition, the whole text has been prepared according to the guidelines of the fifteenth edition of the *Chicago Manual of Style*. This policy has resulted in significant alterations to Challoner's edition, which superabounds in colons and commas, lacks quotation marks and begins each verse on a new line, sometimes making the text difficult to understand. In contrast to most English Bibles, this volume renders all of the text as prose, even the parts that were originally in verse, since neither the Latin nor the English is poetic. The Latin text has been punctuated according to the English translation to allow easy movement between the two languages. In the rare instances when they diverge, the text in each language has been punctuated according to its most natural meaning (see, for example, Gen 31:1–4).

Readers of the Dumbarton Oaks Medieval Library who wish to compare either the English or the Latin version presented here with another Bible should bear in mind that the versification in the Vulgate and the numbering of psalms differ from those in Bibles translated from languages other than Latin. Furthermore, the books in this volume have been selected and ordered according to Challoner's revisions, which follow the Sixto-Clementine Bible. This policy has resulted in the inclusion of some chapters and books commonly considered "apocryphal" or "deuterocanonical" (Tobit, Judith, Wisdom, Ecclesiasticus, Baruch, 1 and 2 Maccabees, Daniel 3:24–90, Daniel 13 and 14) and the omission of others that were relegated to appendices even in early printed versions of the Bible (3 and 4 Ezra and the Prayer of Mannaseh). The names of some books differ from the ones that may be familiar to many readers: for instance, 1 and 2 Kings in this volume are commonly called 1 and 2 Samuel; 3 and 4 Kings are usually 1 and 2 Kings; 1 and 2 Paralipomenon equate to 1 and 2 Chronicles; 1 Ezra is usually simply Ezra, while 2 Ezra is typically Nehemiah; the Canticle of Canticles is also known as the Song of Songs; Ecclesiasticus is Sirach and in some Latin Bibles is known as Iesu Filii Sirach; and, last, the Apocalypse of St. John the Apostle may be known to most readers as the Book of Revelation.

THE LATIN TEXT OF THIS EDITION

The Latin in this edition presents as closely as possible the text from which the Douay-Rheims translators worked. It would have been a version of the Bible known to many Europeans from the eighth through the sixteenth century. Be-

fore Jerome, translations of parts of the Bible into Latin existed; we call these disparate texts the Old Latin Bible. After Jerome finished his work, versions of his Vulgate proliferated. According to one count, a third of the biblical manuscripts we have today dating to about one hundred years after Jerome's death are from the Vulgate, and a century later "manuscripts of the Vulgate start to outnumber those of the Old Latin by about two to one. In the seventh century, the ratio has risen to about six to one."[5] The early ninth century brought the stabilization of a recension that was overseen by Alcuin, the schoolmaster from York who played a major role in the cultural revival promoted by Charlemagne. The so-called Alcuin Bibles, of which some thirty survive, became the standard text outside Italy during the Carolingian period. They were the products of monastic copy centers known as scriptoria. In the thirteenth century, the Alcuin Bibles gave way to the so-called Paris Bibles, which were written by professional scribes. The text of the Paris Bibles, a direct descendent of the Alcuin Bibles, was in turn closely related to the Sixto-Clementine Bibles of the late sixteenth century. In large part, the DOML text corresponds to Robert Weber's edition (2007). Most adjustments to bring the Latin closer to the English coincide with an edition of the Sixto-Clementine Bible (1959) that preserves the majority of the readings from the second Clementine edition (1593) and occasionally replaces that text with readings from the other two Clementine editions, which were very similar to each other. For consistency's sake, the spellings and inflections of adjustments based on the Sixto-Clementine Bible have been brought into line with Weber's text.

When neither the Weber nor the Sixto-Clementine text

provides the reading that the Douay-Rheims translators appear to have seen, the critical apparatuses in Weber and in Quentin's edition (1926– [1995]) have been consulted. Often the readings attested in early printed editions of the Bible, such as the famous "42-line Bible" printed by Johannes Gutenberg in 1454, come closest to the translation. In rare instances it has been necessary to print reconstructions of the text theoretically used by the translators, since neither the Sixto-Clementine, Weber and Quentin editions nor the citations in their apparatus provide a suitable reading. These reconstructions, often closer to the Greek Septuagint than to any Vulgate edition, follow the Old Latin Bible.

In trying to identify the Latin source or sources of the Douay-Rheims translation, some scholars have pointed to the Louvain Bible,[6] an early printed edition that strongly resembles the Sixto-Clementine Version. However, the readings in the Douay-Rheims Version do not support the conclusion that Martin based his translation on either the Louvain Bible of 1547 or the correction of that edition published at Rome in 1574. Furthermore, the preface of the Douay-Rheims Version addressed "To the right vvelbeloved English reader" states (and Greenslade accepts) that the editors of the Old Testament "conformed it to the most perfect Latin Edition"—presumably, given the publication date, the Sixto-Clementine Version.[7] To take just one illustration of the danger of assuming that the translators used a single identifiable source, consider Ex 16:29, which in the Douay translation reads in part, "and let none goe forth": of the many sources considered by Quentin (including the Louvain Bible), only two—both early printed editions and neither of them the Sixto-Clementine or the Louvain edition—begin

the relevant Latin clause with a conjunction. Moreover, while the translators claimed their work was "diligently conferred with the Hebrew, Greeke, and other Editions in diuers languages,"[8] the relative paucity of readings different from well-established Latin sources and the inconsistency in the nature of the divergences suggest that they were working with a now lost Latin text of idiosyncratic nature rather than a still extant one that they chose to ignore from time to time. Since several people collaborated on that translation, the translators may also have followed different editions of the Bible and therefore produced a translation for which there is no single surviving Latin source.

Unlike the Latin as edited by Weber, the Sixto-Clementine edition (to whose family the Douay-Rheims translation belongs) often regularizes the language found in earlier manuscripts. In general, the Sixto-Clementine rarely accepts the *lectio difficilior,* while most editors since the eighteenth century, including Weber, tend to choose the "more difficult reading" from among multiple possibilities. For example, at Gen 32:5, the Weber edition reads, "habeo boves et asinos oves et servos atque ancillas," while the Sixto-Clementine editors preferred to avoid the variations of asyndeton after *asinos* and of *atque,* so their text reads, "Habeo boves et asinos et oves et servos et ancillas." In this instance, the Douay-Rheims translators evidently saw a conjunction between *asinos* and *oves* and also between *servos* and *ancillas.* In this edition, an *et* has been inserted in the former case, but the *atque* has remained in the latter, because we cannot know which of the many options for the English "and" the translators encountered in their Latin.

At times, the translation reflects a base text closer to We-

ber's than to the Sixto-Clementine edition. For example, at Gen 1:14, Weber reads "fiant luminaria in firmamento caeli ut dividant diem ac noctem," while for *ut,* the Sixto-Clementine edition reads *et.* However, the Douay-Rheims translation (as revised by Challoner, but here retaining the grammatical construction of the original) reads, "Let there be lights made in the firmament of heaven to divide the day and the night," clearly translating *ut.* The Sixto-Clementine choice was probably made by analogy to verses like Gen 1:6, which reads in both editions "Fiat firmamentum in medio aquarum, et dividat."

THE ENGLISH TEXT OF THIS EDITION

The "Douay-Rheims Version" is an imperfect name for the translation of the Vulgate Bible used in this volume. Indeed, one anonymous scholar in 1836 went so far as to write that calling a translation similar to the one printed here "the Douay or Rhemish version is an abuse of terms."[9] The English here follows a text that was published in 1899. Although this text has been understood routinely as being the Douay-Rheims Version without any qualification, it in fact offers an English translation that derives not directly from the work of the English College of Douay and Rheims, but rather from a nineteenth-century form of a revision by Challoner. Challoner published at least five revisions of the New Testament and two of the Old (the New Testaments appeared in 1749, 1750, 1752, 1764 and 1772, the Old Testaments in 1750 and 1763–1764); after his death, others produced many more. Since the editions of 1582, 1609 and 1610, many subsequent revisions have purported to be simple reprints.

Indeed, the frontispiece to the 1899 edition has a message of approbation by James Cardinal Gibbons, then archbishop of Baltimore, who writes that the text "is an accurate reprint of the Rheims and Douay edition with Dr. Challoner's notes." But if we are to understand the "Rheims and Douay edition" to mean the translations originally printed in those cities in the late sixteenth and early seventeenth centuries, the text we have is by no means an accurate reprint of that.

Because the versions issued between 1610 and 1899 can be difficult to come by, and because the only work approaching a systematic collation of various "Douay-Rheims" Bibles is a bitterly anti-Catholic work from 1855,[10] many scholars regard the Douay-Rheims translation as a text that has barely changed (if at all) since its first printing. Some are aware of Challoner's extensive revisions in the mid-eighteenth century, which updated the language of the Douay-Rheims Version and toned down the polemical annotations, but few know the extent of his alterations, or that they make it more distant from the Latin Vulgate, or that they took place over several editions or that the editions published after his death often contain the work of other scholars.

Many factors complicate analysis of the modifications that the Douay-Rheims Version has undergone over the past four centuries. The most significant is the doctrinal conservatism of the Catholic Church. Owing to both the primacy of Jerome's Vulgate (another inadequate label, since Jerome hardly produced the Latin text by himself), recognized at the Council of Trent (1545–1563), and the desire of the Church to exert some control over access to scripture, the translation of the Bible into vernacular tongues was dis-

couraged. Yet after Protestant churches made the text of the Bible available to speakers of English and German, it became easier for reformist thinkers to disseminate their teachings. Some English-speaking Catholics then sought to produce their own translation, but since the point of this work was to regulate the message read by the flock, the translation required authorization to insure that it was appropriate. A letter of 1580 from William Allen, the president of the English College at Douay, to a colleague, Professor Jean de Vendeville, expresses the need for papal sanctioning of the translation: "We on our part will undertake, if His Holiness shall think proper, to produce a faithful, pure, and genuine version of the Bible in accordance with the version approved by the Church."[11] The printed edition was approved not by the pope but by three professors at Allen's own college (Douay-Rheims 1609, *Approbatio*).

Conservatism demanded the Church's approbation and made revision difficult. How could a reviser supplant something that had already been declared acceptable to the Church? Revisions required approval of their own, yet they could not directly contradict previously approved editions. For this reason, the only reference to a difference between Challoner's 1750 edition and the printings of 1582, 1609 and 1610 comes on the title page, which describes the work as "Newly revised and corrected, according to the Clementine Edition of the Scriptures." As the phrasing shows, Challoner was careful to note that his version derived from the Latin Bible first authorized by Pope Clement VIII in 1592, ten years after the Rheims New Testament, but he obscured the extent of his revisions. Despite the popularity of Challoner's revision and of the Bibles still in print that descend from it,

the English translations and revisions of scripture were not created under a directive from the Vatican. There is no single, indisputably "official" translation of the Latin Bible into English. All the translations lay claim to official status without criticizing other Catholic versions, and none of them has clear primacy. This confusing (and confused) climate has misled modern readers into believing precisely what the editors and translators of English Catholic Bibles from the sixteenth through the nineteenth century wanted them to think: a single standard English translation of the Bible existed, and the reader in question was holding a copy of it. One well-respected medievalist cautioned against using the King James Version for medieval studies (because it lacks a close relationship to the Vulgate text), implying that the Douay-Rheims Version is preferable. While correct about the King James Version, he shows himself to be unaware of the Douay-Rheims's own modern tradition, writing, "The English translation of [the Vulgate] is the one known as the 'Douai-Rheims' translation . . . also available in many modern editions," and later quoting the translation of Ct 2:4 in the Douay-Rheims as "he set in order charity in me."[12] This quotation comes from Challoner's revision of the translation from 1750; the 1610 translation reads, "he hath ordered in me charitie."

The particular case of Ct 2:4 does not perfectly illustrate the danger of using Challoner's revision of the Douay-Rheims translation, because his rendering still matches the Vulgate text ("ordinavit in me caritatem"). But in many places (italicized in this edition) Challoner strayed from the Latin, usually to revise some particularly awkward phrasing

in the older Douay-Rheims edition. For example, at Gen 6:13, he changed "the earth is replenished with iniquitie from the face of them" to "the earth is filled with iniquity through them." Four points are important about this revision. The first is that Challoner updated the spelling of "iniquitie." Second, here, as elsewhere, he translated very logically an ordinary Latin word *(repleta)* with an equally common English one ("filled"), rather than with a cognate ("replenished"). Thus, he followed a policy that contrasts with the Latinate qualities that pervade the earlier translation. Third, "through" is not found in any Latin edition; while the meaning of "from the face of them" is obscure in English, it is a literal rendition of all the transmitted Vulgate texts of this verse. The fourth point is the trickiest one to address: the preposition "through" instead of "from the face of" is in fact found in the King James Version, which was in Challoner's day the more or less official Anglican (and of course Protestant) Bible.

Gen 6:13 illustrates how Challoner revised the Douay-Rheims Bible on literary grounds. One peculiarity of Bible studies is that many areas of interest are plagued with partisanship, and it can be difficult to make any argument without seeming to side with one religious (or secular) establishment against another. In trying to articulate the relationship between the King James and Douay-Rheims Versions, many otherwise useful sources emphasize the effects of one on the other according to the publisher's disposition: that is to say, Catholic sources underscore the similarities between the 1582 New Testament and the 1611 King James text, while Protestant reference works point to Challoner's alleged in-

debtedness to the King James Version. A notable exception is the anonymous article quoted above, which in its passionate call for a responsible, authorized translation of the Sixto-Clementine Vulgate rightly commented on a difference between the 1582 New Testament and Challoner's revision: "This correction is taken verbatim from the Protestant version."[13] Without delving into the differences in the theological programs of the editors of the Douay-Rheims and King James Versions or calling one preferable to the other, one could argue convincingly (as many have done) that the King James Bible has far greater—or at the very least, more enduring—literary merit than the original Douay-Rheims Version.

To understand the relative qualities of these English Bibles, compare, for example, the translations of Dt 30:19. The Douay-Rheims reads: "I cal for witnesses this day heauen and earth, that I haue proposed to you life and death, blessing and cursing. Choose therefore life, that both thou mayest liue, and thy seede." The King James Version has "I call heauen and earth to record this day against you, that I haue set before you life and death, blessing and cursing: therefore choose life, that both thou and thy seed may liue." Significantly, the King James Version is more natural and memorable; we should also note that the most awkward phrasing in the Douay-Rheims translation ("proposed to") has, in Challoner, been replaced by "set before," the King James reading.

The literary superiority of the King James Version is worth bearing in mind, because Challoner (whose schoolboy nickname, we are told, was Book)[14] revised the Douay-

Rheims text primarily on the basis of literary sensibilities. His version significantly departs from the Douay-Rheims when that text is most stilted, and not infrequently in such instances, Challoner's revision closely matches the sense or wording (or both) of the King James Bible.

A word of caution should be issued to those who would accept the implication of the subtitle of Challoner's Bible: "Newly revised and corrected, according to the Clementine Edition of the Scriptures." This description suggests that Challoner updated the Douay-Rheims translation in light of the standard text of the Bible that had not been available to the translators at the English College. Through oversight, however, his revision skipped a few phrases that the Douay-Rheims translators had missed as well (mostly when similar Latin words appeared on different parts of the page, causing leaps of the eye).[15] These omissions suggest strongly that Challoner's primary task was to make the English of the Douay-Rheims version more readable; it was not a revision on textual grounds. Otherwise, a careful collation of the Douay-Rheims Version with the Sixto-Clementine Bible would have been essential. More often than not, Challoner appears simply to have read the Douay-Rheims and fixed the poor or awkward style, occasionally turning to the King James, Latin, Greek or possibly Hebrew texts for help. He does not seem to have compared the Douay-Rheims systematically with the Latin (or any other version).

If we are not prepared to credit the magnum opus of the Anglican Church as a major source for Challoner, we can say that many of his revisions came from Hebrew and Greek sources (the same texts that the King James editors read,

possibly accounting for the similarities). Why Challoner often turned to sources other than the Latin Vulgate, which had existed in stable and authorized form since 1592, is unclear, especially in view of his title-page statement that he had updated the Douay-Rheims according to the Sixto-Clementine Bible. The period in which Challoner published his first edition of the New Testament (1749) was one of lively productivity for biblical scholars. The monumental edition of the pre-Vulgate Latin Bible credited to Pierre Sabatier, a Benedictine monk, was in production (Rheims 1739, 1749; Paris 1751). This text was meant to reconstruct the Bible as it was known to the Church fathers writing in Latin before the general acceptance of Jerome's text, and it received the approbation of two vicars general and Sabatier's own abbot. It relies frequently on Greek and Hebrew sources, indicating that the study of those texts was not as distasteful to the Church elite in the eighteenth century as it had been in 1609, when the Douay-Rheims translators prefaced their edition with the following words:

> But here an other question may be proposed: VVhy we translate the Latin text, rather than the Hebrew, or Greke, which Protestantes preferre, as the fountaine tongues, wherin holie Scriptures were first written? To this we answer, that if in dede those first pure Editions were now extant, or if such as be extant, were more pure than the Latin, we would also preferre such fountaines before the riuers, in whatsoeuer they should be found to disagree. But the ancient best lerned Fathers, & Doctors of the Church, do much complaine, and

testifie to vs, that both the Hebrew and Greke Editions are fouly corrupted by Iewes, and Heretikes, since the Latin was truly translated out of them, whiles they were more pure.[16]

Indeed, by 1750 the Counter-Reformational motives of the Douay-Rheims Version of 1582, 1609 and 1610 had become largely irrelevant, and the polemical annotations of the first translation were either omitted or stripped of their vehemence. Even the notes in the Old Testament of 1609–1610 contain less vitriol than those in the 1582 New Testament. Strict adherence to the Vulgate Bible mattered less to Challoner than to the original translators, although he still evidently favored literalism in his renderings. Consequently, he may have preferred to replace poorly worded translations with a new literal translation of a different source, rather than to print loose constructions of the Latin text. Nonetheless, the translation on the whole adheres faithfully to the Vulgate, the official Bible of the Catholic Church; after all, Challoner wrote a pamphlet entitled "The Touchstone of the New Religion: or, Sixty Assertions of Protestants, try'd by their own Rule of Scripture alone, and condemned by clear and express Texts of their own Bible" (London 1735). Interestingly, this tract reveals Challoner's familiarity with, or at least access to, the King James Version of the Bible. As one scholar put it, "He sought to establish the Roman Church's credentials out of the mouths of her enemies."[17]

It may be fitting that the DOML Bible is an artificial one. After all, in whatever language or languages the texts collectively called the Bible are read, they are heterogeneous, cobbled together over centuries, having been composed (or re-

vealed) and varied by oral tradition throughout the preceding millennia. With only minor revisions, we use Challoner's edition of the Douay-Rheims Bible because his text preserves the character of the English translation that brings us closest to the end of the medieval period while still being fairly elegant and readable. This edition differs from the 1899 printing in restoring readings from the 1750 and 1752 editions which had been spuriously altered in the 1899 version and in updating the biblical names and the punctuation of the earlier edition. Challoner's notes have been excised, though his chapter summaries remain.

With its rich and somewhat thorny history, Challoner's English is important to scholars of many disciplines, and its proximity to the literal translation of the most important book of the medieval period—namely, the Latin Bible—makes it invaluable to English-speakers studying the Middle Ages.

A Note on the Translation

Every discussion of the Douay-Rheims translation—whether praising or condemning it, whether acknowledging or ignoring Challoner's contribution to the text—affirms its proximity to the Latin. The translation in this volume has, however, a few characteristics that are either difficult for contemporary English-speakers to understand or that make the English less literal than it could be.

Challoner's word choice may sometimes puzzle readers. In the service of literalism, the Douay-Rheims translators and Challoner usually rendered *postquam* by the now obsolete phrase "after that," regardless of whether the Latin

word was a conjunction or an adverb. For example, at Gen 24:22, the translation reads, "And after that the camels had drunk, the man took out golden earrings weighing two sicles and as many bracelets of ten sicles weight," whereas a natural, more modern rendering would eliminate the word "that." Possibly by analogy to the case of *postquam,* or possibly because in the seventeenth century there was little distinction between the meanings of "after" and "after that," the translators occasionally rendered other words as "after that" where the phrase makes little sense in modern usage; see, for example, the temporal *cum* at Gen 8:6. On the whole, though, Challoner avoided trying to fit the square peg of English translation into the round hole of the Latin text. He shied away from the Douay-Rheims tendency to translate Latin words with awkward cognates, such as "invocate" for forms of *invoco* (for example, Gen 4:26); he frequently rendered relative pronouns with a conjunction followed by a demonstrative (Gen 3:1 and elsewhere); and he and his antecedents were free with temporal constructions, rendering, to take one example, *de nocte* as "very early" at Ex 34:4. Furthermore, Challoner translated many conjunctions as "now" that literally mean "and," "but," "moreover" or "therefore" (for example, Gen 16:1 and 3 Rg 1:1); the King James translators were also liberal in their use of "now."

Challoner's breaches of the rule of strict (some have said excessive) literalism also occur in areas other than word choice. The most frequent deviations appear in the translation of participles, the passive voice and especially passive participles. The translation of Nm 20:6 illustrates this program: the verse in Latin begins, "Ingressusque Moses et Aaron dimissa multitudine Tabernaculum Foederis corruerunt"; the 1609 translation reads, "And Moyses and Aaron,

the multitude being dismissed, entering into the tabernacle of couenant, fel"; whereas Challoner, preferring not to employ the passive voice or more than one construction with a participle, rendered the verse (with my punctuation), "And Moses and Aaron leaving the multitude went into the Tabernacle of the Covenant and fell." The many ablatives absolute and other participial constructions that have been modified by Challoner to fit more neatly into his preferred English style have not been signaled by italics in this volume because they do not illuminate anything about the Latin text and because the renderings are not so loose as to make their relationship to the Latin difficult to perceive.

Another systematic abandonment of literal translations appears in Challoner's rendering of oath formulas and other invocations of God, especially those that begin in Latin *vivo* or *vivit Dominus* or that employ constructions similar to "haec faciat mihi Deus et haec addat." Usually the first two formulas are rendered by adding "as" in English before the subject of the verb, and if the next clause begins with a conjunction, it is excised in translation. See, for example, 1 Rg 14:39, which begins in Latin, "Vivit Dominus, salvator Israhel, quia si" and was translated in the 1609 edition as "Our Lord the sauiour of Israel liueth, that if," which was modified by Challoner to read, "As the Lord liveth who is the saviour of Israel, if." The constructions that substantially resemble "haec faciat mihi Deus et haec addat" as at 1 Rg 14:44 were translated predictably in 1609 as "These thinges doe God to me, and these thinges adde he." Challoner rendered the prayer as "May God do so and so to me and add still more." Both of these divergences from the Latin are anticipated in the English of the King James Version, and because such renderings are pervasive, they have

been noted only here and are not mentioned in the Notes to the Text. Challoner's antecedents at Douay and Rheims were also at times a bit lax in their translation. The degrees of adjectives and adverbs are not differentiated: *durius* (Gen 31:29) can be rendered as "roughly," *pessima* (Gen 37:20) as "naughtie." *Haec* (Gen 9:8), especially before verbs of saying, is often translated as "thus." Similar lapses in literalism occur with the verbs *volo* and *debeo,* the future tense, the future perfect tense and the subjunctive mood, which are all often rendered as simple futures in English; yet in most cases when the Douay-Rheims translators stuck to a literal translation and Challoner changed it, his variation and its source have been noted. When the Douay-Rheims translators use a turn of phrase that does not square with the Latin, the divergence has been commented upon only if the translation seems to be a useful key to the Latin they worked from; if they seem simply to have rendered the text loosely, no note appears. The most striking translation choices that the professors from Douay and Rheims made were to translate *utinam* (e.g., Ex 16:3) as "would to God," *absit* (e.g., Gen 44:17) as "God forbid," *salve* (e.g., 2 Rg 18:28) as "God save thee" and *vivat Rex* (e.g., 1 Rg 10:24) as "God save the King," even though there is no reference to the Divine. One other consistent policy of the Douay-Rheims translation was to translate *Dominus* as "our Lord." This practice stemmed from theological rather than philological reasons, and Challoner (like the King James translators) rendered this word as "the Lord." In these cases, there can be no other Latin reading, and since the English is not helpful in illuminating a hitherto unknown Latin text, no note has been made.

Last, the translation and Challoner's revision tried to

avoid enjambment as much as possible. For example, Nm 7:18–19 reads in Latin, "Secundo die, obtulit Nathanahel, filius Suar, dux de tribu Isachar:/acetabulum argenteum," whereas at verses 24–25 of the same chapter we find "Tertio die, princeps filiorum Zabulon, Heliab, filius Helon,/obtulit acetabulum argenteum." Syntactically, the verses are identical (the colon is placed in the Latin only on the basis of the translation), but because in the first example *obtulit* appears in a separate verse from its direct object, the translation reads, "The second day, Nethanel, the son of Zuar, prince of the tribe of Issachar, made his offering:/a silver dish," while at verses 24–25 we have "The third day, the prince of the sons of Zebulun, Eliab, the son of Helon,/offered a silver dish."

Apart from these few deviations and the occasional italicized words and phrases, the Challoner revision is an exceptionally literal and readable translation of the Vulgate Bible, and it has proved helpful over the past quarter millennium to those who find the meaning of the Latin obscure.

A Note on the Psalms

The devotional poems of the Old Testament survive in a staggering number of manuscripts and other witnesses. Before Jerome, Old Latin translations proliferated, and Jerome himself produced three versions of the Psalms, called the Roman, Gallican and Hebrew Psalters. The first two are revisions of Old Latin texts brought into line with the Greek Septuagint. In composing the Gallican Psalter, Jerome referred to Origen's Hexapla ("sixfold"), a monumental edition of the Old Testament from before 254 CE that contains the text in Hebrew, Hebrew transliterated into Greek and

four Greek translations. The Hebrew Psalter is so called because Jerome translated it out of that language into Latin, and until the time of Charlemagne it typically appeared in complete Bibles. Alcuin replaced it in his recension with the Gallican Psalter, the version popular in what is now France (hence its name). Although long after the dissemination of the Alcuinian Bible the Roman Psalter persisted in Britain and in certain liturgical rites and the Hebrew retained popularity in Spain, the Gallic Psalter became the Vulgate one. It is printed in the Sixto-Clementine Bibles and for the most part appears to have provided the basis for the Douay-Rheims translation, although some readings there reflect the Roman, Hebrew or Old Latin Psalters.

Most Latin (and Hebrew) manuscripts contain 150 psalms. The numbering of the psalms in the Gallican Psalter differs from sources translated from Hebrew, such as the King James Version and the New Revised Standard Version. The table below displays the differences:

VULGATE	HEBREW
1–8	1–8
9:22	10:1
10–112	11–113
113:9	115:1
114	116
115:1 (often written as 115:10, without 115:1–9)	116:10
116–45	117–46
147:1–9 (often written as 12–20, without 1–11)	147:12–20
148–50	148–50

I am grateful to the many people who have helped me with this project, including readers George Carlisle, Bob Edgar, Sally Edgar, Jim Halporn, Scott Johnson and Christopher

Osborne; Alexandra Helprin, for her support and encouragement; Terra Dunham, Ian Stevenson and Sharmila Sen at Harvard University Press; Jesse Rainbow, for answering all my questions about Hebrew with clarity, depth, and precision; Christopher Husch, Philip Kim, and Julian Yolles for their excellent proofreading; Maria Ascher, for her thoughtful editing of the Introduction; Andy Kelly, whose generosity was particularly helpful in the introductory paragraphs on Richard Challoner; Michael Herren and Danuta Shanzer for their careful reading and helpful suggestions; Angela Kinney for her invaluable editorial assisstance; and especially Jan Ziolkowski, who conceived of the series, trusted me to see this project through, and supervised my work.

NOTES

1 See Carleton, *The Part of Rheims in the Making of the English Bible*, p. 13.

2 Quentin, *Mémoire sur l'établissement du texte de la Vulgate*, pp. 190–92.

3 Dodd, *The Church History of England*, vol. 2, p. 121, quoted in Pope and Bullough, *English Versions of the Bible*, p. 252.

4 Knox, *The First and Second Diaries of the English College*, p. 145, cited in Carleton, *The Part of Rheims in the Making of the English Bible*, p. 16.

5 de Hamel, *The Book: A History of the Bible*, p. 28.

6 Pope and Bullough, *English Versions of the Bible*, p. 295; Greenslade, *The Cambridge History of the Bible*, p. 163.

7 Greenslade, *The Cambridge History of the Bible*, p. 163.

8 Frontispiece, Douay-Rheims Bible, 1609.

9 A Catholic, "A new Version of the Four Gospels," p. 476, quoted in Cartmell, "English Spiritual Writers," p. 583. Cartmell erroneously cites the passage as appearing on page 276 but attributes it correctly to Nicholas Wiseman, though the review was published anonymously.

10 Cotton, *Rhemes and Doway*.

11 Translated from the Latin by Knox; see Carleton, *The Part of Rheims in the Making of the English Bible*, p. 15.

12 Kaske, *Medieval Christian Literary Imagery,* p. 6.

13 A Catholic, "A new Version of the Four Gospels," p. 476.

14 Duffy, *Challoner and His Church,* p. 6.

15 See Pope and Bullough, *English Versions of the Bible,* pp. 359–71.

16 "To the right vvelbeloved English reader," Douay-Rheims Bible, 1609.

17 Gilley, "Challoner as Controvertionalist," p. 93.

Abbreviations

Gen	Genesis
Ex	Exodus
Lv	Leviticus
Dt	Deuteronomy
Nm	Numbers
Jos	Joshua
Jdg	Judges
Rt	Ruth
1 Kings	1 Kings
2 Kings	2 Kings
3 Kings	3 Kings
4 Kings	4 Kings
1 Par	1 Paralipomenon
2 Par	2 Paralipomenon
1 Ezr	1 Ezra
2 Ezr	2 Ezra
Tb	Tobit
Jdt	Judith
Est	Esther
Job	Job
Ps	Psalms
Prov	Proverbs

Ecl	Ecclesiastes
Ct	Canticle of Canticles
Wis	Wisdom
Sir	Ecclesiasticus
Is	Isaiah
Jer	Jeremiah
Lam	Lamentations
Bar	Baruch
Ez	Ezekiel
Dn	Daniel
Hos	Hosea
Joel	Joel
Am	Amos
Ob	Obadiah
Jon	Jonah
Mi	Micah
Na	Nahum
Hab	Habakkuk
Zeph	Zephaniah
Hag	Haggai
Zech	Zechariah
Mal	Malachi
1 Mcc	1 Maccabees
2 Mcc	2 Maccabees
Mt	Matthew
Mk	Mark
Lk	Luke
John	John
Act	Acts of the Apostles

Rom	Romans
1 Cor	1 Corinthians
2 Cor	2 Corinthians
Gal	Galatians
Eph	Ephesians
Phlp	Philippians
Col	Colossians
1 Th	1 Thessalonians
2 Th	2 Thessalonians
1 Tim	1 Timothy
2 Tim	2 Timothy
Tit	Titus
Phlm	Philemon
Hbr	Hebrews
Ja	James
1 Pt	1 Peter
2 Pt	2 Peter
1 John	1 John
2 John	2 John
3 John	3 John
Jud	Jude
Apc	Apocalypse of St. John the Apostle

LATIN NAMES FOR BOOKS IN THE BIBLE

Gen	Genesis
Ex	Exodi
Lv	Levitici
Nm	Numerorum
Dt	Deuteronomii

Ios	Iosue
Idc	Iudicum
Rt	Ruth
1 Rg	1 Regum
2 Rg	2 Regum
3 Rg	3 Regum
4 Rg	4 Regum
1 Par	1 Paralipomenon
2 Par	2 Paralipomenon
1 Esr	1 Ezrae
2 Esr	2 Ezrae
Tb	Tobiae
Idt	Iudith
Est	Hester
Iob	Iob
Ps	Psalmi
Prv	Proverbiorum
Ecl	Ecclesiastes
Ct	Canticum Canticorum
Sap	Sapientiae
Sir	Sirach (Ecclesiasticus *or* Iesu Filii Sirach)
Is	Isaias
Ier	Hieremias
Lam	Lamentationes
Bar	Baruch
Ez	Hiezechiel
Dn	Danihel
Os	Osee
Ioel	Iohel

Am	Amos
Abd	Abdias
Ion	Iona
Mi	Micha
Na	Naum
Hab	Abacuc
So	Sofonias
Agg	Aggeus
Za	Zaccharias
Mal	Malachi
1 Mcc	1 Macchabeorum
2 Mcc	2 Macchabeorum
Mt	Secundum Mattheum
Mc	Secundum Marcum
Lc	Secundum Lucam
Io	Secundum Iohannem
Act	Actus Apostolorum
Rm	Ad Romanos
1 Cor	Ad Corinthios 1
2 Cor	Ad Corinthios 2
Gal	Ad Galatas
Eph	Ad Ephesios
Phil	Ad Philippenses
Col	Ad Colossenes
1 Th	Ad Thessalonicenses 1
2 Th	Ad Thessalonicenses 2
1 Tim	Ad Timotheum
Tit	Ad Titum
Phlm	Ad Philemonem

Hbr	Ad Hebraeos
Iac	Epistula Iacobi
1 Pt	Epistula Petri 1
2 Pt	Epistula Petri 2
1 Io	Epistula Iohannis 1
2 Io	Epistula Iohannis 2
3 Io	Epistula Iohannis 3
Iud	Epistula Iudae
Apc	Apocalypsis Iohannis

JOB

Caput 1

Vir erat in terra Hus nomine Iob, et erat vir ille simplex et rectus ac timens Deum et recedens a malo. 2 Natique sunt ei septem filii et tres filiae, 3 et fuit possessio eius septem milia ovium et tria milia camelorum, quingenta quoque iuga boum et quingentae asinae ac familia multa nimis, eratque vir ille magnus inter omnes Orientales.

4 Et ibant filii eius et faciebant convivium per domos, unusquisque in die suo. Et mittentes vocabant tres sorores suas ut comederent et biberent cum eis. 5 Cumque in orbem transissent dies convivii mittebat ad eos Iob et sanctificabat illos consurgensque diluculo offerebat holocausta per singulos, dicebat enim, "Ne forte peccaverint filii mei et benedixerint Deo in cordibus suis." Sic faciebat Iob cunctis diebus.

6 Quadam autem die cum venissent filii Dei ut adsisterent coram Domino, adfuit inter eos etiam Satan. 7 Cui dixit Dominus, "Unde venis?"

Qui respondens ait, "Circuivi terram et perambulavi eam."

Chapter 1

Job's virtue and riches. Satan by permission from God strippeth him of all his substance. His patience.

There was a man in the land of Uz whose name was Job, and that man was simple and upright and fearing God and avoiding evil. 2 And there were born to him seven sons and three daughters, 3 and his possession was seven thousand sheep and three thousand camels and five hundred yoke of oxen and five hundred she-asses and a family exceeding great, and this man was great among all the people of the East.

4 And his sons went and made a feast by houses, every one in his day. And sending they called their three sisters to eat and drink with them. 5 And when the days of their feasting were gone about Job sent to them and sanctified them and rising up early offered holocausts for every one of them, for he said, "Lest perhaps my sons have sinned and have *blessed* God in their hearts." So did Job all days.

6 Now on a certain day when the sons of God came to stand before the Lord, Satan also was present among them. 7 And the Lord said to him, "Whence comest thou?"

And he answered and said, "I have gone round about the earth and walked through it."

8 Dixitque Dominus ad eum, "Numquid considerasti servum meum, Iob, quod non sit ei similis in terra, homo simplex et rectus et timens Deum ac recedens a malo?" 9 Cui respondens Satan ait, "Numquid frustra timet Iob Deum? 10 Nonne tu vallasti eum ac domum eius universamque substantiam per circuitum, operibus manuum eius benedixisti, et possessio illius crevit in terra? 11 Sed extende paululum manum tuam, et tange cuncta quae possidet, nisi in faciem benedixerit tibi?"

12 Dixit ergo Dominus ad Satan, "Ecce: universa quae habet in manu tua sunt, tantum in eum ne extendas manum tuam." Egressusque est Satan a facie Domini.

13 Cum autem quadam die filii et filiae eius comederent et biberent vinum in domo fratris sui primogeniti 14 nuntius venit ad Iob qui diceret, "Boves arabant et asinae pascebantur iuxta eos, 15 et inruerunt Sabei tuleruntque omnia et pueros percusserunt gladio, et evasi ego solus ut nuntiarem tibi."

16 Cumque adhuc ille loqueretur venit alter et dixit, "Ignis Dei cecidit e caelo et tactas oves puerosque consumpsit, et effugi ego solus ut nuntiarem tibi."

17 Sed et illo adhuc loquente venit alius et dixit, "Chaldei fecerunt tres turmas et invaserunt camelos et tulerunt eos, necnon et pueros percusserunt gladio, et ego fugi solus ut nuntiarem tibi."

18 Adhuc loquebatur ille, et ecce: alius intravit et dixit, "Filiis tuis et filiabus vescentibus et bibentibus vinum in domo fratris sui primogeniti; 19 repente ventus vehemens

8 And the Lord said to him, "Hast thou considered my servant, Job, that there is none like him in the earth, a simple and upright man and fearing God and avoiding evil?" 9 *And* Satan answering said, "Doth Job fear God in vain? 10 Hast not thou made a fence for him and his house and all his substance round about, blessed the works of his hands, and his possession hath increased on the earth? 11 But stretch forth thy hand a little, and touch all that he hath, *and see if* he blesseth thee *not to thy* face."

12 Then the Lord said to Satan, "Behold: all that he hath is in thy hand, only put not forth thy hand upon his person." And Satan went forth from the presence of the Lord.

13 Now upon a certain day when his sons and daughters were eating and drinking wine in the house of their eldest brother 14 there came a messenger to Job *and* said, "The oxen were ploughing and the asses feeding beside them, 15 and the Sabeans rushed in and took all away and slew the servants with the sword, and I alone have escaped to tell thee."

16 And while he was yet speaking another came and said, "The fire of God fell from heaven and striking the sheep and the servants hath consumed them, and I alone have escaped to tell thee."

17 And while he also was yet speaking there came another and said, "The Chaldeans made three troops and have fallen upon the camels and taken them, moreover they have slain the servants with the sword, and I alone have escaped to tell thee."

18 He was yet speaking, and behold: another came in and said, "Thy sons and daughters were eating and drinking wine in the house of their elder brother; 19 a violent wind came on

inruit a regione deserti et concussit quattuor angulos domus, quae corruens oppressit liberos tuos, et mortui sunt, et effugi ego solus ut nuntiarem tibi." 20 Tunc surrexit Iob et scidit vestimenta sua et tonso capite corruens in terram adoravit 21 et dixit, "Nudus egressus sum de utero matris meae, et nudus revertar illuc. Dominus dedit, et Dominus abstulit; sicut Domino placuit ita factum est. Sit nomen Domini benedictum." 22 In omnibus his non peccavit Iob labiis suis, neque stultum quid contra Deum locutus est.

Caput 2

Factum est autem cum quadam die venissent filii Dei et starent coram Domino, venisset quoque Satan inter eos et staret in conspectu eius, 2 ut diceret Dominus ad Satan, "Unde venis?"

Qui respondens ait, "Circuivi terram et perambulavi eam."

3 Et dixit Dominus ad Satan, "Numquid considerasti servum meum, Iob, quod non sit ei similis in terra, vir simplex et rectus ac timens Deum ac recedens a malo et adhuc reti-

a sudden from the side of the desert and shook the four corners of the house, and it *fell upon* thy children, and they are dead, and I alone have escaped to fell thee."

20 Then Job rose up and rent his garments and having shaven his head fell down upon the ground and worshipped 21 and said, "Naked came I out of my mother's womb, and naked shall I return thither. The Lord gave, and the Lord hath taken away; as it hath pleased the Lord so is it done. Blessed be the name of the Lord." 22 In all these things Job sinned not by his lips, nor spoke he any foolish thing against God.

Chapter 2

Satan by God's permission striketh Job with ulcers from head to foot. His patience is still invincible.

And it came to pass when on a certain day the sons of God came and stood before the Lord and Satan came among them and stood in his sight 2 that the Lord said to Satan, "Whence comest thou?"

And he answered and said, "I have gone round about the earth and walked through it."

3 And the Lord said to Satan, "Hast thou considered my servant, Job, that there is none like him in the earth, a man simple and upright and fearing God and avoiding evil and

nens innocentiam? Tu autem commovisti me adversus eum, ut adfligerem illum frustra."

4 Cui respondens Satan ait, "Pellem pro pelle et cuncta quae habet homo dabit pro anima sua, 5 alioquin mitte manum tuam, et tange os eius et carnem, et tunc videbis quod in facie benedicat tibi."

6 Dixit ergo Dominus ad Satan, "Ecce: in manu tua est, verumtamen animam illius serva."

7 Egressus igitur Satan a facie Domini percussit Iob ulcere pessimo a planta pedis usque ad verticem eius, 8 qui testa saniem deradebat, sedens in sterquilinio. 9 Dixit autem illi uxor sua, "Adhuc tu permanes in simplicitate tua? Benedic Deo, et morere."

10 Qui ait ad illam, "Quasi una de stultis mulieribus locuta es. Si bona suscepimus de manu Dei, quare mala non suscipiamus?" In omnibus his non peccavit Iob labiis suis.

11 Igitur audientes tres amici Iob omne malum quod accidisset ei venerunt, singuli de loco suo, Eliphaz, Themanites, et Baldad, Suites, et Sophar, Naamathites, condixerant enim ut pariter venientes visitarent eum et consolarentur. 12 Cumque levassent procul oculos suos non cognoverunt eum, et exclamantes ploraverunt, scissisque vestibus sparserunt pulverem super caput suum in caelum. 13 Et sederunt cum eo in terram septem diebus et septem noctibus, et nemo loquebatur ei verbum, videbant enim dolorem esse vehementem.

still keeping his innocence? But thou hast moved me against him, that I should afflict him without cause."

4 And Satan answered and said, "Skin for skin and all that a man hath he will give for his life, 5 but put forth thy hand, and touch his bone and his flesh, and then thou shalt see that he will bless thee to thy face."

6 And the Lord said to Satan, "Behold: he is in thy hand, but yet save his life."

7 So Satan went forth from the presence of the Lord and struck Job with a very grievous ulcer from the sole of the foot even to the top of his head, 8 and he *took* a potsherd *and* scraped the corrupt matter, sitting on a dunghill. 9 And his wife said to him, "Dost thou still continue in thy simplicity? Bless God, and die."

10 And he said to her, "Thou hast spoken like one of the foolish women. If we have received good things at the hand of God, why should we not receive evil?" In all these things Job did not sin with his lips.

11 Now when Job's three friends heard all the evil that had befallen him they came, every one from his own place, Eliphaz, the Temanite, and Bildad, the Shuhite, and Zophar, the Naamathite, for they had made an appointment to come together and visit him and comfort him. 12 And when they had lifted up their eyes afar off they knew him not, and crying out they wept, and rending their garments they sprinkled dust upon their heads towards heaven. 13 And they sat with him on the ground seven days and seven nights, and no man spoke to him a word, for they saw that his grief was very great.

Caput 3

Post haec aperuit Iob os suum et maledixit diei suo, 2 et locutus est, 3 "Pereat dies in qua natus sum et nox in qua dictum est, 'Conceptus est homo.' 4 Dies ille vertatur in tenebras. Non requirat eum Deus desuper, et non inlustretur lumine. 5 Obscurent eum tenebrae et umbra mortis. Occupet eum caligo, et involvatur amaritudine. 6 Noctem illam tenebrosus turbo possideat. Non conputetur in diebus anni nec numeretur in mensibus. 7 Sit nox illa solitaria nec laude digna. 8 Maledicant ei qui maledicunt diei, qui parati sunt suscitare Leviathan. 9 Obtenebrentur stellae caligine eius. Expectet lucem et non videat nec ortum surgentis aurorae 10 quia non conclusit ostia ventris qui portavit me nec abstulit mala ab oculis meis.

11 "Quare non in vulva mortuus sum, egressus ex utero non statim perii? 12 Quare exceptus genibus? Cur lactatus uberibus? 13 Nunc enim dormiens silerem et somno meo requiescerem 14 cum regibus et consulibus terrae qui aedificant sibi solitudines 15 aut cum principibus qui possident aurum et replent domos suas argento 16 aut sicut abortivum

Chapter 3

Job expresses his sense of the miseries of man's life by cursing the day of his birth.

After this Job opened his mouth and cursed his day, 2 and he said, 3 "Let the day perish wherein I was born and the night in which it was said, 'A man child is conceived.' 4 Let that day be turned into darkness. Let not God regard it from above, and let not the light shine upon it. 5 Let darkness and the shadow of death cover it. Let a mist overspread it, and let it be wrapped up in bitterness. 6 Let a darksome whirlwind seize upon that night. Let it not be counted in the days of the year nor numbered in the months. 7 Let that night be solitary and not worthy of praise. 8 Let them curse it who curse the day, who are ready to raise up a Leviathan. 9 Let the stars be darkened with the mist thereof. Let it expect light and not see it nor the rising of the dawning of the day 10 because it shut not up the doors of the womb that bore me nor took away evils from my eyes.

11 "Why did I not die in the womb? Why did I not perish when I came out of the belly? 12 Why received upon the knees? Why suckled at the breasts? 13 For now I should have been asleep and still and should have rest in my sleep 14 with kings and consuls of the earth who build themselves solitudes 15 or with princes that possess gold and fill their houses with silver 16 or as a hidden untimely birth—I should not

absconditum—non subsisterem!—vel qui concepti non viderunt lucem. 17 Ibi impii cessaverunt a tumultu, et ibi requieverunt fessi robore. 18 Et quondam vincti pariter sine molestia non audierunt vocem exactoris. 19 Parvus et magnus ibi sunt, et servus liber a domino suo.

20 "Quare data est misero lux, et vita his qui in amaritudine animae sunt, 21 qui expectant mortem—et non venit— quasi effodientes thesaurum, 22 gaudentque vehementer cum invenerint sepulchrum, 23 viro cuius abscondita est via, et circumdedit eum Deus tenebris?

24 "Antequam comedam suspiro, et quasi inundantes aquae sic rugitus meus, 25 quia timor quem timebam evenit mihi et quod verebar accidit. 26 Nonne dissimulavi? Nonne silui? Nonne quievi? Et venit super me indignatio."

Caput 4

Respondens autem Eliphaz, Themanites, dixit, 2 "Si coeperimus loqui tibi, forsitan moleste accipias, sed conceptum sermonem tenere quis possit? 3 Ecce: docuisti multos, et

be!—or as they that being conceived have not seen the light. 17 There the wicked cease from tumult, and there the wearied in strength are at rest. 18 And they sometime bound together without disquiet have not heard the voice of the oppressor. 19 The small and great are there, and the servant is free from his master.

20 "Why is light given to him that is in misery, and life to them that are in bitterness of soul, 21 that look for death—and it cometh not—as they that dig for a treasure, 22 and they rejoice exceedingly when they have found the grave, 23 to a man whose way is hidden, and God hath surrounded him with darkness?

24 "Before I eat I sigh, and as overflowing waters so is my roaring, 25 for the fear which I feared hath come upon me and that which I was afraid of hath befallen me. 26 Have I not dissembled? Have I not kept silence? Have I not been quiet? And indignation is come upon me."

Chapter 4

Eliphaz charges Job with impatience and pretends that God never afflicts the innocent.

Then Eliphaz, the Temanite, answered and said, 2 "If we begin to speak to thee, perhaps thou wilt take it ill, but who can withhold the words he hath conceived? 3 Behold: thou

manus lassas roborasti. 4 Vacillantes confirmaverunt sermones tui, et genua trementia confortasti, 5 nunc autem venit super te plaga, et defecisti. Tetigit te, et conturbatus es. 6 "Ubi est timor tuus, fortitudo tua, patientia tua et perfectio viarum tuarum? 7 Recordare, obsecro te, quis umquam innocens periit? Aut quando recti deleti sunt? 8 Quin potius vidi eos qui operantur iniquitatem et seminant dolores et metunt eos 9 flante Deo perisse et spiritu irae eius esse consumptos. 10 Rugitus leonis et vox leaenae et dentes catulorum leonum contriti sunt. 11 Tigris periit eo quod non haberet praedam, et catuli leonis dissipati sunt.

12 "Porro ad me dictum est verbum absconditum, et quasi furtive suscepit auris mea venas susurri eius. 13 In horrore visionis nocturnae quando solet sopor occupare homines, 14 pavor tenuit me et tremor, et omnia ossa mea perterrita sunt, 15 et cum spiritus me praesente transiret inhorruerunt pili carnis meae. 16 Stetit quidam cuius non agnoscebam vultum, imago coram oculis meis, et vocem quasi aurae lenis audivi: 17 'Numquid homo Dei conparatione iustificabitur, aut factore suo purior erit vir? 18 Ecce: qui serviunt ei non sunt stabiles, et in angelis suis repperit pravitatem. 19 Quanto magis hii qui habitant domos luteas qui terrenum habent fundamentum consumentur velut a tinea? 20 De mane usque ad vesperum succidentur, et quia nullus intellegit in aeternum peribunt. 21 Qui autem reliqui fuerint auferentur ex eis. Morientur, et non in sapientia.'"

hast taught many, and thou hast strengthened the weary hands. 4 Thy words have confirmed them that were staggering, and thou hast strengthened the trembling knees, 5 but now the scourge is come upon thee, and thou faintest. It hath touched thee, and thou art troubled.

6 "Where is thy fear, thy fortitude, thy patience and the perfection of thy ways? 7 Remember, I pray thee, who ever perished being innocent? Or when were the just destroyed? 8 On the contrary I have seen those who work iniquity and sow sorrows and reap them 9 perishing by the blast of God and consumed by the spirit of his wrath. 10 The roaring of the lion and the voice of the lioness and the teeth of the whelps of lions are broken. 11 The tiger hath perished for want of prey, and the young lions are scattered abroad.

12 "Now there was a word spoken to me in private, and my ears by stealth as it were received the veins of its whisper. 13 In the horror of a vision by night when deep sleep is wont to hold men, 14 fear seized upon me and trembling, and all my bones were affrighted, 15 and when a spirit passed before me the hair of my flesh stood up. 16 There stood one whose countenance I knew not, an image before my eyes, and I heard the voice as it were of a gentle wind: 17 'Shall man be justified in comparison of God, or shall a man be more pure than his maker? 18 Behold: they that serve him are not steadfast, and in his angels he found wickedness. 19 How much more shall they that dwell in houses of clay who have an earthly foundation be consumed as with the moth? 20 From morning till evening they shall be cut down, and because no one understandeth they shall perish for ever. 21 And they that shall be left shall be taken away from them. They shall die, and not in wisdom.'"

Caput 5

"Voca ergo, si est qui tibi respondeat, et ad aliquem sanctorum convertere. 2 Vere stultum interficit iracundia, et parvulum occidit invidia. 3 Ego vidi stultum firma radice, et maledixi pulchritudini eius statim. 4 Longe fient filii eius a salute et conterentur in porta, et non erit qui eruat 5 cuius messem famelicus comedet, et ipsum rapiet armatus, et ebibent sitientes divitias eius.

6 "Nihil in terra sine causa fit, et de humo non orietur dolor. 7 Homo ad laborem nascitur et avis ad volatum, 8 quam ob rem ego deprecabor Dominum et ad Deum ponam eloquium meum 9 qui facit magna et inscrutabilia et mirabilia absque numero, 10 qui dat pluviam super faciem terrae et inrigat aquis universa, 11 qui ponit humiles in sublimi et maerentes erigit sospitate, 12 qui dissipat cogitationes malignorum ne possint implere manus eorum quod coeperant, 13 qui adprehendit sapientes in astutia eorum et consilium pravo-

Chapter 5

Eliphaz proceeds in his charge and exhorts Job to acknowledge his sins.

"Call now, if there be any that will answer thee, and turn to some of the saints. 2 Anger indeed killeth the foolish, and envy slayeth the little one. 3 I have seen a fool with a strong root, and I cursed his beauty immediately. 4 His children shall be far from safety and shall be destroyed in the gate, and there shall be none to deliver them 5 whose harvest the hungry shall eat, and the armed man shall take him by violence, and the thirsty shall drink up his riches.

6 "Nothing upon earth is done without a cause, and sorrow *doth* not spring out of the ground. 7 Man is born to labour and the bird to fly, 8 wherefore I will pray to the Lord and address my speech to God 9 who doth great things and unsearchable and wonderful things without number, 10 who giveth rain upon the face of the earth and watereth all things with waters, 11 who setteth up the humble on high and comforteth with health those that mourn, 12 who bringeth to nought the designs of the malignant so that their hands cannot accomplish what they had begun, 13 who catcheth the wise in their craftiness and disappointeth the counsel of

rum dissipat. ¹⁴ Per diem incurrent tenebras et quasi in nocte sic palpabunt in meridie, ¹⁵ porro salvum faciet egenum a gladio oris eorum et de manu violenti pauperem. ¹⁶ Et erit egeno spes, iniquitas autem contrahet os suum.

¹⁷ "Beatus homo qui corripitur a Deo; increpationem ergo Domini ne reprobes, ¹⁸ quia ipse vulnerat et medetur; percutit, et manus eius sanabunt. ¹⁹ In sex tribulationibus liberabit te, et in septima non tanget te malum. ²⁰ In fame eruet te de morte, et in bello de manu gladii. ²¹ A flagello linguae absconderis, et non timebis calamitatem cum venerit. ²² In vastitate et fame ridebis, et bestias terrae non formidabis. ²³ Sed cum lapidibus regionum pactum tuum, et bestiae terrae pacificae erunt tibi. ²⁴ Et scies quod pacem habeat tabernaculum tuum, et visitans speciem tuam non peccabis. ²⁵ Scies quoque quoniam multiplex erit semen tuum et progenies tua quasi herba terrae. ²⁶ Ingredieris in abundantia sepulchrum, sicut infertur acervus tritici in tempore suo. ²⁷ Ecce: hoc ut investigavimus ita est, quod auditum, mente pertracta."

the wicked. 14 They shall meet with darkness in the day and grope at noonday as in the night, 15 but he shall save the needy from the sword of their mouth and the poor from the hand of the violent. 16 And to the needy there shall be hope, but iniquity shall draw in her mouth.

17 "Blessed is the man whom God correcteth; refuse not therefore the chastising of the Lord, 18 for he woundeth and cureth; he striketh, and his hands shall heal. 19 In six troubles he shall deliver thee, and in the seventh evil shall not touch thee. 20 In famine he shall deliver thee from death, and in battle from the hand of the sword. 21 Thou shalt be hidden from the scourge of the tongue, and thou shalt not fear calamity when it cometh. 22 In destruction and famine thou shalt laugh, and thou shalt not be afraid of the beasts of the earth. 23 But thou shalt have a covenant with the stones of the lands, and the beasts of the earth shall be at peace with thee. 24 And thou shalt know that thy tabernacle is in peace, and visiting thy beauty thou shalt not sin. 25 Thou shalt know also that thy seed shall be multiplied and thy offspring like the grass of the earth. 26 Thou shalt enter into the grave in abundance, as a heap of wheat is brought in its season. 27 Behold: this is even so as we have searched out, which thou having heard, consider it thoroughly in thy mind."

Caput 6

Respondens autem Iob dixit, 2 "Utinam adpenderentur peccata mea, quibus iram merui et calamitas quam patior, in statera. 3 Quasi harena maris haec gravior appareret; unde et verba mea dolore sunt plena, 4 quia sagittae Domini in me sunt, quarum indignatio ebibit spiritum meum, et terrores Domini militant contra me.

5 "Numquid rugiet onager cum habuerit herbam? Aut mugiet bos cum ante praesepe plenum steterit? 6 Aut poterit comedi insulsum quod non est sale conditum? Aut potest aliquis gustare quod gustatum adfert mortem? 7 Quae prius tangere nolebat anima mea nunc prae angustia cibi mei sunt.

8 "Quis det ut veniat petitio mea et quod expecto tribuat mihi Deus 9 et qui coepit ipse me conterat, solvat manum suam et succidat me 10 et haec mihi sit consolatio, ut adfligens me dolore non parcat, nec contradicam sermonibus Sancti? 11 Quae est enim fortitudo mea ut sustineam? Aut quis finis meus ut patienter agam? 12 Nec fortitudo lapidum fortitudo mea, nec caro mea aerea est.

Chapter 6

Job maintains his innocence and complains of his friends.

But Job answered and said, 2 "O that my sins, whereby I have deserved wrath and the calamity that I suffer, were weighed in a balance. 3 As the sand of the sea this would appear heavier; therefore my words are full of sorrow, 4 for the arrows of the Lord are in me, the rage whereof drinketh up my spirit, and the terrors of the Lord war against me.

5 "Will the wild ass bray when he hath grass? Or will the ox low when he standeth before a full manger? 6 Or can an unsavoury thing be eaten that is not seasoned with salt? Or can a man taste that which when tasted bringeth death? 7 The things which before my soul would not touch now through anguish are my meats.

8 "Who will grant that my request may come and that God may give me what I look for 9 and that he that hath begun may destroy me, that he may let loose his hand and cut me off 10 and that this may be my comfort, that afflicting me with sorrow he spare not, nor I contradict the words of the Holy One? 11 For what is my strength that I can hold out? Or what is my end that I should keep patience? 12 My strength is not the strength of stones, nor is my flesh of brass.

13 "Ecce: non est auxilium mihi in me, et necessarii quoque mei recesserunt a me. 14 Qui tollit ab amico suo misericordiam timorem Domini derelinquit. 15 Fratres mei praeterierunt me sicut torrens qui raptim transit in convallibus. 16 "Qui timent pruinam, inruet super eos nix. 17 Tempore quo fuerint dissipati peribunt, et ut incaluerit solventur de loco suo. 18 Involutae sunt semitae gressuum eorum; ambulabunt in vacuum et peribunt. 19 Considerate semitas Theman, itinera Saba, et expectate paulisper. 20 Confusi sunt quia speravi; venerunt quoque usque ad me et pudore cooperti sunt.

21 "Nunc venistis, et modo videntes plagam meam timetis. 22 Numquid dixi, 'Adferte mihi, et de substantia vestra donate mihi'? 23 Vel, 'Liberate me de manu hostis, et de manu robustorum eruite me'? 24 Docete me, et ego tacebo. Et si quid forte ignoravi, instruite me.

25 "Quare detraxistis sermonibus veritatis, cum e vobis nullus sit qui possit arguere me? 26 Ad increpandum tantum eloquia concinnatis, et in ventum verba profertis. 27 Super pupillum inruitis, et subvertere nitimini amicum vestrum. 28 Verumtamen, quod coepistis explete; praebete aurem, et videte an mentiar. 29 Respondete, obsecro, absque contentione, et loquentes id quod iustum est iudicate. 30 Et non invenietis in lingua mea iniquitatem, nec in faucibus meis stultitia personabit."

13 "Behold: there is no help for me in myself, and my familiar friends also are departed from me. 14 He that taketh away mercy from his friend forsaketh the fear of the Lord. 15 My brethren have passed by me as the torrent that passeth swiftly in the valleys.

16 "They that fear the hoary frost, the snow shall fall upon them. 17 At the time when they shall be scattered they shall perish, and after it groweth hot they shall be melted out of their place. 18 The paths of their steps are entangled; they shall walk in vain and shall perish. 19 Consider the paths of Tema, the ways of Sheba, and wait a little while. 20 They are confounded because I have hoped; they are come also even unto me and are covered with shame.

21 "Now you are come, and now seeing my affliction you are afraid. 22 Did I say, 'Bring to me, and give me of your substance'? 23 Or, 'Deliver me from the hand of the enemy, and rescue me out of the hand of the mighty'? 24 Teach me, and I will hold my peace. And if I have been ignorant in any thing, instruct me.

25 "Why have you detracted the words of truth, whereas there is none of you that can reprove me? 26 You dress up speeches only to rebuke, and you utter words to the wind. 27 You rush in upon the fatherless, and you endeavour to overthrow your friend. 28 However, finish what you have begun; give ear, and see whether I lie. 29 Answer, I beseech you, without contention, and speaking that which is just judge ye. 30 And you shall not find iniquity in my tongue, neither shall folly sound in my mouth."

Caput 7

"Militia est vita hominis super terram, et sicut dies mercennarii dies eius. 2 Sicut servus desiderat umbram, et sicut mercennarius praestolatur finem operis sui, 3 sic et ego habui menses vacuos et noctes laboriosas enumeravi mihi. 4 Si dormiero, dicam, 'Quando consurgam?' Et rursum expectabo vesperam et replebor doloribus usque ad tenebras.

5 "Induta est caro mea putredine et sordibus pulveris. Cutis mea aruit et contracta est. 6 Dies mei velocius transierunt quam a texente tela succiditur et consumpti sunt absque ulla spe. 7 Memento quia ventus est vita mea, et non revertetur oculus meus ut videat bona, 8 nec aspiciet me visus hominis. Oculi tui in me, et non subsistam. 9 Sicut consumitur nubes et pertransit, sic qui descenderit ad inferos non ascendet, 10 nec revertetur ultra in domum suam, neque cognoscet eum amplius locus eius. 11 Quapropter et ego non parcam ori meo; loquar in tribulatione spiritus mei; confabulabor cum amaritudine animae meae.

12 "Numquid mare sum ego aut cetus, quia circumdedisti me carcere? 13 Si dixero, 'Consolabitur me lectulus meus, et

Chapter 7

Job declares the miseries of man's life and addresses himself to God.

"The life of man upon earth is a warfare, and his days are like the days of a hireling. 2 As a servant longeth for the shade, *as* the hireling looketh for the end of his work, 3 so I also have had empty months and have numbered to myself wearisome nights. 4 If I *lie down to* sleep, I shall say, 'When shall I arise?' And again I shall look for the evening and shall be filled with sorrows even till darkness.

5 "My flesh is clothed with rottenness and the filth of dust. My skin is withered and drawn together. 6 My days have passed more swiftly than the web is cut by the weaver and are consumed without any hope. 7 Remember that my life is *but* wind, and my eyes shall not return to see good things, 8 nor shall the sight of man behold me. Thy eyes are upon me, and I shall be no more. 9 As a cloud is consumed and passeth away, so he that shall go down to hell shall not come up, 10 nor shall he return any more into his house, neither shall his place know him any more. 11 Wherefore *I* will not spare my mouth; I will speak in the affliction of my spirit; I will talk with the bitterness of my soul.

12 "Am I a sea or a whale, that thou hast enclosed me in a prison? 13 If I say, 'My bed shall comfort me, and I shall be

relevabor loquens mecum in strato meo,' 14 terrebis me per somnia et per visiones horrore concuties, 15 quam ob rem elegit suspendium anima mea et mortem ossa mea. 16 Desperavi. Nequaquam ultra iam vivam. Parce mihi, nihil enim sunt dies mei.

17 "Quid est homo quia magnificas eum? Aut quid ponis erga eum cor tuum? 18 Visitas eum diluculo, et subito probas illum. 19 Usquequo non parcis mihi nec dimittis me ut gluttiam salivam meam?

20 "Peccavi. Quid faciam tibi, O custos hominum? Quare posuisti me contrarium tibi et factus sum mihimet ipsi gravis? 21 Cur non tollis peccatum meum, et quare non aufers iniquitatem meam? Ecce: nunc in pulvere dormiam, et si mane me quaesieris, non subsistam."

Caput 8

Respondens autem Baldad, Suites, dixit, 2 "Usquequo loqueris talia et spiritus multiplex sermonis oris tui? 3 Numquid Deus subplantat iudicium, aut Omnipotens subvertit quod iustum est? 4 Etiam si filii tui peccaverunt ei et dimisit

relieved speaking with myself on my couch,' 14 thou wilt frighten me with dreams and *terrify* me with visions, 15 *so that* my soul *rather* chooseth hanging and my bones death. 16 I have done with hope. I shall now live no longer. Spare me, for my days are nothing.

17 "What is a man that thou shouldst magnify him? Or why dost thou set thy heart *upon* him? 18 Thou visitest him early in the morning, and thou provest him suddenly. 19 How long *wilt* thou not spare me nor suffer me to swallow down my spittle?

20 "I have sinned. What shall I do to thee, O keeper of men? Why hast thou set me opposite to thee and I am become burdensome to myself? 21 Why dost thou not remove my sin, and why dost thou not take away my iniquity? Behold: now I shall sleep in the dust, and if thou seek me in the morning, I shall not be."

Chapter 8

Bildad under pretence of defending the justice of God accuses Job and exhorts him to return to God.

Then Bildad, the Shuhite, answered and said, 2 "How long wilt thou speak these things, and how long shall the *words* of thy mouth *be like a strong wind?* 3 Doth God pervert judgment, or doth the Almighty overthrow that which is just? 4 Although thy children have sinned against him and he hath

eos in manu iniquitatis suae, 5 tu tamen si diluculo consur-
rexeris ad Deum et Omnipotentem fueris deprecatus, 6 si
mundus et rectus incesseris, statim evigilabit ad te et paca-
tum reddet habitaculum iustitiae tuae, 7 in tantum ut si
priora tua fuerint parva, novissima tua multiplicentur nimis;
8 interroga enim generationem pristinam, et diligenter investiga patrum memoriam, 9 hesterni quippe sumus et ignora-
mus quoniam sicut umbra dies nostri sunt super terram, 10 et
ipsi docebunt te; loquentur tibi et de corde suo proferent
eloquia.

11 "Numquid virere potest scirpus absque humore, aut
crescere carectum sine aqua? 12 Cum adhuc sit in flore nec
carpatur manu, ante omnes herbas arescit. 13 Sic viae omnium qui obliviscuntur Deum, et spes hypocritae peribit.
14 Non ei placebit vecordia sua, et sicut tela aranearum fiducia eius. 15 Innitetur super domum suam, et non stabit. Ful-
ciet eam, et non consurget. 16 Humectus videtur antequam
veniat sol, et in ortu suo germen eius egredietur. 17 Super
acervum petrarum radices eius densabuntur, et inter lapides
commorabitur. 18 Si absorbuerit eum de loco suo, negabit
eum et dicet, 'Non novi te,' 19 haec est enim laetitia viae eius,
ut rursum de terra alii germinentur.

20 "Deus non proiciet simplicem nec porriget manum
malignis 21 donec impleatur risu os tuum et labia tua iubilo.
22 Qui oderunt te induentur confusione, et tabernaculum
impiorum non subsistet."

left them in the hand of their iniquity, 5 yet if thou wilt arise early to God and wilt beseech the Almighty, 6 if thou wilt walk clean and upright, he will presently awake unto thee and will make the dwelling of thy justice peaceable, 7 insomuch that if thy former things were small, thy latter things would be multiplied exceedingly; 8 for inquire of the former generation, and search diligently into the memory of the fathers, 9 for we are but of yesterday and are ignorant that our days upon earth are but a shadow, 10 and they shall teach thee; they shall speak to thee and utter words out of their hearts.

11 "Can the rush be green without moisture, or a sedgebush grow without water? 12 When it is yet in flower and is not plucked up with the hand, it withereth before all herbs. 13 Even so are the ways of all that forget God, and the hope of the hypocrite shall perish. 14 His folly shall not please him, and his trust shall be like the spider's web. 15 He shall lean upon his house, and it shall not stand. He shall prop it up, and it shall not rise. 16 He seemeth to have moisture before the sun cometh, and at his rising his blossom shall shoot forth. 17 His roots shall be thick upon a heap of stones, and among the stones he shall abide. 18 If one swallow him up out of his place, he shall deny him and shall say, 'I know thee not,' 19 for this is the joy of his way, that others may spring again out of the earth.

20 "God will not cast away the simple nor reach out his hand to the evildoer 21 until thy mouth be filled with laughter and thy lips with rejoicing. 22 They that hate thee shall be clothed with confusion, and the dwelling of the wicked shall not stand."

Caput 9

Et respondens Iob ait, 2 "Vere scio quod ita sit et quod non iustificetur homo conpositus Deo. 3 Si voluerit contendere cum eo, non poterit ei respondere unum pro mille. 4 Sapiens corde est et fortis robore—quis restitit ei et pacem habuit?—5 qui transtulit montes, et nescierunt hii quos subvertit in furore suo; 6 qui commovet terram de loco suo, et columnae eius concutiuntur; 7 qui praecipit soli, et non oritur, et stellas claudit quasi sub signaculo; 8 qui extendit caelos solus et graditur super fluctus maris; 9 qui facit Arcturum et Oriona et Hyadas et interiora austri; 10 qui facit magna et inconprehensibilia et mirabilia quorum non est numerus.

11 "Si venerit ad me, non videbo eum. Si abierit, non intellegam. 12 Si repente interroget, quis respondebit ei? Vel quis dicere potest, 'Cur ita facis?' 13 Deus, cuius resistere irae nemo potest et sub quo curvantur qui portant orbem, 14 quantus ergo sum ego qui respondeam ei et loquar verbis meis cum eo? 15 Qui etiam si habuero quippiam iustum non respondebo sed meum iudicem deprecabor. 16 Et cum invo-

Chapter 9

Job acknowledges God's justice, although he often afflicts the innocent.

And Job answered and said, 2 "Indeed I know it is so and that man cannot be justified compared with God. 3 If he will contend with him, he cannot answer him one for a thousand. 4 He is wise in heart and mighty in strength—who hath resisted him and hath had peace?—5 who hath removed mountains, and they whom he overthrew in his wrath knew it not; 6 who shaketh the earth out of her place, and the pillars thereof tremble; 7 who commandeth the sun, and it riseth not, and shutteth up the stars as it were under a seal; 8 who alone spreadeth out the heavens and walketh upon the waves of the sea; 9 who maketh Arcturus and Orion and Hyades and the inner parts of the south; 10 who doth things great and incomprehensible and wonderful of which there is no number.

11 "If he come to me, I shall not see him. If he depart, I shall not understand. 12 If he examine on a sudden, who shall answer him? Or who can say, 'Why dost thou so?' 13 God, whose wrath no man can resist and under whom they stoop that bear up the world, 14 *what* am I then that I should answer him and *have words* with him? 15 I who although I should have any just thing would not answer but would make supplication to my judge. 16 And *if* he should hear me when I

cantem exaudierit me, non credo quod audierit vocem meam, 17 in turbine enim conteret me et multiplicabit vulnera mea etiam sine causa. 18 Non concedit requiescere spiritum meum, et implet me amaritudinibus.

19 "Si fortitudo quaeritur, robustissimus est. Si aequitas iudicii, nemo pro me audet testimonium dicere. 20 Si iustificare me voluero, os meum condemnabit me; si innocentem ostendero, pravum me conprobabit. 21 Etiam si simplex fuero, hoc ipsum ignorabit anima mea, et taedebit me vitae meae. 22 Unum est quod locutus sum: et innocentem et impium ipse consumit. 23 Si flagellat, occidat semel et non de poenis innocentum rideat. 24 Terra data est in manus impii. Vultum iudicum eius operit. Quod si non ille est, quis ergo est?

25 "Dies mei velociores fuerunt cursore; fugerunt et non viderunt bonum. 26 Pertransierunt quasi naves poma portantes, sicut aquila volans ad escam. 27 Cum dixero, 'Nequaquam ita loquar,' commuto faciem meam et dolore torqueor. 28 Verebar omnia opera mea, sciens quod non parceres delinquenti.

29 "Si autem et sic impius sum, quare frustra laboravi? 30 Si lotus fuero quasi aquis nivis et fulserint velut mundissimae manus meae, 31 tamen sordibus intingues me, et abominabuntur me vestimenta mea, 32 neque enim viro qui similis mei est respondebo nec qui mecum in iudicio ex aequo possit audiri. 33 Non est qui utrumque valeat arguere et ponere manum suam in ambobus. 34 Auferat a me virgam suam, et pavor eius non me terreat. 35 Loquar et non timebo eum, neque enim possum metuens respondere."

call, I should not believe that he had heard my voice, 17 for he shall crush me in a whirlwind and multiply my wounds even without cause. 18 He alloweth not my spirit to rest, and he filleth me with bitterness. 19 "If strength be demanded, he is most strong. If equity of judgment, no man dare bear witness for me. 20 If I would justify myself, my own mouth shall condemn me; if I would shew myself innocent, he shall prove me wicked. 21 Although I should be simple, even this my soul shall be ignorant of, and I shall be weary of my life. 22 One thing there is that I have spoken: both the innocent and the wicked he consumeth. 23 If he scourge, let him kill at once and not laugh at the pains of the innocent. 24 The earth is given into the *hand* of the wicked. He covereth the face of the judges thereof. And if it be not he, who is it then?

25 "My days have been swifter than a post; they have fled away and have not seen good. 26 They have passed by as ships carrying fruits, as an eagle flying to the prey. 27 *If* I say, 'I will not speak so,' I change my face and am tormented with sorrow. 28 I feared all my works, knowing that thou didst not spare the offender.

29 "But if so also I am wicked, why have I laboured in vain? 30 If I be washed as it were with snow-waters and my hands shall shine *never so* clean, 31 yet thou shalt plunge me in filth, and my garments shall abhor me, 32 for I shall not answer a man that is like myself nor one that may be heard with me equally in judgment. 33 There is none that may be able to reprove both and to put his hand between both. 34 Let him take his rod away from me, and let not his fear terrify me. 35 I will speak and will not fear him, for I cannot answer while I am in fear."

Caput 10

"Taedet animam meam vitae meae. Dimittam adversum me eloquium meum; loquar in amaritudine animae meae. 2 Dicam Deo, 'Noli me condemnare. Indica mihi cur me ita iudices. 3 Numquid bonum tibi videtur si calumnieris me et opprimas me, opus manuum tuarum, et consilium impiorum adiuves? 4 Numquid oculi carnei tibi sunt, aut sicut videt homo et tu videbis? 5 Numquid sicut dies hominis dies tui, et anni tui sicut humana sunt tempora, 6 ut quaeras iniquitatem meam et peccatum meum scruteris 7 et scias quia nihil impium fecerim, cum sit nemo qui de manu tua possit eruere? 8 Manus tuae plasmaverunt me et fecerunt me totum in circuitu, et sic repente praecipitas me?

9 "'Memento, quaeso, quod sicut lutum feceris me et in pulverem reduces me. 10 Nonne sicut lac mulsisti me et sicut caseum me coagulasti? 11 Pelle et carnibus vestisti me. Ossibus et nervis conpegisti me. 12 Vitam et misericordiam tribuisti mihi, et visitatio tua custodivit spiritum meum. 13 Licet haec celes in corde tuo, tamen scio quia universorum memineris. 14 Si peccavi et ad horam pepercisti mihi, cur ab

Chapter 10

Job laments his afflictions and begs to be delivered.

"My soul is weary of my life. I will let go my speech against myself; I will speak in the bitterness of my soul. ² I will say to God, 'Do not condemn me. Tell me why thou judgest me so. ³ Doth it seem good to thee that thou shouldst calumniate me and oppress me, the work of thy own hands, and help the counsel of the wicked? ⁴ Hast thou eyes of flesh, or shalt *thou* see as man seeth? ⁵ Are thy days as the days of man, and are thy years as the times of men, ⁶ that thou shouldst inquire after my iniquity and search after my sin ⁷ and shouldst know that I have done no wicked thing, whereas there is no man that can deliver out of thy hand? ⁸ Thy hands have made me and fashioned me wholly round about, and dost thou thus cast me down headlong on a sudden?

⁹ "Remember, I beseech thee, that thou hast made me as the clay and thou wilt bring me into dust again. ¹⁰ Hast thou not milked me as milk and curdled me like cheese? ¹¹ Thou hast clothed me with skin and flesh. Thou hast put me together with bones and sinews. ¹² Thou hast granted me life and mercy, and thy visitation hath preserved my spirit. ¹³ Although thou conceal these things in thy heart, yet I know that thou rememberest all things. ¹⁴ If I have sinned and thou hast spared me for an hour, why dost thou not suffer

iniquitate mea mundum me esse non pateris? 15 Et si impius fuero, vae mihi est, et si iustus, non levabo caput saturatus adflictione et miseria. 16 Et propter superbiam quasi leaenam capies me, reversusque mirabiliter me crucias. 17 Instauras testes tuos contra me et multiplicas iram tuam adversum me, et poenae militant in me.

18 "'Quare de vulva eduxisti me? Qui utinam consumptus essem, ne oculus me videret! 19 Fuissem quasi non essem, de utero translatus ad tumulum. 20 Numquid non paucitas dierum meorum finietur brevi? Dimitte, ergo, me ut plangam paululum dolorem meum 21 antequam vadam et non revertar ad terram tenebrosam et opertam mortis caligine, 22 terram miseriae et tenebrarum ubi umbra mortis et nullus ordo sed sempiternus horror inhabitat.'"

Caput 11

Respondens autem Sophar, Naamathites, dixit, 2 "Numquid qui multa loquitur non et audiet? Aut vir verbosus iustificabitur? 3 Tibi soli tacebunt homines? Et cum ceteros inriseris a nullo confutaberis? 4 Dixisti enim, 'Purus est sermo

me to be clean from my iniquity? 15 And if I be wicked, woe unto me, and if just, I shall not lift up my head being filled with affliction and misery. 16 And for pride thou wilt take me as a lioness, and returning thou tormentest me wonderfully. 17 Thou renewest thy witnesses against me and multipliest thy wrath upon me, and pains war against me.

18 "'Why didst thou bring me forth out of the womb? O that I had been consumed, that eye might not see me! 19 I should have been as if I had not been, carried from the womb to the grave. 20 Shall not the fewness of my days be ended shortly? Suffer me, therefore, that I may lament my sorrow a little 21 before I go and return *no more* to a land that is dark and covered with the mist of death, 22 a land of misery and darkness where the shadow of death and no order but everlasting horror dwelleth.'"

Chapter 11

Zophar reproves Job for justifying himself and invites him to repentance.

Then Zophar, the Naamathite, answered and said, 2 "Shall not he that speaketh much hear also? Or shall a man full of talk be justified? 3 Shall men hold their peace to thee only? And when thou hast mocked others shall no man confute thee? 4 For thou hast said, 'My word is pure, and I am clean

meus, et mundus sum in conspectu tuo.' 5 Atque utinam
Deus loqueretur tecum et aperiret labia sua tibi 6 ut ostenderet tibi secreta sapientiae et quod multiplex esset lex eius,
et intellegeres quod multo minora exigaris ab eo quam me-
retur iniquitas tua.

7 "Forsitan vestigia Dei conprehendes et usque ad perfectum Omnipotentem repperies. 8 Excelsior caelo est, et quid
facies? Profundior inferno, et unde cognosces? 9 Longior
terra mensura eius et latior mari. 10 Si subverterit omnia vel
in unum coartaverit, quis contradicet ei? 11 Ipse enim novit
hominum vanitatem, et videns iniquitatem, nonne considerat? 12 Vir vanus in superbiam erigitur et tamquam pullum
onagri se liberum natum putat, 13 tu autem firmasti cor tuum
et expandisti ad eum manus tuas.

14 "Si iniquitatem quod est in manu tua abstuleris a te et
non manserit in tabernaculo tuo iniustitia, 15 tum levare poteris faciem tuam absque macula, et eris stabilis et non timebis. 16 Miseriae quoque obliviceris et quasi aquarum quae
praeterierint recordaberis, 17 et quasi meridianus fulgor
consurget tibi ad vesperam, et cum te consumptum putave-
ris orieris ut Lucifer. 18 Et habebis fiduciam, proposita tibi
spe, et defossus securus dormies. 19 Requiesces, et non erit
qui te exterreat, et deprecabuntur faciem tuam plurimi.

20 "Oculi autem impiorum deficient, et effugium peribit
ab eis, et spes eorum, abominatio animae."

in thy sight.' 5 And I wish that God would speak with thee and would open his lips to thee 6 that he might shew thee the secrets of wisdom and that his law is manifold, and thou mightest understand that he exacteth much less of thee than thy iniquity deserveth.

7 "Peradventure thou wilt comprehend the steps of God and wilt find out the Almighty perfectly. 8 He is higher than heaven, and what wilt thou do? He is deeper than hell, and how wilt thou know? 9 The measure of him is longer than the earth and broader than the sea. 10 If he shall overturn all things or shall press them together, who shall contradict him? 11 For he knoweth the vanity of men, and when he seeth iniquity, doth he not consider it? 12 A vain man is lifted up into pride and thinketh himself born free like a wild ass's colt, 13 but thou hast hardened thy heart and hast spread thy hands to him.

14 "If thou wilt put away from thee the iniquity that is in thy hand and *let* not injustice remain in thy tabernacle, 15 then mayst thou lift up thy face without spot, and thou shalt be steadfast and shalt not fear. 16 Thou shalt also forget misery and remember it *only* as waters that are passed away, 17 and brightness like that of the noonday shall arise to thee at evening, and when thou shalt think thyself consumed thou shalt rise as the Day Star. 18 And thou shalt have confidence, hope being set before thee, and being buried thou shalt sleep secure. 19 Thou shalt rest, and there shall be none to make thee afraid, and many shall entreat thy face.

20 "But the eyes of the wicked shall decay, and the way to escape shall fail them, and their hope, the abomination of the soul."

Caput 12

Respondens autem Iob dixit, 2 "Ergo vos estis soli homines, et vobiscum morietur sapientia? 3 Et mihi est cor sicut et vobis nec inferior vestri sum, quis enim haec quae nostis ignorat? 4 Qui deridetur ab amico suo sicut ego invocabit Deum, et exaudiet eum, deridetur enim iusti simplicitas. 5 Lampas contempta apud cogitationes divitum parata ad tempus statutum. 6 Abundant tabernacula praedonum, et audacter provocant Deum, cum ipse dederit omnia in manus eorum.

7 "Nimirum interroga iumenta, et docebunt te, et volatilia caeli, et indicabunt tibi. 8 Loquere terrae, et respondebit tibi, et narrabunt pisces maris. 9 Quis ignorat quod omnia haec manus Domini fecerit? 10 In cuius manu anima omnis viventis et spiritus universae carnis hominis? 11 Nonne auris verba diiudicat, et fauces comedentis saporem?

12 "In antiquis est sapientia, et in multo tempore prudentia. 13 Apud ipsum est sapientia et fortitudo. Ipse habet consilium et intellegentiam. 14 Si destruxerit, nemo est qui aedificet. Si incluserit hominem, nullus est qui aperiat. 15 Si continuerit aquas, omnia siccabuntur, et si emiserit eas, subvertent terram. 16 Apud ipsum est fortitudo et sapientia.

Chapter 12

Job's reply to Zophar. He extols God's power and wisdom.

Then Job answered and said, 2 "Are you then men alone, and shall wisdom die with you? 3 I also have a heart as well as *you,* for who is ignorant of these things which you know? 4 He that is mocked by his friend as I shall call upon God, and he will hear him, for the simplicity of the just man is laughed to scorn. 5 The lamp despised in the thoughts of the rich is ready for the time appointed. 6 The tabernacles of robbers abound, and they provoke God boldly, whereas it is he that hath given all into their hands.

7 "*But* ask *now* the beasts, and they shall teach thee, and the birds of the air, and they shall tell thee. 8 Speak to the earth, and it shall answer thee, and the fishes of the sea shall tell. 9 Who is ignorant that the hand of the Lord hath made all these things? 10 In whose hand is the soul of every living thing and the spirit of all flesh of man? 11 Doth not the ear discern words, and the palate of him that eateth the taste?

12 "In the ancient is wisdom, and in *length of days* prudence. 13 With him is wisdom and strength. He hath counsel and understanding. 14 If he pull down, there is no man that can build up. If he shut up a man, there is none that can open. 15 If he withhold the waters, all things shall be dried up, and if he send them out, they shall overturn the earth. 16 With him is strength and wisdom. He knoweth both the

Ipse novit et decipientem et eum qui decipitur. 17 Adducit consiliarios in stultum finem et iudices in stuporem. 18 Balteum regum dissolvit et praecingit fune renes eorum. 19 Ducit sacerdotes inglorios et optimates subplantat. 20 Commutans labium veracium et doctrinam senum auferens. 21 Effundit despectionem super principes, eos qui oppressi fuerant relevans. 22 Qui revelat profunda de tenebris et producit in lucem umbram mortis. 23 Qui multiplicat gentes et perdit eas et subversas in integrum restituit. 24 Qui inmutat cor principum populi terrae et decipit eos ut frustra incedant per invium. 25 Palpabunt quasi in tenebris et non in luce, et errare eos faciet quasi ebrios."

Caput 13

"Ecce: omnia haec vidit oculus meus, et audivit auris mea, et intellexi singula. 2 Secundum scientiam vestram et ego novi, nec inferior vestri sum. 3 Sed tamen ad Omnipotentem loquar, et disputare cum Deo cupio, 4 prius vos ostendens fabricatores mendacii et cultores perversorum dog-

deceiver and him that is deceived. 17 He bringeth counsellors to a foolish end and judges to insensibility. 18 He looseth the belt of kings and girdeth their loins with a cord. 19 He leadeth away priests without glory and overthroweth nobles. 20 He changeth the speech of the true speakers and taketh away the doctrine of the aged. 21 He poureth contempt upon princes and relieveth them that were oppressed. 22 He discovereth deep things out of darkness and bringeth up to light the shadow of death. 23 He multiplieth nations and destroyeth them and restoreth them again after they were overthrown. 24 He changeth the heart of the princes of the people of the earth and deceiveth them that they walk in vain where there is no way. 25 They shall grope as in the dark and not in the light, and he shall make them stagger like men that are drunk."

Chapter 13

Job persists in maintaining his innocence and reproves his friends.

"Behold: my eye hath seen all these things, and my ear hath heard them, and I have understood them all. 2 According to your knowledge I also know, neither am I inferior to you. 3 But yet I will speak to the Almighty, and I desire to reason with God, 4 having first shewn that you are forgers of

matum. 5 Atque utinam taceretis ut putaremini esse sapientes. 6 Audite ergo correptiones meas, et iudicium labiorum meorum adtendite.

7 "Numquid Deus indiget vestro mendacio ut pro illo loquamini dolos? 8 Numquid faciem eius accipitis, et pro Deo iudicare nitimini? 9 Aut placebit ei quem celare nihil potest? Aut decipietur ut homo vestris fraudulentiis? 10 Ipse vos arguet quoniam in abscondito faciem eius accipitis. 11 Statim ut se commoverit turbabit vos, et terror eius inruet super vos. 12 Memoria vestra conparabitur cineri, et redigentur in lutum cervices vestrae. 13 Tacete paulisper ut loquar quodcumque mihi mens suggesserit.

14 "Quare lacero carnes meas dentibus meis et animam meam porto in manibus meis? 15 Etiam si occiderit me, in ipso sperabo, verumtamen vias meas in conspectu eius arguam. 16 Et ipse erit salvator meus, non enim veniet in conspectu eius omnis hypocrita. 17 Audite sermonem meum, et enigmata percipite auribus vestris. 18 Si fuero iudicatus, scio quod iustus inveniar. 19 Quis est qui iudicetur mecum? Veniat. Quare tacens consumor? 20 Duo tantum ne facias mihi, et tunc a facie tua non abscondar: 21 manum tuam longe fac a me, et formido tua non me terreat. 22 Voca me, et respondebo tibi, aut certe loquar, et tu responde mihi.

23 "Quantas habeo iniquitates et peccata? Scelera mea et delicta ostende mihi. 24 Cur faciem tuam abscondis et arbitraris me inimicum tuum? 25 Contra folium quod vento rapitur ostendis potentiam tuam, et stipulam siccam perseque-

lies and maintainers of perverse opinions. 5 And I wish you would hold your peace that you might be thought to be wise men. 6 Hear ye therefore my *reproof,* and attend to the judgment of my lips.

7 "Hath God any need of your lie that you should speak deceitfully for him? 8 Do you accept his person, and do you endeavour to judge for God? 9 Or shall it please him from whom nothing can be concealed? Or shall he be deceived as a man with your deceitful dealings? 10 He shall reprove you because in secret you accept his person. 11 As soon as he shall move himself he shall trouble you, and his dread shall fall upon you. 12 Your remembrance shall be compared to ashes, and your necks shall be brought to clay. 13 Hold your peace a little while that I may speak whatsoever my mind shall suggest to me.

14 "Why do I tear my flesh with my teeth and carry my soul in my hands? 15 Although he should kill me, I will trust in him, but yet I will reprove my ways in his sight. 16 And he shall be my saviour, for no hypocrite shall come before his presence. 17 Hear ye my speech, and receive with your ears hidden truths. 18 If I shall be judged, I know that I shall be found just. 19 Who is he that will plead against me? Let him come. Why am I consumed holding my peace? 20 Two things only do not to me, and then from thy face I shall not be hid: 21 withdraw thy hand far from me, and let not thy dread terrify me. 22 Call me, and I will answer thee, or else I will speak, and do thou answer me.

23 "How many are my iniquities and sins? Make me know my crimes and offences. 24 Why hidest thou thy face and thinkest me thy enemy? 25 Against a leaf that is carried away with the wind thou shewest thy power, and thou pursuest a

ris, 26 scribis enim contra me amaritudines et consumere me vis peccatis adulescentiae meae. 27 Posuisti in nervo pedem meum et observasti omnes semitas meas et vestigia pedum meorum considerasti 28 qui quasi putredo consumendus sum et quasi vestimentum quod comeditur a tinea."

Caput 14

"Homo natus de muliere, brevi vivens tempore, repletur multis miseriis, 2 qui quasi flos egreditur et conteritur et fugit velut umbra et numquam in eodem statu permanet.

3 "Et dignum ducis super huiuscemodi aperire oculos tuos et adducere eum tecum in iudicium? 4 Quis potest facere mundum de inmundo conceptum semine? Nonne tu qui solus es?

5 "Breves dies hominis sunt, et numerus mensuum eius apud te est. Constituisti terminos eius qui praeteriri non poterunt. 6 Recede paululum ab eo ut quiescat donec optata veniat sicut mercennarii dies eius.

dry straw, 26 for thou writest bitter things against me and wilt consume me for the sins of my youth. 27 Thou hast put my feet in the stocks and hast observed all my paths and hast considered the steps of my feet 28 who am to be consumed as rottenness and as a garment that is moth-eaten."

Chapter 14

Job declares the shortness of man's days and professes his belief of a resurrection.

"Man born of a woman, living for a short time, is filled with many miseries, 2 who cometh forth like a flower and is destroyed and fleeth as a shadow and never continueth in the same state.

3 "And dost thou think it meet to open thy eyes upon such an one and to bring him into judgment with thee? 4 Who can make him clean that is conceived of unclean seed? Is it not thou who only art?

5 "The days of man are short, and the number of his months is with thee. Thou hast appointed his bounds which cannot be passed. 6 Depart a little from him that he may rest until his wished for day come as that of the hireling.

7 "Lignum habet spem. Si praecisum fuerit, rursum virescit, et rami eius pullulant. 8 Si senuerit in terra radix eius et in pulvere emortuus fuerit truncus illius, 9 ad odorem aquae germinabit et faciet comam quasi cum primum plantatum est. 10 Homo vero cum mortuus fuerit et nudatus atque consumptus, ubi, quaeso, est? 11 Quomodo si recedant aquae de mari et fluvius vacuefactus arescat, 12 sic homo cum dormierit non resurget. Donec adteratur caelum non evigilabit nec consurget de somno suo.

13 "Quis mihi hoc tribuat, ut in inferno protegas me et abscondas me donec pertranseat furor tuus et constituas mihi tempus in quo recorderis mei? 14 Putasne, mortuus homo rursum vivet? Cunctis diebus quibus nunc milito expecto donec veniat inmutatio mea. 15 Vocabis me, et ego respondebo tibi. Operi manuum tuarum porriges dexteram. 16 Tu quidem gressus meos dinumerasti, sed parces peccatis meis. 17 Signasti quasi in sacculo delicta mea sed curasti iniquitatem meam.

18 "Mons cadens defluit, et saxum transfertur de loco suo. 19 Lapides excavant aquae, et adluvione paulatim terra consumitur, et homines ergo similiter perdes. 20 Roborasti eum paululum ut in perpetuum pertransiret. Inmutabis faciem eius et emittes eum. 21 Sive nobiles fuerint filii eius sive ignobiles non intelleget. 22 Attamen caro eius dum vivet dolebit, et anima illius super semet ipso lugebit."

7 "A tree hath hope. If it be cut, it groweth green again, and the boughs thereof sprout. 8 If its root be old in the earth and its stock be dead in the dust, 9 at the scent of water it shall spring and bring forth leaves as when it was first planted. 10 But man when he shall be dead and stripped and consumed, I pray you, where is he? 11 As if the waters should depart out of the sea and an emptied river should be dried up, 12 so man when he is fallen asleep shall not rise again. Till the heavens be broken he shall not awake nor rise up out of his sleep.

13 "Who will grant me this, that thou mayst protect me in hell and hide me till thy wrath pass and appoint me a time when thou wilt remember me? 14 Shall man that is dead, thinkest thou, live again? All the days in which I am now in warfare I expect until my change come. 15 Thou shalt call me, and I will answer thee. To the work of thy hands thou shalt reach out thy right hand. 16 Thou indeed hast numbered my steps, but *spare* my sins. 17 Thou hast sealed up my offences as it were in a bag but hast cured my iniquity.

18 "A mountain falling cometh to nought, and a rock is removed out of its place. 19 Waters wear away the stones, and with inundation the ground by little and little is washed away, so in like manner thou shalt destroy *man.* 20 Thou hast strengthened him for a little while that he may pass away for ever. Thou shalt change his face and shalt send him away. 21 Whether his children come to honour or dishonour he shall not understand. 22 But yet his flesh while he shall live shall have pain, and his soul shall mourn over him."

Caput 15

Respondens autem Eliphaz, Themanites, dixit, 2 "Numquid sapiens respondebit quasi in ventum loquens et implebit ardore stomachum suum? 3 Arguis verbis eum qui non est aequalis tibi, et loqueris quod tibi non expedit. 4 Quantum in te est evacuasti timorem et tulisti preces coram Deo, 5 docuit enim iniquitas tua os tuum, et imitaris linguam blasphemantium. 6 Condemnabit te os tuum, et non ego, et labia tua respondebunt tibi.

7 "Numquid primus homo tu natus es, et ante colles formatus? 8 Numquid consilium Dei audisti, et inferior te erit eius sapientia? 9 Quid nosti quod ignoremus? Quid intellegis quod nesciamus? 10 Et senes et antiqui sunt in nobis, multo vetustiores quam patres tui. 11 Numquid grande est ut consoletur te Deus? Sed verba tua prava hoc prohibent. 12 Quid te elevat cor tuum, et quasi magna cogitans adtonitos habes oculos? 13 Quid tumet contra Deum spiritus tuus ut proferas de ore tuo huiuscemodi sermones? 14 Quid est homo ut inmaculatus sit et ut iustus appareat natus de mu-

Chapter 15

Eliphaz returns to the charge against Job and describes the wretched state of the wicked.

And Eliphaz, the Temanite, answered and said, 2 "Will a wise man answer as if he were speaking in the wind and fill his stomach with burning heat? 3 Thou reprovest him by words who is not equal to thee, and thou speakest that which is not good for thee. 4 As much as is in thee thou hast made void fear and hast taken away prayers from before God, 5 for thy iniquity hath taught thy mouth, and thou imitatest the tongue of blasphemers. 6 Thy own mouth shall condemn thee, and not I, and thy own lips shall answer thee.

7 "Art thou the first man that was born, *or* wast thou made before the hills? 8 Hast thou heard God's counsel, and shall his wisdom be inferior to thee? 9 What knowest thou that we are ignorant of? What dost thou understand that we know not? 10 There are with us also aged and ancient men, much elder than thy fathers. 11 Is it a great matter that God should comfort thee? But thy wicked words hinder this. 12 Why doth thy heart elevate thee, and why dost thou stare with thy eyes as if they were thinking great things? 13 Why doth thy spirit swell against God to utter such words out of thy mouth? 14 What is man that he should be without spot and he that is born of a woman that he should appear

liere? 15 Ecce: inter sanctos eius nemo inmutabilis, et caeli non sunt mundi in conspectu eius. 16 Quanto magis abominabilis et inutilis homo qui bibit quasi aquam iniquitatem? 17 "Ostendam tibi; audi me; quod vidi narrabo tibi. 18 Sapientes confitentur et non abscondunt patres suos 19 quibus solis data est terra, et non transivit alienus per eos. 20 Cunctis diebus suis impius superbit, et numerus annorum incertus est tyrannidis eius. 21 Sonitus terroris semper in auribus illius, et cum pax sit ille semper insidias suspicatur. 22 Non credit quod reverti possit de tenebris ad lucem, circumspectans undique gladium. 23 Cum se moverit ad quaerendum panem novit quod paratus sit in manu eius tenebrarum dies. 24 Terrebit eum tribulatio, et angustia vallabit eum sicut regem qui praeparatur ad proelium, 25 tetendit enim adversus Deum manum suam et contra Omnipotentem roboratus est. 26 Cucurrit adversus eum erecto collo et pingui cervice armatus est. 27 Operuit faciem eius crassitudo, et de lateribus eius arvina dependet. 28 Habitavit in civitatibus desolatis et in domibus desertis quae in tumulos sunt redactae. 29 Non ditabitur, nec perseverabit substantia eius, nec mittet in terra radicem suam. 30 Non recedet de tenebris. Ramos eius arefaciet flamma, et auferetur spiritu oris sui. 31 Non credet frustra errore deceptus quod aliquo pretio redimendus sit. 32 Antequam dies eius impleantur peribit, et manus eius arescent. 33 Laedetur quasi vinea in primo flore botrus eius et quasi oliva florem suum, 34 congregatio enim

just? 15 Behold: among his saints none is unchangeable, and the heavens are not pure in his sight. 16 How much more is man abominable and unprofitable who drinketh iniquity like water? 17 "I will shew thee; hear me, *and* I will tell thee what I have seen. 18 Wise men confess and hide not their fathers 19 to whom alone the earth was given, and no stranger hath passed among them. 20 The wicked man is proud all his days, and the number of the years of his tyranny is uncertain. 21 The sound of dread is always in his ears, and when there is peace he always suspecteth treason. 22 He believeth not that he may return from darkness to light, looking round about for the sword on every side. 23 When he moveth himself to seek bread he knoweth that the day of darkness is ready at his hand. 24 Tribulation shall terrify him, and distress shall surround him as a king that is prepared for the battle, 25 for he hath stretched out his hand against God and hath strengthened himself against the Almighty. 26 He hath run against him with his neck raised up and is armed with a fat neck. 27 Fatness hath covered his face, and the fat hangeth down on his sides. 28 He hath dwelt in desolate cities and in desert houses that are reduced into heaps. 29 He shall not be enriched, neither shall his substance continue, neither shall he push his root in the earth. 30 He shall not depart out of darkness. The flame shall dry up his branches, and he shall be taken away by the breath of his own month. 31 He shall not believe being vainly deceived by error that he may be redeemed with any price. 32 Before his days be full he shall perish, and his hands shall wither away. 33 He shall be blasted as a vine when its grapes are in the first flower and as an olive tree that casteth its flower, 34 for the congregation of the

hypocritae sterilis et ignis devorabit tabernacula eorum qui munera libenter accipiunt. 35 Concepit dolorem et peperit iniquitatem, et uterus eius praeparat dolos."

Caput 16

Respondens autem Iob dixit, 2 "Audivi frequenter talia; consolatores onerosi omnes vos estis. 3 Numquid habebunt finem verba ventosa? Aut aliquid tibi molestum est si loquaris? 4 Poteram et ego similia vestri loqui, atque utinam esset anima vestra pro anima mea. 5 Consolarer et ego vos sermonibus et moverem caput meum super vos. 6 Roborarem vos ore meo et moverem labia mea quasi parcens vobis.

7 "Sed quid agam? Si locutus fuero, non quiescet dolor meus, et si tacuero, non recedet a me. 8 Nunc autem oppressit me dolor meus, et in nihili redacti sunt omnes artus mei. 9 Rugae meae testimonium dicunt contra me, et suscitatur falsiloquus adversus faciem meam contradicens mihi.

hypocrite is barren and fire shall devour their tabernacles who love to take bribes. 35 He hath conceived sorrow and hath brought forth iniquity, and his womb prepareth deceits."

Chapter 16

Job expostulates with his friends and appeals to the judgment of God.

Then Job answered and said, 2 "I have often heard such things as these; you are all troublesome comforters. 3 Shall windy words have *no* end? Or is it any trouble to thee to speak? 4 I also could speak like you, and would God your soul were for my soul. 5 I would comfort you also with words and would wag my head over you. 6 I would strengthen you with my mouth and would move my lips as sparing you.

7 "But what shall I do? If I speak, my pain will not rest, and if I hold my peace, it will not depart from me. 8 But now my sorrow hath oppressed me, and all my limbs are brought to nothing. 9 My wrinkles bear witness against me, and a false speaker riseth up against my face contradicting me.

10 "Collegit furorem suum in me et comminans mihi infremuit contra me dentibus suis. Hostis meus terribilibus oculis me intuitus est. 11 Aperuerunt super me ora sua, et exprobrantes percusserunt maxillam meam. Satiati sunt poenis meis. 12 Conclusit me Deus apud iniquum et manibus impiorum me tradidit. 13 Ego ille quondam opulentus repente contritus sum. Tenuit cervicem meam; confregit me et posuit me sibi quasi in signum. 14 Circumdedit me lanceis suis; convulneravit lumbos meos; non pepercit et effudit in terra viscera mea. 15 Concidit me vulnere super vulnus. Inruit in me quasi gigans.

16 "Saccum consui super cutem meam et operui cinere carnem meam. 17 Facies mea intumuit a fletu, et palpebrae meae caligaverunt. 18 Haec passus sum absque iniquitate manus meae cum haberem mundas ad Deum preces.

19 "Terra, ne operias sanguinem meum, neque inveniat locum in te latendi clamor meus, 20 ecce enim: in caelo testis meus, et conscius meus in excelsis. 21 Verbosi amici mei. Ad Deum stillat oculus meus. 22 Atque utinam sic iudicaretur vir cum Deo quomodo iudicatur filius hominis cum collega suo! 23 Ecce enim: breves anni transeunt, et semitam per quam non revertar ambulo."

10 "He hath gathered together his fury against me and threatening me he hath gnashed with his teeth upon me. My enemy hath beheld me with terrible eyes. 11 They have opened their mouths upon me, and reproaching me they have struck me on the cheek. They are filled with my pains. 12 God hath shut me up with the unjust man and hath delivered me into the hands of the wicked. 13 I that was formerly *so* wealthy am all on a sudden broken to pieces. He hath taken me by my neck; he hath broken me and hath set me up *to be* his mark. 14 He hath compassed me round about with his lances; he hath wounded my loins; he hath not spared and hath poured out my bowels on the earth. 15 He hath torn me with wound upon wound. He hath rushed in upon me like a giant.

16 "I have sowed sackcloth upon my skin and have covered my flesh with ashes. 17 My face is swollen with weeping, and my eyelids are dim. 18 These things have I suffered without the iniquity of my hand when I offered pure prayers to God.

19 "O earth, cover not thou my blood, neither let my cry find a hiding place in thee, 20 for behold: my witness is in heaven, and he that knoweth my conscience is on high. 21 My friends are full of words. My eye poureth out tears to God. 22 And O that a man might so be judged with God as the son of man is judged with his companion! 23 For behold: short years pass away, and I am walking in a path by which I shall not return."

Caput 17

"Spiritus meus adtenuabitur; dies mei breviabuntur, et solum mihi superest sepulchrum. 2 Non peccavi, et in amaritudinibus moratur oculus meus. 3 Libera me, et pone me iuxta te, et cuiusvis manus pugnet contra me. 4 Cor eorum longe fecisti a disciplina, et propterea non exaltabuntur.

5 "Praedam pollicetur sociis, et oculi filiorum eius deficient. 6 Posuit me quasi in proverbium vulgi, et exemplum sum coram eis. 7 Caligavit ab indignatione oculus meus, et membra mea quasi in nihili redacta sunt. 8 Stupebunt iusti super hoc, et innocens contra hypocritam suscitabitur. 9 Et tenebit iustus viam suam, et mundis manibus addet fortitudinem. 10 Igitur vos omnes convertimini, et venite, et non inveniam in vobis ullum sapientem.

11 "Dies mei transierunt. Cogitationes meae dissipatae sunt, torquentes cor meum. 12 Noctem verterunt in diem, et rursum post tenebras spero lucem. 13 Si sustinuero, infernus domus mea est, et in tenebris stravi lectulum meum. 14 Putredini dixi, 'Pater meus es,' 'Mater mea et soror mea,' vermibus. 15 Ubi est ergo nunc praestolatio mea, et patientiam

Chapter 17

"My spirit shall be wasted; my days shall be shortened, and only the grave remaineth for me. 2 I have not sinned, and my eye abideth in bitterness. 3 Deliver me, *O Lord,* and set me beside thee, and let any man's hand fight against me. 4 Thou hast set their heart far from understanding, *therefore* they shall not be exalted.

5 "He promiseth a prey to his companions, and the eyes of his children shall fail. 6 He hath made me as it were a byword of the people, and I am an example before them. 7 My eye is dim through indignation, and my limbs are brought as it were to nothing. 8 The just shall be astonished at this, and the innocent shall be raised up against the hypocrite. 9 And the just man shall hold on his way, and *he that hath clean hands shall be stronger and stronger.* 10 Wherefore be you all converted, and come, and I shall not find among you any wise man.

11 "My days have passed away. My thoughts are dissipated, tormenting my heart. 12 They have turned night into day, and after darkness I hope for light again. 13 If I wait, hell is my house, and I have made my bed in darkness. 14 I have said to rottenness, 'Thou art my father,' to worms, 'My mother and my sister.' 15 Where is now then my expecta-

meam quis considerat? 16 In profundissimum infernum descendent omnia mea: putasne saltim ibi erit requies mihi?"

Caput 18

Respondens autem Baldad, Suites, dixit, 2 "Usque ad quem finem verba iactabitis? Intellegite prius, et sic loquamur. 3 Quare reputati sumus ut iumenta et sorduimus coram vobis? 4 Qui perdis animam tuam in furore tuo, numquid propter te derelinquetur terra, et transferentur rupes de loco suo? 5 Nonne lux impii extinguetur nec splendebit flamma ignis eius? 6 Lux obtenebrescet in tabernaculo illius, et lucerna quae super eum est extinguetur. 7 Artabuntur gressus virtutis eius, et praecipitabit eum consilium suum, 8 inmisit enim in rete pedes suos et in maculis eius ambulat. 9 Tenebitur planta illius laqueo, et exardescet contra eum sitis. 10 Abscondita est in terra pedica eius et decipula illius super semitam. 11 Undique terrebunt eum formidines et involvent pedes eius.

12 "Adtenuetur fame robur eius, et inedia invadat costas illius. 13 Devoret pulchritudinem cutis eius. Consumat bra-

tion, and who considereth my patience? 16 All that I have shall go down into the deepest pit: thinkest thou that there at least I shall have rest?"

Chapter 18

Bildad again reproves Job and describes the miseries of the wicked.

Then Bildad, the Shuhite, answered and said, 2 "How long will you throw out words? Understand first, and so let us speak. 3 Why are we reputed as beasts and counted vile before you? 4 Thou that destroyest thy soul in thy fury, shall the earth be forsaken for thee, and shall rocks be removed out of their place? 5 Shall not the light of the wicked be extinguished and the flame of his fire not shine? 6 The light shall be dark in his tabernacle, and the lamp that is over him shall be put out. 7 The step of his strength shall be straitened, and his own counsel shall cast him down headlong, 8 for he hath thrust his feet into a net and walketh in its meshes. 9 The sole of his foot shall be held in a snare, and thirst shall burn against him. 10 A gin is hidden for him in the earth and his trap upon the path. 11 Fears shall terrify him on every side and shall entangle his feet.

12 "Let his strength be wasted with famine, and let hunger invade his ribs. 13 Let it devour the beauty of his skin. Let

chia illius primogenita mors. 14 Avellatur de tabernaculo suo fiducia eius, et calcet super eum quasi rex interitus. 15 Habitent in tabernaculo illius socii eius qui non est. Aspergatur in tabernaculo eius sulphur. 16 Deorsum radices eius siccentur sursum autem adteratur messis eius. 17 Memoria illius pereat de terra, et non celebretur nomen eius in plateis. 18 Expellet eum de luce in tenebras et de orbe transferet eum. 19 Non erit semen eius neque progenies in populo suo nec ullae reliquiae in regionibus eius. 20 In die eius stupebunt novissimi, et primos invadet horror. 21 Haec sunt ergo tabernacula iniqui et iste locus eius qui ignorat Deum."

Caput 19

Respondens autem Iob dixit, 2 "Usquequo adfligitis animam meam et adteritis me sermonibus? 3 En: decies confunditis me et non erubescitis opprimentes me, 4 nempe et si ignoravi, mecum erit ignorantia mea. 5 At vos contra me erigimini et arguitis me obprobriis meis. 6 Saltim nunc intelle-

the firstborn death consume his arms. 14 Let his confidence be rooted out of his tabernacle, and let destruction tread upon him like a king. 15 Let the companions of him that is not dwell in his tabernacle. Let brimstone be sprinkled in his tent. 16 Let his roots be dried up beneath and his harvest destroyed above. 17 Let the memory of him perish from the earth, and let not his name be renowned in the streets. 18 He shall drive him out of light into darkness and shall remove him out of the world. 19 His seed shall not subsist nor his offspring among his people nor any remnants in his country. 20 They that come after him shall be astonished at his day, and horror shall fall upon them that went before. 21 These then are the tabernacles of the wicked and this the place of him that knoweth not God."

Chapter 19

Job complains of the cruelty of his friends. He describes his
own sufferings and his belief of a future resurrection.

Then Job answered and said, 2 "How long do you afflict my soul and break me in pieces with words? 3 Behold: these ten times you confound me and are not ashamed to oppress me, 4 for *if* I have been ignorant, my ignorance shall be with me. 5 But you have set yourselves up against me and reprove me with my reproaches. 6 At least now understand

gite quia Deus non aequo iudicio adflixerit me et flagellis suis me cinxerit. 7 Ecce: clamabo vim patiens, et nemo audiet; vociferabor, et non est qui iudicet.

8 "Semitam meam circumsepsit, et transire non possum, et in calle meo tenebras posuit. 9 Spoliavit me gloria mea et abstulit coronam de capite meo. 10 Destruxit me undique, et pereo, et quasi evulsae arbori abstulit spem meam. 11 Iratus est contra me furor eius, et sic me habuit quasi hostem suum. 12 Simul venerunt latrones eius et fecerunt sibi viam per me et obsederunt in gyro tabernaculum meum. 13 Fratres meos longe fecit a me, et noti mei quasi alieni recesserunt a me.

14 "Dereliquerunt me propinqui mei, et qui me noverant obliti sunt mei. 15 Inquilini domus meae et ancillae meae sicut alienum habuerunt me, et quasi peregrinus fui in oculis eorum. 16 Servum meum vocavi, et non respondit; ore proprio deprecabar illum. 17 Halitum meum exhorruit uxor mea, et orabam filios uteri mei. 18 Stulti quoque despiciebant me, et cum ab eis recessissem detrahebant mihi. 19 Abominati sunt me quondam consiliarii mei, et quem maxime diligebam aversatus est me. 20 Pelli meae, consumptis carnibus, adhesit os meum, et derelicta sunt tantummodo labia circa dentes meos.

21 "Miseremini mei. Miseremini mei, saltim vos, amici mei, quia manus Domini tetigit me. 22 Quare persequimini me sicut Deus et carnibus meis saturamini? 23 Quis mihi tribuat ut scribantur sermones mei? Quis mihi det ut exaren-

that God hath not afflicted me with an equal judgment and compassed me with his scourges. 7 Behold: I cry suffering violence, and no one will hear; I shall cry aloud, and there is none to judge.

8 "He hath hedged in my path round about, and I cannot pass, and in my way he hath set darkness. 9 He hath stripped me of my glory and hath taken the crown from my head. 10 He hath destroyed me on every side, and I am lost, and he hath taken away my hope as from a tree that is plucked up. 11 His wrath is kindled against me, and he hath counted me as his enemy. 12 His troops have come together and have made themselves a way by me and have besieged my tabernacle round about. 13 He hath put my brethren far from me, and my acquaintance like strangers have departed from me.

14 "My kinsmen have forsaken me, and they that knew me have forgotten me. 15 They that dwelt in my house and my maidservants have counted me a stranger, and I have been like an alien in their eyes. 16 I called my servant, and he gave me no answer; I entreated him with my own mouth. 17 My wife hath abhorred my breath, and I entreated the children of my womb. 18 Even fools despise me, and when I was gone from them they spoke against me. 19 They that were sometime my counsellors have abhorred me, and he whom I love most is turned against me. 20 The flesh being consumed, my bone hath cleaved to my skin, and nothing but lips are left about my teeth.

21 "Have pity on me. Have pity on me, at least you, my friends, because the hand of the Lord hath touched me. 22 Why do you persecute me as God and glut yourselves with my flesh? 23 Who will grant me that my words may be written? Who will grant me that they may be marked down in a

tur in libro 24 stilo ferreo et plumbi lammina, vel celte sculpantur in silice? 25 Scio enim quod Redemptor meus vivat, et in novissimo die de terra surrecturus sim. 26 Et rursum circumdabor pelle mea, et in carne mea videbo Deum 27 quem visurus sum ego ipse, et oculi mei conspecturi sunt et non alius. Reposita est haec spes mea in sinu meo. 28 "Quare ergo nunc dicitis, 'Persequamur eum, et radicem verbi inveniamus contra eum?' 29 Fugite ergo a facie gladii, quoniam ultor iniquitatum gladius est, et scitote esse iudicium."

Caput 20

Respondens autem Sophar, Naamathites, dixit, 2 "Idcirco cogitationes meae variae succedunt sibi, et mens in diversa rapitur. 3 Doctrinam qua me arguis audiam, et spiritus intellegentiae meae respondebit mihi. 4 Hoc scio a principio, ex quo positus est homo super terram, 5 quod laus impiorum brevis sit, et gaudium hypocritae ad instar puncti. 6 Si ascenderit usque ad caelum superbia eius et caput eius nu-

book 24 with an iron pen and in a plate of lead, or else be graven with an instrument in flint stone? 25 For I know that my Redeemer liveth, and in the last day I shall rise out of the earth. 26 And I shall be clothed again with my skin, and in my flesh I will see *my* God 27 whom I myself shall see, and my eyes shall behold and not another. This my hope is laid up in my bosom.

28 "Why then do you say now, 'Let us persecute him, and let us find occasion of word against him?' 29 Flee then from the face of the sword, for the sword is the revenger of iniquities, and know ye that there is judgment."

Chapter 20

Zophar declares the shortness of the prosperity of the wicked and their sudden downfall.

Then Zophar, the Naamathite, answered and said, 2 "Therefore various thoughts succeed one another *in me,* and my mind is hurried away to different things. 3 The doctrine with which thou reprovest me I will hear, and the spirit of my understanding shall answer for me. 4 This I know from the beginning, since man was placed upon the earth, 5 that the praise of the wicked is short, and the joy of the hypocrite but for a moment. 6 If his pride mount up even to

bes tetigerit, 7 quasi sterquilinium in fine perdetur, et qui eum viderant dicent, 'Ubi est?' 8 Velut somnium avolans non invenietur. Transiet sicut visio nocturna. 9 Oculus qui eum viderat non videbit, neque ultra intuebitur eum locus suus. 10 "Filii eius adterentur egestate, et manus illius reddent ei dolorem suum. 11 Ossa eius implebuntur vitiis adulescentiae eius, et cum eo in pulverem dormient, 12 cum enim dulce fuerit in ore eius malum abscondet illud sub lingua sua. 13 Parcet illi et non derelinquet illud et celabit in gutture suo. 14 Panis eius in utero illius vertetur in fel aspidum intrinsecus. 15 Divitias quas devoravit evomet, et de ventre illius extrahet eas Deus. 16 Caput aspidum suget, et occidet eum lingua viperae. 17 Non videat rivulos fluminis, torrentes mellis et butyri. 18 Luet quae fecit omnia nec tamen consumetur; iuxta multitudinem adinventionum suarum sic et sustinebit 19 quoniam confringens nudavit pauperes. Domum rapuit et non aedificavit eam.

20 "Nec est satiatus venter eius, et cum habuerit quae cupierat possidere non poterit. 21 Non remansit de cibo eius, et propterea nihil permanebit de bonis eius. 22 Cum satiatus fuerit artabitur. Aestuabit, et omnis dolor inruet super eum. 23 Utinam impleatur venter eius ut emittat in eum iram furoris sui et pluat super illum bellum suum. 24 Fugiet arma ferrea et inruet in arcum aereum. 25 Eductus et egrediens de

heaven and his head touch the clouds, 7 in the end he shall be destroyed like a dunghill, and they that had seen him shall say, 'Where is he?' 8 As a dream that fleeth away he shall not be found. He shall pass as a vision of the night. 9 The *eyes* that had seen him shall see him *no more,* neither shall his place any more behold him.

10 "His children shall be oppressed with want, and his hands shall render him his sorrow. 11 His bones shall be filled with the vices of his youth, and they shall sleep with him in the dust, 12 for when evil shall be sweet in his mouth he will hide it under his tongue. 13 He will spare it and not leave it and will hide it in his throat. 14 His bread in his belly shall be turned into the gall of asps within him. 15 The riches which he hath swallowed he shall vomit up, and God shall draw them out of his belly. 16 He shall suck the head of asps, and the viper's tongue shall kill him. 17 Let him not see the streams of the river, the brooks of honey and of butter. 18 He shall be punished for all that he did and yet shall not be consumed; according to the multitude of his devices so also shall he suffer 19 because he broke in and stripped the poor. He hath violently taken away a house which he did not build.

20 "And yet his belly was not filled, and when he hath the things he coveted he shall not be able to possess them. 21 There was nothing left of his meat, and therefore nothing shall continue of his goods. 22 When he shall be filled he shall be straitened. He shall burn, and every sorrow shall fall upon him. 23 May his belly be filled that *God* may send forth the wrath of his indignation upon him and rain down his war upon him. 24 He shall flee from weapons of iron and shall fall upon a bow of brass. 25 The sword is drawn out and cometh

vagina sua et fulgurans in amaritudine sua. Vadent et venient super eum horribiles. 26 "Omnes tenebrae absconditae sunt in occultis eius. Devorabit eum ignis qui non succenditur. Adfligetur relictus in tabernaculo suo. 27 Revelabunt caeli iniquitatem eius, et terra consurget adversus eum. 28 Apertum erit germen domus illius. Detrahetur in die furoris Dei. 29 "Haec est pars hominis impii a Deo et hereditas verborum eius a Domino."

Caput 21

Respondens autem Iob dixit, 2 "Audite, quaeso, sermones meos, et agite paenitentiam. 3 Sustinete me ut et ego loquar, et post mea, si videbitur, verba ridete. 4 Numquid contra hominem disputatio mea est ut merito non debeam contristari? 5 Adtendite me, et obstupescite, et superponite digitum ori vestro. 6 Et ego, quando recordatus fuero, pertimesco, et concutit carnem meam tremor.

7 "Quare ergo impii vivunt, sublevati sunt confortatique divitiis? 8 Semen eorum permanet coram eis, propinquorum

forth from its scabbard and glittereth in his bitterness. The terrible ones shall go and come upon him. 26 "All darkness is hid in his secret places. A fire that is not kindled shall devour him. He shall be afflicted when left in his tabernacle. 27 The heavens shall reveal his iniquity, and the earth shall rise up against him. 28 The offspring of his house shall be exposed. He shall be pulled down in the day of God's wrath.

29 "This is the portion of a wicked man from God and the inheritance of his doings from the Lord."

Chapter 21

Job shews that the wicked often prosper in this world even to the end of their life but that their judgment is in another world.

Then Job answered and said, 2 "Hear, I beseech you, my words, and do penance. 3 Suffer me, *and* I will speak, and after, if you please, laugh at my words. 4 Is my debate against man that I should not have just reason to be troubled? 5 Hearken to me, and be astonished, and lay your finger on your mouth. 6 As for me, when I remember, I am afraid, and trembling taketh hold on my flesh.

7 "Why then do the wicked live, are they advanced and strengthened with riches? 8 Their seed continueth before

turba et nepotum in conspectu eorum. 9 Domus eorum securae sunt et pacatae, et non est virga Dei super illos. 10 Bos eorum concepit et non abortivit; vacca peperit et non est privata fetu suo. 11 Egrediuntur quasi greges parvuli eorum, et infantes eorum exultant lusibus. 12 Tenent tympanum et citharam et gaudent ad sonitum organi. 13 Ducunt in bonis dies suos, et in puncto ad inferna descendunt 14 qui dixerunt Deo, 'Recede a nobis; scientiam viarum tuarum nolumus.' 15 "Quis est Omnipotens ut serviamus ei? Et quid nobis prodest si oraverimus illum? 16 Verumtamen quia non sunt in manu eorum bona sua, consilium impiorum longe sit a me. 17 Quotiens lucerna impiorum extinguetur et superveniet eis inundatio? Et dolores dividet furoris sui. 18 Erunt sicut paleae ante faciem venti et sicut favilla quam turbo dispergit. 19 Deus servabit filiis illius dolorem patris, et cum reddiderit tunc sciet. 20 Videbunt oculi eius interfectionem suam, et de furore Omnipotentis bibet, 21 quid enim ad eum pertinet de domo sua post se, et si numerus mensuum eius dimidietur?

22 "Numquid Deum quispiam docebit scientiam qui excelsos iudicat? 23 Iste moritur robustus et sanus, dives et felix. 24 Viscera eius plena sunt adipe, et medullis ossa illius inrigantur, 25 alius vero moritur in amaritudine animae absque ullis opibus, 26 et tamen simul in pulverem dormient, et vermes operient eos.

27 "Certe novi cogitationes vestras et sententias contra me iniquas, 28 dicitis enim, 'Ubi est domus principis? Et

them, a multitude of kinsmen and of children's children in their sight. 9 Their houses are secure and peaceable, and the rod of God is not upon them. 10 Their cattle have conceived and failed not; their cow has calved and is not deprived of her fruit. 11 Their little ones go out like a flock, and their children dance *and play.* 12 They take the timbrel and the harp and rejoice at the sound of the organ. 13 They spend their days in wealth, and in a moment they go down to hell 14 who have said to God, 'Depart from us; we desire not the knowledge of thy ways.'

15 "Who is the Almighty that we should serve him? And what doth it profit us if we pray to him? 16 Yet because their good things are not in their hand, may the counsel of the wicked be far from me. 17 How often shall the lamp of the wicked be put out and a deluge come upon them? And he shall distribute the sorrows of his wrath. 18 They shall be as chaff before the face of the wind and as ashes which the whirlwind scattereth. 19 God shall lay up the sorrow of the father for his children, and when he shall repay it then shall he know. 20 His eyes shall see his own destruction, and he shall drink of the wrath of the Almighty, 21 for what is it to him *what befalleth* his house after him, and if the number of his months be diminished by one half?

22 "Shall any one teach God knowledge who judgeth those that are high? 23 One man dieth strong and hale, rich and happy. 24 His bowels are full of fat, and his bones are moistened with marrow, 25 but another dieth in bitterness of soul without any riches, 26 and yet they shall sleep together in the dust, and worms shall cover them.

27 "Surely I know your thoughts and your unjust judgments against me, 28 for you say, 'Where is the house of the

ubi tabernacula impiorum?' 29 Interrogate quemlibet de via-
toribus, et haec eadem eum intellegere cognoscetis 30 quia
in diem perditionis servatur malus, et ad diem furoris ducetur. 31 Quis arguet coram eo viam eius? Et quae fecit quis
reddet illi? 32 Ipse ad sepulchra ducetur et in congerie mortuorum vigilabit. 33 Dulcis fuit glareis Cocyti, et post se omnem hominem trahet, et ante se innumerabiles. 34 Quomodo
igitur consolamini me frustra, cum responsio vestra repug-
nare ostensa sit veritati?"

Caput 22

Respondens autem Eliphaz, Themanites, dixit, 2 "Numquid Deo conparari potest homo, etiam cum perfectae fuerit scientiae? 3 Quid prodest Deo si iustus fueris? Aut quid ei
confers si inmaculata fuerit via tua? 4 Numquid timens arguet te et veniet tecum in iudicium 5 et non propter malitiam tuam plurimam et infinitas iniquitates tuas? 6 Abstulisti
enim pignus fratrum tuorum sine causa et nudos spoliasti

prince? And where are the dwelling places of the wicked?'
29 Ask any one of them that go by the way, and you shall perceive that he knoweth these same things 30 because the
wicked man is reserved to the day of destruction, and he
shall be brought to the day of wrath. 31 Who shall reprove
his way to his face? And who shall repay him what he hath
done? 32 He shall be brought to the graves and shall watch in
the heap of the dead. 33 He hath been acceptable to the
gravel of Cocytus, and he shall draw every man after him,
and there are innumerable before him. 34 How then do ye
comfort me in vain, whereas your answer is shewn to be re-
pugnant to truth?"

Chapter 22

*Eliphaz falsely imputes many crimes to Job but promises
him prosperity if he will repent.*

Then Eliphaz, the Temanite, answered and said, 2 "Can
man be compared with God, even though he were of perfect
knowledge? 3 What doth it profit God if thou be just? Or
what dost thou give him if thy way be unspotted? 4 Shall
he reprove thee for fear and come with thee into judgment 5 and not for thy manifold wickedness and thy infinite
iniquities? 6 For thou hast taken away the pledge of thy
brethren without cause and stripped the naked of their

vestibus. 7 Aquam lasso non dedisti, et esurienti subtraxisti panem. 8 In fortitudine brachii tui possidebas terram, et potentissimus obtinebas eam. 9 Viduas dimisisti vacuas, et lacertos pupillorum comminuisti. 10 Propterea circumdatus es laqueis, et conturbat te formido subita.

11 "Et putabas te tenebras non visurum et impetu aquarum inundantium non oppressurum iri? 12 An non cogitas quod Deus excelsior caelo et super stellarum verticem sublimetur? 13 Et dicis, 'Quid enim novit Deus?' et, 'Quasi per caliginem iudicat. 14 Nubes latibulum eius, nec nostra considerat, et circa cardines caeli perambulat.' 15 Numquid semitam saeculorum custodire cupis quam calcaverunt viri iniqui 16 qui sublati sunt ante tempus suum et fluvius subvertit fundamentum eorum, 17 qui dicebant Deo, 'Recede a nobis,' et quasi nihil posset facere Omnipotens aestimabant eum, 18 cum ille implesset domos eorum bonis quorum sententia procul sit a me? 19 Videbunt iusti et laetabuntur, et innocens subsannabit eos. 20 Nonne succisa est erectio eorum, et reliquias eorum devoravit ignis?

21 "Adquiesce igitur ei, et habeto pacem, et per haec habebis fructus optimos. 22 Suscipe ex ore illius legem, et pone sermones eius in corde tuo. 23 Si reversus fueris ad Omnipotentem, aedificaberis et longe facies iniquitatem a tabernaculo tuo. 24 Dabit pro terra silicem et pro silice torrentes aureos. 25 Eritque Omnipotens contra hostes tuos, et argen-

clothing. 7 Thou hast not given water to the weary; *thou* hast withdrawn bread from the hungry. 8 In the strength of thy arm thou didst possess the land, and being the most mighty thou holdest it. 9 Thou hast sent widows away empty, and the arms of the fatherless thou hast broken in pieces. 10 Therefore art thou surrounded with snares, and sudden fear troubleth thee.

11 "And didst thou think that thou shouldst not see darkness and that thou shouldst not be covered with the violence of overflowing waters? 12 Dost not thou think that God is higher than heaven and is elevated above the height of the stars? 13 And thou sayst, *'What* doth God know?' and, 'He judgeth as it were through a mist. 14 The clouds are his covert, and he doth not consider our things, and he walketh about the poles of heaven.' 15 Dost thou desire to keep the path of ages which wicked men have trodden 16 who were taken away before their time and a flood hath overthrown their foundation, 17 who said to God, 'Depart from us,' and looked upon the Almighty as if he could do nothing, 18 whereas he had filled their houses with good things whose way of thinking be far from me? 19 The just shall see and shall rejoice, and the innocent shall laugh them to scorn. 20 Is not their exaltation cut down, and hath not fire devoured the remnants of them?

21 "Submit thyself then to him, and be at peace, and thereby thou shalt have the best fruits. 22 Receive the law of his mouth, and lay up his words in thy heart. 23 If thou wilt return to the Almighty, thou shalt be built up and shalt put away iniquity far from thy tabernacle. 24 He shall give for earth flint and for flint torrents of gold. 25 And the Almighty

tum coacervabitur tibi. 26 Tunc super Omnipotentem deliciis afflues et elevabis ad Deum faciem tuam. 27 Rogabis eum, et exaudiet te, et vota tua reddes. 28 Decernes rem, et veniet tibi, et in viis tuis splendebit lumen, 29 qui enim humiliatus fuerit erit in gloria, et qui inclinaverit oculos suos, ipse salvabitur. 30 Salvabitur innocens, salvabitur autem in munditia manuum suarum."

Caput 23

Respondens autem Iob dixit, 2 "Nunc quoque in amaritudine est sermo meus, et manus plagae meae adgravata est super gemitum meum. 3 Quis mihi tribuat ut cognoscam et inveniam illum et veniam usque ad solium eius? 4 Ponam coram eo iudicium et os meum replebo increpationibus 5 ut sciam verba quae mihi respondeat et intellegam quid loquatur mihi. 6 Nolo multa fortitudine contendat mecum nec magnitudinis suae mole me premat. 7 Proponat aequitatem contra me, et perveniat ad victoriam iudicium meum.

8 "Si ad orientem iero, non apparet; si ad occidentem, non intellegam eum. 9 Si ad sinistram, quid agam? Non adpre-

shall be against thy enemies, and silver shall be heaped together for thee. 26 Then shalt thou abound in delights in the Almighty and shalt lift up thy face to God. 27 Thou shalt pray to him, and he will hear thee, and thou shalt pay vows. 28 Thou shalt decree a thing, and it shall come to thee, and light shall shine in thy ways, 29 for he that hath been humbled shall be in glory, and he that shall bow down his eyes, he shall be saved. 30 The innocent shall be saved, and he shall be saved by the cleanness of his hands."

Chapter 23

Job wishes to be tried at God's tribunal.

Then Job answered and said, 2 "Now also my words are in bitterness, and the hand of my scourge is *more grievous than* my mourning. 3 Who will grant me that I might know and find him and come even to his throne? 4 I would set judgment before him and would fill my mouth with complaints 5 that I might know the words that he would answer me and understand what he would say to me. 6 I would not that he should contend with me with much strength nor overwhelm me with the weight of his greatness. 7 Let him propose equity against me, and let my judgment come to victory.

8 "But if I go to the east, he appeareth not; if to the west, I shall not understand him. 9 If to the left hand, what shall I

hendam eum. Si me vertam ad dextram, non videbo illum. 10 Ipse vero scit viam meam et probavit me quasi aurum quod per ignem transit. 11 Vestigia eius secutus est pes meus. Viam eius custodivi et non declinavi ex ea. 12 A mandatis labiorum eius non recessi, et in sinu meo abscondi verba oris eius, 13 ipse enim solus est et nemo avertere potest cogitationem eius et anima eius quodcumque voluerit, hoc fecit. 14 "Cumque expleverit in me voluntatem suam et alia multa similia praesto sunt ei. 15 Et idcirco a facie eius turbatus sum, et considerans eum timore sollicitor. 16 Deus mollivit cor meum, et Omnipotens conturbavit me, 17 non enim perii propter inminentes tenebras, nec faciem meam operuit caligo."

Caput 24

"Ab Omnipotente non sunt abscondita tempora, qui autem noverunt eum ignorant dies illius. 2 Alii terminos transtulerunt, diripuerunt greges et paverunt eos. 3 Asinum pupillorum abigerunt et abstulerunt pro pignore bovem

do? I shall not take hold on him. If I turn myself to the right hand, I shall not see him. 10 But he knoweth my way and has tried me as gold that passeth through the fire. 11 My foot hath followed his steps. I have kept his way and have not declined from it. 12 I have not departed from the commandments of his lips, and the words of his mouth I have hid in my bosom, 13 for he is alone and no man can turn away his thought and whatsoever his soul hath desired, that hath he done.

14 "And when he shall have fulfilled his will in me many other like things are also at hand with him. 15 And therefore I am troubled at his presence, and when I consider him I am made pensive with fear. 16 God hath softened my heart, and the Almighty hath troubled me, 17 for I have not perished because of the darkness that hangs over me, neither hath the mist covered my face."

Chapter 24

God's providence often suffers the wicked to go on a long time in their sins but punisheth them in another life.

"Times are not hid from the Almighty, but they that know him know not his days. 2 Some have removed landmarks, have taken away flocks by force and fed them. 3 They have driven away the ass of the fatherless and have taken

viduae. 4 Subverterunt pauperum viam et oppresserunt pariter mansuetos terrae. 5 Alii quasi onagri in deserto egrediuntur ad opus suum. Vigilantes ad praedam praeparant panem liberis. 6 Agrum non suum demetunt et vineam eius quem vi oppresserunt vindemiant. 7 Nudos dimittunt homines, indumenta tollentes quibus non est operimentum in frigore, 8 quos imbres montium rigant et non habentes velamen amplexantur lapides. 9 Vim fecerunt depraedantes pupillos et vulgum pauperem spoliaverunt. 10 Nudis et incedentibus absque vestitu et esurientibus tulerunt spicas. 11 Inter acervos eorum meridiati sunt qui calcatis torcularibus sitiunt. 12 De civitatibus fecerunt viros gemere, et anima vulneratorum clamavit, et Deus inultum abire non patitur.

13 "Ipsi fuerunt rebelles lumini; nescierunt vias eius, nec reversi sunt per semitas illius. 14 Mane primo consurgit homicida; interficit egenum et pauperem, per noctem vero erit quasi fur. 15 Oculus adulteri observat caliginem, dicens, 'Non me videbit oculus,' et operiet vultum suum. 16 Perfodit in tenebris domos sicut in die condixerant sibi, et ignoraverunt lucem. 17 Si subito apparuerit aurora, arbitrantur umbram mortis, et sic in tenebris quasi in luce ambulant.

18 "Levis est super faciem aquae. Maledicta sit pars eius in terra. Nec ambulet per viam vinearum. 19 Ad nimium calo-

away the widow's ox for a pledge. 4 They have overturned the way of the poor and have oppressed together the meek of the earth. 5 Others like wild asses in the desert go forth to their work. By watching for a prey they get bread for their children. 6 They reap the field that is not their own and gather the vintage of his vineyard whom by violence they have oppressed. 7 They send men away naked, taking away their clothes who have no covering in the cold, 8 *who are wet with* the showers of the mountains and having no covering embrace the stones. 9 They have violently robbed the fatherless and stripped the poor common people. 10 From the naked and them that go without clothing and from the hungry they have taken away the ears of corn. 11 They have taken their rest at noon among the stores of them who after having trodden the winepresses suffer thirst. 12 Out of the cities they have made men to groan, and the soul of the wounded hath cried out, and God doth not suffer it to pass unrevenged.

13 "They have been rebellious to the light; they have not known his ways, neither have they returned by his paths. 14 The murderer riseth at the very break of day; he killeth the needy and the poor man, but in the night he will be as a thief. 15 The eye of the adulterer observeth darkness, saying, 'No eye shall see me,' and he will cover his face. 16 He diggeth through houses in the dark as in the day they had appointed for themselves, and they have not known the light. 17 If the morning suddenly appear, it is to them the shadow of death, and they walk in darkness as if it were in light.

18 "He is light upon the face of the water. Cursed be his portion on the earth. Let him not walk by the way of the vineyards. 19 Let him pass from the snow-waters to excessive

rem transeat ab aquis nivium et usque ad inferos peccatum illius. ²⁰ Obliviscatur eius misericordia; dulcedo illius vermes; non sit in recordatione sed conteratur quasi lignum infructuosum, ²¹ pavit enim sterilem et quae non parit et viduae bene non fecit. ²² Detraxit fortes in fortitudine sua, et cum steterit non credet vitae suae. ²³ Dedit ei Deus locum paenitentiae, et ille abutitur eo in superbiam, oculi autem eius sunt in viis illius. ²⁴ Elevati sunt ad modicum et non subsistent et humiliabuntur sicut omnia et auferentur, et sicut summitates spicarum conterentur.

²⁵ "Quod si non est ita, quis me potest arguere esse mentitum et ponere ante Deum verba mea?"

Caput 25

Respondens autem Baldad, Suites, dixit, ² "Potestas et terror apud eum est qui facit concordiam in sublimibus suis. ³ Numquid est numerus militum eius? Et super quem non surget lumen illius? ⁴ Numquid iustificari potest homo

heat and his sin even to hell. 20 Let mercy forget him; may worms be his sweetness; let him be remembered *no more* but be broken in pieces as an unfruitful tree, 21 for he hath fed the barren *that* beareth not and to the widow he hath done no good. 22 He hath pulled down the strong by his might, and when he standeth up he shall not trust to his life. 23 God hath given him place for penance, and he abuseth it unto pride, but his eyes are upon his ways. 24 They are lifted up for a little while and shall not stand and shall be brought down as all things and shall be taken away, and as the tops of the ears of corn they shall be broken.

25 "And if it be not so, who can convince me that I have lied and set my words before God?"

Chapter 25

God's providence often suffers the wicked to go on a long time in their sins but punisheth them in another life.

Then Bildad, the Shuhite, answered and said, 2 "Power and terror are with him who maketh peace in his high places. 3 Is there any numbering of his soldiers? And upon whom shall not his light arise? 4 Can man be justified compared

conparatus Deo aut apparere mundus natus de muliere? 5 Ecce: etiam luna non splendet, et stellae non sunt mundae in conspectu eius. 6 Quanto magis homo putredo et filius hominis vermis?"

Caput 26

Respondens autem Iob dixit, 2 "Cuius adiutor es? Numquid inbecilli? Et sustentas brachium eius qui non est fortis? 3 Cui dedisti consilium? Forsitan illi qui non habet sapientiam, et prudentiam tuam ostendisti plurimam. 4 Quem docere voluisti? Nonne eum qui fecit spiramentum?

5 "Ecce: gigantes gemunt sub aquis et qui habitant cum eis. 6 Nudus est infernus coram illo, et nullum est operimentum perditioni. 7 Qui extendit aquilonem super vacuum et adpendit terram super nihilum. 8 Qui ligat aquas in nubibus suis ut non erumpant pariter deorsum. 9 Qui tenet vultum solii sui et expandit super illud nebulam suam. 10 Terminum circumdedit aquis usque dum finiantur lux et tenebrae. 11 Columnae caeli contremescunt et pavent ad nutum eius.

with God or he that is born of a woman appear clean? 5 Behold: even the moon doth not shine, and the stars are not pure in his sight. 6 How much *less* man that is rottenness and the son of man who is a worm?"

Chapter 26

Job declares his sentiments of the wisdom and power of God.

T hen Job answered and said, 2 "Whose helper art thou? Is it of him that is weak? And dost thou hold up the arm of him that has no strength? 3 To whom hast thou given counsel? Perhaps to him that hath no wisdom, and thou hast shewn thy very great prudence. 4 Whom hast thou desired to teach? Was it not him that made life?

5 "Behold: the giants groan under the waters and they that dwell with them. 6 Hell is naked before him, and there is no covering for destruction. 7 He stretched out the north over the empty space and hangeth the earth upon nothing. 8 He bindeth up the waters in his clouds so that they break not out *and fall* down together. 9 He withholdeth the face of his throne and spreadeth his cloud over it. 10 He hath set bounds about the waters till light and darkness come to an end. 11 The pillars of heaven tremble and dread at his beck.

12 In fortitudine illius repente maria congregata sunt, et prudentia eius percussit superbum. 13 Spiritus eius ornavit caelos, et obsetricante manu eius eductus est coluber tortuosus. 14 Ecce: haec ex parte dicta sunt viarum eius, et cum vix parvam stillam sermonis eius audierimus quis poterit tonitruum magnitudinis illius intueri?"

Caput 27

Addidit quoque Iob adsumens parabolam suam et dixit, 2 "Vivit Deus qui abstulit iudicium meum et Omnipotens qui ad amaritudinem adduxit animam meam, 3 quia donec superest halitus in me et spiritus Dei in naribus meis 4 non loquentur labia mea iniquitatem, nec lingua mea meditabitur mendacium.

5 "Absit a me ut iustos vos esse iudicem. Donec deficiam non recedam ab innocentia mea. 6 Iustificationem meam quam coepi tenere non deseram, nec enim reprehendit me

12 By his power the seas are suddenly gathered together, and his wisdom has struck the proud one. 13 His spirit hath adorned the heavens, and his obstetric hand brought forth the winding serpent. 14 Lo: these things are said in part of his ways, and seeing we have heard scarce a little drop of his word who shall be able to behold the thunder of his greatness?"

Chapter 27

Job persists in asserting his own innocence and that hypocrites will be punished in the end.

Job also added taking up his parable and said, 2 "As God liveth who hath taken away my judgment and the Almighty who hath brought my soul to bitterness, 3 as long as breath remaineth in me and the spirit of God in my nostrils 4 my lips shall not speak iniquity, neither shall my tongue contrive lying.

5 "God forbid that I should judge you to be just. Till I die I will not depart from my innocence. 6 My justification which I have begun to hold I will not forsake, for my heart

cor meum in omni vita mea. 7 Sit ut impius inimicus meus et adversarius meus quasi iniquus, 8 quae enim spes est hypocritae si avare rapiat et non liberet Deus animam eius? 9 Numquid clamorem eius Deus audiet cum venerit super illum angustia? 10 Aut poterit in Omnipotente delectari et invocare Deum in omni tempore? 11 "Docebo vos per manum Dei quae Omnipotens habeat, nec abscondam. 12 Ecce: vos omnes nostis, et quid sine causa vana loquimini? 13 Haec est pars hominis impii apud Deum et hereditas violentorum quam ab Omnipotente suscipient. 14 Si multiplicati fuerint filii eius, in gladio erunt, et nepotes eius non saturabuntur pane. 15 Qui reliqui fuerint ex eo sepelientur in interitu, et viduae illius non plorabunt. 16 Si conportaverit quasi terram argentum et sicut lutum praeparaverit vestimenta, 17 praeparabit quidem, sed iustus vestietur illis, et argentum innocens dividet. 18 Aedificavit sicut tinea domum suam, et sicut custos fecit umbraculum. 19 Dives cum dormierit nihil secum auferet. Aperiet oculos suos et nihil inveniet. 20 Adprehendet eum quasi aqua inopia; nocte opprimet eum tempestas. 21 Tollet eum ventus urens et auferet et velut turbo rapiet eum de loco suo. 22 Et mittet super eum et non parcet. De manu eius fugiens fugiet. 23 Stringet super eum manus suas et sibilabit super illum intuens locum eius."

doth not reprehend me in all my life. 7 Let my enemy be as the ungodly and my adversary as the wicked one, 8 for what is the hope of the hypocrite if through covetousness he take by violence and God deliver not his soul? 9 Will God hear his cry when distress shall come upon him? 10 Or can he delight himself in the Almighty and call upon God at all times?

11 "I will teach you by the hand of God what the Almighty hath, and I will not conceal it. 12 Behold: you all know it, and why do you speak vain things without cause? 13 This is the portion of a wicked man with God and the inheritance of the violent which they shall receive of the Almighty. 14 If his sons be multiplied, they shall be for the sword, and his grandsons shall not be filled with bread. 15 They that shall remain of him shall be buried in death, and his widows shall not weep. 16 If he shall heap together silver as earth and prepare raiment as clay, 17 he shall prepare indeed, but the just man shall be clothed with it, and the innocent shall divide the silver. 18 He hath built his house as a moth, and as a keeper he hath made a booth. 19 The rich man when he shall sleep shall take away nothing with him. He shall open his eyes and find nothing. 20 Poverty like water shall take hold on him; a tempest shall oppress him in the night. 21 A burning wind shall take him up and carry him away and as a whirlwind shall snatch him from his place. 22 And he shall cast upon him and shall not spare. Out of his hand he would *willingly* flee. 23 He shall clasp his hands upon him and shall hiss at him beholding his place."

Caput 28

"Habet argentum venarum suarum principia, et auro locus est in quo conflatur. 2 Ferrum de terra tollitur, et lapis solutus calore in aes vertitur. 3 Tempus posuit tenebris, et universorum finem ipse considerat, lapidem quoque caliginis et umbram mortis. 4 Dividit torrens a populo peregrinante eos quos oblitus est pes egentis hominis et invios. 5 Terra de qua oriebatur panis in loco suo igne subversa est. 6 Locus sapphyri lapides eius, et glebae illius aurum. 7 Semitam ignoravit avis, nec intuitus est eam oculus vulturis. 8 Non calcaverunt eam filii institorum, nec pertransivit per eam leaena.

9 "Ad silicem extendit manum suam; subvertit a radicibus montes. 10 In petris rivos excidit, et omne pretiosum vidit oculus eius. 11 Profunda quoque fluviorum scrutatus est, et abscondita produxit in lucem.

12 "Sapientia vero ubi invenitur, et quis est locus intellegentiae? 13 Nescit homo pretium eius, nec invenitur in

Chapter 28

Man's industry searcheth out many things; true wisdom is taught by God alone.

"Silver hath beginnings of its veins, and gold hath a place wherein it is melted. 2 Iron is taken out of the earth, and stone melted with heat is turned into brass. 3 He hath set a time for darkness, and the end of all things he considereth, the stone also that is in the dark and the shadow of death. 4 The flood divideth from the people that are on their journey those whom the foot of the needy man hath forgotten and who cannot be come at. 5 The land out of which bread grew in its place hath been overturned with fire. 6 The stones of it are the place of sapphires, and the clods of it are gold. 7 The bird hath not known the path, neither hath the eye of the vulture beheld it. 8 The children of the merchants have not trodden it, neither hath the lioness passed by it.

9 "He hath stretched forth his hand to the flint; he hath overturned mountains from the roots. 10 In the rocks he hath cut out rivers, and his eye hath seen every precious thing. 11 The depths also of rivers he hath searched, and hidden things he hath brought forth to light.

12 "But where is wisdom to be found, and where is the place of understanding? 13 Man knoweth not the price

terra suaviter viventium. 14 Abyssus dicit, 'Non est in me,' et mare loquitur, 'Non est mecum.' 15 Non dabitur aurum obrizum pro ea, nec adpendetur argentum in commutatione eius. 16 Non conferetur tinctis Indiae coloribus nec lapidi sardonico pretiosissimo vel sapphyro. 17 Non adaequabitur ei aurum vel vitrum, nec commutabuntur pro ea vasa auri. 18 Excelsa et eminentia non memorabuntur conparatione eius, trahitur autem sapientia de occultis. 19 Non adaequabitur ei topazius de Aethiopia, nec tincturae mundissimae conponetur. 20 "Unde ergo sapientia venit? Et quis est locus intellegentiae? 21 Abscondita est ab oculis omnium viventium, volucres quoque caeli latet. 22 Perditio et mors dixerunt, 'Auribus nostris audivimus famam eius.' 23 Deus intellegit viam eius, et ipse novit locum illius, 24 ipse enim fines mundi intuetur et omnia quae sub caelo sunt respicit, 25 qui fecit ventis pondus et aquas adpendit in mensura. 26 Quando ponebat pluviis legem et viam procellis sonantibus, 27 tunc vidit illam et enarravit et praeparavit et investigavit. 28 Et dixit homini, 'Ecce timor Domini; ipsa est sapientia, et recedere a malo intellegentia.'"

thereof, neither is it found in the land of them that live in delights. 14 The depth saith, 'It is not in me,' and the sea saith, 'It is not with me.' 15 The finest gold shall not purchase it, neither shall silver be weighed in exchange for it. 16 It shall not be compared with the dyed colours of India or with the most precious stone sardonyx or the sapphire. 17 Gold or *crystal* cannot equal it, neither shall *any* vessels of gold be changed for it. 18 High and eminent things shall not be mentioned in comparison of it, but wisdom is drawn out of secret places. 19 The topaz of Ethiopia shall not be equal to it, neither shall it be compared to the cleanest dyeing.

20 "Whence then cometh wisdom? And where is the place of understanding? 21 It is hid from the eyes of all living, and the fowls of the air know it not. 22 Destruction and death have said, 'With our ears we have heard the fame thereof.' 23 God understandeth the way of it, and he knoweth the place thereof, 24 for he beholdeth the ends of the world and looketh on all things that are under heaven, 25 who made a weight for the winds and weighed the waters *by* measure. 26 When he gave a law for the rain and a way for the sounding storms, 27 then he saw it and declared and prepared and searched it. 28 And he said to man, 'Behold the fear of the Lord; that is wisdom, and to depart from evil is understanding.'"

Caput 29

Addidit quoque Iob adsumens parabolam suam et dixit, 2 "Quis mihi tribuat ut sim iuxta menses pristinos, secundum dies quibus Deus custodiebat me 3 quando splendebat lucerna eius super caput meum et ad lumen eius ambulabam in tenebris, 4 sicut fui in diebus adulescentiae meae quando secreto Deus erat in tabernaculo meo, 5 quando erat Omnipotens mecum et in circuitu meo pueri mei, 6 quando lavabam pedes meos butyro et petra fundebat mihi rivos olei, 7 quando procedebam ad portam civitatis et in platea parabant cathedram mihi?

8 "Videbant me iuvenes et abscondebantur, et senes adsurgentes stabant. 9 Principes cessabant loqui et digitum superponebant ori suo. 10 Vocem suam cohibebant duces, et lingua eorum gutturi suo adherebat. 11 Auris audiens beatificabat me, et oculus videns testimonium reddebat mihi, 12 eo quod liberassem pauperem vociferantem et pupillum cui non esset adiutor. 13 Benedictio perituri super me veniebat, et cor viduae consolatus sum. 14 Iustitia indutus sum, et vestivi me sicut vestimento et diademate iudicio meo. 15 Oculus fui caeco et pes claudo. 16 Pater eram pauperum,

Chapter 29

Job relates his former happiness and the respect that all men shewed him.

J ob also added taking up his parable and said, 2 "Who will grant me that I might be according to the months past, according to the days in which God kept me 3 when his lamp shined over my head and I walked by his light in darkness, 4 as I was in the days of my youth when God was secretly in my tabernacle, 5 when the Almighty was with me and my servants round about me, 6 when I washed my feet with butter and the rock poured me out rivers of oil, 7 when I went out to the gate of the city and in the street they prepared me a chair?

8 "The young men saw me and hid themselves, and the old men rose up and stood. 9 The princes ceased to speak and laid the finger on their mouth. 10 The rulers held their peace, and their tongue cleaved to their throat. 11 The ear that heard me blessed me, and the eye that saw me gave witness to me, 12 because I had delivered the poor man that cried out and the fatherless that had no helper. 13 The blessing of him that was ready to perish came upon me, and I comforted the heart of the widow. 14 I was clad with justice, and I clothed myself with my judgment as with a robe and a diadem. 15 I was an eye to the blind and a foot to the lame. 16 I was the father of the poor, and the cause which I knew

et causam quam nesciebam diligentissime investigabam.
17 Conterebam molas iniqui, et de dentibus illius auferebam
praedam. 18 "Dicebamque, 'In nidulo meo moriar et sicut palma
multiplicabo dies. 19 Radix mea aperta est secus aquas et ros
morabitur in messione mea. 20 Gloria mea semper innovabi-
tur, et arcus meus in manu mea instaurabitur.' 21 Qui me
audiebant expectabant sententiam et intenti tacebant ad
consilium meum. 22 Verbis meis addere nihil audebant, et
super illos stillabat eloquium meum. 23 Expectabant me
sicut pluviam, et os suum aperiebant quasi ad imbrem sero-
tinum. 24 Si quando ridebam ad eos, non credebant, et lux
vultus mei non cadebat in terram. 25 Si voluissem ire ad eos,
sedebam primus, cumque sederem quasi rex circumstante
exercitu, eram tamen maerentium consolator."

Caput 30

"Nunc autem derident me iuniores tempore quorum
non dignabar patres ponere cum canibus gregis mei, 2 quorum virtus manuum erat mihi pro nihilo, et vita ipsa puta-
bantur indigni, 3 egestate et fame steriles, qui rodebant in

not I searched out most diligently. 17 I broke the jaws of the wicked man, and out of his teeth I took away the prey.

18 "And I said, 'I shall die in my nest and as a palm tree shall multiply my days. 19 My root is opened beside the waters, and dew shall continue in my harvest. 20 My glory shall always be renewed, and my bow in my hand shall be repaired.' 21 They that heard me waited for my sentence and being attentive held their peace at my counsel. 22 To my words they durst add nothing, and my speech dropped upon them. 23 They waited for me as for rain, and they opened their mouth as for a latter shower. 24 If at any time I laughed on them, they believed not, and the light of my countenance fell not on earth. 25 If I had a mind to go to them, I sat first, and when I sat as a king with his army standing about him, yet I was a comforter of them that mourned."

Chapter 30

Job shews the wonderful change of his temporal estate, from welfare to great calamity.

"But now the younger in time scorn me whose fathers I would not have set with the dogs of my flock, 2 the strength of whose hands was to me as nothing, and they were thought unworthy of life itself, 3 barren with want and hunger, who gnawed in the wilderness, disfigured with calamity and mis-

solitudine, squalentes calamitate et miseria, 4 et mandebant herbas et arborum cortices, et radix iuniperorum erat cibus eorum, 5 qui de convallibus ista rapientes; cum singula repperissent ad ea cum clamore currebant. 6 In desertis habitabant torrentium et in cavernis terrae vel super glaream. 7 Qui inter huiuscemodi laetabantur et esse sub sentibus delicias conputabant, 8 filii stultorum et ignobilium et in terra penitus non parentes. 9 "Nunc in eorum canticum versus sum et factus sum eis proverbium. 10 Abominantur me et longe fugiunt a me et faciem meam conspuere non verentur, 11 faretram enim suam aperuit et adflixit me et frenum posuit in os meum. 12 Ad dexteram orientis calamitates meae ilico surrexerunt. Pedes meos subverterunt et oppresserunt quasi fluctibus semitis suis. 13 Dissipaverunt itinera mea. Insidiati sunt mihi, et praevaluerunt, et non fuit qui ferret auxilium. 14 Quasi rupto muro et aperta ianua inruerunt super me et ad meas miserias devoluti sunt.

15 "Redactus sum in nihili. Abstulisti quasi ventus desiderium meum, et velut nubes pertransiit salus mea. 16 Nunc autem in memet ipso marcescit anima mea, et possident me dies adflictionis. 17 Nocte os meum perforatur doloribus, et qui me comedunt non dormiunt. 18 In multitudine eorum consumitur vestimentum meum, et quasi capitio tunicae succinxerunt me. 19 Conparatus sum luto et adsimilatus favillae et cineri.

20 "Clamo ad te, et non exaudis me. Sto, et non respicis me. 21 Mutatus es mihi in crudelem, et in duritia manus tuae

ery, 4 and they ate grass and barks of trees, and the root of junipers was their food, 5 who snatched up these things out of the valleys, *and* when they had found any of them they ran to them with a cry. 6 They dwelt in the desert places of torrents and in caves of earth or upon the gravel. 7 They pleased themselves among these kind of things and counted it delightful to be under the briers, 8 the children of foolish and base men and not appearing at all upon the earth.

9 "Now I am turned into their song and am become their byword. 10 They abhor me and flee far from me and are not afraid to spit in my face, 11 for he hath opened his quiver and hath afflicted me and hath put a bridle into my mouth. 12 At the right hand of my rising my calamities forthwith arose. They have overthrown my feet and have overwhelmed me with their paths as with waves. 13 They have destroyed my ways. They have lain in wait against me, and they have prevailed, and there was none to help. 14 They have rushed in upon me as when a wall is broken and a gate opened and have rolled themselves down to my miseries.

15 "I am brought to nothing. As a wind thou hast taken away my desire, and my prosperity hath passed away like a cloud. 16 And now my soul fadeth within myself, and the days of affliction possess me. 17 In the night my bone is pierced with sorrows, and they that feed upon me do not sleep. 18 With the multitude of them my garment is consumed, and they have girded me about as with the collar of my coat. 19 I am compared to dirt and am likened to embers and ashes.

20 "I cry to thee, and thou hearest me not. I stand up, and thou dost not regard me. 21 Thou art changed to be cruel toward me, and in the hardness of thy hand thou art against

adversaris mihi. 22 Elevasti me et quasi super ventum ponens elisisti me valide. 23 Scio quia morti trades me ubi constituta domus est omni viventi, 24 verumtamen non ad consumptionem eorum emittis manum tuam, et si corruerint, ipse salvabis.

25 "Flebam quondam super eum qui adflictus erat, et conpatiebatur anima mea pauperi. 26 Expectabam bona, et venerunt mihi mala. Praestolabar lucem, et eruperunt tenebrae. 27 Interiora mea efferbuerunt absque ulla requie. Praevenerunt me dies adflictionis. 28 Maerens incedebam sine furore. Consurgens in turba clamavi. 29 Frater fui draconum et socius strutionum. 30 Cutis mea denigrata est super me, et ossa mea aruerunt prae caumate. 31 Versa est in luctum cithara mea et organum meum in vocem flentium."

Caput 31

"Pepigi foedus cum oculis meis ut ne cogitarem quidem de virgine, 2 quam enim partem haberet Deus in me desuper et hereditatem Omnipotens de excelsis? 3 Numquid non perditio est iniquo et alienatio operantibus iniustitiam?

me. 22 Thou hast lifted me up and set me as it were upon the wind, and thou hast mightily dashed me. 23 I know that thou wilt deliver me to death where a house is appointed for every one that liveth, 24 but yet thou stretchest not forth thy hand to their consumption, and if they shall fall down, thou wilt save.

25 "I wept heretofore for him that was afflicted, and my soul had compassion on the poor. 26 I expected good things, and evils are come upon me. I waited for light, and darkness broke out. 27 My inner parts have boiled without any rest. The days of affliction have prevented me. 28 I went mourning without indignation. I rose up and cried in the crowd. 29 I was the brother of dragons and companion of ostriches. 30 My skin is become black upon me, and my bones are dried up with heat. 31 My harp is turned to mourning and my organ into the voice of those that weep."

Chapter 31

Job to defend himself from the unjust judgments of his friends gives a sincere account of his own virtues.

"I made a covenant with my eyes that I would not so much as think upon a virgin, 2 for what part should God from above have in me and what inheritance the Almighty from on high? 3 Is not destruction to the wicked and aver-

4 Nonne ipse considerat vias meas et cunctos gressus meos dinumerat? 5 Si ambulavi in vanitate et festinavit in dolo pes meus, 6 adpendat me in statera iusta, et sciat Deus simplicitatem meam. 7 Si declinavit gressus meus de via et si secutum est oculos meos cor meum et si manibus meis adhesit macula, 8 seram et alius comedat, et progenies mea eradicetur. 9 Si deceptum est cor meum super mulierem et si ad ostium amici mei insidiatus sum, 10 scortum sit alterius uxor mea, et super illam incurventur alii, 11 hoc enim nefas est et iniquitas maxima. 12 Ignis est usque ad perditionem devorans et omnia eradicans genimina.

13 "Si contempsi subire iudicium cum servo meo et ancilla mea cum disceptarent adversum me, 14 quid enim faciam cum surrexerit ad iudicandum Deus et cum quaesierit, quid respondebo illi? 15 Numquid non in utero fecit me qui et illum operatus est, et formavit me in vulva unus? 16 Si negavi quod volebant pauperibus et oculos viduae expectare feci, 17 si comedi buccellam meam solus et non comedit pupillus ex ea, 18 quia ab infantia mea crevit mecum miseratio et de utero matris meae egressa est mecum, 19 si despexi pereuntem eo quod non habuerit indumentum et absque operimento pauperem, 20 si non benedixerunt mihi latera eius et de velleribus ovium mearum calefactus est, 21 si levavi super pupillum manum meam etiam cum viderem me in porta superiorem, 22 umerus meus a iunctura sua cadat, et brachium meum cum suis ossibus confringatur, 23 semper enim quasi

sion to them that work iniquity? 4 Doth not he consider my ways and number all my steps? 5 If I have walked in vanity and my foot hath made haste to deceit, 6 let him weigh me in a just balance, and let God know my simplicity. 7 If my step hath turned out of the way and if my heart hath followed my eyes and if a spot hath cleaved to my hands, 8 then let me sow and let another eat, and let my offspring be rooted out. 9 If my heart hath been deceived upon a woman and if I have laid wait at my friend's door, 10 let my wife be the harlot of another, and let other men lie with her, 11 for this is a heinous crime and a most grievous iniquity. 12 It is a fire that devoureth even to destruction and rooteth up all things that spring.

13 "If I have despised to abide judgment with my manservant *or* my maidservant when they had any controversy against me, 14 for what shall I do when God shall rise to judge and when he shall examine, what shall I answer him? 15 Did not he *that* made me in the *womb* make him also, and did not one *and the same* form me in the womb? 16 If I have denied to the poor what they desired and have made the eyes of the widow wait, 17 if I have eaten my morsel alone and the fatherless hath not eaten thereof, 18 for from my infancy mercy grew up with me and it came out with me from my mother's womb, 19 if I have despised him that was perishing for want of clothing and the poor man that had no covering, 20 if his sides have not blessed me and if he were not warmed with the fleece of my sheep, 21 if I have lifted up my hand against the fatherless even when I saw myself superior in the gate, 22 let my shoulder fall from its joint, and let my arm with its bones be broken, 23 for I have always feared

tumentes super me fluctus timui Deum, et pondus eius ferre non potui.

24 "Si putavi aurum robur meum et obrizae dixi, 'Fiducia mea,' 25 si laetatus sum super multis divitiis meis et quia plurima repperit manus mea, 26 si vidi solem cum fulgeret et lunam incedentem clare 27 et laetatum est in abscondito cor meum et osculatus sum manum meam ore meo, 28 quae est iniquitas maxima et negatio contra Deum altissimum, 29 si gavisus sum ad ruinam eius qui me oderat et exultavi quod invenisset eum malum, 30 non enim dedi ad peccandum guttur meum ut expeterem maledicens animam eius, 31 si non dixerunt viri tabernaculi mei, 'Quis det de carnibus eius ut saturemur?'—32 foris non mansit peregrinus; ostium meum viatori patuit—33 si abscondi quasi homo peccatum meum et celavi in sinu meo iniquitatem meam, 34 si expavi ad multitudinem nimiam et despectio propinquorum terruit me et non magis tacui nec egressus sum ostium, 35 quis mihi tribuat auditorem ut desiderium meum Omnipotens audiat et librum scribat ipse qui iudicat 36 ut in umero meo portem illum et circumdem illum quasi coronam mihi? 37 Per singulos gradus meos pronuntiabo illum et quasi principi offeram eum.

38 "Si adversum me terra mea clamat et cum ipsa sulci eius deflent, 39 si fructus eius comedi absque pecunia et animam agricolarum eius adflixi, 40 pro frumento oriatur mihi tribulus et pro hordeo spina."

Finita sunt verba Iob.

God as waves swelling over me, and his weight I was not able to bear.

24 "If I have thought gold my strength and have said to fine gold, 'My confidence,' 25 if I have rejoiced over my great riches and because my hand had gotten much, 26 if I beheld the sun when it shined and the moon going in brightness 27 and my heart in secret hath rejoiced and I have kissed my hand with my mouth, 28 which is a very great iniquity and a denial against the most high God, 29 if I have been glad at the downfall of him that hated me and have rejoiced that evil had found him, 30 for I have not given my mouth to sin *by wishing a curse to* his soul, 31 if the men of my tabernacle have not said, 'Who will give us of his flesh that we may be filled?'—32 the stranger did not stay without; my door was open to the traveller—33 if as a man I have hid my sin and have concealed my iniquity in my bosom, 34 if I have been afraid at a very great multitude and the contempt of kinsmen hath terrified me and I have not rather held my peace and not gone out of the door, 35 who would grant me a hearer that the Almighty may hear my desire and that he himself that judgeth would write a book 36 that I may carry it on my shoulder and put it about me as a crown? 37 At every step of mine I would pronounce it and offer it as to a prince.

38 "If my land cry against me and with it the furrows thereof mourn, 39 if I have eaten the fruits thereof without money and have afflicted the soul of the tillers thereof, 40 let thistles grow up to me instead of wheat and thorns instead of barley."

The words of Job are ended.

Caput 32

Omiserunt autem tres viri isti respondere Iob eo quod iustus sibi videretur. 2 Et iratus indignatusque Heliu, filius Barachel, Buzites de cognatione Ram. Iratus est autem adversus Iob eo quod iustum se esse diceret coram Deo, 3 porro adversum amicos eius indignatus est eo quod non invenissent responsionem rationabilem sed tantummodo condemnassent Iob. 4 Igitur Heliu expectavit Iob loquentem eo quod seniores se essent qui loquebantur, 5 cum autem vidisset quod tres respondere non potuissent iratus est vehementer. 6 Respondensque Heliu, filius Barachel, Buzites, dixit, "Iunior sum tempore, vos autem antiquiores. Idcirco dimisso capite veritus sum indicare vobis meam sententiam, 7 sperabam enim quod aetas prolixior loqueretur et annorum multitudo doceret sapientiam. 8 Sed, ut video, spiritus est in hominibus, et inspiratio Omnipotentis dat intellegentiam. 9 Non sunt longevi sapientes, nec senes intellegunt iudicium. 10 Ideo dicam. Audite me; ostendam vobis etiam ego meam sapientiam, 11 expectavi enim sermones vestros.

"Audivi prudentiam vestram donec disceptaremini sermonibus 12 et donec putabam vos aliquid dicere considera-

Chapter 32

Elihu is angry with Job and his friends. He boasts of himself.

So these three men ceased to answer Job because he seemed just to himself. 2 And Elihu, the son of Barachel, the Buzite of the kindred of Ram, was angry and was moved to indignation. Now he was angry against Job because he said he was just before God, 3 and he was angry with his friends because they had not found a reasonable answer but only had condemned Job. 4 So Elihu waited while Job was speaking because they were his elders that were speaking, 5 but when he saw that the three were not able to answer he was exceedingly angry. 6 Then Elihu, the son of Barachel, the Buzite, answered and said, "I am younger in days, and you are more ancient. Therefore hanging down my head I was afraid to shew you my opinion, 7 for I hoped that greater age would speak and that a multitude of years would teach wisdom. 8 But, as I see, there is a spirit in men, and the inspiration of the Almighty giveth understanding. 9 They that are aged are not the wise men, neither do the ancients understand judgment. 10 Therefore I will speak. Hearken to me; I also will shew you my wisdom, 11 for I have waited for your words.

"I have given ear to your wisdom as long as you were disputing in words 12 and as long as I thought you said something I considered, but, as I see, there is none of you that

bam, sed, ut video, non est qui arguere possit Iob et respondere ex vobis sermonibus eius. 13 Ne forte dicatis, 'Invenimus sapientiam. Deus proiecit eum, non homo,' 14 nihil locutus est mihi, et ego non secundum vestros sermones respondebo illi. 15 "Extimuerunt nec responderunt ultra, abstuleruntque a se eloquia. 16 Quoniam igitur expectavi et non sunt locuti, steterunt nec responderunt ultra. 17 Respondebo et ego partem meam et ostendam scientiam meam, 18 plenus sum enim sermonibus et coartat me spiritus uteri mei. 19 En: venter meus quasi mustum absque spiraculo, quod lagunculas novas disrumpit. 20 Loquar et respirabo paululum. Aperiam labia mea et respondebo. 21 Non accipiam personam viri, et Deum homini non aequabo, 22 nescio enim quamdiu subsistam et si post modicum tollat me Factor meus."

Caput 33

"Audi, igitur, Iob, eloquia mea, et omnes sermones meos ausculta. 2 Ecce: aperui os meum; loquatur lingua mea in faucibus meis. 3 Simplici corde meo sermones mei, et sententiam labia mea puram loquentur. 4 Spiritus Dei fecit me, et spiraculum Omnipotentis vivificavit me. 5 Si potes, re-

can convince Job and answer his words. 13 Lest you should say, 'We have found wisdom. God hath cast him down, not man,' 14 he hath spoken nothing to me, and I will not answer him according to your words.

15 "They were afraid and answered no more, and they left off speaking. 16 Therefore because I have waited and they have not spoken, they stood and answered no more. 17 I also will answer my part and will shew my knowledge, 18 for I am full of matter to speak of and the spirit of my bowels straiteneth me. 19 Behold: my belly is as new wine which wanteth vent, which bursteth the new vessels. 20 I will speak and take breath a little. I will open my lips and will answer. 21 I will not accept the person of man, and I will not level God with man, 22 for I know not how long I shall continue and whether after a while my Maker may take me away."

Chapter 33

Elihu blames Job for asserting his own innocence.

"Hear, therefore, O Job, my speeches, and hearken to all my words. 2 Behold: *now* I have opened my mouth; let my tongue speak within my jaws. 3 My words are from my upright heart, and my lips shall speak a pure sentence. 4 The spirit of God made me, and the breath of the Almighty gave me life. 5 If thou canst, answer me, and stand up against my

sponde mihi, et adversus faciem meam consiste. 6 Ecce: et
me sicut et te fecit Deus, et de eodem luto ego quoque formatus sum. 7 Verumtamen miraculum meum non te terreat,
et eloquentia mea non sit tibi gravis.

8 "Dixisti ergo in auribus meis, et vocem verborum tuorum audivi, 9 'Mundus sum ego et absque delicto. Inmaculatus, et non est iniquitas in me. 10 Quia querellas in me repperit, ideo arbitratus est me inimicum sibi. 11 Posuit in nervo
pedes meos. Custodivit omnes semitas meas.' 12 Hoc est
ergo in quo non es iustificatus. Respondebo tibi quia maior
sit Deus homine. 13 Adversum eum contendis quod non ad
omnia verba responderit tibi? 14 Semel loquitur Deus et secundo id ipsum non repetit. 15 Per somnium in visione nocturna quando inruit sopor super homines et dormiunt in
lectulo, 16 tunc aperit aures virorum et erudiens eos instruit
disciplina 17 ut avertat hominem ab his quae facit et liberet
eum de superbia, 18 eruens animam eius a corruptione et vitam illius ut non transeat in gladium. 19 Increpat quoque per
dolorem in lectulo, et omnia ossa eius marcescere facit.
20 Abominabilis ei fit in vita sua panis et animae illius cibus
ante desiderabilis. 21 Tabescet caro eius, et ossa quae tecta
fuerant nudabuntur. 22 Adpropinquavit corruptioni anima
eius et vita illius mortiferis.

23 "Si fuerit pro eo angelus loquens, unus de milibus, ut
adnuntiet hominis aequitatem, 24 miserebitur eius et dicet,
'Libera eum, ut non descendat in corruptionem; inveni in
quo ei propitier. 25 Consumpta est caro eius a suppliciis; revertatur ad dies adulescentiae suae.'

face. 6 Behold: God hath made me as well as thee, and of the same clay I also was formed. 7 But yet let not my wonder terrify thee, and let not my eloquence be burdensome to thee.

8 "Now thou hast said in my hearing, and I have heard the voice of thy words, 9 'I am clean and without sin. I am unspotted, and there is no iniquity in me. 10 Because he hath found complaints against me, therefore he hath counted me for his enemy. 11 He hath put my feet in the stocks. He hath observed all my paths.' 12 Now this is the thing in which thou art not justified. I will answer thee that God is greater than man. 13 Dost thou strive against him because he hath not answered thee to all words? 14 God speaketh once and repeateth not the selfsame thing the second time. 15 By a dream in a vision by night when deep sleep falleth upon men and they are sleeping in their beds, 16 then he openeth the ears of men and teaching instructeth them in *what they are to learn* 17 that he may withdraw a man from the things he is doing and may deliver him from pride, 18 rescuing his soul from corruption and his life from passing to the sword. 19 He rebuketh also by sorrow in the bed, and he maketh all his bones to wither. 20 Bread becometh abominable to him in his life and to his soul the meat which before he desired. 21 His flesh shall be consumed away, and his bones that were covered shall be made bare. 22 His soul hath drawn near to corruption and his life to the destroyers.

23 "If there shall be an angel speaking for him, one among thousands, to declare man's uprightness, 24 he shall have mercy on him and shall say, 'Deliver him, that he may not go down to corruption; I have found wherein I may be merciful to him. 25 His flesh is consumed with punishments; let him return to the days of his youth.'

²⁶ "Deprecabitur Deum, et placabilis ei erit, et videbit faciem eius in iubilo, et reddet homini iustitiam suam. ²⁷ Respiciet homines et dicet, 'Peccavi, et vere deliqui, et ut eram dignus non recepi.' ²⁸ Liberavit animam suam ne pergeret in interitum sed vivens lucem videret.

²⁹ "Ecce: haec omnia operatur Deus tribus vicibus per singulos ³⁰ ut revocet animas eorum a corruptione et inluminet luce viventium. ³¹ Adtende, Iob, et audi me, et tace dum ego loquar. ³² Si autem habes quod loquaris, responde mihi; loquere, volo enim te apparere iustum. ³³ Quod si non habes, audi me; tace, et docebo te sapientiam."

Caput 34

Pronuntians itaque Heliu etiam haec locutus est, ² "Audite, sapientes, verba mea, et eruditi, auscultate me, ³ auris enim verba probat, et guttur escas gustu diiudicat. ⁴ Iudicium eligamus nobis, et inter nos videamus quid sit melius, ⁵ quia

26 "He shall pray to God, and he will be gracious to him, and he shall see his face with joy, and he will render to man his justice. 27 He shall look upon men and shall say, 'I have sinned, and indeed I have offended, and I have not received *what* I have deserved.' 28 He hath delivered his soul from going into destruction *that* it *may live* and see the light.

29 "Behold: all these things God worketh three times within every one 30 that he may withdraw their souls from corruption and enlighten them with the light of the living. 31 Attend, Job, and hearken to me, and hold thy peace whilst I speak. 32 But if thou hast any thing to say, answer me; speak, for I would have thee to appear just. 33 And if thou have not, hear me; hold thy peace, and I will teach thee wisdom."

Chapter 34

Elihu charges Job with blasphemy and sets forth the power and justice of God.

*A*nd Elihu *continued his discourse and said,* 2 "Hear ye, wise men, my words, and ye learned, hearken to me, 3 for the ear trieth words, and the mouth discerneth meats by the taste. 4 Let us choose to us judgment, and let us see among ourselves what is the best, 5 for Job hath said, 'I am just, and

dixit Iob, 'Iustus sum, et Deus subvertit iudicium meum, 6 in iudicando enim me mendacium est; violenta sagitta mea absque ullo peccato.' 7 Quis est vir ut est Iob, qui bibit subsannationem quasi aquam, 8 qui graditur cum operantibus iniquitatem et ambulat cum viris impiis? 9 Dixit enim, 'Non placebit vir Deo, etiam si cucurrerit cum eo.' 10 Ideo, viri cordati, audite me: absit a Deo impietas, et ab Omnipotente iniquitas, 11 opus enim hominis reddet ei et iuxta vias singulorum restituet eis, 12 vere enim Deus non condemnabit frustra, nec Omnipotens subvertet iudicium.

13 "Quem constituit alium super terram? Aut quem posuit super orbem quem fabricatus est? 14 Si direxerit ad eum cor suum, spiritum illius et flatum ad se trahet. 15 Deficiet omnis caro simul, et homo in cinerem revertetur. 16 Si habes ergo intellectum, audi quod dicitur, et ausculta vocem eloquii mei. 17 Numquid qui non amat iudicium sanari potest? Et quomodo tu eum qui iustus est in tantum condemnas? 18 Qui dicit regi, 'Apostata qui vocat duces impios'? 19 Qui non accipit personas principum nec cognovit tyrannum cum disceptaret contra pauperem, opus enim manuum eius sunt universi? 20 Subito morientur, et in media nocte turbabuntur populi, et pertransibunt et auferent violentum absque manu, 21 oculi enim eius super vias hominum et omnes gressus eorum considerat. 22 Non sunt tenebrae, et non est umbra mortis ut abscondantur ibi qui operantur iniquitatem, 23 neque enim ultra in hominis potestate est ut veniat ad Deum

God hath overthrown my judgment, 6 for in judging me there is a lie; my arrow is violent without any sin.' 7 What man is there like Job, who drinketh up scorning like water, 8 who goeth in company with them that work iniquity and walketh with wicked men? 9 For he hath said, 'Man shall not please God, although he run with him.' 10 Therefore, ye men of understanding, hear me: far from God be wickedness, and iniquity from the Almighty, 11 for he will render to a man his work and according to the ways of every one he will reward them, 12 for in very deed God will not condemn without cause, neither will the Almighty pervert judgment.

13 "What other hath he appointed over the earth? Or whom hath he set over the world which he made? 14 If he turn his heart to him, he shall draw his spirit and breath unto himself. 15 All flesh shall perish together, and man shall return into ashes. 16 If then thou hast understanding, hear what is said, and hearken to the voice of my words. 17 Can he be healed that loveth not judgment? And how dost thou so far condemn him that is just? 18 Who saith to the king, 'Thou art an apostate who calleth rulers ungodly'? 19 Who accepteth not the persons of princes nor hath regarded the tyrant when he contended against the poor man, for all are the work of his hands? 20 They shall suddenly die, and the people shall be troubled at midnight, and they shall pass and take away the violent without hand, 21 for his eyes are upon the ways of men and he considereth all their steps. 22 There is no darkness, and there is no shadow of death *where* they may be hid who work iniquity, 23 for it is no longer in the power of

in iudicium. 24 Conteret multos et innumerabiles et stare faciet alios pro eis, 25 novit enim opera eorum, et idcirco inducet noctem, et conterentur. 26 Quasi impios percussit eos in loco videntium 27 qui quasi de industria recesserunt ab eo et omnes vias eius intellegere noluerunt 28 ut pervenire facerent ad eum clamorem egeni, et audiret vocem pauperum, 29 ipso enim concedente pacem quis est qui condemnet? Ex quo absconderit vultum, quis est qui contempletur eum, et super gentes et super omnes homines? 30 Qui regnare facit hominem hypocritam propter peccata populi?

31 "Quia ergo ego locutus sum ad Deum te quoque non prohibebo. 32 Si erravi, tu doce me; si iniquitatem locutus sum, ultra non addam. 33 Numquid a te Deus expetit eam quia displicuit tibi? Tu enim coepisti loqui et non ego, quod si quid nosti melius, loquere. 34 Viri intellegentes loquantur mihi, et vir sapiens audiat me. 35 Iob autem stulte locutus est, et verba illius non sonant disciplinam. 36 Pater mi, probetur Iob usque ad finem; ne desinas ab homine iniquitatis. 37 Quia addit super peccata sua blasphemiam, inter nos interim constringatur, et tunc ad iudicium provocet sermonibus suis Deum."

man to enter into judgment with God. 24 He shall break in pieces many and innumerable and shall make others to stand in their stead, 25 for he knoweth their works, and therefore he shall bring night on them, and they shall be destroyed. 26 He hath struck them as being wicked in open sight 27 who as it were on purpose have revolted from him and would not understand all his ways 28 so that they caused the cry of the needy to come to him, and he heard the voice of the poor, 29 for when he granteth peace who is there that can condemn? When he hideth his countenance, who is there that can behold him, *whether it regard* nations *or* all men? 30 Who maketh a man that is a hypocrite to reign for the sins of the people?

31 "Seeing then I have spoken *of* God I will not hinder thee *in thy turn.* 32 If I have erred, teach thou me; if I have spoken iniquity, I will add no more. 33 Doth God require it of thee because it hath displeased thee? For thou begannest to speak and not I, but if thou know any thing better, speak. 34 Let men of understanding speak to me, and let a wise man hearken to me. 35 But Job hath spoken foolishly, and his words sound not discipline. 36 My father, let Job be tried even to the end; cease not from the man of iniquity. 37 Because he addeth blasphemy upon his sins, let him be tied fast in the mean time amongst us, and then let him provoke God to judgment with his speeches."

Caput 35

Igitur Heliu haec rursum locutus est, 2 "Numquid aequa tibi videtur tua cogitatio ut diceres, 'Iustior Deo sum'? 3 Dixisti enim, "Non tibi placet quod rectum est,' vel, 'Quid tibi proderit si ego peccavero?' 4 Itaque ego respondebo sermonibus tuis et amicis tuis tecum.

5 "Suspice caelum, et intuere, et contemplare aethera quod altior te sit. 6 Si peccaveris, quid ei nocebis? Et si multiplicatae fuerint iniquitates tuae, quid facies contra eum? 7 Porro si iuste egeris, quid donabis ei, aut quid de manu tua accipiet? 8 Homini qui similis tui est nocebit impietas tua, et filium hominis adiuvabit iustitia tua. 9 Propter multitudinem calumniatorum clamabunt et heiulabunt propter vim brachii tyrannorum. 10 Et non dixit, 'Ubi est Deus qui fecit me, qui dedit carmina in nocte, 11 qui docet nos super iumenta terrae et super volucres caeli erudit nos?' 12 Ibi clamabunt, et non exaudiet propter superbiam malorum. 13 Non ergo frustra audiet Deus, et Omnipotens singulorum causas intuebitur. 14 Etiam cum dixeris, 'Non considerat,'

Chapter 35

Elihu declares that the good or evil done by man cannot reach God.

*M**oreover* Elihu spoke these words, 2 "Doth thy thought seem right to thee that thou shouldst say, 'I am more just than God'? 3 For thou saidst, 'That which is right doth not please thee,' or, 'What will it profit thee if I sin?' 4 Therefore I will answer thy words and thy friends with thee.

5 "Look up to heaven, and see, and behold the sky that it is higher than thee. 6 If thou sin, what shalt thou hurt him? And if thy iniquities be multiplied, what shalt thou do against him? 7 And if thou do justly, what shalt thou give him, or what shall he receive of thy hand? 8 Thy wickedness *may* hurt a man that is like thee, and thy justice *may* help the son of man. 9 By reason of the multitude of oppressions they shall cry out and shall wail for the violence of the arm of tyrants. 10 And he hath not said, 'Where is God who made me, who hath given songs in the night, 11 who teacheth us more than the beasts of the earth and instructeth us more than the fowls of the air?' 12 There shall they cry, and he will not hear because of the pride of evil men. 13 God therefore will not hear in vain, and the Almighty will look into the causes of every one. 14 Yea when thou shalt say, 'He considereth

iudicare coram eo, et expecta eum, 15 nunc enim non infert furorem suum, nec ulciscitur scelus valde. 16 Ergo Iob frustra aperit os suum et absque scientia verba multiplicat."

Caput 36

Addens quoque Heliu haec locutus est, 2 "Sustine me paululum, et indicabo tibi, adhuc enim habeo quod pro Deo loquar. 3 Repetam scientiam meam a principio, et operatorem meum probabo iustum, 4 vere enim absque mendacio sermones mei et perfecta scientia probabitur tibi.

5 "Deus potentes non abicit, cum et ipse sit potens, 6 sed non salvat impios, et iudicium pauperibus tribuit. 7 Non auferet a iusto oculos suos, et reges in solio conlocat in perpetuum, et illi eriguntur. 8 Et si fuerint in catenis et vinciantur funibus paupertatis, 9 indicabit eis opera eorum et scelera eorum quia violenti fuerint. 10 Revelabit quoque aurem eorum ut corripiat et loquetur ut revertantur ab iniquitate. 11 Si audierint et observaverint, conplebunt dies suos in bono et annos suos in gloria. 12 Si autem non audierint,

not,' be judged before him, and expect him, 15 for he doth not now bring on his fury, neither doth he revenge wickedness exceedingly. 16 Therefore Job openeth his mouth in vain and multiplieth words without knowledge."

Chapter 36

Elihu proceeds in setting forth the justice and power of God.

Elihu also *proceeded and said,* 2 "Suffer me a little, and I will shew thee, for I have yet somewhat to speak in God's behalf. 3 I will repeat my knowledge from the beginning, and I will prove my maker just, 4 for indeed my words are without a lie and perfect knowledge shall be proved to thee.

5 "God doth not cast away the mighty, whereas he himself also is mighty, 6 but he saveth not the wicked, and he giveth judgment to the poor. 7 He will not take away his eyes from the just, and he placeth kings on the throne for ever, and they are exalted. 8 And if they shall be in chains and be bound with the cords of poverty, 9 he shall shew them their works and their wicked deeds because they have been violent. 10 He also shall open their ear to correct them and shall speak that they may return from iniquity. 11 If they shall hear and observe, they shall accomplish their days in good and their years in glory. 12 But if they hear not, they shall pass by

transibunt per gladium et consumentur in stultitia. 13 Simulatores et callidi provocant iram Dei, neque clamabunt cum vincti fuerint. 14 Morietur in tempestate anima eorum et vita eorum inter effeminatos. 15 Eripiet pauperem de angustia sua et revelabit in tribulatione aurem eius.

16 "Igitur salvabit te de ore angusto latissime et non habentis fundamentum subter se, requies autem mensae tuae erit plena pinguedine. 17 Causa tua quasi impii iudicata est; causam iudiciumque recipies. 18 Non te ergo superet ira ut aliquem opprimas, nec multitudo donorum inclinet te. 19 Depone magnitudinem tuam absque tribulatione et omnes robustos fortitudine. 20 Ne protrahas noctem ut ascendant populi pro eis. 21 Cave ne declines ad iniquitatem, hanc enim coepisti sequi post miseriam.

22 "Ecce: Deus excelsus in fortitudine sua, et nullus ei similis in legislatoribus. 23 Quis poterit scrutari vias eius? Aut quis potest ei dicere, 'Operatus es iniquitatem'? 24 Memento quod ignores opus eius de quo cecinerunt viri. 25 Omnes homines vident eum; unusquisque intuetur procul. 26 Ecce: Deus magnus, vincens scientiam nostram; numerus annorum eius inaestimabilis. 27 Qui aufert stillas pluviae et effundit imbres ad instar gurgitum 28 qui de nubibus fluunt quae praetexunt cuncta desuper. 29 Si voluerit extendere nubes quasi tentorium suum 30 et fulgurare lumine suo desuper, cardines quoque maris operiet, 31 per haec enim iudicat populos et dat escas multis mortalibus. 32 In manibus abscondit lucem et praecipit ei ut rursus adveniat. 33 Adnuntiat de ea amico suo quod possessio eius sit et ad eam possit ascendere."

the sword and shall be consumed in folly. 13 Dissemblers and crafty men prove the wrath of God, neither shall they cry when they are bound. 14 Their soul shall die in a storm and their life among the effeminate. 15 He shall deliver the poor out of his distress and shall open his ear in affliction.

16 "Therefore he shall *set thee at large* out of the narrow mouth and which hath no foundation under it, and the rest of thy table shall be full of fatness. 17 Thy cause hath been judged as that of the wicked; cause and judgment thou shalt recover. 18 Therefore let not anger overcome thee to oppress any man, neither let multitude of gifts turn thee aside. 19 Lay down thy greatness without tribulation and all the mighty of strength. 20 Prolong not the night that people may come up for them. 21 Beware thou turn not aside to iniquity, for this thou hast begun to follow after misery.

22 "Behold: God is high in his strength, and none is like him among the lawgivers. 23 Who can search out his ways? Or who can say to him, 'Thou has wrought iniquity'? 24 Remember that thou knowest not his work concerning which men have sung. 25 All men see him; every one beholdeth afar off. 26 Behold: God is great, exceeding our knowledge; the number of his years is inestimable. 27 He lifteth up the drops of rain and poureth out showers like floods 28 which flow from the clouds that cover all above. 29 If he will spread out clouds as his tent 30 and lighten with his light from above, he shall cover also the ends of the sea, 31 for by these he judgeth people and giveth food to many mortals. 32 In his hands he hideth the light and commandeth it to come again. 33 He sheweth his friend concerning it that it is his possession and that he may come up to it."

Caput 37

"Super hoc expavit cor meum et emotum est de loco suo. 2 Audite auditionem in terrore vocis eius et sonum de ore illius procedentem. 3 Subter omnes caelos ipse considerat, et lumen illius super terminos terrae. 4 Post eum rugiet sonitus; tonabit voce magnitudinis suae et non investigabitur cum audita fuerit vox eius. 5 Tonabit Deus in voce sua mirabiliter, qui facit magna et inscrutabilia.

6 "Qui praecipit nivi ut descendat in terram et hiemis pluviis et imbri fortitudinis suae. 7 Qui in manu omnium hominum signat ut noverint singuli opera sua. 8 Ingredietur bestia latibulum et in antro suo morabitur. 9 Ab interioribus egredietur tempestas, et ab Arcturo frigus. 10 Flante Deo concrescit gelu et rursum latissimae funduntur aquae. 11 Frumentum desiderat nubes, et nubes spargunt lumen suum 12 quae lustrant per circuitum quocumque eas voluntas gubernantis duxerit, ad omne quod praeceperit illis super faciem orbis terrarum, 13 sive in una tribu sive in terra sua sive in quocumque loco misericordiae suae eas iusserit inveniri.

14 "Ausculta haec, Iob. Sta, et considera miracula Dei. 15 Numquid scis quando praeceperit Deus pluviis ut osten-

Chapter 37

Elihu goes on in his discourse, shewing God's wisdom and power by his wonderful works.

"At this my heart trembleth and is moved out of its place. 2 Hear ye *attentively* the terror of his voice and the sound that cometh out of his mouth. 3 He beholdeth under all the heavens, and his light is upon the ends of the earth. 4 After it a noise shall roar; he shall thunder with the voice of his majesty and shall not be found out when his voice shall be heard. 5 God shall thunder wonderfully with his voice, he that doth great and unsearchable things.

6 "He commandeth the snow to go down upon the earth and the winter rain and the shower of his strength. 7 He sealeth up the hand of all men that every one may know his works. 8 Then the beast shall go into his covert and shall abide in his den. 9 Out of the inner parts shall a tempest come, and cold out of the *north*. 10 When God bloweth there cometh frost and again the waters are poured out abundantly. 11 Corn desireth clouds, and the clouds spread their light 12 which go round about whithersoever the will of him that governeth them shall lead them, to whatsoever he shall command them upon the face of the whole earth, 13 whether in one tribe or in his own land or in what place soever of his mercy he shall command them to be found.

14 "Hearken to these things, Job. Stand, and consider the wondrous works of God. 15 Dost thou know when God

derent lucem nubium eius? 16 Numquid nosti semitas nubium magnas et perfectas scientias? 17 Nonne vestimenta tua calida sunt cum perflata fuerit terra austro? 18 Tu forsitan cum eo fabricatus es caelos, qui solidissimi quasi aere fusi sunt. 19 Ostende nobis quid dicamus illi, nos quippe involvimur tenebris. 20 Quis narrabit ei quae loquor? Etiam si locutus fuerit homo, devorabitur. 21 At nunc non vident lucem. Subito aer cogetur in nubes, et ventus transiens fugabit eas.

22 "Ab aquilone aurum venit, et ad Deum formidolosa laudatio. 23 Digne eum invenire non possumus. Magnus fortitudine et iudicio et iustitia, et enarrari non potest. 24 Ideo timebunt eum viri, et non audebunt contemplari omnes qui sibi videntur esse sapientes."

Caput 38

Respondens autem Dominus Iob de turbine dixit, 2 "Quis est iste involvens sententias sermonibus inperitis? 3 Accinge sicut vir lumbos tuos! Interrogabo te, et responde mihi.

commanded the rains to shew the light of his clouds? 16 Knowest thou the great paths of the clouds and the perfect knowledges? 17 Are not thy garments hot when the south wind blows upon the earth? 18 Thou perhaps hast made the heavens with him, which are most strong as if they were of molten brass. 19 Shew us what we may say to him, for we are wrapped up in darkness. 20 Who shall tell him the things I speak? Even if a man shall speak, he shall be swallowed up. 21 But now they see not the light. The air on a sudden shall be thickened into clouds, and the wind shall pass and drive them away.

22 "Gold cometh out of the north, and to God praise with fear. 23 We cannot find him worthily. He is great in strength and in judgment and in justice, and he is ineffable. 24 Therefore men shall fear him, and all that seem to themselves to be wise shall not dare to behold him."

Chapter 38

God interposes and shews from the things he hath made
that man cannot comprehend his power and wisdom.

Then the Lord answered Job out of a whirlwind and said, 2 "Who is this that wrappeth up sentences in unskillful words? 3 Gird up thy loins like a man! I will ask thee, and answer thou me.

⁴ "Ubi eras quando ponebam fundamenta terrae? Indica mihi, si habes intellegentiam. ⁵ Quis posuit mensuras eius, si nosti? Vel quis tetendit super eam lineam? ⁶ Super quo bases illius solidatae sunt? Aut quis demisit lapidem angularem eius ⁷ cum me laudarent simul astra matutina et iubilarent omnes filii Dei? ⁸ Quis conclusit ostiis mare quando erumpebat quasi de vulva procedens, ⁹ cum ponerem nubem vestimentum eius et caligine illud quasi pannis infantiae obvolverem?

¹⁰ "Circumdedi illud terminis meis et posui vectem et ostia, ¹¹ et dixi, 'Usque huc venies et non procedes amplius, et hic confringes tumentes fluctus tuos.'

¹² "Numquid post ortum tuum praecepisti diluculo et ostendisti aurorae locum suum? ¹³ Et tenuisti, concutiens, extrema terrae, et excussisti impios ex ea? ¹⁴ Restituetur ut lutum signaculum et stabit sicut vestimentum. ¹⁵ Auferetur ab impiis lux sua, et brachium excelsum confringetur. ¹⁶ Numquid ingressus es profunda maris et in novissimis abyssis deambulasti? ¹⁷ Numquid apertae tibi sunt portae mortis, et ostia tenebrosa vidisti? ¹⁸ Numquid considerasti latitudinem terrae? Indica mihi, si nosti omnia. ¹⁹ In qua via habitet lux, et tenebrarum quis locus sit, ²⁰ ut ducas unumquodque ad terminos suos et intellegas semitas domus eius?

²¹ "Sciebas tunc quod nasciturus esses? Et numerum dierum tuorum noveras? ²² Numquid ingressus es thesauros nivis, aut thesauros grandinis aspexisti ²³ quae praeparavi in

4 "Where wast thou when I laid up the foundations of the earth? Tell me, if thou hast understanding. 5 Who hath laid the measures thereof, if thou knowest? Or who hath stretched the line upon it? 6 Upon what are its bases grounded? Or who laid the corner stone thereof 7 when the morning stars praised me together and all the sons of God made a joyful melody? 8 Who shut up the sea with doors when it broke forth as issuing out of the womb, 9 when I made a cloud the garment thereof and wrapped it in a mist as in swaddling bands?

10 "I set my bounds around it and made it *bars* and doors, 11 and I said, 'Hitherto thou shalt come and shalt go no further, and here thou shalt break thy swelling waves.'

12 "Didst thou since thy birth command the morning and shew the dawning of the day its place? 13 And didst thou hold the extremities of the earth, shaking them, and hast thou shaken the ungodly out of it? 14 The seal shall be restored as clay and shall stand as a garment. 15 From the wicked their light shall be taken away, and the high arm shall be broken. 16 Hast thou entered into the depths of the sea and walked in the lowest parts of the deep? 17 Have the gates of death been opened to thee, and hast thou seen the darksome doors? 18 Hast thou considered the breadth of the earth? Tell me, if thou knowest all things. 19 Where is the way where light dwelleth, and where is the place of darkness, 20 that thou mayst bring every thing to its own bounds and understand the paths of the house thereof?

21 "Didst thou know then that thou shouldst be born? And didst thou know the number of thy days? 22 Hast thou entered into the storehouses of the snow, or has thou beheld the treasures of the hail 23 which I have prepared for the

tempus hostis in diem pugnae et belli? 24 Per quam viam spargitur lux, dividitur aestus super terram? 25 Quis dedit vehementissimo imbri cursum et viam sonantis tonitrui 26 ut plueret super terram absque homine in deserto ubi nullus mortalium commoratur, 27 ut impleret inviam et desolatam et produceret herbas virentes? 28 Quis est pluviae pater? Vel quis genuit stillas roris? 29 De cuius utero egressa est glacies? Et gelu de caelo, quis genuit? 30 In similitudinem lapidis aquae durantur, et superficies abyssi constringitur.

31 "Numquid coniungere valebis micantes stellas, Pliadis, aut gyrum Arcturi poteris dissipare? 32 Numquid producis Luciferum in tempore suo et Vesperum super filios terrae consurgere facis? 33 Numquid nosti ordinem caeli, et pones rationem eius in terra? 34 Numquid elevabis in nebula vocem tuam et impetus aquarum operiet te? 35 Numquid mittes fulgura, et ibunt, et revertentia dicent tibi, 'Adsumus'?

36 "Quis posuit in visceribus hominis sapientiam? Vel quis dedit gallo intellegentiam? 37 Quis enarrabit caelorum rationem, et concentum caeli quis dormire faciet? 38 Quando fundebatur pulvis in terram et glebae conpingebantur?

39 "Numquid capies leaenae praedam et animam catulorum eius implebis 40 quando cubant in antris et in specubus insidiantur? 41 Quis praeparat corvo escam suam quando pulli eius ad Deum clamant vagantes eo quod non habeant cibos?"

time of the enemy against the day of battle and war? 24 By what way is the light spread *and* heat divided upon the earth? 25 Who gave a course to violent showers *or* a way for noisy thunder 26 that it should rain on the earth without man in the wilderness where no mortal dwelleth, 27 that it should fill the desert and desolate land and should bring forth green grass? 28 Who is the father of rain? Or who begot the drops of dew? 29 Out of whose womb came the ice? And the frost from heaven, who hath gendered it? 30 The waters are hardened like a stone, and the surface of the deep is congealed.

31 "Shalt thou be able to join together the shining stars, the Pleiades, or canst thou stop the turning about of Arcturus? 32 Canst thou bring forth the Day Star in its time and make the Evening Star to rise upon the children of the earth? 33 Dost thou know the order of heaven, and canst thou set down the reason thereof on the earth? 34 Canst thou lift up thy voice to the clouds *that* an abundance of waters may cover thee? 35 Canst thou send lightnings, and will they go, and will they return and say to thee, 'Here we are'?

36 "Who hath put wisdom in the heart of man? Or who gave the cock understanding? 37 Who *can* declare the order of the heavens, *or* who *can* make the harmony of heaven to sleep? 38 When was the dust poured on the earth and the clods fastened together?

39 "Wilt thou take the prey for the lioness and satisfy the appetite of her whelps 40 when they couch in the dens and lie in wait in holes? 41 Who provideth *food* for the raven when her young ones cry to God wandering about because they have no meat?"

Caput 39

"Numquid nosti tempus partus hibicum in petris, vel parturientes cervas observasti? 2 Dinumerasti menses conceptus earum, et scisti tempus partus earum? 3 Incurvantur ad fetum, et pariunt et rugitus emittunt. 4 Separantur filii earum et pergunt ad pastum; egrediuntur et non revertuntur ad eas.

5 "Quis dimisit onagrum liberum, et vincula eius quis solvit 6 cui dedi in solitudine domum et tabernacula eius in terra salsuginis? 7 Contemnit multitudinem civitatis. Clamorem exactoris non audit. 8 Circumspicit montes pascuae suae et virentia quaeque perquirit.

9 "Numquid volet rinoceros servire tibi, aut morabitur ad praesepe tuum? 10 Numquid alligabis rinocerota ad arandum loro tuo, aut confringet glebas vallium post te? 11 Numquid fiduciam habebis in magna fortitudine eius et derelinques ei labores tuos? 12 Numquid credes ei quoniam reddat sementem tibi et aream tuam congreget?

13 "Pinna strutionis similis est pinnis herodii et accipitris. 14 Quando derelinquit in terra ova sua tu forsitan in pulvere calefacies ea. 15 Obliviscitur quod pes conculcet ea aut

Chapter 39

The wonders of the power and providence of God in many of his creatures.

"Knowest thou the time when the wild goats bring forth among the rocks, or hast thou observed the hinds when they fawn? 2 Hast thou numbered the months of their conceiving, or knowest thou the time when they bring forth? 3 They bow themselves to bring forth young, and they cast them and send forth roarings. 4 Their young are weaned and go to feed; they go forth and return not to them.

5 "Who hath sent out the wild ass free, and who hath loosed his bonds 6 to whom I have given a house in the wilderness and his dwellings in the barren land? 7 He scorneth the multitude of the city. He heareth not the cry of the driver. 8 He looketh round about the mountains of his pasture and seeketh for every green thing.

9 "Shall the rhinoceros be willing to serve thee, or will he stay at thy crib? 10 Canst thou bind the rhinoceros with thy thong to plough, or will he break the clods of the valleys after thee? 11 Wilt thou have confidence in his great strength and leave thy labours to him? 12 Wilt thou trust him that he will render thee the seed and gather it into thy barnfloor?

13 "The wing of the ostrich is like the wings of the heron and of the hawk. 14 When she leaveth her eggs on the earth thou perhaps wilt warm them in the dust. 15 She forgetteth that the foot may tread upon them or that the beast of the

bestia agri conterat. 16 Duratur ad filios suos quasi non sint sui. Frustra laboravit, nullo timore cogente, 17 privavit enim eam Deus sapientia, nec dedit illi intellegentiam. 18 Cum tempus fuerit, in altum alas erigit. Deridet equum et ascensorem eius.

19 "Numquid praebebis equo fortitudinem aut circumdabis collo eius hinnitum? 20 Numquid suscitabis eum quasi lucustas? Gloria narium eius terror. 21 Terram ungula fodit. Exultat audacter. In occursum pergit armatis. 22 Contemnit pavorem. Nec cedit gladio. 23 Super ipsum sonabit faretra; vibrabit hasta et clypeus. 24 Fervens et fremens sorbet terram, nec reputat tubae sonare clangorem. 25 Ubi audierit bucinam dicit, 'Va!' Procul odoratur bellum, exhortationem ducum et ululatum exercitus.

26 "Numquid per sapientiam tuam plumescit accipiter, expandens alas suas ad austrum? 27 Numquid ad praeceptum tuum elevabitur aquila et in arduis ponet nidum suum? 28 In petris manet et in praeruptis silicibus commoratur atque inaccessis rupibus. 29 Inde contemplatur escam, et de longe oculi eius prospiciunt. 30 Pulli eius lambent sanguinem, et ubicumque cadaver fuerit statim adest."

31 Et adiecit Dominus et locutus est ad Iob, 32 "Numquid qui contendit cum Deo tam facile conquiescit? Utique qui arguit Deum debet respondere ei."

33 Respondens autem Iob Domino dixit, 34 "Qui leviter locutus sum, respondere quid possum? Manum meam ponam super os meum. 35 Unum locutus sum quod utinam non dixissem et alterum quibus ultra non addam."

field may break them. 16 She is hardened against her young ones as though they were not hers. She hath laboured in vain, no fear constraining her, 17 for God hath deprived her of wisdom, neither hath he given her understanding. 18 When time shall be, she setteth up her wings on high. She scorneth the horse and his rider.

19 "Wilt thou give strength to the horse or clothe his neck with neighing? 20 Wilt thou lift him up like the locusts? The glory of his nostrils is terror. 21 He breaketh up the earth with his hoof. He pranceth boldly. He goeth forward to meet armed men. 22 He despiseth fear. He *turneth* not *his back* to the sword. 23 Above him shall the quiver rattle; the spear and shield shall glitter. 24 Chasing and raging he swalloweth the ground, neither doth he make account when the noise of the trumpet soundeth. 25 When he heareth the trumpet he saith, '*Ha, ha!*' He smelleth the battle afar off, the encouraging of the captains and the shouting of the army.

26 "Doth the hawk wax feathered by thy wisdom, spreading her wings to the south? 27 Will the eagle mount up at thy command and make her nest in high places? 28 She abideth among the rocks and dwelleth among cragged flints and stony hills where there is no access. 29 From thence she looketh for the prey, and her eyes behold afar off. 30 Her young ones shall suck up blood, and wheresoever the carcass shall be she is immediately there."

31 And the Lord went on and said to Job, 32 "Shall he that contendeth with God be so easily silenced? Surely he that reproveth God ought to answer him."

33 Then Job answered the Lord and said, 34 "What can I answer, who hath spoken inconsiderately? I will lay my hand upon my mouth. 35 One thing I have spoken which I wish I had not said and another to which I will add no more."

Caput 40

Respondens autem Dominus Iob de turbine ait, 2 "Accinge sicut vir lumbos tuos! Interrogabo te, et indica mihi. 3 Numquid irritum facies iudicium meum et condemnabis me ut tu iustificeris? 4 Et si habes brachium sicut Deus, et si voce simili tonas? 5 Circumda tibi decorem, et in sublime erigere, et esto gloriosus, et speciosis induere vestibus. 6 Disperge superbos in furore tuo, et respiciens omnem arrogantem humilia. 7 Respice cunctos superbos, et confunde eos, et contere impios in loco suo. 8 Absconde eos in pulvere simul, et facies eorum demerge in foveam. 9 Et ego confitebor quod salvare te possit dextera tua.

10 "Ecce Behemoth quem feci tecum; faenum quasi bos comedet. 11 Fortitudo eius in lumbis eius, et virtus illius in umbilico ventris eius. 12 Constringit caudam suam quasi cedrum; nervi testiculorum eius perplexi sunt. 13 Ossa eius velut fistulae aeris, cartilago illius quasi lamminae ferreae. 14 Ipse principium est viarum Dei qui fecit eum. Adplicabit gladium eius. 15 Huic montes herbas ferunt; omnes bestiae agri ludent ibi. 16 Sub umbra dormit in secreto calami et in locis humentibus. 17 Protegunt umbrae umbram eius. Circumdabunt eum salices torrentis. 18 Ecce: absorbebit fluvium

Chapter 40

Of the power of God in the Behemoth and the Leviathan.

And the Lord answering Job out of the whirlwind said, 2 "Gird up thy loins like a man! I will ask thee, and do thou tell me. 3 Wilt thou make void my judgment and condemn me that thou mayst be justified? 4 And hast thou an arm like God, and canst thou thunder with a voice like him? 5 Clothe thyself with beauty, and set thyself up on high, and be glorious, and put on goodly garments. 6 Scatter the proud in thy indignation, and behold every arrogant man, and humble him. 7 Look on all that are proud, and confound them, and crush the wicked in their place. 8 Hide them in the dust together, and plunge their faces into the pit. 9 Then I will confess that thy right hand is able to save thee.

10 "Behold Behemoth whom I made with thee; he eateth grass like an ox. 11 His strength is in his loins, and his force in the navel of his belly. 12 He setteth up his tail like a cedar; the sinews of his testicles are wrapped together. 13 His bones are like pipes of brass, his gristle like plates of iron. 14 He is the beginning of the ways of God who made him. He will apply his sword. 15 To him the mountains bring forth grass; there all the beasts of the field shall play. 16 He sleepeth under the shadow in the covert of the reed and in moist places. 17 The shades cover his shadow. The willows of the brook shall compass him about. 18 Behold: he will drink up a river

et non mirabitur, et habet fiduciam quod influat Iordanis in os eius. 19 In oculis eius quasi hamo capiet eum et in sudibus perforabit nares eius.

20 "An extrahere poteris Leviathan hamo, et fune ligabis linguam eius? 21 Numquid pones circulum in naribus eius aut armilla perforabis maxillam eius? 22 Numquid multiplicabit ad te preces aut loquetur tibi mollia? 23 Numquid feriet tecum pactum, et accipies eum servum sempiternum? 24 Numquid inludes ei quasi avi aut ligabis illum ancillis tuis? 25 Concident eum amici? Divident illum negotiatores? 26 Numquid implebis sagenas pelle eius et gurgustium piscium capite illius? 27 Pone super eum manum tuam; memento belli, nec ultra addas loqui. 28 Ecce: spes eius frustrabitur eum, et videntibus cunctis praecipitabitur."

Caput 41

"Non quasi crudelis suscitabo eum, quis enim resistere potest vultui meo? 2 Quis ante dedit mihi ut reddam ei? Omnia quae sub caelo sunt mea sunt. 3 Non parcam ei et verbis

and not wonder, and he trusteth that the Jordan may run into his mouth. 19 In his eyes as with a hook he shall take him and bore through his nostrils with stakes.

20 "Canst thou draw out the Leviathan with a hook, *or canst* thou tie his tongue with a cord? 21 *Canst* thou put a ring in his nose or bore through his jaw with a buckle? 22 Will he make many supplications to thee or speak soft words to thee? 23 Will he make a covenant with thee, and wilt thou take him to be a servant for ever? 24 Shalt thou play with him as with a bird or tie him up for thy handmaids? 25 Shall friends cut him in pieces? Shall merchants divide him? 26 Wilt thou fill nets with his skin and the cabin of fishes with his head? 27 Lay thy hand upon him; remember the battle, and speak no more. 28 Behold: his hope shall fail him, and in the sight of all he shall be cast down."

Chapter 41

A further description of the Leviathan.

"I will not stir him up like one that is cruel, for who can resist my countenance? 2 Who hath given me before that I should repay him? All things that are under heaven are mine. 3 I will not spare him nor his mighty words and framed to

potentibus et ad deprecandum conpositis. 4 Quis revelabit faciem indumenti eius? Et in medium oris eius quis intrabit? 5 Portas vultus eius quis aperiet? Per gyrum dentium eius formido. 6 Corpus illius quasi scuta fusilia, conpactum squamis se prementibus. 7 Una uni coniungitur, et ne spiraculum quidem incedit per eas. 8 Una alteri adherebit, et tenentes se nequaquam separabuntur. 9 Sternutatio eius splendor ignis et oculi eius ut palpebrae diluculi. 10 De ore eius lampades procedunt sicut taedae ignis accensae. 11 De naribus eius procedit fumus sicut ollae succensae atque ferventis. 12 Halitus eius prunas ardere facit, et flamma de ore eius egreditur. 13 In collo eius morabitur fortitudo, et faciem eius praecedit egestas.

14 "Membra carnium eius coherentia sibi; mittet contra eum fulmina, et ad locum alium non ferentur. 15 Cor eius indurabitur quasi lapis et stringetur quasi malleatoris incus. 16 Cum sublatus fuerit timebunt angeli et territi purgabuntur.

17 "Cum adprehenderit eum gladius, subsistere non poterit, neque hasta, neque torax, 18 reputabit enim quasi paleas ferrum et quasi lignum putridum aes. 19 Non fugabit eum vir sagittarius; in stipulam versi sunt ei lapides fundae. 20 Quasi stipulam aestimabit malleum, et deridebit vibrantem hastam.

21 "Sub ipso erunt radii solis, et sternet sibi aurum quasi lutum. 22 Fervescere faciet quasi ollam profundum mare et ponet quasi cum unguenta bulliunt. 23 Post eum lucebit

make supplication. 4 Who *can* discover the face of his garment? *Or* who *can* go into the midst of his mouth? 5 Who *can* open the doors of his face? His teeth are terrible round about. 6 His body is like molten shields, shut close up with scales pressing upon one another. 7 One is joined to another, and not so much as any air *can* come between them. 8 *They stick one* to another, and they hold one another fast and shall not be separated. 9 His sneezing is like the shining of fire and his eyes like the eyelids of the morning. 10 Out of his mouth go forth lamps like torches of lighted fire. 11 Out of his nostrils goeth smoke like that of a pot heated and boiling. 12 His breath kindleth coals, and a flame cometh forth out of his mouth. 13 In his neck strength shall dwell, and want goeth before his face.

14 "The members of his flesh cleave one to another; he shall send lightnings against him, and they shall not be carried to another place. 15 His heart shall be as hard as a stone and as firm as a smith's anvil. 16 When he shall raise him up the angels shall fear and being affrighted shall purify themselves.

17 "When a sword shall lay at him, it shall not be able to hold, nor a spear, nor a breastplate, 18 for he shall esteem iron as straw and brass as rotten wood. 19 The archer shall not put him to flight; the stones of the sling *are* to him *like* stubble. 20 As stubble will he esteem the hammer, and he will laugh him to scorn who shaketh the spear.

21 "The beams of the sun shall be under him, and he shall strew gold under him like mire. 22 He shall make the deep sea to boil like a pot and shall make it as when ointments boil. 23 A path shall shine after him; he shall esteem the deep

semita; aestimabit abyssum quasi senescentem. 24 Non est super terram potestas quae conparetur ei qui factus est ut nullum timeret. 25 Omne sublime videt; ipse est rex super universos filios superbiae."

Caput 42

Respondens autem Iob Domino dixit, 2 "Scio quia omnia potes et nulla te latet cogitatio. 3 'Quis est iste qui celat consilium absque scientia?' Ideo insipienter locutus sum et quae ultra modum excederent scientiam meam. 4 'Audi, et ego loquar. Interrogabo te, et responde mihi.' 5 Auditu auris audivi te, nunc autem oculus meus videt te. 6 Idcirco ipse me reprehendo et ago paenitentiam in favilla et cinere."

7 Postquam autem locutus est Dominus verba haec ad Iob dixit ad Eliphaz, Themaniten, "Iratus est furor meus in te et in duos amicos tuos quoniam non estis locuti coram me rec-

as growing old. 24 There is no power upon earth that can be compared with him who was made to fear no one. 25 He beholdeth every high thing; he is king over all the children of pride."

Chapter 42

Job submits himself. God pronounces in his favour. Job offers sacrifice for his friends. He is blessed with riches and children and dies happily,

Then Job answered the Lord and said, 2 "I know that thou canst do all things and no thought is hid from thee. 3 'Who is this that hideth counsel without knowledge?' Therefore I have spoken unwisely and things that above measure exceeded my knowledge. 4 'Hear, and I will speak. I will ask thee, and do thou tell me.' 5 With the hearing of the ear I have heard thee, but now my eye seeth thee. 6 Therefore I reprehend myself and do penance in dust and ashes."

7 And after the Lord had spoken these words to Job he said to Eliphaz, the Temanite, "My wrath is kindled against thee and against thy two friends because you have not spoken the thing that is right before me as my servant

tum sicut servus meus Iob. 8 Sumite igitur vobis septem tauros et septem arietes, et ite ad servum meum Iob, et offerte holocaustum pro vobis, Iob autem servus meus orabit pro vobis. Faciem eius suscipiam ut non vobis inputetur stultitia, neque enim locuti estis ad me recta sicut servus meus Iob."

9 Abierunt ergo Eliphaz, Themanites, et Baldad, Suites, et Sophar, Naamathites, et fecerunt sicut locutus fuerat ad eos Dominus, et suscepit Dominus faciem Iob. 10 Dominus quoque conversus est ad paenitentiam Iob cum oraret ille pro amicis suis. Et addidit Dominus omnia quaecumque fuerant Iob duplicia. 11 Venerunt autem ad eum omnes fratres sui et universae sorores suae et cuncti qui noverant eum prius, et comederunt cum eo panem in domo eius et moverunt super eum caput et consolati sunt eum super omni malo quod intulerat Deus super eum. Et dederunt ei unusquisque ovem unam et inaurem auream unam. 12 Dominus autem benedixit novissimis Iob magis quam principio eius. Et facta sunt ei quattuordecim milia ovium et sex milia camelorum et mille iuga boum et mille asinae. 13 Et fuerunt ei septem filii et filiae tres. 14 Et vocavit nomen unius Diem et nomen secundae Cassia et nomen tertiae Cornustibii. 15 Non sunt autem inventae mulieres speciosae sicut filiae Iob in universa terra, deditque eis pater suus hereditatem inter fratres earum.

16 Vixit autem Iob post haec centum quadraginta annis, et vidit filios suos et filios filiorum suorum usque ad quartam generationem, et mortuus est senex et plenus dierum.

Job hath. 8 Take unto you therefore seven oxen and seven rams, and go to my servant Job, and offer for yourselves a holocaust, and my servant Job shall pray for you. His face I will accept that folly be not imputed to you, for you have not spoken right things before me as my servant Job hath."

9 So Eliphaz, the Temanite, and Bildad, the Shuhite, and Zophar, the Naamathite, went and did as the Lord had spoken to them, and the Lord accepted the face of Job. 10 The Lord also was turned at the penance of Job when he prayed for his friends. And the Lord *gave Job twice as much as he had before.* 11 And all his brethren came to him and all his sisters and all that knew him before, and they ate bread with him in his house and *bemoaned* him and comforted him upon all the evil that God had brought upon him. And every man gave him one ewe and one earring of gold. 12 And the Lord blessed the *latter end* of Job more than his beginning. And he had fourteen thousand sheep and six thousand camels and a thousand yoke of oxen and a thousand she-asses. 13 And he had seven sons and three daughters. 14 And he called the name of one Jemimah and the name of the second Keziah and the name of the third Keren-happuch. 15 And there were not found in all the earth women so beautiful as the daughters of Job, and their father gave them inheritance among their brethren.

16 And Job lived after these things a hundred and forty years, and he saw his children and his children's children unto the fourth generation, and he died an old man and full of days.

PSALMS

Psalmus I

Beatus vir qui non abiit in consilio impiorum et in via peccatorum non stetit et in cathedra pestilentiae non sedit, 2 sed in lege Domini voluntas eius, et in lege eius meditabitur die ac nocte. 3 Et erit tamquam lignum quod plantatum est secus decursus aquarum, quod fructum suum dabit in tempore suo. Et folium eius non defluet, et omnia quaecumque faciet prosperabuntur.

4 Non sic impii, non sic, sed tamquam pulvis quem proicit ventus a facie terrae. 5 Ideo non resurgent impii in iudicio neque peccatores in concilio iustorum, 6 quoniam novit Dominus viam iustorum, et iter impiorum peribit.

Psalm 1

Beatus vir. The happiness of the just and the evil state of the wicked.

Blessed is the man who hath not walked in the counsel of the ungodly nor stood in the way of sinners nor sat in the chair of pestilence, 2 but his will is in the law of the Lord, and on his law he shall meditate day and night. 3 And he shall be like a tree which is planted near the *running* waters, which shall bring forth its fruit in due season. And his leaf shall not fall off, and all whatsoever he shall do shall prosper.

4 Not so the wicked, not so, but like the dust which the wind driveth from the face of the earth. 5 Therefore the wicked shall not rise again in judgment nor sinners in the council of the just, 6 for the Lord knoweth the way of the just, and the way of the wicked shall perish.

Psalmus 2

Quare fremuerunt Gentes et populi meditati sunt inania? 2 Adstiterunt reges terrae, et principes convenerunt in unum adversus Dominum et adversus Christum eius. 3 Disrumpamus vincula eorum, et proiciamus a nobis iugum ipsorum. 4 Qui habitat in caelis inridebit eos, et Dominus subsannabit eos. 5 Tunc loquetur ad eos in ira sua et in furore suo conturbabit eos.

6 Ego autem constitutus sum rex ab eo super Sion, montem sanctum eius, praedicans praeceptum eius. 7 Dominus dixit ad me, "Filius meus es tu. Ego hodie genui te. 8 Postula a me, et dabo tibi Gentes hereditatem tuam et possessionem tuam terminos terrae. 9 Reges eos in virga ferrea et tamquam vas figuli confringes eos."

10 Et nunc, reges, intellegite. Erudimini, qui iudicatis terram. 11 Servite Domino in timore, et exultate ei cum tremore. 12 Adprehendite disciplinam nequando irascatur Dominus et pereatis de via iusta. 13 Cum exarserit in brevi ira eius, beati omnes qui confidunt in eo.

Psalm 2

Quare fremuerunt. The vain efforts of persecutors against Christ and his church.

Why have the Gentiles raged and the people devised vain things? 2 The kings of the earth stood up, and the princes met together against the Lord and against his Christ. 3 Let us break their bonds asunder, and let us cast away their yoke from us. 4 He that dwelleth in heaven shall laugh at them, and the Lord shall deride them. 5 Then shall he speak to them in his anger and trouble them in his rage.

6 But I am appointed king by him over Zion, his holy mountain, preaching his commandment. 7 The Lord hath said to me, "Thou art my son. This day have I begotten thee. 8 Ask of me, and I will give thee the Gentiles for thy inheritance and the utmost parts of the earth for thy possession. 9 Thou shalt rule them with a rod of iron and shalt break them in pieces like a potter's vessel."

10 And now, O ye kings, understand. Receive instruction, you that judge the earth. 11 Serve ye the Lord with fear, and rejoice unto him with trembling. 12 Embrace discipline lest at any time the Lord be angry and you perish from the just way. 13 When his wrath shall be kindled in a short time, blessed are all they that trust in him.

Psalmus 3

Psalmus David cum fugeret a facie Abessalon filii sui.
2 Domine, quid multiplicati sunt qui tribulant me? Multi insurgunt adversum me. 3 Multi dicunt animae meae, "Non est salus ipsi in Deo eius." 4 Tu autem, Domine, susceptor meus es, gloria mea et exaltans caput meum. 5 Voce mea ad Dominum clamavi, et exaudivit me de monte sancto suo. 6 Ego dormivi et soporatus sum, et exsurrexi quia Dominus suscepit me.

7 Non timebo milia populi circumdantis me. Exsurge, Domine! Salvum me fac, Deus meus, 8 quoniam tu percussisti omnes adversantes mihi sine causa; dentes peccatorum contrivisti. 9 Domini est salus, et super populum tuum benedictio tua.

Psalm 3

Domine, quid multiplicati. The prophet's danger and delivery from his son Absalom. Mystically, the passion and resurrection of Christ.

The psalm of David when he fled from the face of his son Absalom.

2 Why, O Lord, are they multiplied that afflict me? Many are they who rise up against me. 3 Many say to my soul, "There is no salvation for him in his God." 4 But thou, O Lord, art my protector, my glory and the lifter up of my head. 5 I have cried to the Lord with my voice, and he hath heard me from his holy hill. 6 I have slept and have taken my rest, and I have risen up because the Lord hath protected me.

7 I will not fear thousands of the people surrounding me. Arise, O Lord! Save me, O my God, 8 for thou hast struck all them who are my adversaries without cause; thou hast broken the teeth of sinners. 9 Salvation is of the Lord, and thy blessing is upon thy people.

Psalmus 4

In finem. In carminibus. Psalmus David. 2 Cum invocarem, exaudivit me Deus iustitiae meae. In tribulatione, dilatasti mihi. Miserere mei, et exaudi orationem meam. 3 Filii hominum, usquequo gravi corde? Ut quid diligitis vanitatem et quaeritis mendacium? 4 Et scitote quoniam mirificavit Dominus sanctum suum; Dominus exaudiet me cum clamavero ad eum. 5 Irascimini, et nolite peccare quae dicitis in cordibus vestris. In cubilibus vestris conpungimini. 6 Sacrificate sacrificium iustitiae, et sperate in Domino. Multi dicunt, "Quis ostendit nobis bona?" 7 Signatum est super nos lumen vultus tui, Domine. Dedisti laetitiam in corde meo. 8 A fructu frumenti et vini et olei sui multiplicati sunt. 9 In pace, in id ipsum, dormiam, et requiescam, 10 quoniam tu, Domine, singulariter in spe constituisti me.

Psalm 4

Cum invocarem. The prophet teacheth us to flee to God in
tribulation with confidence in him.

Unto the end. In verses. A psalm for David.

2 When I called *upon him,* the God of my justice heard
me. When I was in distress, thou hast enlarged me. Have
mercy on me, and hear my prayer.

3 O ye sons of men, how long will you be dull of heart?
Why do you love vanity and seek after lying? 4 Know ye also
that the Lord hath made his holy one wonderful; the Lord
will hear me when I shall cry unto him. 5 Be ye angry, and sin
not the things you say in your hearts. Be sorry for them upon
your beds. 6 Offer up the sacrifice of justice, and trust in the
Lord.

Many say, "Who sheweth us good things?"

7 The light of thy countenance, O Lord, is signed upon us.
Thou hast given gladness in my heart. 8 By the fruit of their
corn, *their* wine and oil they are multiplied. 9 In peace, in the
self same, I will sleep, and I will rest, 10 for thou, O Lord,
singularly hast settled me in hope.

Psalmus 5

In finem. Pro ea quae hereditatem consequitur. Psalmus David. ² Verba mea auribus percipe, Domine. Intellege clamorem meum. ³ Intende voci orationis meae, rex meus et Deus meus, ⁴ quoniam ad te orabo, Domine; mane exaudies vocem meam. ⁵ Mane adstabo tibi, et videbo, quoniam non Deus volens iniquitatem tu es.

⁶ Neque habitabit iuxta te malignus, neque permanebunt iniusti ante oculos tuos. ⁷ Odisti omnes qui operantur iniquitatem; perdes omnes qui loquuntur mendacium. Virum sanguinum et dolosum abominabitur Dominus.

⁸ Ego autem, in multitudine misericordiae tuae introibo in domum tuam. Adorabo ad templum sanctum tuum in timore tuo.

⁹ Domine, deduc me in iustitia tua. Propter inimicos meos, dirige in conspectu tuo viam meam, ¹⁰ quoniam non est in ore eorum veritas. Cor eorum vanum est. ¹¹ Sepulchrum patens est guttur eorum. Linguis suis dolose agebant. Iudica illos, Deus. Decidant a cogitationibus suis. Secundum multitudinem impietatum eorum expelle eos, quoniam inritaverunt te, Domine.

Psalm 5

Verba mea auribus. A prayer to God against the iniquities of men.

Unto the end. For her that obtaineth the inheritance. A psalm for David. 2 Give ear, O Lord, to my words. Understand my cry. 3 Hearken to the voice of my prayer, O my king and my God, 4 for to thee will I pray, O Lord; in the morning thou shalt hear my voice. 5 In the morning I will stand before thee, and I will see, because thou art not a God that willest iniquity.

6 Neither shall the wicked dwell near thee, nor shall the unjust abide before thy eyes. 7 Thou hatest all the workers of iniquity; thou wilt destroy all that speak a lie. The bloody and the deceitful man the Lord will abhor.

8 But as for me, in the multitude of thy mercy I will come into thy house. I will worship towards thy holy temple in thy fear.

9 Conduct me, O Lord, in thy justice. Because of my enemies, direct my way in thy sight, 10 for there is no truth in their mouth. Their heart is vain. 11 Their throat is an open sepulchre. They dealt deceitfully with their tongues. Judge them, O God. Let them fall from their devices. According to the multitude of their wickednesses cast them out, for they have provoked thee, O Lord.

12 Et laetentur omnes qui sperant in te. In aeternum exultabunt, et habitabis in eis. Et gloriabuntur in te omnes qui diligunt nomen tuum, 13 quoniam tu benedices iusto, Domine. Ut scuto bonae voluntatis tuae coronasti nos.

Psalmus 6

In finem. In carminibus. Pro octava. Psalmus David.

2 Domine, ne in furore tuo arguas me, neque in ira tua corripias me. 3 Miserere mei, Domine, quoniam infirmus sum. Sana me, Domine, quoniam conturbata sunt ossa mea 4 et anima mea turbata est valde.

Sed tu, Domine, usquequo?

5 Convertere, Domine, et eripe animam meam. Salvum me fac propter misericordiam tuam, 6 quoniam non est in morte qui memor sit tui, in inferno autem quis confitebitur tibi?

7 Laboravi in gemitu meo. Lavabo per singulas noctes lectum meum; lacrimis meis stratum meum rigabo. 8 Turbatus

12 *But* let all them be glad that hope in thee. They shall rejoice for ever, and thou shalt dwell in them. And all they that love thy name shall glory in thee, 13 for thou wilt bless the just, O Lord. Thou hast crowned us as with a shield of thy good will.

Psalm 6

Domine, ne in furore. A prayer of a penitent sinner under the scourge of God. The first penitential psalm.

Unto the end. In verses. A psalm for David. For the octave.

2 O Lord, rebuke me not in thy indignation, nor chastise me in thy wrath. 3 Have mercy on me, O Lord, for I am weak. Heal me, O Lord, for my bones are troubled 4 and my soul is troubled exceedingly.

But thou, O Lord, how long?

5 Turn to me, O Lord, and deliver my soul. O save me for thy mercy's sake, 6 for there is no one in death that is mindful of thee, and who shall confess to thee in hell?

7 I have laboured in my groanings. Every night I will wash my bed; I will water my couch with my tears. 8 My eye is

est a furore oculus meus. Inveteravi inter omnes inimicos meos. ⁹ Discedite a me, omnes qui operamini iniquitatem, quoniam exaudivit Dominus vocem fletus mei. ¹⁰ Exaudivit Dominus deprecationem meam. Dominus orationem meam suscepit. ¹¹ Erubescant et conturbentur vehementer omnes inimici mei. Convertantur et erubescant valde velociter.

Psalmus 7

Psalmus David quem cantavit Domino pro verbis Chusi, filii Iemini.

² Domine, Deus meus, in te speravi; salvum me fac ex omnibus persequentibus me, et libera me ³ nequando rapiat ut leo animam meam dum non est qui redimat neque qui salvum faciat.

⁴ Domine, Deus meus, si feci istud, si est iniquitas in manibus meis, ⁵ si reddidi retribuentibus mihi mala, decidam

troubled through indignation. I have grown old amongst all my enemies. 9 Depart from me, all ye workers of iniquity, for the Lord hath heard the voice of my weeping. 10 The Lord hath heard my supplication. The Lord hath received my prayer. 11 Let all my enemies be ashamed and be very much troubled. Let them be turned back and be ashamed very speedily.

Psalm 7

Domine, Deus meus. David, trusting in the justice of his cause, prayeth for God's help against his enemies.

The psalm of David which he sung to the Lord for the words of Cush, the son of Jemini.

2 O Lord, my God, in thee have I put my trust; save me from all them that persecute me, and deliver me 3 lest at any time he seize upon my soul like a lion while there is no one to redeem me nor to save.

4 O Lord, my God, if I have done this thing, if there be iniquity in my hands, 5 if I have rendered to them that repaid me evils, let me deservedly fall empty before my ene-

merito ab inimicis meis inanis. 6 Persequatur inimicus animam meam et conprehendat et conculcet in terra vitam meam et gloriam meam in pulverem deducat. 7 Exsurge, Domine, in ira tua, et exaltare in finibus inimicorum meorum, et exsurge, Domine, Deus meus, in praecepto quod mandasti, 8 et synagoga populorum circumdabit te, et propter hanc in altum regredere.

9 Dominus iudicat populos. Iudica me, Domine, secundum iustitiam meam et secundum innocentiam meam super me. 10 Consumetur nequitia peccatorum, et diriges iustum, qui scrutaris corda et renes, Deus. 11 Iustum adiutorium meum a Domino, qui salvos facit rectos corde. 12 Deus iudex iustus, fortis et patiens. Numquid irascitur per singulos dies?

13 Nisi conversi fueritis, gladium suum vibrabit; arcum suum tetendit et paravit illum. 14 Et in eo paravit vasa mortis; sagittas suas ardentibus effecit.

15 Ecce: parturiit iniustitiam; concepit dolorem et peperit iniquitatem. 16 Lacum aperuit et effodit eum, et incidit in foveam quam fecit. 17 Convertetur dolor eius in caput eius, et in verticem ipsius iniquitas eius descendet.

18 Confitebor Domino secundum iustitiam eius et psallam nomini Domini, Altissimi.

mies. 6 Let the enemy pursue my soul and take it and tread down my life on the earth and bring down my glory to the dust. 7 Rise up, O Lord, in thy anger, and be thou exalted in the borders of my enemies, and arise, O Lord, my God, in the precept which thou hast commanded, 8 and a congregation of people shall surround thee, and for their sakes return thou on high.

9 The Lord judgeth the people. Judge me, O Lord, according to my justice and according to my innocence in me. 10 The wickedness of sinners shall be brought to nought, and thou shalt direct the just. *The searcher* of hearts and reins *is* God. 11 Just is my help from the Lord, who saveth the upright of heart. 12 God is a just judge, strong and patient. Is he angry every day?

13 Except you will be converted, he will brandish his sword; he hath bent his bow and made it ready. 14 And in it he hath prepared the instruments of death; he hath made ready his arrows for them that burn.

15 Behold: he hath been in labour with injustice; he hath conceived sorrow and brought forth iniquity. 16 He hath opened a pit and dug it, and he is fallen into the hole he made. 17 His sorrow shall be turned on his own head, and his iniquity shall come down upon his crown.

18 I will give glory to the Lord according to his justice and will sing to the name of the Lord, the Most High.

Psalmus 8

In finem. Pro torcularibus. Psalmus David. 2 Domine, Dominus noster, quam admirabile est nomen tuum in universa terra! Quoniam elevata est magnificentia tua super caelos. 3 Ex ore infantium et lactantium perfecisti laudem propter inimicos tuos ut destruas inimicum et ultorem, 4 quoniam videbo caelos tuos, opera digitorum tuorum, lunam et stellas quae tu fundasti.

5 Quid est homo quod memor es eius, aut filius hominis quoniam visitas eum? 6 Minuisti eum paulo minus ab angelis; gloria et honore coronasti eum 7 et constituisti eum super opera manuum tuarum. 8 Omnia subiecisti sub pedibus eius, oves et boves universas, insuper et pecora campi, 9 volucres caeli et pisces maris qui perambulant semitas maris.

10 Domine, Dominus noster, quam admirabile est nomen tuum in universa terra!

Psalm 8

Domine, Dominus noster. God is wonderful in his works, especially in mankind, singularly exalted by the incarnation of Christ.

Unto the end. For the presses. A psalm for David.

2 O Lord, our Lord, how admirable is thy name in the whole earth! For thy magnificence is elevated above the heavens. 3 Out of the mouth of infants and of sucklings thou hast perfected praise because of thy enemies that thou mayst destroy the enemy and the avenger, 4 for I will behold thy heavens, the works of thy fingers, the moon and the stars which thou hast founded.

5 What is man that thou art mindful of him, or the son of man that thou visitest him? 6 Thou hast made him a little less than the angels; thou hast crowned him with glory and honour 7 and hast set him over the works of thy hands. 8 Thou hast subjected all things under his feet, all sheep and oxen, moreover the beasts also of the fields, 9 the birds of the air and the fishes of the sea that pass through the paths of the sea.

10 O Lord, our Lord, how admirable is thy name in the whole earth!

Psalmus 9

In finem. Pro occultis Filii. Psalmus David. 2 Confitebor tibi, Domine, in toto corde meo. Narrabo omnia mirabilia tua. 3 Laetabor et exultabo in te. Psallam nomini tuo, Altissime. 4 In convertendo inimicum meum retrorsum infirmabuntur et peribunt a facie tua, 5 quoniam fecisti iudicium meum et causam meam. Sedisti super thronum, qui iudicas iustitiam. 6 Increpasti Gentes, et periit impius; nomen eorum delisti in aeternum et in saeculum saeculi. 7 Inimici defecerunt frameae in finem, et civitates eorum destruxisti. Periit memoria eorum cum sonitu, 8 et Dominus in aeternum permanet. Paravit in iudicio thronum suum, 9 et ipse iudicabit orbem terrae in aequitate. Iudicabit populos in iustitia.

10 Et factus est Dominus refugium pauperi, adiutor in oportunitatibus in tribulatione. 11 Et sperent in te qui noverunt nomen tuum, quoniam non dereliquisti quaerentes te, Domine. 12 Psallite Domino, qui habitat in Sion; adnuntiate inter Gentes studia eius, 13 quoniam requirens sanguinem eorum recordatus est. Non est oblitus clamorem pauperum.

Psalm 9

Confitebor tibi, Domine. The church praiseth God for his protection against her enemies.

Unto the end. For the hidden things of the Son. A psalm for David. 2 I will give praise to thee, O Lord, with my whole heart. I will relate all thy wonders. 3 I will be glad and rejoice in thee. I will sing to thy name, O thou Most High. 4 When my enemy shall be turned back they shall be weakened and perish before thy face, 5 for thou hast maintained my judgment and my cause. Thou hast sat on the throne, who judgest justice. 6 Thou hast rebuked the Gentiles, and the wicked one hath perished; thou hast blotted out their name for ever and ever. 7 The swords of the enemy have failed unto the end, and their cities thou hast destroyed. Their memory hath perished with a noise, 8 *but* the Lord remaineth for ever. He hath prepared his throne in judgment, 9 and he shall judge the world in equity. He shall judge the people in justice.

10 And the Lord is become a refuge for the poor, a helper in due time in tribulation. 11 And let them trust in thee who know thy name, for thou hast not forsaken them that seek thee, O Lord. 12 Sing ye to the Lord, who dwelleth in Zion; declare his *ways* among the Gentiles, 13 for requiring their blood he hath remembered them. He hath not forgotten the cry of the poor.

14 Miserere mei, Domine! Vide humilitatem meam de inimicis meis, 15 qui exaltas me de portis mortis, ut adnuntiem omnes laudationes tuas in portis filiae Sion. 16 Exultabo in salutari tuo. Infixae sunt Gentes in interitu quem fecerunt; in laqueo isto quem absconderunt conprehensus est pes eorum. 17 Cognoscetur Dominus iudicia faciens. In operibus manuum suarum conprehensus est peccator. 18 Convertantur peccatores in infernum, omnes gentes quae obliviscuntur Deum, 19 quoniam non in finem oblivio erit pauperis; patientia pauperum non peribit in finem. 20 Exsurge, Domine; non confortetur homo; iudicentur Gentes in conspectu tuo. 21 Constitue, Domine, legislatorem super eos, ut sciant Gentes quoniam homines sunt.

Psalmus 10 secundum Hebraeos

Ut quid, Domine, recessisti longe? Dispicis in oportunitatibus, in tribulatione? 2 Dum superbit impius, incenditur pauper. Conprehenduntur in consiliis quibus cogitant, 3 quoniam laudatur peccator in desideriis animae suae et iniquus benedicitur.

14 Have mercy on me, O Lord! See my humiliation which I suffer from my enemies, 15 thou that liftest me up from the gates of death, that I may declare all thy praises in the gates of the daughter of Zion. 16 I will rejoice in thy salvation. The Gentiles have stuck fast in the destruction which they prepared; their foot hath been taken in the very snare which they hid. 17 The Lord shall be known when he executeth judgments. The sinner hath been caught in the works of his own hands. 18 The wicked shall be turned into hell, all the nations that forget God, 19 for the poor man shall not be forgotten to the end; the patience of the poor shall not perish for ever.

20 Arise, O Lord; let not man be strengthened; let the Gentiles be judged in thy sight. 21 Appoint, O Lord, a lawgiver over them, that the Gentiles may know themselves to be *but* men.

Psalm 10 according to the Hebrews

Why, O Lord, hast thou retired afar off? Why dost thou slight us in our wants, in the time of trouble? 2 Whilst the wicked man is proud, the poor is set on fire. They are caught in the counsels which they devise, 3 for the sinner is praised in the desires of his soul and the unjust man is blessed.

4 Exacerbavit Dominum peccator secundum multitudinem irae suae. Non quaeret. 5 Non est Deus in conspectu eius; inquinatae sunt viae illius in omni tempore. Auferuntur iudicia tua a facie eius; omnium inimicorum suorum dominabitur, 6 dixit enim in corde suo, "Non movebor a generatione in generationem sine malo." 7 Cuius maledictione os plenum est et amaritudine et dolo. Sub lingua eius labor et dolor. 8 Sedet in insidiis cum divitibus in occultis ut interficiat innocentem. 9 Oculi eius in pauperem respiciunt; insidiatur, in abscondito, quasi leo in spelunca sua. Insidiatur ut rapiat pauperem, rapere pauperem dum adtrahit eum. 10 In laqueo suo humiliabit eum; inclinabit se et cadet cum dominatus fuerit pauperum, 11 dixit enim in corde suo, "Oblitus est Deus; avertit faciem suam ne videat in finem."

12 Exsurge, Domine Deus! Exaltetur manus tua. Ne obliviscaris pauperum.

13 Propter quid inritavit impius Deum? Dixit enim in corde suo, "Non requiret." 14 Vides, quoniam tu laborem et dolorem consideras ut tradas eos in manus tuas. Tibi derelictus est pauper; orfano tu eris adiutor. 15 Contere brachium peccatoris et maligni. Quaeretur peccatum illius et non invenietur.

4 The sinner hath provoked the Lord according to the multitude of his wrath. He will not seek him. 5 God is not before his eyes; his ways are filthy at all times. Thy judgments are removed from his sight; he shall rule over all his enemies, 6 for he hath said in his heart, "I shall not be moved from generation to generation *and shall be* without evil." 7 His mouth is full of cursing and of bitterness and of deceit. Under his tongue are labour and sorrow. 8 He sitteth in ambush with the rich in private places that he may kill the innocent. 9 His eyes are upon the poor man; he lieth in wait, in secret, like a lion in his den. He lieth in ambush that he may catch the poor man, to catch the poor whilst he draweth him to him. 10 In his net he will bring him down; he will crouch and fall when he shall have power over the poor, 11 for he hath said in his heart, "God hath forgotten; he hath turned away his face not to see to the end."

12 Arise, O Lord God! Let thy hand be exalted. Forget not the poor.

13 Wherefore hath the wicked provoked God? For he hath said in his heart, "He will not require it." 14 Thou seest it, for thou considerest labour and sorrow that thou mayst deliver them into thy hands. To thee is the poor man left; thou wilt be a helper to the orphan. 15 Break thou the arm of the sinner and of the malignant. His sin shall be sought and shall not be found.

16 Dominus regnabit in aeternum et in saeculum saeculi. Peribitis Gentes de terra illius. 17 Desiderium pauperum exaudivit Dominus; praeparationem cordis eorum audivit auris tua 18 iudicare pupillo et humili ut non adponat ultra magnificare se homo super terram.

Psalmus 10

In finem. Psalmus David. 2 In Domino confido. Quomodo dicitis animae meae, "Transmigra in montem, sicut passer"? 3 Quoniam, ecce, peccatores intenderunt arcum; paraverunt sagittas suas in faretra ut sagittent in obscuro rectos corde, 4 quoniam quae perfecisti destruxerunt, iustus autem quid fecit? 5 Dominus in templo sancto suo. Dominus, in caelo sedis eius. Oculi eius in pauperem respiciunt; palpebrae eius interrogant filios hominum. 6 Dominus interrogat iustum et impium, qui autem diligit iniquitatem odit animam suam. 7 Pluet super

16 The Lord shall reign to eternity, yea, for ever and ever. Ye Gentiles shall perish from his land. 17 The Lord hath heard the desire of the poor; thy ear hath heard the preparation of their heart 18 to judge for the fatherless and for the humble that man may no more presume to magnify himself upon earth.

Psalm 10

In Domino confido. The just man's confidence in God in the midst of persecutions.

Unto the end. A psalm for David.
2 In the Lord I put my trust. How then do you say to my soul, *"Get thee away from hence* to the mountain, like a sparrow"? 3 For, lo, the wicked have bent their bow; they have prepared their arrows in the quiver to shoot in the dark the upright of heart, 4 for they have destroyed the things which thou hast made, but what has the just man done? 5 The Lord is in his holy temple. The Lord's throne is in heaven. His eyes look on the poor man; his eyelids examine the sons of men. 6 The Lord trieth the just and the wicked, but he that loveth iniquity hateth his own soul. 7 He shall rain snares

peccatores laqueos; ignis et sulphur et spiritus procellarum pars calicis eorum, 8 quoniam iustus Dominus et iustitias dilexit; aequitatem vidit vultus eius.

Psalmus 11

In finem. Pro octava. Psalmus David.

2 Salvum me fac, Domine, quoniam defecit sanctus, quoniam deminutae sunt veritates a filiis hominum. 3 Vana locuti sunt, unusquisque ad proximum suum. Labia dolosa et in corde et corde locuti sunt. 4 Disperdat Dominus universa labia dolosa et linguam magniloquam, 5 qui dixerunt, "Linguam nostram magnificabimus; labia nostra a nobis sunt; quis noster Dominus est?"

6 "Propter miseriam inopum et gemitum pauperum nunc exsurgam," dicit Dominus. "Ponam in salutari. Fiducialiter agam in eo."

7 Eloquia Domini eloquia casta, argentum igne examina-

upon sinners; fire and brimstone and storms of winds shall be the portion of their cup, 8 for the Lord is just and hath loved justice; his countenance hath beheld righteousness.

Psalm 11

Salvum me fac. The prophet calls for God's help against the wicked.

Unto the end. For the octave. A psalm for David.

2 Save me, O Lord, for there is now no saint. *Truths* are decayed from among the children of men. 3 They have spoken vain things, every one to his neighbour. With deceitful lips *and with a double heart* have they spoken. 4 May the Lord destroy all deceitful lips and the tongue that speaketh proud things, 5 who have said, "We will magnify our tongue; our lips are our own; who is Lord over us?"

6 "By reason of the misery of the needy and the groans of the poor now will I arise," saith the Lord. "I will set him in safety. I will deal confidently in his regard."

7 The words of the Lord are pure words, as silver tried by

tum, probatum terrae, purgatum septuplum. 8 Tu, Domine, servabis nos et custodies nos a generatione hac et in aeternum. 9 In circuitu impii ambulant. Secundum altitudinem tuam multiplicasti filios hominum.

Psalmus 12

In finem. Psalmus David.
Usquequo, Domine, oblivisceris me in finem? Usquequo avertis faciem tuam a me? 2 Quamdiu ponam consilia in anima mea, dolorem in corde meo per diem? 3 Usquequo exaltabitur inimicus meus super me? 4 Respice, et exaudi me, Domine, Deus meus. Inlumina oculos meos ne umquam obdormiam in morte 5 nequando dicat inimicus meus, "Praevalui adversus eum." Qui tribulant me exultabunt si motus fuero, 6 ego autem in misericordia tua speravi. Exultabit cor meum in salutari tuo. Cantabo Domino, qui bona tribuit mihi, et psallam nomini Domini, Altissimi.

the fire, *purged* from the earth, refined seven times. 8 Thou, O Lord, wilt preserve us and keep us from this generation for ever. 9 The wicked walk round about. According to thy highness thou hast multiplied the children of men.

Psalm 12

Usquequo, Domine. A prayer in tribulation.

Unto the end. A psalm for David.

How long, O Lord, wilt thou forget me unto the end? How long dost thou turn away thy face from me? 2 How long shall I take counsels in my soul, sorrow in my heart all the day? 3 How long shall my enemy be exalted over me? 4 Consider, and hear me, O Lord, my God. Enlighten my eyes that I never sleep in death 5 lest at any time my enemy say, "I have prevailed against him." They that trouble me will rejoice *when* I am moved, 6 but I have trusted in thy mercy. My heart shall rejoice in thy salvation. I will sing to the Lord, who giveth me good things. Yea, I will sing to the name of the Lord, the Most High.

Psalmus 13

In finem. Psalmus David.

Dixit insipiens in corde suo, "Non est Deus." Corrupti sunt et abominabiles facti sunt in studiis suis. Non est qui faciat bonum, non est, usque ad unum. 2 Dominus de caelo prospexit super filios hominum ut videat si est intellegens aut requirens Deum. 3 Omnes declinaverunt; simul inutiles facti sunt; non est qui faciat bonum, non est, usque ad unum. Sepulchrum patens est guttur eorum. Linguis suis dolose agebant. Venenum aspidum sub labiis eorum. Quorum os maledictione et amaritudine plenum est. Veloces pedes eorum ad effundendum sanguinem, contritio et infelicitas in viis eorum, et viam pacis non cognoverunt. Non est timor Dei ante oculos eorum.

4 Nonne cognoscent omnes qui operantur iniquitatem, qui devorant plebem meam sicut escam panis? 5 Dominum non invocaverunt. Illic trepidaverunt timore ubi non erat timor, 6 quoniam Dominus in generatione iusta. Consilium inopis confudistis, quoniam Dominus spes eius est.

Psalm 13

Dixit insipiens. The general corruption of man before our redemption by Christ.

Unto the end. A psalm for David.

The fool hath said in his heart, "There is no God." They are corrupt and are become abominable in their *ways*. There is none that doth good, no, not one.

2 The Lord hath looked down from heaven upon the children of men to see if there be any that understand and seek God. 3 They are all gone aside; they are become unprofitable together; there is none that doth good, no, not one. Their throat is an open sepulchre. With their tongues they acted deceitfully. The poison of asps is under their lips. Their mouth is full of cursing and bitterness. Their feet are swift to shed blood, destruction and unhappiness in their ways, and the way of peace they have not known. There is no fear of God before their eyes.

4 Shall not all they know that work iniquity, who devour my people as they eat bread? 5 They have not called upon the Lord. There have they trembled for fear where there was no fear, 6 for the Lord is in the just generation. You have confounded the counsel of the poor man, *but* the Lord is his hope.

7 Quis dabit ex Sion salutare Israhel? Cum averterit Dominus captivitatem plebis suae exultabit Iacob, et laetabitur Israhel.

Psalmus 14

Psalmus David.

Domine, quis habitabit in tabernaculo tuo? Aut quis requiescet in monte sancto tuo? 2 Qui ingreditur sine macula et operatur iustitiam, 3 qui loquitur veritatem in corde suo, qui non egit dolum in lingua sua nec fecit proximo suo malum et obprobrium non accepit adversus proximos suos. 4 Ad nihilum deductus est in conspectu eius malignus, timentes autem Dominum glorificat. Qui iurat proximo suo et non decipit, 5 qui pecuniam suam non dedit ad usuram et munera super innocentes non accepit, qui facit haec non movebitur in aeternum.

7 Who shall give out of Zion the salvation of Israel? When the Lord shall have turned away the captivity of his people Jacob shall rejoice, and Israel shall be glad.

Psalm 14

Domine, quis habitabit. What kind of men shall dwell in the heavenly Zion.

A psalm for David.

Lord, who shall dwell in thy tabernacle? Or who shall rest in thy holy hill? 2 He that walketh without blemish and worketh justice, 3 he that speaketh truth in his heart, who hath not used deceit in his tongue nor hath done evil to his neighbour nor taken up a reproach against his neighbours. 4 In his sight the malignant is brought to nothing, but he glorifieth them that fear the Lord. He that sweareth to his neighbour and deceiveth not, 5 he that hath not put out his money to usury nor taken bribes against the innocent, he that doth these things shall not be moved for ever.

Psalmus 15

Tituli inscriptio ipsi David.

Conserva me, Domine, quoniam in te speravi. 2 Dixi Domino, "Deus meus es tu," quoniam bonorum meorum non eges. 3 Sanctis qui sunt in terra eius mirificavit omnes voluntates meas in eis. 4 Multiplicatae sunt infirmitates eorum; postea adceleraverunt. Non congregabo conventicula eorum de sanguinibus, nec memor ero nominum eorum per labia mea. 5 Dominus pars hereditatis meae et calicis mei; tu es qui restitues hereditatem meam mihi.

6 Funes ceciderunt mihi in praeclaris, etenim hereditas mea praeclara est mihi. 7 Benedicam Domino, qui tribuit mihi intellectum; insuper et usque ad noctem increpaverunt me renes mei. 8 Providebam Dominum in conspectu meo semper, quoniam a dextris est mihi ne commovear. 9 Propter hoc laetatum est cor meum, et exultavit lingua mea. Insuper et caro mea requiescet in spe 10 quoniam non derelinques animam meam in inferno nec dabis sanctum tuum videre corruptionem. Notas mihi fecisti vias vitae. Adimplebis me laetitia cum vultu tuo. Delectationes in dextera tua usque in finem.

Psalm 15

Conserva me, Domine. Christ's future victory and triumph over the world and death.

The inscription of a title to David himself.

Preserve me, O Lord, for I have put my trust in thee. 2 I have said to the Lord, "Thou art my God," for thou hast no need of my goods. 3 To the saints who are in his land he hath made wonderful all my desires in them. 4 Their infirmities were multiplied; afterwards they made haste. I will not gather together their meetings *for blood-offerings,* nor will I be mindful of their names by my lips. 5 The Lord is the portion of my inheritance and of my cup; it is thou that wilt restore my inheritance to me.

6 The lines are fallen unto me in goodly placcs, for my inheritance is goodly to me. 7 I will bless the Lord, who hath given me understanding; moreover my reins also have corrected me even till night. 8 I set the Lord always in my sight, for he is at my right hand that I be not moved. 9 Therefore my heart hath been glad, and my tongue hath rejoiced. Moreover my flesh also shall rest in hope 10 because thou wilt not leave my soul in hell nor wilt thou give thy holy one to see corruption. Thou hast made known to me the ways of life. Thou shalt fill me with joy with thy countenance. At thy right hand are delights even to the end.

Psalmus 16

Oratio David.

Exaudi, Domine, iustitiam meam. Intende deprecationem meam. Auribus percipe orationem meam non in labiis dolosis. 2 De vultu tuo iudicium meum prodeat; oculi tui videant aequitates. 3 Probasti cor meum et visitasti nocte. Igne me examinasti, et non est inventa in me iniquitas. 4 Ut non loquatur os meum opera hominum propter verba labiorum tuorum ego custodivi vias duras. 5 Perfice gressus meos in semitis tuis ut non moveantur vestigia mea.

6 Ego clamavi, quoniam exaudisti me, Deus. Inclina aurem tuam mihi, et exaudi verba mea! 7 Mirifica misericordias tuas. Qui salvos facis sperantes in te 8 a resistentibus dexterae tuae, custodi me ut pupillam oculi. Sub umbra alarum tuarum protege me 9 a facie impiorum qui me adflixerunt. Inimici mei animam meam circumdederunt. 10 Adipem suum concluserunt. Os eorum locutum est superbiam. 11 Proicientes me nunc circumdederunt me. Oculos suos statuerunt declinare in terram. 12 Susceperunt me sicut leo paratus ad praedam et sicut catulus leonis habitans in abditis.

Psalm 16

Exaudi, Domine, iustitiam. A just man's prayer in tribulation against the malice of his enemy.

The prayer of David.

Hear, O Lord, my justice. Attend to my supplication. Give ear unto my prayer *which proceedeth* not *from* deceitful lips. 2 Let my judgment come forth from thy countenance; let thy eyes behold the things that are equitable. 3 Thou hast proved my heart and visited it by night. Thou hast tried me by fire, and iniquity hath not been found in me. 4 That my mouth may not speak the works of men for the sake of the words of thy lips I have kept hard ways. 5 Perfect thou my goings in thy paths that my footsteps be not moved.

6 I have cried to thee, for thou, O God, hast heard me. O incline thy ear unto me, and hear my words! 7 *Shew forth* thy *wonderful* mercies. Thou who savest them that trust in thee 8 from them that resist thy right hand, keep me as the apple of thy eye. Protect me under the shadow of thy wings 9 from the face of the wicked who have afflicted me. My enemies have surrounded my soul. 10 They have shut up their fat. Their mouth hath spoken *proudly.* 11 They have cast me forth, and now they have surrounded me. They have set their eyes bowing down to the earth. 12 They have taken me as a lion prepared for the prey and as a young lion dwelling in secret places.

13 Exsurge, Domine! Praeveni eum, et subplanta eum. Eripe animam meam ab impio, frameam tuam 14 ab inimicis manus tuae. Domine, a paucis de terra divide eos in vita eorum; de absconditis tuis adimpletus est venter eorum. Saturati sunt filiis, et dimiserunt reliquias suas parvulis suis. 15 Ego autem, in iustitia apparebo conspectui tuo; satiabor cum apparuerit gloria tua.

Psalmus 17

In finem. Puero Domini, David, qui locutus est Domino verba cantici huius in die qua eripuit eum Dominus de manu omnium inimicorum eius et de manu Saul, et dixit:
2 Diligam te, Domine, fortitudo mea. 3 Dominus firmamentum meum et refugium meum et liberator meus. Deus meus adiutor meus, et sperabo in eum, protector meus et cornu salutis meae et susceptor meus. 4 Laudans invocabo Dominum, et ab inimicis meis salvus ero.

13 Arise, O Lord! *Disappoint* him, and supplant him. Deliver my soul from the wicked one, thy sword 14 from the enemies of thy hand. O Lord, divide them from the few of the earth in their life; their belly is filled from thy hidden stores. They are full of children, and they have left to their little ones the rest of their substance. 15 But as for me, I will appear before thy sight in justice; I shall be satisfied when thy glory shall appear.

Psalm 17

Diligam te, Domine. David's thanks to God for his delivery from all his enemies.

Unto the end. For David, the servant of the Lord, who spoke to the Lord the words of this canticle in the day that the Lord delivered him from the hand of all his enemies and from the hand of Saul, and he said:

2 I will love thee, O Lord, my strength. 3 The Lord is my firmament, *my* refuge and my deliverer. My God is my helper, and in him will I put my trust, my protector and the horn of my salvation and my support. 4 Praising I will call upon the Lord, and I shall be saved from my enemies.

5 Circumdederunt me dolores mortis, et torrentes iniquitatis conturbaverunt me. 6 Dolores inferni circumdederunt me; praeoccupaverunt me laquei mortis. 7 In tribulatione invocavi Dominum, et ad Deum meum clamavi, et exaudivit de templo sancto suo vocem meam et clamor meus in conspectu eius introivit in aures eius. 8 Commota est et contremuit terra; fundamenta montium conturbata sunt et commota sunt quoniam iratus est eis. 9 Ascendit fumus in ira eius, et ignis a facie eius exarsit; carbones succensi sunt ab eo. 10 Inclinavit caelos et descendit, et caligo sub pedibus eius. 11 Et ascendit super cherubin, et volavit; volavit super pinnas ventorum. 12 Et posuit tenebras latibulum suum, in circuitu eius tabernaculum eius tenebrosa aqua in nubibus aeris. 13 Prae fulgore in conspectu eius nubes transierunt, grando et carbones ignis. 14 Et intonuit de caelo Dominus, et Altissimus dedit vocem suam, grando et carbones ignis. 15 Et misit sagittas suas, et dissipavit eos. Fulgora multiplicavit et conturbavit eos. 16 Et apparuerunt fontes aquarum, et revelata sunt fundamenta orbis terrarum ab increpatione tua, Domine, ab inspiratione spiritus irae tuae.

17 Misit de summo et accepit me et adsumpsit me de aquis multis. 18 Eripuit me de inimicis meis fortissimis et ab his qui oderunt me, quoniam confirmati sunt super me. 19 Praevenerunt me in die adflictionis meae, et factus est Dominus protector meus. 20 Et eduxit me in latitudinem. Salvum me fecit quoniam voluit me.

5 The sorrows of death surrounded me, and the torrents of iniquity troubled me. 6 The sorrows of hell encompassed me, *and* the snares of death prevented me. 7 In my affliction I called upon the Lord, and I cried to my God, and he heard my voice from his holy temple and my cry before him came into his ears. 8 The earth shook and trembled; the foundations of the mountains were troubled and were moved because he was angry with them. 9 There went up a smoke in his wrath, and a fire flamed from his face; coals were kindled by it. 10 He bowed the heavens and came down, and darkness was under his feet. 11 And he ascended upon the cherubim, and he flew; he flew upon the wings of the winds. 12 And he made darkness his covert, his pavilion round about him dark waters in the clouds of the air. 13 At the brightness that was before him the clouds passed, hail and coals of fire. 14 And the Lord thundered from heaven, and the Highest gave his voice, hail and coals of fire. 15 And he sent forth his arrows, and he scattered them. He multiplied lightnings and troubled them. 16 Then the fountains of waters appeared, and the foundations of the world were discovered at thy rebuke, O Lord, at the blast of the spirit of thy wrath.

17 He sent from on high and took me and received me out of many waters. 18 He delivered me from my strongest enemies and from them that hated me, for they were too strong for me. 19 They prevented me in the day of my affliction, and the Lord became my protector. 20 And he brought me forth into a large place. He saved me because he was well pleased with me.

21 Et retribuet mihi Dominus secundum iustitiam meam et secundum puritatem manuum mearum retribuet mihi 22 quia custodivi vias Domini nec impie gessi a Deo meo, 23 quoniam omnia iudicia eius in conspectu meo sunt et iustitias eius non reppuli a me. 24 Et ero inmaculatus cum eo et observabo me ab iniquitate mea. 25 Et retribuet mihi Dominus secundum iustitiam meam et secundum puritatem manuum mearum in conspectu oculorum eius.

26 Cum sancto sanctus eris, et cum viro innocente innocens eris, 27 et cum electo electus eris, et cum perverso perverteris, 28 quoniam tu populum humilem salvum facies et oculos superborum humiliabis, 29 quoniam tu inluminas lucernam meam, Domine. Deus meus, inlumina tenebras meas, 30 quoniam in te eripiar a temptatione et in Deo meo transgrediar murum.

31 Deus meus, inpolluta via eius. Eloquia Domini igne examinata; protector est omnium sperantium in eum, 32 quoniam quis Deus praeter Dominum? Aut quis Deus praeter Deum nostrum? 33 Deus, qui praecinxit me virtute et posuit inmaculatam viam meam, 34 qui perfecit pedes meos tamquam cervorum et super excelsa statuens me, 35 qui docet manus meas ad proelium, et posuisti ut arcum aereum brachia mea.

36 Et dedisti mihi protectionem salutis tuae, et dextera tua suscepit me, et disciplina tua correxit me in finem, et

21 And the Lord will reward me according to my justice and will repay me according to the cleanness of my hands 22 because I have kept the ways of the Lord and have not done wickedly against my God, 23 for all his judgments are in my sight and his justices I have not put away from me. 24 And I shall be spotless with him and shall keep myself from my iniquity. 25 And the Lord will reward me according to my justice and according to the cleanness of my hands before his eyes.

26 With the holy thou wilt be holy, and with the innocent man thou wilt be innocent, 27 and with the elect thou wilt be elect, and with the perverse thou wilt be perverted, 28 for thou wilt save the humble people *but* wilt bring down the eyes of the proud, 29 for thou lightest my lamp, O Lord. O my God, enlighten my darkness, 30 for by thee I shall be delivered from temptation and through my God I shall go over a wall.

31 As for my God, his way is undefiled. The words of the Lord are fire-tried; he is the protector of all that trust in him, 32 for who is God but the Lord? Or who is God but our God? 33 God, who hath girt me with strength and made my way blameless, 34 who hath made my feet like the feet of harts and who setteth me upon high places, 35 who teacheth my hands to war, and thou hast made my arms like a brazen bow.

36 And thou hast given me the protection of thy salvation, and thy right hand hath held me up, and thy discipline hath corrected me unto the end, and thy discipline, the same

disciplina tua, ipsa me docebit. ³⁷ Dilatasti gressus meos subtus me, et non sunt infirmata vestigia mea. ³⁸ Persequar inimicos meos et conprehendam illos, et non convertar donec deficiant. ³⁹ Confringam illos, nec poterunt stare; cadent subtus pedes meos. ⁴⁰ Et praecinxisti me virtute ad bellum et subplantasti insurgentes in me subtus me. ⁴¹ Et inimicos meos dedisti mihi dorsum et odientes me disperdisti. ⁴² Clamaverunt—nec erat qui salvos faceret—ad Dominum, nec exaudivit eos. ⁴³ Et comminuam illos ut pulverem ante faciem venti; ut lutum platearum delebo eos. ⁴⁴ Eripies me de contradictionibus populi. Constitues me in caput Gentium. ⁴⁵ Populus quem non cognovi servivit mihi; in auditu auris oboedivit mihi. ⁴⁶ Filii alieni mentiti sunt mihi; filii alieni inveterati sunt et claudicaverunt a semitis suis. ⁴⁷ Vivit Dominus, et benedictus Deus meus, et exaltetur Deus salutis meae. ⁴⁸ Deus, qui das vindictas mihi et subdis populos sub me, liberator meus de inimicis meis iracundis, ⁴⁹ et ab insurgentibus in me exaltabis me; a viro iniquo eripies me. ⁵⁰ Propterea confitebor tibi in nationibus, Domine, et psalmum dicam nomini tuo, ⁵¹ magnificans salutes regis eius et faciens misericordiam christo suo, David, et semini eius usque in saeculum.

shall teach me. 37 Thou hast enlarged my steps under me, and my feet are not weakened. 38 I will pursue after my enemies and overtake them, and I will not turn again till they *are consumed.* 39 I will break them, and they shall not be able to stand; they shall fall under my feet. 40 And thou hast girded me with strength unto battle and hast subdued under me them that rose up against me. 41 And thou hast made my enemies turn their back upon me and hast destroyed them that hated me.

42 They cried—*but* there was none to save them—to the Lord, *but* he heard them not. 43 And I shall beat them as small as the dust before the wind; I shall bring them to nought like the dirt in the streets. 44 Thou wilt deliver me from the contradictions of the people. Thou wilt make me head of the Gentiles.

45 A people which I knew not hath served me; at the hearing of the ear they have obeyed me. 46 The children that are strangers have lied to me; strange children have *faded away* and have halted from their paths.

47 The Lord liveth, and blessed be my God, and let the God of my salvation be exalted. 48 O God, who avengest me and subduest the people under me, my deliverer from my enraged enemies, 49 and thou wilt lift me up above them that rise up against me; from the unjust man thou wilt deliver me. 50 Therefore will I give glory to thee, O Lord, among the nations, and I will sing a psalm to thy name, 51 *giving great deliverance* to his king and shewing mercy to David, his anointed, and to his seed for ever.

Psalmus 18

In finem. Psalmus David.
² Caeli enarrant gloriam Dei, et opera manuum eius adnuntiat firmamentum. ³ Dies diei eructat verbum, et nox nocti indicat scientiam. ⁴ Non sunt loquellae neque sermones quorum non audiantur voces eorum. ⁵ In omnem terram exivit sonus eorum, et in fines orbis terrae verba eorum. ⁶ In sole posuit tabernaculum suum, et ipse tamquam sponsus procedens de thalamo suo exultavit ut gigans ad currendam viam. ⁷ A summo caeli egressio eius, et occursus eius usque ad summum eius, nec est qui se abscondat a calore eius.

⁸ Lex Domini inmaculata, convertens animas. Testimonium Domini fidele, sapientiam praestans parvulis. ⁹ Iustitiae Domini rectae, laetificantes corda. Praeceptum Domini lucidum, inluminans oculos. ¹⁰ Timor Domini sanctus, permanens in saeculum saeculi. Iudicia Domini vera, iustificata in semet ipsa, ¹¹ desiderabilia super aurum et lapidem pre-

Psalm 18

Caeli enarrant. The works of God shew forth his glory. His law is greatly to be esteemed and loved.

Unto the end. A psalm for David.

2 The heavens shew forth the glory of God, and the firmament declareth the work of his hands. 3 Day to day uttereth speech, and night to night sheweth knowledge. 4 There are no speeches nor languages where their voices are not heard. 5 Their sound hath gone forth into all the earth, and their words unto the ends of the world. 6 He hath set his tabernacle in the sun, and he as a bridegroom coming out of his bridechamber hath rejoiced as a giant to run the way. 7 His going out is from the end of heaven, and his circuit even to the end thereof, and there is no one that can hide himself from his heat.

8 The law of the Lord is unspotted, converting souls. The testimony of the Lord is faithful, giving wisdom to little ones. 9 The justices of the Lord are right, rejoicing hearts. The commandment of the Lord is lightsome, enlightening the eyes. 10 The fear of the Lord is holy, enduring for ever and ever. The judgments of the Lord are true, justified in themselves, 11 more to be desired than gold and many pre-

tiosum multum et dulciora super mel et favum, 12 etenim servus tuus custodit ea in custodiendis illis retributio multa. 13 Delicta quis intellegit? Ab occultis meis munda me, 14 et ab alienis parce servo tuo. Si mei non fuerint dominati, tunc inmaculatus ero, et emundabor a delicto maximo, 15 et erunt ut conplaceant eloquia oris mei et meditatio cordis mei in conspectu tuo semper, Domine, adiutor meus et redemptor meus.

Psalmus 19

In finem. Psalmus David.

2 Exaudiat te Dominus in die tribulationis. Protegat te nomen Dei Iacob. 3 Mittat tibi auxilium de sancto et de Sion tueatur te. 4 Memor sit omnis sacrificii tui, et holocaustum tuum pingue fiat. 5 Tribuat tibi secundum cor tuum et omne consilium tuum confirmet.

6 Laetabimur in salutari tuo, et in nomine Dei nostri magnificabimur. 7 Impleat Dominus omnes petitiones tuas. Nunc cognovi quoniam salvum fecit Dominus christum suum. Exaudiet illum de caelo sancto suo. In potentatibus

cious stones and sweeter than honey and the honeycomb, 12 for thy servant keepeth them and in keeping them there is a great reward.

13 Who can understand sins? From my secret ones cleanse me, *O Lord*, 14 and from those of others spare thy servant. If they shall have no dominion over me, then shall I be without spot, and I shall be cleansed from the greatest sin, 15 and the words of my mouth shall be such as may please, and the meditation of my heart always in thy sight, O Lord, my helper and my redeemer.

Psalm 19

Exaudiat te Dominus. A prayer for the king.

Unto the end. A psalm for David.

2 May the Lord hear thee in the day of tribulation. May the name of the God of Jacob protect thee. 3 May he send thee help from the sanctuary and defend thee out of Zion. 4 May he be mindful of all thy sacrifices, and may thy whole burnt offering be made fat. 5 May he give thee according to thy own heart and confirm all thy counsels.

6 We will rejoice in thy salvation, and in the name of our God we shall be exalted. 7 The Lord fulfil all thy petitions. Now have I known that the Lord hath saved his anointed. He will hear him from his holy heaven. The salvation of his

salus dexterae eius. 8 Hii in curribus et hii in equis, nos autem in nomine Domini, Dei nostri, invocabimus. 9 Ipsi obligati sunt et ceciderunt, nos vero surreximus et erecti sumus.

10 Domine, salvum fac regem, et exaudi nos in die qua invocaverimus te.

Psalmus 20

In finem. Psalmus David.

2 Domine, in virtute tua laetabitur rex, et super salutare tuum exultabit vehementer. 3 Desiderium cordis eius tribuisti ei et voluntate labiorum eius non fraudasti eum, 4 quoniam praevenisti eum in benedictionibus dulcedinis; posuisti in capite eius coronam de lapide pretioso. 5 Vitam petiit a te, et tribuisti ei longitudinem dierum in saeculum et in saeculum saeculi. 6 Magna gloria eius in salutari tuo; gloriam et magnum decorem inpones super eum, 7 quoniam dabis eum benedictionem in saeculum saeculi; laetificabis eum in gaudio cum vultu tuo, 8 quoniam rex sperat in Domino, et in misericordia Altissimi non commovebitur.

right hand is in powers. 8 Some trust in chariots and some in horses, but we will call upon the name of the Lord, our God. 9 They are bound and have fallen, but we are risen and are set upright. 10 O Lord, save the king, and hear us in the day that we shall call upon thee.

Psalm 20

Domine, in virtute. Praise to God for Christ's exaltation after his passion.

U nto the end. A psalm for David.

2 In thy strength, O Lord, the king shall joy, and in thy salvation he shall rejoice exceedingly. 3 Thou hast given him his heart's desire and hast not *withholden from* him the will of his lips, 4 for thou hast prevented him with blessings of sweetness; thou hast set on his head a crown of precious stones. 5 He asked life of thee, and thou hast given him length of days for ever and ever. 6 His glory is great in thy salvation; glory and great beauty shalt thou lay upon him, 7 for thou shalt give him to be a blessing for ever and ever; thou shalt make him joyful in gladness with thy countenance, 8 for the king hopeth in the Lord, and through the mercy of the Most High he shall not be moved.

9 Inveniatur manus tua omnibus inimicis tuis; dextera tua inveniat omnes qui te oderunt. 10 Pones eos ut clibanum ignis. In tempore vultus tui Dominus in ira sua conturbabit eos, et devorabit eos ignis. 11 Fructum eorum de terra perdes et semen eorum a filiis hominum, 12 quoniam declinaverunt in te mala; cogitaverunt consilia quae non potuerunt stabilire, 13 quoniam pones eos dorsum. In reliquis tuis praeparabis vultum eorum.

14 Exaltare, Domine, in virtute tua. Cantabimus et psallemus virtutes tuas.

Psalmus 21

In finem. Pro susceptione matutina. Psalmus David.

2 Deus, Deus meus, respice in me: quare me dereliquisti? Longe a salute mea verba delictorum meorum. 3 Deus meus, clamabo per diem, et non exaudies, et nocte, et non ad insipientiam mihi.

9 Let thy hand be found by all thy enemies; let thy right hand find out all them that hate thee. 10 Thou shalt make them as an oven of fire. In the time of thy *anger* the Lord shall trouble them in his wrath, and fire shall devour them. 11 Their fruit shalt thou destroy from the earth and their seed from among the children of men, 12 for they have intended evils against thee; they have devised counsels which they have not been able to establish, 13 for thou shalt make them turn their back. In thy remnants thou shalt prepare their face.

14 Be thou exalted, O Lord, in thy own strength. We will sing and praise thy power.

Psalm 21

Deus, Deus meus. Christ's passion and the conversion of the Gentiles.

Unto the end. For the morning *protection.* A psalm for David.

2 O God, my God, look upon me: why hast thou forsaken me? Far from my salvation are the words of my sins. 3 O my God, I shall cry by day, and thou wilt not hear, and by night, and it shall not be reputed as folly in me.

4 Tu autem in sancto habitas, laus Israhel. 5 In te speraverunt patres nostri; speraverunt, et liberasti eos. 6 Ad te clamaverunt, et salvi facti sunt; in te speraverunt, et non sunt
confusi. 7 Ego autem sum vermis et non homo, obprobrium
hominum et abiectio plebis. 8 Omnes videntes me deriserunt me; locuti sunt labiis et moverunt caput.

9 Speravit in Domino: eripiat eum; salvum faciat eum,
quoniam vult eum, 10 quoniam tu es qui extraxisti me de
ventre, spes mea ab uberibus matris meae. 11 In te proiectus
sum ex utero. De ventre matris meae Deus meus es tu. 12 Ne
discesseris a me, quoniam tribulatio proxima est, quoniam
non est qui adiuvet.

13 Circumdederunt me vituli multi; tauri pingues obsederunt me. 14 Aperuerunt super me os suum sicut leo rapiens
et rugiens. 15 Sicut aqua effusus sum, et dispersa sunt universa ossa mea. Factum est cor meum tamquam cera liques-
cens in medio ventris mei. 16 Aruit tamquam testa virtus
mea, et lingua mea adhesit faucibus meis, et in pulverem
mortis deduxisti me, 17 quoniam circumdederunt me canes
multi; concilium malignantium obsedit me. Foderunt manus meas et pedes meos. 18 Dinumeraverunt omnia ossa
mea, ipsi vero consideraverunt et inspexerunt me. 19 Divise-
runt sibi vestimenta mea, et super vestem meam miserunt
sortem.

20 Tu autem, Domine, ne elongaveris auxilium tuum a me;
ad defensionem meam conspice. 21 Erue a framea, Deus,
animam meam, et de manu canis unicam meam. 22 Salva me
ex ore leonis et a cornibus unicornium humilitatem meam.
23 Narrabo nomen tuum fratribus meis; in media ecclesia
laudabo te.

4 But thou dwellest in the holy place, the praise of Israel. 5 In thee have our fathers hoped; they have hoped, and thou hast delivered them. 6 They cried to thee, and they were saved; they trusted in thee, and were not confounded. 7 But I am a worm and no man, the reproach of men and the outcast of the people. 8 All they that saw me have laughed me to scorn; they have spoken with the lips and wagged the head.

9 He hoped in the Lord: let him deliver him; let him save him, seeing he delighteth in him, 10 for thou art he that hast drawn me out of the womb, my hope from the breasts of my mother. 11 I was cast upon thee from the womb. From my mother's womb thou art my God. 12 Depart not from me, for tribulation is very near, for there is none to help me.

13 Many calves have surrounded me; fat bulls have besieged me. 14 They have opened their mouths against me as a lion ravening and roaring. 15 I am poured out like water, and all my bones are scattered. My heart is become like wax melting in the midst of my bowels. 16 My strength is dried up like a potsherd, and my tongue hath cleaved to my jaws, and thou hast brought me down into the dust of death, 17 for many dogs have encompassed me; the council of the malignant hath besieged me. They have dug my hands and feet. 18 They have numbered all my bones, and they have looked and stared upon me. 19 They parted my garments amongst them, and upon my vesture they cast lots.

20 But thou, O Lord, remove not thy help to a distance from me; look towards my defence. 21 Deliver, O God, my soul from the sword, *my* only one from the hand of the dog. 22 Save me from the lion's mouth and my lowness from the horns of the unicorns. 23 I will declare thy name to my brethren; in the midst of the church will I praise thee.

24 Qui timetis Dominum, laudate eum; universum semen Iacob, glorificate eum. 25 Timeat eum omne semen Israhel quoniam non sprevit neque dispexit deprecationem pauperis nec avertit faciem suam a me et cum clamarem ad eum exaudivit me. 26 Apud te laus mea in ecclesia magna; vota mea reddam in conspectu timentium eum. 27 Edent pauperes et saturabuntur, et laudabunt Dominum qui requirunt eum; vivent corda eorum in saeculum saeculi. 28 Reminiscentur et convertentur ad Dominum universi fines terrae, et adorabunt in conspectu eius universae familiae Gentium, 29 quoniam Domini est regnum, et ipse dominabitur gentium. 30 Manducaverunt et adoraverunt omnes pingues terrae; in conspectu eius cadent omnes qui descendunt in terram, 31 et anima mea illi vivet, et semen meum serviet ipsi. 32 Adnuntiabitur Domino generatio ventura, et adnuntiabunt caeli iustitiam eius populo qui nascetur quem fecit Dominus.

Psalmus 22

Psalmus David.
Dominus regit me, et nihil mihi deerit. 2 In loco pascuae ibi me conlocavit. Super aquam refectionis educavit me. 3 Animam meam convertit. Deduxit me super semitas iusti-

24 Ye that fear the Lord, praise him; all ye the seed of Jacob, glorify him. 25 Let all the seed of Israel fear him because he hath not slighted nor despised the supplication of the poor man neither hath he turned away his face from me and when I cried to him he heard me. 26 With thee is my praise in a great church; I will pay my vows in the sight of them that fear him. 27 The poor shall eat and shall be filled, and they shall praise the Lord that seek him; their hearts shall live for ever and ever. 28 All the ends of the earth shall remember and shall be converted to the Lord, and all the kindreds of the Gentiles shall adore in his sight, 29 for the kingdom is the Lord's, and he shall have dominion over the nations. 30 All the fat ones of the earth have eaten and have adored; all they that go down to the earth shall fall before him, 31 and to him my soul shall live, and my seed shall serve him. 32 There shall be declared to the Lord a generation to come, and the heavens shall shew forth his justice to a people that shall be born which the Lord hath made.

Psalm 22

Dominus regit me. God's spiritual benefits to faithful souls.

A psalm for David.

The Lord ruleth me, and I shall want nothing. 2 He hath set me in a place of *pasture.* He hath brought me up on the water of refreshment. 3 He hath converted my soul. He hath

tiae propter nomen suum, 4 nam et si ambulavero in medio umbrae mortis non timebo mala, quoniam tu mecum es. Virga tua et baculus tuus, ipsa me consolata sunt. 5 Parasti in conspectu meo mensam adversus eos qui tribulant me. Inpinguasti in oleo caput meum, et calix meus inebrians, quam praeclarus est! 6 Et misericordia tua subsequetur me omnibus diebus vitae meae, et ut inhabitem in domo Domini in longitudinem dierum.

Psalmus 23

Psalmus David. Prima sabbati.

Domini est terra et plenitudo eius, orbis terrarum et universi qui habitant in eo, 2 quia ipse super maria fundavit eum et super flumina praeparavit eum.

3 Quis ascendet in montem Domini, aut quis stabit in loco sancto eius? 4 Innocens manibus et mundo corde qui non accepit in vano animam suam nec iuravit in dolo proximo suo. 5 Hic accipiet benedictionem a Domino et misericordiam a Deo, salvatore suo.

led me on the paths of justice for his own name's sake, 4 for though I should walk in the midst of the shadow of death I will fear no evils, for thou art with me. Thy rod and thy staff, they have comforted me. 5 Thou hast prepared a table before me against them that afflict me. Thou hast anointed my head with oil, and my chalice which inebriateth me, how goodly is it! 6 And thy mercy will follow me all the days of my life, and that I may dwell in the house of the Lord unto length of days.

Psalm 23

Domini est terra. Who are they that shall ascend to heaven?
Christ's triumphant ascension thither.

On the first day of the week. A psalm for David.

The earth is the Lord's and the fulness thereof, the world and all they that dwell therein, 2 for he hath founded it upon the seas and hath prepared it upon the rivers.

3 Who shall ascend into the mountain of the Lord, or who shall stand in his holy place? 4 The innocent in hands and clean of heart who hath not taken his soul in vain nor sworn deceitfully to his neighbour. 5 He shall receive a blessing from the Lord and mercy from God, his saviour.

6 Haec est generatio quaerentium eum, quaerentium faciem Dei Iacob. 7 Adtollite portas, principes, vestras, et elevamini, portae aeternales, et introibit Rex Gloriae. 8 Quis est iste Rex Gloriae? Dominus fortis et potens, Dominus potens in proelio. 9 Adtollite portas, principes, vestras, et elevamini, portae aeternales, et introibit Rex Gloriae. 10 Quis est iste Rex Gloriae? Dominus virtutum, ipse est Rex Gloriae.

Psalmus 24

In finem. Psalmus David.

Ad te, Domine, levavi animam meam. 2 Deus meus, in te confido. Non erubescam, 3 neque inrideant me inimici mei, etenim universi qui sustinent te non confundentur. 4 Confundantur omnes iniqua agentes supervacue. Vias tuas, Domine, demonstra mihi, et semitas tuas doce me. 5 Dirige me

6 This is the generation of them that seek him, of them that seek the face of the God of Jacob. 7 Lift up your gates, O ye princes, and be ye lifted up, O eternal gates, and the King of Glory shall enter in. 8 Who is this King of Glory? The Lord who is strong and mighty, the Lord mighty in battle. 9 Lift up your gates, O ye princes, and be ye lifted up, O eternal gates, and the King of Glory shall enter in. 10 Who is this King of Glory? The Lord of hosts, he is the King of Glory.

Psalm 24

Ad te, Domine, levavi. A prayer for grace, mercy and protection against our enemies.

Unto the end. A psalm for David.

To thee, O Lord, have I lifted up my soul. 2 In thee, O my God, I put my trust. Let me not be ashamed, 3 neither let my enemies laugh at me, for none of them that wait on thee shall be confounded. 4 Let all them be confounded that act unjust things without cause. Shew, O Lord, thy ways to me, and teach me thy paths. 5 Direct me in thy truth, and teach

in veritate tua, et doce me, quoniam tu es Deus, salvator meus, et te sustinui tota die.

6 Reminiscere miserationum tuarum, Domine, et misericordiarum tuarum quae a saeculo sunt; 7 delicta iuventutis meae et ignorantias meas ne memineris. Secundum misericordiam tuam memento mei tu, propter bonitatem tuam, Domine.

8 Dulcis et rectus Dominus, propter hoc legem dabit delinquentibus in via. 9 Diriget mansuetos in iudicio; docebit mites vias suas. 10 Universae viae Domini misericordia et veritas requirentibus testamentum eius et testimonia eius. 11 Propter nomen tuum, Domine, propitiaberis peccato meo, multum est enim.

12 Quis est homo qui timet Dominum? Legem statuit ei in via quam elegit. 13 Anima eius in bonis demorabitur, et semen ipsius hereditabit terram. 14 Firmamentum est Dominus timentibus eum, et testamentum ipsius ut manifestetur illis.

15 Oculi mei semper ad Dominum, quoniam ipse evellet de laqueo pedes meos. 16 Respice in me, et miserere mei, quia unicus et pauper sum ego. 17 Tribulationes cordis mei multiplicatae sunt; de necessitatibus meis erue me. 18 Vide humilitatem meam et laborem meum, et dimitte universa delicta mea. 19 Respice inimicos meos, quoniam multiplicati sunt et odio iniquo oderunt me. 20 Custodi animam meam, et erue me. Non erubescam, quoniam speravi in te. 21 Innocentes et recti adheserunt mihi quia sustinui te. 22 Libera, Deus, Israhel ex omnibus tribulationibus suis.

me, for thou art God, my saviour, and on thee have I waited all the day long.

6 Remember, O Lord, thy *bowels of compassion* and thy mercies that are from *the beginning of the world;* 7 the sins of my youth and my ignorances do not remember. According to thy mercy remember thou me, for thy goodness' sake, O Lord.

8 The Lord is sweet and righteous, therefore he will give a law to sinners in the way. 9 He will guide the mild in judgment; he will teach the meek his ways. 10 All the ways of the Lord are mercy and truth to them that seek after his covenant and his testimonies. 11 For thy name's sake, O Lord, thou wilt pardon my sin, for it is great.

12 Who is the man that feareth the Lord? He hath appointed him a law in the way he hath chosen. 13 His soul shall dwell in good things, and his seed shall inherit the land. 14 The Lord is a firmament to them that fear him, and his covenant shall be made manifest to them.

15 My eyes are ever towards the Lord, for he shall pluck my feet out of the snare. 16 Look thou upon me, and have mercy on me, for I am alone and poor. 17 The troubles of my heart are multiplied; deliver me from my necessities. 18 See my abjection and my labour, and forgive me all my sins. 19 Consider my enemies, for they are multiplied and have hated me with an unjust hatred. 20 Keep thou my soul, and deliver me. I shall not be ashamed, for I have hoped in thee. 21 The innocent and the upright have adhered to me because I have waited on thee. 22 Deliver Israel, O God, from all his tribulations.

Psalmus 25

In finem. Psalmus David.

Iudica me, Domine, quoniam ego in innocentia mea ingressus sum et in Domino sperans non infirmabor. 2 Proba me, Domine, et tempta me. Ure renes meos et cor meum, 3 quoniam misericordia tua ante oculos meos est et conplacui in veritate tua.

4 Non sedi cum concilio vanitatis, et cum iniqua gerentibus non introibo. 5 Odivi ecclesiam malignantium, et cum impiis non sedebo. 6 Lavabo inter innocentes manus meas et circumdabo altare tuum, Domine, 7 ut audiam vocem laudis et enarrem universa mirabilia tua. 8 Domine, dilexi decorem domus tuae et locum habitationis gloriae tuae.

9 Ne perdas cum impiis, Deus, animam meam et cum viris sanguinum vitam meam 10 in quorum manibus iniquitates sunt. Dextera eorum repleta est muneribus, 11 ego autem, in innocentia mea ingressus sum. Redime me, et miserere mei. 12 Pes meus stetit in directo. In ecclesiis benedicam te, Domine.

Psalm 25

Iudica me, Domine. David's prayer to God in his distress to be delivered that he may come to worship him in his tabernacle.

Unto the end. A psalm for David.

Judge me, O Lord, for I have walked in my innocence and I have put my trust in the Lord and shall not be weakened. 2 Prove me, O Lord, and try me. Burn my reins and my heart, 3 for thy mercy is before my eyes and I am well pleased with thy truth.

4 I have not sat with the council of vanity, neither will I go in with the doers of unjust things. 5 I have hated the assembly of the malignant, and with the wicked I will not sit. 6 I will wash my hands among the innocent and will compass thy altar, O Lord, 7 that I may hear the voice of thy praise and tell of all thy wondrous works. 8 I have loved, O Lord, the beauty of thy house and the place where thy glory dwelleth.

9 Take not away my soul, O God, with the wicked nor my life with bloody men 10 in whose hands are iniquities. Their right hand is filled with gifts, 11 but as for me, I have walked in my innocence. Redeem me, and have mercy on me. 12 My foot hath stood in the direct way. In the churches I will bless thee, O Lord.

Psalmus 26

Psalmus David priusquam liniretur.
Dominus inluminatio mea et salus mea: quem timebo?
Dominus protector vitae meae: a quo trepidabo? 2 Dum adpropiant super me nocentes ut edant carnes meas, qui tribulant me inimici mei ipsi infirmati sunt et ceciderunt. 3 Si consistant adversus me castra, non timebit cor meum. Si exsurgat adversus me proelium, in hoc ego sperabo. 4 Unam petii a Domino; hanc requiram, ut inhabitem in domo Domini omnes dies vitae meae, ut videam voluptatem Domini et visitem templum eius, 5 quoniam abscondit me in tabernaculo suo; in die malorum protexit me in abscondito tabernaculi sui. 6 In petra exaltavit me, et nunc exaltavit caput meum super inimicos meos. Circuivi et immolavi in tabernaculo eius hostiam iubilationis. Cantabo et psalmum dicam Domino.

7 Exaudi, Domine, vocem meam qua clamavi ad te. Miserere mei, et exaudi me. 8 Tibi dixit cor meum, "Exquisivit te facies mea." Faciem tuam, Domine, requiram. 9 Ne avertas faciem tuam a me. Ne declines in ira a servo tuo. Adiutor meus esto; ne derelinquas me. Neque dispicias me, Deus, salvator meus, 10 quoniam pater meus et mater mea dereli-

Psalm 26

Dominus inluminatio. David's faith and hope in God.

The psalm of David before he was anointed.

The Lord is my light and my salvation: whom shall I fear? The Lord is the protector of my life: of whom shall I be afraid? 2 Whilst the wicked draw near against me to eat my flesh, my enemies that trouble me have themselves been weakened and have fallen. 3 If armies in camp should stand together against me, my heart shall not fear. If a battle should rise up against me, in this will I be confident. 4 One thing I have asked of the Lord; this will I seek after, that I may dwell in the house of the Lord all the days of my life, that I may see the delight of the Lord and may visit his temple, 5 for he hath hidden me in his tabernacle; in the day of evils he hath protected me in the secret place of his tabernacle. 6 He hath exalted me upon a rock, and now he hath lifted up my head above my enemies. I have gone round and have offered up in his tabernacle a sacrifice of jubilation. I will sing and recite a psalm to the Lord.

7 Hear, O Lord, my voice with which I have cried to thee. Have mercy on me, and hear me. 8 My heart hath said to thee, "My face hath sought thee." Thy face, O Lord, will I *still* seek. 9 Turn not away thy face from me. Decline not in thy wrath from thy servant. Be thou my helper; forsake me not. Do not thou despise me, O God, my saviour, 10 for my

querunt me, Dominus autem adsumpsit me. 11 Legem pone mihi, Domine, in via tua, et dirige me in semita recta propter inimicos meos. 12 Ne tradideris me in animas tribulantium me, quoniam insurrexerunt in me testes iniqui et mentita est iniquitas sibi. 13 Credo videre bona Domini in terra viventium. 14 Expecta Dominum; viriliter age, et confortetur cor tuum, et sustine Dominum.

Psalmus 27

Psalmus ipsi David.

Ad te, Domine, clamabo. Deus meus, ne sileas a me, nequando taceas a me et adsimilabor descendentibus in lacum. 2 Exaudi, Domine, vocem deprecationis meae dum oro ad te, dum extollo manus meas ad templum sanctum tuum. 3 Ne simul trahas me cum peccatoribus, et cum operantibus iniquitatem ne perdas me, qui loquuntur pacem cum proximo suo mala autem in cordibus eorum. 4 Da illis secundum opera ipsorum et secundum nequitiam adinventionum ipsorum. Secundum opera manuum eorum tribue illis; redde retributionem eorum ipsis. 5 Quoniam non intellexerunt

father and my mother have left me, but the Lord hath taken me up. 11 Set me, O Lord, a law in thy way, and guide me in the right path because of my enemies. 12 Deliver me not over to the will of them that trouble me, for unjust witnesses have risen up against me and iniquity hath lied to itself.

13 I believe to see the good things of the Lord in the land of the living. 14 Expect the Lord; do manfully, and let thy heart take courage, and wait thou for the Lord.

Psalm 27

Ad te, Domine, clamabo. David's prayer that his enemies may not prevail over him.

A psalm for David himself.

Unto thee will I cry, O Lord. O my God, be not thou silent to me, lest *if* thou be silent to me *I* become like them that go down into the pit. 2 Hear, O Lord, the voice of my supplication when I pray to thee, when I lift up my hands to thy holy temple. 3 Draw me not away together with the wicked, and with the workers of iniquity destroy me not, who speak peace with their neighbour but evils are in their hearts. 4 Give them according to their works and according to the wickedness of their inventions. According to the works of their hands give thou to them; render to them their reward. 5 Because they have not understood the works of

opera Domini et in opera manuum eius destrues illos et non aedificabis eos.

6 Benedictus Dominus, quoniam exaudivit vocem deprecationis meae. 7 Dominus adiutor meus et protector meus; in ipso speravit cor meum, et adiutus sum, et refloruit caro mea, et ex voluntate mea confitebor ei. 8 Dominus fortitudo plebis suae et protector salvationum christi sui est. 9 Salvam fac plebem tuam, Domine, et benedic hereditati tuae, et rege eos et extolle eos usque in aeternum.

Psalmus 28

Psalmus David in consummatione tabernaculi.

Adferte Domino, filii Dei, adferte Domino filios arietum. 2 Adferte Domino gloriam et honorem; adferte Domino gloriam nomini eius. Adorate Dominum in atrio sancto eius!

3 Vox Domini super aquas; Deus maiestatis intonuit, "Dominus super aquas multas." 4 Vox Domini in virtute, vox Domini in magnificentia. 5 Vox Domini confringentis cedros, et confringet Dominus cedros Libani 6 et comminuet

the Lord and *the operations* of his hands thou shalt destroy them and shalt not build them up.

6 Blessed be the Lord, for he hath heard the voice of my supplication. 7 The Lord is my helper and my protector; in him hath my heart confided, and I have been helped, and my flesh hath flourished again, and with my will I will give praise to him. 8 The Lord is the strength of his people and the protector of the salvation of his anointed. 9 Save, O Lord, thy people, and bless thy inheritance, and rule them and exalt them for ever.

Psalm 28

Adferte Domino. An invitation to glorify God, with a commemoration of his mighty works.

A psalm for David at the finishing of the tabernacle.

Bring to the Lord, O ye children of God, bring to the Lord the offspring of rams. 2 Bring to the Lord glory and honour; bring to the Lord glory to his name. Adore ye the Lord in his holy court!

3 The voice of the Lord is upon the waters; the God of majesty hath thundered, "The Lord is upon many waters." 4 The voice of the Lord is in power, the voice of the Lord in magnificence. 5 The voice of the Lord breaketh the cedars; yea, the Lord shall break the cedars of Lebanon 6 and shall

eas tamquam vitulum Libani et dilectus quemadmodum filius unicornium. 7 Vox Domini intercidentis flammam ignis.
8 Vox Domini concutientis desertum, et commovebit Dominus desertum Cades. 9 Vox Domini praeparantis cervos,
et revelabit condensa, et in templo eius omnis dicet gloriam.
10 Dominus diluvium inhabitare facit, et sedebit Dominus
rex in aeternum. Dominus virtutem populo suo dabit. Dominus benedicet populo suo in pace.

Psalmus 29

Psalmus cantici in dedicatione domus David.
2 Exaltabo te, Domine, quoniam suscepisti me nec delectasti inimicos meos super me. 3 Domine, Deus meus, clamavi ad te, et sanasti me. 4 Domine, eduxisti ab inferno animam meam. Salvasti me a descendentibus in lacum.
5 Psallite Domino, sancti eius, et confitemini memoriae
sanctitatis eius, 6 quoniam ira in indignatione eius et vita in
voluntate eius. Ad vesperum demorabitur fletus, et ad matu-
tinum laetitia. 7 Ego autem dixi in abundantia mea, "Non
movebor in aeternum."

reduce them to pieces as a calf of Lebanon and as the beloved son of unicorns. 7 The voice of the Lord divideth the flame of fire. 8 The voice of the Lord shaketh the desert, and the Lord shall shake the desert of Kadesh. 9 The voice of the Lord prepareth the stags, and he will discover the thick woods, and in his temple all shall speak his glory. 10 The Lord maketh the flood to dwell, and the Lord shall sit king for ever. The Lord will give strength to his people. The Lord will bless his people with peace.

Psalm 29

Exaltabo te, Domine. David praiseth God for his deliverance and his merciful dealings with him.

A psalm of a canticle at the dedication of David's house.

2 I will extol thee, O Lord, for thou hast upheld me and hast not made my enemies to rejoice over me. 3 O Lord, my God, I have cried to thee, and thou hast healed me. 4 Thou hast brought forth, O Lord, my soul from hell. Thou hast saved me from them that go down into the pit.

5 Sing to the Lord, O ye his saints, and give praise to the memory of his holiness, 6 for wrath is in his indignation and life in his good will. In the evening weeping shall have place, and in the morning gladness. 7 And in my abundance I said, "I shall never be moved."

8 Domine, in voluntate tua praestitisti decori meo virtutem. Avertisti faciem tuam a me, et factus sum conturbatus. 9 Ad te, Domine, clamabo, et ad Deum meum deprecabor. 10 Quae utilitas in sanguine meo dum descendo in corruptionem? Numquid confitebitur tibi pulvis aut adnuntiabit veritatem tuam? 11 Audivit Dominus et misertus est mei. Dominus factus est adiutor meus. 12 Convertisti planctum meum in gaudium mihi; conscidisti saccum meum et circumdedisti me laetitia 13 ut cantet tibi gloria mea et non conpungar. Domine, Deus meus, in aeternum confitebor tibi!

Psalmus 30

In finem. Psalmus David pro extasi.

2 In te, Domine, speravi. Non confundar in aeternum; in iustitia tua libera me. 3 Inclina ad me aurem tuam; adcelera ut eruas me. Esto mihi in Deum, protectorem et in domum refugii ut salvum me facias, 4 quoniam fortitudo mea et refugium meum es tu, et propter nomen tuum deduces me et enutries me. 5 Educes me de laqueo hoc quem absconderunt mihi, quoniam tu es protector meus. 6 In manus tuas commendo spiritum meum. Redemisti me, Domine, Deus veritatis. 7 Odisti observantes vanitates supervacue, ego autem

8 O Lord, in thy favour thou gavest strength to my beauty. Thou turnedst away thy face from me, and I became troubled. 9 To thee, O Lord, will I cry, and I will make supplication to my God. 10 What profit is there in my blood whilst I go down to corruption? Shall dust confess to thee or declare thy truth? 11 The Lord hath heard and hath had mercy on me. The Lord became my helper. 12 Thou hast turned for me my mourning into joy; thou hast cut my sackcloth and hast compassed me with gladness 13 to the end that my glory may sing to thee and I may not regret.

O Lord, my God, I will give praise to thee for ever!

Psalm 30

In te, Domine, speravi. A prayer of a just man under affliction.

Unto the end. A psalm for David in an ecstasy.

2 In thee, O Lord, have I hoped. Let me never be confounded; deliver me in thy justice. 3 Bow down thy ear to me; make haste to deliver me. Be thou unto me a God, a protector and a house of refuge to save me, 4 for thou art my strength and my refuge, and for thy name's sake thou wilt lead me and nourish me. 5 Thou wilt bring me out of this snare which they have hidden for me, for thou art my protector. 6 Into thy hands I commend my spirit. Thou hast redeemed me, O Lord, the God of truth. 7 Thou hast hated

in Domino speravi. 8 Exultabo et laetabor in misericordia tua, quoniam respexisti humilitatem meam; salvasti de necessitatibus animam meam. 9 Nec conclusisti me in manibus inimici; statuisti in loco spatioso pedes meos.

10 Miserere mei, Domine, quoniam tribulor; conturbatus est in ira oculus meus, anima mea et venter meus, 11 quoniam defecit in dolore vita mea et anni mei in gemitibus. Infirmata est in paupertate virtus mea, et ossa mea conturbata sunt. 12 Super omnes inimicos meos factus sum obprobrium et vicinis meis valde et timor notis meis. Qui videbant me foras fugerunt a me. 13 Oblivioni datus sum tamquam mortuus a corde. Factus sum tamquam vas perditum, 14 quoniam audivi vituperationem multorum commorantium in circuitu. In eo dum convenirent simul adversus me accipere animam meam consiliati sunt, 15 ego autem in te speravi, Domine. Dixi, "Deus meus es tu."

16 In manibus tuis sortes meae. Eripe me de manibus inimicorum meorum et a persequentibus me. 17 Inlustra faciem tuam super servum tuum; salvum me fac in misericordia tua. 18 Domine, ne confundar, quoniam invocavi te. Erubescant impii et deducantur in infernum. 19 Muta fiant labia dolosa quae loquuntur adversus iustum iniquitatem in superbia et in abusione.

20 Quam magna multitudo dulcedinis tuae, Domine, quam abscondisti timentibus te, perfecisti eis qui sperant in te in conspectu filiorum hominum! 21 Abscondes eos in abdito faciei tuae a conturbatione hominum. Proteges eos in tabernaculo tuo a contradictione linguarum. 22 Benedictus Dominus, quoniam mirificavit misericordiam suam mihi in

them that regard vanities to no purpose, but I have hoped in the Lord. 8 I will be glad and rejoice in thy mercy, for thou hast regarded my humility; thou hast saved my soul out of distresses. 9 And thou hast not shut me up in the hands of the enemy; thou hast set my feet in a spacious place.

10 Have mercy on me, O Lord, for I am afflicted; my eye is troubled with wrath, my soul and my belly, 11 for my life is wasted with grief and my years in sighs. My strength is weakened through poverty, and my bones are disturbed. 12 I am become a reproach among all my enemies and very much to my neighbours and a fear to my acquaintance. They that saw me without fled from me. 13 I am forgotten as one dead from the heart. I am become as a vessel that is destroyed, 14 for I have heard the blame of many that dwell round about. While they assembled together against me they consulted to take away my life, 15 but I have put my trust in thee, O Lord. I said, "Thou art my God."

16 My lots are in thy hands. Deliver me out of the hands of my enemies and from them that persecute me. 17 Make thy face to shine upon thy servant; save me in thy mercy. 18 Let me not be confounded, O Lord, for I have called upon thee. Let the wicked be ashamed and be brought down to hell. 19 Let deceitful lips be made dumb which speak iniquity against the just with pride and abuse.

20 O how great is the multitude of thy sweetness, O Lord, which thou hast hidden for them that fear thee, which thou hast wrought for them that hope in thee in the sight of the sons of men! 21 Thou shalt hide them in the secret of thy face from the disturbance of men. Thou shalt protect them in thy tabernacle from the contradiction of tongues. 22 Blessed be the Lord, for he hath *shewn his wonderful* mercy

civitate munita. 23 Ego autem dixi in excessu mentis meae, "Proiectus sum a facie oculorum tuorum." Ideo exaudisti vocem orationis meae dum clamarem ad te.

24 Diligite Dominum, omnes sancti eius, quoniam veritatem requiret Dominus et retribuet abundanter facientibus superbiam. 25 Viriliter agite, et confortetur cor vestrum, omnes qui speratis in Domino.

Psalmus 31

Ipsi David, intellectus.

Beati quorum remissae sunt iniquitates et quorum tecta sunt peccata. 2 Beatus vir cui non inputavit Dominus peccatum nec est in spiritu eius dolus.

3 Quoniam tacui inveteraverunt ossa mea dum clamarem tota die, 4 quoniam die ac nocte gravata est super me manus tua. Conversus sum in aerumna mea dum configitur spina. 5 Delictum meum cognitum tibi feci, et iniustitiam meam non abscondi. Dixi, "Confitebor adversus me iniustitiam meam Domino," et tu remisisti impietatem peccati mei. 6 Pro hac orabit ad te omnis sanctus in tempore oportuno, verumtamen in diluvio aquarum multarum ad eum non adproximabunt.

7 Tu es refugium meum a tribulatione quae circumdedit

to me in a fortified city. 23 But I said in the excess of my mind, "I am cast away from before thy eyes." Therefore thou hast heard the voice of my prayer when I cried to thee.

24 O love the Lord, all ye his saints, for the Lord will require truth and will repay them abundantly that act proudly. 25 Do ye manfully, and let your heart be strengthened, all ye that hope in the Lord.

Psalm 31

Beati quorum. The second penitential psalm.

To David himself, understanding.

Blessed are they whose iniquities are forgiven and whose sins are covered. 2 Blessed is the man to whom the Lord hath not imputed sin and in whose spirit there is no guile.

3 Because I was silent my bones grew old whilst I cried out all the day long, 4 for day and night thy hand was heavy upon me. I am turned in my anguish whilst the thorn is fastened. 5 I have acknowledged my sin to thee, and my injustice I have not concealed. I said, "I will confess against myself my injustice to the Lord," and thou hast forgiven the wickedness of my sin. 6 For this shall every one that is holy pray to thee in a seasonable time, and yet in a flood of many waters they shall not come nigh unto him.

7 Thou art my refuge from the trouble which hath en-

me, exultatio mea. Erue me a circumdantibus me. 8 Intellectum tibi dabo, et instruam te in via hac qua gradieris. Firmabo super te oculos meos. 9 Nolite fieri sicut equus et mulus quibus non est intellectus; in camo et freno maxillas eorum constringe qui non adproximant ad te. 10 Multa flagella peccatoris, sperantem autem in Domino misericordia circumdabit.

11 Laetamini in Domino, et exultate, iusti, et gloriamini, omnes recti corde!

Psalmus 32

Psalmus David.

Exultate, iusti, in Domino! Rectos decet laudatio. 2 Confitemini Domino in cithara; in psalterio, decem cordarum, psallite illi. 3 Cantate ei canticum novum; bene psallite ei in vociferatione, 4 quia rectum est verbum Domini et omnia opera eius in fide. 5 Diligit misericordiam et iudicium. Mise-

compassed me, my joy. Deliver me from them that surround me. 8 I will give thee understanding, and I will instruct thee in this way in which thou shalt go. I will fix my eyes upon thee. 9 Do not become like the horse and the mule who have no understanding; with bit and bridle bind fast their jaws who come not near unto thee. 10 Many are the scourges of the sinner, but mercy shall encompass him that hopeth in the Lord.

11 Be glad in the Lord, and rejoice, ye just, and glory, all ye right of heart!

Psalm 32

Exultate, iusti. An exhortation to praise God and to trust in him.

A psalm for David.

Rejoice in the Lord, O ye just! Praise becometh the upright. 2 Give praise to the Lord on the harp; sing to him with the psaltery, *the instrument* of ten strings. 3 Sing to him a new canticle; sing well unto him with a loud noise, 4 for the word of the Lord is right and all his works are done with faithfulness. 5 He loveth mercy and judgment. The earth is full of

ricordia Domini plena est terra. 6 Verbo Domini caeli firmati sunt, et spiritu oris eius omnis virtus eorum, 7 congregans sicut in utre aquas maris, ponens in thesauris abyssos.

8 Timeat Dominum omnis terra, ab eo autem commoveantur omnes inhabitantes orbem, 9 quoniam ipse dixit et facta sunt, ipse mandavit et creata sunt. 10 Dominus dissipat consilia gentium, reprobat autem cogitationes populorum et reprobat consilia principum. 11 Consilium autem Domini in aeternum manet, cogitationes cordis eius in generatione et generationem. 12 Beata gens cuius est Dominus Deus eius, populus quem elegit in hereditatem sibi. 13 De caelo respexit Dominus; vidit omnes filios hominum. 14 De praeparato habitaculo suo respexit super omnes qui habitant terram, 15 qui finxit singillatim corda eorum, qui intellegit omnia opera illorum. 16 Non salvatur rex per multam virtutem, et gigans non salvabitur in multitudine virtutis suae. 17 Fallax equus ad salutem, in abundantia autem virtutis suae non salvabitur.

18 Ecce: oculi Domini super metuentes eum et in eis qui sperant super misericordia eius 19 ut eruat a morte animas eorum et alat eos in fame. 20 Anima nostra sustinet Dominum, quoniam adiutor et protector noster est, 21 quia in eo laetabitur cor nostrum, et in nomine sancto eius speravimus.

22 Fiat misericordia tua, Domine, super nos, quemadmodum speravimus in te.

the mercy of the Lord. 6 By the word of the Lord the heavens were established, and all the power of them by the spirit of his mouth, 7 gathering together the waters of the sea as in a vessel, laying up the depths in storehouses.

8 Let all the earth fear the Lord, and let all the inhabitants of the world be in awe of him, 9 for he spoke and they were made, he commanded and they were created. 10 The Lord bringeth to nought the counsels of nations, and he rejecteth the devices of people and casteth away the counsels of princes. 11 But the counsel of the Lord standeth for ever, the thoughts of his heart to all generations.

12 Blessed is the nation whose God is the Lord, the people whom he hath chosen for his inheritance. 13 The Lord hath looked from heaven; he hath beheld all the sons of men. 14 From his habitation which he hath prepared he hath looked upon all that dwell on the earth, 15 he who hath made the hearts of every one of them, who understandeth all their works. 16 The king is not saved by a great army, nor shall the giant be saved by his own *great* strength. 17 Vain is the horse for safety, neither shall he be saved by the abundance of his strength.

18 Behold: the eyes of the Lord are on them that fear him and on them that hope in his mercy 19 to deliver their souls from death and feed them in famine. 20 Our soul waiteth for the Lord, for he is our helper and protector, 21 for in him our heart shall rejoice, and in his holy name we have trusted.

22 Let thy mercy, O Lord, be upon us, as we have hoped in thee.

Psalmus 33

David, cum inmutavit vultum suum coram Abimelech, et dimisit eum, et abiit. 2 Benedicam Dominum in omni tempore; semper laus eius in ore meo. 3 In Domino laudabitur anima mea; audiant mansueti et laetentur. 4 Magnificate Dominum mecum, et exaltemus nomen eius in id ipsum! 5 Exquisivi Dominum, et exaudivit me, et ex omnibus tribulationibus meis eripuit me. 6 Accedite ad eum, et inluminamini, et facies vestrae non confundentur. 7 Iste pauper clamavit, et Dominus exaudivit eum et de omnibus tribulationibus eius salvavit eum. 8 Inmittet angelus Domini in circuitu timentium eum et eripiet eos. 9 Gustate, et videte quoniam suavis est Dominus; beatus vir qui sperat in eo. 10 Timete Dominum, omnes sancti eius, quoniam non est inopia timentibus eum. 11 Divites eguerunt et esurierunt, inquirentes autem Dominum non minuentur omni bono.

12 Venite, filii; audite me; timorem Domini docebo vos. 13 Quis est homo qui vult vitam, diligit videre dies bonos? 14 Prohibe linguam tuam a malo et labia tua ne loquantur dolum. 15 Deverte a malo, et fac bonum; inquire pacem, et persequere eam. 16 Oculi Domini super iustos et aures eius in

Psalm 33

Benedicam Dominum. An exhortation to the praise and service of God.

For David, when he changed his countenance before *Ahimelech, who* dismissed him, and he went his way.

2 I will bless the Lord at all times; his praise shall be always in my mouth. 3 In the Lord shall my soul be praised; let the meek hear and rejoice. 4 O magnify the Lord with me, and let us extol his name together! 5 I sought the Lord, and he heard me, and he delivered me from all my troubles. 6 Come ye to him, and be enlightened, and your faces shall not be confounded. 7 This poor man cried, and the Lord heard him and saved him out of all his troubles. 8 The angel of the Lord shall *encamp* round about them that fear him and shall deliver them. 9 O taste, and see that the Lord is sweet; blessed is the man that hopeth in him. 10 Fear the Lord, all ye his saints, for there is no want to them that fear him. 11 The rich have wanted and have suffered hunger, but they that seek the Lord shall not be deprived of any good.

12 Come, children; hearken to me; I will teach you the fear of the Lord. 13 Who is the man that desireth life, who loveth to see good days? 14 Keep thy tongue from evil and thy lips from speaking guile. 15 Turn away from evil, and do good; seek after peace, and pursue it. 16 The eyes of the Lord

preces eorum, 17 facies autem Domini super facientes mala ut perdat de terra memoriam eorum. 18 Clamaverunt iusti, et Dominus exaudivit eos et ex omnibus tribulationibus eorum liberavit eos. 19 Iuxta est Dominus his qui tribulato sunt corde, et humiles spiritu salvabit. 20 Multae tribulationes iustorum, et de omnibus his liberabit eos Dominus. 21 Dominus custodit omnia ossa eorum; unum ex his non conteretur. 22 Mors peccatorum pessima, et qui oderunt iustum delinquent. 23 Redimet Dominus animas servorum suorum, et non delinquent omnes qui sperant in eum.

Psalmus 34

Ipsi David.

Iudica, Domine, nocentes me; expugna inpugnantes me. 2 Adprehende arma et scutum, et exsurge in adiutorium mihi. 3 Effunde frameam, et conclude adversus eos qui persequuntur me. Dic animae meae, "Salus tua ego sum."

4 Confundantur et revereantur quaerentes animam

are upon the just and his ears unto their prayers, 17 but the countenance of the Lord is against them that do evil things to cut off the remembrance of them from the earth. 18 The just cried, and the Lord heard them and delivered them out of all their troubles. 19 The Lord is nigh unto them that are of a contrite heart, and he will save the humble of spirit. 20 Many are the afflictions of the just, *but* out of them all will the Lord deliver them. 21 The Lord keepeth all their bones; not one of them shall be broken. 22 The death of the wicked is very evil, and they that hate the just shall be guilty. 23 The Lord will redeem the souls of his servants, and none of them that trust in him shall offend.

Psalm 34

Iudica, Domine, nocentes me. David, in the person of Christ, prayeth against his persecutors, prophetically foreshewing the punishments that shall fall upon them.

For David himself.

Judge thou, O Lord, them that wrong me; overthrow them that fight against me. 2 Take hold of arms and shield, and rise up to help me. 3 Bring out the sword, and shut up the way against them that persecute me. Say to my soul, "I am thy salvation."

4 Let them be confounded and ashamed that seek after

meam. Avertantur retrorsum et confundantur cogitantes mihi mala. 5 Fiant tamquam pulvis ante faciem venti, et angelus Domini coartans eos. 6 Fiat via illorum tenebrae et lubricum, et angelus Domini persequens eos, 7 quoniam gratis absconderunt mihi interitum laquei sui, supervacue exprobraverunt animam meam. 8 Veniat illi laqueus quem ignorat, et captio quam abscondit conprehendat eum, et in laqueum cadat in ipsum.

9 Anima autem mea exultabit in Domino et delectabitur super salutari suo. 10 Omnia ossa mea dicent, "Domine, quis similis tibi eripiens inopem de manu fortiorum eius, egenum et pauperem a diripientibus eum?" 11 Surgentes testes iniqui quae ignorabam interrogabant me. 12 Retribuebant mihi mala pro bonis, sterilitatem animae meae. 13 Ego autem, cum mihi molesti essent induebar cilicio. Humiliabam in ieiunio animam meam, et oratio mea in sinum meum convertetur. 14 Quasi proximum quasi fratrem nostrum, sic conplacebam; quasi lugens et contristatus, sic humiliabar. 15 Et adversum me laetati sunt et convenerunt; congregata sunt super me flagella, et ignoravi. 16 Dissipati sunt nec conpuncti; temptaverunt me; subsannaverunt me subsannatione; frenduerunt super me dentibus suis.

17 Domine, quando respicies? Restitue animam meam a malignitate eorum, a leonibus unicam meam. 18 Confitebor tibi in ecclesia magna; in populo gravi laudabo te. 19 Non supergaudeant mihi qui adversantur mihi inique, qui oderunt me gratis et annuunt oculis, 20 quoniam mihi quidem paci-

my soul. Let them be turned back and be confounded that devise evil against me. 5 Let them become as dust before the wind, and let the angel of the Lord straiten them. 6 Let their way become dark and slippery, and let the angel of the Lord pursue them, 7 for without cause they have hidden their net for me unto destruction, without cause they have upbraided my soul. 8 Let the snare which he knoweth not come upon him, and let the net which he hath hidden catch him, and into that very snare let him fall.

9 But my soul shall rejoice in the Lord and shall be delighted in his salvation. 10 All my bones shall say, "Lord, who is like to thee who deliverest the poor from the hand of them that are stronger than he, the needy and the poor from them that strip him?" 11 Unjust witnesses rising up have asked me things I knew not. 12 They repaid me evil for good *to the depriving me* of my soul. 13 But as for me, when they were troublesome to me I was clothed with haircloth. I humbled my soul with fasting, and my prayer shall be turned into my bosom. 14 As a neighbour and as *an own* brother, so did I please; as one mourning and sorrowful, so was I humbled. 15 *But* they rejoiced against me and came together; scourges were gathered together upon me, and I knew not. 16 They were separated and repented not; they tempted me; they scoffed at me with scorn; they gnashed upon me with their teeth.

17 Lord, when wilt thou look *upon me?* Rescue thou my soul from their malice, my only one from the lions. 18 I will give thanks to thee in a great church; I will praise thee in a strong people. 19 Let not them that are my enemies wrongfully rejoice over me, who have hated me without cause and wink with the eyes, 20 for they spoke indeed peaceably to

fice loquebantur, et in iracundia terrae loquentes dolos cogitabant. 21 Et dilataverunt super me os suum; dixerunt, "Euge, euge, viderunt oculi nostri." 22 Vidisti, Domine; ne sileas. Domine, ne discedas a me. 23 Exsurge, et intende iudicio meo, Deus meus et Dominus meus, in causam meam. 24 Iudica me secundum iustitiam tuam, Domine, Deus meus, et non supergaudeant mihi. 25 Non dicant in cordibus suis, "Euge; euge animae nostrae," nec dicant, "Devoravimus eum." 26 Erubescant et revereantur simul qui gratulantur malis meis. Induantur confusione et reverentia qui magna loquuntur super me. 27 Exultent et laetentur qui volunt iustitiam meam, et dicant semper, "Magnificetur Dominus, qui volunt pacem servi eius." 28 Et lingua mea meditabitur iustitiam tuam, tota die laudem tuam.

Psalmus 35

In finem. Servo Domini, ipsi David.

2 Dixit iniustus ut delinquat in semet ipso; non est timor Dei ante oculos eius, 3 quoniam dolose egit in conspectu eius ut inveniatur iniquitas eius ad odium. 4 Verba oris eius

me, and speaking in the anger of the earth they devised guile. 21 And they opened their mouth wide against me; they said, "Well done, well done, our eyes have seen it." 22 Thou hast seen, O Lord; be not thou silent. O Lord, depart not from me. 23 Arise, and be attentive to my judgment, to my cause, my God and my Lord. 24 Judge me, O Lord, my God, according to thy justice, and let them not rejoice over me. 25 Let them not say in their hearts, "It is well; it is well to our mind," neither let them say, "We have swallowed him up." 26 Let them blush and be ashamed together who rejoice at my evils. Let them be clothed with confusion and shame who speak great things against me. 27 Let them rejoice and be glad who are well pleased with my justice, and let them say always, "The Lord be magnified, who delights in the peace of his servant." 28 And my tongue shall meditate thy justice, thy praise all the day long.

Psalm 35

Dixit iniustus. The malice of sinners and the goodness of God.

Unto the end. For the servant of *God,* David himself.

2 The unjust hath said within himself that he would sin; there is no fear of God before his eyes, 3 for in his sight he hath done deceitfully that his iniquity may be found unto hatred. 4 The words of his mouth are iniquity and guile;

iniquitas et dolus; noluit intellegere ut bene ageret. 5 Iniquitatem meditatus est in cubili suo; adstetit omni viae non bonae, malitiam autem non odivit.

6 Domine, in caelo misericordia tua, et veritas tua usque
ad nubes. 7 Iustitia tua sicut montes Dei; iudicia tua abyssus
multa. Homines et iumenta salvabis, Domine. 8 Quemadmodum multiplicasti misericordiam tuam, Deus! Filii autem
hominum in tegmine alarum tuarum sperabunt. 9 Inebria-
buntur ab ubertate domus tuae, et torrente voluptatis tuae
potabis eos, 10 quoniam apud te fons vitae, et in lumine tuo
videbimus lumen. 11 Praetende misericordiam tuam scientibus te et iustitiam tuam his qui recto sunt corde. 12 Non veniat mihi pes superbiae, et manus peccatoris non moveat
me. 13 Ibi ceciderunt qui operantur iniquitatem; expulsi
sunt nec potuerunt stare.

Psalmus 36

Psalmus ipsi David.

Noli aemulari in malignantibus, neque zelaveris facientes
iniquitatem, 2 quoniam tamquam faenum velociter arescent
et quemadmodum holera herbarum cito decident. 3 Spera in

he would not understand that he might do well. 5 He hath devised iniquity on his bed; he hath set himself on every way that is not good, but evil he hath not hated.

6 O Lord, thy mercy is in heaven, and thy truth reacheth even to the clouds. 7 Thy justice is as the mountains of God; thy judgments are a great deep. Men and beasts thou wilt preserve, O Lord. 8 O how hast thou multiplied thy mercy, O God! But the children of men shall put their trust under the covert of thy wings. 9 They shall be inebriated with the plenty of thy house, and thou shalt make them drink of the torrent of thy pleasure, 10 for with thee is the fountain of life, and in thy light we shall see light. 11 Extend thy mercy to them that know thee and thy justice to them that are right in heart. 12 Let not the foot of pride come to me, and let not the hand of the sinner move me. 13 There the workers of iniquity are fallen; they are cast out and could not stand.

Psalm 36

Noli aemulari. An exhortation to despise this world and the short prosperity of the wicked and to trust in Providence.

A psalm for David himself.

Be not emulous of evildoers, nor envy them that work iniquity, 2 for they shall shortly wither away as grass and as the *green* herbs shall quickly fall. 3 Trust in the Lord, and do

Domino, et fac bonitatem, et inhabita terram, et pasceris in divitiis eius. 4 Delectare in Domino, et dabit tibi petitiones cordis tui. 5 Revela Domino viam tuam, et spera in eum, et ipse faciet. 6 Et educet quasi lumen iustitiam tuam et iudicium tuum tamquam meridiem. 7 Subditus esto Domino, et ora eum. Noli aemulari in eo qui prosperatur in via sua, in homine faciente iniustitias. 8 Desine ab ira, et derelinque furorem; noli aemulari ut maligneris, 9 quoniam qui malignantur exterminabuntur, sustinentes autem Dominum, ipsi hereditabunt terram, 10 et adhuc pusillum et non erit peccator, et quaeres locum eius et non invenies, 11 mansueti autem hereditabunt terram et delectabuntur in multitudine pacis.

12 Observabit peccator iustum et stridebit super eum dentibus suis. 13 Dominus autem inridebit eum, quia prospicit quoniam veniet dies eius. 14 Gladium evaginaverunt peccatores; intenderunt arcum suum ut decipiant pauperem et inopem, ut trucident rectos corde. 15 Gladius eorum intret in corda ipsorum, et arcus ipsorum confringatur. 16 Melius est modicum iusto super divitias peccatorum multas, 17 quoniam brachia peccatorum conterentur, confirmat autem iustos Dominus. 18 Novit Dominus dies inmaculatorum, et hereditas eorum in aeternum erit. 19 Non confundentur in tempore malo, et in diebus famis saturabuntur 20 quia peccatores peribunt. Inimici vero Domini mox ut honorificati fuerint et exaltati deficientes quemadmodum fumus deficient. 21 Mutuabitur peccator et non solvet, iustus autem miseretur et tribuet, 22 quia benedicentes ei hereditabunt

good, and dwell in the land, and thou shalt be fed with its riches. 4 Delight in the Lord, and he will give thee the requests of thy heart. 5 *Commit* thy way to the Lord, and trust in him, and he will do it. 6 And he will bring forth thy justice as the light and thy judgment as the noon day. 7 Be subject to the Lord, and pray to him. Envy not the man who prospereth in his way, the man who doth unjust things. 8 Cease from anger, and leave rage; have no emulation to do evil, 9 for evildoers shall be cut off, but they that wait upon the Lord, they shall inherit the land, 10 *for* yet a little while and the wicked shall not be, and thou shalt seek his place and shalt not find it, 11 but the meek shall inherit the land and shall delight in abundance of peace.

12 The sinner shall watch the just man and shall gnash upon him with his teeth. 13 But the Lord shall laugh at him, for he foreseeth that his day shall come. 14 The wicked have drawn out the sword; they have bent their bow to *cast down* the poor and needy, to kill the upright of heart. 15 Let their sword enter into their own hearts, and let their bow be broken. 16 Better is a little to the just than the great riches of the wicked, 17 for the arms of the wicked shall be broken in pieces, but the Lord strengtheneth the just. 18 The Lord knoweth the days of the undefiled, and their inheritance shall be for ever. 19 They shall not be confounded in the evil time, and in the days of famine they shall be filled 20 because the wicked shall perish. And the enemies of the Lord presently after they shall be honoured and exalted shall come to nothing and vanish like smoke. 21 The sinner shall borrow and not pay again, but the just sheweth mercy and shall give, 22 for such as bless him shall inherit the land but such as

terram maledicentes autem ei disperibunt. 23 Apud Dominum gressus hominis dirigentur, et viam eius volet. 24 Cum ceciderit non conlidetur, quia Dominus subponit manum suam.

25 Iunior fui etenim senui, et non vidi iustum derelictum nec semen eius quaerens panes. 26 Tota die miseretur et commodat, et semen illius in benedictione erit. 27 Declina a malo, et fac bonum, et inhabita in saeculum saeculi, 28 quia Dominus amat iudicium et non derelinquet sanctos suos: in aeternum conservabuntur. Iniusti punientur, et semen impiorum peribit, 29 iusti autem hereditabunt terram et inhabitabunt in saeculum saeculi super eam. 30 Os iusti meditabitur sapientiam, et lingua eius loquetur iudicium. 31 Lex Dei eius in corde ipsius, et non subplantabuntur gressus eius. 32 Considerat peccator iustum et quaerit mortificare eum, 33 Dominus autem non derelinquet eum in manus eius nec damnabit eum cum iudicabitur illi. 34 Expecta Dominum, et custodi viam eius, et exaltabit te ut hereditate capias terram. Cum perierint peccatores videbis.

35 Vidi impium superexaltatum, et elevatum sicut cedros Libani, 36 et transivi, et ecce: non erat, et quaesivi eum, et non est inventus locus eius. 37 Custodi innocentiam, et vide aequitatem, quoniam sunt reliquiae homini pacifico. 38 Iniusti autem disperibunt simul; reliquiae impiorum peribunt. 39 Salus autem iustorum a Domino, et protector eorum in tempore tribulationis. 40 Et adiuvabit eos Dominus et liberabit eos, et eruet eos a peccatoribus et salvabit eos quia speraverunt in eo.

curse him shall perish. 23 With the Lord shall the steps of a man be directed, and he shall like well his way. 24 When he shall fall he shall not be bruised, for the Lord putteth his hand under him.

25 I have been young and now am old, and I have not seen the just forsaken nor his seed seeking bread. 26 He sheweth mercy and lendeth all the day long, and his seed shall be in blessing. 27 Decline from evil, and do good, and dwell for ever and ever, 28 for the Lord loveth judgment and will not forsake his saints: they shall be preserved for ever. The unjust shall be punished, and the seed of the wicked shall perish, 29 but the just shall inherit the land and shall dwell therein for evermore. 30 The mouth of the just shall meditate wisdom, and his tongue shall speak judgment. 31 The law of his God is in his heart, and his steps shall not be supplanted. 32 The wicked watcheth the just man and seeketh to put him to death, 33 but the Lord will not leave him in his hands nor condemn him when he shall be judged. 34 Expect the Lord, and keep his way, and he will exalt thee to inherit the land. When the sinners shall perish thou shalt see.

35 I have seen the wicked highly exalted, and lifted up like the cedars of Lebanon, 36 and I passed by, and lo: he was not, and I sought him, and his place was not found. 37 Keep innocence, and behold justice, for there are remnants for the peaceable man. 38 But the unjust shall be destroyed together; the remnants of the wicked shall perish. 39 But the salvation of the just is from the Lord, and he is their protector in the time of trouble. 40 And the Lord will help them and deliver them, and he will rescue them from the wicked and save them because they have hoped in him.

Psalmus 37

Psalmus David. In rememorationem de sabbato.
2 Domine, ne in furore tuo arguas me, neque in ira tua
corripias me, 3 quoniam sagittae tuae infixae sunt mihi, et
confirmasti super me manum tuam. 4 Non est sanitas in
carne mea a facie irae tuae; non est pax ossibus meis a facie
peccatorum meorum, 5 quoniam iniquitates meae super-
gressae sunt caput meum et sicut onus grave gravatae sunt
super me. 6 Putruerunt et corruptae sunt cicatrices meae a
facie insipientiae meae. 7 Miser factus sum et curvatus sum
usque ad finem. Tota die contristatus ingrediebar, 8 quoniam
lumbi mei impleti sunt inlusionibus et non est sanitas in
carne mea. 9 Adflictus sum et humiliatus sum nimis. Rugie-
bam a gemitu cordis mei.
10 Domine, ante te omne desiderium meum, et gemitus
meus a te non est absconditus. 11 Cor meum conturbatum
est; dereliquit me virtus mea, et lumen oculorum meorum et
ipsum non est mecum. 12 Amici mei et proximi mei adversus
me adpropinquaverunt et steterunt, et qui iuxta me erant de
longe steterunt, 13 et vim faciebant qui quaerebant animam
meam, et qui inquirebant mala mihi locuti sunt vanitates et
dolos tota die meditabantur. 14 Ego autem tamquam surdus

Psalm 37

Domine, ne in furore. A prayer of a penitent for the remission of his sins. The third penitential psalm.

A psalm for David. For a remembrance of the sabbath.

2 Rebuke me not, O Lord, in thy indignation, nor chastise me in thy wrath, 3 for thy arrows are fastened in me, and *thy hand hath been strong* upon me. 4 There is no health in my flesh *because* of thy wrath; there is no peace for my bones *because* of my sins, 5 for my iniquities are gone over my head and as a heavy burden are become heavy upon me. 6 My sores are putrified and corrupted *because* of my foolishness. 7 I am become miserable and am bowed down even to the end. I walked sorrowful all the day long, 8 for my loins are filled with illusions and there is no health in my flesh. 9 I am afflicted and humbled exceedingly. I roared with the groaning of my heart.

10 Lord, all my desire is before thee, and my groaning is not hidden from thee. 11 My heart is troubled; my strength hath left me, and the light of my eyes *itself* is not with me. 12 My friends and my neighbours have drawn near and stood against me, and they that were near me stood afar off, 13 and they that sought my soul used violence, and they that sought evils to me spoke vain things and studied deceits all the day long. 14 But I as a deaf man heard not and as a

non audiebam et sicut mutus non aperiens os suum, 15 et factus sum sicut homo non audiens et non habens in ore suo redargutiones, 16 quoniam in te, Domine, speravi. Tu exaudies me, Domine, Deus meus, 17 quia dixi, "Nequando supergaudeant mihi inimici mei et dum commoventur pedes mei super me magna locuti sunt," 18 quoniam ego in flagella paratus et dolor meus in conspectu meo semper, 19 quoniam iniquitatem meam adnuntiabo et cogitabo pro peccato meo.

20 Inimici autem mei vivunt et confirmati sunt super me, et multiplicati sunt qui oderunt me inique. 21 Qui retribuunt mala pro bonis detrahebant mihi quoniam sequebar bonitatem. 22 Non derelinquas me, Domine, Deus meus; ne discesseris a me. 23 Intende in adiutorium meum, Domine, Deus salutis meae.

Psalmus 38

In finem. Ipsi Idithun. Canticum David.

2 Dixi, "Custodiam vias meas ut non delinquam in lingua mea. Posui ori meo custodiam cum consisteret peccator adversum me." 3 Obmutui et humiliatus sum et silui a bonis, et

dumb man not opening his mouth, 15 and I became as a man that heareth not and that hath no reproofs in his mouth, 16 for in thee, O Lord, have I hoped. Thou wilt hear me, O Lord, my God, 17 for I said, "Lest at any time my enemies rejoice over me and whilst my feet are moved they speak great things against me," 18 for I am ready for scourges and my sorrow is continually before me, 19 for I will declare my iniquity and I will think for my sin.

20 But my enemies live and are stronger than I, and they that hate me wrongfully are multiplied. 21 They that render evil for good have detracted me because I followed goodness. 22 Forsake me not, O Lord, my God; do not thou depart from me. 23 Attend unto my help, O Lord, the God of my salvation.

Psalm 38

Dixi, Custodiam. A just man's peace and patience in his sufferings, considering the vanity of the world and the providence of God.

Unto the end. For Jeduthun himself. A canticle of David.
2 I said, "I will take heed to my ways that I sin not with my tongue. I have set a guard to my mouth when the sinner stood against me." 3 I was dumb and was humbled and kept

dolor meus renovatus est. 4 Concaluit cor meum intra me, et in meditatione mea exardescet ignis. 5 Locutus sum in lingua mea; notum fac mihi, Domine, finem meum et numerum dierum meorum quis est, ut sciam quid desit mihi.

6 Ecce: mensurabiles posuisti dies meos, et substantia mea tamquam nihilum ante te. Verumtamen universa vanitas, omnis homo vivens. 7 Verumtamen in imagine pertransit homo, sed et frustra conturbatur. Thesaurizat, et ignorat cui congregabit ea. 8 Et nunc quae est expectatio mea? Nonne Dominus? Et substantia mea apud te est.

9 Ab omnibus iniquitatibus meis erue me; obprobrium insipienti dedisti me. 10 Obmutui, et non aperui os meum quoniam tu fecisti. 11 Amove a me plagas tuas. 12 A fortitudine manus tuae ego defeci in increpationibus. Propter iniquitatem corripuisti hominem, et tabescere fecisti sicut araneam animam eius. Verumtamen vane conturbatur omnis homo.

13 Exaudi orationem meam, Domine, et deprecationem meam; auribus percipe lacrimas meas. Ne sileas, quoniam advena sum apud te et peregrinus sicut omnes patres mei. 14 Remitte mihi ut refrigerer priusquam abeam et amplius non ero.

silence from good things, and my sorrow was renewed. 4 My heart grew hot within me, and in my meditation a fire shall flame out. 5 I spoke with my tongue; O Lord, make me know my end and what is the number of my days, that I may know what is wanting to me.

6 Behold: thou hast made my days measurable, and my substance is as nothing before thee. And indeed all things are vanity, every man living. 7 Surely man passeth as an image, yea, and he is disquieted in vain. He storeth up, and he knoweth not for whom he shall gather these things. 8 And now what is my hope? Is it not the Lord? And my substance is with thee.

9 Deliver thou me from all my iniquities; thou hast made me a reproach to the fool. 10 I was dumb, and I opened not my mouth because thou hast done it. 11 Remove thy scourges from me. 12 The strength of thy hand hath made me faint in rebukes. Thou hast corrected man for iniquity, and thou hast made his soul to waste away like a spider. Surely in vain is *any* man disquieted.

13 Hear my prayer, O Lord, and my supplication; give ear to my tears. Be not silent, for I am a stranger with thee and a sojourner as all my fathers were. 14 O forgive me that I may be refreshed before I go hence and be no more.

Psalmus 39

In finem. Ipsi David psalmus.

2 Expectans expectavi Dominum, et intendit mihi, 3 et exaudivit preces meas et eduxit me de lacu miseriae et de luto fecis, et statuit super petram pedes meos et direxit gressus meos, 4 et inmisit in os meum canticum novum, carmen Deo nostro. Videbunt multi et timebunt, et sperabunt in Domino.

5 Beatus vir cuius est nomen Domini spes ipsius et non respexit in vanitates et insanias falsas. 6 Multa fecisti tu Domine, Deus meus, mirabilia tua, et cogitationibus tuis non est qui similis sit tibi. Adnuntiavi, et locutus sum. Multiplicati sunt super numerum. 7 Sacrificium et oblationem noluisti, aures autem perfecisti mihi. Holocaustum et pro peccato non postulasti, 8 tunc dixi, "Ecce: venio."

In capite libri scriptum est de me 9 ut facerem voluntatem tuam, Deus meus. Volui et legem tuam in medio cordis mei. 10 Adnuntiavi iustitiam tuam in ecclesia magna. Ecce: labia mea non prohibebo, Domine; tu scisti. 11 Iustitiam tuam non abscondi in corde meo; veritatem tuam et salutare tuum dixi; non abscondi misericordiam tuam et veritatem tuam a concilio multo.

12 Tu autem, Domine, ne longe facias miserationes tuas a me; misericordia tua et veritas tua semper susceperunt me, 13 quoniam circumdederunt me mala quorum non est

Psalm 39

Expectans expectavi. Christ's coming and redeeming mankind.

Unto the end. A psalm for David himself.

2 With expectation I have waited for the Lord, and he was attentive to me, 3 and he heard my prayers and brought me out of the pit of misery and the mire of dregs, and he set my feet upon a rock and directed my steps, 4 and he put a new canticle into my mouth, a song to our God. Many shall see and shall fear, and they shall hope in the Lord.

5 Blessed is the man whose trust is in the name of the Lord and who hath not had regard to vanities and lying follies. 6 Thou hast multiplied thy wonderful works, O Lord, my God, and in thy thoughts there is no one like to thee. I have declared, and I have spoken. They are multiplied above number. 7 Sacrifice and oblation thou didst not desire, but thou hast *pierced* ears for me. Burnt offering and sin offering thou didst not require, 8 then said I, "Behold: I come."

In the head of the book it is written of me 9 that I should do thy will, O my God. I have desired it and thy law in the midst of my heart. 10 I have declared thy justice in a great church. Lo: I will not restrain my lips, O Lord; thou knowest it. 11 I have not hid thy justice within my heart; I have declared thy truth and thy salvation; I have not concealed thy mercy and thy truth from a great council.

12 Withhold not thou, O Lord, thy *tender* mercies from me; thy mercy and thy truth have always upheld me, 13 for

numerus. Conprehenderunt me iniquitates meae, et non potui ut viderem. Multiplicatae sunt super capillos capitis mei, et cor meum dereliquit me. 14 Conplaceat tibi, Domine, ut eruas me. Domine, ad adiuvandum me respice.

15 Confundantur et revereantur simul qui quaerunt animam meam ut auferant eam. Convertantur retrorsum et revereantur qui volunt mihi mala. 16 Ferant confestim confusionem suam qui dicunt mihi, "Euge; euge." 17 Exultent et laetentur super te omnes quaerentes te, et dicant semper "Magnificetur Dominus!" qui diligunt salutare tuum.

18 Ego autem mendicus sum et pauper; Dominus sollicitus est mei. Adiutor meus et protector meus tu es, Deus meus; ne tardaveris.

Psalmus 40

In finem. Psalmus ipsi David.

2 Beatus qui intellegit super egenum et pauperem; in die mala liberabit eum Dominus. 3 Dominus conservet eum et

evils without number have surrounded me. My iniquities have overtaken me, and I was not able to see. They are multiplied above the hairs of my head, and my heart hath forsaken me. 14 Be pleased, O Lord, to deliver me. Look down, O Lord, to help me.

15 Let them be confounded and ashamed together that seek after my soul to take it away. Let them be turned backward and be ashamed that desire evils to me. 16 Let them immediately bear their confusion that say to me, "'Tis well; 'tis well." 17 Let all that seek thee rejoice and be glad in thee, and let *such as* love thy salvation say always, "The Lord be magnified!"

18 But I am a beggar and poor; the Lord is careful for me. Thou art my helper and my protector, O my God; be not slack.

Psalm 40

Beatus qui intellegit. The happiness of him that shall believe in Christ, notwithstanding the humility and poverty in which he shall come. The malice of his enemies, especially of the traitor Judas.

Unto the end. A psalm for David himself.

2 Blessed is he that understandeth concerning the needy and the poor; the Lord will deliver him in the evil day. 3 The

vivificet eum et beatum faciat eum in terra et non tradat eum in animam inimicorum eius. 4 Dominus opem ferat illi super lectum doloris eius; universum stratum eius versasti in infirmitate eius. 5 Ego dixi, "Domine, miserere mei; sana animam meam, quoniam peccavi tibi."

6 Inimici mei dixerunt mala mihi: "Quando morietur et peribit nomen eius?" 7 Et si ingrediebatur ut videret, vana loquebatur; cor eius congregavit iniquitatem sibi. Egrediebatur foras et loquebatur in id ipsum. 8 Adversum me susurrabant omnes inimici mei adversus me; cogitabant mala mihi. 9 Verbum iniquum constituerunt adversus me. Numquid qui dormit non adiciet ut resurgat? 10 Etenim homo pacis meae in quo speravi, qui edebat panes meos, magnificavit super me subplantationem. 11 Tu autem, Domine, miserere mei, et resuscita me, et retribuam eis. 12 In hoc cognovi quoniam voluisti me, quoniam non gaudebit inimicus meus super me. 13 Me autem propter innocentiam suscepisti et confirmasti me in conspectu tuo in aeternum.

14 Benedictus Dominus, Deus Israhel, a saeculo et in saeculum. Fiat. Fiat.

Lord preserve him and give him life and make him blessed upon the earth and deliver him not up to the will of his enemies. 4 The Lord help him on his bed of sorrow; thou hast turned all his couch in his sickness. 5 I said, "O Lord, be thou merciful to me; heal my soul, for I have sinned against thee."

6 My enemies have spoken evils against me: "When shall he die and his name perish?" 7 And if he came in to see me, he spoke vain things; his heart gathered together iniquity to itself. He went out and spoke to the same purpose. 8 All my enemies whispered together against me; they devised evils to me. 9 They determined against me an unjust word. Shall he that sleepeth rise again no more? 10 For even the man of my peace in whom I trusted, who ate my bread, hath greatly supplanted me. 11 But thou, O Lord, have mercy on me, and raise me up again, and I will requite them. 12 By this I know that thou hast had a good will for me, because my enemy shall not rejoice over me. 13 But thou hast upheld me by reason of my innocence and hast established me in thy sight for ever.

14 Blessed be the Lord, the God of Israel, from eternity to eternity. So be it. So be it.

Psalmus 41

In finem. Intellectus filiis Core.

2 Quemadmodum desiderat cervus ad fontes aquarum, ita desiderat anima mea ad te, Deus. 3 Sitivit anima mea ad Deum fortem vivum. Quando veniam et parebo ante faciem Dei? 4 Fuerunt mihi lacrimae meae panes die ac nocte dum dicitur mihi cotidie, "Ubi est Deus tuus?" 5 Haec recordatus sum et effudi in me animam meam, quoniam transibo in locum tabernaculi admirabilis, usque ad domum Dei, in voce exultationis et confessionis, sonus epulantis.

6 Quare tristis es, anima mea? Et quare conturbas me? Spera in Deo, quoniam adhuc confitebor illi, salutare vultus mei 7 et Deus meus. Ad me ipsum anima mea conturbata est; propterea memor ero tui de terra Iordanis et Hermoniim, a monte modico. 8 Abyssus abyssum invocat in voce cataractarum tuarum. Omnia excelsa tua et fluctus tui super me transierunt. 9 In die mandavit Dominus misericordiam suam et nocte canticum eius. Apud me oratio Deo vitae meae.

Psalm 41

Quemadmodum desiderat. The fervent desire of the just after God. Hope in afflictions.

Unto the end. Understanding for the sons of Korah. 2 As the hart panteth after the fountains of water, so my soul panteth after thee, O God. 3 My soul hath thirsted after the strong living God. When shall I come and appear before the face of God? 4 My tears have been my bread day and night whilst it is said to me daily, "Where is thy God?" 5 These things I remembered and poured out my soul in me, for I shall go over into the place of the wonderful tabernacle, even to the house of God, with the voice of joy and praise, the noise of one feasting.

6 Why art thou sad, O my soul? And why dost thou trouble me? Hope in God, for I will still give praise to him, the salvation of my countenance 7 and my God. My soul is troubled within my self; therefore will I remember thee from the land of Jordan and Hermoniim, from the little hill. 8 Deep calleth on deep at the noise of thy flood-gates. All thy heights and thy billows have passed over me. 9 In the daytime the Lord hath commanded his mercy and a canticle to him in the night. With me is prayer to the God of my life.

10 Dicam Deo, "Susceptor meus es; quare oblitus es mei? Et quare contristatus incedo dum adfligit me inimicus?" 11 Dum confringuntur ossa mea exprobraverunt mihi qui tribulant me inimici mei, dum dicunt mihi per singulos dies, "Ubi est Deus tuus?"

12 Quare tristis es, anima mea? Et quare conturbas me? Spera in Deum, quoniam adhuc confitebor illi, salutare vultus mei et Deus meus.

Psalmus 42

P salmus David.

Iudica me, Deus, et discerne causam meam de gente non sancta. Ab homine iniquo et doloso erue me, 2 quia tu es Deus, fortitudo mea. Quare me reppulisti? Et quare tristis incedo dum adfligit me inimicus? 3 Emitte lucem tuam et veritatem tuam. Ipsa me deduxerunt et adduxerunt in montem sanctum tuum et in tabernacula tua. 4 Et introibo ad altare Dei, ad Deum qui laetificat iuventutem meam. 5 Confitebor tibi in cithara, Deus, Deus meus.

10 I will say to God, "Thou art my support; why hast thou forgotten me? And why go I mourning whilst my enemy afflicteth me?" 11 Whilst my bones are broken my enemies who trouble me have reproached me, whilst they say to me day by day, "Where is thy God?"

12 Why art thou cast down, O my soul? And why dost thou disquiet me? Hope thou in God, for I will still give praise to him, the salvation of my countenance and my God.

Psalm 42

Iudica me, Deus. The prophet aspireth after the temple and altar of God.

A psalm for David.

Judge me, O God, and distinguish my cause from the nation that is not holy. Deliver me from the unjust and deceitful man, 2 for thou art God, my strength. Why hast thou cast me off? And why do I go sorrowful whilst the enemy afflicteth me? 3 Send forth thy light and thy truth. They have conducted me and brought me unto thy holy hill and into thy tabernacles. 4 And I will go in to the altar of God, to God who giveth joy to my youth. 5 To thee, O God, my God, I will give praise upon the harp.

Quare tristis es, anima mea? Et quare conturbas me? 6 Spera in Deum, quoniam adhuc confitebor illi, salutare vultus mei et Deus meus.

Psalmus 43

In finem. Filiis Core, ad intellectum.

2 Deus, auribus nostris audivimus; patres nostri adnuntiaverunt nobis opus quod operatus es in diebus eorum et in diebus antiquis. 3 Manus tua Gentes disperdit, et plantasti eos; adflixisti populos et expulisti eos, 4 nec enim in gladio suo possederunt terram et brachium eorum non salvavit eos, sed dextera tua et brachium tuum et inluminatio faciei tuae quoniam conplacuisti in eis.

5 Tu es ipse rex meus et Deus meus, qui mandas salutes Iacob. 6 In te inimicos nostros ventilabimus cornu, et in nomine tuo spernemus insurgentes in nobis, 7 non enim in arcu meo sperabo, et gladius meus non salvabit me, 8 salvasti enim nos de adfligentibus nos et odientes nos confudisti.

Why art thou sad, O my soul? And why dost thou disquiet me? 6 Hope in God, for I will still give praise to him, the salvation of my countenance and my God.

Psalm 43

Deus, auribus nostris. The church commemorates former favours and present afflictions under which she prays for succour.

Unto the end. For the sons of Korah, to give understanding.

2 We have heard, O God, with our ears; our fathers have declared to us the work thou hast wrought in their days and in the days of old. 3 Thy hand destroyed the Gentiles, and thou plantedst them; thou didst afflict the people and cast them out, 4 for they got not the possession of the land by their own sword neither did their own arm save them, but thy right hand and thy arm and the light of thy countenance because thou wast pleased with them.

5 Thou art thyself my king and my God, who commandest the saving of Jacob. 6 Through thee we will *push down* our enemies with the horn, and through thy name we will despise them that rise up against us, 7 for I will not trust in my bow, neither shall my sword save me, 8 *but* thou hast saved us from them that afflict us and hast put them to shame that

9 In Deo laudabimur tota die, et in nomine tuo confitebimur in saeculum.

10 Nunc autem reppulisti et confudisti nos, et non egredieris, Deus, in virtutibus nostris. 11 Avertisti nos retrorsum post inimicos nostros, et qui oderunt nos diripiebant sibi. 12 Dedisti nos tamquam oves escarum; et in gentibus dispersisti nos. 13 Vendidisti populum tuum sine pretio, et non fuit multitudo in commutationibus eorum. 14 Posuisti nos obprobrium vicinis nostris, subsannationem et derisum his qui in circuitu nostro. 15 Posuisti nos in similitudinem Gentibus, commotionem capitis in populis.

16 Tota die verecundia mea contra me est, et confusio faciei meae cooperuit me 17 a voce exprobrantis et obloquentis, a facie inimici et persequentis. 18 Haec omnia venerunt super nos, nec obliti sumus te, et inique non egimus in testamento tuo. 19 Et non recessit retrorsum cor nostrum, et declinasti semitas nostras a via tua, 20 quoniam humiliasti nos in loco adflictionis et cooperuit nos umbra mortis.

21 Si obliti sumus nomen Dei nostri, et si expandimus manus nostras ad deum alienum, 22 nonne Deus requiret ista, ipse enim novit abscondita cordis? Quoniam propter te mortificamur omni die; aestimati sumus sicut oves occisionis.

hate us. 9 In God shall we glory all the day long, and in thy name we will give praise for ever.

10 But now thou hast cast us off and put us to shame, and thou, O God, wilt not go out with our armies. 11 Thou hast *made us turn our back to* our enemies, and they that hated us plundered for themselves. 12 Thou hast given us up like sheep to be eaten; thou hast scattered us among the nations. 13 Thou hast sold thy people for no price, and there was no *reckoning* in the *exchange* of them. 14 Thou hast made us a reproach to our neighbours, a scoff and derision to them that are round about us. 15 Thou hast made us a byword among the Gentiles, a shaking of the head among the people.

16 All the day long my shame is before me, and the confusion of my face hath covered me 17 at the voice of him that reprocheth and detracteth me, at the face of the enemy and persecutor. 18 All these things have come upon us, yet we have not forgotten thee, and we have not done wickedly in thy covenant. 19 And our heart hath not turned back, *neither* hast thou turned aside our steps from thy way, 20 for thou hast humbled us in the place of affliction and the shadow of death hath covered us.

21 If we have forgotten the name of our God, and if we have spread forth our hands to a strange god, 22 shall not God search out these things, for he knoweth the secrets of the heart? Because for thy sake we are killed all the day long; we are counted as sheep for the slaughter.

23 Exsurge! Quare dormis, Domine? Exsurge, et ne repellas in finem. 24 Quare faciem tuam avertis, oblivisceris inopiae nostrae et tribulationis nostrae? 25 Quoniam humiliata est in pulvere anima nostra; conglutinatus est in terra venter noster. 26 Exsurge, Domine! Adiuva nos, et redime nos propter nomen tuum.

Psalmus 44

In finem. Pro his qui commutabuntur, filiis Core, ad intellectum. Canticum pro Dilecto.

2 Eructavit cor meum verbum bonum; dico ego opera mea regi; lingua mea calamus scribae velociter scribentis.

3 Speciosus forma prae filiis hominum; diffusa est gratia in labiis tuis; propterea benedixit te Deus in aeternum. 4 Accingere gladio tuo super femur tuum, potentissime. 5 Specie tua et pulchritudine tua intende; prospere procede, et regna propter veritatem et mansuetudinem et iustitiam. Et deducet te mirabiliter dextera tua. 6 Sagittae tuae acutae; populi

23 Arise! Why sleepest thou, O Lord? Arise, and cast us not off to the end. 24 Why turnest thou thy face away *and* forgettest our want and our trouble? 25 For our soul is humbled down to the dust; our belly cleaveth to the earth. 26 Arise, O Lord! Help us, and redeem us for thy name's sake.

Psalm 44

Eructavit cor meum. The excellence of Christ's kingdom and the endowments of his church.

Unto the end. For them that shall be changed, for the sons of Korah, for understanding. A canticle for the Beloved.

2 My heart hath uttered a good word; I speak my works to the king; my tongue is the pen of a scrivener that writeth swiftly.

3 Thou art beautiful above the sons of men; grace is poured abroad in thy lips; therefore hath God blessed thee for ever. 4 Gird thy sword upon thy thigh, O thou most mighty. 5 With thy comeliness and thy beauty set out; proceed prosperously, and reign because of truth and meekness and justice. And thy right hand shall conduct thee wonderfully. 6 Thy arrows are sharp; under thee shall people fall

sub te cadent in corda inimicorum regis. 7 Sedis tua, Deus, in saeculum saeculi; virga directionis virga regni tui.

8 Dilexisti iustitiam et odisti iniquitatem; propterea unxit te Deus, Deus tuus, oleo laetitiae prae consortibus tuis. 9 Murra et gutta et cassia a vestimentis tuis a domibus eburneis ex quibus delectaverunt te 10 filiae regum in honore tuo. Adstetit regina a dextris tuis in vestitu deaurato, circumdata varietate.

11 Audi, filia, et vide, et inclina aurem tuam, et obliviscere populum tuum et domum patris tui, 12 et concupiscet rex decorem tuum, quoniam ipse est Dominus, Deus tuus, et adorabunt eum. 13 Et filiae Tyri in muneribus vultum tuum deprecabuntur, omnes divites plebis. 14 Omnis gloria eius filiae regis ab intus in fimbriis aureis, 15 circumamicta varietatibus. Adducentur regi virgines post eam; proximae eius adferentur tibi. 16 Adferentur in laetitia et exultatione; adducentur in templum regis. 17 Pro patribus tuis, nati sunt tibi filii; constitues eos principes super omnem terram. 18 Memores erunt nominis tui in omni generatione et generatione. Propterea populi confitebuntur tibi in aeternum et in saeculum saeculi.

into the hearts of the king's enemies. 7 Thy throne, O God, is forever and ever; the sceptre of thy kingdom is a sceptre of uprightness.

8 Thou hast loved justice and hated iniquity; therefore God, thy God, hath anointed thee with the oil of gladness above thy fellows. 9 Myrrh and *stacte* and cassia *perfume* thy garments from the ivory houses out of which 10 the daughters of kings have delighted thee in thy glory. The queen stood on thy right hand in gilded clothing, surrounded with variety.

11 Hearken, O daughter, and see, and incline thy ear, and forget thy people and thy father's house, 12 and the king shall greatly desire thy beauty, for he is the Lord, thy God, and him they shall adore. 13 And the daughters of Tyre with gifts, *yea,* all the rich among the people, shall entreat thy countenance. 14 All the glory of the king's daughter is within in golden borders, 15 clothed round about with varieties. After her shall virgins be brought to the king; her neighbours shall be brought to thee. 16 They shall be brought with gladness and rejoicing; they shall be brought into the temple of the king. 17 Instead of thy fathers, sons are born to thee; thou shalt make them princes over all the earth. 18 They shall remember thy name throughout all generations. Therefore shall people praise thee for ever, yea, for ever and ever.

Psalmus 45

In finem. Filiis Core, pro arcanis.

2 Deus noster refugium et virtus, adiutor in tribulationibus, quae invenerunt nos nimis. 3 Propterea non timebimus dum turbabitur terra et transferentur montes in cor maris. 4 Sonaverunt et turbatae sunt aquae eorum; conturbati sunt montes in fortitudine eius. 5 Fluminis impetus laetificat civitatem Dei; sanctificavit tabernaculum suum Altissimus. 6 Deus in medio eius; non commovebitur; adiuvabit eam Deus mane diluculo.

7 Conturbatae sunt gentes, et inclinata sunt regna. Dedit vocem suam; mota est terra. 8 Dominus virtutum nobiscum; susceptor noster Deus Iacob. 9 Venite, et videte opera Domini, quae posuit prodigia super terram, 10 auferens bella usque ad finem terrae. Arcum conteret et confringet arma, et scuta conburet igni.

11 "Vacate, et videte quoniam ego sum Deus; exaltabor in gentibus, et exaltabor in terra."

12 Dominus virtutum nobiscum; susceptor noster Deus Iacob.

Psalm 45

Deus noster refugium. The church in persecution trusteth in the protection of God.

Unto the end. For the sons of Korah, for the hidden.

2 Our God is our refuge and strength, a helper in troubles, which have found us exceedingly. 3 Therefore we will not fear when the earth shall be troubled and the mountains shall be removed into the heart of the sea. 4 Their waters roared and were troubled; the mountains were troubled with his strength. 5 The stream of the river maketh the city of God joyful; the Most High hath sanctified his own tabernacle. 6 God is in the midst thereof; it shall not be moved; God will help it in the morning early.

7 Nations were troubled, and kingdoms were bowed down. He uttered his voice; the earth trembled. 8 The Lord of armies is with us; the God of Jacob is our protector. 9 Come, and behold ye the works of the Lord, what wonders he hath done upon earth, 10 making wars to cease even to the end of the earth. He shall destroy the bow and break the weapons, and the shield he shall burn in the fire.

11 "Be still, and see that I am God; I will be exalted among the nations, and I will be exalted in the earth."

12 The Lord of armies is with us; the God of Jacob is our protector.

Psalmus 46

In finem. Pro filiis Core.

2 Omnes gentes, plaudite manibus! Iubilate Deo in voce exultationis, 3 quoniam Dominus excelsus, terribilis, rex magnus super omnem terram. 4 Subiecit populos nobis et gentes sub pedibus nostris. 5 Elegit nobis hereditatem suam, speciem Iacob quam dilexit. 6 Ascendit Deus in iubilo, et Dominus in voce tubae.

7 Psallite Deo nostro! Psallite! Psallite regi nostro! Psallite, 8 quoniam rex omnis terrae Deus. Psallite sapienter. 9 Regnabit Deus super gentes; Deus sedet super sedem sanctam suam. 10 Principes populorum congregati sunt cum Deo Abraham, quoniam dii fortes terrae vehementer elevati sunt.

Psalm 46

Omnes gentes, plaudite. The Gentiles are invited to praise God for the establishment of the kingdom of Christ.

Unto the end. For the sons of Korah.

2 O clap your hands, all ye nations! Shout unto God with the voice of joy, 3 for the Lord is high, terrible, a great king over all the earth. 4 He hath subdued the people under us and the nations under our feet. 5 He hath chosen for us his inheritance, the beauty of Jacob which he hath loved. 6 God is ascended with jubilee, and the Lord with the sound of trumpet.

7 Sing praises to our God! Sing ye! Sing praises to our king! Sing ye, 8 for God is the king of all the earth. Sing ye wisely. 9 God shall reign over the nations; God sitteth on his holy throne. 10 The princes of the people are gathered together with the God of Abraham, for the strong gods of the earth are exceedingly exalted.

Psalmus 47

Psalmus cantici. Filiis Core secunda sabbati.
2 Magnus Dominus et laudabilis nimis in civitate Dei nostri, in monte sancto eius. 3 Fundatur exultatione universae terrae Mons Sion, latera aquilonis, civitas regis magni. 4 Deus in domibus eius cognoscetur cum suscipiet eam, 5 quoniam ecce: reges terrae congregati sunt; convenerunt in unum. 6 Ipsi videntes sic, admirati sunt; conturbati sunt; commoti sunt; 7 tremor adprehendit eos. Ibi dolores ut parturientis.

8 In spiritu vehementi conteres naves Tharsis. 9 Sicut audivimus, sic vidimus in civitate Domini virtutum, in civitate Dei nostri. Deus fundavit eam in aeternum. 10 Suscepimus, Deus, misericordiam tuam in medio templi tui. 11 Secundum nomen tuum, Deus, sic et laus tua in fines terrae; iustitia plena est dextera tua.

12 Laetetur Mons Sion et exultent filiae Iudae propter iudicia tua, Domine. 13 Circumdate Sion, et conplectimini eam; narrate in turribus eius. 14 Ponite corda vestra in virtute eius, et distribuite domus eius ut enarretis in progeniem

Psalm 47

Magnus Dominus. God is greatly to be praised for the establishment of his church.

A psalm of a canticle. For the sons of Korah on the second day of the week.

2 Great is the Lord and exceedingly to be praised in the city of our God, in his holy mountain. 3 With the joy of the whole earth is Mount Zion founded, on the sides of the north, the city of the great king. 4 In her houses shall God be known when he shall protect her, 5 for behold: the kings of the earth assembled themselves; they gathered together. 6 So they saw, and they wondered; they were troubled; they were moved; 7 trembling took hold of them. There were pains as of a woman in labour.

8 With a vehement wind thou shalt break in pieces the ships of Tarshish. 9 As we have heard, so have we seen in the city of the Lord of hosts, in the city of our God. God hath founded it for ever. 10 We have received thy mercy, O God, in the midst of thy temple. 11 According to thy name, O God, so also is thy praise unto the ends of the earth; thy right hand is full of justice.

12 Let Mount Zion rejoice and the daughters of Judah be glad because of thy judgments, O Lord. 13 Surround Zion, and encompass her; tell ye in her towers. 14 Set your hearts on her strength, and distribute her houses that ye may re-

alteram, 15 quoniam hic est Deus, Deus noster in aeternum et in saeculum saeculi. Ipse reget nos in saecula.

Psalmus 48

In finem. Filiis Core psalmus.

2 Audite haec, omnes gentes! Auribus percipite, omnes qui habitatis orbem, 3 quique terriginae et filii hominum, simul in unum dives et pauper. 4 Os meum loquetur sapientiam, et meditatio cordis mei prudentiam. 5 Inclinabo in parabolam aurem meam; aperiam in psalterio propositionem meam.

6 Cur timebo in die malo? Iniquitas calcanei mei circumdabit me. 7 Qui confidunt in virtute sua et in multitudine divitiarum suarum gloriantur 8 frater non redimit, redimet homo. Non dabit Deo placationem suam 9 et pretium redemptionis animae suae et laborabit in aeternum 10 et vivet adhuc in finem. 11 Non videbit interitum cum viderit sapientes morientes. Simul insipiens et stultus peribunt, et relinquent alienis divitias suas 12 et sepulchra eorum domus illorum in aeternum, tabernacula eorum in progeniem et progeniem. Vocaverunt nomina sua in terris suis.

late it in another generation, 15 for this is God, our God unto eternity and for ever and ever. He shall rule us for ever-more.

Psalm 48

Audite haec, omnes gentes. The folly of worldlings who live on in sin without thinking of death or hell.

Unto the end. A psalm for the sons of Korah.

2 Hear these things, all ye nations! Give ear, all ye inhabitants of the world, 3 all you that are earthborn and you sons of men, both rich and poor together. 4 My mouth shall speak wisdom, and the meditation of my heart understanding. 5 I will incline my ear to a parable; I will open my proposition on the psaltery.

6 Why shall I fear in the evil day? The iniquity of my heel shall encompass me. 7 They that trust in their own strength and glory in the multitude of their riches 8 no brother *can* redeem, *nor* shall man redeem. He shall not give to God his ransom 9 nor the price of the redemption of his soul and shall labour for ever 10 and shall still live unto the end. 11 He shall not see destruction when he shall see the wise dying. The senseless and the fool shall perish together, and they shall leave their riches to strangers 12 and their sepulchres shall be their houses for ever, their dwelling places to all generations. They have called their lands by their names.

13 Et homo cum in honore esset non intellexit; conparatus est iumentis insipientibus et similis factus est illis. 14 Haec via illorum scandalum ipsis, et postea in ore suo conplacebunt. 15 Sicut oves in inferno positi sunt; mors depascet eos. Et dominabuntur eorum iusti in matutino, et auxilium eorum veterescet in inferno a gloria eorum. 16 Verumtamen Deus redimet animam meam de manu inferi cum acceperit me.

17 Ne timueris cum dives factus fuerit homo et cum multiplicata fuerit gloria domus eius, 18 quoniam cum interierit non sumet omnia neque descendet cum eo gloria eius, 19 quia anima eius in vita ipsius benedicetur; confitebitur tibi cum benefeceris ei. 20 Introibit usque in progenies patrum suorum, et usque in aeternum non videbit lumen. 21 Homo in honore cum esset non intellexit; conparatus est iumentis insipientibus et similis factus est illis.

Psalmus 49

Psalmus Asaph.

Deus deorum, Dominus, locutus est, et vocavit terram a solis ortu usque ad occasum. 2 Ex Sion species decoris eius. 3 Deus manifeste veniet; Deus noster et non silebit. Ignis

13 And man when he was in honour did not understand; he is compared to senseless beasts and is become like to them. 14 This way of theirs is a stumbling block to them, and afterwards they shall delight in their mouth. 15 They are laid in hell like sheep; death shall feed upon them. And the just shall have dominion over them in the morning, and their help shall decay in hell from their glory. 16 But God will redeem my soul from the hand of hell when he shall receive me.

17 Be not thou afraid when a man shall be made rich and when the glory of his house shall be increased, 18 for when he shall die he shall take nothing away nor shall his glory descend with him, 19 for in his lifetime his soul will be blessed *and* he will praise thee when thou shalt do well to him. 20 He shall go in to the generations of his fathers, and he shall never see light. 21 Man when he was in honour did not understand; he hath been compared to senseless beasts and made like to them.

Psalm 49

Deus deorum. The coming of Christ, who prefers virtue and inward purity before the blood of victims.

A psalm for Asaph.
    The God of gods, the Lord, hath spoken, and he hath called the earth from the rising of the sun to the going down *thereof.* 2 Out of Zion the loveliness of his beauty. 3 God shall

in conspectu eius exardescet, et in circuitu eius tempestas valida. 4 Advocabit caelum desursum et terram discernere populum suum. 5 Congregate illi sanctos eius qui ordinant testamentum eius super sacrificia, 6 et adnuntiabunt caeli iustitiam eius, quoniam Deus iudex est.

7 "Audi, populus meus, et loquar; Israhel, et testificabor tibi. Deus, Deus tuus, ego sum. 8 Non in sacrificiis tuis arguam te, holocausta autem tua in conspectu meo sunt semper. 9 Non accipiam de domo tua vitulos neque de gregibus tuis hircos, 10 quoniam meae sunt omnes ferae silvarum, iumenta in montibus et boves. 11 Cognovi omnia volatilia caeli, et pulchritudo agri mecum est. 12 Si esuriero, non dicam tibi, meus est enim orbis terrae et plenitudo eius. 13 Numquid manducabo carnes taurorum? Aut sanguinem hircorum potabo? 14 Immola Deo sacrificium laudis, et redde Altissimo vota tua, 15 et invoca me in die tribulationis; eruam te, et honorificabis me."

16 Peccatori autem dixit Deus, "Quare tu enarras iustitias meas et adsumis testamentum meum per os tuum, 17 tu vero odisti disciplinam et proiecisti sermones meos retrorsum? 18 Si videbas furem, currebas cum eo, et cum adulteris portionem tuam ponebas. 19 Os tuum abundavit malitia, et lingua tua concinnabat dolos. 20 Sedens adversus fratrem tuum loquebaris et adversus filium matris tuae ponebas scandalum. 21 Haec fecisti, et tacui. Existimasti inique quod ero tui similis; arguam te et statuam contra faciem tuam. 22 Intellegite haec, qui obliviscimini Deum, nequando rapiat et non

come manifestly; our God *shall come* and shall not keep silence. A fire shall burn before him, and a mighty tempest shall be round about him. 4 He shall call heaven from above and the earth to judge his people. 5 Gather ye together his saints to him who set his covenant before sacrifices, 6 and the heavens shall declare his justice, for God is judge.

7 "Hear, O my people, and I will speak; O Israel, and I will testify to thee. I am God, thy God. 8 I will not reprove thee for thy sacrifices, and thy burnt offerings are always in my sight. 9 I will not take calves out of thy house nor he-goats out of thy flocks, 10 for all the beasts of the woods are mine, the cattle on the hills and the oxen. 11 I know all the fowls of the air, and with me is the beauty of the field. 12 If I should be hungry, I would not tell thee, for the world is mine and the fulness thereof. 13 Shall I eat the flesh of bullocks? Or shall I drink the blood of goats? 14 Offer to God the sacrifice of praise, and pay thy vows to the Most High, 15 and call upon me in the day of trouble; I will deliver thee, and thou shalt glorify me."

16 But to the sinner God hath said, "Why dost thou declare my justices and take my covenant in thy mouth, 17 *seeing* thou hast hated discipline and hast cast my words behind thee? 18 If thou didst see a thief, thou didst run with him, and with adulterers thou *hast been a partaker.* 19 Thy mouth hath abounded with evil, and thy tongue framed deceits. 20 Sitting thou didst speak against thy brother and didst lay a scandal against thy mother's son. 21 These things hast thou done, and I was silent. Thou thoughtest unjustly that I should be like to thee, *but* I will reprove thee and set before thy face. 22 Understand these things, you that forget God,

sit qui eripiat. 23 Sacrificium laudis honorificabit me, et illic iter quo ostendam illi salutare Dei."

Psalmus 50

In finem. Psalmus David 2 cum venit ad eum Nathan, propheta, quando cum Bethsabee peccavit.

3 Miserere mei, Deus, secundum magnam misericordiam tuam, et secundum multitudinem miserationum tuarum dele iniquitatem meam. 4 Amplius lava me ab iniquitate mea, et a peccato meo munda me, 5 quoniam iniquitatem meam ego cognosco et peccatum meum contra me est semper. 6 Tibi soli peccavi et malum coram te feci ut iustificeris in sermonibus tuis et vincas cum iudicaris, 7 ecce enim: in iniquitatibus conceptus sum, et in peccatis concepit me mater mea, 8 ecce enim: veritatem dilexisti; incerta et occulta sapientiae tuae manifestasti mihi.

9 Asparges me hysopo, et mundabor; lavabis me, et super nivem dealbabor. 10 Auditui meo dabis gaudium et laetitiam, et exultabunt ossa humiliata. 11 Averte faciem tuam a pecca-

lest he snatch you away and there be none to deliver you. 23 The sacrifice of praise shall glorify me, and there is the way by which I will shew him the salvation of God."

Psalm 50

Miserere. The repentance and confession of David after his sin. The fourth penitential psalm.

Unto the end. A psalm of David 2 when Nathan, the prophet, came to him after he had sinned with Bathsheba.

3 Have mercy on me, O God, according to thy great mercy, and according to the multitude of thy *tender* mercies blot out my iniquity. 4 Wash me yet more from my iniquity, and cleanse me from my sin, 5 for I know my iniquity and my sin is always before me. 6 To thee only have I sinned and have done evil before thee that thou mayst be justified in thy words and mayst overcome when thou art judged, 7 for behold: I was conceived in iniquities, and in sins did my mother conceive me, 8 for behold: thou hast loved truth; the uncertain and hidden things of thy wisdom thou hast made manifest to me.

9 Thou shalt sprinkle me with hyssop, and I shall be cleansed; thou shalt wash me, and I shall be made whiter than snow. 10 To my hearing thou shalt give joy and gladness, and the bones that have been humbled shall rejoice. 11 Turn away thy face from my sins, and blot out all my iniq-

tis meis, et omnes iniquitates meas dele. 12 Cor mundum crea in me, Deus, et spiritum rectum innova in visceribus meis. 13 Ne proicias me a facie tua, et spiritum sanctum tuum ne auferas a me. 14 Redde mihi laetitiam salutaris tui, et spiritu principali confirma me. 15 Docebo iniquos vias tuas, et impii ad te convertentur. 16 Libera me de sanguinibus, Deus, Deus salutis meae, et exultabit lingua mea iustitiam tuam. 17 Domine, labia mea aperies, et os meum adnuntiabit laudem tuam, 18 quoniam si voluisses sacrificium, dedissem utique; holocaustis non delectaberis. 19 Sacrificium Deo spiritus contribulatus; cor contritum et humiliatum, Deus, non despicies.

20 Benigne fac, Domine, in bona voluntate tua Sion, ut aedificentur muri Hierusalem. 21 Tunc acceptabis sacrificium iustitiae, oblationes et holocausta; tunc inponent super altare tuum vitulos.

Psalmus 51

In finem. Intellectus David. 2 Cum venit Doec, Idumeus, et adnuntiavit Saul, "Venit David in domum Achimelech."

3 Quid gloriaris in malitia, qui potens es iniquitate? 4 Tota die iniustitiam cogitavit lingua tua. Sicut novacula acuta,

uities. 12 Create a clean heart in me, O God, and renew a right spirit within my bowels. 13 Cast me not away from thy face, and take not thy holy spirit from me. 14 Restore unto me the joy of thy salvation, and strengthen me with a *perfect* spirit. 15 I will teach the unjust thy ways, and the wicked shall be converted to thee. 16 Deliver me from blood, O God, thou God of my salvation, and my tongue shall extol thy justice. 17 O Lord, thou wilt open my lips, and my mouth shall declare thy praise, 18 for if thou hadst desired sacrifice, I would indeed have given it; with burnt offerings thou wilt not be delighted. 19 A sacrifice to God is an afflicted spirit; a contrite and humbled heart, O God, thou wilt not despise.

20 Deal favourably, O Lord, in thy good will with Zion that the walls of Jerusalem may be built up. 21 Then shalt thou accept the sacrifice of justice, oblations and whole burnt offerings; then shall they lay calves upon thy altar.

Psalm 51

Quid gloriaris. David condemneth the wickedness of Doeg, and foretelleth his destruction.

Unto the end. Understanding for David. 2 When Doeg, the Edomite, came and told Saul, "David went to the house of Ahimelech."

3 Why dost thou glory in malice, thou that art mighty in iniquity? 4 All the day long thy tongue hath devised injus-

fecisti dolum. 5 Dilexisti malitiam super benignitatem, iniquitatem magis quam loqui aequitatem. 6 Dilexisti omnia verba praecipitationis, linguam dolosam. 7 Propterea Deus destruet te in finem; evellet te et emigrabit te de tabernaculo tuo et radicem tuam de terra viventium. 8 Videbunt iusti et timebunt et super eum ridebunt et dicent, 9 "Ecce: homo qui non posuit Deum adiutorem suum sed speravit in multitudine divitiarum suarum et praevaluit in vanitate sua." 10 Ego autem, sicut oliva fructifera in domo Dei, speravi in misericordia Dei in aeternum et in saeculum saeculi.

11 Confitebor tibi in saeculum quia fecisti, et expectabo nomen tuum, quoniam bonum in conspectu sanctorum tuorum.

Psalmus 52

In finem. Pro Maeleth, intellegentiae David.

Dixit insipiens in corde suo, "Non est Deus." 2 Corrupti sunt et abominabiles facti sunt in iniquitatibus; non est qui faciat bonum. 3 Deus de caelo prospexit super filios homi-

tice. As a sharp razor, thou hast wrought deceit. 5 Thou hast loved malice more than goodness *and* iniquity rather than to speak righteousness. 6 Thou hast loved all the words of ruin, *O* deceitful tongue. 7 Therefore will God destroy thee for ever; he will pluck thee out and remove thee from thy dwelling place and thy root out of the land of the living. 8 The just shall see and fear and shall laugh at him and say, 9 "Behold: the man that made not God his helper but trusted in the abundance of his riches and prevailed in his vanity." 10 But I, as a fruitful olive tree in the house of God, have hoped in the mercy of God for ever, yea, for ever and ever.

11 I will praise thee for ever because thou hast done it, and I will wait on thy name, for it is good in the sight of thy saints.

Psalm 52

Dixit insipiens. The general corruption of man before the coming of Christ.

Unto the end. For Mahalath, understandings to David.

The fool said in his heart, "There is no God." 2 They are corrupted and become abominable in iniquities; there is none that doth good. 3 God looked down from heaven on

num ut videat si est intellegens aut requirens Deum. 4 Omnes declinaverunt; simul inutiles facti sunt; non est qui faciat bonum, non est, usque ad unum.

5 Nonne scient omnes qui operantur iniquitatem qui devorant plebem meam ut cibum panis? 6 Deum non invocaverunt; illic trepidaverunt timore ubi non fuit timor, quoniam Deus dissipavit ossa eorum qui hominibus placent. Confusi sunt quoniam Deus sprevit eos.

7 Quis dabit ex Sion salutare Israhel? Cum converterit Deus captivitatem plebis suae exultabit Iacob, et laetabitur Israhel.

Psalmus 53

In finem. In carminibus. Intellectus David 2 cum venissent Ziphei et dixissent ad Saul, "Nonne David absconditus est apud nos?"

3 Deus, in nomine tuo salvum me fac, et in virtute tua iudica me. 4 Deus, exaudi orationem meam; auribus percipe verba oris mei, 5 quoniam alieni insurrexerunt adversum me et fortes quaesierunt animam meam et non proposuerunt Deum ante oculos suos, 6 ecce enim: Deus adiuvat me,

the children of men to see if there were any that did understand or did seek God. 4 All have gone aside; they are become unprofitable together; there is none that doth good, no, not one.

5 Shall not all the workers of iniquity know who eat up my people as *they eat* bread? 6 They have not called upon God; there have they trembled for fear where there was no fear, for God hath scattered the bones of them that please men. They have been confounded because God hath despised them.

7 Who will give out of Zion the salvation of Israel? When God shall bring back the captivity of his people Jacob shall rejoice, and Israel shall be glad.

Psalm 53

Deus, in nomine tuo. A prayer for help in distress.

Unto the end. In verses. Understanding for David 2 when the men of Ziph had come and said to Saul, "Is not David hidden with us?"

3 Save me, O God, by thy name, and judge me in thy strength. 4 O God, hear my prayer; give ear to the words of my mouth, 5 for strangers have risen up against me and the mighty have sought after my soul and they have not set God before their eyes, 6 for behold: God is my helper, and the

et Dominus susceptor animae meae. 7 Averte mala inimicis meis, et in veritate tua disperde illos. 8 Voluntarie sacrificabo tibi et confitebor nomini tuo, Domine, quoniam bonum, 9 quoniam ex omni tribulatione eripuisti me et super inimicos meos despexit oculus meus.

Psalmus 54

In finem. In carminibus. Intellectus David.

2 Exaudi, Deus, orationem meam, et ne despexeris deprecationem meam. 3 Intende mihi, et exaudi me. Contristatus sum in exercitatione mea et conturbatus sum 4 a voce inimici et a tribulatione peccatoris, quoniam declinaverunt in me iniquitates et in ira molesti erant mihi. 5 Cor meum conturbatum est in me, et formido mortis cecidit super me. 6 Timor et tremor venerunt super me, et contexit me tenebra. 7 Et dixi, "Quis dabit mihi pinnas sicut columbae? Et volabo et requiescam." 8 Ecce: elongavi fugiens, et mansi in solitudine. 9 Expectabam eum qui salvum me fecit a pusillanimitate spiritus et tempestate.

Lord is the protector of my soul. 7 Turn back the evils upon my enemies, and cut them off in thy truth. 8 I will freely sacrifice to thee and will give praise, O *God,* to thy name because it is good, 9 for thou hast delivered me out of all trouble and my eye hath looked down upon my enemies.

Psalm 54

Exaudi, Deus. A prayer of a just man under persecution from the wicked. It agrees to Christ persecuted by the Jews and betrayed by Judas.

Unto the end. In verses. Understanding for David.

2 Hear, O God, my prayer, and despise not my supplication. 3 Be attentive to me, and hear me. I am grieved in my exercise and am troubled 4 at the voice of the enemy and at the tribulation of the sinner, for they have cast iniquities upon me and in wrath they were troublesome to me. 5 My heart is troubled within me, and the fear of death is fallen upon me. 6 Fear and trembling are come upon me, and darkness hath covered me. 7 And I said, "Who will give me wings like a dove? And I will fly and be at rest." 8 Lo: I have gone far off flying away, and I abode in the wilderness. 9 I waited for him that hath saved me from pusillanimity of spirit and a storm.

10 Praecipita, Domine, et divide linguas eorum, quoniam vidi iniquitatem et contradictionem in civitate. 11 Die et nocte circumdabit eam super muros eius iniquitas, et labor in medio eius 12 et iniustitia, et non defecit de plateis eius usura et dolus, 13 quoniam si inimicus meus maledixisset mihi sustinuissem utique et si is qui oderat me super me magna locutus fuisset abscondissem me forsitan ab eo. 14 Tu vero, homo unianimis, dux meus et notus meus, 15 qui simul mecum dulces capiebas cibos, in domo Dei ambulavimus cum consensu. 16 Veniat mors super illos, et descendant in infernum viventes, quoniam nequitiae in habitaculis eorum, in medio eorum.

17 Ego autem ad Deum clamavi, et Dominus salvabit me. 18 Vespere et mane et meridie narrabo et adnuntiabo, et exaudiet vocem meam. 19 Redimet in pace animam meam ab his qui adpropinquant mihi, quoniam inter multos erant mecum. 20 Exaudiet Deus, et humiliabit illos qui est ante saecula, non enim est illis commutatio et non timuerunt Deum. 21 Extendit manum suam in retribuendo. Contaminaverunt testamentum eius. 22 Divisi sunt ab ira vultus eius, et adpropinquavit cor illius. Molliti sunt sermones eius super oleum, et ipsi sunt iacula.

23 Iacta super Dominum curam tuam, et ipse te enutriet; non dabit in aeternum fluctuationem iusto. 24 Tu vero, Deus, deduces eos in puteum interitus. Viri sanguinum et doli non dimidiabunt dies suos, ego autem sperabo in te, Domine.

10 Cast down, O Lord, and divide their tongues, for I have seen iniquity and contradiction in the city. 11 Day and night shall iniquity surround it upon its walls, and in the midst thereof are labour 12 and injustice, and usury and deceit have not departed from its streets, 13 for if my enemy had reviled me I would verily have borne with it and if he that hated me had spoken great things against me I would perhaps have hidden my self from him. 14 But thou, a man of one mind, my guide and my familiar, 15 who didst take sweet meats together with me, in the house of God we walked with consent. 16 Let death come upon them, and let them go down alive into hell, for there is wickedness in their dwellings, in the midst of them.

17 But I have cried to God, and the Lord will save me. 18 Evening and morning and at noon I will speak and declare, and he shall hear my voice. 19 He shall redeem my soul in peace from them that draw near to me, for among many they were with me. 20 God shall hear, and *the Eternal* shall humble them, for there is no change with them and they have not feared God. 21 He hath stretched forth his hand to repay. They have defiled his covenant. 22 They are divided by the wrath of his countenance, and his heart hath drawn near. His words are smoother than oil, and the same are darts.

23 Cast thy care upon the Lord, and he shall sustain thee; he shall not suffer the just to waver for ever. 24 But thou, O God, shalt bring them down into the pit of destruction. Bloody and deceitful men shall not live out half their days, but I will trust in thee, O Lord.

Psalmus 55

In finem. Pro populo qui a sanctis longe factus est, David, in tituli inscriptione cum tenuerunt eum Allophili in Geth. 2 Miserere mei, Deus, quoniam conculcavit me homo; tota die, inpugnans, tribulavit me. 3 Conculcaverunt me inimici mei tota die, quoniam multi bellantes adversum me. 4 Ab altitudine diei timebo, ego vero in te sperabo. 5 In Deo laudabo sermones meos; in Deo speravi; non timebo quid faciat mihi caro.

6 Tota die verba mea execrabantur; adversum me omnia cogitationes eorum in malum. 7 Inhabitabunt et abscondent; ipsi calcaneum meum observabunt sicut sustinuerunt animam meam. 8 Pro nihilo salvos facies illos; in ira populos confringes. Deus, 9 vitam meam adnuntiavi tibi; posuisti lacrimas meas in conspectu tuo. Sicut et in promissione tua, 10 tunc convertentur inimici mei retrorsum. In quacumque die invocavero te, ecce: cognovi quoniam Deus meus es. 11 In Deo laudabo verbum; in Domino laudabo sermonem. In Deo speravi; non timebo quid faciat mihi homo. 12 In me sunt, Deus, vota tua quae reddam, laudationes tibi, 13 quoniam eripuisti animam meam de morte et pedes meos de lapsu, ut placeam coram Deo, in lumine viventium.

Psalm 55

Miserere mei, Deus. A prayer of David in danger and distress.

Unto the end. For a people that is *removed at a distance* from the *sanctuary,* for David, for an inscription of a title *or pillar* when the Philistines held him in Gath.

2 Have mercy on me, O God, for man hath trodden me under foot; all the day long he hath afflicted me, fighting against me. 3 My enemies have trodden on me all the day long, for they are many that make war against me. 4 From the height of the day I shall fear, but I will trust in thee. 5 In God I will praise my words; in God I have put my trust; I will not fear what flesh can do against me.

6 All the day long they detested my words; all their thoughts were against me unto evil. 7 They will dwell and hide themselves; they will watch my heel as they have waited for my soul. 8 For nothing shalt thou save them; in *thy* anger thou shalt break the people in pieces. O God, 9 I have declared to thee my life; thou hast set my tears in thy sight. As also in thy promise, 10 then shall my enemies be turned back. In what day soever I shall call upon thee, behold: I know thou art my God. 11 In God will I praise the word; in the Lord will I praise his speech. In God have I hoped; I will not fear what man can do to me. 12 In me, O God, are vows to thee which I will pay, praises to thee, 13 because thou hast delivered my soul from death, *my* feet from falling, that I may please in the sight of God, in the light of the living.

Psalmus 56

In finem. Ne disperdas, David, in tituli inscriptione, cum fugeret a facie Saul in speluncam.

2 Miserere mei, Deus; miserere mei, quoniam in te confidit anima mea, et in umbra alarum tuarum sperabo donec transeat iniquitas. 3 Clamabo ad Deum, Altissimum, Deum qui benefecit mihi. 4 Misit de caelo et liberavit me; dedit in obprobrium conculcantes me. Misit Deus misericordiam suam et veritatem suam, 5 et eripuit animam meam de medio catulorum leonum. Dormivi conturbatus. Filii hominum, dentes eorum arma et sagittae et lingua eorum gladius acutus. 6 Exaltare super caelos, Deus, et in omnem terram gloria tua. 7 Laqueum paraverunt pedibus meis, et incurvaverunt animam meam. Foderunt ante faciem meam foveam, et inciderunt in eam. 8 Paratum cor meum, Deus; paratum cor meum. Cantabo et psalmum dicam.

9 Exsurge, gloria mea! Exsurge, psalterium et cithara! Exsurgam diluculo. 10 Confitebor tibi in populis, Domine, et psalmum dicam tibi in gentibus, 11 quoniam magnificata est usque ad caelos misericordia tua et usque ad nubes veritas tua. 12 Exaltare super caelos, Deus, et super omnem terram gloria tua.

Psalm 56

Miserere mei, Deus. The prophet prays in his affliction and praises God for his delivery.

Unto the end. Destroy not, for David, for an inscription of a title, when he fled *from* Saul into the cave.

2 Have mercy on me, O God; have mercy on me, for my soul trusteth in thee, and in the shadow of thy wings will I hope until iniquity pass away. 3 I will cry to God, the Most High, to God who hath done good to me. 4 He hath sent from heaven and delivered me; he hath made them a reproach that trod upon me. God hath sent his mercy and his truth, 5 and he hath delivered my soul from the midst of the young lions—I slept troubled—the sons of men *whose* teeth are weapons and arrows and their tongue a sharp sword. 6 Be thou exalted, O God, above the heavens, and thy glory *above* all the earth. 7 They prepared a snare for my feet, and they bowed down my soul. They dug a pit before my face, and they are fallen into it. 8 My heart is ready, O God; my heart is ready. I will sing and rehearse a psalm.

9 Arise, O my glory! Arise, psaltery and harp! I will arise early. 10 I will give praise to thee, O Lord, among the people; *I* will sing a psalm to thee among the nations, 11 for thy mercy is magnified even to the heavens and thy truth unto the clouds. 12 Be thou exalted, O God, above the heavens, and thy glory above all the earth.

Psalmus 57

In finem. Ne disperdas, David, in tituli inscriptione. 2 Si vere utique iustitiam loquimini, recta iudicate, filii hominum, 3 etenim in corde iniquitates operamini; in terra iniustitiam manus vestrae concinnant. 4 Alienati sunt peccatores a vulva; erraverunt ab utero; locuti sunt falsa. 5 Furor illis secundum similitudinem serpentis, sicut aspidis surdae et obturantis aures suas, 6 quae non exaudiet vocem incantantium et venefici incantantis sapienter. 7 Deus conteret dentes eorum in ore ipsorum; molas leonum confringet Dominus. 8 Ad nihilum devenient, tamquam aqua decurrens; intendit arcum suum donec infirmentur. 9 Sicut cera quae fluit auferentur; supercecidit ignis, et non viderunt solem. 10 Priusquam intellegerent spinae vestrae ramnum sicut viventes sic in ira absorbet eos. 11 Laetabitur iustus cum viderit vindictam; manus suas lavabit in sanguine peccatoris, 12 et dicet homo, "Si utique est fructus iusto, utique est Deus iudicans eos in terra."

Psalm 57

Si vere utique. David reproveth the wicked and foretelleth their punishment.

Unto the end. Destroy not, for David, for an inscription of a title.

2 If in very deed ye speak justice, judge right things, ye sons of men, 3 for in your heart you work iniquity; your hands forge injustice in the earth. 4 The wicked are alienated from the womb; they have gone astray from the womb; they have spoken false things. 5 Their madness is according to the likeness of a serpent, like the deaf asp *that* stoppeth her ears, 6 which will not hear the voice of the charmers nor of the wizard that charmeth wisely. 7 God shall break in pieces their teeth in their mouth; the Lord shall break the grinders of the lions. 8 They shall come to nothing, like water running down; he hath bent his bow till they be weakened. 9 Like wax that melteth they shall be taken away; fire hath fallen on them, and they *shall* not *see* the sun. 10 Before your thorns *could know* the brier he swalloweth them up as alive in his wrath. 11 The just shall rejoice when he shall see the revenge; he shall wash his hands in the blood of the sinner, 12 and man shall say, "If indeed there be fruit to the just, there is indeed a God that judgeth them on the earth."

Psalmus 58

In finem. Ne disperdas, David, in tituli inscriptione, quando misit Saul et custodivit domum eius ut interficeret eum. 2 Eripe me de inimicis meis, Deus meus, et ab insurgentibus in me protege me. 3 Eripe me de operantibus iniquitatem, et de viris sanguinum salva me, 4 quia ecce: ceperunt animam meam; inruerunt in me fortes, 5 neque iniquitas mea neque peccatum meum, Domine. Sine iniquitate cucurri et direxi. 6 Exsurge in occursum meum, et vide, et tu, Domine, Deus virtutum, Deus Israhel. Intende ad visitandas omnes gentes; non misearis omnibus qui operantur iniquitatem. 7 Convertentur ad vesperam et famem patientur ut canes et circuibunt civitatem. 8 Ecce: loquentur in ore suo, et gladius in labiis eorum, quoniam quis audivit? 9 Et tu, Domine, deridebis eos; ad nihilum deduces omnes gentes.

10 Fortitudinem meam ad te custodiam, quia tu susceptor meus es. 11 Deus meus, misericordia tua praeveniet me. 12 Deus ostendet mihi super inimicos meos; ne occidas eos, nequando obliviscantur populi mei. Disperge illos in virtute tua, et depone eos, protector meus, Domine, 13 delictum

Psalm 58

Eripe me. A prayer to be delivered from the wicked, with confidence in God's help and protection. It agrees to Christ and his enemies, the Jews.

Unto the end. Destroy not, for David, for an inscription of a title, when Saul sent and watched his house to kill him.

2 Deliver me from my enemies, O my God, and defend me from them that rise up against me. 3 Deliver me from them that work iniquity, and save me from bloody men, 4 for behold: they have caught my soul; the mighty have rushed in upon me, 5 neither is it my iniquity nor my sin, O Lord. Without iniquity have I run and directed *my steps*. 6 Rise up thou to meet me, and behold, even thou, O Lord, the God of hosts, the God of Israel. Attend to visit all the nations; have no mercy on all them that work iniquity. 7 They shall return at evening and shall suffer hunger like dogs and shall go round about the city. 8 Behold: they shall speak with their mouth, and a sword is in their lips, for "Who," *say they*, "hath heard *us?*" 9 *But* thou, O Lord, shalt laugh at them; thou shalt bring all the nations to nothing.

10 I will keep my strength to thee, for thou art my protector. 11 My God, *his* mercy shall prevent me. 12 God shall let me see over my enemies; slay them not, lest at any time my people forget. Scatter them by thy power, and bring them down, O Lord, my protector, 13 *for* the sin of their mouth

oris eorum, sermonem labiorum ipsorum, et conprehendantur in superbia sua. Et de execratione et mendacio adnuntiabuntur 14 in consummatione, in ira consummationis, et non erunt. Et scient quia Deus dominabitur Iacob et finium terrae. 15 Convertentur ad vesperam et famem patientur ut canes et circuibunt civitatem. 16 Ipsi dispergentur ad manducandum si vero non fuerint saturati et murmurabunt. 17 Ego autem cantabo fortitudinem tuam et exultabo mane misericordiam tuam, quia factus es susceptor meus et refugium meum in die tribulationis meae. 18 Adiutor meus, tibi psallam, quia Deus, susceptor meus, es, Deus meus, misericordia mea.

Psalmus 59

In finem. Pro his qui inmutabuntur, in tituli inscriptione, ipsi David, in doctrina, 2 cum succendit Mesopotamiam Syriae et Sobal et convertit Ioab et percussit Idumaeam in Valle Salinarum duodecim milia.

3 Deus, reppulisti nos et destruxisti nos; iratus es et misertus es nobis. 4 Commovisti terram et turbasti eam; sana

and the word of their lips, and let them be taken in their pride. And for their cursing and lying they shall be talked of 14 when they are consumed, when they are consumed by thy wrath, and they shall be no more. And they shall know that God will rule Jacob and all the ends of the earth. 15 They shall return at evening and shall suffer hunger like dogs and shall go round about the city. 16 They shall be scattered abroad to eat and shall *murmur* if they be not filled. 17 But I will sing thy strength and will extol thy mercy in the morning, for thou art become my support and my refuge in the day of my trouble. 18 Unto thee, O my helper, will I sing, for thou art God, my defence, my God, my mercy.

Psalm 59

Deus, reppulisti nos. After many afflictions the church of Christ shall prevail.

Unto the end. For them that shall be changed, for the inscription of a title, to David himself, for doctrine, 2 when he set fire to Mesopotamia of Syria and Sobal and Joab returned and slew of Edom in the Vale of the Saltpits twelve thousand men.

3 O God, thou hast cast us off and hast destroyed us; thou hast been angry and hast had mercy on us. 4 Thou hast moved the earth and hast troubled it; heal thou the breaches

contritiones eius, quia commota est. ⁵ Ostendisti populo tuo dura; potasti nos vino conpunctionis. ⁶ Dedisti metuentibus te significationem, ut fugiant a facie arcus, ut liberentur dilecti tui. ⁷ Salvum fac dextera tua, et exaudi me.

⁸ Deus locutus est in sancto suo; laetabor, et partibor Sicima et Convallem Tabernaculorum metibor. ⁹ Meus est Galaad, et meus est Manasses, et Effraim fortitudo capitis mei. Iuda rex meus; ¹⁰ Moab olla spei meae. In Idumeam extendam calciamentum meum; mihi alienigenae subditi sunt.

¹¹ Quis deducet me in civitatem munitam? Quis deducet me usque in Idumeam? ¹² Nonne tu, Deus, qui reppulisti nos? Et non egredieris, Deus, in virtutibus nostris? ¹³ Da nobis auxilium de tribulatione, quia vana salus hominis. ¹⁴ In Deo faciemus virtutem, et ipse ad nihilum deducet tribulantes nos.

Psalmus 60

Ιn finem. In hymnis, David.

² Exaudi, Deus, deprecationem meam; intende orationi meae. ³ A finibus terrae ad te clamavi dum anxiaretur cor

thereof, for it has been moved. 5 Thou hast shewn thy people hard things; thou hast made us drink the wine of sorrow. 6 Thou hast given a warning to them that fear thee, that they may flee from before the bow, that thy beloved may be delivered. 7 Save me with thy right hand, and hear me.

8 God hath spoken in his holy place; I will rejoice, and I will divide Shechem and will mete out the Vale of Tabernacles. 9 Gilead is mine, and Manasseh is mine, and Ephraim is the strength of my head. Judah is my king; 10 Moab is the pot of my hope. Into Edom will I stretch out my shoe; to me the foreigners are made subject.

11 Who will bring me into the strong city? Who will lead me into Edom? 12 Wilt not thou, O God, who hast cast us off? And wilt not thou, O God, go out with our armies? 13 Give us help from trouble, for vain is the salvation of man. 14 Through God we shall do mightily, and he shall bring to nothing them that afflict us.

Psalm 60

Exaudi, Deus. A prayer for the coming of the kingdom of Christ, which shall have no end.

Unto the end. In hymns, for David.

2 Hear, O God, my supplication; be attentive to my prayer. 3 To thee have I cried from the ends of the earth when my heart was in anguish; thou hast exalted me on a

meum; in petra exaltasti me. Deduxisti me, 4 quia factus es spes mea, turris fortitudinis a facie inimici. 5 Inhabitabo in tabernaculo tuo in saecula; protegar in velamento alarum tuarum, 6 quoniam tu, Deus meus, exaudisti orationem meam; dedisti hereditatem timentibus nomen tuum. 7 Dies super dies regis adicies, annos eius usque in diem generationis et generationis. 8 Permanet in aeternum in conspectu Dei; misericordiam et veritatem quis requiret eius? 9 Sic psalmum dicam nomini tuo in saeculum saeculi ut reddam vota mea de die in diem.

Psalmus 61

In finem. Pro Idithun. Psalmus David.

2 Nonne Deo subiecta erit anima mea? Ab ipso enim salutare meum, 3 nam et ipse Deus meus et salutaris meus; susceptor meus. Non movebor amplius. 4 Quousque inruitis in hominem? Interficitis universi vos tamquam parieti inclinato et maceriae depulsae, 5 verumtamen pretium meum cogitaverunt repellere. Cucurri in siti; ore suo benedicebant et corde suo maledicebant. 6 Verumtamen Deo subiecta esto, anima mea, quoniam ab ipso patientia mea, 7 quia ipse Deus meus et salvator meus. Adiutor meus; non emigrabo.

rock. Thou hast conducted me, 4 for thou hast been my hope, a tower of strength against the face of the enemy. 5 In thy tabernacle I shall dwell for ever; I shall be protected under the covert of thy wings, 6 for thou, my God, hast heard my prayer; thou hast given an inheritance to them that fear thy name. 7 Thou wilt add days to the days of the king, his years even to *generation* and generation. 8 He abideth for ever in the sight of God; his mercy and truth who shall search? 9 So will I sing a psalm to thy name for ever and ever that I may pay my vows from day to day.

Psalm 61

Nonne Deo. The prophet encourageth himself and all others to trust in God and serve him.

Unto the end. For Jeduthun. A psalm of David.

2 Shall not my soul be subject to God? For from him is my salvation, 3 for he is my God and my saviour; he is my protector. I shall be moved no more. 4 How long do you rush in upon a man? You all kill as if *you were thrusting down* a leaning wall and a *tottering* fence, 5 but they have thought to cast away my price. I ran in thirst; they blessed with their mouth *but* cursed with their heart. 6 But be thou, O my soul, subject to God, for from him is my patience, 7 for he is my God and my saviour. He is my helper; I shall not be moved.

8 In Deo salutare meum et gloria mea; Deus auxilii mei, et spes mea in Deo est.

9 Sperate in eo, omnis congregatio populi; effundite coram illo corda vestra. Deus adiutor noster in aeternum. 10 Verumtamen vani filii hominum; mendaces filii hominum in stateris ut decipiant ipsi de vanitate in id ipsum. 11 Nolite sperare in iniquitate, et rapinas nolite concupiscere. Divitiae si affluant, nolite cor adponere.

12 Semel locutus est Deus. Duo haec audivi: quia potestas Dei, 13 et tibi, Domine, misericordia, quia tu reddes unicuique iuxta opera sua.

Psalmus 62

P salmus David cum esset in deserto Iudaeae.

2 Deus, Deus meus, ad te de luce vigilo. Sitivit in te anima mea—quam multipliciter!—tibi caro mea, 3 in terra deserta et invia et inaquosa. Sic in sancto apparui tibi ut viderem virtutem tuam et gloriam tuam, 4 quoniam melior est misericordia tua super vitas. Labia mea laudabunt te. 5 Sic benedicam te in vita mea, et in nomine tuo levabo manus meas.

6 Sicut adipe et pinguidine repleatur anima mea, et labiis exultationis laudabit os meum. 7 Si memor fui tui super stra-

8 In God is my salvation and my glory; he is the God of my help, and my hope is in God.

9 Trust in him, all ye congregation of people; pour out your hearts before him. God is our helper for ever. 10 But vain are the sons of men; the sons of men are liars in the balances that by vanity they may together deceive. 11 Trust not in iniquity, and covet not robberies. If riches abound, set not your heart upon them.

12 God hath spoken once. These two things have I heard: that power belongeth to God, 13 and mercy to thee, O Lord, for thou wilt render to every man according to his works.

Psalm 62

Deus, Deus meus, ad te. The prophet aspireth after God.

A psalm of David while he was in the desert of *Edom*.

2 O God, my God, to thee do I watch at break of day. For thee my soul hath thirsted, for thee my flesh—O how many ways!—3 in a desert land and where there is no way and no water. So in the sanctuary have I come before thee to see thy power and thy glory, 4 for thy mercy is better than lives. Thee my lips will praise. 5 Thus will I bless thee *all* my life *long,* and in thy name I will lift up my hands.

6 Let my soul be filled as with marrow and fatness, and my mouth shall praise thee with joyful lips. 7 If I have remem-

tum meum, in matutinis meditabor in te, 8 quia fuisti adiutor meus. Et in velamento alarum tuarum exultabo.

9 Adhesit anima mea post te; me suscepit dextera tua. 10 Ipsi vero in vanum quaesierunt animam meam; introibunt in inferiora terrae; 11 tradentur in manus gladii; partes vulpium erunt. 12 Rex vero laetabitur in Deo. Laudabitur omnis qui iurat in eo, quia obstructum est os loquentium iniqua.

Psalmus 63

In finem. Psalmus David.

2 Exaudi, Deus, orationem meam cum deprecor; a timore inimici eripe animam meam.

3 Protexisti me a conventu malignantium, a multitudine operantium iniquitatem, 4 quia exacuerunt ut gladium linguas suas; intenderunt arcum, rem amaram, 5 ut sagittent in occultis inmaculatum. 6 Subito sagittabunt eum et non timebunt; firmaverunt sibi sermonem nequam. Narraverunt

bered thee upon my bed, I will meditate on thee in the morning, 8 because thou hast been my helper. And I will rejoice under the covert of thy wings.

9 My soul hath stuck close to thee; thy right hand hath received me. 10 But they have sought my soul in vain; they shall go into the lower parts of the earth; 11 they shall be delivered into the hands of the sword; they shall be the portions of foxes. 12 But the king shall rejoice in God. All *they* shall be praised that swear by him, because the mouth is stopped of them that speak wicked things.

Psalm 63

Exaudi, Deus, orationem. A prayer in affliction with confidence in God that he will bring to naught the machinations of persecutors.

Unto the end. A psalm for David.

2 Hear, O God, my prayer when I make supplication *to thee;* deliver my soul from the fear of the enemy.

3 Thou hast protected me from the assembly of the malignant, from the multitude of the workers of iniquity, 4 for they have whetted their tongues like a sword; they have bent their bow, a bitter thing, 5 to shoot in secret the undefiled. 6 They will shoot at him on a sudden and will not fear; they *are resolute in wickedness.* They have talked of hiding snares.

ut absconderent laqueos. Dixerunt, "Quis videbit eos?"
7 Scrutati sunt iniquitates; defecerunt scrutantes scrutinio.
Accedet homo ad cor altum, 8 et exaltabitur Deus. Sagittae
parvulorum factae sunt plagae eorum, 9 et infirmatae sunt
contra eos linguae eorum. Conturbati sunt omnes qui videbant eos, 10 et timuit omnis homo. Et adnuntiaverunt opera
Dei et facta eius intellexerunt. 11 Laetabitur iustus in Domino et sperabit in eo, et laudabuntur omnes recti corde.

Psalmus 64

In finem. Psalmus David. Canticum Hieremiae et Ezechielis populo transmigrationis quando incipiebant proficisci.
2 Te decet hymnus, Deus, in Sion, et tibi reddetur votum
in Hierusalem. 3 Exaudi orationem meam; ad te omnis caro
veniet. 4 Verba iniquorum praevaluerunt super nos, et im-
pietatibus nostris tu propitiaberis. 5 Beatus quem elegisti et
adsumpsisti; inhabitabit in atriis tuis. Replebimur in bonis
domus tuae; sanctum est templum tuum, 6 mirabile in aequitate.
Exaudi nos, Deus, salutaris noster, spes omnium finium

They have said, "Who shall see them?" 7 They have searched after iniquities; they have failed in their search. Man shall come to a deep heart, 8 and God shall be exalted. The arrows of children are their wounds, 9 and their tongues against them are made weak. All that saw them were troubled, 10 and every man was afraid. And they declared the works of God and understood his doings. 11 The just shall rejoice in the Lord and shall hope in him, and all the upright in heart shall be praised.

Psalm 64

Te decet. God is to be praised in his church, to which all nations shall be called.

To the end. A psalm of David. The canticle of Jeremiah and Ezekiel to the people of the captivity when they began to go out.

2 A hymn, O God, becometh thee in Zion, and a vow shall be paid to thee in Jerusalem. 3 O hear my prayer; all flesh shall come to thee. 4 The words of the wicked have prevailed over us, and thou wilt pardon our transgressions. 5 Blessed is he whom thou hast chosen and taken *to thee;* he shall dwell in thy courts. We shall be filled with the good things of thy house; holy is thy temple, 6 wonderful in justice.

Hear us, O God, our saviour, who art the hope of all the

terrae et in mari longe. 7 Praeparans montes in virtute tua, accinctus potentia, 8 qui conturbas profundum maris, sonum fluctuum eius. Turbabuntur Gentes, 9 et timebunt qui inhabitant terminos a signis tuis; exitus matutini et vespere delectabis. 10 Visitasti terram et inebriasti eam; multiplicasti locupletare eam. Flumen Dei repletum est aquis; parasti cibum illorum, quoniam ita est praeparatio eius. 11 Rivos eius inebria; multiplica genimina eius. In stillicidiis eius laetabitur germinans. 12 Benedices coronae anni benignitatis tuae, et campi tui replebuntur ubertate. 13 Pinguescent speciosa deserti, et exultatione colles accingentur. 14 Induti sunt arietes ovium, et valles abundabunt frumento. Clamabunt, etenim hymnum dicent.

Psalmus 65

In finem. Canticum psalmi resurrectionis.

Iubilate Deo, omnis terra, 2 psalmum dicite nomini eius; date gloriam laudi eius! 3 Dicite Deo, "Quam terribilia sunt

ends of the earth and in the sea afar off. 7 Thou who preparest the mountains by thy strength, being girded with power, 8 who troublest the depth of the sea, the noise of its waves. The Gentiles shall be troubled, 9 and they that dwell in the *uttermost* borders shall be afraid at thy signs; thou shalt make the outgoings of the morning and of the evening to be joyful. 10 Thou hast visited the earth and hast plentifully watered it; thou hast many ways enriched it. The river of God is filled with water; thou hast prepared their food, for so is its preparation. 11 Fill up plentifully the streams thereof; multiply its fruits. It shall spring up and rejoice in its showers. 12 Thou shalt bless the crown of the year of thy goodness, and thy fields shall be filled with plenty. 13 The beautiful places of the wilderness shall grow fat, and the hills shall be girded about with joy. 14 The rams of the flock are clothed, and the vales shall abound with corn. They shall shout; yea, they shall sing a hymn.

Psalm 65

Iubilate Deo. An invitation to praise God.

Unto the end. A canticle of a psalm of the resurrection.

Shout with joy to God, all the earth, 2 sing ye a psalm to his name; give glory to his praise! 3 Say unto God, "How ter-

opera tua, Domine! In multitudine virtutis tuae mentientur tibi inimici tui. 4 Omnis terra adoret te et psallat tibi; psalmum dicat nomini tuo." 5 Venite, et videte opera Dei, terribilis in consiliis super filios hominum, 6 qui convertit mare in aridam—in flumine pertransibunt pede; ibi laetabimur in ipso—7 qui dominatur in virtute sua in aeternum; oculi eius super gentes respiciunt. Qui exasperant non exaltentur in semet ipsis.

8 Benedicite, Gentes, Deum nostrum, et auditam facite vocem laudis eius, 9 qui posuit animam meam ad vitam et non dedit in commotionem pedes meos, 10 quoniam probasti nos, Deus; igne nos examinasti sicut examinatur argentum. 11 Induxisti nos in laqueum; posuisti tribulationes in dorso nostro. 12 Inposuisti homines super capita nostra. Transivimus per ignem et aquam, et eduxisti nos in refrigerium. 13 Introibo in domum tuam in holocaustis; reddam tibi vota mea 14 quae distinxerunt labia mea et locutum est os meum in tribulatione mea. 15 Holocausta medullata offeram tibi cum incensu arietum; offeram tibi boves cum hircis.

16 Venite; audite, et narrabo, omnes qui timetis Deum, quanta fecit animae meae. 17 Ad ipsum ore meo clamavi, et exaltavi sub lingua mea. 18 Iniquitatem si aspexi in corde

rible are thy works, O Lord! In the multitude of thy strength thy enemies shall lie to thee. 4 Let all the earth adore thee and sing to thee; let it sing a psalm to thy name." 5 Come, and see the works of God, who is terrible in his counsels over the sons of men, 6 who turneth the sea into dry land—in the river they shall pass on foot; there shall we rejoice in him—7 who by his power ruleth for ever; his eyes behold the nations. Let not them that provoke him be exalted in themselves.

8 O bless our God, ye Gentiles, and make the voice of his praise to be heard, 9 who hath set my soul to live and hath not suffered my feet to be moved, 10 for thou, O God, hast proved us; thou hast tried us by fire as silver is tried. 11 Thou hast brought us into a net; thou hast laid afflictions on our back. 12 Thou hast set men over our heads. We have passed through fire and water, and thou hast brought us out into a refreshment. 13 I will go into thy house with burnt offerings; I will pay thee my vows 14 which my lips have uttered and my mouth hath spoken when I was in trouble. 15 I will offer up to thee holocausts full of marrow with burnt offerings of rams; I will offer to thee bullocks with goats.

16 Come, *and* hear, all ye that fear God, and I will tell you what great things he hath done for my soul. 17 I cried to him with my mouth, and I extolled him with my tongue. 18 If I have looked at iniquity in my heart, the Lord will not hear

meo, non exaudiet Dominus. 19 Propterea exaudivit Deus et adtendit voci deprecationis meae. 20 Benedictus Deus, qui non amovit orationem meam et misericordiam suam a me.

Psalmus 66

In finem. In hymnis. Psalmus cantici David.

2 Deus misereatur nostri et benedicat nobis; inluminet vultum suum super nos, et misereatur nostri 3 ut cognoscamus in terra viam tuam, in omnibus gentibus salutare tuum.

4 Confiteantur tibi populi, Deus; confiteantur tibi populi omnes. 5 Laetentur et exultent gentes, quoniam iudicas populos in aequitate et gentes in terra dirigis. 6 Confiteantur tibi populi, Deus; confiteantur tibi populi omnes.

7 Terra dedit fructum suum. Benedicat nos Deus, Deus noster. 8 Benedicat nos Deus, et metuant eum omnes fines terrae.

me. 19 Therefore hath God heard me and hath attended to the voice of my supplication. 20 Blessed be God, who hath not turned away my prayer nor his mercy from me.

Psalm 66

Deus misereatur. A prayer for the propagation of the church.

Unto the end. In hymns. A psalm of a canticle for David.

2 May God have mercy on us and bless us; may he cause the light of his countenance to shine upon us, and may he have mercy on us 3 that we may know thy way upon earth, thy salvation in all nations.

4 Let people confess to thee, O God; let all people give praise to thee. 5 Let the nations be glad and rejoice, for thou judgest the people with justice and directest the nations upon earth. 6 Let the people, O God, confess to thee; let all the people give praise to thee.

7 The earth hath yielded her fruit. May God, our God, bless us. 8 May God bless us, and all the ends of the earth fear him.

Psalmus 67

In finem. Ipsi David psalmus cantici.

2 Exsurgat Deus, et dissipentur inimici eius, et fugiant qui oderunt eum a facie eius! 3 Sicut deficit fumus, deficiant; sicut fluit cera a facie ignis, sic pereant peccatores a facie Dei. 4 Et iusti epulentur et exultent in conspectu Dei et delectentur in laetitia.

5 Cantate Deo! Psalmum dicite nomini eius; iter facite ei qui ascendit super occasum; Dominus nomen illi. Exultate in conspectu eius. Turbabuntur a facie eius, 6 patris orfanorum et iudicis viduarum, Deus in loco sancto suo, 7 Deus inhabitare facit unius moris in domo, qui educit vinctos in fortitudine, similiter eos qui exasperant, qui habitant in sepulchris.

8 Deus, cum egredereris in conspectu populi tui, cum pertransieris in deserto, 9 terra mota est, etenim caeli distillaverunt a facie Dei Sina, a facie Dei Israhel. 10 Pluviam voluntariam segregabis, Deus, hereditati tuae, et infirmata

Psalm 67

Exsurgat Deus. The glorious establishment of the church of the New Testament, prefigured by the benefits bestowed on the people of Israel.

Unto the end. A psalm of a canticle for David himself.

2 Let God arise, and let his enemies be scattered, and let them that hate him flee from before his face! 3 As smoke vanisheth, so let them vanish away; as wax melteth before the fire, so let the wicked perish at the presence of God. 4 And let the just feast and rejoice before God and be delighted with gladness.

5 Sing ye to God! Sing a psalm to his name; make a way for him who ascendeth upon the west; the Lord is his name. Rejoice ye before him. *But the wicked* shall be troubled at his presence, 6 who is the father of orphans and the judge of widows, God in his holy place, 7 God who maketh men of one manner to dwell in a house, who bringeth out them that were bound in strength, in like manner them that provoke, that dwell in sepulchres.

8 O God, when thou didst go forth in the sight of thy people, when thou didst pass through the desert, 9 the earth was moved, and the heavens dropped at the presence of the God of Sinai, at the presence of the God of Israel. 10 Thou shalt set aside for thy inheritance a free rain, O God, and it was

est, tu vero perfecisti eam. 11 Animalia tua habitabunt in ea; parasti in dulcedine tua pauperi, Deus.

12 Dominus dabit verbum evangelizantibus virtute multa. 13 Rex virtutum dilecti, dilecti, et speciei domus dividere spolia. 14 Si dormiatis inter medios cleros, pinnae columbae deargentatae et posteriora dorsi eius in pallore auri. 15 Dum discernit caelestis reges super eam, nive dealbabuntur in Selmon.

16 Mons Dei mons pinguis, mons coagulatus, mons pinguis—17 ut quid suspicamini montes coagulatos?—mons in quo beneplacitum est Deo habitare, in eo etenim Dominus habitabit in finem. 18 Currus Dei decem milibus multiplex, milia laetantium. Dominus in eis in Sina, in sancto.

19 Ascendisti in altum; cepisti captivitatem; accepisti dona in hominibus, etenim non credentes inhabitare Dominum Deum.

20 Benedictus Dominus die cotidie; prosperum iter faciet nobis Deus salutarium nostrorum. 21 Deus noster Deus salvos faciendi, et Domini, Domini exitus mortis. 22 Verumtamen Deus confringet capita inimicorum suorum, verticem

weakened, but thou hast made it perfect. 11 In it shall thy animals dwell; in thy sweetness, O God, thou hast provided for the poor.

12 The Lord shall give the word to them that preach good tidings with great power. 13 The king of powers is of the beloved, of the beloved, and *the beauty of the house shall divide* spoils. 14 If you sleep among the midst of lots, you shall be as the wings of a dove covered with silver and the hinder parts of her back with the paleness of gold. 15 When he that is in heaven appointeth kings over her, they shall be whited with snow in Zalmon.

16 The mountain of God is a fat mountain, a curdled mountain, a fat mountain—17 why suspect ye curdled mountains?—a mountain in which God is well pleased to dwell, for there the Lord shall dwell unto the end. 18 The chariot of God is *attended by* ten thousands, thousands of them that rejoice. The Lord is among them in Sinai, in the holy place.

19 Thou hast ascended on high; thou hast led captivity captive; thou hast received gifts in men, yea, *for those also that do not believe, the dwelling of* the Lord God.

20 Blessed be the Lord day by day; the God of our salvation will make our journey prosperous to us. 21 Our God is the God of salvation, and of the Lord, of the Lord are the issues from death. 22 But God shall break the heads of his enemies, the hairy crown of them that walk on in their

capilli perambulantium in delictis suis. 23 Dixit Dominus, "Ex Basan convertam; convertam in profundum maris, 24 ut intinguatur pes tuus in sanguine, lingua canum tuorum, ex inimicis, ab ipso." 25 Viderunt ingressus tui, Deus, ingressus Dei mei, regis mei qui est in sancto. 26 Praevenerunt principes coniuncti psallentibus in medio iuvencularum tympanistriarum. 27 In ecclesiis benedicite Deum, Dominum, de fontibus Israhel.

28 Ibi Beniamin, adulescentulus, in mentis excessu. Principes Iuda duces eorum, principes Zabulon, principes Nepthali. 29 Manda, Deus, virtutem tuam! Confirma, Deus, hoc quod operatus es in nobis. 30 A templo tuo in Hierusalem tibi adferent reges munera. 31 Increpa feras harundinis, congregatio taurorum in vaccis populorum ut excludant eos qui probati sunt argento. Dissipa gentes quae bella volunt. 32 Venient legati ex Aegypto; Aethiopia praeveniet manus eius Deo.

33 Regna terrae, cantate Deo! Psallite Domino! Psallite Deo, 34 qui ascendit super caelum caeli, ad orientem. Ecce: dabit voci suae vocem virtutis. 35 Date gloriam Deo super Israhel, magnificentia eius et virtus eius in nubibus. 36 Mirabilis Deus in sanctis suis; Deus Israhel, ipse dabit virtutem et fortitudinem plebi suae. Benedictus Deus.

sins. 23 The Lord said, "I will turn them from Bashan; I will turn them into the depth of the sea, 24 that thy foot may be dipped in the blood of thy enemies, the tongue of thy dogs be red with the same." 25 They have seen thy goings, O God, the goings of my God, of my king who is in his sanctuary. 26 Princes went before joined with singers in the midst of young damsels playing on timbrels. 27 In the churches bless ye God, the Lord, from the fountains of Israel.

28 There is Benjamin, a youth, in ecstasy of mind. The princes of Judah are their leaders, the princes of Zebulun, the princes of Naphtali. 29 Command thy strength, O God! Confirm, O God, what thou hast wrought in us. 30 From thy temple in Jerusalem kings shall offer presents to thee. 31 Rebuke the wild beasts of the reeds, the congregation of bulls with the kine of the people who seek to exclude them who are tried with silver. Scatter thou the nations that delight in wars. 32 Ambassadors shall come out of Egypt; Ethiopia shall *soon* stretch out her hands to God.

33 Sing to God, ye kingdoms of the earth! Sing ye to the Lord! Sing ye to God, 34 who mounteth above the heaven of heavens, to the east. Behold: he will give to his voice the voice of power. 35 Give ye glory to God for Israel, his magnificence and his power is in the clouds. 36 God is wonderful in his saints; the God of Israel *is* he *who* will give power and strength to his people. Blessed be God.

Psalmus 68

In finem. Pro his qui commutabuntur. David. 2 Salvum me fac, Deus, quoniam intraverunt aquae usque ad animam meam. 3 Infixus sum in limum profundi, et non est substantia. Veni in altitudinem maris, et tempestas demersit me. 4 Laboravi clamans; raucae factae sunt fauces meae; defecerunt oculi mei dum spero in Deum meum.

5 Multiplicati sunt super capillos capitis mei qui oderunt me gratis. Confortati sunt qui persecuti sunt me inimici mei iniuste; quae non rapui tunc exsolvebam. 6 Deus, tu scis insipientiam meam, et delicta mea a te non sunt abscondita. 7 Non erubescant in me qui expectant te, Domine, Domine virtutum. Non confundantur super me qui quaerunt te, Deus Israhel. 8 Quoniam propter te sustinui obprobrium, operuit confusio faciem meam. 9 Extraneus factus sum fratribus meis et peregrinus filiis matris meae, 10 quoniam zelus domus tuae comedit me et obprobria exprobrantium tibi ceciderunt super me. 11 Et operui in ieiunio animam meam,

Psalm 68

Salvum me fac, Deus. Christ in his passion declareth the
greatness of his sufferings and the malice of his persecutors,
the Jews, and foretelleth their reprobation.

Unto the end. For them that shall be changed. For
David.

2 Save me, O God, for the waters are come in even unto
my soul. 3 I stick fast in the mire of the deep, and there is no
sure standing. I am come into the depth of the sea, and a tempest hath overwhelmed me. 4 I have laboured with crying;
my jaws are become hoarse; my eyes have failed whilst I
hope in my God.

5 They are multiplied above the hairs of my head who
hate me without cause. My enemies are grown strong who
have wrongfully persecuted me; then did I pay that which I
took not away. 6 O God, thou knowest my foolishness, and
my offences are not hidden from thee. 7 Let not them be
ashamed for me who look for thee, O Lord, the Lord of
hosts. Let them not be confounded on my account who seek
thee, O God of Israel. 8 Because for thy sake I have borne
reproach, shame hath covered my face. 9 I am become a
stranger to my brethren and an alien to the sons of my
mother, 10 for the zeal of thy house hath eaten me up and
the reproaches of them that reproached thee are fallen upon
me. 11 And I covered my soul in fasting, and it was made a

et factum est in obprobrium mihi. 12 Et posui vestimentum meum cilicium, et factus sum illis in parabolam. 13 Adversum me loquebantur qui sedebant in porta, et in me psallebant qui bibebant vinum. 14 Ego vero, orationem meam ad te, Domine, tempus beneplaciti, Deus. In multitudine misericordiae tuae exaudi me, in veritate salutis tuae. 15 Eripe me de luto ut non infigar; libera me ab his qui oderunt me et de profundis aquarum. 16 Non me demergat tempestas aquae neque absorbeat me profundum, neque urgeat super me puteus os suum. 17 Exaudi me, Domine, quoniam benigna est misericordia tua; secundum multitudinem miserationum tuarum respice ad me. 18 Et ne avertas faciem tuam a puero tuo, quoniam tribulor; velociter exaudi me. 19 Intende animae meae, et libera eam; propter inimicos meos eripe me.

20 Tu scis inproperium meum et confusionem meam et reverentiam meam. 21 In conspectu tuo sunt omnes qui tribulant me; inproperium expectavit cor meum et miseriam. Et sustinui qui simul contristaretur, et non fuit, et qui consolaretur, et non inveni. 22 Et dederunt in escam meam fel, et in siti mea potaverunt me aceto. 23 Fiat mensa eorum coram ipsis in laqueum et in retributiones et in scandalum. 24 Obscurentur oculi eorum ne videant, et dorsum eorum semper incurva. 25 Effunde super eos iram tuam, et furor irae tuae conprehendat eos. 26 Fiat habitatio eorum deserta, et in tabernaculis eorum non sit qui inhabitet 27 quoniam quem tu percussisti persecuti sunt et super dolorem vulnerum meorum addiderunt. 28 Adpone iniquitatem super iniquitatem

reproach to me. 12 And I made haircloth my garment, and I became a byword to them. 13 They that sat in the gate spoke against me, and they that drank wine made me their song. 14 But as for me, my prayer is to thee, O Lord, for the time of thy good pleasure, O God. In the multitude of thy mercy hear me, in the truth of thy salvation. 15 Draw me out of the mire that I may not stick fast; deliver me from them that hate me and out of the deep waters. 16 Let not the tempest of water drown me nor the deep water swallow me up, and let not the pit shut her mouth upon me. 17 Hear me, O Lord, for thy mercy is kind; look upon me according to the multitude of thy *tender* mercies. 18 And turn not away thy face from thy servant, for I am in trouble; hear me speedily. 19 Attend to my soul, and deliver it; save me because of my enemies.

20 Thou knowest my reproach and my confusion and my shame. 21 In thy sight are all they that afflict me; my heart hath expected reproach and misery. And I *looked for* one that would grieve together with me, *but* there was none, and for one that would comfort me, and I found none. 22 And they gave me gall for my food, and in my thirst they gave me vinegar to drink. 23 Let their table become as a snare before them and a recompense and a stumbling block. 24 Let their eyes be darkened that they see not, and their back bend thou down always. 25 Pour out thy indignation upon them, and let thy wrathful anger take hold of them. 26 Let their habitation be made desolate, and let there be none to dwell in their tabernacles 27 because they have persecuted him whom thou hast smitten and they have added to the grief of my wounds. 28 Add thou iniquity upon their iniquity, and let

eorum, et non intrent in iustitiam tuam. 29 Deleantur de libro viventium, et cum iustis non scribantur.

30 Ego sum pauper et dolens. Salus tua, Deus, suscepit me. 31 Laudabo nomen Dei cum cantico, et magnificabo eum in laude. 32 Et placebit Deo super vitulum novellum cornua producentem et ungulas. 33 Videant pauperes et laetentur; quaerite Deum, et vivet anima vestra, 34 quoniam exaudivit pauperes Dominus et vinctos suos non despexit. 35 Laudent illum caeli et terra, mare et omnia reptilia in eis, 36 quoniam Deus salvam faciet Sion, et aedificabuntur civitates Iuda. Et inhabitabunt ibi et hereditate adquirent eam. 37 Et semen servorum eius possidebit eam, et qui diligunt nomen eius habitabunt in ea.

Psalmus 69

In finem. Psalmus David. In rememoratione quod salvum fecit Dominus.

2 Deus, in adiutorium meum intende; Domine, ad adiuvandum me festina. 3 Confundantur et revereantur qui quaerunt animam meam. 4 Avertantur retrorsum et erubescant qui volunt mihi mala. Avertantur statim erubescentes qui

them not come into thy justice. 29 Let them be blotted out of the book of the living, and with the just let them not be written.

30 But I am poor and sorrowful. Thy salvation, O God, hath set me up. 31 I will praise the name of God with a canticle, and I will magnify him with praise. 32 And it shall please God better than a young calf that bringeth forth horns and hoofs. 33 Let the poor see and rejoice; seek ye God, and your soul shall live, 34 for the Lord hath heard the poor and hath not despised his prisoners. 35 Let the heavens and the earth praise him, the sea and every thing that creepeth therein, 36 for God will save Zion, and the cities of Judah shall be built up. And they shall dwell there and acquire it by inheritance. 37 And the seed of his servants shall possess it, and they that love his name shall dwell therein.

Psalm 69

Deus, in adiutorium. A prayer in persecution.

Unto the end. A psalm for David. To bring to remembrance that the Lord saved him.

2 O God, come to my assistance; O Lord, make haste to help me. 3 Let them be confounded and ashamed that seek my soul. 4 Let them be turned backward and blush for shame that desire evils to me. Let them be presently turned away

dicunt mihi, "Euge; euge." 5 Exultent et laetentur in te omnes qui quaerunt te, et dicant semper, "Magnificetur Dominus!" qui diligunt salutare tuum. 6 Ego vero egenus et pauper; Deus, adiuva me. Adiutor meus et liberator meus es tu; Domine, ne moreris.

Psalmus 70

David psalmus. Filiorum Ionadab et priorum captivorum.

In te, Domine, speravi; non confundar in aeternum. 2 In iustitia tua libera me, et eripe me. Inclina ad me aurem tuam, et salva me. 3 Esto mihi in Deum, protectorem et in locum munitum ut salvum me facias, quoniam firmamentum meum et refugium meum es tu. 4 Deus meus, eripe me de manu peccatoris et de manu contra legem agentis et iniqui, 5 quoniam tu es patientia mea, Domine, Domine, spes mea a iuventute mea. 6 In te confirmatus sum ex utero; de ventre matris meae tu es protector meus. In te cantatio mea semper.

7 Tamquam prodigium factus sum multis, et tu adiutor fortis. 8 Repleatur os meum laude ut cantem gloriam tuam,

blushing for shame that say to me, "'Tis well; 'tis well." 5 Let all that seek thee rejoice and be glad in thee, and let *such as* love thy salvation say always, "The Lord be magnified!" 6 But I am needy and poor; O God, help me. Thou art my helper and my deliverer; O Lord, make no delay.

Psalm 70

In te, Domine. A prayer for perseverance.

A psalm for David. Of the sons of Jonadab and the former captives.

In thee, O Lord, I have hoped; let me never be put to confusion. 2 Deliver me in thy justice, and rescue me. Incline thy ear unto me, and save me. 3 Be thou unto me a God, a protector and a place of strength that thou mayst make me safe, for thou art my firmament and my refuge. 4 Deliver me, O my God, out of the hand of the sinner and out of the hand of the transgressor of the law and of the unjust, 5 for thou art my patience, O Lord, my hope, O Lord, from my youth. 6 By thee have I been confirmed from the womb; from my mother's womb thou art my protector. *Of thee shall I continually sing.*

7 I am become unto many as a wonder, *but* thou art a strong helper. 8 Let my mouth be filled with praise that I

tota die magnitudinem tuam. [9] Non proicias me in tempore senectutis; cum deficiet virtus mea ne derelinquas me, [10] quia dixerunt inimici mei mihi, et qui custodiebant animam meam consilium fecerunt in unum, [11] dicentes, "Deus dereliquit eum; persequimini, et conprehendite eum, quia non est qui eripiat." [12] Deus, ne elongeris a me; Deus meus, in adiutorium meum respice. [13] Confundantur et deficiant detrahentes animae meae; operiantur confusione et pudore qui quaerunt mala mihi.

[14] Ego autem semper sperabo et adiciam super omnem laudem tuam. [15] Os meum adnuntiabit iustitiam tuam, tota die salutem tuam. Quoniam non cognovi litteraturam [16] introibo in potentias Domini. Domine, memorabor iustitiae tuae solius. [17] Deus, docuisti me ex iuventute mea, et usque nunc pronuntiabo mirabilia tua. [18] Et usque in senectam et senium, Deus, ne derelinquas me donec adnuntiem brachium tuum generationi omni quae ventura est, potentiam tuam [19] et iustitiam tuam, Deus, usque in altissima quae fecisti magnalia.

Deus, quis similis tibi? [20] Quantas ostendisti mihi tribulationes, multas et malas, et conversus vivificasti me et de abyssis terrae iterum reduxisti me. [21] Multiplicasti magnificentiam tuam, et conversus consolatus es me, [22] nam et ego confitebor tibi in vasis psalmi veritatem tuam, Deus; psallam tibi in cithara, sanctus Israhel. [23] Exultabunt labia mea cum cantavero tibi et anima mea quam redemisti. [24] Sed et lingua mea tota die meditabitur iustitiam tuam cum confusi et reveriti fuerint qui quaerunt mala mihi.

may sing thy glory, thy greatness all the day long. 9 Cast me not off in the time of old age; when my strength shall fail do not thou forsake me, 10 for my enemies have spoken *against* me, and they that watched my soul have consulted together, 11 saying, "God hath forsaken him; pursue, and take him, for there is none to deliver him." 12 O God, be not thou far from me; O my God, *make haste* to my help. 13 Let them be confounded and come to nothing that detract my soul; let them be covered with confusion and shame that seek my hurt.

14 But I will always hope and will add to all thy praise. 15 My mouth shall shew forth thy justice, thy salvation all the day long. Because I have not known learning 16 I will enter into the powers of the Lord. O Lord, I will be mindful of thy justice alone. 17 Thou hast taught me, O God, from my youth, and till now I will declare thy wonderful works. 18 And unto old age and grey hairs, O God, forsake me not until I shew forth thy arm to all the generation that is to come, thy power 19 and thy justice, O God, even to the highest great things thou hast done.

O God, who is like to thee? 20 How great troubles hast thou shewn me, many and grievous, and turning thou hast brought me to life and hast brought me back again from the depths of the earth. 21 Thou hast multiplied thy magnificence, and turning to me thou hast comforted me, 22 for I will also confess to thee thy truth with the instruments of psaltery, O God; I will sing to thee with the harp, thou holy one of Israel. 23 My lips shall greatly rejoice when I shall sing to thee and my soul which thou hast redeemed. 24 Yea, and my tongue shall meditate on thy justice all the day when they shall be confounded and put to shame that seek evils to me.

Psalmus 71

In Salomonem.

2 Deus, iudicium tuum regi da, et iustitiam tuam filio regis iudicare populum tuum in iustitia et pauperes tuos in iudicio. 3 Suscipiant montes pacem populo et colles iustitiam. 4 Iudicabit pauperes populi, et salvos faciet filios pauperum, et humiliabit calumniatorem. 5 Et permanebit cum sole et ante lunam in generatione et generationem. 6 Descendet sicut pluvia in vellus et sicut stillicidia stillantia super terram. 7 Orietur in diebus eius iustitia et abundantia pacis donec auferatur luna. 8 Et dominabitur a mari usque ad mare et a flumine usque ad terminos orbis terrarum. 9 Coram illo procident Aethiopes, et inimici eius terram lingent. 10 Reges Tharsis et insulae munera offerent; reges Arabum et Saba dona adducent, 11 et adorabunt eum omnes reges terrae. Omnes gentes servient ei, 12 quia liberabit pauperem a potente et pauperem cui non erat adiutor. 13 Parcet pauperi et inopi, et animas pauperum salvas faciet. 14 Ex usuris et iniquitate redimet animas eorum, et honorabile nomen eorum coram illo. 15 Et vivet, et dabitur ei de auro Arabiae, et orabunt de ipso semper. Tota die benedicent ei.

Psalm 71

Deus, iudicium tuum. A prophecy of the coming of Christ and
of his kingdom prefigured by Solomon and his happy reign.

A psalm on Solomon.
2 Give to the king thy judgment, O God, and to the king's
son thy justice to judge thy people with justice and thy poor
with judgment. 3 Let the mountains receive peace for the
people and the hills justice. 4 He shall judge the poor of the
people, and he shall save the children of the poor, and he
shall humble the oppressor. 5 And he shall continue with the
sun and before the moon throughout all generations. 6 He
shall come down like rain upon the fleece and as showers
falling gently upon the earth. 7 In his days shall justice spring
up and abundance of peace till the moon be taken away.
8 And he shall rule from sea to sea and from the river unto
the ends of the earth. 9 Before him the Ethiopians shall fall
down, and his enemies shall lick the ground. 10 The kings of
Tarshish and the islands shall offer presents; the kings of the
Arabians and of Seba shall bring gifts, 11 and all kings of the
earth shall adore him. All nations shall serve him, 12 for he
shall deliver the poor from the mighty and the needy that
had no helper. 13 He shall spare the poor and needy, and
he shall save the souls of the poor. 14 He shall redeem their
souls from usuries and iniquity, and their name shall be
honourable in his sight. 15 And he shall live, and to him shall
be given of the gold of Arabia, *for* him they shall always
adore. They shall bless him all the day.

16 Et erit firmamentum in terra in summis montium. Superextolletur super Libanum fructus eius, et florebunt de civitate sicut faenum terrae. 17 Sit nomen eius benedictum in saecula; ante solem permanet nomen eius. Et benedicentur in ipso omnes tribus terrae; omnes gentes magnificabunt eum. 18 Benedictus Dominus, Deus Israhel, qui facit mirabilia solus. 19 Et benedictum nomen maiestatis eius in aeternum, et replebitur maiestate eius omnis terra. Fiat. Fiat. 20 Defecerunt laudes David, filii Iesse.

Psalmus 72

Psalmus Asaph.

Quam bonus Israhel Deus his qui recto sunt corde! 2 Mei autem paene moti sunt pedes; paene effusi sunt gressus mei 3 quia zelavi super iniquis, pacem peccatorum videns, 4 quia non est respectus morti eorum et firmamentum in plaga eorum. 5 In labore hominum non sunt, et cum hominibus non

16 And there shall be a firmament on the earth on the tops of mountains. Above Lebanon shall the fruit thereof be exalted, and they of the city shall flourish like the grass of the earth. 17 Let his name be blessed for evermore; his name continueth before the sun. And in him shall all the tribes of the earth be blessed; all nations shall magnify him.

18 Blessed be the Lord, the God of Israel, who alone doth wonderful things. 19 And blessed be the name of his majesty for ever, and the whole earth shall be filled with his majesty. So be it. So be it.

20 The praises of David, the son of Jesse, are ended.

Psalm 72

Quam bonus Israhel Deus. The temptation of the weak upon seeing the prosperity of the wicked is overcome by the consideration of the justice of God, who will quickly render to every one according to his works.

A psalm for Asaph.

How good is God to Israel to them that are of a right heart! 2 But my feet were almost moved; my steps had well nigh slipped 3 because I had a zeal on occasion of the wicked, seeing the prosperity of sinners, 4 for there is no regard to their death nor is there strength in their *stripes.* 5 They are not in the labour of men, neither shall they be scourged

flagellabuntur. 6 Ideo tenuit eos superbia; operti sunt iniquitate et impietate sua. 7 Prodiit quasi ex adipe iniquitas eorum; transierunt in affectum cordis. 8 Cogitaverunt et locuti
sunt nequitiam; iniquitatem in excelso locuti sunt. 9 Posuerunt in caelum os suum, et lingua eorum transivit in terra.
10 Ideo convertetur populus meus hic, et dies pleni invenientur in eis.

11 Et dixerunt, "Quomodo scit Deus?" et, "Si est scientia
in Excelso?" 12 Ecce: ipsi peccatores, et abundantes in saeculo obtinuerunt divitias. 13 Et dixi, "Ergo sine causa iustifi-
cavi cor meum et lavi inter innocentes manus meas." 14 Et
fui flagellatus tota die, et castigatio mea in matutinis. 15 Si
dicebam, "Narrabo sic," ecce: nationem filiorum tuorum re-
probavi. 16 Existimabam ut cognoscerem hoc; labor est ante
me 17 donec intrem in sanctuarium Dei et intellegam in novissimis eorum, 18 verumtamen propter dolos posuisti eis;
deiecisti eos dum adlevarentur. 19 Quomodo facti sunt in
desolationem? Subito defecerunt; perierunt propter iniquitatem suam. 20 Velut somnium surgentium, Domine, in civitate tua imaginem ipsorum ad nihilum rediges, 21 quia in-
flammatum est cor meum et renes mei commutati sunt 22 et
ego ad nihilum redactus sum et nescivi. 23 Ut iumentum factus sum apud te, et ego semper tecum.

24 Tenuisti manum dexteram meam, et in voluntate tua
deduxisti me, et cum gloria suscepisti me, 25 quid enim mihi
est in caelo? Et a te quid volui super terram? 26 Defecit caro

like other men. 6 Therefore pride hath held them fast; they are covered with their iniquity and their wickedness. 7 Their iniquity hath come forth as it were from fatness; they have passed into the affection of the heart. 8 They have thought and spoken wickedness; they have spoken iniquity on high. 9 They have set their mouth against heaven, and their tongue hath passed through the earth. 10 Therefore will my people return here, and full days shall be found in them.

11 And they said, "How doth God know?" and, "Is there knowledge in the Most High?" 12 Behold: these are sinners, and yet abounding in the world they have obtained riches. 13 And I said, "Then have I *in vain* justified my heart and washed my hands among the innocent." 14 And I have been scourged all the day, and my chastisement hath been in the mornings. 15 If I said, "I will speak thus," behold: I should condemn the *generation* of thy children. 16 I studied that I might know this thing; it is a labour in my sight 17 until I go into the sanctuary of God and understand concerning their last ends, 18 but indeed for deceits thou hast put it to them; when they were lifted up thou hast cast them down. 19 How are they brought to desolation? They have suddenly ceased to be; they have perished by reason of their iniquity. 20 As the dream of them that awake, O Lord, so in thy city thou shalt bring their image to nothing, 21 for my heart hath been inflamed and my reins have been changed 22 and I am brought to nothing and I knew not. 23 I am become as a beast before thee, and I am always with thee.

24 Thou hast held me by my right hand, and by thy will thou hast conducted me, and with thy glory thou hast received me, 25 for what have I in heaven? And besides thee what *do I desire* upon earth? 26 *For thee* my flesh and my heart

mea et cor meum; Deus cordis mei et pars mea Deus in aeternum, 27 quia ecce: qui elongant se a te peribunt; perdidisti
omnem qui fornicatur abs te. 28 Mihi autem adherere Deo
bonum est, ponere in Domino Deo spem meam, ut adnuntiem omnes praedicationes tuas in portis filiae Sion.

Psalmus 73

Intellectus Asaph.

Ut quid, Deus, reppulisti in finem; iratus est furor tuus
super oves pascuae tuae? 2 Memor esto congregationis tuae
quam possedisti ab initio. Redemisti virgam hereditatis
tuae, Mons Sion in quo habitasti in eo. 3 Leva manus tuas in
superbias eorum in finem; quanta malignatus est inimicus in
sancto. 4 Et gloriati sunt qui oderunt te in medio sollemnitatis tuae. Posuerunt signa sua signa, 5 et non cognoverunt
sicut in exitu super summum. Quasi in silva lignorum secu-
ribus 6 exciderunt ianuas eius in id ipsum; in securi et ascia
deiecerunt eam. 7 Incenderunt igni sanctuarium tuum; in

hath fainted away; thou art the God of my heart and the God that is my portion for ever, 27 for behold: they that go far from thee shall perish; thou hast destroyed all *them* that are disloyal to thee. 28 But it is good for me to adhere to my God, to put my hope in the Lord God, that I may declare all thy praises in the gates of the daughter of Zion.

Psalm 73

Ut quid, Deus. A prayer of the church under grievous persecutions.

Understanding for Asaph.

O God, why hast thou cast us off unto the end; why is thy wrath enkindled against the sheep of thy pasture? 2 Remember thy congregation which thou hast possessed from the beginning, the sceptre of thy inheritance *which* thou hast redeemed, Mount Zion in which thou hast dwelt. 3 Lift up thy hands against their pride unto the end; *see what* things the enemy hath done wickedly in the sanctuary. 4 And they that hate thee have made their boasts in the midst of thy solemnity. They have set up their ensigns for signs, 5 and they knew not *both* in the going out *and* on the highest top. As with axes in a wood of trees 6 they have cut down *at once* the gates thereof; with axe and hatchet they have brought it down. 7 They have set fire to thy sanctuary; they have de-

terra polluerunt tabernaculum nominis tui. 8 Dixerunt in corde suo, cognatio eorum simul, "Quiescere faciamus omnes dies festos Dei a terra. 9 Signa nostra non vidimus; iam non est propheta, et nos non cognoscet amplius."

10 Usquequo, Deus, inproperabit inimicus? Inritat adversarius nomen tuum in finem? 11 Ut quid avertis manum tuam et dexteram tuam de medio sinu tuo in finem? 12 Deus autem rex noster ante saecula; operatus est salutem in medio terrae. 13 Tu confirmasti in virtute tua mare; contribulasti capita draconum in aquis. 14 Tu confregisti capita draconis; dedisti eum escam populis Aethiopum. 15 Tu disrupisti fontes et torrentes; tu siccasti fluvios Aetham. 16 Tuus est dies, et tua est nox; tu fabricatus es auroram et solem. 17 Tu fecisti omnes terminos terrae; aestatem et ver tu plasmasti ea.

18 Memor esto huius: inimicus inproperavit Dominum, et populus insipiens incitavit nomen tuum. 19 Ne tradas bestiis animas confitentes tibi, et animas pauperum tuorum ne obliviscaris in finem. 20 Respice in testamentum tuum, quia repleti sunt qui obscurati sunt terrae domibus iniquitatum. 21 Ne avertatur humilis factus confusus. Pauper et inops laudabunt nomen tuum. 22 Exsurge, Deus! Iudica causam tuam; memor esto inproperiorum tuorum eorum quae ab insipiente sunt tota die. 23 Ne obliviscaris voces inimicorum tuorum. Superbia eorum qui te oderunt ascendit semper.

filed the dwelling place of thy name on the earth. 8 They said in their heart, the whole kindred of them together, "Let us abolish all the festival days of God from the land. 9 Our signs we have not seen; there is now no prophet, and he will know us no more."

10 How long, O God, shall the enemy reproach? Is the adversary to provoke thy name for ever? 11 Why dost thou turn away thy hand and thy right hand out of the midst of thy bosom for ever? 12 But God is our king before ages; he hath wrought salvation in the midst of the earth. 13 Thou by thy strength didst make the sea firm; thou didst crush the heads of the dragons in the waters. 14 Thou hast broken the heads of the dragon; thou hast given him to be meat for the people of the Ethiopians. 15 Thou hast broken up the fountains and the torrents; thou hast dried up the Ethan rivers. 16 Thine is the day, and thine is the night; thou hast made the morning light and the sun. 17 Thou hast made all the borders of the earth; the summer and the spring *were formed by thee.*

18 Remember this: the enemy hath reproached the Lord, and a foolish people hath provoked thy name. 19 Deliver not up to beasts the souls that confess to thee, and forget not to the end the souls of thy poor. 20 Have regard to thy covenant, for they that are the obscure of the earth have been filled with dwellings of iniquity. 21 Let not the humble be turned away with confusion. The poor and needy shall praise thy name. 22 Arise, O God! Judge thy own cause; remember *thy* reproaches *with which the foolish man hath reproached thee* all the day. 23 Forget not the voices of thy enemies. The pride of them that hate thee ascendeth continually.

Psalmus 74

In finem. Ne corrumpas. Psalmus Asaph cantici.
2 Confitebimur tibi, Deus! Confitebimur, et invocabimus nomen tuum. Narrabimus mirabilia tua. 3 Cum accepero tempus, ego iustitias iudicabo.

4 Liquefacta est terra et omnes qui habitant in ea. Ego confirmavi columnas eius. 5 Dixi iniquis, "Nolite inique facere," et delinquentibus, "Nolite exaltare cornu. 6 Nolite extollere in altum cornu vestrum; nolite loqui adversus Deum iniquitatem, 7 quia neque ab oriente neque ab occidente neque a desertis montibus, 8 quoniam Deus iudex est. Hunc humiliat, et hunc exaltat, 9 quia calix in manu Domini vini meri plenus mixto. Et inclinavit ex hoc in hoc, verumtamen fex eius non est exinanita; bibent omnes peccatores terrae.

10 Ego autem adnuntiabo in saeculum; cantabo Deo Iacob. 11 Et omnia cornua peccatorum confringam, et exaltabuntur cornua iusti.

Psalm 74

Confitebimur tibi. There is a just judgment to come, therefore let the wicked take care.

Unto the end. Corrupt not. A psalm of a canticle for Asaph.

2 We will praise thee, O God! We will praise, and we will call upon thy name. We will relate thy wondrous works. 3 When I shall take a time, I will judge justices.

4 The earth is melted and all that dwell therein. I have established the pillars thereof. 5 I said to the wicked, "Do not act wickedly," and to the sinners, "Lift not up the horn. 6 Lift not up your horn on high; speak not iniquity against God, 7 for neither from the east nor from the west nor from the desert hills, 8 for God is the judge. One he putteth down, and another he lifteth up, 9 for in the hand of the Lord there is a cup of strong wine full of mixture. And he hath poured it out from this to that, but the dregs thereof are not emptied; all the sinners of the earth shall drink.

10 But I will declare for ever; I will sing to the God of Jacob. 11 And I will break all the horns of sinners, *but* the horns of the just shall be exalted.

Psalmus 75

In finem. In laudibus. Psalmus Asaph. Canticum ad Assyrios.

2 Notus in Iudaea Deus; in Israhel magnum nomen eius, 3 et factus est in pace locus eius, et habitatio eius in Sion. 4 Ibi confregit potentias arcuum, scutum, gladium et bellum.

5 Inluminas tu mirabiliter de montibus aeternis. 6 Turbati sunt omnes insipientes corde. Dormierunt somnum suum, et nihil invenerunt omnes viri divitiarum manibus suis. 7 Ab increpatione tua, Deus Iacob, dormitaverunt qui ascenderunt equos. 8 Tu terribilis es, et quis resistet tibi? Ex tunc, ira tua. 9 De caelo auditum fecisti iudicium; terra tremuit et quievit 10 cum exsurgeret in iudicium Deus ut salvos faceret omnes mansuetos terrae, 11 quoniam cogitatio hominis confitebitur tibi et reliquiae cogitationis diem festum agent tibi.

12 Vovete, et reddite Domino, Deo vestro; omnes qui in circuitu eius adfertis munera terribili, 13 et ei qui aufert spiritum principum, terribili apud reges terrae.

Psalm 75

Notus in Iudaea. God is known in his church and exerts his power in protecting it. It alludes to the slaughter of the Assyrians in the days of King Hezekiah.

Unto the end. In praises. A psalm for Asaph. A canticle to the Assyrians.

2 In Judea God is known; his name is great in Israel, 3 and his place is in peace, and his abode in Zion. 4 There hath he broken the powers of bows, the shield, the sword and the battle.

5 Thou enlightenest wonderfully from the everlasting hills. 6 All the foolish of heart were troubled. They have slept their sleep, and all the men of riches have found nothing in their hands. 7 At thy rebuke, O God of Jacob, they have all slumbered that mounted on horseback. 8 Thou art terrible, and who shall resist thee? From that time, thy wrath. 9 Thou hast caused judgment to be heard from heaven; the earth trembled and was still 10 when God arose in judgment to save all the meek of the earth, 11 for the thought of man shall give praise to thee and the remainders of the thought shall keep holiday to thee.

12 Vow ye, and pay to the Lord, your God; all you that are round about him bring presents to him that is terrible, 13 even to him who taketh away the spirit of princes, to the terrible with the kings of the earth.

Psalmus 76

In finem. Pro Idithun. Psalmus Asaph.

2 Voce mea ad Dominum clamavi, voce mea ad Deum, et intendit mihi. 3 In die tribulationis meae Deum exquisivi manibus meis nocte contra eum, et non sum deceptus. Rennuit consolari anima mea. 4 Memor fui Dei et delectatus sum et exercitatus sum, et defecit spiritus meus. 5 Anticipaverunt vigilias oculi mei; turbatus sum, et non sum locutus. 6 Cogitavi dies antiquos, et annos aeternos in mente habui. 7 Et meditatus sum nocte cum corde meo, et exercitabar, et scobebam spiritum meum.

8 Numquid in aeternum proiciet Deus? Aut non adponet ut conplacitior sit adhuc? 9 Aut in finem misericordiam suam abscidet, a generatione in generationem? 10 Aut obliviscetur misereri Deus? Aut continebit in ira sua misericordias suas?

11 Et dixi, "Nunc coepi; haec mutatio dexterae Excelsi." 12 Memor fui operum Domini, quia memor ero ab initio mirabilium tuorum. 13 Et meditabor in omnibus operibus tuis et in adinventionibus tuis exercebor. 14 Deus, in sancto via tua. Quis Deus magnus sicut Deus noster? 15 Tu es Deus qui facis mirabilia. Notam fecisti in populis virtutem tuam.

Psalm 76

Voce mea. The faithful have recourse to God in trouble of mind, with confidence in his mercy and power.

Unto the end. For Jeduthun. A psalm of Asaph
2 I cried to the Lord with my voice, to God with my voice, and he *gave ear* to me. 3 In the day of my trouble I sought God with my hands *lifted up to* him in the night, and I was not deceived. My soul refused to be comforted. 4 I remembered God and was delighted and was exercised, and my spirit swooned away. 5 My eyes prevented the watches; I was troubled, and I spoke not. 6 I thought upon the days of old, and I had in my mind the eternal years. 7 And I meditated in the night with my own heart, and I was exercised, and I *swept* my spirit.

8 Will God then cast off for ever? Or will he never be more favourable again? 9 Or will he cut off his mercy for ever, from generation to generation? 10 Or will God forget to shew mercy? Or will he in his anger shut up his mercies?

11 And I said, "Now have I begun; this is the change of the right hand of the Most High." 12 I remembered the works of the Lord, for I will be mindful of thy wonders from the beginning. 13 And I will meditate on all thy works and will be employed in thy inventions. 14 Thy way, O God, is in the holy place. Who is the great God like our God? 15 Thou art the God that dost wonders. Thou hast made thy power

16 Redemisti in brachio tuo populum tuum, filios Iacob et Ioseph. 17 Viderunt te aquae, Deus; viderunt te aquae, et timuerunt, et turbatae sunt abyssi. 18 Multitudo sonitus aquarum; vocem dederunt nubes, etenim sagittae tuae transeunt, 19 vox tonitrui tui in rota. Inluxerunt coruscationes tuae orbi terrae; commota est et contremuit terra. 20 In mari via tua et semitae tuae in aquis multis, et vestigia tua non cognoscentur. 21 Deduxisti sicut oves populum tuum in manu Mosi et Aaron.

Psalmus 77

Intellectus Asaph.

Adtendite, populus meus, legem meam; inclinate aurem vestram in verba oris mei. 2 Aperiam in parabolis os meum; eloquar propositiones ab initio. 3 Quanta audivimus et cognovimus ea et patres nostri narraverunt nobis! 4 Non sunt occultata a filiis eorum in generationem alteram, narrantes laudes Domini et virtutes eius et mirabilia eius quae fecit. 5 Et suscitavit testimonium in Iacob et legem posuit in Israhel. Quanta mandavit patribus nostris, nota facere ea filiis

known among the nations. 16 With thy arm thou hast redeemed thy people, the children of Jacob and of Joseph. 17 The waters saw thee, O God; the waters saw thee, and they were afraid, and the depths were troubled. 18 Great was the noise of the waters; the clouds sent out a sound, for thy arrows pass, 19 the voice of thy thunder in a wheel. Thy lightnings enlightened the world; the earth shook and trembled. 20 Thy way is in the sea and thy paths in many waters, and thy footsteps shall not be known. 21 Thou hast conducted thy people like sheep by the hand of Moses and Aaron.

Psalm 77

Adtendite. God's great benefits to the people of Israel, notwithstanding their ingratitude.

Understanding for Asaph.

Attend, O my people, to my law; incline your ears to the words of my mouth. 2 I will open my mouth in parables; I will utter propositions from the beginning. 3 How great things have we heard and known and our fathers have told us! 4 They have not been hidden from their children in another generation, declaring the praises of the Lord and his powers and his wonders which he hath done. 5 And he set up a testimony in Jacob and made a law in Israel. How great things he commanded our fathers, that they should make

suis, 6 ut cognoscat generatio altera, filii qui nascentur et exsurgent et narrabunt filiis suis 7 ut ponant in Deo spem suam et non obliviscantur opera Dei et mandata eius exquirant, 8 ne fiant sicut patres eorum, generatio prava et exasperans, generatio quae non direxit cor suum; non est creditus cum Deo spiritus eius.

9 Filii Effrem intendentes et mittentes arcum, conversi sunt in die belli. 10 Non custodierunt testamentum Dei, et in lege eius noluerunt ambulare. 11 Et obliti sunt benefactorum eius et mirabilium eius quae ostendit eis. 12 Coram patribus eorum fecit mirabilia in terra Aegypti, in campo Taneos. 13 Interrupit mare et perduxit eos, et statuit aquas quasi in utre, 14 et deduxit eos in nube diei, et tota nocte in inluminatione ignis. 15 Interrupit petram in heremo et adaquavit eos velut in abysso multa. 16 Et eduxit aquam de petra et deduxit tamquam flumina aquas. 17 Et adposuerunt adhuc peccare ei; in iram excitaverunt Excelsum in inaquoso. 18 Et temptaverunt Deum in cordibus suis ut peterent escas animabus suis. 19 Et male locuti sunt de Deo; dixerunt, "Numquid poterit Deus parare mensam in deserto? 20 Quoniam percussit petram et fluxerunt aquae et torrentes inundaverunt, numquid et panem potest dare aut parare mensam populo suo?"

21 Ideo audivit Dominus et distulit, et ignis accensus est in Iacob, et ira ascendit in Israhel 22 quia non crediderunt in

the same known to their children, 6 that another generation might know them, the children that should be born and should rise up and declare them to their children 7 that they may put their hope in God and may not forget the works of God and may seek his commandments, 8 that they may not become like their fathers, a perverse and exasperating generation, a generation that set not their heart aright *and whose* spirit was not faithful to God.

9 The sons of Ephraim who bend and shoot with the bow, they have turned back in the day of battle. 10 They kept not the covenant of God, and in his law they would not walk. 11 And they forgot his benefits and his wonders that he had shewn them. 12 Wonderful things did he do in the sight of their fathers in the land of Egypt, in the field of Tanis. 13 He divided the sea and brought them through, and he made the waters to stand as in a vessel, 14 and he conducted them with a cloud by day, and all the night with a light of fire. 15 He struck the rock in the wilderness and gave them to drink as out of the great deep. 16 *He* brought forth water out of the rock and made streams run down as rivers. 17 And they added yet more sin against him; they provoked the Most High to wrath in the place without water. 18 And they tempted God in their hearts by asking meat for their desires. 19 And they spoke ill of God; they said, "Can God furnish a table in the wilderness? 20 Because he struck the rock and the waters gushed out and the streams overflowed, can he also give bread or provide a table for his people?"

21 Therefore the Lord heard and *was angry,* and a fire was kindled against Jacob, and wrath came up against Israel 22 because they believed not in God and trusted not in his

Deo nec speraverunt in salutare eius. 23 Et mandavit nubibus desuper et ianuas caeli aperuit 24 et pluit illis manna ad manducandum et panem caeli dedit eis. 25 Panem angelorum manducavit homo; cibaria misit eis in abundantiam. 26 Transtulit austrum de caelo et induxit in virtute sua africum. 27 Et pluit super eos sicut pulverem carnes et sicut harenam maris volatilia pinnata. 28 Et ceciderunt in medio castrorum eorum circa tabernacula eorum. 29 Et manducaverunt et saturati sunt nimis, et desiderium eorum adtulit eis; 30 non sunt fraudati a desiderio suo. Adhuc escae eorum erant in ore ipsorum, 31 et ira Dei ascendit super eos, et occidit pingues eorum et electos Israhel inpedivit.

32 In omnibus his peccaverunt adhuc, et non crediderunt mirabilibus eius. 33 Et defecerunt in vanitate dies eorum et anni eorum cum festinatione. 34 Cum occideret eos, quaerebant eum, et revertebantur et diluculo veniebant ad eum. 35 Et rememorati sunt quia Deus adiutor est eorum et Deus excelsus redemptor eorum est. 36 Et dilexerunt eum in ore suo, et lingua sua mentiti sunt ei, 37 cor autem ipsorum non erat rectum cum eo, nec fideles habiti sunt in testamento eius.

38 Ipse autem est misericors et propitius fiet peccatis eorum et non perdet eos. Et abundavit ut averteret iram suam et non accendit omnem iram suam. 39 Et recordatus est quia

salvation. 23 And he *had* commanded the clouds from above and *had* opened the doors of heaven 24 and *had* rained down manna upon them to eat and *had given* them the bread of heaven. 25 Man ate the bread of angels; he sent them provisions in abundance. 26 He removed the south wind from heaven and by his power brought in the southwest wind. 27 And he rained upon them flesh as dust and feathered fowls like as the sand of the sea. 28 And they fell in the midst of their camp round about their pavilions. 29 *So* they did eat and were filled exceedingly, and he gave them their desire; 30 they were not defrauded of that which they craved. As yet their meat was in their mouth, 31 and the wrath of God came upon them, and he slew the fat ones amongst them and brought down the chosen men of Israel.

32 In all these things they sinned still, and they believed not *for* his wondrous works. 33 And their days were consumed in vanity and their years in haste. 34 When he slew them, then they sought him, and they returned and came to him early in the morning. 35 And they remembered that God was their helper and the most high God their redeemer. 36 And they loved him with their mouth, and with their tongue they lied unto him, 37 but their heart was not right with him, nor were they counted faithful in his covenant.

38 But he is merciful and will forgive their sins and will not destroy them. And many a time did he turn away his anger and did not kindle all his wrath. 39 And he remembered

caro sunt, spiritus vadens et non rediens. 40 Quotiens exacerbaverunt eum in deserto, in iram concitaverunt eum in inaquoso! 41 Et conversi sunt et temptaverunt Deum et sanctum Israhel exacerbaverunt.

42 Non sunt recordati manus eius die qua redemit eos de manu tribulantis, 43 sicut posuit in Aegypto signa sua et prodigia sua in campo Taneos. 44 Et convertit in sanguine flumina eorum et imbres eorum ne biberent. 45 Misit in eos coenomyiam et comedit eos et ranam et disperdit eos. 46 Et dedit erugini fructus eorum et labores eorum lucustae. 47 Et occidit in grandine vineas eorum et moros eorum in pruina. 48 Et tradidit grandini iumenta eorum et possessionem eorum igni. 49 Misit in eos iram indignationis suae, indignationem et iram et tribulationem, inmissiones per angelos malos. 50 Viam fecit semitae irae suae; non pepercit a morte animabus eorum, et iumenta eorum in morte conclusit. 51 Et percussit omne primogenitum in terra Aegypti, primitias omnis laboris eorum in tabernaculis Cham.

52 Et abstulit sicut oves populum suum et perduxit eos tamquam gregem in deserto. 53 Et deduxit eos in spe, et non timuerunt, et inimicos eorum operuit mare. 54 Et induxit eos in montem sanctificationis suae, montem quem adquisivit dextera eius. Et eiecit a facie eorum Gentes et sorte divisit eis terram in funiculo distributionis, 55 et habitare fecit in tabernaculis eorum tribus Israhel.

that they are flesh, a wind that goeth and returneth not. 40 How often did they provoke him in the desert *and* move him to wrath in the place without water! 41 And they turned back and tempted God and grieved the holy one of Israel.

42 They remembered not his hand in the day that he redeemed them from the hand of him that afflicted them, 43 *how* he wrought his signs in Egypt and his wonders in the field of Tanis. 44 And he turned their rivers into blood and their showers that they might not drink. 45 He sent amongst them *divers sorts of flies which* devoured them and *frogs which* destroyed them. 46 And he gave up their fruits to the blast and their labours to the locust. 47 And he destroyed their vineyards with hail and their mulberry trees with hoarfrost. 48 And he gave up their cattle to the hail and their stock to the fire. 49 *And* he sent upon them the wrath of his indignation, indignation and wrath and trouble, which he sent by evil angels. 50 He made a way for a path to his anger; he spared not their souls from death, and their cattle he shut up in death. 51 And he killed all the firstborn in the land of Egypt, the firstfruits of all their labour in the tabernacles of Ham.

52 And he took away his own people as sheep and guided them in the wilderness like a flock. 53 And he brought them out in hope, and they feared not, and the sea overwhelmed their enemies. 54 And he brought them into the mountain of his sanctuary, the mountain which his right hand had purchased. And he cast out the Gentiles before them and by lot divided to them their land by a line of distribution, 55 and he made the tribes of Israel to dwell in their tabernacles.

56 Et temptaverunt et exacerbaverunt Deum excelsum, et testimonia eius non custodierunt. 57 Et averterunt se et non servaverunt pactum; quemadmodum patres eorum conversi sunt in arcum pravum. 58 In iram concitaverunt eum in collibus suis et in sculptilibus suis ad aemulationem eum provocaverunt. 59 Audivit Deus et sprevit, et ad nihilum redegit valde Israhel. 60 Et reppulit tabernaculum Selo, tabernaculum suum ubi habitavit in hominibus. 61 Et tradidit in captivitatem virtutem eorum et pulchritudinem eorum in manus inimici. 62 Et conclusit in gladio populum suum, et hereditatem suam sprevit. 63 Iuvenes eorum comedit ignis, et virgines eorum non sunt lamentatae. 64 Sacerdotes eorum in gladio ceciderunt, et viduae eorum non plorabantur. 65 Et excitatus est tamquam dormiens Dominus, tamquam potens crapulatus a vino. 66 Et percussit inimicos suos in posteriora; obprobrium sempiternum dedit illis.

67 Et reppulit tabernaculum Ioseph et tribum Effrem non elegit, 68 sed elegit tribum Iuda, Montem Sion quem dilexit. 69 Et aedificavit sicut unicornium sanctificium suum in terra quam fundavit in saecula. 70 Et elegit David servum suum et sustulit eum de gregibus ovium; de post fetantes accepit eum 71 pascere Iacob, servum suum, et Israhel, hereditatem suam. 72 Et pavit eos in innocentia cordis sui et in intellectibus manuum suarum deduxit eos.

56 *Yet* they tempted and provoked the most high God, and they kept not his testimonies. 57 And they turned away and kept not the covenant; even like their fathers they were turned aside as a crooked bow. 58 They provoked him to anger on their hills and moved him to jealousy with their graven things. 59 God heard and despised them, and he reduced Israel exceedingly *as it were* to nothing. 60 And he put away the tabernacle of Shiloh, his tabernacle where he dwelt among men. 61 And he delivered their strength into captivity and their beauty into the hands of the enemy. 62 And he shut up his people under the sword, and he despised his inheritance. 63 Fire consumed their young men, and their maidens were not lamented. 64 Their priests fell by the sword, and their widows *did not mourn*. 65 And the Lord was awaked as one out of sleep *and* like a mighty man that hath been surfeited with wine. 66 And he smote his enemies on the hinder parts; he put them to an everlasting reproach.

67 And he rejected the tabernacle of Joseph and chose not the tribe of Ephraim, 68 but he chose the tribe of Judah, Mount Zion which he loved. 69 And he built his sanctuary as of unicorns in the land which he founded for ever. 70 And he chose his servant David and took him from the flocks of sheep; he brought him from *following the ewes great with young* 71 to feed Jacob, his servant, and Israel, his inheritance. 72 And he fed them in the innocence of his heart and conducted them by the skilfulness of his hands.

Psalmus 78

Psalmus Asaph.

Deus, venerunt Gentes in hereditatem tuam; polluerunt templum sanctum tuum; posuerunt Hierusalem in pomorum custodiam. 2 Posuerunt morticina servorum tuorum escas volatilibus caeli, carnes sanctorum tuorum bestiis terrae. 3 Effuderunt sanguinem ipsorum tamquam aquam in circuitu Hierusalem, et non erat qui sepeliret.

4 Facti sumus obprobrium vicinis nostris, subsannatio et inlusio his qui circum nos sunt. 5 Usquequo, Domine, irasceris in finem? Accendetur velut ignis zelus tuus? 6 Effunde iram tuam in gentes quae te non noverunt et in regna quae nomen tuum non invocaverunt 7 quia comederunt Iacob et locum eius desolaverunt. 8 Ne memineris iniquitatum nostrarum antiquarum; cito anticipent nos misericordiae tuae, quia pauperes facti sumus nimis. 9 Adiuva nos, Deus, salutaris noster, et propter gloriam nominis tui, Domine, libera nos, et propitius esto peccatis nostris propter nomen

Psalm 78

Deus, venerunt Gentes. The church in time of persecution prayeth for relief. It seems to belong to the time of the Maccabees.

A psalm for Asaph.

O God, the heathens are come into thy inheritance; they have defiled thy holy temple; they have made Jerusalem as a place to keep fruit. 2 They have given the dead bodies of thy servants to be meat for the fowls of the air, the flesh of thy saints for the beasts of the earth. 3 They have poured out their blood as water round about Jerusalem, and there was none to bury them.

4 We are become a reproach to our neighbours, a scorn and derision to them that are round about us. 5 How long, O Lord, wilt thou be angry for ever? Shall thy zeal be kindled like a fire? 6 Pour out thy wrath upon the nations that have not known thee and upon the kingdoms that have not called upon thy name 7 because they have devoured Jacob and have laid waste his place. 8 Remember not our former iniquities; let thy mercies speedily prevent us, for we are become exceeding poor. 9 Help us, O God, our saviour, and for the glory of thy name, O Lord, deliver us, and forgive us our sins

tuum, 10 ne forte dicant in Gentibus, "Ubi est Deus eorum?"
Et innotescat in nationibus coram oculis nostris ultio sanguinis servorum tuorum qui effusus est. 11 Introeat in
conspectu tuo gemitus conpeditorum. Secundum magnitudinem brachii tui posside filios mortificatorum. 12 Et redde
vicinis nostris septuplum in sinu eorum inproperium ipsorum quod exprobraverunt tibi, Domine.

13 Nos autem, populus tuus, et oves pascuae tuae, confitebimur tibi in saeculum. In generationem et generationem
adnuntiabimus laudem tuam.

Psalmus 79

In finem. Pro his qui commutabuntur. Testimonium
Asaph. Psalmus.

2 Qui regis Israhel, intende, qui deducis tamquam ovem
Ioseph. Qui sedes super cherubin, manifestare 3 coram Effraim, Beniamin et Manasse. Excita potentiam tuam, et veni
ut salvos facias nos. 4 Deus, converte nos, et ostende faciem

for thy name's sake, 10 lest they should *say* among the Gentiles, "Where is their God?" And let *him* be made known among the nations before our eyes *by the revenging* the blood of thy servants which hath been shed. 11 Let the sighing of the prisoners come in before thee. According to the greatness of thy arm take possession of the children of them that have been put to death. 12 And render to our neighbours sevenfold in their bosom *the* reproach wherewith they have reproached thee, O Lord.

13 But we, thy people, and the sheep of thy pasture, will give thanks to thee for ever. We will shew forth thy praise unto generation and generation.

Psalm 79

Qui regis Israhel. A prayer for the church in tribulation, commemorating God's former favours.

Unto the end. For them that shall be changed. A testimony for Asaph. A psalm.

2 Give ear, O thou that rulest Israel, thou that leadest Joseph like a sheep. Thou that sittest upon the cherubims, shine forth 3 before Ephraim, Benjamin and Manasseh. Stir up thy might, and come to save us. 4 Convert us, O God, and

tuam, et salvi erimus. 5 Domine, Deus virtutum, quousque irasceris super orationem servi tui, 6 cibabis nos pane lacrimarum et potum dabis nobis in lacrimis in mensura? 7 Posuisti nos in contradictionem vicinis nostris, et inimici nostri subsannaverunt nos. 8 Deus virtutum, converte nos, et ostende faciem tuam, et salvi erimus.

9 Vineam de Aegypto transtulisti; eiecisti Gentes et plantasti eam. 10 Dux itineris fuisti in conspectu eius; plantasti radices eius, et implevit terram. 11 Operuit montes umbra eius, et arbusta eius cedros Dei. 12 Extendit palmites suos usque ad mare et usque ad flumen propagines eius. 13 Ut quid destruxisti maceriam eius et vindemiant eam omnes qui praetergrediuntur viam? 14 Exterminavit eam aper de silva, et singularis ferus depastus est eam. 15 Deus virtutum, convertere; respice de caelo, et vide, et visita vineam istam, 16 et perfice eam quam plantavit dextera tua et super filium hominis quem confirmasti tibi. 17 Incensa igni et suffossa ab increpatione vultus tui peribunt. 18 Fiat manus tua super virum dexterae tuae et super filium hominis quem confirmasti tibi. 19 Et non discedimus a te; vivificabis nos, et nomen tuum invocabimus. 20 Domine, Deus virtutum, converte nos, et ostende faciem tuam, et salvi erimus.

shew us thy face, and we shall be saved. 5 O Lord, God of hosts, how long wilt thou be angry against the prayer of thy servant? 6 How long wilt thou feed us with the bread of tears and give us for our drink tears in measure? 7 Thou hast made us to be a contradiction to our neighbours, and our enemies have scoffed at us. 8 O God of hosts, convert us, and shew thy face, and we shall be saved.

9 Thou hast brought a vineyard out of Egypt; thou hast cast out the Gentiles and planted it. 10 Thou wast the guide of its journey in its sight; thou plantedst the roots thereof, and it filled the land. 11 The shadow of it covered the hills, and the branches thereof the cedars of God. 12 It stretched forth its branches unto the sea and its boughs unto the river. 13 Why hast thou broken down the hedge thereof *so that* all they who pass by the way do pluck it? 14 The boar out of the wood hath laid it waste, and a singular wild beast hath devoured it. 15 Turn again, O God of hosts; look down from heaven, and see, and visit this vineyard, 16 and perfect *the same* which thy right hand hath planted and upon the son of man whom thou hast confirmed for thyself. 17 Things set on fire and dug down shall perish at the rebuke of thy countenance. 18 Let thy hand be upon the man of thy right hand and upon the son of man whom thou hast confirmed for thyself. 19 And we depart not from thee; thou shalt quicken us, and we will call upon thy name. 20 O Lord, God of hosts, convert us, and shew thy face, and we shall be saved.

Psalmus 80

In finem. Pro torcularibus. Psalmus ipsi Asaph.

2 Exultate Deo, adiutori nostro; iubilate Deo Iacob! 3 Sumite psalmum, et date tympanum, psalterium iucundum cum cithara. 4 Bucinate in neomenia tuba, in insigni die sollemnitatis vestrae, 5 quia praeceptum in Israhel est et iudicium Deo Iacob. 6 Testimonium in Ioseph posuit illud.

Cum exiret de terra Aegypti linguam quam non noverat audivit. 7 Devertit ab oneribus dorsum eius; manus eius in cofino servierunt. 8 "In tribulatione invocasti me, et liberavi te; exaudivi te in abscondito tempestatis; probavi te apud Aquam Contradictionis. 9 'Audi, populus meus, et contestabor te, Israhel, si audieris me. 10 Non erit in te deus recens, nec adorabis deum alienum, 11 ego enim sum Dominus, Deus tuus, qui eduxi te de terra Aegypti. Dilata os tuum, et implebo illud.'

12 "Et non audivit populus meus vocem meam, et Israhel non intendit mihi. 13 Et dimisi illos secundum desideria cordis eorum; ibunt in adinventionibus suis. 14 Si populus meus audisset me, Israhel si in viis meis ambulasset, 15 pro nihilo forsitan inimicos eorum humiliassem et super tribulantes eos misissem manum meam."

Psalm 80

Exultate Deo. An invitation to a solemn praising of God.

Unto the end. For the winepresses. A psalm for Asaph himself.

2 Rejoice to God, our helper; sing aloud to the God of Jacob! 3 Take a psalm, and bring hither the timbrel, the pleasant psaltery with the harp. 4 Blow up the trumpet on the new moon, on the noted day of your solemnity, 5 for it is a commandment in Israel and a judgment to the God of Jacob. 6 He ordained it for a testimony in Joseph.

When he came out of the land of Egypt he heard a tongue which he knew not. 7 He removed his back from the burdens; his hands *had* served in baskets. 8 "Thou calledst upon me in affliction, and I delivered thee; I heard thee in the secret place of tempest; I proved thee at the *Waters* of Contradiction. 9 'Hear, O my people, and I will testify to thee, O Israel, if thou wilt hearken to me. 10 There shall be no new god in thee, neither shalt thou adore a strange god, 11 for I am the Lord, thy God, who brought thee out of the land of Egypt. Open thy mouth wide, and I will fill it.'

12 *"But* my people heard not my voice, and Israel hearkened not to me. 13 *So* I let them go according to the desires of their heart; they shall walk in their own inventions. 14 If my people had heard me, if Israel had walked in my ways, 15 I should *soon* have humbled their enemies and laid my hand on them that troubled them."

16 Inimici Domini mentiti sunt ei, et erit tempus eorum in saeculo. 17 Et cibavit illos ex adipe frumenti et de petra melle saturavit illos.

Psalmus 81

Psalmus Asaph.

Deus stetit in synagoga deorum, in medio autem deos deiudicat. 2 "Usquequo iudicatis iniquitatem et facies peccatorum sumitis? 3 Iudicate egeno et pupillo; humilem et pauperem iustificate. 4 Eripite pauperem, et egenum de manu peccatoris liberate."

5 Nescierunt neque intellexerunt; in tenebris ambulant. Movebuntur omnia fundamenta terrae.

6 Ego dixi, "Dii estis, et filii Excelsi omnes. 7 Vos autem sicut homines moriemini et sicut unus de principibus cadetis."

8 Surge, Deus! Iudica terram, quoniam tu hereditabis in omnibus gentibus.

16 The enemies of the Lord have lied to him, and their time shall be for ever. 17 And he fed them with the fat of wheat and filled them with honey out of the rock.

Psalm 81

Deus stetit. An exhortation to judges and men in power.

A psalm for Asaph.

God hath stood in the congregation of gods, and being in the midst of them he judgeth gods. 2 "How long will you judge *unjustly* and accept the persons of the wicked? 3 Judge for the needy and fatherless; do justice to the humble and the poor. 4 Rescue the poor, and deliver the needy out of the hand of the sinner."

5 They have not known nor understood; they walk on in darkness. All the foundations of the earth shall be moved.

6 I have said, "You are gods, and all of you the sons of the Most High. 7 But you like men shall die and shall fall like one of the princes."

8 Arise, O God! Judge thou the earth, for thou shalt inherit among all the nations.

Psalmus 82

Canticum psalmi Asaph.

2 Deus, quis similis erit tibi? Ne taceas, neque conpesca-
ris, Deus, 3 quoniam ecce, inimici tui sonaverunt, et qui oderunt te extulerunt caput. 4 Super populum tuum malignave-
runt consilium et cogitaverunt adversus sanctos tuos.
5 Dixerunt, "Venite, et disperdamus eos de gente, et non
memoretur nomen Israhel ultra," 6 quoniam cogitaverunt
unianimiter; simul adversum te testamentum disposuerunt,
7 tabernacula Idumeorum et Ismahelitae, Moab et Aggareni,
8 Gebal et Ammon et Amalech, alienigenae cum habitantibus Tyrum, 9 etenim Assur venit cum illis; facti sunt in
adiutorium filiis Loth. 10 Fac illis sicut Madiam et Sisarae, sicut Iabin in torrente Cison; 11 disperierunt in Endor; facti
sunt ut stercus terrae. 12 Pone principes eorum sicut Oreb
et Zeb et Zebee et Salmana. Omnes principes eorum
13 qui dixerunt, "Hereditate possideamus sanctuarium Dei,"
14 Deus meus, pone illos ut rotam et sicut stipulam ante faciem venti. 15 Sicut ignis qui conburit silvam et sicut flamma
conburens montes, 16 ita persequeris illos in tempestate tua

Psalm 82

Deus, quis similis. A prayer against the enemies of God's church.

A canticle of a psalm for Asaph.

2 O God, who shall be like to thee? Hold not thy peace, neither be thou still, O God, 3 for lo, thy enemies have made a noise, and they that hate thee have lifted up the head. 4 They have taken a malicious counsel against thy people and have consulted against thy saints. 5 They have said, "Come, and let us destroy them *so that they be not* a nation, and let the name of Israel be remembered no more," 6 for they have contrived with one consent; they have made a covenant together against thee, 7 the tabernacles of the Edomites and the Ishmaelites, Moab and the Hagrites, 8 Gebal and Ammon and Amalek, the *Philistines* with the inhabitants of Tyre, 9 yea, and the Assyrian also is *joined* with them; they are come to the aid of the sons of Lot. 10 Do to them as thou didst to Midian and to Sisera, as to Jabin at the brook of Kishon 11 *who* perished at En-dor *and* became as dung for the earth. 12 Make their princes like Oreb and Zeeb and Zebah and Zalmunna. All their princes 13 who have said, "Let us possess the sanctuary of God for an inheritance," 14 O my God, make them like a wheel and as stubble before the wind. 15 As fire which burneth the wood and as a flame burning mountains, 16 so shalt thou pursue them with thy tempest

et in ira tua turbabis eos. 17 Imple facies illorum ignominia, et quaerent nomen tuum, Domine. 18 Erubescant et conturbentur in saeculum saeculi, et confundantur et pereant. 19 Et cognoscant quia nomen tibi Dominus; tu solus Altissimus in omni terra.

Psalmus 83

In finem. Pro torcularibus. Filiis Core psalmus.

2 Quam dilecta tabernacula tua, Domine virtutum! 3 Concupiscit et deficit anima mea in atria Domini. Cor meum et caro mea exultavit in Deum vivum, 4 etenim passer invenit sibi domum et turtur nidum sibi ubi ponat pullos suos, altaria tua, Domine virtutum, rex meus et Deus meus.

5 Beati qui habitant in domo tua, Domine; in saecula saeculorum laudabunt te. 6 Beatus vir cuius est auxilium abs te; ascensiones in corde suo disposuit 7 in valle lacrimarum, in

and shalt trouble them in thy wrath. 17 Fill their faces with shame, and they shall seek thy name, O Lord. 18 Let them be ashamed and troubled for ever and ever, and let them be confounded and perish. 19 And let them know that the Lord is thy name; thou alone art the Most High over all the earth.

Psalm 83

Quam dilecta. The soul aspireth after heaven, rejoicing in the mean time in being in the communion of God's church upon earth.

Unto the end. For the winepresses. A psalm for the sons of Korah.

2 How lovely are thy tabernacles, O Lord of hosts! 3 My soul longeth and fainteth for the courts of the Lord. My heart and my flesh have rejoiced in the living God, 4 for the sparrow hath found herself a house and the turtle a nest for herself where she may lay her young ones, thy altars, O Lord of hosts, my king and my God.

5 Blessed are they that dwell in thy house, O Lord; they shall praise thee for ever and ever. 6 Blessed is the man whose help is from thee; in his heart he hath disposed *to ascend by steps* 7 in the vale of tears, in the place which he hath set,

loco quem posuit, 8 etenim benedictionem dabit legis dator; ibunt de virtute in virtutem; videbitur Deus deorum in Sion.

9 Domine, Deus virtutum, exaudi orationem meam; auribus percipe, Deus Iacob. 10 Protector noster, aspice, Deus, et respice in faciem Christi tui, 11 quia melior est dies una in atriis tuis super milia. Elegi abiectus esse in domo Dei mei magis quam habitare in tabernaculis peccatorum, 12 quia misericordiam et veritatem diligit Deus; gratiam et gloriam dabit Dominus. 13 Non privabit bonis eos qui ambulant in innocentia. Domine virtutum, beatus vir qui sperat in te.

Psalmus 84

In finem. Filiis Core. Psalmus.

2 Benedixisti, Domine, terram tuam; avertisti captivitatem Iacob. 3 Remisisti iniquitatem plebis tuae; operuisti omnia peccata eorum. 4 Mitigasti omnem iram tuam; avertisti ab ira indignationis tuae. 5 Converte nos, Deus, salutaris noster, et averte iram tuam a nobis.

6 Numquid in aeternum irasceris nobis, aut extendes iram tuam a generatione in generationem? 7 Deus, tu conversus

8 for the lawgiver shall give a blessing; they shall go from virtue to virtue; the God of gods shall be seen in Zion.

9 O Lord, God of hosts, hear my prayer; give ear, O God of Jacob. 10 Behold, O God, our protector, and look on the face of thy Christ, 11 for better is one day in thy courts above thousands. I have chosen to be an abject in the house of my God rather than to dwell in the tabernacles of sinners, 12 for God loveth mercy and truth; the Lord will give grace and glory. 13 He will not deprive of good things them that walk in innocence. O Lord of hosts, blessed is the man that trusteth in thee.

Psalm 84

Benedixisti, Domine. The coming of Christ to bring peace and salvation to man.

U nto the end. For the sons of Korah. A psalm.

2 Lord, thou hast blessed thy land; thou hast turned away the captivity of Jacob. 3 Thou hast forgiven the iniquity of thy people; thou hast covered all their sins. 4 Thou hast mitigated all thy anger; thou hast turned away from the wrath of thy indignation. 5 Convert us, O God, our saviour, and turn off thy anger from us.

6 Wilt thou be angry with us for ever, or wilt thou extend thy wrath from generation to generation? 7 Thou wilt turn,

vivificabis nos, et plebs tua laetabitur in te. 8 Ostende nobis, Domine, misericordiam tuam, et salutare tuum da nobis. 9 Audiam quid loquatur in me Dominus Deus, quoniam loquetur pacem in plebem suam et super sanctos suos et in eos qui convertuntur ad cor.

10 Verumtamen prope timentes eum salutare ipsius, ut inhabitet gloria in terra nostra. 11 Misericordia et veritas obviaverunt sibi; iustitia et pax osculatae sunt. 12 Veritas de terra orta est, et iustitia de caelo prospexit, 13 etenim Dominus dabit benignitatem et terra nostra dabit fructum suum. 14 Iustitia ante eum ambulabit et ponet in via gressus suos.

Psalmus 85

Oratio ipsi David.

Inclina, Domine, aurem tuam, et exaudi me, quoniam inops et pauper sum ego. 2 Custodi animam meam, quoniam sanctus sum; salvum fac servum tuum, Deus meus, sperantem in te. 3 Miserere mei, Domine, quoniam ad te clamavi tota die. 4 Laetifica animam servi tui, quoniam ad te, Do-

O God, and bring us to life, and thy people shall rejoice in thee. 8 Shew us, O Lord, thy mercy, and grant us thy salvation. 9 I will hear what the Lord God will speak in me, for he will speak peace unto his people and unto his saints and unto them that are converted to the heart.

10 Surely his salvation is near to them that fear him, that glory may dwell in our land. 11 Mercy and truth have met each other; justice and peace have kissed. 12 Truth is sprung out of the earth, and justice hath looked down from heaven, 13 for the Lord will give goodness and our earth shall yield her fruit. 14 Justice shall walk before him and shall set his steps in the way.

Psalm 85

Inclina, Domine. A prayer for God's grace to assist us to the end.

A prayer for David himself.

Incline thy ear, O Lord, and hear me, for I am needy and poor. 2 Preserve my soul, for I am holy; save thy servant, O my God, that trusteth in thee. 3 Have mercy on me, O Lord, for I have cried to thee all the day. 4 Give joy to the soul of thy servant, for to thee, O Lord, I have lifted up my

mine, animam meam levavi, 5 quoniam tu, Domine, suavis et mitis et multae misericordiae omnibus invocantibus te. 6 Auribus percipe, Domine, orationem meam, et intende voci deprecationis meae. 7 In die tribulationis meae clamavi ad te quia exaudisti me.

8 Non est similis tui in diis, Domine, et non est secundum opera tua. 9 Omnes gentes quascumque fecisti venient et adorabunt coram te, Domine, et glorificabunt nomen tuum, 10 quoniam magnus es tu et faciens mirabilia; tu es Deus solus.

11 Deduc me, Domine, in via tua, et ingrediar in veritate tua; laetetur cor meum ut timeat nomen tuum. 12 Confitebor tibi, Domine, Deus meus, in toto corde meo, et glorificabo nomen tuum in aeternum, 13 quia misericordia tua magna est super me et eruisti animam meam ex inferno inferiori.

14 Deus, iniqui insurrexerunt super me, et synagoga potentium quaesierunt animam meam, et non proposuerunt te in conspectu suo. 15 Et tu, Domine, Deus miserator et misericors, patiens et multae misericordiae et verax. 16 Respice in me, et miserere mei; da imperium tuum puero tuo, et salvum fac filium ancillae tuae. 17 Fac mecum signum in bono et videant qui oderunt me et confundantur quoniam tu, Domine, adiuvasti me et consolatus es me.

soul, 5 for thou, O Lord, art sweet and mild and plenteous in mercy to all that call upon thee. 6 Give ear, O Lord, to my prayer, and attend to the voice of my petition. 7 I have called upon thee in the day of my trouble because thou hast heard me.

8 There is none among the gods like unto thee, O Lord, and there is none according to thy works. 9 All the nations thou hast made shall come and adore before thee, O Lord, and they shall glorify thy name, 10 for thou art great and dost wonderful things; thou art God alone.

11 Conduct me, O Lord, in thy way, and I will walk in thy truth; let my heart rejoice that it may fear thy name. 12 I will praise thee, O Lord, my God, with my whole heart, and I will glorify thy name for ever, 13 for thy mercy is great towards me and thou hast delivered my soul out of the lower hell.

14 O God, the wicked are risen up against me, and the assembly of the mighty have sought my soul, and they have not set thee *before* their *eyes*. 15 And thou, O Lord, art a God of compassion and merciful, patient and of much mercy and true. 16 O look upon me, and have mercy on me; give thy command to thy servant, and save the son of thy handmaid. 17 *Shew me* a token *for good* that they who hate me may see and be confounded because thou, O Lord, hast helped me and hast comforted me.

Psalmus 86

Filiis Core. Psalmus cantici.

Fundamenta eius in montibus sanctis; 2 diligit Dominus portas Sion super omnia tabernacula Iacob. 3 Gloriosa dicta sunt de te, civitas Dei.

4 Memor ero Raab et Babylonis scientium me. Ecce alienigenae et Tyrus et populus Aethiopum; hii fuerunt illic. 5 Numquid Sion dicet, "Homo et homo natus est in ea?" Et ipse fundavit eam Altissimus. 6 Dominus narrabit in scripturis populorum et principum horum qui fuerunt in ea. 7 Sicut laetantium omnium habitatio in te.

Psalmus 87

Canticum psalmi. Filiis Core. In finem. Pro Maeleth, ad respondendum intellectus Eman, Ezraitae.

Psalm 86

Fundamenta eius. The glory of the church of Christ.

For the sons of Korah. A psalm of a canticle.

The foundations thereof are in the holy mountains; 2 the Lord loveth the gates of Zion above all the tabernacles of Jacob. 3 Glorious things are said of thee, O city of God.

4 I will be mindful of Rahab and of Babylon knowing me. Behold the foreigners and Tyre and the people of the Ethiopians; these were there. 5 Shall not Zion say, "This man and that man is born in her?" And the Highest himself hath founded her. 6 The Lord shall tell in his writings of peoples and of princes of them that have been in her. 7 The dwelling in thee is as it were of all rejoicing.

Psalm 87

Domine, Deus salutis. A prayer of one under grievous affliction, it agrees to Christ in his passion and alludes to his death and burial.

A canticle of a psalm. For the sons of Korah. Unto the end. For Mahalath, to answer understanding of Heman, the Ezrahite.

2 Domine, Deus salutis meae, in die clamavi et nocte coram te. 3 Intret in conspectu tuo oratio mea; inclina aurem tuam ad precem meam, 4 quia repleta est malis anima mea et vita mea inferno adpropinquavit. 5 Aestimatus sum cum descendentibus in lacum; factus sum sicut homo sine adiutorio, 6 inter mortuos liber, sicut vulnerati dormientes in sepulchris quorum non es memor amplius et ipsi de manu tua repulsi sunt.

7 Posuerunt me in lacu inferiori, in tenebrosis et in umbra mortis. 8 Super me confirmatus est furor tuus, et omnes fluctus tuos induxisti super me. 9 Longe fecisti notos meos a me; posuerunt me abominationem sibi. Traditus sum et non egrediebar. 10 Oculi mei languerunt prae inopia. Clamavi ad te, Domine, tota die; expandi ad te manus meas. 11 Numquid mortuis facies mirabilia? Aut medici suscitabunt et confitebuntur tibi? 12 Numquid narrabit aliquis in sepulchro misericordiam tuam et veritatem tuam in perditione? 13 Numquid cognoscentur in tenebris mirabilia tua et iustitia tua in terra oblivionis? 14 Et ego ad te, Domine, clamavi, et mane oratio mea praeveniet te.

15 Ut quid, Domine, repellis orationem meam; avertis faciem tuam a me? 16 Pauper sum ego et in laboribus a iuventute mea exaltatus autem humiliatus sum et conturbatus. 17 In me transierunt irae tuae, et terrores tui conturbaverunt me. 18 Circuierunt me sicut aqua tota die; circumdederunt me simul. 19 Elongasti a me amicum et proximum et notos meos a miseria.

2 O Lord, the God of my salvation, I have cried in the day and in the night before thee. 3 Let my prayer come in before thee; incline thy ear to my petition, 4 for my soul is filled with evils and my life hath drawn nigh to hell. 5 I am counted among them that go down to the pit; I am become as a man without help, 6 free among the dead, like the slain sleeping in the sepulchres whom thou rememberest no more and they are cast off from thy hand.

7 They have laid me in the lower pit, in the dark places and in the shadow of death. 8 Thy wrath is strong over me, and all thy waves thou hast brought in upon me. 9 Thou hast put away my acquaintance far from me; they have set me an abomination to themselves. I was delivered up and came not forth. 10 My eyes languished through poverty. All the day I cried to thee, O Lord; I stretched out my hands to thee. 11 Wilt thou shew wonders to the dead? Or shall physicians raise to life and give praise to thee? 12 Shall any one in the sepulchre declare thy mercy and thy truth in destruction? 13 Shall thy wonders be known in the dark and thy justice in the land of forgetfulness? 14 *But* I, O Lord, have cried to thee, and in the morning my prayer shall prevent thee.

15 Lord, why castest thou off my prayer; why turnest thou away thy face from me? 16 I am poor and in labours from my youth and being exalted have been humbled and troubled. 17 Thy wrath hath come upon me, and thy terrors have troubled me. 18 They have come round about me like water all the day; they have compassed me about together. 19 Friend and neighbour thou hast put far from me and my acquaintance because of misery.

Psalmus 88

Intellectus. Aethan, Ezraitae.

2 Misericordias Domini in aeternum cantabo. In generationem et generationem adnuntiabo veritatem tuam in ore meo, 3 quoniam dixisti, "In aeternum misericordia aedificabitur in caelis." Praeparabitur veritas tua in eis.

4 "Disposui testamentum electis meis; iuravi David, servo meo, 5 'Usque in aeternum praeparabo semen tuum, et aedificabo in generationem et generationem sedem tuam.'"

6 Confitebuntur caeli mirabilia tua, Domine, etenim veritatem tuam in ecclesia sanctorum, 7 quoniam quis in nubibus aequabitur Domino, similis erit Deo in filiis Dei? 8 Deus, qui glorificatur in consilio sanctorum, magnus et terribilis super omnes qui in circuitu eius sunt. 9 Domine, Deus virtutum, quis similis tibi? Potens es, Domine, et veritas tua in circuitu tuo. 10 Tu dominaris potestatis maris motum autem fluctuum eius tu mitigas. 11 Tu humiliasti sicut vulneratum

Psalm 88

Misericordias Domini. The perpetuity of the church of Christ in consequence of the promise of God, which notwithstanding, God permits her to suffer sometimes most grievous afflictions.

Of understanding. For Ethan, the Ezrahite.

2 The mercies of the Lord I will sing for ever. I will shew forth thy truth with my mouth to generation and generation, 3 for thou hast said, "Mercy shall be built up for ever in the heavens." Thy truth shall be prepared in them.

4 "I have made a covenant with my elect; I have sworn to David, my servant, 5 'Thy seed will I *settle* for ever, and I will build up thy throne unto generation and generation.'"

6 The heavens shall confess thy wonders, O Lord, and thy truth in the church of the saints, 7 for who in the clouds *can be compared* to the Lord, *or who* among the sons of God shall be like to God? 8 God, who is glorified in the assembly of the saints, great and terrible above all them that are about him. 9 O Lord, God of hosts, who is like to thee? Thou art mighty, O Lord, and thy truth is round about thee. 10 Thou rulest the power of the sea and appeasest the motion of the waves thereof. 11 Thou hast humbled the proud one as one that is

superbum; in brachio virtutis tuae dispersisti inimicos tuos. 12 Tui sunt caeli, et tua est terra; orbem terrae et plenitudinem eius tu fundasti. 13 Aquilonem et mare tu creasti. Thabor et Hermon in nomine tuo exultabunt. 14 Tuum brachium cum potentia. Firmetur manus tua et exaltetur dextera tua. 15 Iustitia et iudicium praeparatio sedis tuae. Misericordia et veritas praecedent faciem tuam.

16 Beatus populus qui scit iubilationem. Domine, in lumine vultus tui ambulabunt, 17 et in nomine tuo exultabunt tota die, et in iustitia tua exaltabuntur, 18 quoniam gloria virtutis eorum tu es, et in beneplacito tuo exaltabitur cornu nostrum, 19 quia Domini est adsumptio nostra et sancti Israhel, regis nostri.

20 Tunc locutus es in visione sanctis tuis et dixisti, "Posui adiutorium in potentem et exaltavi electum de plebe mea. 21 Inveni David, servum meum; oleo sancto meo linui eum, 22 manus enim mea auxiliabitur ei et brachium meum confirmabit eum. 23 Nihil proficiet inimicus in eo et filius iniquitatis non adponet nocere eum. 24 Et concidam a facie ipsius inimicos eius, et odientes eum in fugam convertam. 25 Et veritas mea et misericordia mea cum ipso, et in nomine meo exaltabitur cornu eius. 26 Et ponam in mari manum eius et in fluminibus dexteram eius. 27 Ipse invocabit me, 'Pater meus es tu, Deus meus, et susceptor salutis meae.' 28 Et ego primogenitum ponam illum, excelsum prae regibus terrae. 29 In aeternum servabo illi misericordiam meam et testamentum meum fidele ipsi. 30 Et ponam in saeculum saeculi semen

slain; with the arm of thy strength thou hast scattered thy enemies. 12 Thine are the heavens, and thine is the earth; the world and the fulness thereof thou hast founded. 13 The north and the sea thou hast created. Tabor and Hermon shall rejoice in thy name. 14 Thy arm is with might. Let thy hand be strengthened and thy right hand exalted. 15 Justice and judgment are the preparation of thy throne. Mercy and truth shall go before thy face.

16 Blessed is the people that knoweth jubilation. They shall walk, O Lord, in the light of thy countenance, 17 and in thy name they shall rejoice all the day, and in thy justice they shall be exalted, 18 for thou art the glory of their strength, and in thy good pleasure shall our horn be exalted, 19 for our protection is of the Lord and of our king, the holy one of Israel.

20 Then thou spokest in a vision to thy saints and saidst, "I have laid help upon one that is mighty and have exalted one chosen out of my people. 21 I have found David, my servant; with my holy oil I have anointed him, 22 for my hand shall help him and my arm shall strengthen him. 23 The enemy shall have no advantage over him nor the son of iniquity *have power* to hurt him. 24 And I will cut down his enemies before his face, and them that hate him I will put to flight. 25 And my truth and my mercy shall be with him, and in my name shall his horn be exalted. 26 And I will set his hand in the sea and his right hand in the rivers. 27 He shall cry out to me, 'Thou art my father, my God, and the support of my salvation.' 28 And I will make him my firstborn, high above the kings of the earth. 29 I will keep my mercy for him for ever and my covenant faithful to him. 30 And I will make his seed

eius et thronum eius sicut dies caeli. 31 Si autem dereliquerint filii eius legem meam et in iudiciis meis non ambulaverint, 32 si iustitias meas profanaverint et mandata mea non custodierint, 33 visitabo in virga iniquitates eorum et in verberibus peccata eorum, 34 misericordiam autem meam non auferam ab eo, neque nocebo in veritate mea, 35 neque profanabo testamentum meum, et quae procedunt de labiis meis non faciam irrita. 36 Semel iuravi in sancto meo, si David mentiar, 37 semen eius in aeternum manebit 38 et thronus eius sicut sol in conspectu meo et sicut luna perfecta in aeternum et testis in caelo fidelis."

39 Tu vero reppulisti et despexisti; distulisti christum tuum. 40 Evertisti testamentum servi tui; profanasti in terram sanctuarium eius. 41 Destruxisti omnes sepes eius; posuisti firmamentum eius formidinem. 42 Diripuerunt eum omnes transeuntes viam; factus est obprobrium vicinis suis. 43 Exaltasti dexteram deprimentium eum; laetificasti omnes inimicos eius. 44 Avertisti adiutorium gladii eius et non es auxiliatus ei in bello. 45 Destruxisti eum ab emundatione, et sedem eius in terram conlisisti. 46 Minorasti dies temporis eius; perfudisti eum confusione.

47 Usquequo, Domine, avertis in finem? Exardescet sicut ignis ira tua? 48 Memorare quae mea substantia, numquid enim vane constituisti omnes filios hominum? 49 Quis est homo qui vivet et non videbit mortem, eruet animam suam de manu inferi? 50 Ubi sunt misericordiae tuae antiquae, Domine, sicut iurasti David in veritate tua? 51 Memor esto, Do-

to endure for evermore and his throne as the days of heaven. 31 And if his children forsake my law and walk not in my judgments, 32 if they profane my justices and keep not my commandments, 33 I will visit their iniquities with a rod and their sins with stripes, 34 but my mercy I will not take away from him, nor will I *suffer my truth to fail,* 35 neither will I profane my covenant, and the words that proceed from my mouth I will not make void. 36 Once have I sworn by my holiness, *I will not lie* unto David. 37 His seed shall endure for ever 38 and his throne as the sun before me and as the moon perfect for ever and a faithful witness in heaven."

39 But thou hast rejected and despised; thou hast *been angry with* thy anointed. 40 Thou hast overthrown the covenant of thy servant; thou hast profaned his sanctuary on the earth. 41 Thou hast broken down all his hedges; thou hast made his strength fear. 42 All that pass by the way have robbed him; he is become a reproach to his neighbours. 43 Thou hast set up the right hand of them that oppress him; thou hast made all his enemies to rejoice. 44 Thou hast turned away the help of his sword and hast not assisted him in battle. 45 Thou hast *made his purification to cease,* and thou hast cast his throne down to the ground. 46 Thou hast shortened the days of his time; thou hast covered him with confusion.

47 How long, O Lord, turnest thou away unto the end? Shall thy anger burn like fire? 48 Remember what my substance is, for hast thou made all the children of men in vain? 49 Who is the man that shall live and not see death, that shall deliver his soul from the hand of hell? 50 Lord, where are thy ancient mercies according to what thou didst swear to David in thy truth? 51 Be mindful, O Lord, of the

mine, obprobrii servorum tuorum quod continui in sinu meo multarum gentium 52 quod exprobraverunt inimici tui, Domine, quod exprobraverunt commutationem christi tui. 53 Benedictus Dominus in aeternum. Fiat. Fiat.

Psalmus 89

Oratio Mosi, hominis Dei.

Domine, refugium tu factus es nobis a generatione in generationem. 2 Priusquam montes fierent aut formaretur terra et orbis, a saeculo usque in saeculum tu es Deus; 3 ne avertas hominem in humilitatem. Et dixisti, "Convertimini, filii hominum," 4 quoniam mille anni ante oculos tuos tamquam dies hesterna quae praeteriit et custodia in nocte. 5 Quae pro nihilo habentur eorum anni erunt. 6 Mane sicut herba transeat; mane floreat et transeat; vespere decidat, induret et arescat, 7 quia defecimus in ira tua et in furore tuo turbati sumus.

8 Posuisti iniquitates nostras in conspectu tuo, saeculum nostrum in inluminatione vultus tui, 9 quoniam omnes dies nostri defecerunt, et in ira tua defecimus. Anni nostri sicut

reproach of thy servants which I have held in my bosom of many nations 52 wherewith thy enemies have reproached, O Lord, wherewith they have reproached the change of thy anointed.

53 Blessed be the Lord for evermore. So be it. So be it.

Psalm 89

Domine, refugium. A prayer for the mercy of God, recounting the shortness and miseries of the days of man.

A prayer of Moses, the man of God.

Lord, thou hast been our refuge from generation to generation. 2 Before the mountains were made or the earth and the world was formed, from eternity *and* to eternity thou art God; 3 turn not man away to be brought low. And thou hast said, "Be converted, O ye sons of men," 4 for a thousand years in thy sight are as yesterday which is past and as a watch in the night. 5 Things that are counted nothing shall their years be. 6 In the morning man shall grow up like grass; in the morning he shall flourish and pass away; in the evening he shall fall, grow dry and wither, 7 for in thy wrath we have fainted away and are troubled in thy indignation.

8 Thou hast set our iniquities *before* thy *eyes,* our *life* in the light of thy countenance, 9 for all our days are spent, and in thy wrath we have fainted away. Our years shall be consid-

aranea meditabuntur. 10 Dies annorum nostrorum, in ipsis septuaginta anni, si autem in potentatibus octoginta anni, et amplius eorum labor et dolor, quoniam supervenit mansuetudo et corripiemur.

11 Quis novit potestatem irae tuae et prae timore tuo iram tuam 12 dinumerare? Dexteram tuam sic notam fac et eruditos corde, in sapientia. 13 Convertere, Domine—usquequo? —et deprecare esto super servos tuos. 14 Repleti sumus mane misericordia tua, et exultavimus et delectati sumus omnibus diebus nostris. 15 Laetati sumus pro diebus quibus nos humiliasti, annis quibus vidimus mala. 16 Respice in servos tuos et in opera tua, et dirige filios eorum. 17 Et sit splendor Domini, Dei nostri, super nos, et opera manuum nostrarum dirige super nos, et opus manuum nostrarum dirige.

Psalmus 90

Laus cantici David.

Qui habitat in adiutorio Altissimi in protectione Dei caeli commorabitur. 2 Dicet Domino, "Susceptor meus es tu

ered as a spider. 10 The days of our years, in them are three-score and ten years, but if in the strong they be fourscore years, and what is more of them is labour and sorrow, for mildness is come upon us and we shall be corrected.

11 Who knoweth the power of thy anger and for thy fear 12 can number thy wrath? So make thy right hand known and men learned in heart, in wisdom. 13 Return, O Lord—how long?—and be entreated in favour of thy servants. 14 We are filled in the morning with thy mercy, and we have rejoiced and are delighted all our days. 15 We have rejoiced for the days in which thou hast humbled us, for the years in which we have seen evils. 16 Look upon thy servants and upon their works, and direct their children. 17 And let the brightness of the Lord, our God, be upon us, and direct thou the works of our hands over us; yea, the work of our hands do thou direct.

Psalm 90

Qui habitat. The just is secure under the protection of God.

The praise of a canticle for David.

He that dwelleth in the aid of the Most High shall abide under the protection of the God of *Jacob.* 2 He shall say to the Lord, "Thou art my protector and my refuge, my God;

et refugium meum, Deus meus; sperabo in eum, 3 quoniam ipse liberavit me de laqueo venantium et a verbo aspero."

4 In scapulis suis obumbrabit te, et sub pinnis eius sperabis. 5 Scuto circumdabit te veritas eius; non timebis a timore nocturno, 6 a sagitta volante in die, a negotio perambulante in tenebris, ab incursu et daemonio meridiano. 7 Cadent a latere tuo mille et decem milia a dextris tuis, ad te autem non adpropinquabit.

8 Verumtamen oculis tuis considerabis et retributionem peccatorum videbis 9 quoniam tu, Domine, spes mea.

Altissimum posuisti refugium tuum. 10 Non accedet ad te malum, et flagellum non adpropinquabit tabernaculo tuo, 11 quoniam angelis suis mandavit de te ut custodiant te in omnibus viis tuis. 12 In manibus portabunt te ne forte offendas ad lapidem pedem tuum. 13 Super aspidem et basiliscum ambulabis, et conculcabis leonem et draconem. 14 Quoniam in me speravit liberabo eum; protegam eum quia cognovit nomen meum. 15 Clamabit ad me, et exaudiam eum; cum ipso sum in tribulatione; eripiam eum, et glorificabo eum. 16 Longitudine dierum replebo eum, et ostendam illi salutare meum.

in him will I trust, 3 for he hath delivered me from the snare of the hunters and from the sharp word."

4 He will overshadow thee with his shoulders, and under his wings thou shalt trust. 5 His truth shall compass thee with a shield; thou shalt not be afraid of the terror of the night, 6 of the arrow that flieth in the day, of the business that walketh about in the dark, of invasion or of the noonday devil. 7 A thousand shall fall at thy side and ten thousand at thy right hand, but it shall not come nigh thee.

8 But thou shalt consider with thy eyes and shalt see the reward of the wicked 9 because thou, O Lord, art my hope.

Thou hast made the Most High thy refuge. 10 There shall no evil come to thee, nor shall the scourge come near thy dwelling, 11 for he hath given his angels charge over thee to keep thee in all thy ways. 12 In their hands they shall bear thee up *lest* thou dash thy foot against a stone. 13 Thou shalt walk upon the asp and the basilisk, and thou shalt trample under foot the lion and the dragon. 14 Because he hoped in me I will deliver him; I will protect him because he hath known my name. 15 He shall cry to me, and I will hear him; I am with him in tribulation; I will deliver him, and I will glorify him. 16 I will fill him with length of days, and I will shew him my salvation.

Psalmus 91

Psalmus cantici in die sabbati.

2 Bonum est confiteri Domino et psallere nomini tuo, Altissime, 3 ad adnuntiandum mane misericordiam tuam et veritatem tuam per noctem 4 in decacordo, psalterio, cum cantico in cithara, 5 quia delectasti me, Domine, in factura tua, et in operibus manuum tuarum exultabo!

6 Quam magnificata sunt opera tua, Domine! Nimis profundae factae sunt cogitationes tuae. 7 Vir insipiens non cognoscet, et stultus non intelleget haec 8 cum exorti fuerint peccatores sicut faenum et apparuerint omnes qui operantur iniquitatem ut intereant in saeculum saeculi. 9 Tu autem, Altissimus in aeternum, Domine, 10 quoniam ecce, inimici tui, Domine, quoniam ecce: inimici tui peribunt, et dispergentur omnes qui operantur iniquitatem. 11 Et exaltabitur sicut unicornis cornu meum et senectus mea in misericordia uberi. 12 Et despexit oculus meus inimicis meis, et insurgentibus in me malignantibus audiet auris mea.

13 Iustus ut palma florebit; ut cedrus Libani multiplicabitur. 14 Plantati in domo Domini in atriis domus Dei nostri

Psalm 91

Bonum est confiteri. God is to be praised for his wondrous works.

A psalm of a canticle on the sabbath day.

2 It is good to give praise to the Lord and to sing to thy name, O Most High, 3 to shew forth thy mercy in the morning and thy truth in the night 4 upon an instrument of ten strings, upon the psaltery, with a canticle upon the harp, 5 for thou hast given me, O Lord, a delight in thy doings, and in the works of thy hands I shall rejoice!

6 O Lord, how great are thy works! Thy thoughts are exceeding deep. 7 The senseless man shall not know, nor will the fool understand these things 8 when the wicked shall spring up as grass and all the workers of iniquity shall appear that they may perish for ever and ever. 9 But thou, O Lord, art Most High for evermore, 10 for behold, thy enemies, O Lord, for behold: thy enemies shall perish, and all the workers of iniquity shall be scattered. 11 *But* my horn shall be exalted like that of the unicorn and my old age in plentiful mercy. 12 My eye also hath looked down upon my enemies, and my ear shall hear *of the downfall* of the malignant that rise up against me.

13 The just shall flourish like the palm tree; he shall *grow up* like the cedar of Lebanon. 14 They that are planted in the house of the Lord shall flourish in the courts of the house of

florebunt. 15 Adhuc multiplicabuntur in senecta uberi et bene patientes erunt 16 ut adnuntient quoniam rectus Dominus, Deus noster, et non est iniquitas in eo.

Psalmus 92

Laus cantici ipsi David in die ante sabbatum, quando fundata est terra.

Dominus regnavit. Decorem indutus est; indutus est Dominus fortitudinem et praecinxit se, etenim firmavit orbem terrae qui non commovebitur. 2 Parata sedis tua ex tunc; a saeculo tu es. 3 Elevaverunt flumina, Domine; elevaverunt flumina vocem suam; elevaverunt flumina fluctus suos 4 a vocibus aquarum multarum. Mirabiles elationes maris; mirabilis in altis Dominus! 5 Testimonia tua credibilia facta sunt nimis; domum tuam decet sanctitudo, Domine, in longitudine dierum.

our God. 15 They shall still increase in a fruitful old age and shall be well treated 16 that they may shew that the Lord, our God, is righteous, and there is no iniquity in him.

Psalm 92

Dominus regnavit. The glory and stability of the kingdom, that is, of the church of Christ.

P raise *in the way* of a canticle for David himself on the day before the sabbath, when the earth was founded.

The Lord hath reigned. He is clothed with beauty; the Lord is clothed with strength and hath girded himself, for he hath established the world which shall not be moved. 2 Thy throne is prepared from of old; thou art from everlasting. 3 The floods have lifted up, O Lord; the floods have lifted up their voice; the floods have lifted up their waves 4 with the noise of many waters. Wonderful are the surges of the sea; wonderful is the Lord on high! 5 Thy testimonies are become exceedingly credible; holiness becometh thy house, O Lord, unto length of days.

Psalmus 93

Psalmus ipsi David quarta sabbati.

Deus ultionum Dominus; Deus ultionum libere egit. 2 Exaltare, qui iudicas terram; redde retributionem superbis. 3 Usquequo peccatores, Domine, usquequo peccatores gloriabuntur? 4 Effabuntur et loquentur iniquitatem? Loquentur omnes qui operantur iniustitiam?

5 Populum tuum, Domine, humiliaverunt, et hereditatem tuam vexaverunt. 6 Viduam et advenam interfecerunt, et pupillos occiderunt. 7 Et dixerunt, "Non videbit Dominus, nec intelleget Deus Iacob."

8 Intellegite, insipientes in populo, et, stulti, aliquando sapite. 9 Qui plantavit aurem, non audiet? Aut qui finxit oculum, non considerat? 10 Qui corripit gentes, non arguet, qui docet hominem scientiam? 11 Dominus scit cogitationes hominum, quoniam vanae sunt.

12 Beatus homo quem tu erudieris, Domine, et de lege tua docueris eum 13 ut mitiges ei a diebus malis donec fodiatur peccatori fovea, 14 quia non repellet Dominus plebem suam,

Psalm 93

Deus ultionum. God shall judge and punish the oppressors of his people.

A psalm for David himself on the fourth day of the week.

The Lord is the God *to whom revenge belongeth;* the God of revenge hath acted freely. 2 Lift up thyself, thou that judgest the earth; render a reward to the proud. 3 How long shall sinners, O Lord, how long shall sinners glory? 4 Shall they utter and speak iniquity? Shall all speak who work injustice?

5 Thy people, O Lord, they have brought low, and they have afflicted thy inheritance. 6 They have slain the widow and the stranger, and they have murdered the fatherless. 7 And they have said, "The Lord shall not see, neither shall the God of Jacob understand."

8 Understand, ye senseless among the people, and, you fools, be wise at last. 9 He that planted the ear, shall he not hear? Or he that formed the eye, doth he not consider? 10 He that chastiseth nations, shall he not rebuke, he that teacheth man knowledge? 11 The Lord knoweth the thoughts of men, that they are vain.

12 Blessed is the man whom thou shalt instruct, O Lord, and shalt teach him out of thy law 13 that thou mayst give him rest from the evil days till a pit be dug for the wicked, 14 for the Lord will not cast off his people, neither will he

et hereditatem suam non derelinquet 15 quoadusque iustitia convertatur in iudicium et qui iuxta illam omnes qui recto sunt corde.

16 Quis consurget mihi adversus malignantes? Aut quis stabit mecum adversus operantes iniquitatem? 17 Nisi quia Dominus adiuvit me paulo minus habitasset in inferno anima mea. 18 Si dicebam, "Motus est pes meus," misericordia tua, Domine, adiuvabat me. 19 Secundum multitudinem dolorum meorum in corde meo consolationes tuae laetificaverunt animam meam. 20 Numquid adherit tibi sedis iniquitatis qui fingis laborem in praecepto? 21 Captabunt in animam iusti et sanguinem innocentem condemnabunt. 22 Et factus est Dominus mihi in refugium, et Deus meus in adiutorium spei meae, 23 et reddet illis iniquitatem ipsorum, et in malitia eorum disperdet eos; disperdet illos Dominus, Deus noster.

Psalmus 94

Laus cantici ipsi David.

Venite; exultemus Domino! Iubilemus Deo, salutari nostro. 2 Praeoccupemus faciem eius in confessione et in psalmis iubilemus ei, 3 quoniam Deus magnus Dominus et rex

forsake his own inheritance 15 until justice be turned into judgment and they that are near it are all the upright in heart.

16 Who shall rise up for me against the evildoers? Or who shall stand with me against the workers of iniquity? 17 Unless the Lord had been my helper my soul had almost dwelt in hell. 18 If I said, "My foot is moved," thy mercy, O Lord, assisted me. 19 According to the multitude of my sorrows in my heart thy comforts have given joy to my soul. 20 Doth the seat of iniquity stick to thee who framest labour in commandment? 21 They will hunt after the soul of the just and will condemn innocent blood. 22 *But* the Lord is my refuge, and my God the help of my hope, 23 and he will render them their iniquity, and in their malice he will destroy them; the Lord, our God, will destroy them.

Psalm 94

Venite; exultemus. An invitation to adore and serve God and to hear his voice.

Praise of a canticle for David himself.

Come; let us praise the Lord with joy! Let us joyfully sing to God, our saviour. 2 Let us come before his presence with thanksgiving and make a joyful noise to him with psalms, 3 for the Lord is a great God and a great king above

magnus super omnes deos, 4 quia in manu eius fines terrae, et altitudines montium ipsius sunt, 5 quoniam ipsius est mare, et ipse fecit illud, et siccam manus eius formaverunt.

6 Venite; adoremus et procidamus et ploremus ante Dominum qui fecit nos, 7 quia ipse est Dominus, Deus noster, et nos populus pascuae eius et oves manus eius. 8 Hodie si vocem eius audieritis, nolite obdurare corda vestra 9 sicut in inritatione secundum diem temptationis in deserto ubi temptaverunt me patres vestri. Probaverunt me et viderunt opera mea. 10 Quadraginta annis offensus fui generationi illi, et dixi, "Semper hi errant corde," 11 et, "Isti non cognoverunt vias meas," ut iuravi in ira mea si intrabunt in requiem meam.

Psalmus 95

Quando domus aedificabatur post captivitatem canticum ipsi David.

Cantate Domino canticum novum! Cantate Domino, omnis terra! 2 Cantate Domino, et benedicite nomini eius. Adnuntiate de die in diem salutare eius. 3 Adnuntiate inter Gentes gloriam eius, in omnibus populis mirabilia eius, 4 quoniam magnus Dominus et laudabilis nimis; terribilis est super omnes deos, 5 quoniam omnes dii Gentium dae-

all gods, 4 for in his hand are *all* the ends of the earth, and the heights of the mountains are his, 5 for the sea is his, and he made it, and his hands formed the dry land.

6 Come; let us adore and fall down and weep before the Lord that made us, 7 for he is the Lord, our God, and we are the people of his pasture and the sheep of his hand. 8 Today if you shall hear his voice, harden not your hearts 9 as in the provocation according to the day of temptation in the wilderness where your fathers tempted me. They proved me and saw my works. 10 Forty years long was I offended with that generation, and I said, "These always err in heart," 11 and, "These men have not known my ways," so I swore in my wrath that they shall not enter into my rest.

Psalm 95

Cantate Domino. An exhortation to praise God for the coming of Christ and his kingdom.

A canticle for David himself when the house was built after the captivity.

Sing ye to the Lord a new canticle! Sing to the Lord, all the earth! 2 Sing ye to the Lord, and bless his name. Shew forth his salvation from day to day. 3 Declare his glory among the Gentiles, his wonders among all people, 4 for the Lord is great and exceedingly to be praised; he is to be feared above all gods, 5 for all the gods of the Gentiles are devils, but the

monia, Dominus autem caelos fecit. 6 Confessio et pulchritudo in conspectu eius, sanctimonia et magnificentia in sanctificatione eius.

7 Adferte Domino, patriae Gentium, adferte Domino gloriam et honorem. 8 Adferte Domino gloriam nomini eius. Tollite hostias, et introite in atria eius. 9 Adorate Dominum in atrio sancto eius. Commoveatur a facie eius universa terra. 10 Dicite in Gentibus quia Dominus regnavit, etenim correxit orbem terrae qui non movebitur. Iudicabit populos in aequitate. 11 Laetentur caeli, et exultet terra; commoveatur mare et plenitudo eius. 12 Gaudebunt campi et omnia quae in eis sunt. Tunc exultabunt omnia ligna silvarum 13 a facie Domini quia venit, quoniam venit iudicare terram. Iudicabit orbem terrae in aequitate et populos in veritate sua.

Psalmus 96

Huic David quando terra eius restituta est ei.

Dominus regnavit; exultet terra; laetentur insulae multae! 2 Nubes et caligo in circuitu eius; iustitia et iudicium correc-

Lord made the heavens. 6 Praise and beauty are before him, holiness and majesty in his sanctuary.

7 Bring ye to the Lord, O ye kindreds of the Gentiles, bring ye to the Lord glory and honour. 8 Bring to the Lord glory unto his name. Bring up sacrifices, and come into his courts. 9 Adore ye the Lord in his holy court. Let all the earth be moved at his presence. 10 Say ye among the Gentiles, "*The* Lord hath reigned," for he hath corrected the world which shall not be moved. He will judge the people with justice. 11 Let the heavens rejoice, and let the earth be glad; let the sea be moved and the fulness thereof. 12 The fields and all things that are in them shall be joyful. Then shall all the trees of the woods rejoice 13 before the face of the Lord because he cometh, because he cometh to judge the earth. He shall judge the world with justice and the people with his truth.

Psalm 96

Dominus regnavit. All are invited to rejoice at the glorious coming and reign of Christ.

For *the same* David when his land was restored again to him.

The Lord hath reigned; let the earth rejoice; let many islands be glad! 2 Clouds and darkness are round about him; justice and judgment are the *establishment* of his throne.

tio sedis eius. 3 Ignis ante ipsum praecedet et inflammabit in circuitu inimicos eius. 4 Adluxerunt fulgora eius orbi terrae; vidit et commota est terra. 5 Montes sicut cera fluxerunt a facie Domini, a facie Domini omnis terra. 6 Adnuntiaverunt caeli iustitiam eius, et viderunt omnes populi gloriam eius. 7 Confundantur omnes qui adorant sculptilia et qui gloriantur in simulacris suis. Adorate eum, omnes angeli eius.

8 Audivit et laetata est Sion. Et exultaverunt filiae Iudae propter iudicia tua, Domine, 9 quoniam tu Dominus altissimus super omnem terram; nimis exaltatus es super omnes deos.

10 Qui diligitis Dominum, odite malum. Custodit Dominus animas sanctorum suorum; de manu peccatoris liberabit eos. 11 Lux orta est iusto et rectis corde laetitia. 12 Laetamini, iusti, in Domino, et confitemini memoriae sanctificationis eius.

Psalmus 97

Psalmus ipsi David.

Cantate Domino canticum novum quoniam mirabilia fecit! Salvavit sibi dextera eius, et brachium sanctum eius. 2 Notum fecit Dominus salutare suum; in conspectu Gen-

3 A fire shall go before him and shall burn his enemies round about. 4 His lightnings have shone forth to the world; the earth saw and trembled. 5 The mountains melted like wax at the presence of the Lord, at the presence of the Lord, all the earth. 6 The heavens declared his justice, and all people saw his glory. 7 Let them be all confounded that adore graven things and that glory in their idols. Adore him, all you his angels.

8 Zion heard and was glad. And the daughters of Judah rejoiced because of thy judgments, O Lord, 9 for thou art the most high Lord over all the earth; thou art exalted exceedingly above all gods.

10 You that love the Lord, hate evil. The Lord preserveth the souls of his saints; he will deliver them out of the hand of the sinner. 11 Light is risen to the just and joy to the right of heart. 12 Rejoice, ye just, in the Lord, and give praise to the remembrance of his holiness.

Psalm 97

Cantate Domino. All are again invited to praise the Lord for the victories of Christ.

A psalm for David himself.

Sing ye to the Lord a new canticle because he hath done wonderful things! His right hand hath wrought for him salvation, and his arm is holy. 2 The Lord hath made known

tium revelavit iustitiam suam. 3 Recordatus est misericordiae suae et veritatem suam domui Israhel. Viderunt omnes termini terrae salutare Dei nostri.

4 Iubilate Deo, omnis terra! Cantate, et exultate, et psallite! 5 Psallite Domino in cithara, in cithara et voce psalmi, 6 in tubis ductilibus et voce tubae corneae. Iubilate in conspectu regis, Domini. 7 Moveatur mare et plenitudo eius, orbis terrarum et qui habitant in eo. 8 Flumina plaudent manu; simul montes exultabunt 9 a conspectu Domini quoniam venit iudicare terram. Iudicabit orbem terrarum in iustitia et populos in aequitate.

Psalmus 98

Psalmus ipsi David.

Dominus regnavit—irascantur populi—qui sedet super cherubin; moveatur terra. 2 Dominus in Sion magnus et excelsus super omnes populos. 3 Confiteantur nomini tuo magno, quoniam terribile et sanctum est 4 et honor regis iudicium diligit. Tu parasti directiones; iudicium et iustitiam

his salvation; he hath revealed his justice in the sight of the Gentiles. 3 He hath remembered his mercy and his truth toward the house of Israel. All the ends of the earth have seen the salvation of our God.

4 Sing joyfully to God, all the earth! Make melody, *rejoice, and sing!* 5 Sing praise to the Lord on the harp, on the harp and with the voice of a psalm, 6 with long trumpets and sound of cornet. Make a joyful noise before the Lord, *our* king. 7 Let the sea be moved and the fullness thereof, the world and they that dwell therein. 8 The rivers shall clap their hands; the mountains shall rejoice together 9 at the presence of the Lord because he cometh to judge the earth. He shall judge the world with justice and the people with equity.

Psalm 98

Dominus regnavit. The reign of the Lord in Zion, that is, of Christ in his church.

A psalm for David himself.

The Lord hath reigned—let the people be angry—he that sitteth on the cherubims; let the earth be moved. 2 The Lord is great in Zion and high above all people. 3 Let them give praise to thy great name, for it is terrible and holy 4 and the king's honour loveth judgment. Thou hast prepared direc-

in Iacob tu fecisti. 5 Exaltate Dominum, Deum nostrum, et adorate scabillum pedum eius, quoniam sanctum est.

6 Moses et Aaron in sacerdotibus eius et Samuhel inter eos qui invocant nomen eius, invocabant Dominum, et ipse exaudiebat illos. 7 In columna nubis loquebatur ad eos. Custodiebant testimonia eius et praeceptum quod dedit illis. 8 Domine, Deus noster, tu exaudiebas illos; Deus tu propitius fuisti eis et ulciscens in omnes adinventiones eorum. 9 Exaltate Dominum, Deum nostrum, et adorate in monte sancto eius, quoniam sanctus Dominus, Deus noster.

Psalmus 99

P salmus in confessione.

2 Iubilate Deo, omnis terra! Servite Domino in laetitia. Introite in conspectu eius in exultatione. 3 Scitote quoniam Dominus, ipse est Deus; ipse fecit nos et non ipsi nos. Populus eius et oves pascuae eius. 4 Introite portas eius in confessione, atria eius in hymnis; confitemini illi. Laudate nomen eius, 5 quoniam suavis Dominus; in aeternum misericordia eius et usque in generationem et generationem veritas eius.

tions; thou hast done judgment and justice in Jacob. 5 Exalt ye the Lord, our God, and adore his footstool, for it is holy.

6 Moses and Aaron among his priests and Samuel among them that call upon his name, they called upon the Lord, and he heard them. 7 He spoke to them in the pillar of the cloud. They kept his testimonies and the commandment which he gave them. 8 Thou didst hear them, O Lord, our God; thou wast a merciful God to them and taking vengeance on all their inventions. 9 Exalt ye the Lord, our God, and adore at his holy mountain, for the Lord, our God, is holy.

Psalm 99

Iubilate Deo. All are invited to rejoice in God, the creator of all.

A psalm of praise.

2 Sing joyfully to God, all the earth! Serve ye the Lord with gladness. Come in before his presence with exceeding great joy. 3 Know ye that the Lord, he is God; he made us and not we ourselves. We are his people and the sheep of his pasture. 4 Go ye into his gates with praise, into his courts with hymns, *and* give glory to him. Praise ye his name, 5 for the Lord is sweet; his mercy endureth for ever and his truth to generation and generation.

Psalmus 100

Ipsi David psalmus.

Misericordiam et iudicium cantabo tibi, Domine. Psallam, 2 et intellegam in via inmaculata quando venies ad me. Perambulabam in innocentia cordis mei, in medio domus meae. 3 Non proponebam ante oculos meos rem iniustam; facientes praevaricationes odivi. Non adhesit mihi 4 cor pravum; declinantem a me malignum non cognoscebam. 5 Detrahentem secreto proximo suo, hunc persequebar. Superbo oculo et insatiabili corde cum hoc non edebam. 6 Oculi mei ad fideles terrae ut sedeant mecum. Ambulans in via inmaculata, hic mihi ministrabat. 7 Non habitabit in medio domus meae qui facit superbiam; qui loquitur iniqua non direxit in conspectu oculorum meorum. 8 In matutino interficiebam omnes peccatores terrae ut disperderem de civitate Domini omnes operantes iniquitatem.

Psalm 100

Misericordiam et iudicium. The prophet exhorteth all by his example to follow mercy and justice.

A psalm for David himself.

Mercy and judgment I will sing to thee, O Lord. I will sing, 2 and I will understand in the unspotted way when thou shalt come to me. I walked in the innocence of my heart, in the midst of my house. 3 I did not set before my eyes any unjust thing; I hated the workers of iniquities. 4 The perverse heart did not cleave to me, *and* the malignant that turned aside from me I would not know. 5 The man that in private detracted his neighbour, him did I persecute. With him that had a proud eye and an unsatiable heart I would not eat. 6 My eyes *were* upon the faithful of the earth to sit with me. The man that walked in the perfect way, he served me. 7 He that worketh pride shall not dwell in the midst of my house; he that speaketh unjust things did not prosper before my eyes. 8 In the morning I put to death all the wicked of the land that I might cut off all the workers of iniquity from the city of the Lord.

Psalmus 101

Oratio pauperis cum anxius fuerit et coram Domino effuderit precem suam.

2 Domine, exaudi orationem meam, et clamor meus ad te veniat. 3 Non avertas faciem tuam a me in quacumque die tribulor. Inclina ad me aurem tuam. In quacumque die invocavero te, velociter exaudi me, 4 quia defecerunt sicut fumus dies mei et ossa mea sicut gremium aruerunt. 5 Percussus sum ut faenum, et aruit cor meum, quia oblitus sum comedere panem meum. 6 A voce gemitus mei adhesit os meum carni meae. 7 Similis factus sum pelicano solitudinis; factus sum sicut nycticorax in domicilio. 8 Vigilavi et factus sum sicut passer solitarius in tecto. 9 Tota die exprobrabant mihi inimici mei, et qui laudabant me adversus me iurabant, 10 quia cinerem tamquam panem manducavi et poculum meum cum fletu miscebam 11 a facie irae et indignationis tuae, quia elevans adlisisti me. 12 Dies mei sicut umbra declinaverunt, et ego sicut faenum arui.

13 Tu autem, Domine, in aeternum permanes et memoriale tuum in generationem et generationem. 14 Tu exsurgens

Psalm 101

Domine, exaudi. A prayer for one in affliction. The fifth penitential psalm.

The prayer of the poor man when he was anxious and poured out his supplication before the Lord.

2 Hear, O Lord, my prayer, and let my cry come to thee. 3 Turn not away thy face from me in the day when I am in trouble. Incline thy ear to me. In what day soever I shall call upon thee, hear me speedily, 4 for my days are vanished like smoke and my bones are grown dry like fuel for the fire. 5 I am smitten as grass, and my heart is withered, because I forgot to eat my bread. 6 Through the voice of my groaning my bone hath cleaved to my flesh. 7 I am become like to a pelican of the wilderness; I am like a night raven in the house. 8 I have watched and am become as a sparrow all alone on the housetop. 9 All the day long my enemies reproached me, and they that praised me did swear against me, 10 for I did eat ashes like bread and mingled my drink with weeping 11 because of thy anger and indignation, for having lifted me up thou hast thrown me down. 12 My days have declined like a shadow, and I am withered like grass.

13 But thou, O Lord, endurest for ever and thy memorial to all generations. 14 Thou shalt arise and have mercy on

misereberis Sion, quia tempus miserendi eius, quia venit tempus, 15 quoniam placuerunt servis tuis lapides eius, et terrae eius miserebuntur. 16 Et timebunt Gentes nomen tuum, Domine, et omnes reges terrae gloriam tuam, 17 quia aedificavit Dominus Sion, et videbitur in gloria sua. 18 Respexit in orationem humilium, et non sprevit precem eorum.

19 Scribantur haec in generationem alteram, et populus qui creabitur laudabit Dominum 20 quia prospexit de excelso sancto suo. Dominus de caelo in terram aspexit 21 ut audiret gemitus conpeditorum, ut solvat filios interemptorum, 22 ut adnuntient in Sion nomen Domini et laudem suam in Hierusalem 23 in conveniendo populos in unum et reges ut serviant Domino.

24 Respondit ei in via virtutis suae. Paucitatem dierum meorum nuntia mihi. 25 Ne revoces me in dimidio dierum meorum; in generationem et generationem anni tui. 26 Initio tu, Domine, terram fundasti, et opera manuum tuarum sunt caeli. 27 Ipsi peribunt, tu autem permanes, et omnes sicut vestimentum veterescent, et sicut opertorium mutabis eos, et mutabuntur, 28 tu autem idem ipse es, et anni tui non deficient. 29 Filii servorum tuorum habitabunt, et semen eorum in saeculum dirigetur.

Zion, for it is time to have mercy on it, for the time is come, 15 for the stones thereof have pleased thy servants, and they shall have pity on the earth thereof. 16 And the Gentiles shall fear thy name, O Lord, and all the kings of the earth thy glory, 17 for the Lord hath built up Zion, and he shall be seen in his glory. 18 He hath had regard to the prayer of the humble, and he hath not despised their petition.

19 Let these things be written unto another generation, and the people that shall be created shall praise the Lord 20 because he hath looked forth from his high sanctuary. From heaven the Lord hath looked upon the earth 21 that he might hear the groans of them that are in fetters, that he might release the children of the slain, 22 that they may declare the name of the Lord in Zion and his praise in Jerusalem 23 when the people assemble together and kings to serve the Lord.

24 He answered him in the way of his strength. Declare unto me the fewness of my days. 25 Call me not away in the midst of my days; thy years are unto generation and generation. 26 In the beginning, O Lord, thou foundedst the earth, and the heavens are the works of thy hands. 27 They shall perish, but thou remainest, and all of them shall grow old like a garment, and as a vesture thou shalt change them, and they shall be changed, 28 but thou art always the selfsame, and thy years shall not fail. 29 The children of thy servants shall *continue,* and their seed shall be directed for ever.

Psalmus 102

Ipsi David.

Benedic, anima mea, Domino, et omnia quae intra me sunt nomini sancto eius! 2 Benedic, anima mea, Domino, et noli oblivisci omnes retributiones eius 3 qui propitiatur omnibus iniquitatibus tuis, qui sanat omnes infirmitates tuas, 4 qui redimit de interitu vitam tuam, qui coronat te in misericordia et miserationibus, 5 qui replet in bonis desiderium tuum. Renovabitur ut aquilae iuventus tua.

6 Faciens misericordias Dominus et iudicium omnibus iniuriam patientibus; 7 notas fecit vias suas Mosi, filiis Israhel voluntates suas. 8 Miserator et misericors Dominus, longanimis et multum misericors. 9 Non in perpetuum irascetur, neque in aeternum comminabitur. 10 Non secundum peccata nostra fecit nobis nec secundum iniquitates nostras retribuit nobis, 11 quoniam secundum altitudinem caeli a terra corroboravit misericordiam suam super timentes se. 12 Quantum distat ortus ab occidente longe fecit a nobis iniquitates nostras. 13 Quomodo miseretur pater filiorum misertus est Dominus timentibus se, 14 quoniam ipse cognovit figmentum nostrum. Recordatus est quoniam pulvis sumus.

Psalm 102

Benedic, anima. Thanksgiving to God for his mercies.

For David himself.

Bless the Lord, O my soul, and *let* all that is within me *praise* his holy name! 2 Bless the Lord, O my soul, and *never* forget all *he hath done for thee* 3 who forgiveth all thy iniquities, who healeth all thy diseases, 4 who redeemeth thy life from destruction, who crowneth thee with mercy and compassion, 5 who satisfieth thy desire with good things. Thy youth shall be renewed like the eagle's.

6 The Lord doth mercies and judgment for all that suffer wrong; 7 he hath made his ways known to Moses, his wills to the children of Israel. 8 The Lord is compassionate and merciful, longsuffering and plenteous in mercy. 9 He will not always be angry, nor will he threaten for ever. 10 He hath not dealt with us according to our sins nor rewarded us according to our iniquities, 11 for according to the height of the heaven above the earth he hath strengthened his mercy towards them that fear him. 12 As far as the east is from the west, so far hath he removed our iniquities from us. 13 As a father hath compassion on his children, so hath the Lord compassion on them that fear him, 14 for he knoweth our frame. He remembereth that we are dust.

15 Homo sicut faenum dies eius. Tamquam flos agri, sic efflorebit, 16 quoniam spiritus pertransibit in illo et non subsistet et non cognoscet amplius locum suum. 17 Misericordia autem Domini ab aeterno et usque in aeternum super timentes eum, et iustitia illius in filios filiorum 18 his qui servant testamentum eius et memores sunt mandatorum ipsius ad faciendum ea. 19 Dominus in caelo paravit sedem suam, et regnum ipsius omnibus dominabitur.

20 Benedicite Domino, omnes angeli eius, potentes virtute, facientes verbum illius ad audiendam vocem sermonum eius. 21 Benedicite Domino, omnes virtutes eius, ministri eius qui facitis voluntatem eius. 22 Benedicite Domino, omnia opera eius, in omni loco dominationis ipsius. Benedic, anima mea, Domino!

Psalmus 103

Ipsi David.

Benedic, anima mea, Domino. Domine, Deus meus, magnificatus es vehementer. Confessionem et decorem induisti 2 amictus lumine sicut vestimento, extendens caelum sicut

15 *Man's* days are as grass. As the flower of the field, so shall he flourish, 16 for the spirit shall pass in him and he shall not be and he shall know his place no more. 17 But the mercy of the Lord is from eternity and unto eternity upon them that fear him, and his justice unto children's children 18 to *such as* keep his covenant and are mindful of his commandments to do them. 19 The Lord hath prepared his throne in heaven, and his kingdom shall rule over all.

20 Bless the Lord, all ye his angels, you that are mighty in strength, and execute his word, *hearkening* to the voice of his *orders*. 21 Bless the Lord, all ye his hosts, you ministers of his that do his will. 22 Bless the Lord, all his works, in every place of his dominion. O my soul, bless thou the Lord!

Psalm 103

Benedic, anima. God is to be praised for his mighty works and wonderful providence.

For David himself.

Bless the Lord, O my soul. O Lord, my God, thou art exceedingly great. Thou hast put on praise and beauty 2 and art clothed with light as with a garment, who stretchest out

pellem, 3 qui tegis aquis superiora eius, qui ponis nubem ascensum tuum, qui ambulas super pinnas ventorum, 4 qui facis angelos tuos spiritus et ministros tuos ignem urentem, 5 qui fundasti terram super stabilitatem suam. Non inclinabitur in saeculum saeculi.

6 Abyssus, sicut vestimentum amictus eius; super montes stabunt aquae. 7 Ab increpatione tua fugient; a voce tonitrui tui formidabunt. 8 Ascendunt montes, et descendunt campi in locum quem fundasti eis. 9 Terminum posuisti quem non transgredientur, neque convertentur operire terram. 10 Qui emittis fontes in convallibus; inter medium montium pertransibunt aquae.

11 Potabunt omnes bestiae agri; expectabunt onagri in siti sua. 12 Super ea volucres caeli habitabunt; de medio petrarum dabunt voces. 13 Rigans montes de superioribus suis, de fructu operum tuorum satiabitur terra, 14 producens faenum iumentis et herbam servituti hominum ut educas panem de terra 15 et vinum laetificet cor hominis, ut exhilaret faciem in oleo et panis cor hominis confirmet. 16 Saturabuntur ligna campi, et cedri Libani quas plantavit, 17 illic passeres nidificabunt. Erodii domus dux est eorum. 18 Montes excelsi cervis, petra refugium erinaciis.

the heaven like a pavilion, 3 who coverest the higher rooms thereof with water, who makest the *clouds thy chariot,* who walkest upon the wings of the winds, 4 who makest thy angels spirits and thy ministers a burning fire, 5 who hast founded the earth upon its own *bases.* It shall not be moved for ever and ever.

6 The deep, like a garment is its clothing; above the mountains shall the waters stand. 7 At thy rebuke they shall flee; at the voice of thy thunder they shall fear. 8 The mountains ascend, and the plains descend into the place which thou hast founded for them. 9 Thou hast set a bound which they shall not pass over, neither shall they return to cover the earth. 10 Thou sendest forth springs in the vales; between the midst of the hills the waters shall pass.

11 All the beasts of the field shall drink; the wild asses shall expect in their thirst. 12 Over them the birds of the air shall dwell; from the midst of the rocks they shall give forth their voices. 13 Thou waterest the hills from *thy* upper rooms; the earth shall be filled with the fruit of thy works, 14 bringing forth grass for cattle and herb for the service of men that thou mayst bring bread out of the earth 15 and that wine may cheer the heart of man, that he may make the face cheerful with oil and that bread may strengthen man's heart. 16 The trees of the field shall be filled, and the cedars of Lebanon which he hath planted, 17 there the sparrows shall make their nests. The *highest* of them is the house of the heron. 18 The high hills are a refuge for the harts, the rock for the irchins.

19 Fecit lunam in tempora; sol cognovit occasum suum.
20 Posuisti tenebras, et facta est nox. In ipsa pertransibunt omnes bestiae silvae, 21 catuli leonum rugientes ut rapiant et quaerant a Deo escam sibi. 22 Ortus est sol, et congregati sunt, et in cubilibus suis conlocabuntur. 23 Exibit homo ad opus suum et ad operationem suam usque ad vesperum.

24 Quam magnificata sunt opera tua, Domine! Omnia in sapientia fecisti; impleta est terra possessione tua, 25 hoc mare magnum et spatiosum. Illic reptilia quorum non est numerus, animalia pusilla cum magnis; 26 illic naves pertransibunt, draco iste quem formasti ad inludendum ei. 27 Omnia a te expectant ut des illis escam in tempore. 28 Dante te illis colligent. Aperiente te manum tuam omnia implebuntur bonitate. 29 Avertente autem te faciem, turbabuntur; auferes spiritum eorum, et deficient et in pulverem suum revertentur. 30 Emittes spiritum tuum, et creabuntur, et renovabis faciem terrae.

31 Sit gloria Domini in saeculum! Laetabitur Dominus in operibus suis. 32 Qui respicit terram et facit eam tremere. Qui tangit montes, et fumigant. 33 Cantabo Domino in vita mea. Psallam Deo meo quamdiu sum. 34 Iucundum sit ei eloquium meum, ego vero delectabor in Domino. 35 Deficiant peccatores a terra, et iniqui ita ut non sint. Benedic, anima mea, Domino!

19 He hath made the moon for seasons; the sun knoweth his going down. 20 Thou hast appointed darkness, and it is night. In it shall all the beasts of the woods go about, 21 the young lions roaring *after their prey* and *seeking* their meat from God. 22 The sun ariseth, and they are gathered together, and they shall lie down in their dens. 23 Man shall go forth to his work and to his labour until the evening.

24 How great are thy works, O Lord! Thou hast made all things in wisdom; the earth is filled with thy riches. 25 *So is* this great sea, *which stretcheth wide its arms.* There are creeping things without number, creatures little *and* great; 26 there the ships shall go, this sea dragon which thou hast formed to play therein. 27 All expect of thee that thou give them food in season. 28 *What thou givest* to them they shall gather up. When thou openest thy hand they shall all be filled with good. 29 But if thou turnest away thy face, they shall be troubled; thou shalt take away their breath, and they shall fail and shall return to their dust. 30 Thou shalt send forth thy spirit, and they shall be created, and thou shalt renew the face of the earth.

31 May the glory of the Lord endure for ever! The Lord shall rejoice in his works. 32 He looketh upon the earth and maketh it tremble. He toucheth the mountains, and they smoke. 33 I will sing to the Lord *as long as I live.* I will sing praise to my God *while I have my being.* 34 Let my speech be acceptable to him, but I will take delight in the Lord. 35 Let sinners *be consumed* out of the earth, and the unjust so that they be no more. O my soul, bless thou the Lord!

Psalmus 104

Alleluia.

Confitemini Domino, et invocate nomen eius! Adnuntiate inter Gentes opera eius. 2 Cantate ei, et psallite ei. Narrate omnia mirabilia eius. 3 Laudamini in nomine sancto eius; laetetur cor quaerentium Dominum. 4 Quaerite Dominum, et confirmamini. Quaerite faciem eius semper. 5 Mementote mirabilium eius quae fecit, prodigia eius et iudicia oris eius, 6 semen Abraham, servi eius, filii Iacob, electi eius.

7 Ipse Dominus, Deus noster; in universa terra iudicia eius. 8 Memor fuit in saeculum testamenti sui, verbi quod mandavit in mille generationes, 9 quod disposuit ad Abraham et iuramenti sui ad Isaac. 10 Et statuit illud Iacob in praeceptum et Israhel in testamentum aeternum, 11 dicens, "Tibi dabo terram Chanaan, funiculum hereditatis vestrae," 12 cum essent numero brevi, paucissimi et incolae eius. 13 Et pertransierunt de gente in gentem et de regno ad populum alterum. 14 Non reliquit hominem nocere eis, et corripuit pro eis reges. 15 "Nolite tangere christos meos, et in prophetis meis nolite malignari." 16 Et vocavit famem super terram, et omne firmamentum panis contrivit.

Psalm 104

Confitemini Domino. A thanksgiving to God for his benefits to his people Israel.

Alleluia.

Give glory to the Lord, and call upon his name! Declare his deeds among the Gentiles. 2 Sing to him; yea, sing praises to him. Relate all his wondrous works. 3 Glory ye in his holy name; let the heart of them rejoice that seek the Lord. 4 Seek ye the lord, and be strengthened. Seek his face evermore. 5 Remember his marvellous works which he hath done, his wonders and the judgments of his mouth, 6 O ye seed of Abraham, his servant, ye sons of Jacob, his chosen.

7 He is the Lord, our God; his judgments are in all the earth. 8 He hath remembered his covenant for ever, the word which he commanded to a thousand generations, 9 which he made to Abraham and his oath to Isaac. 10 And he appointed *the same* to Jacob for a law and to Israel for an everlasting testament, 11 saying, "To thee will I give the land of Canaan, the lot of your inheritance," 12 when they were *but* a small number, *yea,* very few and sojourners therein. 13 And they passed from nation to nation and from one kingdom to another people. 14 He suffered no man to hurt them, and he reproved kings for their sakes. 15 "Touch ye not my anointed, and do no evil to my prophets." 16 And he called a famine upon the land, and he broke in pieces all the support of bread.

17 Misit ante eos virum. In servum venundatus est Ioseph. 18 Humiliaverunt in conpedibus pedes eius; ferrum pertransiit animam eius 19 donec veniret verbum eius. Eloquium Domini inflammavit eum. 20 Misit rex, et solvit eum, princeps populorum, et dimisit eum. 21 Constituit eum dominum domus suae et principem omnis possessionis suae 22 ut erudiret principes eius sicut semet ipsum et senes eius prudentiam doceret.

23 Et intravit Israhel in Aegyptum, et Iacob accola fuit in terra Cham. 24 Et auxit populum eius vehementer et firmavit eum super inimicos eius. 25 Convertit cor eorum ut odirent populum eius et dolum facerent in servos eius. 26 Misit Mosen, servum suum, Aaron, quem elegit ipsum. 27 Posuit in eis verba signorum suorum et prodigiorum in terra Cham. 28 Misit tenebras et obscuravit et non exacerbavit sermones suos. 29 Convertit aquas eorum in sanguinem et occidit pisces eorum. 30 Edidit terra eorum ranas in penetralibus regum ipsorum. 31 Dixit, et venit coenomyia et scinifes in omnibus finibus eorum. 32 Posuit pluvias eorum grandinem, ignem conburentem in terra ipsorum. 33 Et percussit vineas eorum et ficulneas eorum, et contrivit lignum finium eorum. 34 Dixit, et venit lucusta et bruchus cuius non erat numerus. 35 Et comedit omne faenum in terra eorum et comedit omnem fructum terrae eorum. 36 Et percussit omne primogenitum in terra eorum, primitias omnis laboris eorum.

37 Et eduxit eos cum argento et auro, et non erat in tribubus eorum infirmus. 38 Laetata est Aegyptus in profectione eorum, quia incubuit timor eorum super eos. 39 Expandit nubem in protectionem eorum et ignem ut luceret

17 He sent a man before them, Joseph, *who* was sold for a slave. 18 They humbled his feet in fetters; the iron pierced his soul 19 until his word came. The word of the Lord inflamed him. 20 The king sent, and he released him, the ruler of the people, and he set him at liberty. 21 He made him master of his house and ruler of all his possession 22 that he might instruct his princes as himself and teach his ancients wisdom.

23 And Israel went into Egypt, and Jacob was a sojourner in the land of Ham. 24 And he increased his people exceedingly and strengthened them over their enemies. 25 He turned their heart to hate his people and to deal deceitfully with his servants. 26 He sent Moses, his servant, Aaron, the man whom he had chosen. 27 *He gave them power to shew* his signs and his wonders in the land of Ham. 28 He sent darkness and made it obscure and grieved not his words. 29 He turned their waters into blood and destroyed their fish. 30 Their land brought forth frogs in the inner chambers of their kings. 31 He spoke, and there came *divers sorts of flies* and sciniphs in all their coasts. 32 He *gave them hail for rain,* a burning fire in their land. 33 And he destroyed their vineyards and their fig trees, and he broke in pieces the *trees* of their coasts. 34 He spoke, and the locust came and the bruchus of which there was no number. 35 And they devoured all the grass in their land and consumed all the fruit of their ground. 36 And he slew all the firstborn in their land, the firstfruits of all their labour.

37 And he brought them out with silver and gold, and there was not among their tribes one that was feeble. 38 Egypt was glad when they departed, for the fear of them lay upon them. 39 He spread a cloud for their protection and

eis per noctem. 40 Petierunt, et venit coturnix, et pane caeli saturavit eos. 41 Disrupit petram, et fluxerunt aquae; abierunt in sicco flumina 42 quoniam memor fuit verbi sancti sui quod habuit ad Abraham puerum suum. 43 Et eduxit populum suum in exultatione et electos suos in laetitia. 44 Et dedit illis regiones Gentium, et labores populorum possederunt 45 ut custodiant iustificationes eius et legem eius requirant.

Psalmus 105

Alleluia.

Confitemini Domino, quoniam bonus, quoniam in saeculum misericordia eius! 2 Quis loquetur potentias Domini? Auditas faciet omnes laudes eius? 3 Beati qui custodiunt iudicium et faciunt iustitiam in omni tempore.

4 Memento nostri, Domine, in beneplacito populi tui. Visita nos in salutari tuo 5 ad videndum in bonitate electorum tuorum, ad laetandum in laetitia gentis tuae, ut lauderis cum hereditate tua. 6 Peccavimus cum patribus nostris; iniuste egimus; iniquitatem fecimus. 7 Patres nostri in Aegypto non

fire to give them light in the night. 40 They asked, and the quail came, and he filled them with the bread of heaven. 41 He opened the rock, and waters flowed; rivers ran down in the dry land 42 because he remembered his holy word which he had spoken to his servant Abraham. 43 And he brought forth his people with joy and his chosen with gladness. 44 And he gave them the lands of the Gentiles, and they possessed the labours of the people 45 that they might observe his justifications and seek after his law.

Psalm 105

Confitemini Domino. A confession of the manifold sins and ingratitudes of the Israelites.

Alleluia.

Give glory to the Lord, for he is good, for his mercy endureth for ever! 2 Who shall declare the powers of the Lord? *Who* shall *set forth* all his praises? 3 Blessed are they that keep judgment and do justice at all times.

4 Remember us, O Lord, in the favour of thy people. Visit us with thy salvation 5 that we may see the good of thy chosen, that we may rejoice in the joy of thy nation, that thou mayst be praised with thy inheritance. 6 We have sinned with our fathers; we have acted unjustly; we have wrought iniquity. 7 Our fathers understood not thy wonders in Egypt;

intellexerunt mirabilia tua; non fuerunt memores multitudinis misericordiae tuae, et inritaverunt ascendentes in mare, Mare Rubrum. 8 Et salvavit eos propter nomen suum ut notam faceret potentiam suam. 9 Et increpuit Mare Rubrum, et exsiccatum est, et deduxit eos in abyssis sicut in deserto. 10 Et salvavit eos de manu odientium, et redemit eos de manu inimici. 11 Et operuit aqua tribulantes eos; unus ex eis non remansit. 12 Et crediderunt verbis eius, et laudaverunt laudem eius.

13 Cito fecerunt; obliti sunt operum eius, et non sustinuerunt consilium eius. 14 Et concupierunt concupiscentiam in deserto, et temptaverunt Deum in inaquoso. 15 Et dedit eis petitionem ipsorum et misit saturitatem in animas eorum. 16 Et inritaverunt Mosen in castris, Aaron, sanctum Domini. 17 Aperta est terra et degluttivit Dathan et operuit super congregationem Abiron. 18 Et exarsit ignis in synagoga eorum; flamma conbusit peccatores. 19 Et fecerunt vitulum in Choreb, et adoraverunt sculptile. 20 Et mutaverunt gloriam suam in similitudinem vituli comedentis faenum. 21 Obliti sunt Deum qui salvavit eos, qui fecit magnalia in Aegypto, 22 mirabilia in terra Cham, terribilia in Mari Rubro.

23 Et dixit ut disperderet eos, si non Moses, electus eius, stetisset in confractione in conspectu eius ut averteret iram eius ne disperderet eos. 24 Et pro nihilo habuerunt terram desiderabilem. Non crediderunt verbo eius, 25 et murmuraverunt in tabernaculis suis. Non exaudierunt vocem Domini. 26 Et elevavit manum suam super eos ut prosterneret eos in deserto 27 et ut deiceret semen eorum in nationibus et

they remembered not the multitude of thy *mercies,* and they provoked to wrath going up to the sea, *even* the Red Sea. 8 And he saved them for his own name's sake that he might make his power known. 9 And he rebuked the Red Sea and it was dried up, and he led them through the depths as in a wilderness. 10 And he saved them from the hand of them that hated them, and he redeemed them from the hand of the enemy. 11 And the water covered them that afflicted them; there was not one of them left. 12 And they believed his words, and they sang his praises.

13 They had quickly done; they forgot his works, and they waited not for his counsel. 14 And they coveted their desire in the desert, and they tempted God in the place without water. 15 And he gave them their request and sent fulness into their souls. 16 And they provoked Moses in the camp, Aaron, the holy one of the Lord. 17 The earth opened and swallowed up Dathan and covered the congregation of Abiram. 18 And a fire was kindled in their congregation; the flame burned the wicked. 19 They made also a calf in Horeb, and they adored the graven thing. 20 And they changed their glory into the likeness of a calf that eateth grass. 21 They forgot God who saved them, who had done great things in Egypt, 22 wondrous works in the land of Ham, terrible things in the Red Sea.

23 And he said that he would destroy them, had not Moses, his chosen, stood before him in the breach to turn away his wrath lest he should destroy them. 24 And they set at nought the desirable land. They believed not his word, 25 and they murmured in their tents. They hearkened not to the voice of the Lord. 26 And he lifted up his hand over them to overthrow them in the desert 27 and to cast down their seed

dispergeret eos in regionibus. 28 Et initiati sunt Beelphegor et comederunt sacrificia mortuorum. 29 Et inritaverunt eum in adinventionibus suis, et multiplicata est in eis ruina. 30 Et stetit Finees et placavit, et cessavit quassatio. 31 Et reputatum est ei in iustitiam, in generatione et generationem usque in sempiternum. 32 Et inritaverunt eum ad Aquas Contradictionis, et vexatus est Moses propter eos 33 quia exacerbaverunt spiritum eius et distinxit in labiis suis. 34 Non disperdiderunt gentes quas dixit Dominus illis. 35 Et commixti sunt inter Gentes et didicerunt opera eorum 36 et servierunt sculptilibus eorum, et factum est illis in scandalum. 37 Et immolaverunt filios suos et filias suas daemoniis. 38 Et effuderunt sanguinem innocentem, sanguinem filiorum suorum et filiarum suarum quas sacrificaverunt sculptilibus Chanaan. Et infecta est terra in sanguinibus 39 et contaminata est in operibus eorum, et fornicati sunt in adinventionibus suis. 40 Et iratus est furore Dominus in populo suo, et abominatus est hereditatem suam. 41 Et tradidit eos in manus gentium, et dominati sunt eorum qui oderant eos. 42 Et tribulaverunt eos inimici eorum, et humiliati sunt sub manibus eorum.

43 Saepe liberavit eos, ipsi autem exacerbaverunt eum in consilio suo, et humiliati sunt in iniquitatibus suis. 44 Et vidit cum tribularentur, et audivit orationem eorum. 45 Et memor fuit testamenti sui et paenituit eum secundum multitudinem misericordiae suae. 46 Et dedit eos in misericordias in conspectu omnium qui ceperant eos.

among the nations and to scatter them in the countries. 28 They also were initiated to Baalpeor and ate the sacrifices of the dead. 29 And they provoked him with their inventions, and destruction was multiplied among them. 30 Then Phinehas stood up and pacified him, and the slaughter ceased. 31 And it was reputed to him unto justice, to generation and generation for evermore. 32 They provoked him also at the Waters of Contradiction, and Moses was afflicted for their sakes 33 because they exasperated his spirit and he distinguished with his lips.

34 They did not destroy the nations of which the Lord spoke unto them. 35 And they were mingled among the heathens and learned their works 36 and served their idols, and it became a stumbling block to them. 37 And they sacrificed their sons and their daughters to devils. 38 And they shed innocent blood, the blood of their sons and of their daughters which they sacrificed to the idols of Canaan. And the land was polluted with blood 39 and was defiled with their works, and they went aside after their own inventions. 40 And the Lord was *exceedingly angry* with his people, and he abhorred his inheritance. 41 And he delivered them into the hands of the nations, and they that hated them had dominion over them. 42 And their enemies afflicted them, and they were humbled under their hands.

43 Many times did he deliver them, but they provoked him with their counsel, and they were brought low by their iniquities. 44 And he saw when they were in tribulation, and he heard their prayer. 45 And he was mindful of his covenant and repented according to the multitude of his mercies. 46 And he gave them unto mercies in the sight of all those that had made them captives.

47 Salvos fac nos, Domine, Deus noster, et congrega nos de nationibus ut confiteamur nomini tuo sancto et gloriemur in laude tua. 48 Benedictus Dominus, Deus Israhel, a saeculo et usque in saeculum, et dicet omnis populus, "Fiat; fiat."

Psalmus 106

Alleluia.

Confitemini Domino, quoniam bonus, quoniam in saeculum misericordia eius. 2 Dicant qui redempti sunt a Domino, quos redemit de manu inimici et de regionibus congregavit eos 3 a solis ortu et occasu, ab aquilone et mari.

4 Erraverunt in solitudine, in inaquoso. Viam civitatis habitaculi non invenerunt. 5 Esurientes et sitientes; anima eorum in ipsis defecit. 6 Et clamaverunt ad Dominum cum tribularentur, et de necessitatibus eorum eripuit eos. 7 Et deduxit eos in viam rectam ut irent in civitatem habitationis. 8 Confiteantur Domino misericordiae eius et mirabilia

47 Save us, O Lord, our God, and gather us from among the nations that we may give thanks to thy holy name and may glory in thy praise. 48 Blessed be the Lord, the God of Israel, from everlasting to everlasting, and let all the people say, "So be it; so be it."

Psalm 106

Confitemini Domino. All are invited to give thanks to God for his perpetual providence over men.

Alleluia.

Give glory to the Lord, for he is good, for his mercy endureth for ever. 2 Let them say so that have been redeemed by the Lord, whom he hath redeemed from the hand of the enemy and gathered out of the countries 3 from the rising and from the setting of the sun, from the north and from the sea.

4 They wandered in a wilderness, in a place without water. They found not the way of a city for their habitation. 5 They were hungry and thirsty; their soul fainted in them. 6 And they cried to the Lord in their tribulation, and he delivered them out of their distresses. 7 And he led them into the right way that they might go to a city of habitation. 8 Let the mercies of the Lord give glory to him and his wonderful works

eius filiis hominum, 9 quia satiavit animam inanem et animam esurientem satiavit bonis, 10 sedentes in tenebris et umbra mortis, vinctos in mendicitate et ferro. 11 Quia exacerbaverunt eloquia Dei et consilium Altissimi inritaverunt 12 et humiliatum est in laboribus cor eorum, infirmati sunt nec fuit qui adiuvaret. 13 Et clamaverunt ad Dominum cum tribularentur, et de necessitatibus eorum liberavit eos. 14 Et eduxit eos de tenebris et umbra mortis et vincula eorum disrupit.

15 Confiteantur Domino misericordiae eius et mirabilia eius filiis hominum 16 quia contrivit portas aereas et vectes ferreos confregit. 17 Suscepit eos de via iniquitatis eorum, propter iniustitias enim suas humiliati sunt. 18 Omnem escam abominata est anima eorum, et adpropinquaverunt usque ad portas mortis. 19 Et clamaverunt ad Dominum cum tribularentur, et de necessitatibus eorum liberavit eos. 20 Misit verbum suum et sanavit eos et eripuit eos de interitionibus eorum.

21 Confiteantur Domino misericordiae eius et mirabilia eius filiis hominum. 22 Et sacrificent sacrificium laudis et adnuntient opera eius in exultatione. 23 Qui descendunt mare in navibus, facientes operationem in aquis multis, 24 ipsi viderunt opera Domini et mirabilia eius in profundo. 25 Dixit, et stetit spiritus procellae, et exaltati sunt fluctus eius. 26 Ascendunt usque ad caelos, et descendunt usque ad abyssos. Anima eorum in malis tabescebat. 27 Turbati sunt et moti

to the children of men, 9 for he hath satisfied the empty soul and hath filled the hungry soul with good things, 10 *such as* sat in darkness and in the shadow of death, bound in want and in iron. 11 Because they had exasperated the words of God and provoked the counsel of the Most High 12 and their heart was humbled with labours, they were weakened, and there was none to help them. 13 Then they cried to the Lord in their affliction, and he delivered them out of their distresses. 14 And he brought them out of darkness and the shadow of death and broke their bonds in sunder.

15 Let the mercies of the Lord give glory to him and his wonderful works to the children of men 16 because he hath broken gates of brass and burst iron bars. 17 He took them out of the way of their iniquity, for they were brought low for their injustices. 18 Their soul abhorred all manner of meat, and they drew nigh even to the gates of death. 19 And they cried to the Lord in their affliction, and he delivered them out of their distresses. 20 He sent his word and healed them and delivered them from their destructions.

21 Let the mercies of the Lord give glory to him and his wonderful works to the children of men. 22 And let them sacrifice the sacrifice of praise and declare his works with joy. 23 They that go down to the sea in ships, doing business in the great waters, 24 these have seen the works of the Lord and his wonders in the deep. 25 He said *the word,* and there arose a storm of wind, and the waves thereof were lifted up. 26 They mount up to the heavens, and they go down to the depths. Their soul pined away with evils. 27 They were trou-

sunt sicut ebrius, et omnis sapientia eorum devorata est. 28 Et clamaverunt ad Dominum cum tribularentur, et de necessitatibus eorum eduxit eos, 29 et statuit procellam eius in auram, et siluerunt fluctus eius. 30 Et laetati sunt quia siluerunt, et deduxit eos in portum voluntatis eorum.

31 Confiteantur Domino misericordiae eius et mirabilia eius filiis hominum. 32 Et exaltent eum in ecclesia plebis et in cathedra seniorum laudent eum. 33 Posuit flumina in desertum et exitus aquarum in sitim, 34 terram fructiferam in salsuginem, a malitia inhabitantium in ea. 35 Posuit desertum in stagna aquarum et terram sine aqua in exitus aquarum 36 et conlocavit illic esurientes, et constituerunt civitatem habitationis. 37 Et seminaverunt agros et plantaverunt vineas, et fecerunt fructum nativitatis. 38 Et benedixit eis, et multiplicati sunt nimis, et iumenta eorum non minoravit. 39 Et pauci facti sunt, et vexati sunt a tribulatione malorum et dolore. 40 Effusa est contemptio super principes, et errare fecit eos in invio et non in via. 41 Et adiuvit pauperem de inopia et posuit sicut oves familias.

42 Videbunt recti et laetabuntur, et omnis iniquitas oppilabit os suum. 43 Quis sapiens et custodiet haec et intelleget misericordias Domini?

bled and reeled like a drunken man, and all their wisdom was swallowed up. 28 And they cried to the Lord in their affliction, and he brought them out of their distresses, 29 and he turned the storm into a breeze, and its waves were still. 30 And they rejoiced because they were still, and he brought them to the haven which they wished for.

31 Let the mercies of the Lord give glory to him and his wonderful works to the children of men. 32 And let them exalt him in the church of the people and praise him in the chair of the ancients. 33 He hath turned rivers into a wilderness and the sources of waters into dry ground, 34 a fruitful land into barrenness, for the wickedness of them that dwell therein. 35 He hath turned a wilderness into pools of waters and a *dry* land into water springs 36 and hath placed there the hungry, and they made a city for their habitation. 37 And they sowed fields and planted vineyards, and they yielded fruit of birth. 38 And he blessed them, and they were multiplied exceedingly, and their cattle he *suffered* not *to* decrease. 39 Then they were brought to be few, and they were afflicted through the trouble of evils and sorrow. 40 Contempt was poured forth upon their princes, and he caused them to wander where there was no passing and out of the way. 41 And he helped the poor out of poverty and made him families like *a flock of* sheep.

42 The just shall see and shall rejoice, and all iniquity shall stop her mouth. 43 Who is wise and will keep these things and will understand the mercies of the Lord?

Psalmus 107

Canticum psalmi ipsi David.

2 Paratum cor meum, Deus. Paratum cor meum; cantabo et psallam in gloria mea. 3 Exsurge, gloria mea! Exurge psalterium et cithara! Exsurgam diluculo. 4 Confitebor tibi in populis, Domine, et psallam tibi in nationibus, 5 quia magna super caelos misericordia tua et usque ad nubes veritas tua. 6 Exaltare super caelos, Deus, et super omnem terram gloria tua 7 ut liberentur dilecti tui. Salvum fac dextera tua, et exaudi me.

8 Deus locutus est in sancto suo. Exaltabo, et dividam Sicima, et Convallem Tabernaculorum dimetiar. 9 Meus est Galaad, et meus est Manasse, et Effraim susceptio capitis mei. Iuda rex meus, 10 Moab lebes spei meae. In Idumeam extendam calciamentum meum. Mihi alienigenae amici facti sunt.

11 Quis deducet me in civitatem munitam? Quis deducet me usque in Idumeam? 12 Nonne tu, Deus, qui reppulisti

Psalm 107

Paratum cor meum. The prophet praiseth God for benefits received.

A canticle of a psalm for David himself.

2 My heart is ready, O God. My heart is ready; I will sing and will give praise with my glory. 3 Arise, my glory! Arise, psaltery and harp! I will arise in the morning early. 4 I will praise thee, O Lord, among the people, and I will sing unto thee among the nations, 5 for thy mercy is great above the heavens and thy truth even unto the clouds. 6 Be thou exalted, O God, above the heavens and thy glory over all the earth 7 that thy beloved may be delivered. Save with thy right hand, and hear me.

8 God hath spoken in his holiness. I will rejoice, and I will divide Shechem, and I will mete out the Vale of Tabernacles. 9 Gilead is mine, and Manasseh is mine, and Ephraim the protection of my head. Judah is my king, 10 Moab the pot of my hope. Over Edom I will stretch out my shoe. The aliens are become my friends.

11 Who will bring me into the strong city? Who will lead me into Edom? 12 Wilt not thou, O God, who hast cast

nos? Et non exibis, Deus, in virtutibus nostris? 13 Da nobis auxilium de tribulatione, quia vana salus hominis. 14 In
Deo faciemus virtutem, et ipse ad nihilum deducet inimicos
nostros.

Psalmus 108

In finem. David psalmus.

2 Deus, laudem meam ne tacueris, quia os peccatoris et
os dolosi super me apertum est. 3 Locuti sunt adversum me
lingua dolosa, et sermonibus odii circuierunt me et expugnaverunt me gratis. 4 Pro eo ut me diligerent, detrahebant
mihi, ego autem orabam. 5 Et posuerunt adversus me mala
pro bonis et odium pro dilectione mea.

6 Constitue super eum peccatorem, et diabulus stet a dextris eius. 7 Cum iudicatur, exeat condemnatus, et oratio eius
fiat in peccatum. 8 Fiant dies eius pauci, et episcopatum eius

us off? And wilt not thou, O God, go forth with our armies? 13 O grant us help from trouble, for vain is the help of man. 14 Through God we shall do mightily, and he will bring our enemies to nothing.

Psalm 108

Deus, laudem meam. David in the person of Christ prayeth against his persecutors, more especially the traitor Judas, foretelling and approving his just punishment for his obstinacy in sin and final impenitence.

U nto the end. A psalm for David.

2 O God, be not thou silent in my praise, for the mouth of the wicked and the mouth of the deceitful man is opened against me. 3 They have spoken against me with deceitful tongues, and they have compassed me about with words of hatred and have fought against me without cause. 4 Instead of *making me a return of love,* they detracted me, but I *gave myself to prayer.* 5 And they repaid me evil for good and hatred for my love.

6 Set thou the sinner over him, and may the devil stand at his right hand. 7 When he is judged, may he go out condemned, and may his prayer be turned to sin. 8 May his days

accipiat alter. 9 Fiant filii eius orfani et uxor eius vidua. 10 Nutantes transferantur filii eius et mendicent, et eiciantur de habitationibus suis. 11 Scrutetur fenerator omnem substantiam eius, et diripiant alieni labores eius. 12 Non sit illi adiutor nec sit qui misereatur pupillis eius. 13 Fiant nati eius in interitum; in generatione una deleatur nomen eius. 14 In memoriam redeat iniquitas patrum eius in conspectu Domini, et peccatum matris eius non deleatur. 15 Fiant contra Dominum semper, et dispereat de terra memoria eorum 16 pro eo quod non est recordatus facere misericordiam 17 et persecutus est hominem inopem et mendicum et conpunctum corde, mortificare. 18 Et dilexit maledictionem, et veniet ei, et noluit benedictionem, et elongabitur ab eo. Et induit maledictionem sicut vestimentum, et intravit sicut aqua in interiora eius et sicut oleum in ossibus eius. 19 Fiat ei sicut vestimentum quo operitur et sicut zona qua semper praecingitur.

20 Hoc opus eorum qui detrahunt mihi apud Dominum et qui loquuntur mala adversus animam meam. 21 Et tu, Domine, Domine, fac mecum propter nomen tuum quia suavis misericordia tua. Libera me, 22 quia egenus et pauper ego sum et cor meum turbatum est intra me. 23 Sicut umbra cum declinat ablatus sum, et excussus sum sicut lucustae. 24 Genua mea infirmata sunt a ieiunio, et caro mea inmutata est propter oleum. 25 Et ego factus sum obprobrium illis;

be few, and his bishopric let another take. 9 May his children be fatherless and his wife a widow. 10 Let his children be carried about vagabonds and beg, and let them be cast out of their dwellings. 11 May the usurer search all his substance, and let strangers plunder his labours. 12 May there be none to help him nor none to pity his fatherless offspring. 13 May his *posterity be cut off;* in one generation may his name be blotted out. 14 May the iniquity of his fathers be remembered in the sight of the Lord, and let not the sin of his mother be blotted out. 15 May they be before the Lord continually, and let the memory of them perish from the earth 16 because he remembered not to shew mercy 17 but persecuted the poor man and the beggar and the broken in heart, to put him to death. 18 And he loved cursing, and it shall come unto him, and he would not have blessing, and it shall be far from him. And he put on cursing like a garment, and it went in like water into his entrails and like oil in his bones. 19 May it be unto him like a garment which covereth him and like a girdle with which he is girded continually.

20 This is the work of them who detract me before the Lord and who speak evils against my soul. 21 *But* thou, O Lord, Lord, do with me for thy name's sake because thy mercy is sweet. Do thou deliver me, 22 for I am poor and needy and my heart is troubled within me. 23 I am taken away like the shadow when it declineth, and I am shaken off as locusts. 24 My knees are weakened through fasting, and my flesh is changed for oil. 25 And I am become a reproach

viderunt me, et moverunt capita sua. 26 Adiuva me, Domine, Deus meus; salvum fac me secundum misericordiam tuam. 27 Et sciant quia manus tua haec et tu, Domine, fecisti eam. 28 Maledicent illi, et tu benedices. Qui insurgunt in me confundantur, servus autem tuus laetabitur. 29 Induantur qui detrahunt mihi pudore, et operiantur sicut deploide confusione sua. 30 Confitebor Domino nimis in ore meo, et in medio multorum laudabo eum 31 quia adstetit a dextris pauperis ut salvam faceret a persequentibus animam meam.

Psalmus 109

David psalmus.

Dixit Dominus Domino meo, "Sede a dextris meis donec ponam inimicos tuos scabillum pedum tuorum. 2 Virgam virtutis tuae emittet Dominus ex Sion; dominare in medio

to them; they saw me, and they shaked their heads. 26 Help me, O Lord, my God; save me according to thy mercy. 27 And let them know that this is thy hand and that thou, O Lord, hast done it. 28 They will curse, and thou wilt bless. Let them that rise up against me be confounded, but thy servant shall rejoice. 29 Let them that detract me be clothed with shame, and let them be covered with their confusion as with a double cloak. 30 I will give great thanks to the Lord with my mouth, and in the midst of many I will praise him 31 because he hath stood at the right hand of the poor to save my soul from persecutors.

Psalm 109

Dixit Dominus. Christ's exaltation and everlasting priesthood.

A psalm for David.

The Lord said to my Lord, "Sit thou at my right hand until I make thy enemies thy footstool. 2 The Lord will send forth the sceptre of thy power out of Zion; rule thou in the

inimicorum tuorum. 3 Tecum principium in die virtutis tuae, in splendoribus sanctorum; ex utero ante Luciferum genui te."

4 Iuravit Dominus, et non paenitebit eum, "Tu es sacerdos in aeternum secundum ordinem Melchisedech." 5 Dominus a dextris tuis confregit in die irae suae reges. 6 Iudicabit in nationibus; implebit cadavera; conquassabit capita in terra multorum. 7 De torrente in via bibet; propterea exaltabit caput.

Psalmus 110

Alleluia.

Confitebor tibi, Domine, in toto corde meo in consilio iustorum et congregatione. 2 Magna opera Domini, exquisita in omnes voluntates eius. 3 Confessio et magnificentia opus eius, et iustitia eius manet in saeculum saeculi. 4 Memoriam fecit mirabilium suorum, misericors et miserator Dominus. 5 Escam dedit timentibus se. Memor erit in saeculum testamenti sui. 6 Virtutem operum suorum adnuntia-

midst of thy enemies. 3 With thee is the principality in the day of thy strength, in the brightness of the saints; from the womb before the Day Star I begot thee."

4 The Lord hath sworn, and he will not repent, "Thou art a priest for ever according to the order of Melchizedek." 5 The Lord at thy right hand hath broken kings in the day of his wrath. 6 He shall judge among nations; he shall fill ruins; he shall crush the heads in the land of many. 7 He shall drink of the torrent in the way; therefore shall he lift up the head.

Psalm 110

Confitebor tibi, Domine. God is to be praised for his graces and benefits to his church.

Alleluia.

I will praise thee, O Lord, with my whole heart in the council of the just and in the congregation. 2 Great are the works of the Lord, sought out according to all his wills. 3 His work is praise and magnificence, and his justice continueth for ever and ever. 4 He hath made a remembrance of his wonderful works, being a merciful and gracious Lord. 5 He hath given food to them that fear him. He will be mindful for ever of his covenant. 6 He will shew forth to his people

bit populo suo [7] ut det illis hereditatem Gentium. Opera manuum eius veritas et iudicium. [8] Fidelia omnia mandata eius, confirmata in saeculum saeculi, facta in veritate et aequitate. [9] Redemptionem misit populo suo; mandavit in aeternum testamentum suum. Sanctum et terribile nomen eius. [10] Initium sapientiae timor Domini, intellectus bonus omnibus facientibus eum. Laudatio eius manet in saeculum saeculi.

Psalmus III

Alleluia. Reversionis Aggei et Zacchariae.

Beatus vir qui timet Dominum. In mandatis eius volet nimis. [2] Potens in terra erit semen eius; generatio rectorum benedicetur. [3] Gloria et divitiae in domo eius, et iustitia eius manet in saeculum saeculi. [4] Exortum est in tenebris lumen rectis; misericors et miserator et iustus. [5] Iucundus homo qui miseretur et commodat; disponet sermones suos in iudicio [6] quia in aeternum non commovebitur. [7] In memoria aeterna erit iustus; ab auditione mala non timebit. Paratum

the power of his works 7 that he may give them the inheritance of the Gentiles. The works of his hands are truth and judgment. 8 All his commandments are faithful, confirmed for ever and ever, made in truth and equity. 9 He hath sent redemption to his people; he hath commanded his covenant for ever. Holy and terrible is his name. 10 The fear of the Lord is the beginning of wisdom, a good understanding to all that do it. His praise continueth for ever and ever.

Psalm 111

Beatus vir. The good man is happy.

Alleluia. Of the returning of Haggai and Zechariah.

Blessed is the man that feareth the Lord. He shall delight exceedingly in his commandments. 2 His seed shall be mighty upon earth; the generation of the righteous shall be blessed. 3 Glory and wealth shall be in his house, and his justice remaineth for ever and ever. 4 To the righteous a light is risen up in darkness; he is merciful and compassionate and just. 5 Acceptable is the man that sheweth mercy and lendeth; he shall order his words with judgment 6 because he shall not be moved for ever. 7 The just shall be in everlasting remembrance; he shall not fear the evil hearing. His heart is

cor eius sperare in Domino. 8 Confirmatum est cor eius; non commovebitur donec dispiciat inimicos suos. 9 Dispersit; dedit pauperibus. Iustitia eius manet in saeculum saeculi. Cornu eius exaltabitur in gloria. 10 Peccator videbit et irascetur; dentibus suis fremet et tabescet. Desiderium peccatorum peribit.

Psalmus 112

Alleluia.

Laudate, pueri, Dominum! Laudate nomen Domini. 2 Sit nomen Domini benedictum ex hoc, nunc et usque in saeculum. 3 A solis ortu usque ad occasum, laudabile nomen Domini. 4 Excelsus super omnes gentes Dominus et super caelos gloria eius.

5 Quis sicut Dominus, Deus noster, qui in altis habitat 6 et humilia respicit in caelo et in terra, 7 suscitans a terra inopem et de stercore erigens pauperem 8 ut conlocet eum

ready to hope in the Lord. 8 His heart is strengthened; he shall not be moved until he look over his enemies. 9 He hath distributed; he hath given to the poor. His justice remaineth for ever and ever. His horn shall be exalted in glory. 10 The wicked shall see and shall be angry; he shall gnash with his teeth and pine away. The desire of the wicked shall perish.

Psalm 112

Laudate, pueri. God is to be praised for his regard to the poor and humble.

Alleluia.

Praise the Lord, ye children! Praise ye the name of the Lord. 2 Blessed be the name of the Lord from henceforth, now and for ever. 3 From the rising of the sun unto the going down *of the same,* the name of the Lord is worthy of praise. 4 The Lord is high above all nations and his glory above the heavens.

5 Who is as the Lord, our God, who dwelleth on high 6 and looketh down on the low things in heaven and in earth, 7 raising up the needy from the earth and lifting up the poor out of the dunghill 8 that he may place him with princes,

cum principibus, cum principibus populi sui, 9 qui habitare facit sterilem in domo matrem filiorum laetantem?

Psalmus 113

Alleluia.

In exitu Israhel de Aegypto, domus Iacob de populo bar-baro, 2 facta est Iudaea sanctificatio eius, Israhel potestas eius. 3 Mare vidit et fugit; Iordanis conversus est retrorsum. 4 Montes exultaverunt ut arietes et colles sicut agni ovium. 5 Quid est tibi, mare, quod fugisti, et tu, Iordanis, quia conversus es retrorsum, 6 montes, exultastis sicut arietes, et colles, sicut agni ovium? 7 A facie Domini mota est terra, a facie Dei Iacob, 8 qui convertit petram in stagna aquarum et rupem in fontes aquarum.

9 Non nobis, Domine, non nobis sed nomini tuo da gloriam 10 super misericordia tua et veritate tua, nequando dicant

with the princes of his people, 9 who maketh a barren woman to dwell in a house the joyful mother of children?

Psalm 113

In exitu Israel. God hath shewn his power in delivering his people. Idols are vain. The Hebrews divide this into two psalms.

Alleluia.

When Israel went out of Egypt, the house of Jacob from a barbarous people, 2 Judea was made his sanctuary, Israel his dominion. 3 The sea saw and fled; Jordan was turned back. 4 The mountains skipped like rams and the hills like the lambs of the flock. 5 What ailed thee, O thou sea, that thou didst flee, and thou, O Jordan, that thou wast turned back, 6 ye mountains, that ye skipped like rams, and ye hills, like lambs of the flock? 7 At the presence of the Lord the earth was moved, at the presence of the God of Jacob, 8 who turned the rock into pools of water and the stony hill into fountains of waters.

Here the Hebrews begin Psalm 115

9 Not to us, O Lord, not to us, but to thy name give glory 10 for thy mercy and for thy truth's sake, lest the Gen-

Gentes, "Ubi est Deus eorum?" 11 Deus autem noster in caelo; omnia quaecumque voluit fecit. 12 Simulacra Gentium argentum et aurum, opera manuum hominum. 13 Os habent et non loquentur; oculos habent et non videbunt. 14 Aures habent et non audient; nares habent et non odorabuntur. 15 Manus habent et non palpabunt; pedes habent et non ambulabunt, non clamabunt in gutture suo. 16 Similes illis fiant qui faciunt ea et omnes qui confidunt in eis.

17 Domus Israhel speravit in Domino; adiutor eorum et protector eorum est. 18 Domus Aaron speravit in Domino; adiutor eorum et protector eorum est. 19 Qui timent Dominum speraverunt in Domino; adiutor eorum et protector eorum est. 20 Dominus memor fuit nostri et benedixit nobis. Benedixit domui Israhel; benedixit domui Aaron. 21 Benedixit omnibus qui timent Dominum, pusillis cum maioribus.

22 Adiciat Dominus super vos, super vos et super filios vestros. 23 Benedicti vos a Domino, qui fecit caelum et terram. 24 Caelum caeli Domino, terram autem dedit filiis hominum. 25 Non mortui laudabunt te, Domine, neque omnes qui descendunt in infernum, 26 sed nos qui vivimus benedicimus Domino, ex hoc nunc et usque in saeculum.

tiles should say, "Where is their God?" 11 But our God is in heaven; he hath done all things whatsoever he would. 12 The idols of the Gentiles are silver and gold, the works of the hands of men. 13 They have mouths and *speak* not; they have eyes and *see* not. 14 They have ears and *hear* not; they have noses and *smell* not. 15 They have hands and *feel* not; they have feet and *walk* not, neither shall they cry out through their throat. 16 Let them that make them become like unto them and all such as trust in them.

17 The house of Israel hath hoped in the Lord; he is their helper and their protector. 18 The house of Aaron hath hoped in the Lord; he is their helper and their protector. 19 They that fear the Lord have hoped in the Lord; he is their helper and their protector. 20 The Lord hath been mindful of us and hath blessed us. He hath blessed the house of Israel; he hath blessed the house of Aaron. 21 He hath blessed all that fear the Lord, *both* little *and* great.

22 May the Lord add *blessings* upon you, upon you and upon your children. 23 Blessed be you of the Lord, who made heaven and earth. 24 The heaven of heaven is the Lord's, but the earth he has given to the children of men. 25 The dead shall not praise thee, O Lord, nor any of them that go down to hell, 26 but we that live bless the Lord, from this time now and for ever.

Psalmus 114

Alleluia.

Dilexi quoniam exaudiet Dominus vocem orationis meae, 2 quia inclinavit aurem suam mihi, et in diebus meis invocabo. 3 Circumdederunt me dolores mortis, et pericula inferni invenerunt me. Tribulationem et dolorem inveni, 4 et nomen Domini invocavi. O Domine, libera animam meam. 5 Misericors Dominus et iustus, et Deus noster miseretur. 6 Custodiens parvulos Dominus. Humiliatus sum, et liberavit me. 7 Convertere, anima mea, in requiem tuam, quia Dominus benefecit tibi, 8 quia eripuit animam meam de morte, oculos meos a lacrimis, pedes meos a lapsu. 9 Placebo Domino in regione vivorum.

Psalm 114

Dilexi. The prayer of a just man in affliction with a lively confidence in God.

Alleluia.

I have loved because the Lord will hear the voice of my prayer, 2 because he hath inclined his ear unto me, and in my days I will call upon him. 3 The sorrows of death have compassed me, and the perils of hell have found me. I met with trouble and sorrow, 4 and I called upon the name of the Lord. O Lord, deliver my soul. 5 The Lord is merciful and just, and our God sheweth mercy. 6 The Lord is the keeper of little ones. I was humbled, and he delivered me. 7 Turn, O my soul, into thy rest, for the Lord hath been bountiful to thee, 8 for he hath delivered my soul from death, my eyes from tears, my feet from falling. 9 I will please the Lord in the land of the living.

Psalmus 115

Alleluia.

Credidi; propter quod locutus sum, ego autem humiliatus sum nimis. 2 Ego dixi in excessu meo, "Omnis homo mendax." 3 Quid retribuam Domino pro omnibus quae retribuit mihi? 4 Calicem salutaris accipiam, et nomen Domini invocabo. 5 Vota mea Domino reddam coram omni populo eius.

6 Pretiosa in conspectu Domini mors sanctorum eius, 7 O Domine, quia ego servus tuus; ego servus tuus et filius ancillae tuae. Disrupisti vincula mea. 8 Tibi sacrificabo hostiam laudis, et nomen Domini invocabo. 9 Vota mea Domino reddam in conspectu omnis populi eius, 10 in atriis domus Domini, in medio tui, Hierusalem.

Psalm 115

Credidi. This in the Hebrew is joined with the foregoing psalm and continues to express the faith and gratitude of the psalmist.

Alleluia.

I have believed; therefore have I spoken, but I have been humbled exceedingly. 2 I said in my excess, "Every man is a liar." 3 What shall I render to the Lord for all the things that he hath rendered to me? 4 I will take the chalice of salvation, and I will call upon the name of the Lord. 5 I will pay my vows to the Lord before all his people.

6 Precious in the sight of the Lord is the death of his saints, 7 O Lord, for I am thy servant; I am thy servant and the son of thy handmaid. Thou hast broken my bonds. 8 I will sacrifice to thee the sacrifice of praise, and I will call upon the name of the Lord. 9 I will pay my vows to the Lord in the sight of all his people, 10 in the courts of the house of the Lord, in the midst of thee, O Jerusalem.

Psalmus 116

Alleluia.

Laudate Dominum, omnes gentes! Laudate eum, omnes populi! 2 Quoniam confirmata est super nos misericordia eius, et veritas Domini manet in saeculum.

Psalmus 117

Alleluia.

Confitemini Domino, quoniam bonus, quoniam in saeculum misericordia eius. 2 Dicat nunc Israhel quoniam bonus, quoniam in saeculum misericordia eius. 3 Dicat nunc domus Aaron quoniam in saeculum misericordia eius. 4 Dicant nunc qui timent Dominum quoniam in saeculum misericordia eius.

Psalm 116

Laudate Dominum. All nations are called upon to praise God
for his mercy and truth.

Alleluia.
   O Praise the Lord, all ye nations! Praise him, all ye people!
2 For his mercy is confirmed upon us, and the truth of the
Lord remaineth for ever.

Psalm 117

Confitemini Domino. The psalmist praiseth God for his delivery from evils, putteth his whole trust in him and foretelleth the coming of Christ.

Alleluia.
   Give praise to the Lord, for he is good, for his mercy endureth for ever. 2 Let Israel now say that he is good, that his
mercy endureth for ever. 3 Let the house of Aaron now say
that his mercy endureth for ever. 4 Let them that fear the
Lord now say that his mercy endureth for ever.

5 De tribulatione invocavi Dominum, et exaudivit me in latitudinem Dominus. 6 Dominus mihi adiutor; non timebo quid faciat mihi homo. 7 Dominus mihi adiutor, et ego despiciam inimicos meos. 8 Bonum est confidere in Domino quam confidere in homine. 9 Bonum est sperare in Domino quam sperare in principibus. 10 Omnes gentes circumierunt me, et in nomine Domini ultus sum in eos. 11 Circumdantes circumdederunt me, in nomine autem Domini ultus sum in eos. 12 Circumdederunt me sicut apes, et exarserunt sicut ignis in spinis, et in nomine Domini ultus sum in eos. 13 Inpulsus eversus sum ut caderem, et Dominus suscepit me.

14 Fortitudo mea et laudatio mea Dominus, et factus est mihi in salutem.

15 Vox exultationis et salutis in tabernaculis iustorum.

16 Dextera Domini fecit virtutem; dextera Domini exaltavit me; dextera Domini fecit virtutem. 17 Non moriar sed vivam et narrabo opera Domini.

18 Castigans castigavit me Dominus, et morti non tradidit me.

19 Aperite mihi portas iustitiae; ingressus in eas confitebor Domino. 20 Haec porta Domini; iusti intrabunt in eam.

21 Confitebor tibi quoniam exaudisti me et factus es mihi in salutem. 22 Lapidem quem reprobaverunt aedificantes, hic factus est in caput anguli. 23 A Domino factum est istud, et est mirabile in oculis nostris.

24 Haec est dies quam fecit Dominus; exultemus et laete-

5 In my trouble I called upon the Lord, and the Lord heard me *and enlarged me.* 6 The Lord is my helper; I will not fear what man can do unto me. 7 The Lord is my helper, and I will look over my enemies. 8 It is good to confide in the Lord rather than to have confidence in man. 9 It is good to trust in the Lord rather than to trust in princes. 10 All nations compassed me about, and in the name of the Lord I have been revenged on them. 11 Surrounding me they compassed me about, and in the name of the Lord I have been revenged on them. 12 They surrounded me like bees, and they burned like fire among thorns, and in the name of the Lord I was revenged on them. 13 Being pushed I was overturned that I might fall, but the Lord supported me.

14 The Lord is my strength and my praise, and he is become my salvation.

15 The voice of rejoicing and of salvation is in the tabernacles of the just.

16 The right hand of the Lord hath wrought strength; the right hand of the Lord hath exalted me; the right hand of the Lord hath wrought strength. 17 I shall not die but live and shall declare the works of the Lord.

18 The Lord chastising hath chastised me, but he hath not delivered me over to death.

19 Open ye to me the gates of justice; I will go in to them and give praise to the Lord. 20 This is the gate of the Lord; the just shall enter into it.

21 I will give glory to thee because thou hast heard me and art become my salvation. 22 The stone which the builders rejected, the same is become the head of the corner. 23 This is the Lord's doing, and it is wonderful in our eyes.

24 This is the day which the Lord hath made; let us be glad

mur in ea. 25 O Domine, salvum me fac. O Domine, bene prosperare.

26 Benedictus qui venit in nomine Domini. Benediximus vobis de domo Domini. 27 Deus Dominus, et inluxit nobis. Constituite diem sollemnem in condensis, usque ad cornu altaris.

28 Deus meus es tu, et confitebor tibi! Deus meus es tu, et exaltabo te. Confitebor tibi quoniam exaudisti me et factus es mihi in salutem.

29 Confitemini Domino, quoniam bonus, quoniam in saeculum misericordia eius.

Psalmus 118

Alleluia.

Aleph.

Beati inmaculati in via qui ambulant in lege Domini. 2 Beati qui scrutantur testimonia eius, in toto corde exquirunt eum, 3 non enim qui operantur iniquitatem in viis eius ambulaverunt. 4 Tu mandasti mandata tua custodiri nimis. 5 Utinam

and rejoice therein. 25 O Lord, save me. O Lord, give good success.

26 Blessed be he that cometh in the name of the Lord. We have blessed you out of the house of the Lord. 27 The Lord is God, and he hath shone upon us. Appoint a solemn day with shady boughs, even to the horn of the altar.

28 Thou art my God, and I will praise thee! Thou art my God, and I will exalt thee. I will praise thee because thou hast heard me and art become my salvation.

29 O praise ye the Lord, for he is good, for his mercy endureth for ever.

Psalm 118

Beati immaculati. Of the excellence of virtue consisting in
the love and observance of the commandments of God.

A lleluia.

ALEPH.

Blessed are the undefiled in the way who walk in the law of the Lord. 2 Blessed are they that search his testimonies, that seek him with their whole heart, 3 for they that work iniquity have not walked in his ways. 4 Thou hast commanded thy commandments to be kept most diligently. 5 O that

dirigantur viae meae ad custodiendas iustificationes tuas!
6 Tunc non confundar cum perspexero in omnibus mandatis
tuis. 7 Confitebor tibi in directione cordis in eo quod didici
iudicia iustitiae tuae. 8 Iustificationes tuas custodiam; non
me derelinquas usquequaque!

BETH.

9 In quo corrigit adulescentior viam suam? In custodiendo
sermones tuos. 10 In toto corde meo exquisivi te; non repellas me a mandatis tuis. 11 In corde meo abscondi eloquia tua
ut non peccem tibi. 12 Benedictus es, Domine; doce me iustificationes tuas. 13 In labiis meis pronuntiavi omnia iudicia oris tui. 14 In via testimoniorum tuorum delectatus sum
sicut in omnibus divitiis. 15 In mandatis tuis exercebor, et
considerabo vias tuas. 16 In iustificationibus tuis meditabor;
non obliviscar sermones tuos.

GIMEL.

17 Retribue servo tuo; vivifica me, et custodiam sermones
tuos. 18 Revela oculos meos, et considerabo mirabilia de lege
tua. 19 Incola ego sum in terra; non abscondas a me mandata
tua. 20 Concupivit anima mea desiderare iustificationes tuas
in omni tempore. 21 Increpasti superbos; maledicti qui de-
clinant a mandatis tuis. 22 Aufer a me obprobrium et
contemptum quia testimonia tua exquisivi, 23 etenim sederunt principes et adversum me loquebantur, servus autem

my ways may be directed to keep thy justifications! 6 Then shall I not be confounded when I shall look into all thy commandments. 7 I will praise thee with uprightness of heart when I shall have learned the judgments of thy justice. 8 I will keep thy justifications; O do not thou utterly forsake me!

BETH.

9 By what doth a young man correct his way? By observing thy words. 10 With my whole heart have I sought after thee; *let me* not *stray* from thy commandments. 11 Thy words have I hidden in my heart that I may not sin against thee. 12 Blessed art thou, O Lord; teach me thy justifications. 13 With my lips I have pronounced all the judgments of thy mouth. 14 I have been delighted in the way of thy testimonies as in all riches. 15 I will meditate on thy commandments, and I will consider thy ways. 16 I will think of thy justifications; I will not forget thy words.

GIMEL.

17 Give *bountifully* to thy servant; enliven me, and I shall keep thy words. 18 Open thou my eyes, and I will consider the wondrous things of thy law. 19 I am a sojourner on the earth; hide not thy commandments from me. 20 My soul hath coveted to long for thy justifications at all times. 21 Thou hast rebuked the proud; they are cursed who decline from thy commandments. 22 Remove from me reproach and contempt because I have sought after thy testimonies, 23 for princes sat and spoke against me, but thy servant was em-

tuus exercebatur in iustificationibus tuis, 24 nam et testimonia tua meditatio mea et consilium meum iustificationes
tuae.

DELETH.

25 Adhesit pavimento anima mea; vivifica me secundum verbum tuum. 26 Vias meas enuntiavi, et exaudisti me. Doce me
iustificationes tuas. 27 Viam iustificationum tuarum instrue
me, et exercebor in mirabilibus tuis. 28 Dormitavit anima
mea prae taedio; confirma me in verbis tuis. 29 Viam iniquitatis amove a me, et de lege tua miserere mei. 30 Viam veritatis elegi; iudicia tua non sum oblitus. 31 Adhesi testimoniis
tuis, Domine; noli me confundere. 32 Viam mandatorum
tuorum cucurri cum dilatasti cor meum.

HE.

33 Legem pone mihi, Domine, viam iustificationum tuarum,
et exquiram eam semper. 34 Da mihi intellectum, et scrutabor legem tuam, et custodiam illam in toto corde meo.
35 Deduc me in semitam mandatorum tuorum; quia ipsam
volui. 36 Inclina cor meum in testimonia tua et non in avaritiam. 37 Averte oculos meos ne videant vanitatem; in via tua
vivifica me. 38 Statue servo tuo eloquium tuum in timore
tuo. 39 Amputa obprobrium meum quod suspicatus sum,
quia iudicia tua iucunda. 40 Ecce: concupivi mandata tua; in
aequitate tua vivifica me.

ployed in thy justifications, 24 for thy testimonies are my meditation and thy justifications my counsel.

DALETH.

25 My soul hath cleaved to the pavement; quicken thou me according to thy word. 26 I have declared my ways, and thou hast heard me. Teach me thy justifications. 27 Make me to understand the way of thy justifications, and I shall be exercised in thy wondrous works. 28 My soul hath slumbered through *heaviness;* strengthen thou me in thy words. 29 Remove from me the way of iniquity, and out of thy law have mercy on me. 30 I have chosen the way of truth; thy judgments I have not forgotten. 31 I have stuck to thy testimonies, O Lord; put me not to shame. 32 I have run the way of thy commandments when thou didst enlarge my heart.

HE.

33 Set before me for a law the way of thy justifications, O Lord, and I will always seek after it. 34 Give me understanding, and I will search thy law, and I will keep it with my whole heart. 35 Lead me into the path of thy commandments; for this same I have desired. 36 Incline my heart into thy testimonies and not to covetousness. 37 Turn away my eyes that they may not behold vanity; quicken me in thy way. 38 Establish thy word to thy servant in thy fear. 39 Turn away my reproach which I have apprehended, for thy judgments are delightful. 40 Behold: I have longed after thy precepts; quicken me in thy justice.

Vav.

41 Et veniat super me misericordia tua, Domine, salutare tuum secundum eloquium tuum. 42 Et respondebo exprobrantibus mihi verbum: quia speravi in sermonibus tuis. 43 Et ne auferas de ore meo verbum veritatis usquequaque, quia in iudiciis tuis supersperavi. 44 Et custodiam legem tuam semper, in saeculum et in saeculum saeculi. 45 Et ambulabam in latitudine quia mandata tua exquisivi. 46 Et loquebar de testimoniis tuis in conspectu regum, et non confundebar. 47 Et meditabar in mandatis tuis, quae dilexi. 48 Et levavi manus meas ad mandata tua, quae dilexi, et exercebar in iustificationibus tuis.

Zai.

49 Memor esto verbi tui servo tuo in quo mihi spem dedisti. 50 Haec me consolata est in humilitate mea quia eloquium tuum vivificavit me. 51 Superbi inique agebant usquequaque, a lege autem tua non declinavi. 52 Memor fui iudiciorum tuorum a saeculo, Domine, et consolatus sum. 53 Defectio tenuit me prae peccatoribus derelinquentibus legem tuam. 54 Cantabiles mihi erant iustificationes tuae in loco peregrinationis meae. 55 Memor fui in nocte nominis tui, Domine, et custodivi legem tuam. 56 Haec facta est mihi quia iustificationes tuas exquisivi.

Vau.

41 Let thy mercy also come upon me, O Lord, thy salvation according to thy word. 42 *So* shall I answer them that reproach me *in any thing:* that I have trusted in thy words. 43 And take not thou the word of truth utterly out of my mouth, for in thy words I have hoped exceedingly. 44 *So* shall I always keep thy law, for ever and ever. 45 And I walked at large because I have sought after thy commandments. 46 And I spoke of thy testimonies before kings, and I was not ashamed. 47 I meditated also on thy commandments, which I loved. 48 And I lifted up my hands to thy commandments, which I loved, and I was exercised in thy justifications.

Zain.

49 Be thou mindful of thy word to thy servant in which thou hast given me hope. 50 This hath comforted me in my humiliation because thy word hath enlivened me. 51 The proud did iniquitously altogether, but I declined not from thy law. 52 I remembered, O Lord, thy judgments of old, and I was comforted. 53 A fainting hath taken hold of me because of the wicked that forsake thy law. 54 Thy justifications were the subject of my song in the place of my pilgrimage. 55 In the night I have remembered thy name, O Lord, and have kept thy law. 56 This happened to me because I sought after thy justifications.

Нетн.

57 Portio mea, Domine, dixi custodire legem tuam. 58 Deprecatus sum faciem tuam in toto corde meo; miserere mei secundum eloquium tuum. 59 Cogitavi vias meas et converti pedes meos in testimonia tua. 60 Paratus sum et non sum turbatus ut custodiam mandata tua. 61 Funes peccatorum circumplexi sunt me, et legem tuam non sum oblitus. 62 Media nocte surgebam ad confitendum tibi super iudicia iustificationis tuae. 63 Particeps ego sum omnium timentium te et custodientium mandata tua. 64 Misericordia tua, Domine, plena est terra; iustificationes tuas doce me.

Тетн.

65 Bonitatem fecisti cum servo tuo, Domine, secundum verbum tuum. 66 Bonitatem et disciplinam et scientiam doce me, quia mandatis tuis credidi. 67 Priusquam humiliarer ego deliqui; propterea eloquium tuum custodivi. 68 Bonus es tu, et in bonitate tua doce me iustificationes tuas. 69 Multiplicata est super me iniquitas superborum, ego autem in toto corde scrutabor mandata tua. 70 Coagulatum est sicut lac cor eorum, ego vero legem tuam meditatus sum. 71 Bonum mihi quia humiliasti me ut discam iustificationes tuas. 72 Bonum mihi lex oris tui super milia auri et argenti.

HETH.

57 O Lord, my portion, I have said I would keep thy law. 58 I entreated thy face with all my heart; have mercy on me according to thy word. 59 I have thought on my ways and turned my feet unto thy testimonies. 60 I am ready and am not troubled that I may keep thy commandments. 61 The cords of the wicked have encompassed me, *but* I have not forgotten thy law. 62 I rose at midnight to give praise to thee for the judgments of thy justification. 63 I am a partaker with all them that fear thee and that keep thy commandments. 64 The earth, O Lord, is full of thy mercy; teach me thy justifications.

TETH.

65 Thou hast done well with thy servant, O Lord, according to thy word. 66 Teach me goodness and discipline and knowledge, for I have believed thy commandments. 67 Before I was humbled I offended; therefore have I kept thy word. 68 Thou art good, and in thy goodness teach me thy justifications. 69 The iniquity of the proud hath been multiplied over me, but I will seek thy commandments with my whole heart. 70 Their heart is curdled like milk, but I have meditated on thy law. 71 It is good for me that thou hast humbled me that I may learn thy justifications. 72 The law of thy mouth is good to me above thousands of gold and silver.

Ioth.

73 Manus tuae fecerunt me et plasmaverunt me; da mihi intellectum, et discam mandata tua. 74 Qui timent te videbunt me et laetabuntur quia in verba tua supersperavi. 75 Cognovi, Domine, quia aequitas iudicia tua, et in veritate humiliasti me. 76 Fiat misericordia tua ut consoletur me secundum eloquium tuum servo tuo! 77 Veniant mihi miserationes tuae, et vivam, quia lex tua meditatio mea est. 78 Confundantur superbi quia iniuste fecerunt in me, ego autem exercebor in mandatis tuis. 79 Convertantur mihi timentes te et qui noverunt testimonia tua. 80 Fiat cor meum inmaculatum in iustificationibus tuis ut non confundar.

Caf.

81 Defecit in salutare tuum anima mea, et in verbum tuum supersperavi. 82 Defecerunt oculi mei in eloquium tuum, dicentes, "Quando consolaberis me?" 83 quia factus sum sicut uter in pruina. Iustificationes tuas non sum oblitus. 84 Quot sunt dies servi tui? Quando facies de persequentibus me iudicium? 85 Narraverunt mihi iniqui fabulationes sed non ut lex tua. 86 Omnia mandata tua veritas; inique persecuti sunt me; adiuva me. 87 Paulo minus consummaverunt me in terra, ego autem non dereliqui mandata tua. 88 Secundum misericordiam tuam vivifica me, et custodiam testimonia oris tui.

JOD.

73 Thy hands have made me and formed me; give me understanding, and I will learn thy commandments. 74 They that fear thee shall see me and shall be glad because I have greatly hoped in thy words. 75 I know, O Lord, that thy judgments are equity, and in thy truth thou hast humbled me. 76 O let thy mercy be for my comfort according to thy word unto thy servant! 77 Let thy *tender* mercies come unto me, and I shall live, for thy law is my meditation. 78 Let the proud be ashamed because they have done unjustly towards me, but I will be employed in thy commandments. 79 Let them that fear thee turn to me and they that know thy testimonies. 80 Let my heart be undefiled in thy justifications that I may not be confounded.

CAPH.

81 My soul hath fainted after thy salvation, and in thy word I have very much hoped. 82 My eyes have failed for thy word, saying, "When wilt thou comfort me?" 83 for I am become like a bottle in the frost. I have not forgotten thy justifications. 84 How many are the days of thy servant? When wilt thou execute judgment on them that persecute me? 85 The wicked have told me fables but not as thy law. 86 All thy statutes are truth; they have persecuted me unjustly; do thou help me. 87 They had almost made an end of me upon earth, but I have not forsaken thy commandments. 88 Quicken thou me according to thy mercy, and I shall keep the testimonies of thy mouth.

LAMED.

89 In aeternum, Domine, verbum tuum permanet in caelo, 90 in generationem et generationem veritas tua. Fundasti terram, et permanet. 91 Ordinatione tua perseverat dies, quoniam omnia serviunt tibi. 92 Nisi quod lex tua meditatio mea est, tunc forte perissem in humilitate mea. 93 In aeternum non obliviscar iustificationes tuas, quia in ipsis vivificasti me. 94 Tuus sum; ego salvum me fac, quoniam iustificationes tuas exquisivi. 95 Me expectaverunt peccatores ut perderent me; testimonia tua intellexi. 96 Omnis consummationis vidi finem; latum mandatum tuum nimis.

MEM.

97 Quomodo dilexi legem tuam, Domine! Tota die meditatio mea est. 98 Super inimicos meos prudentem me fecisti mandato tuo, quia in aeternum mihi est. 99 Super omnes docentes me intellexi quia testimonia tua meditatio mea est. 100 Super senes intellexi quia mandata tua quaesivi. 101 Ab omni via mala prohibui pedes meos ut custodiam verba tua. 102 A iudiciis tuis non declinavi quia tu legem posuisti mihi. 103 Quam dulcia faucibus meis eloquia tua! Super mel ori meo. 104 A mandatis tuis intellexi. Propterea odivi omnem viam iniquitatis.

LAMED.

89 For ever, O Lord, thy word standeth firm in heaven, 90 thy truth unto all generations. Thou hast founded the earth, and it continueth. 91 By thy ordinance the day goeth on, for all things serve thee. 92 Unless thy law had been my meditation, I had then perhaps perished in my abjection. 93 Thy justifications I will never forget, for by them thou hast given me life. 94 I am thine; save thou me, for I have sought thy justifications. 95 The wicked have waited for me to destroy me, *but* I have understood thy testimonies. 96 I have seen an end of all perfection; thy commandment is exceeding broad.

MEM.

97 O how have I loved thy law, O Lord! It is my meditation all the day. 98 Through thy commandment thou hast made me wiser than my enemies, for it is ever with me. 99 I have understood more than all my teachers because thy testimonies are my meditation. 100 I have had understanding above ancients because I have sought thy commandments. 101 I have restrained my feet from every evil way that I may keep thy words. 102 I have not declined from thy judgments because thou hast set me a law. 103 How sweet are thy words to my palate! More than honey to my mouth. 104 By thy commandments I have had understanding. Therefore have I hated every way of iniquity.

Nun.

105 Lucerna pedibus meis verbum tuum et lumen semitis meis. 106 Iuravi et statui custodire iudicia iustitiae tuae. 107 Humiliatus sum usquequaque, Domine. Vivifica me secundum verbum tuum. 108 Voluntaria oris mei beneplacita fac, Domine, et iudicia tua doce me. 109 Anima mea in manibus meis semper, et legem tuam non sum oblitus. 110 Posuerunt peccatores laqueum mihi, et de mandatis tuis non erravi. 111 Hereditate adquisivi testimonia tua in aeternum, quia exultatio cordis mei sunt. 112 Inclinavi cor meum ad faciendas iustificationes tuas in aeternum propter retributionem.

Samech.

113 Iniquos odio habui et legem tuam dilexi. 114 Adiutor et susceptor meus es tu, et in verbum tuum supersperavi. 115 Declinate a me, maligni, et scrutabor mandata Dei mei. 116 Suscipe me secundum eloquium tuum, et vivam, et non confundas me ab expectatione mea. 117 Adiuva me, et salvus ero, et meditabor in iustificationibus tuis semper. 118 Sprevisti omnes discedentes a iudiciis tuis, quia iniusta cogitatio eorum. 119 Praevaricantes reputavi omnes peccatores terrae; ideo dilexi testimonia tua. 120 Confige timore tuo carnes meas, a iudiciis enim tuis timui.

Nun.

105 Thy word is a lamp to my feet and a light to my paths.
106 I have sworn and am determined to keep the judgments
of thy justice. 107 I have been humbled, O Lord, exceedingly.
Quicken thou me according to thy word. 108 The free offerings of my mouth make acceptable, O Lord, and teach me
thy judgments. 109 My soul is continually in my hands, and I
have not forgotten thy law. 110 Sinners have laid a snare for
me, but I have not erred from thy precepts. 111 I have purchased thy testimonies for an inheritance for ever, because
they are the joy of my heart. 112 I have inclined my heart to
do thy justifications for ever for the reward.

Samech.

113 I have hated the unjust and have loved thy law. 114 Thou
art my helper and my protector, and in thy word I have
greatly hoped. 115 Depart from me, ye malignant, and I will
search the commandments of my God. 116 Uphold me according to thy word, and I shall live, and *let me not be confounded in* my expectation. 117 Help me, and I shall be saved,
and I will meditate always on thy justifications. 118 Thou
hast despised all them that fall off from thy judgments, for
their thought is unjust. 119 I have accounted all the sinners
of the earth prevaricators; therefore have I loved thy testimonies. 120 Pierce thou my flesh with thy fear, for I am afraid
of thy judgments.

AIN.

121 Feci iudicium et iustitiam; non tradas me calumniantibus me. 122 Suscipe servum tuum in bonum; non calumnientur me superbi. 123 Oculi mei defecerunt in salutare tuum et in eloquium iustitiae tuae. 124 Fac cum servo tuo secundum misericordiam tuam, et iustificationes tuas doce me. 125 Servus tuus sum ego; da mihi intellectum ut sciam testimonia tua. 126 Tempus faciendi, Domine. Dissipaverunt legem tuam. 127 Ideo dilexi mandata tua super aurum et topazion. 128 Propterea ad omnia mandata tua dirigebar. Omnem viam iniquam odio habui.

FE.

129 Mirabilia testimonia tua; ideo scrutata est ea anima mea. 130 Declaratio sermonum tuorum inluminat et intellectum dat parvulis. 131 Os meum aperui et adtraxi spiritum quia mandata tua desiderabam. 132 Aspice in me, et miserere mei secundum iudicium diligentium nomen tuum. 133 Gressus meos dirige secundum eloquium tuum, et non dominetur mei omnis iniustitia. 134 Redime me a calumniis hominum ut custodiam mandata tua. 135 Faciem tuam inlumina super servum tuum, et doce me iustificationes tuas. 136 Exitus aquarum deduxerunt oculi mei quia non custodierunt legem tuam.

AIN.

121 I have done judgment and justice; give me not up to them that slander me. 122 Uphold thy servant unto good; let not the proud calumniate me. 123 My eyes have fainted after thy salvation and for the word of thy justice. 124 Deal with thy servant according to thy mercy, and teach me thy justifications. 125 I am thy servant; give me understanding that I may know thy testimonies. 126 It is time, O Lord, to do. They have dissipated thy law. 127 Therefore have I loved thy commandments above gold and the topaz. 128 Therefore was I directed to all thy commandments. I have hated all wicked ways.

PHE.

129 Thy testimonies are wonderful; therefore my soul hath sought them. 130 The declaration of thy words giveth light and giveth understanding to little ones. 131 I opened my mouth and panted because I longed for thy commandments. 132 Look thou upon me, and have mercy on me according to the judgment of them that love thy name. 133 Direct my steps according to thy word, and let no iniquity have dominion over me. 134 Redeem me from the calumnies of men that I may keep thy commandments. 135 Make thy face to shine upon thy servant, and teach me thy justifications. 136 My eyes have sent forth springs of water because they have not kept thy law.

SADE.

137 Iustus es, Domine, et rectum iudicium tuum. 138 Mandasti iustitiam, testimonia tua et veritatem tuam nimis. 139 Tabescere me fecit zelus meus quia obliti sunt verba tua inimici mei. 140 Ignitum eloquium tuum vehementer, et servus tuus dilexit illud. 141 Adulescentulus sum ego et contemptus; iustificationes tuas non sum oblitus. 142 Iustitia tua iustitia in aeternum, et lex tua veritas. 143 Tribulatio et angustia invenerunt me; mandata tua meditatio mea. 144 Aequitas testimonia tua in aeternum. Intellectum da mihi, et vivam.

COF.

145 Clamavi in toto corde, "Exaudi me, Domine! Iustificationes tuas requiram." 146 Clamavi te, "Salvum me fac ut custodiam mandata tua!" 147 Praeveni in maturitate et clamavi quia in verba tua supersperavi. 148 Praevenerunt oculi mei ad te diluculo ut meditarer eloquia tua. 149 Vocem meam audi secundum misericordiam tuam, Domine, et secundum iudicium tuum vivifica me. 150 Adpropinquaverunt persequentes me iniquitati, a lege autem tua longe facti sunt. 151 Prope es tu, Domine, et omnes viae tuae veritas. 152 Initio cognovi de testimoniis tuis quia in aeternum fundasti ea.

SADE.

137 Thou art just, O Lord, and thy judgment is right. 138 Thou hast commanded justice, thy testimonies and thy truth exceedingly. 139 My zeal hath made me pine away because my enemies forgot thy words. 140 Thy word is exceedingly refined, and thy servant hath loved it. 141 I am very young and despised, *but* I forget not thy justifications. 142 Thy justice is justice for ever, and thy law is the truth. 143 Trouble and anguish have found me; thy commandments are my meditation. 144 Thy testimonies are justice for ever. Give me understanding, and I shall live.

COPH.

145 I cried with my whole heart, "Hear me, O Lord! I will seek thy justifications." 146 I cried unto thee, "Save me that I may keep thy commandments!" 147 I prevented *the dawning of the day* and cried because in thy words I very much hoped. 148 My eyes to thee have prevented *the morning* that I might meditate on thy words. 149 Hear thou my voice, O Lord, according to thy mercy, and quicken me according to thy judgment. 150 They that persecute me have drawn nigh to iniquity, but they are gone far off from thy law. 151 Thou art near, O Lord, and all thy ways are truth. 152 I have known from the beginning concerning thy testimonies that thou hast founded them for ever.

Res.

153 Vide humilitatem meam, et eripe me, quia legem tuam non sum oblitus. 154 Iudica iudicium meum, et redime me; propter eloquium tuum vivifica me. 155 Longe a peccatoribus salus quia iustificationes tuas non exquisierunt. 156 Misericordiae tuae multae, Domine; secundum iudicium tuum vivifica me. 157 Multi qui persequuntur me et tribulant me; a testimoniis tuis non declinavi. 158 Vidi praevaricantes et tabescebam quia eloquia tua non custodierunt. 159 Vide quoniam mandata tua dilexi, Domine; in misericordia tua vivifica me. 160 Principium verborum tuorum veritas; in aeternum omnia iudicia iustitiae tuae.

Sen.

161 Principes persecuti sunt me gratis, et a verbis tuis formidavit cor meum. 162 Laetabor ego super eloquia tua sicut qui invenit spolia multa. 163 Iniquitatem odio habui et abominatus sum, legem autem tuam dilexi. 164 Septies in die laudem dixi tibi super iudicia iustitiae tuae. 165 Pax multa diligentibus legem tuam, et non est illis scandalum. 166 Expectabam salutare tuum, Domine, et mandata tua dilexi. 167 Custodivit anima mea testimonia tua et dilexit ea vehementer. 168 Servavi mandata tua et testimonia tua quia omnes viae meae in conspectu tuo.

Res.

153 See my humiliation, and deliver me, for I have not forgotten thy law. 154 Judge my judgment, and redeem me; quicken thou me for thy word's sake. 155 Salvation is far from sinners because they have not sought thy justifications. 156 Many, O Lord, are thy mercies; quicken me according to thy judgment. 157 Many are they that persecute me and afflict me, *but* I have not declined from thy testimonies. 158 I beheld the transgressors and pined away because they kept not thy word. 159 *Behold:* I have loved thy commandments, O Lord; quicken me thou in thy mercy. 160 The beginning of thy words is truth; all the judgments of thy justice are for ever.

Sin.

161 Princes have persecuted me without cause, and my heart hath been in awe of thy words. 162 I will rejoice at thy words as one that hath found great spoil. 163 I have hated and abhorred iniquity, but I have loved thy law. 164 Seven times a day I have given praise to thee for the judgments of thy justice. 165 Much peace have they that love thy law, and to them there is no stumbling block. 166 I looked for thy salvation, O Lord, and I loved thy commandments. 167 My soul hath kept thy testimonies and hath loved them exceedingly. 168 I have kept thy commandments and thy testimonies because all my ways are in thy sight.

THAV.

169 Adpropinquet deprecatio mea in conspectu tuo, Domine. Iuxta eloquium tuum da mihi intellectum. 170 Intret postulatio mea in conspectu tuo; secundum eloquium tuum eripe me. 171 Eructabunt labia mea hymnum cum docueris me iustificationes tuas. 172 Pronuntiabit lingua mea eloquium tuum quia omnia mandata tua aequitas. 173 Fiat manus tua ut salvet me, quoniam mandata tua elegi. 174 Concupivi salutare tuum, Domine, et lex tua meditatio mea. 175 Vivet anima mea et laudabit te, et iudicia tua adiuvabunt me. 176 Erravi sicut ovis quae periit; quaere servum tuum quia mandata tua non sum oblitus.

Psalmus 119

Canticum graduum.

Ad Dominum cum tribularer clamavi, et exaudivit me. 2 Domine, libera animam meam a labiis iniquis et a lingua dolosa. 3 Quid detur tibi aut quid adponatur tibi ad linguam

TAU.

169 Let my supplication, O Lord, come near in thy sight. Give me understanding according to thy word. 170 Let my request come in before thee; deliver thou me according to thy word. 171 My lips shall utter a hymn when thou shalt teach me thy justifications. 172 My tongue shall pronounce thy word because all thy commandments are justice. 173 Let thy hand be *with me* to save me, for I have chosen thy precepts. 174 I have longed for thy salvation, O Lord, and thy law is my meditation. 175 My soul shall live and shall praise thee, and thy judgments shall help me. 176 I have gone astray like a sheep that is lost; seek thy servant because I have not forgotten thy commandments.

Psalm 119

Ad Dominum. A prayer in tribulation.

A gradual canticle.

In my trouble I cried to the Lord, and he heard me. 2 O Lord, deliver my soul from wicked lips and a deceitful tongue. 3 What shall be given to thee or what shall be added

dolosam? 4 Sagittae potentis acutae cum carbonibus desolatoriis. 5 Heu mihi quia incolatus meus prolongatus est! Habitavi cum habitantibus Cedar; 6 multum incola fuit anima mea. 7 Cum his qui oderant pacem eram pacificus; cum loquebar illis inpugnabant me gratis.

Psalmus 120

Canticum graduum.

Levavi oculos meos in montes unde veniet auxilium mihi. 2 Auxilium meum a Domino, qui fecit caelum et terram.

3 Non det in commotionem pedem tuum, neque dormiet qui custodit te. 4 Ecce: non dormitabit neque dormiet qui custodit Israhel. 5 Dominus custodit te; Dominus protectio tua super manum dexteram tuam. 6 Per diem sol non uret te neque luna per noctem. 7 Dominus custodit te ab omni malo; custodiat animam tuam Dominus. 8 Dominus

to thee to a deceitful tongue? 4 The sharp arrows of the mighty with coals that lay waste. 5 Woe is me that my sojourning is prolonged! I have dwelt with the inhabitants of Kedar; 6 my soul hath been long a sojourner. 7 With them that hated peace I was peaceable; when I spoke to them they fought against me without cause.

Psalm 120

Levavi oculos. God is the keeper of his servants.

A gradual canticle.

I have lifted up my eyes to the mountains from whence help shall come to me. 2 My help is from the Lord, who made heaven and earth.

3 May he not suffer thy foot to be moved, neither let him slumber that keepeth thee. 4 Behold: he shall neither slumber nor sleep that keepeth Israel. 5 The Lord is thy keeper; the Lord is thy protection upon thy right hand. 6 The sun shall not burn thee by day nor the moon by night. 7 The Lord keepeth thee from all evil; may the Lord keep thy soul. 8 May

custodiat introitum tuum et exitum tuum ex hoc, nunc et usque in saeculum.

Psalmus 121

Canticum graduum.

Laetatus sum in his quae dicta sunt mihi, "In domum Domini ibimus." 2 Stantes erant pedes nostri in atriis tuis, Hierusalem, 3 Hierusalem, quae aedificatur ut civitas, cuius participatio eius in id ipsum, 4 illuc enim ascenderunt tribus, tribus Domini, testimonium Israhel, ad confitendum nomini Domini. 5 Quia illic sederunt sedes in iudicium, sedes super domum David, 6 rogate quae ad pacem sunt Hierusalem et abundantia diligentibus te. 7 Fiat pax in virtute tua et abundantia in turribus tuis. 8 Propter fratres meos et proximos meos loquebar pacem de te. 9 Propter domum Domini, Dei nostri, quaesivi bona tibi.

the Lord keep thy coming in and thy going out from henceforth, now and for ever.

Psalm 121

Laetatus sum in his. The desire and hope of the just for the
coming of the kingdom of God and the peace of his church.

A gradual canticle.

I rejoiced at the things that were said to me, "We shall
go into the house of the Lord." 2 Our feet were standing in
thy courts, O Jerusalem, 3 Jerusalem, which is built as a city,
which is *compact* together, 4 for thither did the tribes go up,
the tribes of the Lord, the testimony of Israel, to praise the
name of the Lord. 5 Because there seats have sat in judgment, seats upon the house of David, 6 pray ye for the things
that are for the peace of Jerusalem and abundance for them
that love thee. 7 Let peace be in thy strength and abundance
in thy towers. 8 For the sake of my brethren and of my neighbours I spoke peace of thee. 9 Because of the house of the
Lord, our God, I have sought good things for thee.

Psalmus 122

Canticum graduum.

Ad te levavi oculos meos qui habitas in caelis. 2 Ecce: si-cut oculi servorum in manibus dominorum suorum, sicut oculi ancillae in manibus dominae eius, ita oculi nostri ad Dominum, Deum nostrum, donec misereatur nostri.

3 Miserere nostri, Domine; miserere nostri, quia multum repleti sumus despectione, 4 quia multum repleta est anima nostra. Obprobrium abundantibus et despectio superbis.

Psalmus 123

Canticum graduum.

"Nisi quia Dominus erat in nobis," dicat nunc Israhel, 2 "nisi quia Dominus erat in nobis cum exsurgerent in nos homines, 3 forte vivos degluttissent nos, cum irasceretur

Psalm 122

Ad te levavi. A prayer in affliction with confidence in God.

A gradual canticle.

To thee have I lifted up my eyes who dwellest in heaven. 2 Behold: as the eyes of servants are on the hands of their masters, as the eyes of the handmaid are on the hands of her mistress, so are our eyes unto the Lord, our God, until he have mercy on us.

3 Have mercy on us, O Lord; have mercy on us, for we are greatly filled with contempt, 4 for our soul is greatly filled. We are a reproach to the rich and contempt to the proud.

Psalm 123

Nisi quia Dominus. The church giveth glory to God for her deliverance from the hands of her enemies.

A gradual canticle.

"If it had not been that the Lord was with us," let Israel now say, 2 "if it had not been that the Lord was with us when men rose up against us, 3 perhaps they had swallowed us up

furor eorum in nos, 4 forsitan aqua absorbuisset nos. 5 Torrentem pertransivit anima nostra, forsitan pertransisset anima nostra aquam intolerabilem."

6 Benedictus Dominus qui non dedit nos in captionem dentibus eorum. 7 Anima nostra sicut passer erepta est de laqueo venantium. Laqueus contritus est, et nos liberati sumus. 8 Adiutorium nostrum in nomine Domini, qui fecit caelum et terram.

Psalmus 124

Canticum graduum.

Qui confidunt in Domino sicut Mons Sion; non commovebitur in aeternum qui habitat 2 in Hierusalem. Montes in circuitu eius, et Dominus in circuitu populi sui ex hoc, nunc et usque in saeculum, 3 quia non relinquet Dominus virgam peccatorum super sortem iustorum ut non extendant iusti ad iniquitatem manus suas.

alive, when their fury was enkindled against us, 4 perhaps the waters had swallowed us up. 5 Our soul hath passed through a torrent, perhaps our soul had passed through a water insupportable."

6 Blessed be the Lord who hath not given us to be a prey to their teeth. 7 Our soul hath been delivered as a sparrow out of the snare of the fowlers. The snare is broken, and we are delivered. 8 Our help is in the name of the Lord, who made heaven and earth.

Psalm 124

Qui confidunt. The just are always under God's protection.

A gradual canticle.

They that trust in the Lord shall be as Mount Zion; he shall not be moved for ever that dwelleth 2 in Jerusalem. Mountains are round about it, *so* the Lord is round about his people from henceforth, now and for ever, 3 for the Lord will not leave the rod of sinners upon the lot of the just that the just may not stretch forth their hands to iniquity.

4 Benefac, Domine, bonis et rectis corde, 5 declinantes autem in obligationes adducet Dominus cum operantibus iniquitatem.

Pax super Israhel.

Psalmus 125

Canticum graduum.

In convertendo Dominus captivitatem Sion facti sumus sicut consolati. 2 Tunc repletum est gaudio os nostrum et lingua nostra exultatione. Tunc dicent inter Gentes, "Magnificavit Dominus facere cum eis." 3 Magnificavit Dominus facere nobiscum; facti sumus laetantes. 4 Converte, Domine, captivitatem nostram sicut torrens in austro. 5 Qui seminant in lacrimis in exultatione metent. 6 Euntes ibant et flebant, mittentes semina sua, 7 venientes autem venient cum exultatione, portantes manipulos suos.

4 Do good, O Lord, to those that are good and to the upright of heart, 5 but such as turn aside into bonds the Lord shall lead out with the workers of iniquity.

Peace upon Israel.

Psalm 125

In convertendo. The people of God rejoice at their delivery from captivity.

A gradual canticle.

When the Lord brought back the captivity of Zion we became like men comforted. 2 Then was our mouth filled with gladness and our tongue with joy. Then shall they say among the Gentiles, "The Lord hath done great things for them." 3 The Lord hath done great things for us; we are become joyful. 4 Turn again our captivity, O Lord, as a stream in the south. 5 They that sow in tears shall reap in joy. 6 Going they went and wept, casting their seeds, 7 but coming they shall come with joyfulness, carrying their sheaves.

Psalmus 126

Canticum graduum Salomonis.

Nisi Dominus aedificaverit domum in vanum laboraverunt qui aedificant eam. Nisi Dominus custodierit civitatem frustra vigilat qui custodit eam. 2 Vanum est vobis ante lucem surgere; surgite postquam sederitis, qui manducatis panem doloris. Cum dederit dilectis suis somnum, 3 ecce: hereditas Domini filii, mercis fructus ventris. 4 Sicut sagittae in manu potentis, ita filii excussorum. 5 Beatus vir qui implevit desiderium suum ex ipsis; non confundetur cum loquetur inimicis suis in porta.

Psalmus 127

Canticum graduum.

Beati omnes qui timent Dominum, qui ambulant in viis eius. 2 Labores manuum tuarum quia manducabis, beatus es,

Psalm 126

Nisi Dominus. Nothing can be done without God's grace and blessing.

A gradual canticle of Solomon.
Unless the Lord build the house they *labour* in vain that build it. Unless the Lord keep the city he watcheth in vain that keepeth it. 2 It is vain for you to rise before light; rise ye after you have sitten, you that eat the bread of sorrow. When he shall give sleep to his beloved, 3 behold: the inheritance of the Lord are children, the reward the fruit of the womb. 4 As arrows in the hand of the mighty, so the children of them that have been shaken. 5 Blessed is the man that hath filled the desire with them; he shall not be confounded when he shall speak to his enemies in the gate.

Psalm 127

Beati omnes. The fear of God is the way to happiness.

A gradual canticle.
Blessed are all they that fear the Lord, that walk in his ways. 2 For thou shalt eat the labours of thy hands, blessed

et bene tibi erit. 3 Uxor tua sicut vitis abundans in lateribus domus tuae, filii tui sicut novellae olivarum in circuitu mensae tuae. 4 Ecce: sic benedicetur homo qui timet Dominum. 5 Benedicat te Dominus ex Sion, et videas bona Hierusalem omnibus diebus vitae tuae, 6 et videas filios filiorum tuorum, pax super Israhel.

Psalmus 128

Canticum graduum.

"Saepe expugnaverunt me a iuventute mea," dicat nunc Israhel, 2 "Saepe expugnaverunt me a iuventute mea, etenim non potuerunt mihi. 3 Supra dorsum meum fabricaverunt peccatores; prolongaverunt iniquitatem suam."

4 Dominus iustus concidet cervices peccatorum. 5 Confundantur et convertantur retrorsum omnes qui oderunt Sion. 6 Fiant sicut faenum tectorum quod priusquam evellatur exaruit, 7 de quo non implevit manum suam qui metit et sinum suum qui manipulos colligit. 8 Et non dixerunt qui praeteribant, "Benedictio Domini super vos; benediximus vobis in nomine Domini."

art thou, and it shall be well with thee. 3 Thy wife as a fruitful vine on the sides of thy house, thy children as *olive plants* round about thy table. 4 Behold: thus shall the man be blessed that feareth the Lord. 5 May the Lord bless thee out of Zion, and mayst thou see the good things of Jerusalem all the days of thy life, 6 and mayst thou see thy children's children *and* peace upon Israel.

Psalm 128

Saepe expugnaverunt. The church of God is invincible. Her persecutors come to nothing.

A gradual canticle.

"Often have they fought against me from my youth," let Israel now say, 2 "Often have they fought against me from my youth, but they could not prevail over me. 3 The wicked have wrought upon my back; they have lengthened their iniquity."

4 The Lord who is just will cut the necks of sinners. 5 Let them all be confounded and turned back that hate Zion. 6 Let them be as grass upon the tops of houses which withereth before it be plucked up, 7 who with the mower filleth not his hand nor he that gathereth sheaves his bosom. 8 And they that passed by have not said, "The blessing of the Lord be upon you; we have blessed you in the name of the Lord."

Psalmus 129

Canticum graduum.

De profundis clamavi ad te, Domine. 2 Domine, exaudi vocem meam. Fiant aures tuae intendentes in vocem deprecationis meae. 3 Si iniquitates observabis, Domine, Domine, quis sustinebit? 4 Quia apud te propitiatio est, et propter legem tuam sustinui te, Domine. Sustinuit anima mea in verbum eius; 5 speravit anima mea in Domino. 6 A custodia matutina usque ad noctem speret Israhel in Domino 7 quia apud Dominum misericordia et copiosa apud eum redemptio, 8 et ipse redimet Israhel ex omnibus iniquitatibus eius.

Psalmus 130

Canticum graduum David.

Domine, non est exaltatum cor meum, neque elati sunt oculi mei, neque ambulavi in magnis neque in mirabilibus

Psalm 129

De profundis. A prayer of a sinner trusting in the mercies of
God. The sixth penitential psalm.

A gradual canticle.

Out of the depths I have cried to thee, O Lord. 2 Lord,
hear my voice. Let thy ears be attentive to the voice of my
supplication. 3 If thou, O Lord, wilt mark iniquities, Lord,
who shall stand it? 4 For with thee there is *merciful forgiveness,* and by reason of thy law I have waited for thee, O Lord.
My soul hath relied on his word; 5 my soul hath hoped in the
Lord. 6 From the morning watch even until night let Israel
hope in the Lord, 7 because with the Lord there is mercy
and with him plentiful redemption, 8 and he shall redeem Israel from all his iniquities.

Psalm 130

Domine, non est. The prophet's humility.

A gradual canticle of David.

Lord, my heart is not exalted, nor are my eyes lofty, neither have I walked in great matters nor in wonderful things

super me. 2 Si non humiliter sentiebam sed exaltavi animam meam, sicut ablactatus est super matrem suam, ita retributio in anima mea. 3 Speret Israhel in Domino ex hoc, nunc et usque in saeculum.

Psalmus 131

Canticum graduum.

Memento, Domine, David et omnis mansuetudinis eius, 2 sicut iuravit Domino. Votum vovit Deo Iacob, 3 "Si introiero in tabernaculum domus meae, si ascendero in lectum strati mei, 4 si dedero somnum oculis meis et palpebris meis dormitationem 5 et requiem temporibus meis, donec inveniam locum Domino, tabernaculum Deo Iacob." 6 Ecce: audivimus eam in Efrata; invenimus eam in campis silvae. 7 Introibimus in tabernaculum eius; adorabimus in loco ubi steterunt pedes eius.

8 Surge, Domine, in requiem tuam, tu et arca sanctificationis tuae. 9 Sacerdotes tui induantur iustitia, et sancti tui exultent. 10 Propter David servum tuum, non avertas faciem christi tui.

above me. 2 If I was not humbly minded but exalted my soul, as a child that is weaned is towards his mother, so reward in my soul. 3 Let Israel hope in the Lord from henceforth, now and for ever.

Psalm 131

Memento, Domine. A prayer for the fulfilling of the promise made to David.

A gradual canticle.

O Lord, remember David and all his meekness, 2 *how* he swore to the Lord. He vowed a vow to the God of Jacob, 3 "If I shall enter into the tabernacle of my house, if I shall go up into the bed wherein I lie, 4 if I shall give sleep to my eyes *or* slumber to my eyelids 5 or rest to my temples, until I find out a place for the Lord, a tabernacle for the God of Jacob." 6 Behold: we have heard of it in Ephrathah; we have found it in the fields of the wood. 7 We will go into his tabernacle; we will adore in the place where his feet stood.

8 Arise, O Lord, into thy resting place, thou and the ark *which thou hast sanctified.* 9 Let thy priests be clothed with justice, and let thy saints rejoice. 10 For thy servant David's sake, turn not away the face of thy anointed.

11 Iuravit Dominus David veritatem, et non frustrabit eam, "De fructu ventris tui ponam super sedem tuam. 12 Si custodierint filii tui testamentum meum et testimonia mea haec quae docebo eos, et filii eorum usque in saeculum sedebunt super sedem tuam," 13 quoniam elegit Dominus Sion; elegit eam in habitationem sibi. 14 "Haec requies mea in saeculum saeculi; hic habitabo, quoniam elegi eam. 15 Viduam eius benedicens benedicam; pauperes eius saturabo panibus. 16 Sacerdotes eius induam salutari et sancti eius exultatione exultabunt. 17 Illuc producam cornu David; paravi lucernam christo meo. 18 Inimicos eius induam confusione, super ipsum autem efflorebit sanctificatio mea."

Psalmus 132

Canticum graduum David.

Ecce quam bonum et quam iucundum habitare fratres in unum, 2 sicut unguentum in capite quod descendit in barbam, barbam Aaron, quod descendit in oram vestimenti eius, 3 sicut ros Hermon, qui descendit in Montem Sion, quoniam illic mandavit Dominus benedictionem et vitam usque in saeculum.

11 The Lord hath sworn truth to David, and he will not make it void, "Of the fruit of thy womb I will set upon thy throne. 12 If thy children will keep my covenant and these my testimonies which I shall teach them, their children also for evermore shall sit upon thy throne," 13 for the Lord hath chosen Zion; he hath chosen it for his dwelling. 14 "This is my rest for ever and ever; here will I dwell, for I have chosen it. 15 Blessing I will bless her widow; I will satisfy her poor with bread. 16 I will clothe her priests with salvation and her saints shall rejoice with exceeding great joy. 17 There will I bring forth a horn to David; I have prepared a lamp for my anointed. 18 His enemies I will clothe with confusion, but upon him shall my sanctification flourish."

Psalm 132

Ecce quam bonum. The happiness of brotherly love and concord.

A gradual canticle of David.

Behold how good and how pleasant it is for brethren to dwell *together in unity,* 2 like the *precious* ointment on the head that ran down upon the beard, the beard of Aaron, which ran down to the skirt of his garment, 3 as the dew of Hermon, which descendeth upon Mount Zion, for there the Lord hath commanded blessing and life for evermore.

Psalmus 133

Canticum graduum.

Ecce: nunc benedicite Dominum, omnes servi Domini qui statis in domo Domini, in atriis domus Dei nostri. 2 In noctibus extollite manus vestras in sancta, et benedicite Domino. 3 Benedicat te Dominus ex Sion, qui fecit caelum et terram.

Psalmus 134

Alleluia.

Laudate nomen Domini! Laudate, servi, Dominum, 2 qui statis in domo Domini, in atriis domus Dei nostri. 3 Laudate Dominum, quia bonus Dominus; psallite nomini eius,

Psalm 133

Ecce: nunc benedicite. An exhortation to praise God continually.

A gradual canticle.

Behold: now bless ye the Lord, all ye servants of the Lord who stand in the house of the Lord, in the courts of the house of our God. 2 In the nights lift up your hands to the holy places, and bless ye the Lord. 3 May the Lord out of Zion bless thee, he that made heaven and earth.

Psalm 134

Laudate nomen. An exhortation to praise God. The vanity of idols.

Alleluia.

Praise ye the name of the Lord! O you his servants, praise the Lord, 2 you that stand in the house of the Lord, in the courts of the house of our God. 3 Praise ye the Lord, for the

quoniam suave, 4 quoniam Iacob elegit sibi Dominus, Israhel in possessionem sibi, 5 quia ego cognovi quod magnus est Dominus et Deus noster prae omnibus diis.

6 Omnia quaecumque voluit Dominus fecit in caelo, in terra, in mare et in omnibus abyssis. 7 Educens nubes ab extremo terrae, fulgora in pluviam fecit. Qui producit ventos de thesauris suis. 8 Qui percussit primogenita Aegypti ab homine usque ad pecus. 9 Emisit signa et prodigia in medio tui, Aegypte, in Pharaonem et in omnes servos eius. 10 Qui percussit gentes multas et occidit reges fortes, 11 Seon, regem Amorreorum, et Og, regem Basan, et omnia regna Chanaan 12 et dedit terram eorum hereditatem, hereditatem Israhel populo suo.

13 Domine, nomen tuum in aeternum, Domine, memoriale tuum in generationem et generationem, 14 quia iudicabit Dominus populum suum et in servis suis deprecabitur.

15 Simulacra Gentium argentum et aurum, opera manuum hominum. 16 Os habent, et non loquentur; oculos habent, et non videbunt. 17 Aures habent, et non audient, neque enim est spiritus in ore eorum. 18 Similes illis fiant qui faciunt ea et omnes qui confidunt in eis.

19 Domus Israhel, benedicite Domino! Domus Aaron, benedicite Domino! 20 Domus Levi, benedicite Domino! Qui timetis Dominum, benedicite Domino! 21 Benedictus Dominus ex Sion, qui habitat in Hierusalem.

Lord is good; sing ye to his name, for it is sweet, 4 for the Lord hath chosen Jacob unto himself, Israel for his own possession, 5 for I have known that the Lord is great and our God is above all gods.

6 Whatsoever the Lord pleased he hath done in heaven, in earth, in the sea and in all the deeps. 7 He bringeth up clouds from the end of the earth; he hath made lightnings for the rain. He bringeth forth winds out of his stores. 8 He slew the firstborn of Egypt from man even unto beast. 9 He sent forth signs and wonders in the midst of thee, O Egypt, upon Pharaoh and upon all his servants. 10 He smote many nations and slew mighty kings, 11 Sihon, king of the Amorites, and Og, king of Bashan, and all the kingdoms of Canaan 12 and gave their land for an inheritance, for an inheritance to his people Israel.

13 Thy name, O Lord, is for ever, thy memorial, O Lord, unto all generations, 14 for the Lord will judge his people and will be entreated in favour of his servants.

15 The idols of the Gentiles are silver and gold, the works of men's hands. 16 They have a mouth, *but* they *speak not;* they have eyes, *but* they *see not.* 17 They have ears, *but* they *hear not, neither* is there any breath in their mouths. 18 Let them that make them be like to them and every one that trusteth in them.

19 Bless the Lord, O house of Israel! Bless the Lord, O house of Aaron! 20 Bless the Lord, O house of Levi! You that fear the Lord, bless the Lord! 21 Blessed be the Lord out of Zion, who dwelleth in Jerusalem.

Psalmus 135

Alleluia.

Confitemini Domino, quoniam bonus, quoniam in aeternum misericordia eius! 2 Confitemini Deo deorum, quoniam in aeternum misericordia eius. 3 Confitemini Domino dominorum, quoniam in aeternum misericordia eius, 4 qui facit mirabilia magna solus, quoniam in aeternum misericordia eius, 5 qui fecit caelos in intellectu, quoniam in aeternum misericordia eius, 6 qui firmavit terram super aquas, quoniam in aeternum misericordia eius, 7 qui fecit luminaria magna, quoniam in aeternum misericordia eius, 8 solem in potestatem diei, quoniam in aeternum misericordia eius, 9 lunam et stellas in potestatem noctis, quoniam in aeternum misericordia eius, 10 qui percussit Aegyptum cum primogenitis eorum, quoniam in aeternum misericordia eius, 11 qui eduxit Israhel de medio eorum, quoniam in aeternum misericordia eius, 12 in manu potenti et brachio excelso, quoniam in aeternum misericordia eius, 13 qui divisit Rubrum Mare in divisiones, quoniam in aeternum misericordia eius, 14 et eduxit Israhel per medium eius, quoniam in aeternum misericordia eius, 15 et excussit Pharaonem et virtutem eius in Mari Rubro, quoniam in aeternum misericordia eius, 16 qui transduxit populum suum per desertum, quoniam in

Psalm 135

Confitemini Domino. God is to be praised for his wonderful works.

Alleluia.

Praise the Lord, for he is good, for his mercy endureth for ever! 2 Praise ye the God of gods, for his mercy endureth for ever. 3 Praise ye the Lord of lords, for his mercy endureth for ever, 4 who alone doth great wonders, for his mercy endureth for ever, 5 who made the heavens in understanding, for his mercy endureth for ever, 6 who established the earth above the waters, for his mercy endureth for ever, 7 who made the great lights, for his mercy endureth for ever, 8 the sun to rule the day, for his mercy endureth for ever, 9 the moon and the stars to rule the night, for his mercy endureth for ever, 10 who smote Egypt with their firstborn, for his mercy endureth for ever, 11 who brought out Israel from among them, for his mercy endureth for ever, 12 with a mighty hand and with a *stretched out* arm, for his mercy endureth for ever, 13 who divided the Red Sea into parts, for his mercy endureth for ever, 14 and brought out Israel through the midst thereof, for his mercy endureth for ever, 15 and overthrew Pharaoh and his host in the Red Sea, for his mercy endureth for ever, 16 who led his people through

aeternum misericordia eius, [17] qui percussit reges magnos, quoniam in aeternum misericordia eius, [18] et occidit reges fortes, quoniam in aeternum misericordia eius, [19] Seon, regem Amorreorum, quoniam in aeternum misericordia eius, [20] et Og, regem Basan, quoniam in aeternum misericordia eius. [21] Et dedit terram eorum hereditatem, quoniam in aeternum misericordia eius, [22] hereditatem Israhel servo suo, quoniam in aeternum misericordia eius, [23] quia in humilitate nostra memor fuit nostri, quoniam in aeternum misericordia eius, [24] et redemit nos ab inimicis nostris, quoniam in aeternum misericordia eius, [25] qui dat escam omni carni, quoniam in aeternum misericordia eius.

[26] Confitemini Deo caeli, quoniam in aeternum misericordia eius. Confitemini Domino dominorum, quoniam in aeternum misericordia eius!

Psalmus 136

Psalmus David Hieremiae.

Super flumina Babylonis, illic sedimus et flevimus cum recordaremur Sion. [2] In salicibus in medio eius suspendimus organa nostra, [3] quia illic interrogaverunt nos qui captivos duxerunt nos verba cantionum et qui abduxerunt nos,

the desert, for his mercy endureth for ever, 17 who smote great kings, for his mercy endureth for ever, 18 and slew strong kings, for his mercy endureth for ever, 19 Sihon, king of the Amorites, for his mercy endureth for ever, 20 and Og, king of Bashan, for his mercy endureth for ever. 21 And he gave their land for an inheritance, for his mercy endureth for ever, 22 for an inheritance to his servant Israel, for his mercy endureth for ever, 23 for he was mindful of us in our affliction, for his mercy endureth for ever, 24 and he redeemed us from our enemies, for his mercy endureth for ever, 25 who giveth food to all flesh, for his mercy endureth for ever.

26 Give glory to the God of heaven, for his mercy endureth for ever. 27 Give glory to the Lord of lords, for his mercy endureth for ever!

Psalm 136

Super flumina. The lamentation of the people of God in their captivity in Babylon.

A psalm of David for Jeremiah.

Upon the rivers of Babylon, there we sat and wept when we remembered Zion. 2 On the willows in the midst thereof we hung up our instruments, 3 for there they that led us into captivity required of us the words of songs and they that

"Hymnum cantate nobis de canticis Sion." 4 Quomodo cantabimus canticum Domini in terra aliena? 5 Si oblitus fuero tui, Hierusalem, oblivioni detur dextera mea. 6 Adhereat lingua mea faucibus meis, si non meminero tui, si non praeposuero Hierusalem in principio laetitiae meae.

7 Memor esto, Domine, filiorum Edom in die Hierusalem qui dicunt, "Exinanite; exinanite usque ad fundamentum in ea." 8 Filia Babylonis, misera, beatus qui retribuet tibi retributionem tuam quam retribuisti nobis. 9 Beatus qui tenebit et adlidet parvulos tuos ad petram.

Psalmus 137

Ipsi David.

Confitebor tibi, Domine, in toto corde meo, quoniam audisti verba oris mei. In conspectu angelorum psallam tibi. 2 Adorabo ad templum sanctum tuum, et confitebor nomini tuo super misericordia tua et veritate tua, quoniam magnificasti super omne nomen sanctum tuum. 3 In quacumque die invocavero te, exaudi me; multiplicabis in anima mea virtutem. 4 Confiteantur tibi Domine omnes reges terrae, quia

carried us away *said,* "Sing ye to us a hymn of the songs of Zion." 4 How shall we sing the song of the Lord in a strange land? 5 If I forget thee, O Jerusalem, let my right hand be forgotten. 6 Let my tongue cleave to my jaws, if I do not remember thee, if I make not Jerusalem the beginning of my joy.

7 Remember, O Lord, the children of Edom in the day of Jerusalem who say, "Rase it; rase it even to the foundation thereof." 8 O daughter of Babylon, miserable, blessed shall he be who shall repay thee thy payment which thou hast paid us. 9 Blessed be he that shall take and dash thy little ones against the rock.

Psalm 137

Confitebor tibi. Thanksgiving to God for his benefits.

F or David himself.

I will praise thee, O Lord, with my whole heart, for thou hast heard the words of my mouth. I will sing praise to thee in the sight of the angels. 2 I will worship towards thy holy temple, and I will give glory to thy name for thy mercy and for thy truth, for thou hast magnified thy holy name above all. 3 In what day soever I shall call upon thee, hear me; thou shalt multiply strength in my soul. 4 May all the kings of the *earth* give glory to thee, for they have heard all the words of

audierunt omnia verba oris tui. 5 Et cantent in viis Domini, quoniam magna gloria Domini, 6 quoniam excelsus Dominus et humilia respicit, et alta a longe cognoscit. 7 Si ambulavero in medio tribulationis, vivificabis me, et super iram inimicorum meorum extendisti manum tuam, et salvum me fecit dextera tua. 8 Dominus retribuet pro me. Domine, misericordia tua in saeculum. Opera manuum tuarum ne dispicias!

Psalmus 138

In finem. David psalmus.

Domine, probasti me et cognovisti me. 2 Tu cognovisti sessionem meam et surrectionem meam. 3 Intellexisti cogitationes meas de longe; semitam meam et funiculum meum investigasti, 4 et omnes vias meas praevidisti, quia non est sermo in lingua mea. 5 Ecce, Domine: tu cognovisti omnia, novissima et antiqua; tu formasti me et posuisti super me manum tuam. 6 Mirabilis facta est scientia tua ex me; confortata est, et non potero ad eam.

thy mouth. 5 And let them sing in the ways of the Lord, for great is the glory of the Lord, 6 for the Lord is high and looketh on the low, and the high he knoweth afar off. 7 If I shall walk in the midst of tribulation, thou wilt quicken me, and thou hast stretched forth thy hand against the wrath of my enemies, and thy right hand hath saved me. 8 The Lord will repay for me. Thy mercy, O Lord, endureth for ever. O despise not the works of thy hands!

Psalm 138

Domine, probasti. God's special providence over his servants.

Unto the end. A psalm of David.

Lord, thou hast proved me and known me. 2 Thou hast known my sitting down and my rising up. 3 Thou hast understood my thoughts afar off; my path and my line thou hast searched out, 4 and thou hast foreseen all my ways, for there is no speech in my tongue. 5 Behold, O Lord: thou hast known all things, the last and those of old; thou hast formed me and hast laid thy hand upon me. 6 Thy knowledge is become wonderful to me; it is *high,* and I cannot reach to it.

7 Quo ibo ab spiritu tuo? Et quo a facie tua fugiam? 8 Si ascendero in caelum, tu illic es; si descendero in infernum, ades. 9 Si sumpsero pinnas meas diluculo et habitavero in extremis maris, 10 etenim illuc manus tua deducet me, et tenebit me dextera tua. 11 Et dixi, "Forsitan tenebrae conculcabunt me, et nox inluminatio mea in deliciis meis." 12 Quia tenebrae non obscurabuntur a te, et nox sicut dies inluminabitur. Sicut tenebrae eius ita et lumen eius, 13 quia tu possedisti renes meos; suscepisti me de utero matris meae. 14 Confitebor tibi, quia terribiliter magnificatus es; mirabilia opera tua, et anima mea cognoscit nimis. 15 Non est occultatum os meum a te quod fecisti in occulto et substantia mea in inferioribus terrae. 16 Inperfectum meum viderunt oculi tui, et in libro tuo omnes scribentur. Dies formabuntur et nemo in eis. 17 Mihi autem nimis honorificati sunt amici tui, Deus. Nimis confortatus est principatus eorum. 18 Dinumerabo eos, et super harenam multiplicabuntur. Exsurrexi et adhuc sum tecum. 19 Si occideris, Deus, peccatores, viri sanguinum, declinate a me, 20 quia dicitis in cogitatione, "Accipient in vanitate civitates tuas."

21 Nonne qui oderunt te, Domine, oderam et super inimicos tuos tabescebam? 22 Perfecto odio oderam illos; inimici facti sunt mihi. 23 Proba me, Deus, et scito cor meum; interroga me, et cognosce semitas meas. 24 Et vide si via iniquitatis in me est, et deduc me in via aeterna.

7 Whither shall I go from thy spirit? *Or* whither shall I flee from thy face? 8 If I ascend into heaven, thou art there; if I descend into hell, thou art present. 9 If I take my wings early in the morning and dwell in the uttermost parts of the sea, 10 even there also shall thy hand lead me, and thy right hand shall hold me. 11 And I said, "Perhaps darkness shall cover me, and night shall be my light in my pleasures." 12 *But* darkness shall not be dark to thee, and night shall be light all the day. *The darkness thereof and the light thereof are alike to thee,* 13 for thou hast possessed my reins; thou hast protected me from my mother's womb. 14 I will praise thee, for thou art fearfully magnified; wonderful are thy works, and my soul knoweth right well. 15 My bone is not hidden from thee which thou hast made in secret and my substance in the lower parts of the earth. 16 Thy eyes did see my imperfect being, and in thy book all shall be written. Days shall be formed and no one in them. 17 But to me thy friends, O God, are made exceedingly honourable. Their principality is exceedingly strengthened. 18 I will number them, and they shall be multiplied above the sand. I rose up and am still with thee. 19 If thou wilt kill the wicked, O God, ye men of blood, depart from me, 20 because you say in thought, "They shall receive thy cities in vain."

21 Have I not hated them, O Lord, that hated thee and pined away because of thy enemies? 22 I have hated them with a perfect hatred, *and* they are become enemies to me. 23 Prove me, O God, and know my heart; examine me, and know my paths. 24 And see if there be in me the way of iniquity, and lead me in the eternal way.

Psalmus 139

In finem. Psalmus David.

2 Eripe me, Domine, ab homine malo; a viro iniquo eripe me, 3 qui cogitaverunt iniquitates in corde; tota die constituebant proelia. 4 Acuerunt linguas suas sicut serpentis; venenum aspidum sub labiis eorum. 5 Custodi me, Domine, de manu peccatoris, et ab hominibus iniquis eripe me, qui cogitaverunt subplantare gressus meos.

6 Absconderunt superbi laqueum mihi, et funes extenderunt in laqueum. Iuxta iter scandalum posuerunt mihi. Diapsalma. 7 Dixi Domino, "Deus meus es tu; exaudi, Domine, vocem deprecationis meae." 8 Domine, Domine, virtus salutis meae, obumbrasti super caput meum in die belli. 9 Non tradas me, Domine, a desiderio meo peccatori. Cogitaverunt contra me; ne derelinquas me, ne forte exaltentur. 10 Caput circuitus eorum, labor labiorum ipsorum operiet eos. 11 Cadent super eos carbones; in ignem deicies eos. In miseriis non subsistent. 12 Vir linguosus non dirigetur in terra; virum iniustum mala capient in interitu.

Psalm 139

Eripe me, Domine. A prayer to be delivered from the wicked.

Unto the end. A psalm of David.

2 Deliver me, O Lord, from the evil man; rescue me from the unjust man, 3 who have devised iniquities in their hearts; all the day long they designed battles. 4 They have sharpened their tongues like *a* serpent; the venom of asps is under their lips. 5 Keep me, O Lord, from the hand of the wicked, and from unjust men deliver me, who have proposed to supplant my steps.

6 The proud have hidden a net for me, and they have stretched out cords for a snare. They have laid for me a stumbling block by the wayside. 7 I said to the Lord, "Thou art my God; hear, O Lord, the voice of my supplication." 8 O Lord, Lord, the strength of my salvation, thou hast overshadowed my head in the day of battle. 9 Give me not up, O Lord, from my desire to the wicked. They have plotted against me; do not thou forsake me, *lest* they should triumph. 10 The head of their compassing me about, the labour of their lips shall overwhelm them. 11 Burning coals shall fall upon them; thou wilt cast them down into the fire. In miseries they shall not be able to stand. 12 A man full of tongue shall not be established in the earth; evil shall catch the unjust man unto destruction.

13 Cognovi quia faciet Dominus iudicium inopis et vindictam pauperum. 14 Verumtamen iusti, confitebuntur nomini tuo, et habitabunt recti cum vultu tuo.

Psalmus 140

Psalmus David.
Domine, clamavi ad te. Exaudi me; intende voci meae
cum clamavero ad te. 2 Dirigatur oratio mea sicut incensum
in conspectu tuo, elevatio manuum mearum sacrificium
vespertinum. 3 Pone, Domine, custodiam ori meo et ostium
circumstantiae labiis meis. 4 Non declines cor meum in
verba malitiae, ad excusandas excusationes in peccatis cum
hominibus operantibus iniquitatem, et non communicabo
cum electis eorum. 5 Corripiet me iustus in misericordia et
increpabit me, oleum autem peccatoris non inpinguet caput
meum, quoniam adhuc et oratio mea in beneplacitis eorum.
6 Absorti sunt iuncti petrae iudices eorum. Audient verba
mea, quoniam potuerunt, 7 sicut crassitudo terrae erupta est
super terram. Dissipata sunt ossa nostra secus infernum.
8 Quia ad te, Domine, Domine, oculi mei. In te speravi;

13 I know that the Lord will do justice to the needy and will revenge the poor. 14 But as for the just, they shall give glory to thy name, and the upright shall dwell with thy countenance.

Psalm 140

Domine, clamavi. A prayer against sinful words and deceitful flatterers.

A psalm of David.

I have cried to thee, O Lord. Hear me; hearken to my voice when I cry to thee. 2 Let my prayer be directed as incense in thy sight, the lifting up of my hands as evening sacrifice. 3 Set a watch, O Lord, before my mouth and a door round about my lips. 4 Incline not my heart to evil words, to make excuses in sins with men that work iniquity, and I will not communicate with the choicest of them. 5 The just man shall correct me in mercy and shall reprove me, but let not the oil of the sinner fatten my head, for my prayer shall still be against the things with which they are well pleased. 6 Their judges *falling upon* the rock have been swallowed up. They shall hear my words, for they have prevailed, 7 as when the thickness of the earth is broken up upon the ground. Our bones are scattered by the side of hell. 8 *But* to thee, O Lord, Lord, are my eyes. In thee have I put my trust; take

non auferas animam meam. 9 Custodi me a laqueo quem statuerunt mihi et ab scandalis operantium iniquitatem. 10 Cadent in retiaculo eius peccatores. Singulariter sum ego donec transeam.

Psalmus 141

Intellectus. David. Cum esset in spelunca oratio.

2 Voce mea ad Dominum clamavi; voce mea ad Dominum deprecatus sum. 3 Effundo in conspectu eius deprecationem meam, et tribulationem meam ante ipsum pronuntio. 4 In deficiendo ex me spiritum meum, et tu cognovisti semitas meas. In via hac qua ambulabam absconderunt laqueum mihi. 5 Considerabam ad dexteram et videbam, et non erat qui cognosceret me. Periit fuga a me, et non est qui requirat animam meam. 6 Clamavi ad te, Domine. Dixi, "Tu es spes mea, portio mea in terra viventium." 7 Intende ad deprecationem meam, quia humiliatus sum nimis. Libera me a persequentibus me, quia confortati sunt super me. 8 Educ de custodia animam meam ad confitendum nomini tuo. Me expectant iusti donec retribuas mihi.

not away my soul. 9 Keep me from the snare which they have laid for me and from the stumbling blocks of them that work iniquity. 10 The wicked shall fall in his net. I am alone until I pass.

Psalm 141

Voce mea. A prayer of David in extremity of danger.

Of understanding. For David. A prayer when he was in the cave.

2 I cried to the Lord with my voice; with my voice I made supplication to the Lord. 3 In his sight I pour out my prayer, and before him I declare my trouble. 4 When my spirit failed me, *then* thou knewest my paths. In this way wherein I walked they have hidden a snare for me. 5 I looked on my right hand and beheld, and there was no one that would know me. Flight hath failed me, and there is no one that hath regard to my soul. 6 I cried to thee, O Lord. I said, "Thou art my hope, my portion in the land of the living." 7 Attend to my supplication, for I am brought very low. Deliver me from my persecutors, for they are stronger than I. 8 Bring my soul out of prison that I may praise thy name. The just wait for me until thou reward me.

Psalmus 142

Psalmus David quando Absalom filius eius eum persequebatur.

Domine, exaudi orationem meam! Auribus percipe obsecrationem meam in veritate tua; exaudi me in tua iustitia, 2 et non intres in iudicium cum servo tuo, quia non iustificabitur in conspectu tuo omnis vivens, 3 quia persecutus est inimicus animam meam; humiliavit in terra vitam meam. Conlocavit me in obscuris sicut mortuos saeculi, 4 et anxiatus est super me spiritus meus. In me turbatum est cor meum.

5 Memor fui dierum antiquorum; meditatus sum in omnibus operibus tuis; in factis manuum tuarum meditabar. 6 Expandi manus meas ad te; anima mea sicut terra sine aqua tibi. 7 Velociter exaudi me, Domine; defecit spiritus meus. Non avertas faciem tuam a me et similis ero descendentibus in lacum. 8 Auditam mihi fac mane misericordiam tuam, quia in te speravi. Notam fac mihi viam in qua ambulem, quia ad te levavi animam meam. 9 Eripe me de inimicis meis, Domine; ad te confugi. 10 Doce me facere voluntatem tuam, quia Deus meus es tu. Spiritus tuus bonus deducet me in viam rectam. 11 Propter nomen tuum, Domine, vivificabis

Psalm 142

Domine, exaudi. The psalmist in tribulation calleth upon God for his delivery. The seventh penitential psalm.

A psalm of David when his son Absalom pursued him.

Hear, O Lord, my prayer! Give ear to my supplication in thy truth; hear me in thy justice, 2 and enter not into judgment with thy servant, for in thy sight no man living shall be justified, 3 for the enemy hath persecuted my soul; he hath brought down my life to the earth. He hath made me to dwell in darkness as those that have been dead of old, 4 and my spirit is in anguish within me. My heart within me is troubled.

5 I remembered the days of old; I meditated on all thy works; I meditated upon the works of thy hands. 6 I stretched forth my hands to thee; my soul is as earth without water unto thee. 7 Hear me speedily, O Lord; my spirit hath fainted away. Turn not away thy face from me *lest I be* like unto them that go down into the pit. 8 Cause me to hear thy mercy in the morning, for in thee have I hoped. Make the way known to me wherein I should walk, for I have lifted up my soul to thee. 9 Deliver me from my enemies, O Lord; to thee have I fled. 10 Teach me to do thy will, for thou art my God. Thy good spirit shall lead me into the right *land.* 11 For thy name's sake, O Lord, thou wilt quicken me in thy

me in aequitate tua. Educes de tribulatione animam meam, 12 et in misericordia tua disperdes inimicos meos. Et perdes omnes qui tribulant animam meam, quoniam ego servus tuus sum.

Psalmus 143

Psalmus David adversus Goliad.

Benedictus Dominus, Deus meus, qui docet manus meas ad proelium et digitos meos ad bellum. 2 Misericordia mea et refugium meum, susceptor meus et liberator meus, protector meus, et in eo speravi, qui subdit populum meum sub me.

3 Domine, quid est homo quia innotuisti ei? Aut filius hominis, quia reputas eum? 4 Homo vanitati similis factus est; dies eius sicut umbra praetereunt. 5 Domine, inclina caelos tuos, et descende; tange montes, et fumigabunt. 6 Fulgora coruscationem, et dissipabis eos; emitte sagittas tuas, et conturbabis eos. 7 Emitte manum tuam de alto; eripe me, et libera me de aquis multis, de manu filiorum alienorum 8 quorum os locutum est vanitatem, et dextera eorum dextera iniquitatis.

justice. Thou wilt bring my soul out of trouble, 12 and in thy mercy thou wilt destroy my enemies. And thou wilt *cut off* all them that afflict my soul, for I am thy servant.

Psalm 143

Benedictus Dominus. The prophet praiseth God and prayeth to be delivered from his enemies. No worldly happiness is to be compared with that of serving God.

A psalm of David against Goliath.

Blessed be the Lord, my God, who teacheth my hands to fight and my fingers to war. 2 My mercy and my refuge, my support and my deliverer, my protector, and I have hoped in him, who subdueth my people under me.

3 Lord, what is man, that thou art made known to him? Or the son of man, that thou makest account of him? 4 Man is like to vanity; his days pass away like a shadow. 5 Lord, bow down thy heavens, and descend; touch the mountains, and they shall smoke. 6 *Send forth* lightning, and thou shalt scatter them; shoot out thy arrows, and thou shalt trouble them. 7 Put forth thy hand from on high; take me out, and deliver me from many waters, from the hand of strange children 8 whose mouth hath spoken vanity, and their right hand is the right hand of iniquity.

9 Deus, canticum novum cantabo tibi; in psalterio deca-cordo psallam tibi 10 qui das salutem regibus, qui redimisti David servum tuum de gladio maligno. 11 Eripe me, et erue me de manu filiorum alienorum quorum os locutum est va-nitatem, et dextera eorum dextera iniquitatis, 12 quorum filii sicut novellae plantationes in iuventute sua. Filiae eorum conpositae, circumornatae ut similitudo templi, 13 promp-tuaria eorum plena, eructantia ex hoc in illud, oves eorum fetosae, abundantes in egressibus suis, 14 boves eorum crassi. Non est ruina maceriae neque transitus, neque clamor in plateis eorum. 15 Beatum dixerunt populum cui haec sunt; beatus populus cuius Dominus Deus eius.

Psalmus 144

Laudatio ipsi David.

Exaltabo te, Deus, meus rex, et benedicam nomini tuo in saeculum et in saeculum saeculi. 2 Per singulos dies benedi-cam tibi, et laudabo nomen tuum in saeculum et in saeculum

9 To thee, O God, I will sing a new canticle; on the psaltery *and an instrument* of ten strings I will sing praises to thee 10 who givest salvation to kings, who hast redeemed thy servant David from the malicious sword. 11 Deliver me, and rescue me out of the hand of strange children whose mouth hath spoken vanity, and their right hand is the right hand of iniquity, 12 whose sons are as new plants in their youth. Their daughters decked out, adorned round about after the similitude of a temple, 13 their storehouses full, flowing out of this into that, their sheep fruitful in young, abounding in their goings forth, 14 their oxen fat. There is no breach of wall nor passage nor crying out in their streets. 15 They have called the people happy that hath these things, *but* happy is that people whose God is the Lord.

Psalm 144

Exaltabo te, Deus. A psalm of praise to the infinite majesty of God.

P raise for David himself.

I will extol thee, O God, my king, and I will bless thy name for ever, yea, for ever and ever. 2 Every day will I bless thee, and I will praise thy name for ever, yea, for ever and

saeculi. 3 Magnus Dominus et laudabilis nimis, et magnitudinis eius non est finis. 4 Generatio et generatio laudabit opera tua, et potentiam tuam pronuntiabunt. 5 Magnificentiam gloriae sanctitatis tuae loquentur et mirabilia tua narrabunt. 6 Et virtutem terribilium tuorum dicent et magnitudinem tuam narrabunt. 7 Memoriam abundantiae suavitatis tuae eructabunt et iustitia tua exultabunt.

8 Miserator et misericors Dominus, patiens et multum misericors. 9 Suavis Dominus universis, et miserationes eius super omnia opera eius. 10 Confiteantur tibi, Domine, omnia opera tua, et sancti tui benedicant tibi. 11 Gloriam regni tui dicent et potentiam tuam loquentur 12 ut notam faciant filiis hominum potentiam tuam et gloriam magnificentiae regni tui. 13 Regnum tuum regnum omnium saeculorum, et dominatio tua in omni generatione et generationem.

Fidelis Dominus in omnibus verbis suis et sanctus in omnibus operibus suis. 14 Adlevat Dominus omnes qui corruunt et erigit omnes elisos. 15 Oculi omnium in te sperant, Domine, et tu das escam illorum in tempore oportuno. 16 Aperis tu manum tuam et imples omne animal benedictione. 17 Iustus Dominus in omnibus viis suis et sanctus in omnibus operibus suis. 18 Prope est Dominus omnibus invocantibus eum, omnibus invocantibus eum in veritate. 19 Voluntatem timentium se faciet, et deprecationem eorum exaudiet et salvos faciet eos. 20 Custodit Dominus omnes

ever. 3 Great is the Lord and greatly to be praised, and of his greatness there is no end. 4 Generation and generation shall praise thy works, and they shall declare thy power. 5 They shall speak of the magnificence of the glory of thy holiness and shall tell thy wondrous works. 6 And they shall speak of the might of thy terrible acts and shall declare thy greatness. 7 They shall publish the memory of the abundance of thy sweetness and shall rejoice in thy justice.

8 The Lord is gracious and merciful, patient and plenteous in mercy. 9 The Lord is sweet to all, and his *tender* mercies are over all his works. 10 Let all thy works, O Lord, praise thee, and let thy saints bless thee. 11 They shall speak of the glory of thy kingdom and shall tell of thy power 12 to make thy might known to the sons of men and the glory of the magnificence of thy kingdom. 13 Thy kingdom is a kingdom of all ages, and thy dominion endureth throughout all generations.

The Lord is faithful in all his words and holy in all his works. 14 The Lord lifteth up all that fall and setteth up all that are cast down. 15 The eyes of all hope in thee, O Lord, and thou givest them meat in due season. 16 Thou openest thy hand and fillest with blessing every living creature. 17 The Lord is just in all his ways and holy in all his works. 18 The Lord is nigh unto all them that call upon him, to all that call upon him in truth. 19 He will do the will of them that fear him, and he will hear their prayer and save them. 20 The Lord keepeth all them that love him, *but* all the

diligentes se, et omnes peccatores disperdet. 21 Laudationem Domini loquetur os meum, et benedicat omnis caro nomini sancto eius in saeculum et in saeculum saeculi!

Psalmus 145

Alleluia. Aggei et Zacchariae.
2 Lauda, anima mea, Dominum! Laudabo Dominum in vita mea. Psallam Deo meo quamdiu fuero. Nolite confidere in principibus, 3 in filiis hominum, in quibus non est salus. 4 Exibit spiritus eius, et revertetur in terram suam; in illa die peribunt omnes cogitationes eorum. 5 Beatus cuius Deus Iacob adiutor eius; spes eius in Domino, Deo ipsius, 6 qui fecit caelum et terram, mare et omnia quae in eis, 7 qui custodit veritatem in saeculum, facit iudicium iniuriam patientibus, dat escam esurientibus.

Dominus solvit conpeditos. 8 Dominus inluminat caecos. Dominus erigit adlisos. Dominus diligit iustos. 9 Dominus custodit advenas. Pupillum et viduam suscipiet, et vias

wicked he will destroy. 21 My mouth shall speak the praise of
the Lord, and let all flesh bless his holy name forever, yea,
for ever and ever!

Psalm 145

Lauda, anima. We are not to trust in men, but in God alone.

Alleluia. Of Haggai and Zechariah.

2 Praise the Lord, O my soul! In my life I will praise the
Lord. I will sing to my God as long as I shall be. Put not your
trust in princes, 3 in the children of men, in whom there is
no salvation. 4 His spirit shall go forth, and he shall return
into his earth; in that day all their thoughts shall perish.
5 Blessed is he who hath the God of Jacob for his helper,
whose hope is in the Lord, his God, 6 who made heaven and
earth, the sea and all things that are in them, 7 who keepeth
truth for ever, who executeth judgment for them that suffer
wrong, who giveth food to the hungry.

The Lord looseth them that are fettered. 8 The Lord enlighteneth the blind. The Lord lifteth up them that are cast
down. The Lord loveth the just. 9 The Lord keepeth the
strangers. He will support the fatherless and the widow, and

peccatorum disperdet. 10 Regnabit Dominus in saecula, Deus tuus, Sion, in generationem et generationem.

Psalmus 146

Alleluia.

Laudate Dominum, quoniam bonum psalmus! Deo nostro sit iucunda decoraque laudatio. 2 Aedificans Hierusalem Dominus, dispersiones Israhel congregabit, 3 qui sanat contritos corde et alligat contritiones illorum, 4 qui numerat multitudinem stellarum et omnibus eis nomina vocat. 5 Magnus Dominus noster, et magna virtus eius, et sapientiae eius non est numerus, 6 suscipiens mansuetos Dominus, humilians autem peccatores usque ad terram.

7 Praecinite Domino in confessione! Psallite Deo nostro in cithara, 8 qui operit caelum nubibus et parat terrae pluviam, qui producit in montibus faenum et herbam servituti hominum, 9 qui dat iumentis escam ipsorum et pullis corvo-

the ways of sinners he will destroy. 10 The Lord shall reign for ever, thy God, O Zion, unto generation and generation.

Psalm 146

Laudate Dominum. An exhortation to praise God for his benefits.

Alleluia.

Praise ye the Lord, because psalm is good! To our God be joyful and comely praise. 2 The Lord buildeth up Jerusalem; he will gather together the dispersed of Israel, 3 who healeth the broken of heart and bindeth up their bruises, 4 who *telleth the number* of the stars and calleth them all by their names. 5 Great is our Lord, and great is his power, and of his wisdom there is no number. 6 The Lord lifteth up the meek, and bringeth the wicked down even to the ground.

7 Sing ye to the Lord with praise! Sing to our God upon the harp, 8 who covereth the heaven with clouds and prepareth rain for the earth, who maketh grass to grow on the mountains and herbs for the service of men, 9 who giveth to beasts their food and to the young ravens that call upon

rum invocantibus eum. 10 Non in fortitudine equi voluntatem habebit nec in tibiis viri beneplacitum erit ei. 11 Beneplacitum est Domino super timentes eum et in eis qui sperant super misericordia eius.

Psalmus 147

Alleluia.

Lauda, Hierusalem, Dominum! Lauda Deum tuum, Sion! 2 Quoniam confortavit seras portarum tuarum, benedixit filiis tuis in te, 3 qui posuit fines tuos pacem et adipe frumenti satiat te, 4 qui emittit eloquium suum terrae—velociter currit sermo eius—5 qui dat nivem sicut lanam, nebulam sicut cinerem spargit. 6 Mittit cristallum suum sicut buccellas. Ante faciem frigoris eius quis sustinebit? 7 Emittet verbum suum et liquefaciet ea; flabit spiritus eius et fluent aquae. 8 Qui adnuntiat verbum suum Iacob, iustitias et iudicia sua Israhel, 9 non fecit taliter omni nationi, et iudicia sua non manifestavit eis.

Alleluia.

him. 10 He shall not delight in the strength of the horse nor take pleasure in the legs of a man. 11 The Lord taketh pleasure in them that fear him and in them that hope in his mercy.

Psalm 147

Lauda, Hierusalem. The church is called upon to praise God for his peculiar graces and favours to his people. In the Hebrew, this psalm is joined to the foregoing.

Alleluia.

Praise the Lord, O Jerusalem! Praise thy God, O Zion! 2 Because he hath strengthened the bolts of thy gates, he hath blessed thy children within thee, 3 who hath placed peace in thy borders and filleth thee with the fat of corn, 4 who sendeth forth his speech to the earth—his word runneth swiftly—5 who giveth snow like wool, scattereth mists like ashes. 6 He sendeth his crystal like morsels. Who shall stand before the face of his cold? 7 He shall send out his word and shall melt them; his wind shall blow and the waters shall run. 8 Who declareth his word to Jacob, his justices and his judgments to Israel, 9 he hath not done in like manner to every nation, and his judgments he hath not made manifest to them.

Alleluia.

Psalmus 148

Alleluia.

Laudate Dominum de caelis! Laudate eum in excelsis! 2 Laudate eum, omnes angeli eius! Laudate eum, omnes virtutes eius! 3 Laudate eum, sol et luna! Laudate eum, omnes stellae et lumen! 4 Laudate eum, caeli caelorum, et aquae quae super caelos sunt 5 laudent nomen Domini, quia ipse dixit, et facta sunt; ipse mandavit, et creata sunt. 6 Statuit ea in saeculum et in saeculum saeculi; praeceptum posuit, et non praeteribit.

7 Laudate Dominum de terra, dracones et omnes abyssi, 8 ignis, grando, nix, glacies, spiritus procellarum, quae faciunt verbum eius, 9 montes et omnes colles, ligna fructifera et omnes cedri, 10 bestiae et universa pecora, serpentes et volucres pinnatae, 11 reges terrae et omnes populi, principes et omnes iudices terrae, 12 iuvenes et virgines! Senes cum iunioribus laudent nomen Domini, 13 quia exaltatum est nomen eius solius.

Psalm 148

Laudate Dominum de caelis. All creatures are invited to praise their Creator.

Alleluia.

Praise ye the Lord from the heavens! Praise ye him in the high places! 2 Praise ye him, all his angels! Praise ye him, all his hosts! 3 Praise ye him, O sun and moon! Praise him, all ye stars and light! 4 Praise him, ye heavens of heavens, and let all the waters that are above the heavens 5 praise the name of the Lord, for he spoke, and they were made; he commanded, and they were created. 6 He hath established them for ever and for ages of ages; he hath made a decree, and it shall not pass away.

7 Praise the Lord from the earth, ye dragons and all ye deeps, 8 fire, hail, snow, ice, stormy winds, which fulfil his word, 9 mountains and all hills, fruitful trees and all cedars, 10 beasts and all cattle, serpents and feathered fowls, 11 kings of the earth and all people, princes and all judges of the earth, 12 young men and maidens! Let the old with the younger praise the name of the Lord, 13 for his name alone is exalted.

14 Confessio eius super caelum et terram, et exaltavit cornu populi sui, hymnus omnibus sanctis eius, filiis Israhel, populo adpropinquanti sibi.
Alleluia.

Psalmus 149

Alleluia.

Cantate Domino canticum novum; laus eius in ecclesia sanctorum. 2 Laetetur Israhel in eo qui fecit eum, et filii Sion exultent in rege suo. 3 Laudent nomen eius in choro; in tympano et psalterio psallant ei, 4 quia beneplacitum est Domino in populo suo et exaltabit mansuetos in salutem. 5 Exultabunt sancti in gloria; laetabuntur in cubilibus suis. 6 Exaltationes Dei in gutture eorum et gladii ancipites in manibus eorum 7 ad faciendam vindictam in nationibus, increpationes in populis, 8 ad alligandos reges eorum in conpedibus et nobiles eorum in manicis ferreis, 9 ut faciant in eis iudicium conscriptum. Gloria haec est omnibus sanctis eius.
Alleluia.

14 The praise of him is above heaven and earth, and he hath exalted the horn of his people, a hymn to all his saints, to the children of Israel, a people approaching to him. Alleluia.

Psalm 149

Cantate Domino. The church is particularly bound to praise God.

Alleluia.

Sing ye to the Lord a new canticle; let his praise be in the church of the saints. 2 Let Israel rejoice in him that made him, and let the children of Zion be joyful in their king. 3 Let them praise his name in choir; let them sing to him with the timbrel and the psaltery, 4 for the Lord is well pleased with his people and he will exalt the meek unto salvation. 5 The saints shall rejoice in glory; they shall be joyful in their beds. 6 The high praises of God shall be in their mouth and two-edged swords in their hands 7 to execute vengeance upon the nations, chastisements among the people, 8 to bind their kings with fetters and their nobles with manacles of iron, 9 to execute upon them the judgment that is written. This glory is to all his saints. Alleluia.

Psalmus 150

Alleluia.

Laudate Dominum in sanctis eius! Laudate eum in firmamento virtutis eius! 2 Laudate eum in virtutibus eius! Laudate eum secundum multitudinem magnitudinis eius! 3 Laudate eum in sono tubae! Laudate eum in psalterio et cithara! 4 Laudate eum in tympano et choro! Laudate eum in cordis et organo! 5 Laudate eum in cymbalis bene sonantibus! Laudate eum in cymbalis iubilationis!

6 Omnis spiritus laudet Dominum!

Alleluia.

Psalm 150

Laudate Dominum in sanctis. An exhortation to praise God with all sorts of instruments.

Alleluia.

Praise ye the Lord in his holy places! Praise ye him in the firmament of his power! 2 Praise ye him for his mighty acts! Praise ye him according to the multitude of his greatness! 3 Praise him with the sound of trumpet! Praise him with psaltery and harp! 4 Praise him with timbrel and choir! Praise him with strings and organs! 5 Praise him on *high* sounding cymbals! Praise him on cymbals of joy!

6 Let every spirit praise the Lord!

Alleluia.

PROVERBS

Caput 1

Parabolae Salomonis, filii David, regis Israhel, 2 ad sciendam sapientiam et disciplinam, 3 ad intellegenda verba prudentiae et suscipiendam eruditionem doctrinae, iustitiam et iudicium et aequitatem, 4 ut detur parvulis astutia, adulescenti scientia et intellectus.

5 Audiens sapiens sapientior erit, et intellegens gubernacula possidebit. 6 Animadvertet parabolam et interpretationem, verba sapientium et enigmata eorum. 7 Timor Domini principium sapientiae. Sapientiam atque doctrinam stulti despiciunt.

8 Audi, fili mi, disciplinam patris tui, et ne dimittas legem matris tuae, 9 ut addatur gratia capiti tuo et torques aurea collo tuo. 10 Fili mi, si te lactaverint peccatores, ne adquiescas eis. 11 Si dixerint, "Veni nobiscum; insidiemur sanguini; abscondamus tendiculas contra insontem frustra; 12 degluttiamus eum sicut infernus viventem et integrum quasi de-

Chapter 1

The use and end of the proverbs. An exhortation to flee
the company of the wicked and to hearken to the voice of
wisdom.

The parables of Solomon, the son of David, king of Israel,
2 to know wisdom and instruction, 3 to understand the
words of prudence and to receive the instruction of doctrine, justice and judgment and equity, 4 to give subtilty to
little ones, to the young man knowledge and understanding.

5 A wise man shall hear and shall be wiser, and he that
understandeth shall possess governments. 6 He shall understand a parable and the interpretation, the words of the wise
and their mysterious sayings. 7 The fear of the Lord is the
beginning of wisdom. Fools despise wisdom and instruction.

8 My son, hear the instruction of thy father, and forsake
not the law of thy mother, 9 that grace may be added to
thy head and a chain of gold to thy neck. 10 My son, if sinners shall entice thee, consent not to them. 11 If they shall
say, "Come with us; let us lie in wait for blood; let us hide
snares for the innocent without cause; 12 let us swallow him
up alive like hell and whole as one that goeth down into

scendentem in lacum. 13 Omnem pretiosam substantiam repperiemus; implebimus domos nostras spoliis. 14 Sortem mitte nobiscum; marsuppium unum sit omnium nostrum," 15 fili mi, ne ambules cum eis; prohibe pedem tuum a semitis eorum, 16 pedes enim illorum ad malum currunt et festinant ut effundant sanguinem. 17 Frustra autem iacitur rete ante oculos pinnatorum, 18 ipsi quoque contra sanguinem suum insidiantur et moliuntur fraudes contra animas suas. 19 Sic semitae omnis avari animas possidentium rapiunt.

20 Sapientia foris praedicat; in plateis dat vocem suam. 21 In capite turbarum clamitat; in foribus portarum urbis profert verba sua, dicens, 22 "Usquequo, parvuli, diligitis infantiam et stulti ea quae sibi sunt noxia cupiunt et inprudentes odibunt scientiam? 23 Convertimini ad correptionem meam. En: proferam vobis spiritum meum et ostendam vobis verba mea. 24 Quia vocavi et rennuistis, extendi manum meam, et non fuit qui aspiceret. 25 Despexistis omne consilium meum et increpationes meas neglexistis. 26 Ego quoque in interitu vestro ridebo et subsannabo cum vobis id quod timebatis advenerit. 27 Cum inruerit repentina calamitas et interitus quasi tempestas ingruerit, quando venerit super vos tribulatio et angustia, 28 tunc invocabunt me, et non exaudiam; mane consurgent et non invenient me, 29 eo quod exosam habuerint disciplinam et timorem Domini non susceperint 30 nec adquieverint consilio meo et detraxerint universae correptioni meae. 31 Comedent igitur fructus viae suae suisque consiliis saturabuntur. 32 Aversio parvulorum

the pit. 13 We shall find all precious substance; we shall fill our houses with spoils. 14 Cast in thy lot with us; let us all have one purse," 15 my son, walk not thou with them; restrain thy foot from their paths, 16 for their feet run to evil and make haste to shed blood. 17 But a net is spread in vain before the eyes of them that have wings, 18 and they themselves lie in wait for their own blood and practise deceits against their own souls. 19 So the ways of every covetous man destroy the souls of the possessors.

20 Wisdom preacheth abroad; she uttereth her voice in the streets. 21 At the head of multitudes she crieth out; in the entrance of the gates of the city she uttereth her words, saying, 22 "O children, how long will you love childishness and fools covet those things which are hurtful to themselves and the unwise hate knowledge? 23 Turn ye at my reproof. Behold: I will utter my spirit to you and will shew you my words. 24 Because I called and you refused, I stretched out my hand, and there was none that regarded. 25 You have despised all my counsel and have neglected my reprehensions. 26 I also will laugh in your destruction and will mock when that shall come to you which you feared. 27 When sudden calamity shall fall on you and destruction as a tempest shall be at hand, when tribulation and distress shall come upon you, 28 then shall they call upon me, and I will not hear; they shall rise in the morning and shall not find me, 29 because they have hated instruction and received not the fear of the Lord 30 nor consented to my counsel *but* despised all my reproof. 31 Therefore they shall eat the fruit of their own way and shall be filled with their own devices. 32 The turning

interficiet eos, et prosperitas stultorum perdet illos. 33 Qui autem me audierit absque terrore requiescet et abundantia perfruetur malorum timore sublato."

Caput 2

Fili mi, si susceperis sermones meos et mandata mea absconderis penes te 2 ut audiat sapientiam auris tua, inclina cor tuum ad noscendam prudentiam, 3 si enim sapientiam invocaveris et inclinaveris cor tuum prudentiae, 4 si quaesieris eam quasi pecuniam et sicut thesauros effoderis illam, 5 tunc intelleges timorem Domini et scientiam Dei invenies 6 quia Dominus dat sapientiam, et ex ore eius scientia et prudentia. 7 Custodiet rectorum salutem et proteget gradientes simpliciter, 8 servans semitas iustitiae et vias sanctorum custodiens. 9 Tunc intelleges iustitiam et iudicium et aequitatem et omnem semitam bonam.

10 Si intraverit sapientia cor tuum et scientia animae tuae placuerit, 11 consilium custodiet te, et prudentia servabit te 12 ut eruaris de via mala et ab homine qui perversa loquitur,

away of little ones shall kill them, and the prosperity of fools shall destroy them. 33 But he that shall hear me shall rest without terror and shall enjoy abundance *without* fear of evils."

Chapter 2

The advantages of wisdom and the evils from which it delivers.

My son, if thou wilt receive my words and wilt hide my commandments with thee 2 that thy ear may hearken to wisdom, incline thy heart to know prudence, 3 for if thou shalt call for wisdom and incline thy heart to prudence, 4 if thou shalt seek her as money and shalt dig for her as for a treasure, 5 then shalt thou understand the fear of the Lord and shalt find the knowledge of God 6 because the Lord giveth wisdom, and out of his mouth cometh prudence and knowledge. 7 He wilt keep the salvation of the righteous and protect them that walk in simplicity, 8 keeping the paths of justice and guarding the ways of saints. 9 Then shalt thou understand justice and judgment and equity and every good path.

10 If wisdom shall enter into thy heart and knowledge please thy soul, 11 counsel shall keep thee, and prudence shall preserve thee, 12 that thou mayst be delivered from the evil way and from the man that speaketh perverse things,

13 qui relinquunt iter rectum et ambulant per vias tenebrosas, 14 qui laetantur cum malefecerint et exultant in rebus pessimis, 15 quorum viae perversae et infames gressus eorum, 16 ut eruaris a muliere aliena et ab extranea quae mollit sermones suos 17 et relinquit ducem pubertatis suae 18 et pacti Dei sui oblita est, inclinata est enim ad mortem domus eius et ad inferos semitae ipsius—19 omnes qui ingrediuntur ad eam non revertentur, nec adprehendent semitas vitae—20 ut ambules in via bona et calles iustorum custodias, 21 qui enim recti sunt habitabunt in terra, et simplices permanebunt in ea. 22 Impii vero de terra perdentur, et qui inique agunt auferentur ex ea.

Caput 3

Fili mi, ne obliviscaris legis meae, et praecepta mea custodiat cor tuum, 2 longitudinem enim dierum et annos vitae et pacem adponent tibi. 3 Misericordia et veritas non te deserant; circumda eas gutturi tuo, et describe in tabulis cordis tui, 4 et invenies gratiam et disciplinam bonam coram Deo et hominibus. 5 Habe fiduciam in Domino ex toto corde tuo,

13 who leave the right way and walk by dark ways, 14 who are glad when they have done evil and rejoice in the most wicked things, 15 whose ways are perverse and their steps infamous, 16 that thou mayst be delivered from the strange woman and from the stranger who softeneth her words 17 and forsaketh the guide of her youth 18 and hath forgotten the covenant of her God, for her house inclineth unto death and her paths to hell—19 none that go in unto her shall return again, neither shall they take hold of the paths of life—20 that thou mayst walk in a good way and mayst keep the paths of the just, 21 for they that are upright shall dwell in the earth, and the simple shall continue in it. 22 But the wicked shall be destroyed from the earth, and they that do unjustly shall be taken away from it.

Chapter 3

An exhortation to the practice of virtue.

My son, forget not my law, and let thy heart keep my commandments, 2 for they shall add to thee length of days and years of life and peace. 3 Let not mercy and truth leave thee; put them about thy neck, and write them in the tables of thy heart, 4 and thou shalt find grace and good understanding before God and men. 5 Have confidence in the Lord with all thy heart, and lean not upon thy own

et ne innitaris prudentiae tuae. 6 In omnibus viis tuis cogita illum, et ipse diriget gressus tuos. 7 Ne sis sapiens apud temet ipsum; time Deum, et recede a malo, 8 sanitas quippe erit umbilico tuo et inrigatio ossuum tuorum. 9 Honora Dominum de tua substantia, et de primitiis omnium frugum tuarum da ei, 10 et implebuntur horrea tua saturitate, et vino torcularia tua redundabunt. 11 Disciplinam Domini, fili mi, ne abicias, nec deficias cum ab eo corriperis, 12 quem enim diligit Dominus, corripit, et quasi pater in filio conplacet sibi.

13 Beatus homo qui invenit sapientiam et qui affluit prudentia: 14 melior est adquisitio eius negotiatione argenti et auro primo et purissimo fructus eius. 15 Pretiosior est cunctis opibus, et omnia quae desiderantur huic non valent conparari. 16 Longitudo dierum in dextera eius, et in sinistra illius divitiae et gloria 17 Viae eius viae pulchrae, et omnes semitae illius pacificae. 18 Lignum vitae est his qui adprehenderint eam, et qui tenuerit eam beatus. 19 Dominus sapientia fundavit terram, stabilivit caelos prudentia. 20 Sapientia illius eruperunt abyssi et nubes rore concrescunt. 21 Fili mi, ne effluant haec ab oculis tuis; custodi legem atque consilium, 22 et erit vita animae tuae et gratia faucibus tuis. 23 Tunc ambulabis fiducialiter in via tua, et pes tuus non inpinget. 24 Si dormieris, non timebis; quiesces, et suavis erit somnus tuus. 25 Ne paveas repentino terrore et inruentes tibi potentias impiorum, 26 Dominus enim erit in latere tuo et custodiet pedem tuum ne capiaris.

prudence. 6 In all thy ways think on him, and he will direct thy steps. 7 Be not wise in thy own conceit; fear God, and depart from evil, 8 for it shall be health to thy navel and moistening to thy bones. 9 Honour the Lord with thy substance, and give him of the first of all thy fruits, 10 and thy barns shall be filled with abundance, and thy presses shall run over with wine. 11 My son, reject not the correction of the Lord, and do not faint when thou art chastised by him, 12 for whom the Lord loveth, he chastiseth, and as a father in the son he pleaseth himself.

13 Blessed is the man that findeth wisdom and is rich in prudence: 14 the purchasing thereof is better than the merchandise of silver and her fruit than the chief and purest gold. 15 She is more precious than all riches, and all the things that are desired are not to be compared to her. 16 Length of days is in her right hand, and in her left hand riches and glory. 17 Her ways are beautiful ways, and all her paths are peaceable. 18 She is a tree of life to them that lay hold on her, and he that shall retain her is blessed. 19 The Lord by wisdom hath founded the earth, hath established the heavens by prudence. 20 By his wisdom the depths have broken out and the clouds grow thick with dew. 21 My son, let not these things depart from thy eyes; keep the law and counsel, 22 and there shall be life to thy soul and grace to thy mouth. 23 Then shalt thou walk confidently in thy way, and thy foot shall not stumble. 24 If thou sleep, thou shalt not fear; thou shalt rest, and thy sleep shall be sweet. 25 Be not afraid of sudden fear nor of the power of the wicked falling upon thee, 26 for the Lord will be at thy side and will keep thy foot that thou be not taken.

27 Noli prohibere benefacere eum qui potest; si vales, et ipse benefac. 28 Ne dicas amico tuo, "Vade, et revertere, et cras dabo tibi," cum statim possis dare. 29 Ne moliaris amico tuo malum cum ille in te habeat fiduciam. 30 Ne contendas adversus hominem frustra cum ipse tibi nihil mali fecerit. 31 Ne aemuleris hominem iniustum, nec imiteris vias eius, 32 quia abominatio Domini est omnis inlusor, et cum simplicibus sermocinatio eius. 33 Egestas a Domino in domo impii, habitacula autem iustorum benedicentur. 34 Inlusores ipse deludet, et mansuetis dabit gratiam. 35 Gloriam sapientes possidebunt; stultorum exaltatio ignominia.

Caput 4

Audite, filii, disciplinam patris, et adtendite, ut sciatis prudentiam. 2 Donum bonum tribuam vobis; legem meam ne derelinquatis, 3 nam et ego filius fui patris mei, tenellus, et unigenitus coram matre mea. 4 Et docebat me atque dicebat, "Suscipiat verba mea cor tuum; custodi praecepta mea, et vives. 5 Posside sapientiam; posside prudentiam; ne obli-

27 Do not withhold him from doing good who is able; if thou art able, do good thyself also. 28 Say not to thy friend, "Go, and come again, and tomorrow I will give to thee," when thou canst give at present. 29 Practise not evil against thy friend when he hath confidence in thee. 30 Strive not against a man without cause when he hath done thee no evil. 31 Envy not the unjust man, and do not follow his ways, 32 for every mocker is an abomination to the Lord, and his communication is with the simple. 33 Want is from the Lord in the house of the wicked, but the habitations of the just shall be blessed. 34 He shall scorn the scorners, and to the meek he will give grace. 35 The wise shall possess glory; the promotion of fools is disgrace.

Chapter 4

A further exhortation to seek after wisdom.

Hear, ye children, the instruction of a father, and attend, that you may know prudence. 2 I will give you a good gift; forsake not my law, 3 for I also was my father's son, tender, and as an only son in the sight of my mother. 4 And he taught me and said, "Let thy heart receive my words; keep my commandments, and thou shalt live. 5 Get wisdom; get prudence; forget not, neither decline from the words

viscaris, neque declines a verbis oris mei. 6 Ne dimittas eam, et custodiet te; dilige eam, et servabit te."

7 Principium sapientiae: posside sapientiam, et in omni possessione tua adquire prudentiam. 8 Arripe illam, et exaltabit te; glorificaberis ab ea cum eam fueris amplexatus. 9 Dabit capiti tuo augmenta gratiarum et corona inclita proteget te.

10 Audi, fili mi, et suscipe verba mea, ut multiplicentur tibi anni vitae. 11 Viam sapientiae monstrabo tibi; ducam te per semitas aequitatis, 12 quas cum ingressus fueris, non artabuntur gressus tui, et currens non habebis offendiculum. 13 Tene disciplinam; ne dimittas eam; custodi illam, quia ipsa est vita tua. 14 Ne delecteris in semitis impiorum, nec tibi placeat malorum via. 15 Fuge ab ea, nec transeas per illam; declina, et desere eam, 16 non enim dormiunt nisi malefecerint, et capitur somnus ab eis nisi subplantaverint. 17 Comedunt panem impietatis et vinum iniquitatis bibunt. 18 Iustorum autem semita quasi lux splendens procedit et crescit usque ad perfectam diem. 19 Via impiorum tenebrosa; nesciunt ubi corruant.

20 Fili mi, ausculta sermones meos, et ad eloquia mea inclina aurem tuam. 21 Ne recedant ab oculis tuis; custodi ea in medio cordis tui, 22 vita enim sunt invenientibus ea et universae carni sanitas. 23 Omni custodia serva cor tuum quia ex ipso vita procedit. 24 Remove a te os pravum, et detrahentia labia sint procul a te. 25 Oculi tui recta videant, et palpebrae tuae praecedant gressus tuos. 26 Dirige semitam pedibus tuis, et omnes viae tuae stabilientur. 27 Ne declines ad

of my mouth. 6 Forsake her not, and she shall keep thee; love her, and she shall preserve thee."

7 The beginning of wisdom: get wisdom, and with all thy possession purchase prudence. 8 Take hold on her, and she shall exalt thee; thou shalt be glorified by her when thou shalt embrace her. 9 She shall give to thy head increase of graces and protect thee with a noble crown.

10 Hear, O my son, and receive my words, that years of life may be multiplied to thee. 11 I will shew thee the way of wisdom; I will lead thee by the paths of equity, 12 which when thou shalt have entered, thy steps shall not be straitened, and when thou runnest thou shalt not meet a stumbling block. 13 Take hold on instruction; leave it not; keep it, because it is thy life. 14 Be not delighted in the paths of the wicked, neither let the way of evil men please thee. 15 Flee from it; pass *not* by it; go aside, and forsake it, 16 for they sleep not except they have done evil, and *their sleep is taken away* unless they have made *some* to fall. 17 They eat the bread of wickedness and drink the wine of iniquity. 18 But the path of the just as a shining light goeth forwards and increaseth even to perfect day. 19 The way of the wicked is darksome; they know not where they fall.

20 My son, hearken to my words, and incline thy ear to my sayings. 21 Let them not depart from thy eyes; keep them in the midst of thy heart, 22 for they are life to those that find them and health to all flesh. 23 With all watchfulness keep thy heart because life issueth out from it. 24 Remove from thee a froward mouth, and let detracting lips be far from thee. 25 Let thy eyes look straight on, and let thy eyelids go before thy steps. 26 Make straight the path for thy feet, and all thy ways shall be established. 27 Decline not to the right

dexteram neque ad sinistram; averte pedem tuum a malo, vias enim quae a dextris sunt novit Dominus, perversae vero sunt quae a sinistris sunt. Ipse autem rectos faciet cursus tuos, initera autem tua in pace producet.

Caput 5

Fili mi, adtende sapientiam meam, et prudentiae meae inclina aurem tuam 2 ut custodias cogitationes et disciplinam labia tua conservent. Ne adtendas fallaciae mulieris, 3 favus enim distillans labia meretricis et nitidius oleo guttur eius, 4 novissima autem illius amara quasi absinthium et acuta quasi gladius biceps. 5 Pedes eius descendunt in mortem, et ad inferos gressus illius penetrant. 6 Per semitam vitae non ambulant. Vagi sunt gressus eius et investigabiles. 7 Nunc, ergo, fili mi, audi me, et ne recedas a verbis oris mei. 8 Longe fac ab ea viam tuam, et ne adpropinques foribus domus eius. 9 Ne des alienis honorem tuum et annos tuos crudeli 10 ne forte impleantur extranei viribus tuis et labores tui sint in domo aliena 11 et gemas in novissimis quando consumpseris carnes tuas et corpus tuum et dicas, 12 "Cur detestatus sum disciplinam et increpationibus non adquievit cor meum 13 nec audivi vocem docentium me et magistris non inclinavi

hand nor to the left; turn away thy foot from evil, for the Lord knoweth the ways that are on the right hand, but those are perverse which are on the left hand. But he will make thy courses straight; he will bring forward thy ways in peace.

Chapter 5

An exhortation to fly unlawful lust and the occasions of it.

My son, attend to my wisdom, and incline thy ear to my prudence 2 that thou mayst keep thoughts and thy lips may preserve instruction. Mind not the deceit of a woman, 3 for the lips of a harlot are like a honeycomb dropping and her throat is smoother than oil, 4 but her end is bitter as wormwood and sharp as a two-edged sword. 5 Her feet go down into death, and her steps go in as far as hell. 6 They walk not by the path of life. Her steps are wandering and unaccountable. 7 Now, therefore, my son, hear me, and depart not from the words of my mouth. 8 Remove thy way far from her, and come not nigh the doors of her house. 9 Give not thy honour to strangers and thy years to the cruel 10 *lest* strangers be filled with thy strength and thy labours be in another man's house 11 and thou mourn at the last when thou shalt have spent thy flesh and thy body and say, 12 "Why have I hated instruction and my heart consented not to reproof 13 and have not heard the voice of them that taught me and have

aurem meam? 14 Paene fui in omni malo in medio ecclesiae et synagogae." 15 Bibe aquam de cisterna tua et fluenta putei tui. 16 Deriventur fontes tui foras, et in plateis aquas tuas divide. 17 Habeto eas solus, nec sint alieni participes tui. 18 Sit vena tua benedicta, et laetare cum muliere adulescentiae tuae. 19 Cerva carissima et gratissimus hinulus. Ubera eius inebrient te omni tempore; in amore illius delectare iugiter.

20 Quare seduceris, fili mi, ab aliena et foveris sinu alterius? 21 Respicit Dominus vias hominis et omnes gressus illius considerat. 22 Iniquitates suae capiunt impium, et funibus peccatorum suorum constringitur. 23 Ipse morietur quia non habuit disciplinam, et in multitudine stultitiae suae decipietur.

Caput 6

Fili mi, si spoponderis pro amico tuo, defixisti apud extraneum manum tuam; 2 inlaqueatus es verbis oris tui et captus propriis sermonibus. 3 Fac, ergo, quod dico, fili mi, et temet

not inclined my ear to masters? 14 I have almost been in all evil in the midst of the church and of the congregation."

15 Drink water out of thy own cistern and the streams of thy own well. 16 Let thy fountains be conveyed abroad, and in the streets divide thy waters. 17 Keep them to thyself alone, neither let strangers be partakers with thee. 18 Let thy vein be blessed, and rejoice with the wife of thy youth. 19 Let her be thy dearest hind and most agreeable fawn. Let her breasts inebriate thee at all times; be thou delighted continually with her love.

20 Why art thou seduced, my son, by a strange woman and art cherished in the bosom of another? 21 The Lord beholdeth the ways of man and considereth all his steps. 22 His own iniquities catch the wicked, and he is fast bound with the ropes of his own sins. 23 He shall die because he hath not received instruction, and in the multitude of his folly he shall be deceived.

Chapter 6

Documents on several heads.

My son, if thou be surety for thy friend, thou hast engaged fast thy hand to a stranger; 2 thou art ensnared with the words of thy mouth and caught with thy own words. 3 Do, therefore, my son, what I say, and deliver thyself,

ipsum libera, quia incidisti in manum proximi tui. Discurre; festina; suscita amicum tuum; 4 ne dederis somnum oculis tuis, nec dormitent palpebrae tuae. 5 Eruere quasi dammula de manu et quasi avis de manu aucupis.

6 Vade ad formicam, O piger, et considera vias eius, et disce sapientiam, 7 quae, cum non habeat ducem nec praeceptorem nec principem, 8 parat aestate cibum sibi et congregat in messe quod comedat. 9 Usquequo, piger, dormies? Quando consurges ex somno tuo? 10 Paululum dormies; paululum dormitabis; paululum conseres manus ut dormias, 11 et veniet tibi quasi viator egestas, et pauperies quasi vir armatus. Si vero impiger fueris, veniet ut fons messis tua, et egestas longe fugiet a te.

12 Homo apostata, vir inutilis, graditur ore perverso. 13 Annuit oculis, terit pede, digito loquitur. 14 Pravo corde machinatur malum, et in omni tempore iurgia seminat. 15 Huic extemplo veniet perditio sua, et subito contereretur nec habebit ultra medicinam.

16 Sex sunt quae odit Dominus, et septimum detestatur anima eius: 17 oculos sublimes, linguam mendacem, manus effundentes innoxium sanguinem, 18 cor machinans cogitationes pessimas, pedes veloces ad currendum in malum, 19 proferentem mendacia testem fallacem et eum qui seminat inter fratres discordias.

because thou art fallen into the hand of thy neighbour. Run about; make haste; stir up thy friend; 4 give not sleep to thy eyes, neither let thy eyelids slumber. 5 Deliver thyself as a doe from the hand and as a bird from the hand of the fowler.

6 Go to the ant, O sluggard, and consider her ways, and learn wisdom, 7 which, although she hath no guide nor master nor captain, 8 provideth her meat for herself in the summer and gathereth *her food* in the harvest. 9 How long wilt thou sleep, O sluggard? When wilt thou arise out of thy sleep? 10 Thou wilt sleep a little; thou wilt slumber a little; thou wilt fold thy hands a little to sleep, 11 and want shall come upon thee as a traveller, and poverty as a man armed. But if thou be diligent, thy harvest shall come as a fountain, and want shall flee far from thee.

12 A man that is an apostate, an unprofitable man, walketh with a perverse mouth. 13 He winketh with the eyes, presseth with the foot, speaketh with the finger. 14 With a wicked heart he deviseth evil, and at all times he soweth discord. 15 To *such a one* his destruction shall presently come, and he shall suddenly be destroyed and shall no longer have any remedy.

16 Six things there are which the Lord hateth, and the seventh his soul detesteth: 17 haughty eyes, a lying tongue, hands that shed innocent blood, 18 a heart that deviseth wicked plots, feet that are swift to run into mischief, 19 a deceitful witness that uttereth lies and him that soweth discord among brethren.

20 Conserva, fili mi, praecepta patris tui, et ne dimittas legem matris tuae. 21 Liga ea in corde tuo iugiter, et circumda gutturi tuo. 22 Cum ambulaveris, gradiantur tecum; cum dormieris, custodiant te, et evigilans loquere cum eis, 23 quia mandatum lucerna est et lex lux et via vitae increpatio disciplinae, 24 ut custodiant te a muliere mala et a blanda lingua extraneae. 25 Non concupiscat pulchritudinem eius cor tuum; nec capiaris nutibus illius, 26 pretium enim scorti vix unius est panis, mulier autem viri pretiosam animam capit.

27 Numquid abscondere potest homo ignem in sinu suo ut vestimenta illius non ardeant? 28 Aut ambulare super prunas ut non conburantur plantae eius? 29 Sic qui ingreditur ad mulierem proximi sui non erit mundus cum tetigerit eam. 30 Non grandis est culpa cum quis furatus fuerit, furatur enim ut esurientem impleat animam. 31 Deprehensus quoque, reddet septuplum et omnem substantiam domus suae tradet. 32 Qui autem adulter est, propter cordis inopiam perdet animam suam. 33 Turpitudinem et ignominiam congregat sibi, et obprobrium illius non delebitur 34 quia zelus et furor viri non parcet in die vindictae, 35 nec adquiescet cuiusquam precibus, nec suscipiet pro redemptione dona plurima.

20 My son, keep the commandments of thy father, and forsake not the law of thy mother. 21 Bind them in thy heart continually, and put them about thy neck. 22 When thou walkest, let them go with thee; when thou sleepest, let them keep thee, and when thou awakest, talk with them, 23 bcause the commandment is a lamp and the law a light and reproofs of instruction are the way of life, 24 that they may keep thee from the evil woman and from the flattering tongue of the stranger. 25 Let not thy heart covet her beauty; be not caught with her winks, 26 for the price of a harlot is scarce one loaf, but the woman catcheth the precious soul of a man.

27 Can a man hide fire in his bosom *and* his garments not burn? 28 Or can he walk upon hot coals *and* his feet not be burnt? 29 So he that goeth in to his neighbour's wife shall not be clean when he shall touch her. 30 The fault is not *so* great when a man hath stolen, for he stealeth to fill his hungry soul. 31 And if he be taken, he shall restore sevenfold and shall give up all the substance of his house. 32 But he that is an adulterer, for the folly of his heart shall destroy his own soul. 33 He gathereth to himself shame and dishonour, and his reproach shall not be blotted out 34 because the jealousy and rage of the husband will not spare in the day of revenge, 35 nor will he yield to any man's prayers, nor will he accept for satisfaction ever so many gifts.

Caput 7

Fili mi, custodi sermones meos, et praecepta mea reconde tibi. Fili, 2 serva mandata mea—et vives—et legem meam quasi pupillam oculi tui. 3 Liga eam in digitis tuis; scribe illam in tabulis cordis tui. 4 Dic sapientiae, "Soror mea es," et prudentiam voca amicam tuam 5 ut custodiat te a muliere extranea et ab aliena quae verba sua dulcia facit.

6 De fenestra enim domus meae per cancellos prospexi, 7 et video parvulos. Considero vecordem iuvenem 8 qui transit per plateas iuxta angulum et propter viam domus illius graditur 9 in obscuro advesperascente die, in noctis tenebris et caligine. 10 Et ecce: mulier occurrit illi ornatu meretricio, praeparata ad capiendas animas, garrula et vaga, 11 quietis inpatiens, nec valens in domo consistere pedibus suis, 12 nunc foris, nunc in plateis, nunc iuxta angulos insidians. 13 Adprehensumque deosculatur iuvenem et procaci vultu blanditur, dicens, 14 "Victimas pro salute vovi; hodie reddidi vota mea. 15 Idcirco egressa sum in occursum tuum, desiderans te videre, et repperi. 16 Intexui funibus lectum meum; stravi tapetibus pictis ex Aegypto. 17 Aspersi cubile

Chapter 7

The love of wisdom is the best preservative from being led astray by temptation.

My son, keep my words, and lay up my precepts with thee. Son, 2 keep my commandments—and thou shalt live— and my law as the apple of thy eye. 3 Bind it upon thy fingers; write it upon the tables of thy heart. 4 Say to wisdom, "Thou art my sister," and call prudence thy friend 5 that she may keep thee from the woman that is not thine and from the stranger who sweeteneth her words.

6 For I looked out of the window of my house through the lattice, 7 and I see little ones. I behold a foolish young man 8 who passeth through the *street* by the corner and goeth nigh the way of her house 9 in the dark when it grows late, in the darkness and obscurity of the night. 10 And behold: a woman meeteth him in harlot's attire, prepared to deceive souls, talkative and wandering, 11 not bearing to be quiet, not able to abide *still* at home, 12 now abroad, now in the streets, now lying in wait near the corners. 13 And catching the young man she kisseth him and with an impudent face flattereth, saying, 14 "I vowed victims for prosperity; this day I have paid my vows. 15 Therefore I am come out to meet thee, desirous to see thee, and I have found thee. 16 I have woven my bed with cords; I have covered it with painted tapestry brought from Egypt. 17 I have *perfumed* my bed

meum murra, aloe et cinnamomo. 18 Veni; inebriemur uberibus, et fruamur cupitis amplexibus donec inlucescat dies, 19 non est enim vir in domo sua; abiit via longissima; 20 sacculum pecuniae secum tulit; in die plenae lunae reversurus est domum suam."

21 Inretivit eum multis sermonibus et blanditiis labiorum protraxit illum. 22 Statim eam sequitur quasi bos ductus ad victimam et quasi agnus lasciviens et ignorans quod ad vincula stultus trahatur 23 donec transfigat sagitta iecur eius velut si avis festinet ad laqueum et nescit quia de periculo animae illius agitur.

24 Nunc, ergo, fili mi, audi me, et adtende verba oris mei. 25 Ne abstrahatur in viis illius mens tua, neque decipiaris semitis eius, 26 multos enim vulneratos deiecit, et fortissimi quique interfecti sunt ab ea. 27 Viae inferi domus eius, penetrantes in interiora mortis.

Caput 8

Numquid non sapientia clamitat et prudentia dat vocem suam? 2 In summis excelsisque verticibus super viam, in mediis semitis stans, 3 iuxta portas civitatis, in ipsis foribus

with myrrh, aloes and cinnamon. 18 Come; let us be inebriated with the breasts, and let us enjoy the desired embraces till the day appear, 19 for my husband is not at home; he is gone a very long journey; 20 he took with him a bag of money; he will return home the day of the full moon."

21 She entangled him with many words and drew him away with the flattery of her lips. 22 Immediately he followeth her as an ox led to be a victim and as a lamb playing the wanton and not knowing that he is drawn like a fool to bonds 23 till the arrow pierce his liver as if a bird should make haste to the snare and knoweth not that his life is in danger.

24 Now, therefore, my son, hear me, and attend to the words of my mouth. 25 Let not thy mind be drawn away in her ways, neither be thou deceived with her paths, 26 for she hath cast down many wounded, and *the* strongest have been slain by her. 27 Her house is the *way* to hell, reaching even to the inner chambers of death.

Chapter 8

The preaching of wisdom. Her excellence.

Doth not wisdom cry aloud and prudence put forth her voice? 2 Standing in the *top of the highest places by* the way, in the midst of the paths, 3 beside the gates of the city, in the

loquitur, dicens, 4 "O viri, ad vos clamito, et vox mea ad filios hominum. 5 Intellegite, parvuli, astutiam, et, insipientes, animadvertite. 6 Audite, quoniam de rebus magnis locutura sum, et aperientur labia mea ut recta praedicent. 7 Veritatem meditabitur guttur meum, et labia mea detestabuntur impium. 8 Iusti sunt omnes sermones mei; non est in eis pravum quid neque perversum. 9 Recti sunt intellegentibus et aequi invenientibus scientiam. 10 Accipite disciplinam meam et non pecuniam; doctrinam magis quam aurum eligite, 11 melior est enim sapientia cunctis pretiosissimis, et omne desiderabile ei non potest conparari.

12 "Ego, sapientia, habito in consilio et eruditis intersum cogitationibus. 13 Timor Domini odit malum; arrogantiam et superbiam et viam pravam et os bilingue detestor. 14 Meum est consilium et aequitas; mea est prudentia; mea est fortitudo. 15 Per me reges regnant et legum conditores iusta decernunt. 16 Per me principes imperant et potentes decernunt iustitiam. 17 Ego diligentes me diligo, et qui mane vigilant ad me invenient me. 18 Mecum sunt divitiae et gloria, opes superbae et iustitia, 19 melior est enim fructus meus auro et pretioso lapide, et genimina mea argento electo. 20 In viis iustitiae ambulo, in medio semitarum iudicii, 21 ut ditem diligentes me et thesauros eorum repleam.

22 "Dominus possedit me in initio viarum suarum antequam quicquam faceret a principio. 23 Ab aeterno ordinata sum et ex antiquis, antequam terra fieret. 24 Nondum erant abyssi, et ego iam concepta eram, necdum fontes aquarum eruperant. 25 Necdum montes gravi mole constiterant.

very doors she speaketh, saying, 4 "O ye men, to you I call, and my voice is to the sons of men. 5 O little ones, understand subtlety, and, ye unwise, take notice. 6 Hear, for I will speak of great things, and my lips shall be opened to preach right things. 7 My mouth shall meditate truth, and my lips shall hate wickedness. 8 All my words are just; there is nothing wicked nor perverse in them. 9 They are right to them that understand and just to them that find knowledge. 10 Receive my instruction and not money; choose knowledge rather than gold, 11 for wisdom is better than all the most precious things, and whatsoever may be desired cannot be compared to it.

12 "I, wisdom, dwell in counsel and am present in learned thoughts. 13 The fear of the Lord hateth evil; I hate arrogance and pride and *every* wicked way and a mouth with a double tongue. 14 Counsel and equity is mine; prudence is mine; strength is mine. 15 By me kings reign and lawgivers decree just things. 16 By me princes rule and the mighty decree justice. 17 I love them that love me, and they that in the morning early watch for me shall find me. 18 With me are riches and glory, glorious riches and justice, 19 for my fruit is better than gold and the precious stone, and my blossoms than choice silver. 20 I walk in the *way* of justice, in the midst of the paths of judgment, 21 that I may enrich them that love me and may fill their treasures.

22 "The Lord possessed me in the beginning of his ways before he made any thing from the beginning. 23 I was set up from eternity and of old, before the earth was made. 24 The depths were not as yet, and I was already conceived, neither had the fountains of waters as yet sprung out. 25 The mountains with their huge bulk had not as yet been established.

Ante colles ego parturiebar. 26 Adhuc terram non fecerat et flumina et cardines orbis terrae. 27 Quando praeparabat caelos aderam, quando certa lege et gyro vallabat abyssos, 28 quando aethera firmabat sursum et librabat fontes aquarum, 29 quando circumdabat mari terminum suum et legem ponebat aquis ne transirent fines suos, quando adpendebat fundamenta terrae. 30 Cum eo eram cuncta conponens et delectabar per singulos dies, ludens coram eo omni tempore, 31 ludens in orbe terrarum, et deliciae meae esse cum filiis hominum.

32 "Nunc, ergo, filii, audite me: beati qui custodiunt vias meas. 33 Audite disciplinam, et estote sapientes, et nolite abicere eam. 34 Beatus homo qui audit me et qui vigilat ad fores meas cotidie et observat ad postes ostii mei. 35 Qui me invenerit inveniet vitam et hauriet salutem a Domino. 36 Qui autem in me peccaverit laedet animam suam. Omnes qui me oderunt diligunt mortem."

Caput 9

Sapientia aedificavit sibi domum; excidit columnas septem. 2 Immolavit victimas suas, miscuit vinum et proposuit mensam suam. 3 Misit ancillas suas ut vocarent ad arcem et ad moenia civitatis.

Before the hills I was brought forth. 26 He had not yet made the earth nor the rivers nor the poles of the world. 27 When he prepared the heavens I was present, when with a certain law and compass he enclosed the depths, 28 when he established the sky above and poised the fountains of waters, 29 when he compassed the sea with its bounds and set a law to the waters that they should not pass their limits, when he balanced the foundations of the earth. 30 I was with him forming all things and was delighted every day, playing before him at all times, 31 playing in the world, and my delights were to be with the children of men.

32 "Now, therefore, ye children, hear me: blessed are they that keep my ways. 33 Hear instruction, and be wise, and refuse it not. 34 Blessed is the man that heareth me and that watcheth daily at my gates and waiteth at the posts of my doors. 35 He that shall find me shall find life and shall *have* salvation from the Lord. 36 But he that shall sin against me shall hurt his own soul. All that hate me love death."

Chapter 9

Wisdom invites all to her feast. Folly calls another way.

Wisdom hath built herself a house; she hath hewn her out seven pillars. 2 She hath slain her victims, mingled her wine and set forth her table. 3 She hath sent her maids to invite to the tower and to the walls of the city.

4 "Si quis est parvulus, veniat ad me." Et insipientibus locuta est, 5 "Venite; comedite panem meum, et bibite vinum quod miscui vobis. 6 Relinquite infantiam, et vivite, et ambulate per vias prudentiae.

7 "Qui erudit derisorem ipse sibi facit iniuriam, et qui arguit impium generat maculam sibi. 8 Noli arguere derisorem ne oderit te. Argue sapientem, et diliget te. 9 Da sapienti occasionem, et addetur ei sapientia. Doce iustum, et festinabit accipere.

10 "Principium sapientiae timor Domini, et scientia sanctorum prudentia, 11 per me enim multiplicabuntur dies tui, et addentur tibi anni vitae. 12 Si sapiens fueris, tibimet ipsi eris; si autem inlusor, solus portabis malum."

13 Mulier stulta et clamosa plenaque inlecebris et nihil omnino sciens 14 sedit in foribus domus suae super sellam in excelso urbis loco 15 ut vocaret transeuntes per viam et pergentes itinere suo. 16 "Qui est parvulus, declinet ad me." Et vecordi locuta est, 17 "Aquae furtivae dulciores sunt, et panis absconditus suavior." 18 Et ignoravit quod gigantes ibi sint et in profundis inferni convivae eius.

4 *"Whosoever* is a little one, let him come to me." And to the unwise she said, 5 "Come; eat my bread, and drink the wine which I have mingled for you. 6 Forsake childishness, and live, and walk by the ways of prudence.

7 "He that teacheth a scorner doth an injury to himself, and he that rebuketh a wicked man getteth himself a blot. 8 Rebuke not a scorner lest he hate thee. Rebuke a wise man, and he will love thee. 9 Give an occasion to a wise man, and wisdom shall be added to him. Teach a just man, and he shall make haste to receive it.

10 "The fear of the Lord is the beginning of wisdom, and the knowledge of the holy is prudence, 11 for by me shall thy days be multiplied, and years of life shall be added to thee. 12 If thou be wise, thou shalt be so to thyself, and if a scorner, thou alone shalt bear the evil."

13 A foolish woman and clamorous and full of allurements and knowing nothing at all 14 sat at the door of her house upon a seat in a high place of the city 15 to call them that pass by the way and go on their journey. 16 "He that is a little one, let him turn to me." And to the fool she said, 17 "Stolen waters are sweeter, and hidden bread is more pleasant." 18 And he did not know that giants are there and that her guests are in the depths of hell.

Caput 10

Filius sapiens laetificat patrem, filius vero stultus maestitia est matris suae.

2 Nil proderunt thesauri impietatis, iustitia vero liberabit a morte. 3 Non adfliget Dominus fame animam iusti, et insidias impiorum subvertet.

4 Egestatem operata est manus remissa, manus autem fortium divitias parat. Qui nititur mendaciis, hic pascit ventos, idem autem ipse sequitur aves volantes. 5 Qui congregat in messe filius sapiens est, qui autem stertit aestate filius confusionis.

6 Benedictio Domini super caput iusti, os autem impiorum operit iniquitas. 7 Memoria iusti cum laudibus, et nomen impiorum putrescet.

8 Sapiens corde praecepta suscipiet; stultus caeditur labiis. 9 Qui ambulat simpliciter ambulat confidenter, qui autem depravat vias suas manifestus erit. 10 Qui annuit oculo

Chapter 10

In the twenty following chapters are contained many wise sayings and axioms relating to wisdom and folly, virtue and vice.

A wise son maketh the father glad, but a foolish son is the sorrow of his mother.

2 Treasures of wickedness shall profit nothing, but justice shall deliver from death. 3 The Lord will not afflict the soul of the just with famine, and he will disappoint the deceitful practices of the wicked.

4 The slothful hand hath wrought poverty, but the hand of the *industrious* getteth riches. He that trusteth to lies feedeth the winds, and the same runneth after birds that fly away. 5 He that gathereth in the harvest is a wise son, but he that snorteth in the summer is the son of confusion.

6 The blessing of the Lord is upon the head of the just, but iniquity covereth the mouth of the wicked. 7 The memory of the just is with praises, and the name of the wicked shall rot.

8 The wise of heart *receiveth* precepts; a fool is beaten with lips. 9 He that walketh sincerely walketh confidently, but he that perverteth his ways shall be manifest. 10 He that

dabit dolorem, et stultus labiis verberabitur. 11 Vena vitae os iusti, et os impiorum operit iniquitatem. 12 Odium suscitat rixas, et universa delicta operit caritas. 13 In labiis sapientis invenitur sapientia et virga in dorso eius qui indiget corde. 14 Sapientes abscondunt scientiam, os autem stulti confusioni proximum est.

15 Substantia divitis urbs fortitudinis eius; pavor pauperum egestas eorum. 16 Opus iusti ad vitam, fructus autem impii ad peccatum. 17 Via vitae custodienti disciplinam, qui autem increpationes relinquit errat.

18 Abscondunt odium labia mendacia; qui profert contumeliam insipiens est. 19 In multiloquio peccatum non deerit, qui autem moderatur labia sua prudentissimus est. 20 Argentum electum lingua iusti; cor autem impiorum pro nihilo. 21 Labia iusti erudiunt plurimos, qui autem indocti sunt in cordis egestate morientur.

22 Benedictio Domini divites facit, nec sociabitur eis adflictio.

23 Quasi per risum stultus operatur scelus, sapientia autem est viro prudentia.

24 Quod timet impius veniet super eum; desiderium suum iustis dabitur. 25 Quasi tempestas transiens, non erit impius, iustus autem quasi fundamentum sempiternum. 26 Sicut acetum dentibus et fumus oculis, sic piger his qui miserunt eum. 27 Timor Domini adponet dies, et anni impiorum breviabuntur. 28 Expectatio iustorum laetitia, spes autem impiorum peribit. 29 Fortitudo simplicis via Domini et pavor

winketh with the eye shall cause sorrow, and the foolish in lips shall be beaten. 11 The mouth of the just is a vein of life, and the mouth of the wicked covereth iniquity. 12 Hatred stirreth up strifes, and charity covereth all sins. 13 In the lips of the wise is wisdom found and a rod on the back of him that wanteth sense. 14 Wise men lay up knowledge, but the mouth of the fool is next to confusion.

15 The substance of a rich man is the city of his strength; the fear of the poor is their poverty. 16 The work of the just is unto life, but the fruit of the wicked unto sin. 17 The way of life to him that observeth correction, but he that forsaketh reproofs goeth astray.

18 Lying lips hide hatred; he that uttereth reproach is foolish. 19 In the multitude of words there shall not want sin, but he that refraineth his lips is most wise. 20 The tongue of the just is as choice silver, but the heart of the wicked is nothing worth. 21 The lips of the just teach many, but they that are ignorant shall die in the want of understanding.

22 The blessing of the Lord maketh men rich, neither shall affliction be joined to them.

23 A fool worketh mischief as it were for sport, but wisdom is prudence to a man.

24 That which the wicked feareth shall come upon him; to the just their desire shall be given. 25 As a tempest that passeth, *so* the wicked shall be no more, but the just is as an everlasting foundation. 26 As vinegar to the teeth and smoke to the eyes, so is the sluggard to them that sent him. 27 The fear of the Lord shall prolong days, and the years of the wicked shall be shortened. 28 The expectation of the just is joy, but the hope of the wicked shall perish. 29 The strength of the upright is the way of the Lord and fear to them that work

his qui operantur malum. 30 Iustus in aeternum non commovebitur, impii autem non habitabunt in terram. 31 Os iusti parturiet sapientiam; lingua pravorum peribit. 32 Labia iusti considerant placita, et os impiorum perversa.

Caput 11

Statera dolosa abominatio apud Dominum, et pondus aequum voluntas eius.

2 Ubi fuerit superbia, ibi erit et contumelia, ubi autem humilitas, ibi et sapientia. 3 Simplicitas iustorum diriget eos, et subplantatio perversorum vastabit illos.

4 Non proderunt divitiae in die ultionis, iustitia autem liberabit a morte. 5 Iustitia simplicis diriget viam eius, et in impietate sua corruet impius. 6 Iustitia rectorum liberabit eos, et in insidiis suis capientur iniqui. 7 Mortuo homine impio nulla erit ultra spes, et expectatio sollicitorum peribit. 8 Iustus de angustia liberatus est, et tradetur impius pro eo. 9 Simulator ore decipit amicum suum, iusti autem liberabuntur scientia. 10 In bonis iustorum exultabit civitas, et in perditione impiorum erit laudatio. 11 Benedictione iustorum exaltabitur civitas, et ore impiorum subvertetur.

evil. 30 The just shall never be moved, but the wicked shall not dwell on the earth. 31 The mouth of the just shall bring forth wisdom; the tongue of the perverse shall perish. 32 The lips of the just consider what is acceptable, and the mouth of the wicked *uttereth* perverse things.

Chapter 11

A deceitful balance is an abomination before the Lord, and a just weight is his will.

2 Where pride is, there also shall be reproach, but where humility is, there also is wisdom. 3 The simplicity of the just shall guide them, and the deceitfulness of the wicked shall destroy them.

4 Riches shall not profit in the day of revenge, but justice shall deliver from death. 5 The justice of the upright shall make his way prosperous, and the wicked man shall fall by his own wickedness. 6 The justice of the righteous shall deliver them, and the unjust shall be caught in their own snares. 7 When the wicked man is dead there shall be no hope any more, and the expectation of the solicitous shall perish. 8 The just is delivered out of distress, and the wicked shall be given up for him. 9 The dissembler with his mouth deceiveth his friend, but the just shall be delivered by knowledge. 10 When it goeth well with the just the city shall rejoice, and when the wicked perish there shall be praise. 11 By the blessing of the just the city shall be exalted, and by the mouth of the wicked it shall be overthrown.

12 Qui despicit amicum suum indigens corde est, vir autem prudens tacebit. 13 Qui ambulat fraudulenter revelat arcana, qui autem fidelis est celat amici commissum.

14 Ubi non est gubernator populus corruet, salus autem ubi multa consilia. 15 Adfligetur malo qui fidem facit pro extraneo, qui autem cavet laqueos securus erit.

16 Mulier gratiosa inveniet gloriam, et robusti habebunt divitias. 17 Benefacit animae suae vir misericors, qui autem crudelis est et propinquos abicit.

18 Impius facit opus instabile, seminanti autem iustitiam merces fidelis.

19 Clementia praeparat vitam, et sectatio malorum, mortem.

20 Abominabile Domino pravum cor, et voluntas eius in his qui simpliciter ambulant.

21 Manus in manu non erit innocens malus, semen autem iustorum salvabitur.

22 Circulus aureus in naribus suis, mulier pulchra et fatua.

23 Desiderium iustorum omne bonum est; praestolatio impiorum furor.

24 Alii dividunt propria et ditiores fiunt; alii rapiunt non sua et semper in egestate sunt. 25 Anima quae benedicit inpinguabitur, et qui inebriat ipse quoque inebriabitur. 26 Qui abscondit frumenta maledicetur in populis, benedictio autem super caput vendentium. 27 Bene consurgit diluculo qui quaerit bona, qui autem investigator malorum est

12 He that despiseth his friend is mean of heart, but the wise man will hold his peace. 13 He that walketh deceitfully revealeth secrets, but he that is faithful concealeth the thing committed to him by his friend.

14 Where there is no governor the people shall fall, but there is safety where there is much counsel. 15 He shall be afflicted with evil that is surety for a stranger, but he that is aware of snares shall be secure.

16 A gracious woman shall find glory, and the strong shall have riches. 17 A merciful man doth good to his own soul, but he that is cruel casteth off even his own kindred.

18 The wicked maketh an unsteady work, but to him that soweth justice there is a faithful reward.

19 Clemency prepareth life, and the pursuing of evil things, death.

20 A perverse heart is abominable to the Lord, and his will is in them that walk sincerely.

21 Hand in hand the evil man shall not be innocent, but the seed of the just shall be saved.

22 A golden ring in a swine's snout, a woman fair and foolish.

23 The desire of the just is all good; the expectation of the wicked is indignation.

24 Some distribute their own goods and grow richer; others take away what is not their own and are always in want. 25 The soul that blesseth shall be made fat, and he that inebriateth shall be inebriated also himself. 26 He that hideth up corn shall be cursed among the people, but a blessing upon the head of them that sell. 27 Well doth he rise early who seeketh good things, but he that seeketh after evil

opprimetur ab eis. 28 Qui confidit in divitiis suis corruet, iusti autem quasi virens folium germinabunt.

29 Qui conturbat domum suam possidebit ventos, et qui stultus est serviet sapienti. 30 Fructus iusti lignum vitae, et qui suscipit animas sapiens est. 31 Si iustus in terra recipit, quanto magis impius et peccator!

Caput 12

Qui diligit disciplinam diligit scientiam, qui autem odit increpationes insipiens est. 2 Qui bonus est hauriet a Domino gratiam, qui autem confidit cogitationibus suis impie agit. 3 Non roborabitur homo ex impietate, et radix iustorum non commovebitur. 4 Mulier diligens corona viro suo, et putredo in ossibus eius quae confusione res dignas gerit.

5 Cogitationes iustorum iudicia, et consilia impiorum fraudulenta. 6 Verba impiorum insidiantur sanguini; os iustorum liberabit eos. 7 Verte impios, et non erunt, domus autem iustorum permanebit. 8 Doctrina sua noscetur vir, qui autem vanus et excors est patebit contemptui. 9 Melior est pauper et sufficiens sibi quam gloriosus et indigens pane. 10 Novit iustus animas iumentorum suorum, viscera autem

things shall be oppressed by them. 28 He that trusteth in his riches shall fall, but the just shall spring up as a green leaf.

29 He that troubleth his own house shall inherit the winds, and the fool shall serve the wise. 30 The fruit of the just man is a tree of life, and he that gaineth souls is wise. 31 If the just man receive in the earth, how much more the wicked and the sinner!

Chapter 12

He that loveth correction loveth knowledge, but he that hateth reproof is foolish. 2 He that is good shall draw grace from the Lord, but he that trusteth in his own devices doth wickedly. 3 Man shall not be strengthened by wickedness, and the root of the just shall not be moved. 4 A diligent woman is a crown to her husband, and she that doth things worthy of confusion is as rottenness in his bones.

5 The thoughts of the just are judgments, and the counsels of the wicked are deceitful. 6 The words of the wicked lie in wait for blood; the mouth of the just shall deliver them. 7 Turn the wicked, and they shall not be, but the house of the just shall stand firm. 8 A man shall be known by his learning, but he that is vain and foolish shall be exposed to contempt. 9 Better is the poor man that provideth for himself than he that is glorious and wanteth bread. 10 The just regardeth the lives of his beasts, but the bowels of the wicked are

impiorum crudelia. 11 Qui operatur terram suam saturabitur panibus, qui autem sectatur otium stultissimus est. Qui suavis est in vini demorationibus in suis munitionibus relinquit contumeliam.

12 Desiderium impii munimentum est pessimorum, radix autem iustorum proficiet. 13 Propter peccata labiorum ruina proximat malo, effugiet autem iustus de angustia. 14 De fructu oris sui unusquisque replebitur bonis, et iuxta opera manuum suarum retribuetur ei.

15 Via stulti recta in oculis eius, qui autem sapiens est audit consilia. 16 Fatuus statim indicat iram suam, qui autem dissimulat iniuriam callidus est. 17 Qui quod novit loquitur index iustitiae est, qui autem mentitur testis est fraudulentus. 18 Est qui promittit et quasi gladio pungitur conscientiae, lingua autem sapientium sanitas est.

19 Labium veritatis firmum erit in perpetuum, qui autem testis est repentinus concinnat linguam mendacii. 20 Dolus in corde cogitantium mala, qui autem ineunt pacis consilia sequitur eos gaudium.

21 Non contristabit iustum quicquid ei acciderit, impii autem replebuntur malo. 22 Abominatio Domino labia mendacia, qui autem fideliter agunt placent ei. 23 Homo versutus celat scientiam, et cor insipientium provocat stultitiam. 24 Manus fortium dominabitur, quae autem remissa est tributis serviet.

cruel. 11 He that tilleth his land shall be satisfied with bread, but he that pursueth idleness is very foolish. He that is delighted in passing his time over wine leaveth a reproach in his strong holds.

12 The desire of the wicked is the fortification of evil men, but the root of the just shall prosper. 13 For the sins of the lips ruin draweth nigh to the evil man, but the just shall escape out of distress. 14 By the fruit of his own mouth shall a man be filled with good things, and according to the works of his hands it shall be repaid him.

15 The way of a fool is right in his own eyes, but he that is wise hearkeneth unto counsels. 16 A fool immediately sheweth his anger, but he that dissembleth injuries is wise. 17 He that speaketh that which he knoweth sheweth forth justice, but he that lieth is a deceitful witness. 18 There is that promiseth and is pricked as it were with a sword of conscience, but the tongue of the wise is health.

19 The lip of truth shall be steadfast for ever, but he that is a hasty witness frameth a lying tongue. 20 Deceit is in the heart of them that think evil things, but joy followeth them that take counsels of peace.

21 Whatsoever shall befall the just man shall not make him sad, but the wicked shall be filled with mischief. 22 Lying lips are an abomination to the Lord, but they that deal faithfully please him. 23 A cautious man concealeth knowledge, and the heart of fools publisheth folly. 24 The hand of the valiant shall bear rule, but that which is slothful shall be under tribute.

25 Maeror in corde viri humiliabit illum, et sermone bono laetificabitur. 26 Qui neglegit damnum propter amicum iustus est, iter autem impiorum decipiet eos. 27 Non inveniet fraudulentus lucrum, et substantia hominis erit auri pretium. 28 In semita iustitiae vita, iter autem devium ducit ad mortem.

Caput 13

Filius sapiens doctrina patris, qui autem inlusor est non audit cum arguitur. 2 De fructu oris sui homo saturabitur bonis, anima autem praevaricatorum iniqua. 3 Qui custodit os suum custodit animam suam, qui autem inconsideratus est ad loquendum sentiet mala.

4 Vult et non vult piger, anima autem operantium inpinguabitur.

5 Verbum mendax iustus detestabitur, impius autem confundit et confundetur. 6 Iustitia custodit innocentis viam, impietas vero peccatorem subplantat. 7 Est quasi dives cum nihil habeat et est quasi pauper cum in multis divitiis sit. 8 Redemptio animae viri divitiae suae, qui autem pauper est increpationem non sustinet.

9 Lux iustorum laetificat, lucerna autem impiorum extinguetur.

25 Grief in the heart of a man shall bring him low, *but* with a good word he shall be made glad. 26 He that neglecteth a loss for the sake of a friend is just, but the way of the wicked shall deceive them. 27 The deceitful man shall not find gain, *but* the substance of a *just* man shall be precious gold. 28 In the path of justice is life, but the bye-way leadeth to death.

Chapter 13

A wise son heareth the doctrine of his father, but he that is a scorner heareth not when he is reproved. 2 Of the fruit of his own mouth shall a man be filled with good things, but the soul of transgressors is wicked. 3 He that keepeth his mouth keepeth his soul, but he that hath no guard on his speech shall meet with evils.

4 The sluggard willeth and willeth not, but the soul of them that work shall be made fat.

5 The just shall hate a lying word, but the wicked confoundeth and shall be confounded. 6 Justice keepeth the way of the innocent, but wickedness overthroweth the sinner. 7 One is as it were rich when he hath nothing and another is as it were poor when he hath great riches. 8 The ransom of a man's life are his riches, but he that is poor beareth not reprehension.

9 The light of the just giveth joy, but the lamp of the wicked shall be put out.

10 Inter superbos semper iurgia sunt, qui autem agunt cuncta consilio reguntur sapientia.

11 Substantia festinata minuetur, quae autem paulatim colligitur manu multiplicabitur. 12 Spes quae differtur adfligit animam; lignum vitae desiderium veniens.

13 Qui detrahit alicui rei ipse se in futurum obligat, qui autem timet praeceptum in pace versabitur. Animae dolosae errant in peccatis, iusti autem misericordes sunt et miserantur.

14 Lex sapientis fons vitae ut declinet a ruina mortis. 15 Doctrina bona dabit gratiam; in itinere contemptorum vorago. 16 Astutus omnia agit cum consilio, qui autem fatuus est aperit stultitiam. 17 Nuntius impii cadet in malum, legatus autem fidelis sanitas.

18 Egestas et ignominia ei qui deserit disciplinam, qui autem adquiescit arguenti glorificabitur.

19 Desiderium si conpleatur delectat animam; detestantur stulti eos qui fugiunt mala.

20 Qui cum sapientibus graditur sapiens erit; amicus stultorum efficietur similis. 21 Peccatores persequitur malum, et iustis retribuentur bona. 22 Bonus relinquit heredes, filios et nepotes, et custoditur iusto substantia peccatoris.

23 Multi cibi in novalibus patrum, et aliis congregantur absque iudicio. 24 Qui parcit virgae odit filium suum, qui autem diligit illum instanter erudit.

10 Among the proud there are always contentions, but they that do all things with counsel are ruled by wisdom.

11 Substance *got in haste* shall be diminished, but that which by little and little is gathered with the hand shall increase. 12 Hope that is deferred afflicteth the soul; desire when it cometh is a tree of life.

13 Whosoever speaketh ill of any thing bindeth himself for the time to come, but he that feareth the commandment shall dwell in peace. Deceitful souls go astray in sins; *the* just are merciful and shew mercy.

14 The law of the wise is a fountain of life that he may decline from the ruin of death. 15 Good instruction shall give grace; in the way of scorners is a deep pit. 16 The prudent man doth all things with counsel, but he that is a fool layeth open his folly. 17 The messenger of the wicked shall fall into mischief, but a faithful ambassador is health.

18 Poverty and shame to him that refuseth instruction, but he that yieldeth to reproof shall be glorified.

19 The desire *that is* accomplished delighteth the soul; fools hate them that flee from evil things.

20 He that walketh with the wise shall be wise; a friend of fools shall become like to them. 21 Evil pursueth sinners, and to the just good shall be repaid. 22 The good man leaveth heirs, sons and grandsons, and the substance of the sinner is kept for the just.

23 Much food is in the tillage of fathers, *but* for others it is gathered without judgment. 24 He that spareth the rod hateth his son, but he that loveth him correcteth him betimes.

25 Iustus comedit et replet animam suam, venter autem impiorum insaturabilis.

Caput 14

Sapiens mulier aedificat domum suam; insipiens instructam quoque destruet manibus.

2 Ambulans recto itinere et timens Deum despicitur ab eo qui infami graditur via.

3 In ore stulti virga superbiae, labia autem sapientium custodiunt eos.

4 Ubi non sunt boves praesepe vacuum est, ubi autem plurimae segetes ibi manifesta fortitudo bovis.

5 Testis fidelis non mentietur, profert autem mendacium testis dolosus.

6 Quaerit derisor sapientiam et non invenit; doctrina prudentium facilis. 7 Vade contra virum stultum, et nescit labia prudentiae. 8 Sapientia callidi est intellegere viam suam, et inprudentia stultorum errans. 9 Stultus inludet peccatum, et inter iustos morabitur gratia.

10 Cor quod novit amaritudinem animae suae, in gaudio eius non miscebitur extraneus.

11 Domus impiorum delebitur; tabernacula iustorum germinabunt.

12 Est via quae videtur homini iusta, novissima autem eius deducunt ad mortem. 13 Risus dolore miscebitur, et extrema gaudii luctus occupat.

25 The just eateth and filleth his soul, but the belly of the wicked *is never to be filled.*

Chapter 14

A wise woman buildeth her house, *but* the foolish will pull down with her hands that also which is built.

2 He that walketh in the right way and feareth God is despised by him that goeth by an infamous way.

3 In the mouth of a fool is the rod of pride, but the lips of the wise preserve them.

4 Where there are no oxen the crib is empty, but where there is much corn there the strength of the ox is manifest.

5 A faithful witness will not lie, but a deceitful witness uttereth a lie.

6 A scorner seeketh wisdom and findeth it not; the learning of the wise is easy. 7 Go against a foolish man, and he knoweth not the lips of prudence. 8 The wisdom of a discreet man is to understand his way, and the imprudence of fools erreth. 9 A fool will laugh at sin, *but* among the just grace shall abide.

10 The heart that knoweth the bitterness of his own soul, in his joy the stranger shall not intermeddle.

11 The house of the wicked shall be destroyed, *but* the tabernacles of the just shall flourish.

12 There is a way which seemeth just to a man, but the ends thereof lead to death. 13 Laughter shall be mingled with sorrow, and mourning taketh hold of the ends of joy.

14 Viis suis replebitur stultus, et super eum erit vir bonus.

15 Innocens credit omni verbo; astutus considerat gressus suos. 16 Sapiens timet et declinat a malo; stultus transilit et confidit. 17 Inpatiens operabitur stultitiam, et vir versutus odiosus est. 18 Possidebunt parvuli stultitiam, et astuti expectabunt scientiam. 19 Iacebunt mali ante bonos, et impii ante portas iustorum. 20 Etiam proximo suo pauper odiosus erit, amici vero divitum multi.

21 Qui despicit proximum suum peccat, qui autem miseretur pauperi beatus erit. 22 Errant qui operantur malum; misericordia et veritas praeparant bona.

23 In omni opere erit abundantia, ubi autem verba sunt plurima ibi frequenter egestas. 24 Corona sapientium divitiae eorum, fatuitas stultorum, inprudentia.

25 Liberat animas testis fidelis, et profert mendacia versipellis.

26 In timore Domini fiducia fortitudinis, et filiis eius erit spes. 27 Timor Domini fons vitae ut declinet a ruina mortis.

28 In multitudine populi dignitas regis, et in paucitate plebis ignominia principis.

29 Qui patiens est multa gubernatur prudentia, qui autem inpatiens exaltat stultitiam suam.

14 A fool shall be filled with his own ways, and the good man shall be above him.

15 The innocent believeth every word; the discreet man considereth his steps. *No good shall come to the deceitful son, but the wise servant shall prosper in his dealings, and his way shall be made straight.* 16 A wise man feareth and declineth from evil; the fool leapeth over and is confident. 17 The impatient man shall work folly, and the crafty man is hateful. 18 The childish shall possess folly, and the prudent shall look for knowledge. 19 The evil shall fall down before the good, and the wicked before the gates of the just. 20 The poor man shall be hateful even to his own neighbour, but the friends of the rich are many.

21 He that despiseth his neighbour sinneth, but he that sheweth mercy to the poor shall be blessed. *He that believeth in the Lord loveth mercy.* 22 They err that work evil, *but* mercy and truth prepare good things.

23 In much work there shall be abundance, but where there are many words there is oftentimes want. 24 The crown of the wise is their riches, the folly of fools, imprudence.

25 A faithful witness delivereth souls, and the double dealer uttereth lies.

26 In the fear of the Lord is confidence of strength, and there shall be hope for his children. 27 The fear of the Lord is a fountain of life to decline from the ruin of death.

28 In the multitude of people is the dignity of the king, and in the small number of the people the dishonour of the prince.

29 He that is patient is governed with much wisdom, but he that is impatient exalteth his folly.

³⁰ Vita carnium sanitas cordis; putredo ossuum invidia.

³¹ Qui calumniatur egentem exprobrat factori eius, honorat autem eum qui miseretur pauperis.

³² In malitia sua expelletur impius, sperat autem iustus in morte sua.

³³ In corde prudentis requiescit sapientia, et indoctos quosque erudiet.

³⁴ Iustitia elevat gentem, miseros autem facit populos peccatum.

³⁵ Acceptus est regi minister intellegens; iracundiam eius inutilis sustinebit.

Caput 15

Responsio mollis frangit iram; sermo durus suscitat furorem. ² Lingua sapientium ornat scientiam; os fatuorum ebullit stultitiam. ³ In omni loco oculi Domini contemplantur malos et bonos. ⁴ Lingua placabilis lignum vitae, quae autem inmoderata est conteret spiritum.

⁵ Stultus inridet disciplinam patris sui, qui autem custodit increpationes astutior fiet.

In abundanti iustitia virtus maxima est, cogitationes autem impiorum eradicabuntur. ⁶ Domus iusti plurima fortitudo, et in fructibus impii conturbatio.

30 Soundness of heart is the life of the flesh, *but* envy is the rottenness of the bones.

31 He that *oppresseth* the poor upbraideth his maker, but he that hath pity on the poor honoureth him.

32 The wicked man shall be driven out in his wickedness, but the just hath hope in his death.

33 In the heart of the prudent resteth wisdom, and it shall instruct all the ignorant.

34 Justice exalteth a nation, but sin maketh nations miserable.

35 A wise servant is acceptable to the king; he that is good for nothing shall feel his anger.

Chapter 15

A mild answer breaketh wrath, *but* a harsh word stirreth up fury. 2 The tongue of the wise adorneth knowledge, *but* the mouth of fools bubbleth out folly. 3 The eyes of the Lord in every place behold the good and the evil. 4 A peaceable tongue is a tree of life, but that which is immoderate shall crush the spirit.

5 A fool laugheth at the instruction of his father, but he that regardeth reproofs shall become prudent.

In abundant justice there is the greatest strength, but the devices of the wicked shall be rooted out. 6 The house of the just is very much strength, and in the fruits of the wicked is trouble.

7 Labia sapientium disseminabunt scientiam; cor stultorum dissimile erit.

8 Victimae impiorum abominabiles Domino; vota iustorum placabilia. 9 Abominatio est Domino via impii; qui sequitur iustitiam diligitur ab eo.

10 Doctrina mala deserenti viam vitae; qui increpationes odit morietur.

11 Infernus et perditio coram Domino; quanto magis corda filiorum hominum?

12 Non amat pestilens eum qui se corripit, nec ad sapientes graditur.

13 Cor gaudens exhilarat faciem; in maerore animi deicitur spiritus. 14 Cor sapientis quaerit doctrinam, et os stultorum pascitur inperitia.

15 Omnes dies pauperis mali; secura mens quasi iuge convivium.

16 Melius est parum cum timore Domini quam thesauri magni et insatiabiles. 17 Melius est vocari ad holera cum caritate quam ad vitulum saginatum cum odio.

18 Vir iracundus provocat rixas; qui patiens est mitigat suscitatas.

19 Iter pigrorum quasi sepes spinarum; via iustorum absque offendiculo.

20 Filius sapiens laetificat patrem, et stultus homo despicit matrem suam. 21 Stultitia gaudium stulto, et vir prudens dirigit gressus.

22 Dissipantur cogitationes ubi non est consilium, ubi vero plures sunt consiliarii, confirmantur.

7 The lips of the wise shall disperse knowledge; the heart of fools shall be unlike.

8 The victims of the wicked are abominable to the Lord; the vows of the just are acceptable. 9 The way of the wicked is an abomination to the Lord; he that followeth justice is beloved by him.

10 Instruction is grievous to him that forsaketh the way of life; he that hateth reproof shall die.

11 Hell and destruction are before the Lord; how much more the hearts of the children of men?

12 A corrupt man loveth not one that reproveth him, nor will he go to the wise.

13 A glad heart maketh a cheerful countenance, *but by* grief of mind the spirit is cast down. 14 The heart of the wise seeketh instruction, and the mouth of fools feedeth on foolishness.

15 All the days of the poor are evil; a secure mind is like a continual feast.

16 Better is a little with the fear of the Lord than great treasures *without content.* 17 It is better to be invited to herbs with love than to a fatted calf with hatred.

18 A passionate man stirreth up strifes; he that is patient appeaseth those that are stirred up.

19 The way of the slothful is as a hedge of thorns; the way of the just is without offence.

20 A wise son maketh a father joyful, *but* the foolish man despiseth his mother. 21 Folly is joy to the fool, and the wise man maketh straight his steps.

22 Designs are brought to nothing where there is no counsel, but where there are many counsellors, they are established.

23 Laetatur homo in sententia oris sui, et sermo oportunus est optimus.

24 Semita vitae super eruditum ut declinet de inferno novissimo.

25 Domum superborum demolietur Dominus et firmos faciet terminos viduae. 26 Abominatio Domini cogitationes malae, et purus sermo pulcherrimus firmabitur ab eo.

27 Conturbat domum suam qui sectatur avaritiam, qui autem odit munera vivet. Per misericordiam et fidem purgantur peccata, per timorem autem Domini declinat omnis a malo.

28 Mens iusti meditatur oboedientiam; os impiorum redundat malis. 29 Longe est Dominus ab impiis, et orationes iustorum exaudiet.

30 Lux oculorum laetificat animam; fama bona inpinguat ossa. 31 Auris quae audit increpationes vitae in medio sapientium commorabitur.

32 Qui abicit disciplinam despicit animam suam, qui autem adquiescit increpationibus possessor est cordis.

33 Timor Domini disciplina sapientiae, et gloriam praecedit humilitas.

Caput 16

Hominis est animam praeparare et Domini gubernare linguam. 2 Omnes viae hominis patent oculis eius; spirituum ponderator est Dominus. 3 Revela Domino opera tua, et

23 A man rejoiceth in the sentence of his mouth, and a word in due time is best.

24 The path of life is above *for* the wise that he may decline from the lowest hell.

25 The Lord will destroy the house of the proud and will strengthen the borders of the widow. 26 Evil thoughts are an abomination to the Lord, and pure words most beautiful shall be confirmed by him.

27 He that is *greedy of gain* troubleth his own house, but he that hateth bribes shall live. By mercy and faith sins are purged away, and by the fear of the Lord every one declineth from evil.

28 The mind of the just studieth obedience; the mouth of the wicked overfloweth with evils. 29 The Lord is far from the wicked, and he will hear the prayers of the just.

30 The light of the eyes rejoiceth the soul; a good name maketh the bones fat. 31 The ear that heareth the reproofs of life shall abide in the midst of the wise.

32 He that rejecteth instruction despiseth his own soul, but he that yieldeth to reproof possesseth understanding.

33 The fear of the Lord is the lesson of wisdom, and humility goeth before glory.

Chapter 16

It is the part of man to prepare the soul and of the Lord to govern the tongue. 2 All the ways of a man are open to his eyes; the Lord is the weigher of spirits. 3 Lay open thy

dirigentur cogitationes tuae. 4 Universa propter semet ipsum operatus est Dominus, impium quoque ad diem malum. 5 Abominatio Domini omnis arrogans; etiam si manus ad manum fuerit, non est innocens. Initium viae bonae facere iustitiam, accepta est autem apud Deum magis quam immolare hostias.

6 Misericordia et veritate redimitur iniquitas, et in timore Domini declinatur a malo. 7 Cum placuerint Domino viae hominis, inimicos quoque eius convertet ad pacem.

8 Melius est parum cum iustitia quam multi fructus cum iniquitate.

9 Cor hominis disponit viam suam, sed Domini est dirigere gressus eius.

10 Divinatio in labiis regis; in iudicio non errabit os eius. 11 Pondus et statera iudicia Domini sunt, et opera eius omnes lapides sacculi. 12 Abominabiles regi qui agunt impie, quoniam iustitia firmatur solium. 13 Voluntas regum labia iusta; qui recta loquitur diligetur. 14 Indignatio regis nuntii mortis, et vir sapiens placabit eam. 15 In hilaritate vultus regis vita, et clementia eius quasi imber serotinus.

16 Posside sapientiam quia auro melior est, et adquire prudentiam, quia pretiosior est argento.

17 Semita iustorum declinat mala; custos animae suae servat viam suam.

18 Contritionem praecedit superbia, et ante ruinam exaltatur spiritus.

works to the Lord, and thy thoughts shall be directed. 4 The Lord hath made all things for himself, the wicked also for the evil day. 5 Every proud man is an abomination to the Lord; though hand should be joined to hand, he is not innocent. The beginning of a good way is to do justice, and this is more acceptable with God than to offer sacrifices.

6 By mercy and truth iniquity is redeemed, and by the fear of the Lord men depart from evil. 7 When the ways of man shall please the Lord, he will convert even his enemies to peace.

8 Better is a little with justice than great revenues with iniquity.

9 The heart of man disposeth his way, but *the Lord must* direct his steps.

10 Divination is in the lips of the king; his mouth shall not err in judgment. 11 Weight and balance are judgments of the Lord, and his work all the weights of the bag. 12 They that act wickedly are abominable to the king, for the throne is established by justice. 13 Just lips are the delight of kings; he that speaketh right things shall be loved. 14 The wrath of a king is as messengers of death, and the wise man will pacify it. 15 In the cheerfulness of the king's countenance is life, and his clemency is like the latter rain.

16 Get wisdom because it is better than gold, and purchase prudence, for it is more precious than silver.

17 The path of the just departeth from evils; he that keepeth his soul keepeth his way.

18 Pride goeth before destruction, and the spirit is lifted up before a fall.

¹⁹ Melius est humiliari cum mitibus quam dividere spolia cum superbis.

²⁰ Eruditus in verbo repperiet bona, et qui in Domino sperat beatus est. ²¹ Qui sapiens corde est appellabitur prudens, et qui dulcis eloquio maiora percipiet. ²² Fons vitae eruditio possidentis; doctrina stultorum fatuitas. ²³ Cor sapientis erudiet os eius et labiis illius addet gratiam. ²⁴ Favus mellis verba conposita, dulcedo animae, sanitas ossuum.

²⁵ Est via quae videtur homini recta, et novissima eius ducunt ad mortem.

²⁶ Anima laborantis laborat sibi quia conpulit eum os suum.

²⁷ Vir impius fodit malum, et in labiis eius ignis ardescit. ²⁸ Homo perversus suscitat lites, et verbosus separat principes. ²⁹ Vir iniquus lactat amicum suum et ducit eum per viam non bonam. ³⁰ Qui adtonitis oculis cogitat prava, mordens labia sua, perficit malum.

³¹ Corona dignitatis senectus quae in viis iustitiae repperietur. ³² Melior est patiens viro forte, et qui dominatur animo suo expugnatore urbium.

³³ Sortes mittuntur in sinum, sed a Domino temperantur.

19 It is better to be humbled with the meek than to divide spoils with the proud.

20 The learned in word shall find good things, and he that trusteth in the Lord is blessed. 21 The wise in heart shall be called prudent, and he that is sweet in words shall attain to greater things. 22 Knowledge is a fountain of life to him that possesseth it; the instruction of fools is foolishness. 23 The heart of the wise shall instruct his mouth and shall add grace to his lips. 24 Well ordered words are as a honeycomb, sweet to the soul *and* health to the bones.

25 There is a way that seemeth to a man right, and the ends thereof lead to death.

26 The soul of him that laboureth laboureth for himself because his mouth hath obliged him to it.

27 The wicked man diggeth evil, and in his lips is a burning fire. 28 A perverse man stirreth up quarrels, and one full of words separateth princes. 29 An unjust man allureth his friend and leadeth him into a way that is not good. 30 He that with fixed eyes deviseth wicked things, biting his lips, bringeth evil to pass.

31 Old age is a crown of dignity when it is found in the ways of justice. 32 The patient man is better than the valiant, and he that ruleth his spirit than he that taketh cities.

33 Lots are cast into the lap, but they are *disposed* of by the Lord.

Caput 17

Melior est buccella sicca cum gaudio quam domus plena victimis cum iurgio.

2 Servus sapiens dominabitur filiis stultis et inter fratres hereditatem dividet.

3 Sicut igne probatur argentum et aurum camino, ita corda probat Dominus.

4 Malus oboedit linguae iniquae, et fallax obtemperat labiis mendacibus.

5 Qui despicit pauperem exprobrat factori eius, et qui ruina laetatur alterius non erit inpunitus.

6 Corona senum filii filiorum, et gloria filiorum patres sui.

7 Non decent stultum verba conposita, nec principem labium mentiens.

8 Gemma gratissima expectatio praestolantis; quocumque se vertit prudenter intellegit.

9 Qui celat delictum quaerit amicitias; qui altero sermone repetit separat foederatos.

10 Plus proficit correptio apud prudentem quam centum plagae apud stultum.

11 Semper iurgia quaerit malus, angelus autem crudelis mittetur contra eum.

12 Expedit magis ursae occurrere raptis fetibus quam fatuo confidenti sibi in stultitia sua.

13 Qui reddit mala pro bonis, non recedet malum de domo eius.

Chapter 17

Better is a dry morsel with joy than a house full of victims with strife.

2 A wise servant shall rule over foolish sons and shall divide the inheritance among the brethren.

3 As silver is tried by fire and gold in the furnace, so the Lord trieth the hearts.

4 The evil man obeyeth an unjust tongue, and the deceitful hearkeneth to lying lips.

5 He that despiseth the poor reproacheth his maker, and he that rejoiceth at another man's ruin shall not be unpunished.

6 Children's children are the crown of old men, and the glory of children are their fathers.

7 Eloquent words do not become a fool, nor lying lips a prince.

8 The expectation of him that expecteth is a most acceptable jewel; whithersoever he turneth himself he understandeth wisely.

9 He that concealeth a transgression seeketh friendships; he that repeateth it *again* separateth friends.

10 A reproof availeth more with a wise man than a hundred stripes with a fool.

11 An evil man always seeketh quarrels, but a cruel angel shall be sent against him.

12 It is better to meet a bear robbed of her whelps than a fool trusting *in* his own folly.

13 He that rendereth evil for good, evil shall not depart from his house.

14 Qui dimittit aquam caput est iurgiorum, et antequam patiatur contumeliam, iudicium deserit.

15 Qui iustificat impium et qui condemnat iustum, abominabilis est uterque apud Deum.

16 Quid prodest habere divitias stultum, cum sapientiam emere non possit? Qui altam facit domum suam quaerit ruinam, et qui evitat discere incidet in mala.

17 Omni tempore diligit qui amicus est, et frater in angustiis conprobatur. 18 Homo stultus plaudet manibus cum sponderit pro amico suo. 19 Qui meditatur discordias diligit rixas, et qui exaltat ostium quaerit ruinam.

20 Qui perversi cordis est non inveniet bonum, et qui vertit linguam incidet in malum.

21 Natus est stultus in ignominiam suam, sed nec pater in fatuo laetabitur.

22 Animus gaudens aetatem floridam facit; spiritus tristis exsiccat ossa.

23 Munera de sinu impius accipit ut pervertat semitas iudicii.

24 In facie prudentis lucet sapientia; oculi stultorum in finibus terrae. 25 Ira patris filius stultus et dolor matris quae genuit eum.

26 Non est bonum damnum inferre iusto nec percutere principem qui recta iudicat.

27 Qui moderatur sermones suos doctus et prudens est, et pretiosi spiritus vir eruditus. 28 Stultus quoque, si tacuerit, sapiens reputabitur, et si conpresserit labia sua, intellegens.

14 The beginning of quarrels is as when one letteth out water, and before he suffereth reproach, he forsaketh judgment.

15 He that justifieth the wicked and he that condemneth the just, both are abominable before God.

16 What doth it avail a fool to have riches, *seeing* he cannot buy wisdom? He that maketh his house high seeketh a downfall, and he that refuseth to learn shall fall into evils.

17 He that is a friend loveth at all times, and a brother is proved in distress. 18 A foolish man will clap hands when he is surety for his friend. 19 He that studieth discords loveth quarrels, and he that exalteth his door seeketh ruin.

20 He that is of a perverse heart shall not find good, and he that perverteth his tongue shall fall into evil.

21 A fool is born to his own disgrace, and even his father shall not rejoice in a fool.

22 A joyful mind maketh age flourishing; a sorrowful spirit drieth up the bones.

23 The wicked man taketh gifts out of the bosom that he may pervert the paths of judgment.

24 Wisdom shineth in the face of the wise; the eyes of fools are in the ends of the earth. 25 A foolish son is the anger of the father and the sorrow of the mother that bore him.

26 It is no good thing to do hurt to the just nor to strike the prince who judgeth right.

27 He that setteth bounds to his words is knowing and wise, and the man of understanding is of a precious spirit. 28 Even a fool, if he will hold his peace, shall be counted wise, and if he close his lips, a man of understanding.

Caput 18

Occasiones quaerit qui vult recedere ab amico; omni tempore erit exprobrabilis. 2 Non recipit stultus verba prudentiae nisi ea dixeris quae versantur in corde eius.

3 Impius cum in profundum venerit peccatorum contemnit, sed sequitur eum ignominia et obprobrium.

4 Aqua profunda verba ex ore viri, et torrens redundans fons sapientiae.

5 Accipere personam impii non est bonum ut declines a veritate iudicii.

6 Labia stulti inmiscunt se rixis, et os eius iurgia provocat. 7 Os stulti contritio eius, et labia illius ruina animae eius. 8 Verba bilinguis quasi simplicia, et ipsa perveniunt usque ad interiora ventris.

Pigrum deicit timor, animae autem effeminatorum esurient. 9 Qui mollis et dissolutus est in opere suo frater est sua opera dissipantis.

10 Turris fortissima nomen Domini; ad ipsum currit iustus et exaltabitur. 11 Substantia divitis urbs roboris eius et quasi murus validus circumdans eum.

12 Antequam conteratur exaltatur cor hominis, et antequam glorificetur humiliatur.

Chapter 18

He that hath a mind to depart from a friend seeketh occasions; he shall ever be subject to reproach. 2 A fool receiveth not the words of prudence unless thou say those things which are in his heart.

3 The wicked man when he is come into the depths of sins contemneth, but ignominy and reproach follow him.

4 Words from the mouth of a man are as deep water, and the fountain of wisdom is an overflowing stream.

5 It is not good to accept the person of the wicked to decline from the truth of judgment.

6 The lips of a fool intermeddle with strife, and his mouth provoketh quarrels. 7 The mouth of a fool is his destruction, and his lips are the ruin of his soul. 8 The words of the double tongued are as if they were harmless, and they reach even to the inner parts of the bowels.

Fear casteth down the slothful, and the souls of the effeminate shall be hungry. 9 He that is loose and slack in his work is the brother of him that wasteth his own works.

10 The name of the Lord is a strong tower; the just runneth to it and shall be exalted. 11 The substance of the rich man is the city of his strength and as a strong wall compassing him about.

12 Before destruction the heart of a man is exalted, and before he be glorified it is humbled.

¹³ Qui prius respondet quam audiat stultum se esse demonstrat et confusione dignum.

¹⁴ Spiritus viri sustentat inbecillitatem suam, spiritum vero ad irascendum facilem, quis poterit sustinere?

¹⁵ Cor prudens possidebit scientiam, et auris sapientium quaerit doctrinam.

¹⁶ Donum hominis dilatat viam eius et ante principes spatium ei facit.

¹⁷ Iustus prior est accusator sui; venit amicus eius et investigabit eum.

¹⁸ Contradictiones conprimit sors et inter potentes quoque diiudicat.

¹⁹ Frater qui adiuvatur a fratre quasi civitas firma, et iudicia quasi vectes urbium.

²⁰ De fructu oris viri replebitur venter eius, et genimina labiorum illius saturabunt eum. ²¹ Mors et vita in manu linguae; qui diligunt eam comedent fructus eius.

²² Qui invenit mulierem bonam invenit bonum et hauriet iucunditatem a Domino.

²³ Cum obsecrationibus loquetur pauper, et dives effabitur rigide.

²⁴ Vir amicalis ad societatem magis amicus erit quam frater.

13 He that answereth before he heareth sheweth himself to be a fool and worthy of confusion.

14 The spirit of a man upholdeth his infirmity, but a spirit that is easily angered, who can bear?

15 A wise heart shall acquire knowledge, and the ear of the wise seeketh instruction.

16 A man's gift enlargeth his way and maketh him room before princes.

17 The just is first accuser of himself; his friend cometh and shall search him.

18 The lot suppresseth contentions and determineth even between the mighty.

19 A brother that is helped by his brother is like a strong city, and judgments are like the bars of cities.

20 Of the fruit of a man's mouth shall his belly be satisfied, and the offspring of his lips shall fill him. 21 Death and life are in the power of the tongue; they that love it shall eat the fruits thereof.

22 He that hath found a good wife hath found a good thing and shall receive a pleasure from the Lord. *He that driveth away a good wife driveth away a good thing, but he that keepeth an adulteress is foolish and wicked.*

23 The poor will speak with supplications, and the rich will speak roughly.

24 A man amiable in society shall be more friendly than a brother.

Caput 19

Melior est pauper qui ambulat in simplicitate sua quam dives torquens labia sua et insipiens.

2 Ubi non est scientia animae non est bonum, et qui festinus est pedibus offendet. 3 Stultitia hominis subplantat gressus eius, et contra Deum fervet animo suo.

4 Divitiae addunt amicos plurimos, a paupere autem et hii quos habuit separantur.

5 Testis falsus non erit inpunitus, et qui mendacia loquitur non effugiet.

6 Multi colunt personam potentis et amici sunt dona tribuenti. 7 Fratres hominis pauperis oderunt eum, insuper et amici procul recesserunt ab eo.

Qui tantum verba sectatur nihil habebit, 8 qui autem possessor est mentis diligit animam suam, et custos prudentiae inveniet bona.

9 Testis falsus non erit inpunitus, et qui loquitur mendacia peribit.

10 Non decent stultum deliciae, nec servum dominari principibus.

11 Doctrina viri per patientiam noscitur, et gloria eius est iniqua praetergredi.

12 Sicut fremitus leonis, ita et regis ira, et sicut ros super herbam ita et hilaritas eius.

Chapter 19

Better is the poor man that walketh in his simplicity than a rich man that is perverse in his lips and unwise.

2 Where there is no knowledge of the soul there is no good, and he that is hasty with his feet shall stumble. 3 The folly of a man supplanteth his steps, and he fretteth in his mind against God.

4 Riches make many friends, but from the poor man even they whom he had depart.

5 A false witness shall not be unpunished, and he that speaketh lies shall not escape.

6 Many honour the person of him that is mighty and are friends of him that giveth gifts. 7 The brethren of the poor man hate him, moreover also his friends have departed far from him.

He that followeth after words only shall have nothing, 8 but he that possesseth a mind loveth his own soul, and he that keepeth prudence shall find good things.

9 A false witness shall not be unpunished, and he that speaketh lies shall perish.

10 Delicacies are not seemly for a fool, nor for a servant to have rule over princes.

11 The learning of a man is known by patience, and his glory is to pass over wrongs.

12 As the roaring of a lion, so also is the anger of a king, and *his* cheerfulness as the dew upon the grass.

¹³ Dolor patris filius stultus, et tecta iugiter perstillantia litigiosa mulier. ¹⁴ Domus et divitiae dantur a parentibus, a Domino autem proprie uxor prudens.

¹⁵ Pigredo inmittit soporem, et anima dissoluta esuriet.

¹⁶ Qui custodit mandatum custodit animam suam, qui autem neglegit viam suam mortificabitur.

¹⁷ Feneratur Domino qui miseretur pauperis, et vicissitudinem suam reddet ei.

¹⁸ Erudi filium tuum; ne desperes, ad interfectionem autem eius ne ponas animam tuam.

¹⁹ Qui inpatiens est sustinebit damnum, et cum rapuerit aliud adponet.

²⁰ Audi consilium, et suscipe disciplinam, ut sis sapiens in novissimis tuis.

²¹ Multae cogitationes in corde viri, voluntas autem Domini permanebit.

²² Homo indigens misericors est, et melior pauper quam vir mendax.

²³ Timor Domini ad vitam, et in plenitudine commorabitur absque visitatione pessima.

²⁴ Abscondit piger manum suam sub ascella nec ad os suum adplicat eam.

²⁵ Pestilente flagellato, stultus sapientior erit, sin autem corripueris sapientem, intelleget disciplinam.

²⁶ Qui adfligit patrem et fugat matrem ignominiosus est et infelix.

²⁷ Non cesses, fili, audire doctrinam, nec ignores sermones scientiae.

13 A foolish son is the grief of his father, and a wrangling wife is like a roof continually dropping through. 14 House and riches are given by parents, but a prudent wife is properly from the Lord.

15 Slothfulness casteth into a deep sleep, and an idle soul shall suffer hunger.

16 He that keepeth the commandment keepeth his own soul, but he that neglecteth his own way shall die.

17 He that hath mercy on the poor lendeth to the Lord, and he will repay him.

18 Chastise thy son; despair not, but to the killing of him set not thy soul.

19 He that is impatient shall suffer damage, and when he shall take away he shall add another thing.

20 Hear counsel, and receive instruction, that thou mayst be wise in thy latter end.

21 There are many thoughts in the heart of a man, but the will of the Lord shall stand firm.

22 A needy man is merciful, and better is the poor than the lying man.

23 The fear of the Lord is unto life, and he shall abide in the fulness without *being visited with evil.*

24 The slothful hideth his hand under his armpit and *will* not so much as bring it to his mouth.

25 The wicked man being scourged, the fool shall be wiser, but if thou rebuke a wise man, he will understand discipline.

26 He that afflicteth his father and chaseth away his mother is infamous and unhappy.

27 Cease not, O my son, to hear instruction, and be not ignorant of the words of knowledge.

28 Testis iniquus deridet iudicium, et os impiorum devorat iniquitatem. 29 Parata sunt derisoribus iudicia et mallei percutientes stultorum corporibus.

Caput 20

Luxuriosa res vinum, et tumultuosa ebrietas; quicumque his delectatur non erit sapiens.

2 Sicut rugitus leonis, ita et terror regis; qui provocat eum peccat in animam suam.

3 Honor est homini qui separat se a contentionibus, omnes autem stulti miscentur contumeliis.

4 Propter frigus piger arare noluit; mendicabit ergo aestate, et non dabitur ei.

5 Sicut aqua profunda sic consilium in corde viri, sed homo sapiens exhauriet illud.

6 Multi homines misericordes vocantur, virum autem fidelem quis inveniet?

7 Iustus qui ambulat in simplicitate sua beatos post se filios derelinquet.

8 Rex qui sedet in solio iudicii dissipat omne malum intuitu suo.

9 Quis potest dicere, "Mundum est cor meum; purus sum a peccato"?

10 Pondus et pondus, mensura et mensura, utrumque abominabile est apud Deum.

11 Ex studiis suis intellegitur puer, si munda et recta sint opera eius.

28 An unjust witness scorneth judgment, and the mouth of the wicked devoureth iniquity. 29 Judgments are prepared for scorners and striking hammers for the bodies of fools.

Chapter 20

Wine is a luxurious thing, and drunkenness riotous; whosoever is delighted therewith shall not be wise.

2 As the roaring of a lion, so also is the dread of a king; he that provoketh him sinneth against his own soul.

3 It is an honour for a man *to* separate himself from quarrels, but all fools are meddling with reproaches.

4 Because of the cold the sluggard would not plough; he shall beg therefore in the summer, and it shall not be given him.

5 Counsel in the heart of a man is like deep water, but a wise man will draw it out.

6 Many men are called merciful, but who shall find a faithful man?

7 The just that walketh in his simplicity shall leave behind him blessed children.

8 The king that sitteth on the throne of judgment scattereth away all evil with his look.

9 Who can say, "My heart is clean; I am pure from sin"?

10 *Diverse weights and diverse measures,* both are abominable before God.

11 By his inclinations a child is known, if his works be clean and right.

12 Aurem audientem et oculum videntem, Dominus fecit utrumque.

13 Noli diligere somnum ne te egestas opprimat; aperi oculos tuos, et saturare panibus.

14 "Malum est; malum est," dicit omnis emptor, et cum recesserit, tunc gloriabitur. 15 Est aurum et multitudo gemmarum, vas autem pretiosum labia scientiae.

16 Tolle vestimentum eius qui fideiussor extitit alieni, et pro extraneis aufer pignus ab eo.

17 Suavis est homini panis mendacii, et postea implebitur os eius calculo.

18 Cogitationes consiliis roborantur, et gubernaculis tractanda sunt bella.

19 Ei qui revelat mysteria et ambulat fraudulenter et dilatat labia sua ne commiscearis.

20 Qui maledicit patri suo et matri, extinguetur lucerna eius in mediis tenebris.

21 Hereditas ad quam festinatur in principio in novissimo benedictione carebit.

22 Ne dicas, "Reddam malum." Expecta Dominum, et liberabit te.

23 Abominatio est apud Dominum pondus et pondus; statera dolosa non est bona.

24 A Domino diriguntur gressus viri, quis autem hominum intellegere potest viam suam?

25 Ruina est homini devorare sanctos et post vota retractare.

26 Dissipat impios rex sapiens et curvat super eos fornicem.

27 Lucerna Domini spiraculum hominis, quae investigat

12 The hearing ear and the seeing eye, the Lord hath made them both.

13 Love not sleep lest poverty oppress thee; open thy eyes, and be filled with bread.

14 "It is naught; it is naught," saith every buyer, and when he is gone away, then he will boast. 15 There is gold and a multitude of jewels, but the lips of knowledge are a precious vessel.

16 Take away the garment of him that is surety for a stranger, and take a pledge from him for strangers.

17 The bread of lying is sweet to a man, *but* afterwards his mouth shall be filled with gravel.

18 Designs are strengthened by counsels, and wars are to be managed by governments.

19 Meddle not with him that revealeth secrets and walketh deceitfully and openeth wide his lips.

20 He that curseth his father and mother, his lamp shall be put out in the midst of darkness.

21 The inheritance *gotten hastily* in the beginning in the end shall be without a blessing.

22 Say not, "I will return evil." Wait for the Lord, and he will deliver thee.

23 *Diverse weights* are an abomination before the Lord; a deceitful balance is not good.

24 The steps of men are guided by the Lord, but who is the man that can understand his own way?

25 It is ruin to a man to devour holy ones and after vows to retract.

26 A wise king scattereth the wicked and *bringeth over them the wheel.*

27 The spirit of a man is the lamp of the Lord, which

omnia secreta ventris. 28 Misericordia et veritas custodiunt regem, et roboratur clementia thronus eius. 29 Exultatio iuvenum fortitudo eorum, et dignitas senum, canities. 30 Livor vulneris absterget mala et plagae in secretioribus ventris.

Caput 21

Sicut divisiones aquarum, ita cor regis in manu Domini: quocumque voluerit inclinabit illud. 2 Omnis via viri recta sibi videtur, adpendit autem corda Dominus. 3 Facere misericordiam et iudicium magis placet Domino quam victimae.

4 Exaltatio oculorum est dilatatio cordis; lucerna impiorum peccatum.

5 Cogitationes robusti semper in abundantia, omnis autem piger semper in egestate. 6 Qui congregat thesauros lingua mendacii vanus et excors est et inpingetur ad laqueos mortis. 7 Rapinae impiorum detrahent eos quia noluerunt facere iudicium.

8 Perversa via viri aliena est, qui autem mundus est, rectum opus eius.

9 Melius est sedere in angulo domatis quam cum muliere litigiosa et in domo communi.

10 Anima impii desiderat malum; non miserebitur proximo suo.

searcheth all the hidden things of the bowels. 28 Mercy and truth preserve the king, and his throne is strengthened by clemency. 29 The joy of young men is their strength, and the dignity of old men, their grey hairs.

30 The blueness of a wound shall wipe away evils and stripes in the more inward parts of the belly.

Chapter 21

As the divisions of waters, so the heart of the king is in the hand of the Lord: whithersoever he will he shall turn it. 2 Every way of a man seemeth right to himself, but the Lord weigheth the hearts. 3 To do mercy and judgment pleaseth the Lord more than victims.

4 Haughtiness of the eyes is the enlarging of the heart; the lamp of the wicked is sin.

5 The thoughts of the industrious always *bring forth* abundance, but every sluggard is always in want. 6 He that gathereth treasures by a lying tongue is vain and foolish and shall stumble upon the snares of death. 7 The robberies of the wicked shall be their downfall because they would not do judgment.

8 The perverse way of a man is strange, but as for him that is pure, his work is right.

9 It is better to sit in a corner of the housetop than with a brawling woman and in a common house.

10 The soul of the wicked desireth evil; he will not have pity on his neighbour.

11 Multato pestilente, sapientior erit parvulus, et si sectetur sapientem, sumet scientiam.

12 Excogitat iustus de domo impii ut detrahat impios a malo.

13 Qui obturat aurem suam ad clamorem pauperis et ipse clamabit et non exaudietur.

14 Munus absconditum extinguit iras, et donum in sinu, indignationem maximam.

15 Gaudium iusto est facere iudicium et pavor operantibus iniquitatem.

16 Vir qui erraverit a via doctrinae in coetu gigantum commorabitur.

17 Qui diligit epulas in egestate erit; qui amat vinum et pinguia non ditabitur.

18 Pro iusto datur impius, et pro rectis iniquus.

19 Melius est habitare in terra deserta quam cum muliere rixosa et iracunda.

20 Thesaurus desiderabilis et oleum in habitaculo iusti, et inprudens homo dissipabit illud.

21 Qui sequitur iustitiam et misericordiam inveniet vitam, iustitiam et gloriam.

22 Civitatem fortium ascendit sapiens et destruxit robur fiduciae eius.

23 Qui custodit os suum et linguam suam custodit ab angustiis animam suam.

24 Superbus et arrogans vocatur indoctus, qui in ira operatur superbiam.

25 Desideria occidunt pigrum, noluerunt enim quicquam manus eius operari. 26 Tota die concupiscit et desiderat, qui autem iustus est tribuet et non cessabit.

11 When a pestilent man is punished, the little one will be wiser, and if he follow the wise, he will receive knowledge.

12 The just considereth seriously the house of the wicked that he may withdraw the wicked from evil.

13 He that stoppeth his ear against the cry of the poor shall also cry himself and shall not be heard.

14 A secret present quencheth anger, and a gift in the bosom, the greatest wrath.

15 It is joy to the just to do judgment and dread to them that work iniquity.

16 A man that shall wander out of the way of doctrine shall abide in the company of the giants.

17 He that loveth good cheer shall be in want; he that loveth wine and fat things shall not be rich.

18 The wicked is delivered up for the just, and the unjust for the righteous.

19 It is better to dwell in a wilderness than with a quarrelsome and passionate woman.

20 There is a treasure to be desired and oil in the dwelling of the just, and the foolish man shall spend it.

21 He that followeth justice and mercy shall find life, justice and glory.

22 The wise man hath scaled the city of the strong and hath cast down the strength of the confidence thereof.

23 He that keepeth his mouth and his tongue keepeth his soul from distress.

24 The proud and the arrogant is called ignorant, who in anger worketh pride.

25 Desires kill the slothful, for his hands have refused to work at all. 26 He longeth and desireth all the day, but he that is just will give and will not cease.

27 Hostiae impiorum abominabiles quia offeruntur ex scelere.

28 Testis mendax peribit; vir oboediens loquetur victoriam.

29 Vir impius procaciter obfirmat vultum suum, qui autem rectus est corrigit viam suam.

30 Non est sapientia, non est prudentia, non est consilium contra Dominum.

31 Equus paratur ad diem belli, Dominus autem salutem tribuit.

Caput 22

Melius est nomen bonum quam divitiae multae; super argentum et aurum gratia bona. 2 Dives et pauper obviaverunt sibi; utriusque operator est Dominus.

3 Callidus vidit malum et abscondit se; innocens pertransiit et adflictus est damno.

4 Finis modestiae timor Domini, divitiae et gloria et vita.

5 Arma et gladii in via perversi, custos autem animae suae longe recedit ab eis.

6 Proverbium est: adulescens iuxta viam suam, etiam cum senuerit, non recedet ab ea.

7 Dives pauperibus imperat, et qui accipit mutuum servus est fenerantis.

8 Qui seminat iniquitatem metet mala, et virga irae suae consummabitur. 9 Qui pronus est ad misericordiam benedi-

27 The sacrifices of the wicked are abominable because they are offered of wickedness.

28 A lying witness shall perish; an obedient man shall speak of victory.

29 The wicked man impudently hardeneth his face, but he that is righteous correcteth his way.

30 There is no wisdom, there is no prudence, there is no counsel against the Lord.

31 The horse is prepared for the day of battle, but the Lord giveth safety.

Chapter 22

A good name is better than great riches, *and* good favour is above silver and gold. 2 The rich and poor have met one another; the Lord is the maker of them both.

3 The prudent man saw the evil and hid himself; the simple passed on and suffered loss.

4 The fruit of humility is the fear of the Lord, riches and glory and life. 5 Arms and swords are in the way of the perverse, but he that keepeth his own soul departeth far from them.

6 It is a proverb: a young man according to his way, even when he is old, he will not depart from it.

7 The rich ruleth over the poor, and the borrower is servant to him that lendeth.

8 He that soweth iniquity shall reap evils, and with the rod of his anger he shall be consumed. 9 He that is inclined

cetur, de panibus enim suis dedit pauperi. Victoriam et honorem acquiret qui dat munera, animam autem aufert accipientium.

10 Eice derisorem, et exibit cum eo iurgium, cessabuntque causae et contumeliae.

11 Qui diligit cordis munditiam propter gratiam labiorum suorum habebit amicum regem.

12 Oculi Domini custodiunt scientiam, et subplantantur verba iniqui.

13 Dicit piger, "Leo foris; in medio platearum occidendus sum."

14 Fovea profunda os alienae; cui iratus est Dominus incidet in eam.

15 Stultitia conligata est in corde pueri, et virga disciplinae fugabit eam.

16 Qui calumniatur pauperem ut augeat divitias suas dabit ipse ditiori et egebit.

17 Inclina aurem tuam, et audi verba sapientium, adpone autem cor ad doctrinam meam, 18 quae pulchra erit tibi, cum servaveris eam in ventre tuo, et redundabit in labiis tuis 19 ut sit in Domino fiducia tua, unde et ostendi eam tibi hodie. 20 Ecce: descripsi eam tibi tripliciter, in cogitationibus et scientia, 21 ut ostenderem tibi firmitatem, et eloquia veritatis, respondere ex his illis qui miserunt te.

22 Non facias violentiam pauperi, quia pauper est, neque conteras egenum in porta, 23 quia Dominus iudicabit causam eius et configet eos qui confixerint animam eius. 24 Noli esse amicus homini iracundo, neque ambules cum viro furioso, 25 ne forte discas semitas eius et sumas scandalum animae tuae. 26 Noli esse cum his qui defigunt manus suas et qui

to mercy shall be blessed, for of his bread he hath given to the poor. He that *maketh* presents shall purchase victory and honour, but he carrieth away the souls of the receivers.

10 Cast out the scoffer, and contention shall go out with him, and quarrels and reproaches shall cease.

11 He that loveth cleanness of heart for the grace of his lips shall have the king for his friend.

12 The eyes of the Lord preserve knowledge, and the words of the unjust are overthrown.

13 The slothful man saith, "There is a lion without; I shall be slain in the midst of the streets."

14 The mouth of a strange woman is a deep pit; he whom the Lord is angry with shall fall into it.

15 Folly is bound up in the heart of a child, and the rod of correction shall drive it away.

16 He that oppresseth the poor to increase his own riches shall himself give to one that is richer and shall be in need.

17 Incline thy ear, and hear the words of the wise, and apply thy heart to my doctrine, 18 which shall be beautiful for thee, *if* thou keep it in thy bowels, and it shall flow in thy lips 19 that thy trust may be in the Lord, wherefore I have also shewn it to thee this day. 20 Behold: I have described it to thee three manner of ways, in thoughts and knowledge, 21 that I might shew thee the certainty, and the words of truth, to answer out of these to them that sent thee.

22 Do no violence to the poor, because he is poor, and do not oppress the needy in the gate, 23 because the Lord will judge his cause and will afflict them that have afflicted his soul. 24 Be not a friend to an angry man, and do not walk with a furious man, 25 lest perhaps thou learn his ways and take scandal to thy soul. 26 Be not with them that fasten

vades se offerunt pro debitis, 27 si enim non habes unde res-
tituas, quid causae est ut tollat operimentum de cubili tuo?
28 Ne transgrediaris terminos antiquos quos posuerunt patres tui. 29 Vidisti virum velocem in opere suo? Coram regibus stabit nec erit ante ignobiles.

Caput 23

Quando sederis ut comedas cum principe, diligenter adtende quae posita sunt ante faciem tuam, 2 et statue cultrum
in gutture tuo, si tamen habes in potestate animam tuam.
3 Ne desideres de cibis eius in quo est panis mendacii. 4 Noli
laborare ut diteris, sed prudentiae tuae pone modum. 5 Ne
erigas oculos tuos ad opes quas habere non potes, quia facient sibi pinnas quasi aquilae et volabunt in caelum. 6 Ne
comedas cum homine invido, et ne desideres cibos eius,
7 quoniam, in similitudinem arioli et coniectoris, aestimat
quod ignorat. "Comede, et bibe," dicet tibi, et mens eius
non est tecum. 8 Cibos quos comederas evomes et perdes
pulchros sermones tuos.

9 In auribus insipientium ne loquaris quia despicient doctrinam eloquii tui. 10 Ne adtingas terminos parvulorum, et
agrum pupillorum ne introeas, 11 propinquus enim eorum
fortis est, et ipse iudicabit contra te causam illorum.

down their hands and that offer themselves sureties for debts, 27 for if thou have not wherewith to restore, what cause is there that he should take the covering from thy bed? 28 Pass not beyond the ancient bounds which thy fathers have set. 29 Hast thou seen a man swift in his work? He shall stand before kings and shall not be before those that are obscure.

Chapter 23

When thou shalt sit to eat with a prince, consider diligently what is set before thy face, 2 and put a knife to thy throat, if *it be so that* thou have thy soul in thy own power. 3 Be not desirous of his meats in which is the bread of deceit. 4 Labour not to be rich, but set bounds to thy prudence. 5 Lift not up thy eyes to riches which thou canst not have, because they shall make themselves wings like those of an eagle and shall fly towards heaven. 6 Eat not with an envious man, and desire not his meats, 7 because, like a soothsayer and diviner, he thinketh that which he knoweth not. "Eat, and drink," will he say to thee, and his mind is not with thee. 8 The meats which thou hadst eaten thou shalt vomit up and shalt lose thy beautiful words.

9 Speak not in the ears of fools because they will despise the instruction of thy speech. 10 Touch not the bounds of little ones, and enter not into the field of the fatherless, 11 for their near kinsman is strong, and he will judge their cause against thee.

12 Ingrediatur ad doctrinam cor tuum et aures tuae ad verba scientiae.

13 Noli subtrahere a puero disciplinam, si enim percusseris eum virga, non morietur. 14 Tu virga percuties eum et animam eius de inferno liberabis.

15 Fili mi, si sapiens fuerit animus tuus, gaudebit tecum cor meum, 16 et exultabunt renes mei cum locuta fuerint rectum labia tua. 17 Non aemuletur cor tuum peccatores, sed in timore Domini esto tota die, 18 quia habebis spem in novissimo, et praestolatio tua non auferetur. 19 Audi, fili mi, et esto sapiens, et dirige in via animum tuum. 20 Noli esse in conviviis potatorum nec in comesationibus eorum qui carnes ad vescendum conferunt, 21 quia vacantes potibus et dantes symbola consumentur, et vestietur pannis dormitatio.

22 Audi patrem tuum qui genuit te, et ne contemnas cum senuerit mater tua. 23 Veritatem eme, et noli vendere sapientiam et doctrinam et intellegentiam. 24 Exultat gaudio pater iusti; qui sapientem genuit laetabitur in eo. 25 Gaudeat pater tuus et mater tua, et exultet quae genuit te. 26 Praebe, fili mi, cor tuum mihi, et oculi tui vias meas custodiant, 27 fovea enim profunda est meretrix, et puteus angustus aliena. 28 Insidiatur in via quasi latro, et quos incautos viderit interficiet.

29 Cui vae? Cuius patri vae? Cui rixae? Cui foveae? Cui sine causa vulnera? Cui suffusio oculorum? 30 Nonne his qui morantur in vino et student calicibus epotandis? 31 Ne intuearis vinum quando flavescit, cum splenduerit in vitro co-

12 Let thy heart apply itself to instruction and thy ears to words of knowledge.

13 Withhold not correction from a child, for if thou strike him with the rod, he shall not die. 14 Thou shalt beat him with the rod and deliver his soul from hell.

15 My son, if thy mind be wise, my heart shall rejoice with thee, 16 and my reins shall rejoice when thy lips shall speak what is right. 17 Let not thy heart envy sinners, but be thou in the fear of the Lord all the day long, 18 because thou shalt have hope in the latter end, and thy expectation shall not be taken away. 19 Hear thou, my son, and be wise, and guide thy mind in the way. 20 Be not in the feasts of great drinkers nor in their revellings who contribute flesh to eat, 21 because they that give themselves to drinking and that *club together* shall be consumed, and drowsiness shall be clothed with rags.

22 Hearken to thy father that begot thee, and despise not thy mother when she is old. 23 Buy truth, and do not sell wisdom and instruction and understanding. 24 The father of the just rejoiceth *greatly;* he that hath begotten a wise son shall have joy in him. 25 Let thy father and thy mother be joyful, and let her rejoice that bore thee. 26 My son, give me thy heart, and let thy eyes keep my ways, 27 for a harlot is a deep ditch, and a strange woman is a narrow pit. 28 She lieth in wait in the way as a robber, and him whom she shall see unwary she will kill.

29 Who hath woe? Whose father hath woe? Who hath contentions? Who *falls into* pits? Who hath wounds without cause? Who hath *redness* of eyes? 30 Surely they that pass their time in wine and study to drink off their cups. 31 Look not upon the wine when it is yellow, when the colour thereof

lor eius: ingreditur blande, 32 sed in novissimo mordebit ut coluber et sicut regulus venena diffundet. 33 Oculi tui videbunt extraneas, et cor tuum loquetur perversa. 34 Et eris sicut dormiens in medio mari et quasi sopitus gubernator amisso clavo. 35 Et dices, "Verberaverunt me, sed non dolui; traxerunt me, et ego non sensi. Quando evigilabo et rursum vina repperiam?"

Caput 24

Ne aemuleris viros malos, nec desideres esse cum eis, 2 quia rapinas meditatur mens eorum, et fraudes labia eorum loquuntur.

3 Sapientia aedificabitur domus, et prudentia roborabitur. 4 In doctrina replebuntur cellaria universa substantia pretiosa et pulcherrima.

5 Vir sapiens fortis est et vir doctus robustus et validus, 6 quia cum dispositione initur bellum, et erit salus ubi multa consilia sunt.

7 Excelsa stulto sapientia; in porta non aperiet os suum. 8 Qui cogitat mala facere stultus vocabitur. 9 Cogitatio stulti peccatum est, et abominatio hominum detractor.

10 Si desperaveris, lassus in die angustiae, inminuetur fortitudo tua. 11 Erue eos qui ducuntur ad mortem, et qui tra-

shineth in the glass: it goeth in pleasantly, 32 but in the end it will bite like a snake and will spread abroad poison like a basilisk. 33 Thy eyes shall behold strange women, and thy heart shall utter perverse things. 34 And thou shalt be as one sleeping in the midst of the sea and as a pilot fast asleep when the stern is lost. 35 And thou shalt say, "They have beaten me, but I was not sensible of pain; they drew me, and I felt not. When shall I awake and find wine again?"

Chapter 24

Seek not to be like evil men, neither desire to be with them, 2 because their mind studieth robberies, and their lips speak deceits.

3 By wisdom the house shall be built, and by prudence it shall be strengthened. 4 By instruction the storerooms shall be filled with all precious and most beautiful wealth.

5 A wise man is strong and a knowing man stout and valiant, 6 because war is managed by due ordering, and there shall be safety where there are many counsels.

7 Wisdom is too high for a fool; in the gate he shall not open his mouth. 8 He that deviseth to do evils shall be called a fool. 9 The thought of a fool is sin, and the detractor is the abomination of men.

10 If thou lose hope, being weary in the day of distress, thy strength shall be diminished. 11 Deliver them that are led to death, and those that are drawn to death forbear

huntur ad interitum liberare ne cesses. 12 Si dixeris, "Vires non suppetunt," qui inspector est cordis, ipse intellegit, et servatorem animae tuae nihil fallit, reddetque homini iuxta opera sua.

13 Comede, fili mi, mel, quia bonum est, et favum dulcissimum gutturi tuo. 14 Sic et doctrina sapientiae animae tuae, quam cum inveneris habebis in novissimis spem, et spes tua non peribit. 15 Ne insidieris et quaeras impietatem in domo iusti, neque vastes requiem eius, 16 septies enim cadet iustus et resurget, impii autem corruent in malum. 17 Cum ceciderit inimicus tuus, ne gaudeas, et in ruina eius ne exultet cor tuum 18 ne forte videat Dominus et displiceat ei et auferat ab eo iram suam. 19 Ne contendas cum pessimis, nec aemuleris impios, 20 quoniam non habent futurorum spem mali, et lucerna impiorum extinguetur.

21 Time Dominum, fili mi, et regem, et cum detractoribus non commiscearis, 22 quoniam repente consurget perditio eorum, et ruinam utriusque quis novit?

23 Haec quoque sapientibus: cognoscere personam in iudicio non est bonum.

24 Qui dicunt impio, "Iustus es," maledicent eis populi, et detestabuntur eos tribus. 25 Qui arguunt eum laudabuntur, et super ipsos veniet benedictio. 26 Labia deosculabitur qui recta verba respondet.

27 Praepara foris opus tuum, et diligenter exerce agrum tuum ut postea aedifices domum tuam. 28 Ne sis testis frustra contra proximum tuum, nec lactes quemquam labiis

not to deliver. 12 If thou say, "I have not strength enough," he that seeth into the heart, he understandeth, and nothing deceiveth the keeper of thy soul, and he shall render to a man according to his works.

13 Eat honey, my son, because it is good, and the honeycomb most sweet to thy throat. 14 So also is the doctrine of wisdom to thy soul, which when thou hast found thou shalt have hope in the end, and thy hope shall not perish. 15 Lie not in wait, nor seek after wickedness in the house of the just, nor spoil his rest, 16 for a just man shall fall seven times and shall rise again, but the wicked shall fall down into evil. 17 When thy enemy shall fall, be not glad, and in his ruin let not thy heart rejoice 18 lest the Lord see and it displease him and he turn away his wrath from him. 19 Contend not with the wicked, nor seek to be like the ungodly, 20 for evil men have no hope of things to come, and the lamp of the wicked shall be put out.

21 My son, fear the Lord and the king, and have nothing to do with detractors, 22 for their destruction shall rise suddenly, and who knoweth the ruin of both?

23 These things also to the wise: it is not good to have respect to persons in judgment.

24 They that say to the wicked man, "Thou art just," *shall be cursed by the people,* and the tribes shall abhor them. 25 They that rebuke him shall be praised, and a blessing shall come upon them. 26 He shall kiss the lips who answereth right words.

27 Prepare thy work without, and diligently till thy ground that afterward thou mayst build thy house. 28 Be not witness without cause against thy neighbour, and deceive not any

tuis. 29 Ne dicas, "Quomodo fecit mihi sic faciam ei; reddam unicuique secundum opus suum."

30 Per agrum hominis pigri transivi et per vineam viri stulti, 31 et ecce: totum repleverant urticae, et operuerant superficiem eius spinae, et maceria lapidum destructa erat. 32 Quod cum vidissem posui in corde meo, et exemplo didici disciplinam. 33 "Parum," inquam, "dormies. Modicum dormitabis; pauxillum manus conseres ut quiescas. 34 Et veniet tibi quasi cursor egestas et mendicitas quasi vir armatus."

Caput 25

Hae quoque parabolae Salomonis quas transtulerunt viri Ezechiae, regis Iuda.

2 Gloria Dei celare verbum et gloria regum investigare sermonem. 3 Caelum sursum et terra deorsum et cor regum inscrutabile. 4 Aufer robiginem de argento, et egredietur vas purissimum. 5 Aufer impietatem de vultu regis, et firmabitur iustitia thronus eius. 6 Ne gloriosus appareas coram rege, et in loco magnorum ne steteris, 7 melius est enim ut dicatur tibi, "Ascende huc," quam ut humilieris coram principe.

8 Quae viderunt oculi tui ne proferas in iurgio cito ne

man with thy lips. 29 Say not, "I will do to him as he hath done to me; I will render to every one according to his work."

30 I passed by the field of the slothful man and by the vineyard of the foolish man, 31 and behold: *it was all filled with nettles,* and thorns had covered the face thereof, and the stone wall was broken down. 32 Which when I had seen I laid it up in my heart, and by the example I received instruction. 33 "Thou wilt sleep a little," said I, "Thou wilt slumber a little; thou wilt fold thy hands a little to rest. 34 And poverty shall come to thee as a runner and beggary as an armed man."

Chapter 25

These are also parables of Solomon which the men of Hezechiah, king of Judah, copied out.

2 It is the glory of God to conceal the word and the glory of kings to search out the speech. 3 The heaven above and the earth beneath and the heart of kings is unsearchable. 4 Take away the rust from silver, and there shall come forth a most pure vessel. 5 Take away wickedness from the face of the king, and his throne shall be established with justice. 6 Appear not glorious before the king, and stand not in the place of great men, 7 for it is better that it should be said to thee, "Come up hither," than that thou shouldst be humbled before the prince.

8 The things which thy eyes have seen utter not hastily

postea emendare non possis cum dehonestaveris amicum tuum. 9 Causam tuam tracta cum amico tuo, et secretum extraneo non reveles, 10 ne forte insultet tibi cum audierit et exprobrare non cesset. Gratia et amicitia liberant; quas tibi serva ne exprobrabilis fias.

11 Mala aurea in lectis argenteis qui loquitur verbum in tempore suo. 12 Inauris aurea et margaritum fulgens qui arguit sapientem et aurem oboedientem. 13 Sicut frigus nivis in die messis, ita legatus fidelis ei qui misit eum; animam illius requiescere facit. 14 Nubes et ventus et pluviae non sequentes, vir gloriosus et promissa non conplens.

15 Patientia lenietur princeps, et lingua mollis confringet duritiam.

16 Mel invenisti: comede quod sufficit tibi ne forte saturatus evomas illud. 17 Subtrahe pedem tuum de domo proximi tui nequando satiatus oderit te. 18 Iaculum et gladius et sagitta acuta homo qui loquitur contra proximum suum testimonium falsum. 19 Dens putridus et pes lassus qui sperat super infideli in die angustiae 20 et amittit pallium in die frigoris. Acetum in nitro, qui cantat carmina cordi pessimo. Sicut tinea vestimento et vermis ligno, ita tristitia viri nocet cordi.

21 Si esurierit inimicus tuus, ciba illum; si sitierit, da ei aquam bibere, 22 prunas enim congregabis super caput eius, et Dominus reddet tibi. 23 Ventus aquilo dissipat pluvias, et facies tristis linguam detrahentem.

in a quarrel lest afterward thou mayst not be able to make amends when thou hast dishonoured thy friend. 9 Treat thy cause with thy friend, and discover not the secret to a stranger, 10 *lest* he insult over thee when he hath heard it and cease not to upbraid thee. Grace and friendship deliver *a man;* keep *these* for thyself lest thou fall under reproach.

11 *To speak* a word in due time is like apples of gold on beds of silver. 12 As an earring of gold and a bright pearl, *so* is he that reproveth the wise and the obedient ear. 13 As the cold of snow in the time of harvest, so is a faithful messenger to him that sent him, *for he refresheth* his soul. 14 As clouds and wind *when no rain followeth, so* is the man that boasteth and doth not fulfil his promises.

15 By patience a prince shall be appeased, and a soft tongue shall break hardness.

16 Thou hast found honey: eat what is sufficient for thee *lest* being glutted therewith thou vomit it up. 17 Withdraw thy foot from the house of thy neighbour lest having his fill he hate thee. 18 A man that beareth false witness against his neighbour is like a dart and a sword and a sharp arrow. 19 *To trust* in an unfaithful man in the time of trouble is like a rotten tooth and weary foot 20 and one that loseth his garment in cold weather. As vinegar upon nitre, *so* is he that singeth songs to a very evil heart. As a moth doth *by* a garment and a worm *by* the wood, so the sadness of a man consumeth the heart.

21 If thy enemy be hungry, give him to eat; if he thirst, give him water to drink, 22 for thou shalt heap hot coals upon his head, and the Lord will reward thee. 23 The north wind driveth away rain; *so* doth a sad countenance a backbiting tongue.

24 Melius est sedere in angulo domatis quam cum muliere litigiosa et in domo communi.

25 Aqua frigida animae sitienti, et nuntius bonus de terra longinqua.

26 Fons turbatus pede et vena corrupta iustus cadens coram impio.

27 Sicut qui mel multum comedit non est ei bonum, sic qui scrutator est maiestatis opprimetur a gloria. 28 Sicut urbs patens et absque murorum ambitu, ita vir qui non potest in loquendo cohibere spiritum suum.

Caput 26

Quomodo nix aestate et pluvia in messe, sic indecens est stulto gloria. 2 Sicut avis ad alia transvolans et passer quolibet vadens, sic maledictum frustra prolatum in quempiam superveniet. 3 Flagellum equo et camus asino et virga in dorso inprudentium. 4 Ne respondeas stulto iuxta stultitiam suam ne efficiaris ei similis. 5 Responde stulto iuxta stultitiam suam ne sibi sapiens esse videatur.

6 Claudus pedibus et iniquitatem bibens qui mittit verba per nuntium stultum. 7 Quomodo pulchras frustra habet claudus tibias, sic indecens est in ore stultorum parabola. 8 Sicut qui mittit lapidem in acervum Mercurii, ita qui tribuit insipienti honorem. 9 Quomodo si spina nascatur in manu temulenti, sic parabola in ore stultorum.

24 It is better to sit in a corner of the housetop than with a brawling woman and in a common house.

25 As cold water to a thirsty soul, *so* are good tidings from a far country.

26 A just man falling down before the wicked is as a fountain troubled with the foot and a corrupted spring.

27 As it is not good for a man to eat much honey, so he that is a searcher of majesty shall be overwhelmed by glory.

28 As a city that lieth open and is not compassed with walls, so is a man that cannot refrain his own spirit in speaking.

Chapter 26

As snow in summer and rain in harvest, so glory is not seemly for a fool. 2 As a bird flying to other places and a sparrow going here or there, so a curse uttered without cause shall come upon a man. 3 A whip for a horse and a snaffle for an ass and a rod for the back of fools. 4 Answer not a fool according to his folly lest thou be made like him. 5 Answer a fool according to his folly lest he imagine himself to be wise.

6 He that sendeth words by a foolish messenger is lame of feet and drinketh iniquity. 7 As a lame man hath fair legs in vain, so a parable is unseemly in the mouth of fools. 8 As he that casteth a stone into the heap of Mercury, so is he that giveth honour to a fool. 9 As if a thorn should grow in the hand of a drunkard, so is a parable in the mouth of fools.

¹⁰ Iudicium determinat causas, et qui inponit stulto silentium iras mitigat.

¹¹ Sicut canis qui revertitur ad vomitum suum, sic inprudens qui iterat stultitiam suam.

¹² Vidisti hominem sapientem sibi videri? Magis illo spem habebit stultus.

¹³ Dicit piger, "Leo est in via et leaena in itineribus." ¹⁴ Sicut ostium vertitur in cardine suo, ita piger in lectulo suo. ¹⁵ Abscondit piger manum sub ascella sua, et laborat si ad os suum eam converterit. ¹⁶ Sapientior sibi piger videtur septem viris loquentibus sententias.

¹⁷ Sicut qui adprehendit auribus canem, sic qui transit inpatiens et commiscetur rixae alterius. ¹⁸ Sicut noxius est qui mittit lanceas et sagittas in mortem, ¹⁹ sic vir qui fraudulenter nocet amico suo, et cum fuerit deprehensus dicit, "Ludens feci."

²⁰ Cum defecerint ligna extinguetur ignis, et susurrone subtracto, iurgia conquiescunt. ²¹ Sicut carbones ad prunas et ligna ad ignem, sic homo iracundus suscitat rixas.

²² Verba susurronis quasi simplicia, et ipsa perveniunt ad intima ventris. ²³ Quomodo si argento sordido ornare velis vas fictile sic labia tumentia cum pessimo corde sociata. ²⁴ Labiis suis intellegitur inimicus cum in corde tractaverit dolos. ²⁵ Quando submiserit vocem suam, ne credideris ei, quoniam septem nequitiae sunt in corde illius.

10 Judgment determineth causes, and he that putteth a fool to silence appeaseth anger.

11 As a dog that returneth to his vomit, so is the fool that repeateth his folly.

12 Hast thou seen a man wise in his own conceit? *There shall be more hope of a fool* than of him.

13 The slothful man saith, "There is a lion in the way and a lioness in the roads." 14 As the door turneth upon its hinges, so doth the slothful upon his bed 15 The slothful hideth his hand under his armpit, and it grieveth him to turn it to his mouth. 16 The sluggard is wiser in his own conceit than seven men that speak sentences.

17 As he that taketh a dog by the ears, so is he that passeth by *in anger* and meddleth with another man's quarrel. 18 As he is guilty that shooteth arrows and lances unto death, 19 so is the man that hurteth his friend deceitfully, and when he is taken saith, "I did it in jest."

20 When the wood faileth the fire shall go out, and when the talebearer is taken away, contentions *shall* cease. 21 As coals are to burning coals and wood to fire, so an angry man stirreth up strife.

22 The words of a talebearer are as it were simple, *but* they reach to the innermost parts of the belly. 23 Swelling lips joined with a corrupt heart *are like* an earthern vessel *adorned* with silver dross. 24 An enemy is known by his lips when in his heart he entertaineth deceit. 25 When he shall speak low, trust him not, because there are seven mischiefs in his heart.

26 Qui operit odium fraudulenter, revelabitur malitia eius in concilio. 27 Qui fodit foveam incidet in eam, et qui volvit lapidem, revertetur ad eum.

28 Lingua fallax non amat veritatem, et os lubricum operatur ruinas.

Caput 27

Ne glorieris in crastinum, ignorans quid superventura pariat dies.

2 Laudet te alienus et non os tuum, extraneus et non labia tua.

3 Grave est saxum et onerosa harena, sed ira stulti utroque gravior. 4 Ira non habet misericordiam nec erumpens furor, et impetum concitati ferre quis poterit?

5 Melior est manifesta correptio quam amor absconditus.

6 Meliora sunt vulnera diligentis quam fraudulenta odientis oscula.

7 Anima saturata calcabit favum, et anima esuriens et amarum pro dulce sumet.

8 Sicut avis transmigrans de nido suo, sic vir qui relinquit locum suum.

9 Unguento et variis odoribus delectatur cor, et bonis amici consiliis anima dulcoratur. 10 Amicum tuum et amicum patris tui ne dimiseris, et domum fratris tui ne ingre-

26 He that covereth hatred deceitfully, his malice shall be laid open in the public assembly. 27 He that diggeth a pit shall fall into it, and he that rolleth a stone, it shall return to him.

28 A deceitful tongue loveth not truth, and a slippery mouth worketh ruin.

Chapter 27

Boast not for to morrow, for thou knowest not what the day to come may bring forth.

2 Let another praise thee and not thy own mouth, a stranger and not thy own lips.

3 A stone is heavy and sand weighty, but the anger of a fool is heavier than them both. 4 Anger hath no mercy nor fury when it breaketh forth, and who can bear the violence of one provoked?

5 Open rebuke is better than hidden love.

6 Better are the wounds of a friend than the deceitful kisses of an enemy.

7 A soul that is full shall tread upon the honeycomb, and a soul that is hungry shall take even bitter for sweet.

8 As a bird that wandereth from her nest, so is a man that leaveth his place.

9 Ointment and *perfumes* rejoice the heart, and the good counsels of a friend are sweet to the soul. 10 Thy own friend and thy father's friend forsake not, and go not into thy

diaris in die adflictionis tuae. Melior est vicinus iuxta quam frater procul.

11 Stude sapientiae, fili mi, et laetifica cor meum ut possis exprobranti respondere sermonem.

12 Astutus videns malum absconditus est; parvuli transeuntes sustinuere dispendia.

13 Tolle vestimentum eius qui spopondit pro extraneo, et pro alienis aufer ei pignus.

14 Qui benedicit proximo suo voce grandi de nocte consurgens maledicenti similis erit.

15 Tecta perstillantia in die frigoris et litigiosa mulier conparantur. 16 Qui retinet eam quasi qui ventum teneat et oleum dexterae suae vocabit.

17 Ferrum ferro acuitur, et homo exacuit faciem amici sui. 18 Qui servat ficum comedet fructus eius, et qui custos est domini sui glorificabitur. 19 Quomodo in aquis resplendent vultus prospicientium, sic corda hominum manifesta sunt prudentibus. 20 Infernus et perditio numquam replentur, similiter et oculi hominum insatiabiles. 21 Quomodo probatur in conflatorio argentum et in fornace aurum, sic probatur homo ore laudantis. Cor iniqui inquirit mala, cor autem rectum inquirit scientiam.

22 Si contuderis stultum in pila quasi tisanas feriente desuper pilo, non auferetur ab eo stultitia eius. 23 Diligenter agnosce vultum pecoris tui, tuosque greges considera, 24 non enim habebis iugiter potestatem, sed corona tribuetur in generationem et generationem. 25 Aperta sunt prata, et apparuerunt herbae virentes, et collecta sunt faena de montibus. 26 Agni ad vestimentum tuum, et hedi agri pre-

brother's house in the day of thy affliction. Better is a neighbour that is near than a brother afar off.

11 Study wisdom, my son, and make my heart joyful that thou mayst give an answer to him that reproacheth.

12 The prudent man seeing evil hideth himself; little ones passing on have suffered losses.

13 Take away his garment that hath been surety for a stranger, and take from him a pledge for strangers.

14 He that blesseth his neighbour with a loud voice rising in the night shall be like to him that curseth.

15 Roofs dropping through in a cold day and a contentious woman are alike. 16 He that retaineth her is as he that would hold the wind and shall call the oil of his right hand.

17 Iron sharpeneth iron; *so* a man sharpeneth the countenance of his friend. 18 He that keepeth the fig tree shall eat the fruit thereof, and he that is the keeper of his master shall be glorified. 19 As the faces of them that look therein shine in the water, so the hearts of men are laid open to the wise. 20 Hell and destruction are never filled, so the eyes of men are never satisfied. 21 As silver is tried in the fining-pot and gold in the furnace, so a man is tried by the mouth of him that praiseth. The heart of the wicked seeketh after evils, but the righteous heart seeketh after knowledge.

22 Though thou shouldst bray a fool in the mortar as when a pestle striketh upon *sodden* barley, his folly would not be taken from him. 23 Be diligent to know the countenance of thy cattle, and consider thy own flocks, 24 for thou shalt not always have power, but a crown shall be given to generation and generation. 25 The meadows are open, and the green herbs have appeared, and the hay is gathered out of the mountains. 26 Lambs are for thy clothing, and kids *for*

tium. 27 Sufficiat tibi lac caprarum in cibos tuos et in necessaria domus tuae et ad victum ancillis tuis.

Caput 28

Fugit impius nemine persequente, iustus autem, quasi leo
confidens, absque terrore erit.

2 Propter peccata terrae multi principes eius, et propter
hominis sapientiam et horum scientiam quae dicuntur vita
ducis longior erit.

3 Vir pauper calumnians pauperes similis imbri vehementi
in quo paratur fames.

4 Qui derelinquunt legem laudant impium; qui custodiunt succenduntur contra eum. 5 Viri mali non cogitant iudicium, qui autem requirunt Dominum animadvertunt omnia. 6 Melior est pauper ambulans in simplicitate sua quam
dives pravis itineribus. 7 Qui custodit legem filius sapiens
est, qui autem pascit comesatores confundit patrem suum.
8 Qui coacervat divitias usuris et fenore liberali in pauperes
congregat eas. 9 Qui declinat aures suas ne audiat legem,
oratio eius erit execrabilis. 10 Qui decipit iustos in via mala
in interitu suo corruet, et simplices possidebunt bona eius.

11 Sapiens sibi videtur vir dives, pauper autem prudens
scrutabitur eum. 12 In exultatione iustorum multa gloria est;

the price of the field. 27 Let the milk of the goats be enough for thy food and for the necessities of thy house and for maintenance for thy handmaids.

Chapter 28

The wicked man fleeth when no man pursueth, but the just, bold as a lion, shall be without dread.

2 For the sins of the land many are the princes thereof, and for the wisdom of a man and the knowledge of those things that are said the life of the prince shall be prolonged.

3 A poor man that oppresseth the poor is like a violent shower which bringeth a famine.

4 They that forsake the law praise the wicked man; they that keep it are incensed against him. 5 Evil men think not on judgment, but they that seek after the Lord take notice of all things. 6 Better is the poor man walking in his simplicity than the rich in crooked ways. 7 He that keepeth the law is a wise son, but he that feedeth gluttons shameth his father. 8 He that heapeth together riches by usury and loan gathereth them for him that will be bountiful to the poor. 9 He that turneth away his ears from hearing the law, his prayer shall be an abomination. 10 He that deceiveth the just in a wicked way shall fall in his own destruction, and the upright shall possess his goods.

11 The rich man seemeth to himself wise, but the poor man that is prudent shall search him out. 12 In the joy of the just there is great glory; when the wicked reign men are ru-

regnantibus impiis ruinae hominum. 13 Qui abscondit scelera sua non dirigetur, qui autem confessus fuerit et reliquerit ea misericordiam consequetur.

14 Beatus homo qui semper est pavidus, qui vero mentis est durae corruet in malum.

15 Leo rugiens et ursus esuriens, princeps impius super populum pauperem. 16 Dux indigens prudentia multos opprimet per calumniam, qui autem odit avaritiam, longi fient dies eius.

17 Hominem qui calumniatur animae sanguinem, si usque ad lacum fugerit, nemo sustinet. 18 Qui ambulat simpliciter salvus erit; qui perversis graditur viis concidet semel. 19 Qui operatur terram suam saturabitur panibus, qui autem sectatur otium replebitur egestate. 20 Vir fidelis multum laudabitur, qui autem festinat ditari non erit innocens. 21 Qui cognoscit in iudicio faciem non facit bene; iste et pro buccella panis deserit veritatem. 22 Vir qui festinat ditari et aliis invidet ignorat quod egestas superveniet ei. 23 Qui corripit hominem gratiam postea inveniet apud eum magis quam ille qui per linguae blandimenta decipit. 24 Qui subtrahit aliquid a patre suo et a matre et dicit hoc non esse peccatum particeps homicidae est. 25 Qui se iactat et dilatat iurgia concitat; qui sperat in Domino sanabitur. 26 Qui confidit in corde suo stultus est, qui autem graditur sapienter salvus erit. 27 Qui dat pauperi non indigebit; qui despicit deprecantem sustinebit penuriam.

28 Cum surrexerint impii abscondentur homines; cum illi perierint multiplicabuntur iusti.

ined. 13 He that hideth his sins shall not prosper, but he that shall confess and forsake them shall obtain mercy.

14 Blessed is the man that is always fearful, but he that is hardened in mind shall fall into evil.

15 As a roaring lion and a hungry bear, so is a wicked prince over the poor people. 16 A prince void of prudence shall oppress many by calumny, but he that hateth covetousness *shall prolong his days.*

17 A man that doth violence to the blood of a person, if he flee even to the pit, no man *will stay* him. 18 He that walketh uprightly shall be saved; he that *is perverse in his* ways shall fall at once. 19 He that tilleth his ground shall be filled with bread, but he that followeth idleness shall be filled with poverty. 20 A faithful man shall be much praised, but he that maketh haste to be rich shall not be innocent. 21 He that hath respect to a person in judgment doth not well; *such* a man even for a morsel of bread forsaketh the truth. 22 A man that maketh haste to be rich and envieth others is ignorant that poverty shall come upon him. 23 He that rebuketh a man shall afterward find favour with him more than he that by a flattering tongue deceiveth him. 24 He that stealeth any thing from his father *or* from his mother and saith this is no sin is the partner of a murderer. 25 He that boasteth and puffeth up himself stirreth up quarrels, but he that trusteth in the Lord shall be healed. 26 He that trusteth in his own heart is a fool, but he that walketh wisely, he shall be saved. 27 He that giveth to the poor shall not want; he that despiseth his entreaty shall suffer indigence.

28 When the wicked rise up men shall hide themselves; when they perish the just shall be multiplied.

Caput 29

Viro qui corripientem dura cervice contemnit repentinus ei superveniet interitus, et eum sanitas non sequetur.

2 In multiplicatione iustorum laetabitur vulgus; cum impii sumpserint principatum gemet populus.

3 Vir qui amat sapientiam laetificat patrem suum, qui autem nutrit scorta perdet substantiam. 4 Rex iustus erigit terram; vir avarus destruet eam. 5 Homo qui blandis fictisque sermonibus loquitur amico suo rete expandit gressibus eius. 6 Peccantem virum iniquum involvet laqueus, et iustus laudabit atque gaudebit. 7 Novit iustus causam pauperum; impius ignorat scientiam. 8 Homines pestilentes dissipant civitatem, sapientes vero avertunt furorem.

9 Vir sapiens si cum stulto contenderit, sive irascatur sive rideat, non inveniet requiem.

10 Viri sanguinum oderunt simplicem, iusti autem quaerunt animam eius.

11 Totum spiritum suum profert stultus; sapiens differt et reservat in posterum.

12 Princeps qui libenter audit verba mendacii omnes ministros habet impios.

13 Pauper et creditor obviam fuerunt sibi; utriusque inluminator est Dominus. 14 Rex qui iudicat in veritate pauperes, thronus eius in aeternum firmabitur.

Chapter 29

The man that with a stiff neck despiseth him that reproveth him *shall suddenly be destroyed,* and health shall not follow him.

2 When just men increase the people shall rejoice; when the wicked shall bear rule the people shall mourn.

3 A man that loveth wisdom rejoiceth his father, but he that maintaineth harlots shall squander away his substance. 4 A just king setteth up the land; a covetous man shall destroy it. 5 A man that speaketh to his friend with flattering and dissembling words spreadeth a net for his feet. 6 A snare shall entangle the wicked man when he sinneth, and the just shall praise and rejoice. 7 The just taketh notice of the cause of the poor; the wicked is *void* of knowledge. 8 Corrupt men bring a city to ruin, but wise men turn away wrath.

9 If a wise man contend with a fool, whether he be angry or laugh, he shall find no rest.

10 Bloodthirsty men hate the upright, but just men seek his soul.

11 A fool uttereth all his mind; a wise man deferreth and keepeth it till afterwards.

12 A prince that gladly heareth lying words hath all his servants wicked.

13 The poor man and the creditor have met one another; the Lord is the enlightener of them both. 14 The king that judgeth the poor in truth, his throne shall be established for ever.

15 Virga atque correptio tribuit sapientiam, puer autem qui dimittitur voluntati suae confundit matrem suam.

16 In multiplicatione impiorum multiplicabuntur scelera, et iusti ruinas eorum videbunt.

17 Erudi filium tuum et refrigerabit te et dabit delicias animae tuae.

18 Cum prophetia defecerit dissipabitur populus, qui vero custodit legem beatus est.

19 Servus verbis non potest erudiri quia quod dicis intellegit et respondere contemnit. 20 Vidisti hominem velocem ad loquendum? Stultitia magis speranda est quam illius correptio. 21 Qui delicate a pueritia nutrit servum suum postea illum sentiet contumacem.

22 Vir iracundus provocat rixas, et qui ad indignandum facilis est erit ad peccandum proclivior. 23 Superbum sequitur humilitas, et humilem spiritu suscipiet gloria. 24 Qui cum fure partitur odit animam suam; adiurantem audit et non indicat. 25 Qui timet hominem cito corruet; qui sperat in Domino sublevabitur.

26 Multi requirunt faciem principis, et a Domino iudicium egreditur singulorum.

27 Abominantur iusti virum impium, et abominantur impii eos qui in recta sunt via. Verbum custodiens filius extra perditionem erit.

15 The rod and reproof give wisdom, but the child that is left to his own will bringeth his mother to shame.

16 When the wicked are multiplied crimes shall be multiplied, *but* the just shall see their downfall.

17 Instruct thy son and he shall refresh thee and shall give delight to thy soul.

18 When prophecy shall fail the people shall be scattered abroad, but he that keepeth the law is blessed.

19 A slave *will* not be corrected by words because he understandeth what thou sayest and *will not* answer. 20 Hast thou seen a man hasty to speak? Folly is rather to be looked for than his amendment. 21 He that nourisheth his servant delicately from his childhood afterwards shall find him stubborn.

22 A passionate man provoketh quarrels, and he that is easily stirred up to wrath shall be more prone to sin. 23 Humiliation followeth the proud, and glory shall uphold the humble of spirit. 24 He that is partaker with a thief hateth his own soul; he heareth one putting him to his oath and discovereth not. 25 He that feareth man shall quickly fall; he that trusteth in the Lord shall be set on high.

26 Many seek the face of the prince, but the judgment of every one cometh forth from the Lord.

27 The just abhor a wicked man, and the wicked loathe them that are in the right way. The son that keepeth the word shall be free from destruction.

Caput 30

Verba Congregantis, filii Vomentis.

Visio quam locutus est vir cum quo est Deus et qui Deo secum morante confortatus ait, 2 "Stultissimus sum virorum, et sapientia hominum non est mecum. 3 Non didici sapientiam et non novi sanctorum scientiam. 4 Quis ascendit in caelum atque descendit? Quis continuit spiritum in manibus suis? Quis conligavit aquas quasi in vestimento? Quis suscitavit omnes terminos terrae? Quod nomen eius, et quod nomen filii eius, si nosti?"

5 Omnis sermo Dei ignitus; clypeus est sperantibus in se. 6 Ne addas quicquam verbis illius et arguaris inveniarisque mendax. 7 Duo rogavi te; ne deneges mihi antequam moriar. 8 Vanitatem et verba mendacia longe fac a me. Mendicitatem et divitias ne dederis mihi; tribue tantum victui meo necessaria, 9 ne forte saturatus inliciar ad negandum et dicam, "Quis est Dominus?" aut egestate conpulsus furer et peierem nomen Dei mei. 10 Ne accuses servum ad dominum suum ne forte maledicat tibi et corruas.

11 Generatio quae patri suo maledicit et quae non benedicit matri suae, 12 generatio quae sibi munda videtur et tamen

Chapter 30

The wise man thinketh humbly of himself. His prayer and
sentiments upon certain virtues and vices.

T he words of Gatherer, the son of Vomiter.

The vision which the man spoke with whom God is and
who being strengthened by God abiding with him said, 2 "I
am the most foolish of men, and the wisdom of men is not
with me. 3 I have not learned wisdom and have not known
the science of saints. 4 Who hath ascended up into heaven
and descended? Who hath held the wind in his hands? Who
hath bound up the waters together as in a garment? Who
hath raised up all the borders of the earth? What is his name,
and what is the name of his son, if thou knowest?"

5 Every word of God is fire tried; he is a buckler to them
that hope in him. 6 Add not any thing to his words *lest* thou
be reproved and found a liar. 7 Two things I have asked of
thee; deny them not to me before I die. 8 Remove far from
me vanity and lying words. Give me neither beggary nor
riches; give me only the necessaries of life, 9 lest perhaps being filled I should be tempted to deny and say, "Who is the
Lord?" or being compelled by poverty I should steal and forswear the name of my God. 10 Accuse not a servant to his
master *lest* he curse thee and thou fall.

11 There is a generation that curseth their father and doth
not bless their mother, 12 a generation that are pure in their

non est lota a sordibus suis, 13 generatio cuius excelsi sunt oculi et palpebrae eius in alta subrectae, 14 generatio quae pro dentibus gladios habet et commandit molaribus suis ut comedat inopes de terra et pauperes ex hominibus.

15 Sanguisugae duae sunt filiae dicentes, "Adfer; adfer." Tria sunt insaturabilia, et quartum numquam dicit, "Sufficit." 16 Infernus et os vulvae et terra quae non satiatur aqua, ignis vero numquam dicit, "Sufficit."

17 Oculum qui subsannat patrem et qui despicit partum matris suae, effodiant eum corvi de torrentibus et comedant illum filii aquilae. 18 Tria sunt difficilia mihi, et quartum penitus ignoro. 19 Viam aquilae in caelo, viam colubri super petram, viam navis in medio mari et viam viri in adulescentia. 20 Talis est et via mulieris adulterae quae comedit et tergens os suum dicit, "Non sum operata malum."

21 Per tria movetur terra, et quartum non potest sustinere. 22 Per servum cum regnaverit, per stultum cum saturatus fuerit cibo, 23 per odiosam mulierem cum in matrimonio fuerit adsumpta et per ancillam cum heres fuerit dominae suae.

24 Quattuor sunt minima terrae, et ipsa sunt sapientiora sapientibus: 25 formicae, populus infirmus qui praeparat in messe cibum sibi; 26 lepusculus, plebs invalida quae conlocat in petra cubile suum; 27 regem lucusta non habet, et egreditur universa per turmas suas; 28 stilio manibus nititur et moratur in aedibus regis.

29 Tria sunt quae bene gradiuntur et quartum quod ince-

own eyes and yet are not washed from their filthiness, 13 a generation whose eyes are lofty and their eyelids lifted up on high, 14 a generation that for teeth hath swords and grindeth with their jaw teeth to devour the needy from off the earth and the poor from among men.

15 The horseleech hath two daughters that say, "Bring; bring." There are three things that never are satisfied, and the fourth never saith, "It is enough." 16 Hell and the mouth of the womb and the earth which is not satisfied with water, and the fire never saith, "It is enough."

17 The eye that mocketh at his father and that despiseth the labour of his mother in bearing him, let the ravens of the brooks pick it out and the young eagles eat it. 18 Three things are hard to me, and the fourth I am utterly ignorant of. 19 The way of an eagle in the air, the way of a serpent upon a rock, the way of a ship in the midst of the sea and the way of a man in youth. 20 Such also is the way of an adulterous woman who eateth and wipeth her mouth and saith, "I have done no evil."

21 By three things the earth is disturbed, and the fourth it cannot bear. 22 By a slave when he reigneth, by a fool when he is filled with meat, 23 by an odious woman when she is married and by a bondwoman when she is heir to her mistress.

24 There are four very little things of the earth, and they are wiser than the wise: 25 the ants, a feeble people which provide themselves food in the harvest; 26 the rabbit, a weak people which maketh its bed in the rock; 27 the locust hath no king, *yet* they all go out by their bands; 28 the stellio supporteth itself on hands and dwelleth in kings' houses.

29 There are three things which go well and the fourth

dit feliciter: 30 leo, fortissimus bestiarum, ad nullius pavebit occursum; 31 gallus succinctus lumbos; et aries; et rex qui resistat ei.

32 Est qui stultus apparuit postquam elatus est in sublime, si enim intellexisset, ori inposuisset manum. 33 Qui autem fortiter premit ubera ad eliciendum lac exprimit butyrum, et qui vehementer emungit elicit sanguinem, et qui provocat iras producit discordias.

Caput 31

Verba Lamuhel Regis. Visio qua erudivit eum mater sua.

2 Quid, dilecte mi, quid, dilecte uteri mei, quid, dilecte votorum meorum? 3 Ne dederis mulieribus substantiam tuam et divitias tuas ad delendos reges. 4 Noli regibus, O Lamuhel, noli regibus dare vinum quia nullum secretum est ubi regnat ebrietas 5 et ne forte bibant et obliviscantur iudiciorum et mutent causam filiorum pauperis. 6 Date siceram maerentibus et vinum his qui amaro sunt animo. 7 Bibant et obliviscantur egestatis suae et doloris sui non recordentur amplius.

that walketh happily: 30 a lion, the strongest of beasts, *who* hath no fear of any thing he meeteth; 31 a cock girded about the loins; and a ram; and a king whom none can resist.

32 There is that hath appeared a fool after he was lifted up on high, for if he had understood, he would have laid his hand upon his mouth. 33 And he that strongly squeezeth the paps to bring out milk straineth out butter, and he that violently bloweth his nose bringeth out blood, and he that provoketh wrath bringeth forth strife.

Chapter 31

An exhortation to chastity, temperance and works of mercy with the praise of a wise woman.

The words of King Lemuel. The vision wherewith his mother instructed him.

2 What, O my beloved, what, O the beloved of my womb, what, O the beloved of my vows? 3 Give not thy substance to women and thy riches to destroy kings. 4 Give not to kings, O Lemuel; give not wine to kings because there is no secret where drunkenness reigneth 5 and *lest* they drink and forget judgments and pervert the cause of the children of the poor. 6 Give strong drink to them that are sad and wine to them that are grieved in mind. 7 Let them drink and forget their want and remember their sorrow no more.

8 Aperi os tuum muto et causis omnium filiorum qui pertranseunt. 9 Aperi os tuum; decerne quod iustum est, et iudica inopem et pauperem.

10 Mulierem fortem quis inveniet? Procul et de ultimis finibus pretium eius. 11 Confidit in ea cor viri sui, et spoliis non indigebit. 12 Reddet ei bonum et non malum omnibus diebus vitae suae. 13 Quaesivit lanam et linum et operata est consilio manuum suarum. 14 Facta est quasi navis institoris; de longe portans panem suum, 15 et de nocte surrexit deditque praedam domesticis suis et cibaria ancillis suis. 16 Consideravit agrum et emit eum. De fructu manuum suarum plantavit vineam. 17 Accinxit fortitudine lumbos suos et roboravit brachium suum. 18 Gustavit et vidit quia bona est negotiatio eius. Non extinguetur in nocte lucerna illius. 19 Manum suam misit ad fortia, et digiti eius adprehenderunt fusum. 20 Manum suam aperuit inopi et palmas suas extendit ad pauperem. 21 Non timebit domui suae a frigoribus nivis, omnes enim domestici eius vestiti duplicibus. 22 Stragulam vestem fecit sibi, byssus, et purpura indumentum eius. 23 Nobilis in portis vir eius quando sederit cum senatoribus terrae. 24 Sindonem fecit et vendidit et cingulum tradidit Chananeo. 25 Fortitudo et decor indumentum eius, et ridebit in die novissimo. 26 Os suum aperuit sapientiae, et lex clementiae in lingua eius. 27 Consideravit semitas domus suae et panem otiosa non comedit. 28 Surrexerunt filii eius et beatissimam praedicaverunt, vir eius, et laudavit eam.

8 Open thy mouth for the dumb and for the causes of all the children that pass. 9 Open thy mouth; decree that which is just, and do justice to the needy and poor.

10 Who shall find a valiant woman? Far, and from the uttermost coasts is the price of her. 11 The heart of her husband trusteth in her, and he shall have no need of spoils. 12 She will render him good and not evil all the days of her life. 13 She hath sought wool and flax and hath wrought by the counsel of her hands. 14 She is like the merchant's ship; she bringeth her bread from afar, 15 and she hath risen in the night and given a prey to her household and victuals to her maidens. 16 She hath considered a field and bought it. With the fruit of her hands she hath planted a vineyard. 17 She hath girded her loins with strength and hath strengthened her arm. 18 She hath tasted and seen that her traffic is good. Her lamp shall not be put out in the night. 19 She hath put out her hand to strong things, and her fingers have taken hold of the spindle. 20 She hath opened her hand to the needy and stretched out her hands to the poor. 21 She shall not fear for her house in the cold of snow, for all her domestics are clothed with double garments. 22 She hath made for herself clothing of tapestry, fine linen, and purple is her covering. 23 Her husband is honourable in the gates when he sitteth among the senators of the land. 24 She made fine linen and sold it and delivered a girdle to the Canaanite. 25 Strength and beauty are her clothing, and she shall laugh in the latter day. 26 She hath opened her mouth to wisdom, and the law of clemency is on her tongue. 27 She hath looked well on the paths of her house and hath not eaten her bread idle. 28 Her children rose up and called her blessed, her husband, and he praised her.

29 Multae filiae congregaverunt divitias; tu supergressa es universas. 30 Fallax gratia, et vana est pulchritudo; mulier timens Dominum, ipsa laudabitur. 31 Date ei de fructu manuum suarum, et laudent eam in portis opera eius.

29 Many daughters have gathered together riches; thou hast surpassed them all. 30 Favour is deceitful, and beauty is vain; the woman that feareth the Lord, she shall be praised. 31 Give her of the fruit of her hands, and let her works praise her in the gates.

ECCLESIASTES

Caput 1

Verba Ecclesiastes, filii David, regis Hierusalem.

2 "Vanitas vanitatum," dixit Ecclesiastes, "Vanitas vanitatum, et omnia vanitas!"

3 Quid habet amplius homo de universo labore suo quo laborat sub sole? 4 Generatio praeterit, et generatio advenit, terra vero in aeternum stat. 5 Oritur sol et occidit et ad locum suum revertitur, ibique renascens, 6 gyrat per meridiem et flectitur ad aquilonem. Lustrans universa in circuitu pergit, spiritus, et in circulos suos regreditur. 7 Omnia flumina intrant in mare, et mare non redundat. Ad locum unde exeunt flumina revertuntur ut iterum fluant.

8 Cunctae res difficiles; non potest eas homo explicare sermone. Non saturatur oculus visu, nec auris impletur auditu.

Chapter 1

The vanity of all temporal things.

The words of Ecclesiastes, the son of David, king of Jerusalem.

2 "Vanity of vanities," said Ecclesiastes, "Vanity of vanities, and all is vanity!"

3 What hath a man more of all his labour *that* he *taketh* under the sun? 4 *One* generation passeth away, and *another* generation cometh, but the earth standeth for ever. 5 The sun riseth and goeth down and returneth to his place, and there rising again, 6 maketh his round by the south and turneth again to the north. The spirit goeth forward, surveying all places round about, and returneth to his circuits. 7 All the rivers run into the sea, *yet* the sea doth not overflow. Unto the place from whence the rivers come they return to flow again.

8 All things are hard; man cannot explain them by word. The eye is not filled with seeing, neither is the ear filled with hearing.

9 Quid est quod fuit? Ipsum quod futurum est. Quid est quod factum est? Ipsum quod fiendum est. 10 Nihil sub sole novum, nec valet quisquam dicere, "Ecce: hoc recens est," iam enim praecessit in saeculis quae fuerunt ante nos. 11 Non est priorum memoria, sed nec eorum quidem quae postea futura sunt erit recordatio apud eos qui futuri sunt in novissimo.

12 Ego, Ecclesiastes, fui rex Israhel in Hierusalem, 13 et proposui in animo meo quaerere et investigare sapienter de omnibus quae fiunt sub sole. Hanc occupationem pessimam dedit Deus filiis hominum ut occuparentur in ea. 14 Vidi quae fiunt cuncta sub sole, et ecce: universa vanitas et adflictio spiritus. 15 Perversi difficile corriguntur, et stultorum infinitus est numerus.

16 Locutus sum in corde meo, dicens, "Ecce: magnus effectus sum et praecessi sapientia omnes qui fuerunt ante me in Hierusalem, et mens mea contemplata est multa sapienter, et didici." 17 Dedique cor meum ut scirem prudentiam atque doctrinam erroresque et stultitiam, et agnovi quod in his quoque esset labor et adflictio spiritus 18 eo quod in multa sapientia multa sit indignatio, et qui addit scientiam addit et laborem.

9 What is it that hath been? The same thing that shall be. What is it that hath been done? The same that shall be done. 10 Nothing under the sun is new, neither is any man able to say, "Behold: this is new," for it hath already gone before in the ages that were before us. 11 There is no remembrance of former things, nor indeed of those things which hereafter are to come shall there be any remembrance with them that shall be in the latter end.

12 I, Ecclesiastes, was king over Israel in Jerusalem, 13 and I proposed in my mind to seek and search out wisely concerning all things that are done under the sun. This painful occupation hath God given to the children of men to be exercised therein. 14 I have seen all things that are done under the sun, and behold: all is vanity and vexation of spirit. 15 The perverse are *hard to be* corrected, and the number of fools is infinite.

16 I have spoken in my heart, saying, "Behold: I am become great and have gone beyond all in wisdom that were before me in Jerusalem, and my mind hath contemplated many things wisely, and I have learned." 17 And I have given my heart to know prudence and learning and errors and folly, and I have perceived that in these also there was labour and vexation of spirit 18 because in much wisdom there is much indignation, and he that addeth knowledge addeth also labour.

Caput 2

Dixi ego in corde meo, "Vadam et affluam deliciis et fruar bonis." Et vidi quod hoc quoque esset vanitas. 2 Risum reputavi errorem, et gaudio dixi, "Quid frustra deciperis?" 3 Cogitavi in corde meo abstrahere a vino carnem meam ut animum meum transferrem ad sapientiam devitaremque stultitiam donec viderem quid esset utile filiis hominum quod facto opus est sub sole numero dierum vitae suae. 4 Magnificavi opera mea. Aedificavi mihi domos et plantavi vineas. 5 Feci hortos et pomaria et consevi ea cuncti generis arboribus, 6 et extruxi mihi piscinas aquarum ut irrigarem silvam lignorum germinantium. 7 Possedi servos et ancillas multamque familiam habui armenta quoque et magnos ovium greges ultra omnes qui fuerunt ante me in Hierusalem. 8 Coacervavi mihi argentum et aurum et substantias regum ac provinciarum. Feci mihi cantores et cantrices et delicias filiorum hominum, scyphos et urceos in ministerio ad vina fundenda, 9 et supergressus sum opibus omnes qui fuerunt ante me in Hierusalem. Sapientia quoque perseveravit mecum. 10 Et omnia quae desideraverunt oculi mei, non negavi eis, nec prohibui cor meum quin omni voluptate frueretur et oblectaret se in his quae paraveram et hanc ra-

Chapter 2

The vanity of pleasures, riches and worldly labours.

I said in my heart, "I will go and abound with delights and enjoy good things." And I saw that this also was vanity. 2 Laughter I counted error, and to mirth I said, "Why art thou vainly deceived?" 3 I thought in my heart to withdraw my flesh from wine that I might turn my mind to wisdom and might avoid folly till I might see what was profitable for the children of men and what they ought to do under the sun all the days of their life. 4 I *made me great* works. I built me houses and planted vineyards. 5 I made gardens and orchards and set them with trees of all kinds, 6 and I made me ponds of water to water *therewith* the wood of the young trees. 7 I got me menservants and maidservants and had a great family and herds of oxen and great flocks of sheep above all that were before me in Jerusalem. 8 I heaped together for myself silver and gold and the wealth of kings and provinces. I made me singing men and singing women and the delights of the sons of men, cups and vessels to serve to pour out wine, 9 and I surpassed in riches all that were before me in Jerusalem. *My* wisdom also remained with me. 10 And whatsoever my eyes desired, I refused them not, and I withheld not my heart from enjoying every pleasure and delighting itself in the things which I had prepared and esteemed this my portion, to make use of my own la-

tus sum partem meam, si uterer labore meo. 11 Cumque me convertissem ad universa opera quae fecerant manus meae et ad labores in quibus frustra sudaveram, vidi in omnibus vanitatem et adflictionem animi et nihil permanere sub sole.

12 Transivi ad contemplandam sapientiam erroresque et stultitiam. "Quid est," inquam, "homo ut sequi possit regem, factorem suum?" 13 Et vidi quia tantum praecederet sapientia stultitiam quantum differt lux tenebris. 14 Sapientis oculi in capite eius; stultus in tenebris ambulat, et didici quod unus utriusque esset interitus. 15 Et dixi in corde meo, "Si unus stulti et meus occasus erit, quid mihi prodest quod maiorem sapientiae dedi operam?" Locutusque cum mente mea animadverti quod hoc quoque esset vanitas, 16 non enim erit memoria sapientis similiter ut stulti in perpetuum, et futura tempora oblivione cuncta pariter obruent. Moritur doctus similiter et indoctus.

17 Et idcirco taeduit me vitae meae videntem mala esse universa sub sole et cuncta vanitatem atque adflictionem spiritus. 18 Rursum detestatus sum omnem industriam meam qua sub sole studiosissime laboravi, habiturus heredem post me 19 quem ignoro utrum sapiens an stultus futurus sit, et dominabitur in laboribus meis quibus desudavi et sollicitus fui, et est quicquam tam vanum? 20 Unde cessavi renuntiavitque cor meum ultra laborare sub sole, 21 nam cum alius laboret in sapientia et doctrina et sollicitudine, homini otioso quaesita dimittit, et hoc ergo vanitas et magnum malum, 22 quid enim proderit homini de universo labore suo et adflictione spiritus qua sub sole cruciatus est? 23 Cuncti dies eius doloribus et aerumnis pleni sunt; nec per

bour. 11 And when I turned myself to all the works which my hands had wrought and to the labours wherein I had laboured in vain, I saw in all things vanity and vexation of mind and that nothing was lasting under the sun.

12 I passed further to behold wisdom and errors and folly. "What is man," said I, "that he can follow the king, his maker?" 13 And I saw that wisdom excelled folly as much as light differeth from darkness. 14 The eyes of a wise man are in his head; the fool walketh in darkness, and I learned that *they were to die both alike.* 15 And I said in my heart, "If the death of the fool and mine shall be one, what doth it avail me that I have *applied myself more to the study of* wisdom?" And speaking with my own mind I perceived that this also was vanity, 16 for there shall be no remembrance of the wise no more than of the fool for ever, and the times to come shall cover all things together with oblivion. The learned dieth in like manner as the unlearned.

17 And therefore I was weary of my life when I saw that all things under the sun are evil and all vanity and vexation of spirit. 18 Again I hated all my application wherewith I had earnestly laboured under the sun, being like to have an heir after me 19 whom I know not whether he will be a wise man or a fool, and he shall have rule over all my labours with which I have laboured and been solicitous, and is there any thing so vain? 20 Wherefore I left off and my heart renounced labouring any more under the sun, 21 for when a man laboureth in wisdom and knowledge and carefulness, he leaveth what he hath gotten to an idle man, so this also is vanity and a great evil, 22 for what profit shall a man have of all his labour and vexation of spirit with which he hath been tormented under the sun? 23 All his days are full of sorrows

noctem mente requiescit, et hoc nonne vanitas est? 24 Nonne melius est comedere et bibere et ostendere animae suae bona de laboribus suis? Et hoc de manu Dei est.

25 Quis ita vorabit et deliciis affluet ut ego? 26 Homini bono in conspectu suo dedit Deus sapientiam et scientiam et laetitiam, peccatori autem dedit adflictionem et curam superfluam ut addat et congreget et tradat ei qui placuit Deo, sed et hoc vanitas et cassa sollicitudo mentis.

Caput 3

Omnia tempus habent, et suis spatiis transeunt universa sub caelo: 2 tempus nascendi et tempus moriendi; tempus plantandi et tempus evellendi quod plantatum est; 3 tempus occidendi et tempus sanandi; tempus destruendi et tempus aedificandi; 4 tempus flendi et tempus ridendi; tempus plangendi et tempus saltandi; 5 tempus spargendi lapides et tempus colligendi; tempus amplexandi et tempus longe fieri a conplexibus; 6 tempus adquirendi et tempus perdendi; tem-

and miseries; even in the night he doth not rest in mind, and is not this vanity? 24 Is it not better to eat and drink and to shew his soul good things of his labours? And this is from the hand of God.

25 Who shall so feast and abound with delights as I? 26 God hath given to a man that is good in his sight wisdom and knowledge and joy, but to the sinner he hath given vexation and superfluous care to heap up and to gather together and to give it to him that hath pleased God, but this also is vanity and a fruitless solicitude of the mind.

Chapter 3

All human things are liable to perpetual changes. We are to rest on God's providence and cast away fruitless cares.

All things have their season, and in their times all things pass under heaven: 2 a time to be born and a time to die; a time to plant and a time to pluck up that which is planted; 3 a time to kill and a time to heal; a time to destroy and a time to build; 4 a time to weep and a time to laugh; a time to mourn and a time to dance; 5 a time to scatter stones and a time to gather; a time to embrace and a time to be far from embraces; 6 a time to get and a time to lose; a time to keep

pus custodiendi et tempus abiciendi; 7 tempus scindendi et tempus consuendi; tempus tacendi et tempus loquendi; 8 tempus dilectionis et tempus odii; tempus belli et tempus pacis.

9 Quid habet amplius homo de labore suo? 10 Vidi adflictionem quam dedit Deus filiis hominum ut distendantur in ea. 11 Cuncta fecit bona in tempore suo et mundum tradidit disputationi eorum ut non inveniat homo opus quod operatus est Deus ab initio usque ad finem. 12 Et cognovi quod non esset melius nisi laetari et facere bene in vita sua, 13 omnis enim homo qui comedit et bibit et videt bonum de labore suo, hoc donum Dei est.

14 Didici quod omnia opera quae fecit Deus perseverent in perpetuum; non possumus eis quicquam addere nec auferre quae fecit Deus ut timeatur. 15 Quod factum est, ipsum permanet; quae futura sunt iam fuerunt, et Deus instaurat quod abiit.

16 Vidi sub sole in loco iudicii impietatem, et in loco iustitiae iniquitatem. 17 Et dixi in corde meo, "Iustum et impium iudicabit Deus, et tempus omnis rei tunc erit." 18 Dixi in corde meo de filiis hominum ut probaret eos Deus et ostenderet similes esse bestiis. 19 Idcirco unus interitus est hominis et iumentorum, et aequa utriusque condicio: sicut moritur homo, sic et illa moriuntur. Similiter spirant omnia, et nihil habet homo iumento amplius. Cuncta subiacent vanitati, 20 et omnia pergunt ad unum locum. De terra facta sunt, et in terram pariter revertuntur. 21 Quis novit si spiritus

and a time to cast away; 7 a time to rend and a time to sew; a time to keep silence and a time to speak; 8 a time of love and a time of hatred; a time of war and a time of peace.

9 What hath man more of his labour? 10 I have seen the trouble which God hath given the sons of men to be exercised in it. 11 He hath made all things good in their time and hath delivered the world to their consideration so that man cannot find out the work which God hath made from the beginning to the end. 12 And I have known that there was no better thing than to rejoice and to do well in his life, 13 for every man that eateth and drinketh and seeth good of his labour, this is the gift of God.

14 I have learned that all the works which God hath made continue for ever; we cannot add any thing nor take away from those things which God hath made that he may be feared. 15 That which hath been made, the same continueth; the things that shall be have already been, and God restoreth that which is past.

16 I saw under the sun in the place of judgment wickedness, and in the place of justice iniquity. 17 And I said in my heart, "God shall judge both the just and the wicked, and then shall be the time of every thing." 18 I said in my heart concerning the sons of men that God would prove them and shew them to be like beasts. 19 Therefore the death of man and of beasts is one, and the condition of them both is equal: as man dieth, so they also die. All things breathe alike, and man hath nothing more than beast. All things are subject to vanity, 20 and all things go to one place. Of earth they were made, and into earth they return together. 21 Who knoweth

filiorum Adam ascendat sursum et si spiritus iumentorum descendat deorsum?

22 Et deprehendi nihil esse melius quam laetari hominem in opere suo, et hanc esse partem illius, quis enim eum adducet ut post se futura cognoscat?

Caput 4

Verti me ad alia, et vidi calumnias quae sub sole geruntur et lacrimas innocentum. Et consolatorem neminem, nec posse resistere eorum violentiae, cunctorum auxilio destitutos. 2 Et laudavi magis mortuos quam viventes, 3 et feliciorem utroque iudicavi qui necdum natus est nec vidit mala quae sub sole fiunt.

4 Rursum contemplatus omnes labores hominum, et industrias animadverti patere invidiae proximi, et in hoc ergo vanitas et cura superflua est. 5 Stultus conplicat manus suas et comedit carnes suas, dicens, 6 "Melior est pugillus cum requie quam plena utraque manus cum labore et adflictione animi."

if the spirit of the children of Adam ascend upward and if the spirit of the beasts descend downward?

22 And I have found that nothing is better than for a man to rejoice in his work, and that this is his portion, for who shall bring him to know the things that shall be after him?

Chapter 4

Other instances of human miseries.

I turned myself to other things, and I saw the oppressions that are done under the sun and the tears of the innocent. And they had no comforter, and they were not able to resist their violence, being destitute of help from any. 2 And I praised the dead rather than the living, 3 and I judged him happier than them both that is not yet born nor hath seen the evils that are done under the sun.

4 Again I considered all the labours of men, and I remarked that their industries are exposed to the envy of their neighbour, so in this also there is vanity and fruitless care. 5 The fool foldeth his hands together and eateth his own flesh, saying, 6 "Better is a handful with rest than both hands full with labour and vexation of mind."

7 Considerans repperi et aliam vanitatem sub sole: 8 unus est, et secundum non habet, non filium, non fratrem, et tamen laborare non cessat, nec satiantur oculi eius divitiis, nec recogitat, dicens, "Cui laboro et fraudo animam meam bonis?" In hoc quoque vanitas est et adflictio pessima. 9 Melius ergo est duos simul esse quam unum, habent enim emolumentum societatis suae. 10 Si unus ceciderit, ab altero fulcietur. Vae soli, quia cum ruerit, non habet sublevantem se. 11 Et si dormierint duo, fovebuntur mutuo. Unus quomodo calefiet? 12 Et si quispiam praevaluerit contra unum, duo resistunt ei. Funiculus triplex difficile rumpitur.

13 Melior est puer pauper et sapiens rege sene et stulto, qui nescit praevidere in posterum, 14 quod de carcere catenisque interdum quis egrediatur ad regnum, et alius natus in regno inopia consumatur.

15 Vidi cunctos viventes qui ambulant sub sole cum adulescente secundo qui consurget pro eo. 16 Infinitus numerus est populi omnium qui fuerunt ante eum, et qui postea futuri sunt non laetabuntur in eo, sed et hoc vanitas et adflictio spiritus.

17 Custodi pedem tuum ingrediens domum Dei, et adpropinqua ut audias, multo enim melior est oboedientia quam stultorum victimae qui nesciunt quid faciant mali.

7 Considering I found also another vanity under the sun: 8 there is *but* one, and he hath not a second, no child, no brother, and yet he ceaseth not to labour, neither are his eyes satisfied with riches, neither doth he reflect, saying, "For whom do I labour and defraud my soul of good things?" In this also is vanity and a grievous vexation. 9 It is better therefore that two should be together than one, for they have the advantage of their society. 10 If one fall, he shall be supported by the other. Woe to him that is alone, for when he falleth, he hath none to lift him up. 11 And if two lie together, they shall warm one another. How shall one alone be warmed? 12 And if a man prevail against one, two *shall* withstand him. A threefold cord is not easily broken.

13 Better is a child that is poor and wise than a king that is old and foolish, who knoweth not to foresee for hereafter, 14 because out of prison and chains sometimes a man cometh forth to a kingdom, and another born king is consumed with poverty.

15 I saw all men living that walk under the sun with the second young man who shall rise up in his place. 16 The number of the people of all that were before him is infinite, and they that shall come afterwards shall not rejoice in him, but this also is vanity and vexation of spirit.

17 Keep thy foot when thou goest into the house of God, and draw nigh to hear, for much better is obedience than the victims of fools who know not what evil they do.

Caput 5

Ne temere quid loquaris, neque cor tuum sit velox ad proferendum sermonem coram Deo, Deus enim in caelo et tu super terram; idcirco sint pauci sermones tui. 2 Multas curas sequuntur somnia, et in multis sermonibus invenietur stultitia. 3 Si quid vovisti Deo, ne moreris reddere, displicet enim ei infidelis et stulta promissio, sed quodcumque voveris redde. 4 Multoque melius est non vovere quam post votum promissa non conplere. 5 Ne dederis os tuum ut peccare faciat carnem tuam, neque dicas coram angelo, "Non est providentia," ne forte iratus Deus contra sermones tuos dissipet cuncta opera manuum tuarum.

6 Ubi multa sunt somnia, plurimae vanitates et sermones innumeri, tu vero Deum time. 7 Si videris calumnias egenorum et violenta iudicia et subverti iustitiam in provincia, non mireris super hoc negotio, quia excelso alius excelsior est, et super hos quoque eminentiores sunt alii; 8 et insuper universae terrae rex imperat servienti. 9 Avarus non implebitur pecunia, et qui amat divitias fructum non capiet ex eis, et hoc ergo vanitas.

Chapter 5

Caution in words. Vows are to be paid. Riches are often pernicious; the moderate use of them is the gift of God.

Speak not any thing rashly, and let not thy heart be hasty to utter a word before God, for God is in heaven and thou upon earth; therefore let thy words be few. 2 Dreams follow many cares, and in many words shall be found folly. 3 If thou hast vowed any thing to God, defer not to pay it, for an unfaithful and foolish promise displeaseth him, but whatsoever thou hast vowed, pay it. 4 And it is much better not to vow than after a vow not to perform the things promised. 5 Give not thy mouth to cause thy flesh to sin, and say not before the angel, "There is no providence," *lest* God be angry at thy words and destroy all the works of thy hands.

6 Where there are many dreams, there are many vanities and words without number, but do thou fear God. 7 If thou shalt see the oppressions of the poor and violent judgments and justice perverted in the province, wonder not at this matter, for he that is high hath another higher, and there are others still higher than these; 8 *moreover there is the king that* reigneth over all the land subject to him. 9 A covetous man shall not be satisfied with money, and he that loveth riches shall reap no fruit from them, so this also is vanity.

10 Ubi multae sunt opes, multi et qui comedant eas. Et quid prodest possessori nisi quod cernit divitias oculis suis? 11 Dulcis est somnus operanti sive parum sive multum comedat, saturitas autem divitis non sinit dormire eum. 12 Est et alia infirmitas pessima quam vidi sub sole: divitiae conservatae in malum domini sui, 13 pereunt enim in adflictione pessima. Generavit filium qui in summa egestate erit. 14 Sicut egressus est nudus de utero matris suae, sic revertetur et nihil auferet secum de labore suo. 15 Miserabilis prorsus infirmitas: quomodo venit, sic revertetur. Quid ergo prodest ei quod laboravit in ventum? 16 Cunctis diebus vitae suae comedit in tenebris et in curis multis et in aerumna atque tristitia. 17 Hoc itaque mihi visum est bonum: ut comedat quis et bibat et fruatur laetitia ex labore suo quo laboravit ipse sub sole numerum dierum vitae suae, quos dedit ei Deus, et haec est pars illius. 18 Et omni homini cui dedit Deus divitias atque substantiam potestatemque ei tribuit ut comedat ex eis et fruatur parte sua et laetetur de labore suo, hoc est donum Dei, 19 non enim satis recordabitur dierum vitae suae, eo quod Deus occupet deliciis cor eius.

10 Where there are great riches, there are also many to eat them. And what doth it profit the owner but that he seeth the riches with his eyes? 11 Sleep is sweet to a labouring man whether he eat little or much, but the fulness of the rich will not suffer him to sleep. 12 There is also another grievous evil which I have seen under the sun: riches kept to the hurt of the owner, 13 for they are lost with very great affliction. He hath begotten a son who shall be in extremity of want. 14 As he came forth naked from his mother's womb, so shall he return and shall take nothing away with him of his labour. 15 A most deplorable evil: as he came, so shall he return. What then doth it profit him that he hath laboured for the wind? 16 All the days of his life he eateth in darkness and in many cares and in misery and sorrow. 17 This therefore hath seemed good to me: that a man should eat and drink and enjoy the fruit of his labour wherewith he hath laboured under the sun *all* the days of his life, which God hath given him, and this is his portion. 18 And every man to whom God hath given riches and substance and hath given him power to eat thereof and to enjoy his portion and to rejoice of his labour, this is the gift of God, 19 for he shall not much remember the days of his life, because God entertaineth his heart with delight.

Caput 6

Est et aliud malum quod vidi sub sole, et quidem frequens apud homines: 2 vir cui dedit Deus divitias et substantiam et honorem, et nihil deest animae eius ex omnibus quae desiderat, nec tribuit ei potestatem Deus ut comedat ex eo, sed homo extraneus vorabit illud. Hoc vanitas et magna miseria est.

3 Si genuerit quispiam centum liberos et vixerit multos annos et plures dies aetatis habuerit et anima illius non utatur bonis substantiae suae sepulturaque careat, de hoc ego pronuntio quod melior illo sit abortivus, 4 frustra enim venit et pergit ad tenebras, et oblivione delebitur nomen eius. 5 Non vidit solem neque cognovit distantiam boni et mali. 6 Etiam si duobus milibus annis vixerit et non fuerit perfruitus bonis, nonne ad unum locum properant omnia? 7 Omnis labor hominis in ore eius, sed anima illius non implebitur.

8 Quid habet amplius sapiens ab stulto? Et quid pauper nisi ut pergat illuc ubi est vita? 9 Melius est videre quod cupias quam desiderare quod nescias. Sed et hoc vanitas est et praesumptio spiritus. 10 Qui futurus est, iam vocatum est nomen eius, et scitur quod homo sit et non possit contra fortiorem se in iudicio contendere. 11 Verba sunt plurima multam in disputando habentia vanitatem.

Chapter 6

The misery of the covetous man.

There is also another evil which I have seen under the sun, and that frequent among men: 2 a man to whom God hath given riches and substance and honour, and his soul wanteth nothing of all that he desireth, yet God doth not give him power to eat thereof, but a stranger shall eat it up. This is vanity and a great misery.

3 If a man beget a hundred children and live many years and *attain to a great* age and his soul make no use of the goods of his substance and he be without burial, of this man I pronounce that the untimely born is better than he, 4 for he came in vain and goeth to darkness, and his name shall be wholly forgotten. 5 He hath not seen the sun nor known the distance of good and evil. 6 Although he lived two thousand years and hath not enjoyed good things, do not all make haste to one place? 7 All the labour of man is for his mouth, but his soul shall not be filled.

8 What hath the wise man more than the fool? And what the poor man but to go thither where there is life? 9 Better it is to see what thou mayst desire than to desire that which thou canst not know. But this also is vanity and presumption of spirit. 10 He that shall be, his name is already called, and it is known that he is man and cannot contend in judgment with him that is stronger than himself. 11 There are many words that have much vanity in disputing.

Caput 7

Quid necesse est homini maiora se quaerere, cum ignoret quid conducat sibi in vita sua numero dierum peregrinationis suae et tempore quo velut umbra praeterit? Aut quis ei poterit indicare quid post eum futurum sub sole sit? 2 Melius est nomen bonum quam unguenta pretiosa, et dies mortis die nativitatis. 3 Melius est ire ad domum luctus quam ad domum convivii, in illa enim finis cunctorum admonetur hominum et vivens cogitat quid futurum sit. 4 Melior est ira risu, quia per tristitiam vultus corrigitur animus delinquentis. 5 Cor sapientium ubi tristitia est, et cor stultorum ubi laetitia. 6 Melius est a sapiente corripi quam stultorum adulatione decipi, 7 quia sicut sonitus spinarum ardentium sub olla, sic risus stulti; sed et hoc vanitas.

8 Calumnia conturbat sapientem et perdet robur cordis illius. 9 Melior est finis orationis quam principium. Melior est patiens arrogante. 10 Ne velox sis ad irascendum, quia ira in sinu stulti requiescit. 11 Ne dicas, "Quid putas causae est quod priora tempora meliora fuere quam nunc sunt?" stulta est enim huiuscemodi interrogatio.

Chapter 7

Prescriptions against worldly vanities, mortification, patience and seeking wisdom.

What needeth a man to seek things that are above him, whereas he knoweth not what is profitable for him in his life in *all* the days of his pilgrimage and the time that passeth like a shadow? Or who can tell him what shall be after him under the sun? 2 A good name is better than precious ointments, and the day of death than the day of one's birth. 3 It is better to go to the house of mourning than to the house of feasting, for in that we are put in mind of the end of *all* and the living thinketh what is to come. 4 Anger is better than laughter, because by the sadness of the countenance the mind of the offender is corrected. 5 The heart of the wise is where there is mourning, and the heart of fools where there is mirth. 6 It is better to be rebuked by a wise man than to be deceived by the flattery of fools, 7 for as the crackling of thorns burning under a pot, so is the laughter of a fool; now this also is vanity.

8 Oppression troubleth the wise and shall destroy the strength of his heart. 9 Better is the end of a speech than the beginning. Better is the patient man than the presumptuous. 10 Be not quickly angry, for anger resteth in the bosom of a fool. 11 Say not, "What thinkest thou is the cause that former times were better than they are now?" for this manner of question is foolish.

12 Utilior est sapientia cum divitiis et magis prodest videntibus solem, 13 sicut enim protegit sapientia, sic protegit pecunia, hoc autem plus habet eruditio et sapientia: quod vitam tribuunt possessori suo. 14 Considera opera Dei, quod nemo possit corrigere quem ille despexerit. 15 In die bona fruere bonis, et malam diem praecave, sicut enim hanc sic et illam fecit Deus, ut non inveniat homo contra eum iustas querimonias.

16 Haec quoque vidi in diebus vanitatis meae: iustus perit in iustitia sua, et impius multo vivit tempore in malitia sua. 17 Noli esse iustus multum, neque plus sapias quam necesse est, ne obstupescas. 18 Ne impie agas multum, et noli esse stultus, ne moriaris in tempore non tuo.

19 Bonum est te sustentare iustum, sed et ab illo ne subtrahas manum tuam, quia qui Deum timet nihil neglegit. 20 Sapientia confortavit sapientem super decem principes civitatis, 21 non est enim homo iustus in terra qui faciat bonum et non peccet. 22 Sed et cunctis sermonibus qui dicuntur ne accommodes cor tuum ne forte audias servum tuum maledicentem tibi, 23 scit enim tua conscientia quia et tu crebro maledixisti aliis.

24 Cuncta temptavi in sapientia. Dixi, "Sapiens efficiar," et ipsa longius recessit a me, 25 multo magis quam erat et alta profunditas; quis inveniet eam? 26 Lustravi universa animo meo ut scirem et considerarem et quaererem sapientiam et rationem et ut cognoscerem impietatem stulti et errorem inprudentium, 27 et inveni amariorem morte mulierem quae laqueus venatorum est, et sagena cor eius; vincula sunt ma-

12 Wisdom with riches is more profitable and bringeth more advantage to them that see the sun, 13 for as wisdom is a defence, so money is a defence, but learning and wisdom *excel in this:* that they give life to him that possesseth them. 14 Consider the works of God, that no man can correct whom he hath despised. 15 In the good day enjoy good things, and beware beforehand of the evil day, for God hath made both the one and the other, that man may not find against him *any just complaint.*

16 These things also I saw in the days of my vanity: a just man perisheth in his justice, and a wicked man liveth a long time in his wickedness. 17 Be not over just, and be not more wise than is necessary, lest thou become stupid. 18 Be not overmuch wicked, and be not foolish, lest thou die *before* thy time.

19 It is good that thou shouldst hold up the just, yea and from him withdraw not thy hand, for he that feareth God neglecteth nothing. 20 Wisdom hath strengthened the wise more than ten princes of the city, 21 for there is no just man upon earth that doth good and sinneth not. 22 But do not apply thy heart to all words that are spoken lest perhaps thou hear thy servant reviling thee, 23 for thy conscience knoweth that thou also hast often spoken evil of others.

24 I have tried all things in wisdom. I have said, "I will be wise," and it departed farther from me, 25 much more than it was. *It is* a great depth; who shall find it out? 26 I have surveyed all things with my mind to know and consider and seek out wisdom and reason and to know the wickedness of the fool and the error of the imprudent, 27 and I have found a woman more bitter than death who is the hunters' snare, and her heart is a net, *and* her hands are bands. He that

nus illius. Qui placet Deo effugiet eam, qui autem peccator est capietur ab illa.

28 "Ecce: hoc inveni," dixit Ecclesiastes, "unum et alterum ut invenirem rationem, 29 quam adhuc quaerit anima mea, et non inveni. Virum de mille unum repperi; mulierem ex omnibus non inveni. 30 Solummodo hoc inveni: quod fecerit Deus hominem rectum, et ipse se infinitis miscuerit quaestionibus."

Quis talis ut sapiens est? Et quis cognovit solutionem verbi?

Caput 8

Sapientia hominis lucet in vultu eius, et potentissimus faciem illius commutabit. 2 Ego os regis observo et praecepta iuramenti Dei. 3 Ne festines recedere a facie eius, neque permaneas in opere malo, quia omne quod voluerit faciet, 4 et sermo illius potestate plenus est, nec dicere ei quisquam potest, "Quare ita facis?" 5 Qui custodit praeceptum non experietur quicquam mali. Tempus et responsionem cor sapientis intellegit.

pleaseth God shall escape from her, but he that is a sinner shall be caught by her.

28 "Lo: this have I found," said Ecclesiastes, *"weighing* one thing *after* another that I might find out the account, 29 which yet my soul seeketh, and I have not found it. One man among a thousand I have found; a woman among them all I have not found. 30 Only this I have found: that God made man right, and he hath entangled himself with an infinity of questions."

Who is as the wise man? And who hath known the resolution of the word?

Chapter 8

True wisdom is to observe God's commandments. The ways of God are unsearchable.

The wisdom of a man shineth in his countenance, and the most mighty will change his face. 2 I observe the mouth of the king and the commandments of the oath of God. 3 Be not hasty to depart from his face, and do not continue in an evil work, for he will do all that pleaseth him, 4 and his word is full of power, neither can any man say to him, "Why dost thou so?" 5 He that keepeth the commandment shall find no evil. The heart of a wise man understandeth time and answer.

6 Omni negotio tempus est et oportunitas, et multa hominis adflictio 7 quia ignorat praeterita, et ventura nullo scire potest nuntio. 8 Non est in hominis dicione prohibere spiritum, nec habet potestatem in die mortis, nec sinitur quiescere ingruente bello, neque salvabit impietas impium. 9 Omnia haec consideravi et dedi cor meum in cunctis operibus quae fiunt sub sole. Interdum dominatur homo homini in malum suum.

10 Vidi impios sepultos, qui etiam cum adhuc viverent in loco sancto erant et laudabantur in civitate quasi iustorum operum, sed et hoc vanitas est, 11 etenim quia non profertur cito contra malos sententia, absque ullo timore filii hominum perpetrant mala. 12 Attamen ex eo quod peccator centies facit malum et per patientiam sustentatur, ego cognovi quod erit bonum timentibus Deum qui verentur faciem eius. 13 Non sit bonum impio, nec prolongentur dies eius, sed quasi umbra transeant qui non timent faciem Domini.

14 Est et alia vanitas quae fit super terram. Sunt iusti quibus mala proveniunt quasi opera egerint impiorum, et sunt impii qui ita securi sunt quasi iustorum facta habeant, sed et hoc vanissimum iudico. 15 Laudavi igitur laetitiam, quod non esset homini bonum sub sole nisi quod comederet et biberet atque gauderet, et hoc solum secum auferret de labore suo in diebus vitae suae quos dedit ei Deus sub sole.

16 Et adposui cor meum ut scirem sapientiam et intellegerem distentionem quae versatur in terra; est homo qui diebus ac noctibus somnum oculis non capit. 17 Et intellexi

6 There is a time and opportunity for every business, and great affliction for man 7 because he is ignorant of things past, and things to come he cannot know by any messenger. 8 It is not in man's power to stop the spirit, neither hath he power in the day of death, neither is he suffered to rest when war is at hand, neither shall wickedness save the wicked. 9 All these things I have considered and applied my heart to all the works that are done under the sun. Sometimes *one* man ruleth over *another* to his own hurt.

10 I saw the wicked buried, who also when they were yet living were in the holy place and were praised in the city as men of just works, but this also is vanity, 11 for because sentence is not speedily pronounced against the evil, the children of men commit evils without any fear. 12 But though a sinner do evil a hundred times and by patience be borne withal, I know *from thence* that it shall be well with them that fear God who dread his face. 13 *But* let it not be well with the wicked, neither let his days be prolonged, but as a shadow let them pass away that fear not the face of the Lord.

14 There is also another vanity which is done upon the earth. There are just men to whom evils happen as though they had done the works of the wicked, and there are wicked men who are as secure as though they had the deeds of the just, but this also I judge most vain. 15 Therefore I commended mirth, because there was no good for a man under the sun but to eat and drink and be merry, and that he should take nothing else with him of his labour in the days of his life which God hath given him under the sun.

16 And I applied my heart to know wisdom and to understand the distraction that is upon earth, *for there are some* that day and night take no sleep with their eyes. 17 And I un-

quod omnium operum Dei nullam possit homo invenire rationem eorum quae fiunt sub sole, et quanto plus laboraverit
ad quaerendum, tanto minus inveniat. Etiam si dixerit sapiens se nosse, non poterit repperire.

Caput 9

Omnia haec tractavi in corde meo ut curiose intellegerem. Sunt iusti atque sapientes, et opera eorum in manu
Dei, et tamen nescit homo utrum amore an odio dignus sit,
2 sed omnia in futuro servantur incerta, eo quod universa aeque eveniant iusto et impio, bono et malo, mundo et inmundo, immolanti victimas et sacrificia contemnenti. Sicut
bonus, sic et peccator, ut periurus, ita et ille qui verum deie-
rat. 3 Hoc est pessimum inter omnia quae sub sole fiunt,
quia eadem cunctis eveniunt, unde et corda filiorum hominum implentur malitia et contemptu in vita sua, et post haec
ad inferos deducentur. 4 Nemo est qui semper vivat et qui
huius rei habeat fiduciam; melior est canis vivens leone mor-

derstood that man can find no reason of all those works of God that are done under the sun, and the more he shall labour to seek, so much the less shall he find. Yea though the wise man shall say that he knoweth it, he shall not be able to find it.

Chapter 9

Man knows not certainly that he is in God's grace. After death no more work or merit.

All these things have I considered in my heart that I might carefully understand them. There are just men and wise men, and their works are in the hand of God, and yet man knoweth not whether he be worthy of love or hatred, 2 but all things are kept uncertain for the time to come, because all things equally happen to the just and to the wicked, to the good and to the evil, to the clean and to the unclean, to him that offereth victims and to him that despiseth sacrifices. As the good is, so also is the sinner, as the perjured, so he also that sweareth truth. 3 This is a very great evil among all things that are done under the sun, that the same things happen to all men, whereby also the hearts of the children of men are filled with evil and with contempt while they live, and afterwards they shall be brought down to hell. 4 There is no man that liveth always *or* that *hopeth* for this; a living dog

tuo, 5 viventes enim sciunt se esse morituros, mortui vero nihil noverunt amplius, nec habent ultra mercedem, quia oblivioni tradita est memoria eorum. 6 Amor quoque et odium et invidiae simul perierunt, nec habent partem in hoc saeculo et in opere quod sub sole geritur.

7 Vade ergo, et comede in laetitia panem tuum, et bibe cum gaudio vinum tuum, quia Deo placent opera tua. 8 Omni tempore sint vestimenta tua candida, et oleum de capite tuo non deficiat. 9 Perfruere vita cum uxore quam diligis cunctis diebus vitae instabilitatis tuae qui dati sunt tibi sub sole, omni tempore vanitatis tuae, haec est enim pars in vita, et in labore tuo quo laboras sub sole. 10 Quodcumque potest manus tua facere, instanter operare, quia nec opus nec ratio nec scientia nec sapientia erunt apud inferos, quo tu properas.

11 Verti me alio, vidique sub sole nec velocium esse cursum nec fortium bellum nec sapientium panem nec doctorum divitias nec artificum gratiam, sed tempus casumque in omnibus. 12 Nescit homo finem suum, sed sicut pisces capiuntur hamo et sicut aves conprehenduntur laqueo, sic capiuntur homines in tempore malo cum eis extemplo supervenerit.

13 Hanc quoque vidi sub sole sapientiam, et probavi maximam: 14 civitas parva et pauci in ea viri, venit contra eam rex magnus et vallavit eam extruxitque munitiones per gyrum, et perfecta est obsidio. 15 Inventusque est in ea vir pauper et sapiens, et liberavit urbem per sapientiam suam, et nullus

is better than a dead lion, 5 for the living know that they shall die, but the dead know nothing more, neither have they a reward any more, for the memory of them is forgotten. 6 Their love also and their hatred and their envy are all perished, neither have they *any* part in this world and in the work that is done under the sun.

7 Go then, and eat thy bread with joy, and drink thy wine with gladness, because thy works please God. 8 At all times let thy garments be white, and let not oil depart from thy head. 9 Live joyfully with the wife whom thou lovest all the days of thy unsteady life which are given to thee under the sun, all the time of thy vanity, for this is thy portion in life, and in thy labour wherewith thou labourest under the sun. 10 Whatsoever thy hand is able to do, do it earnestly, for neither work nor reason nor wisdom nor knowledge shall be in hell, whither thou art hastening.

11 I turned me to another thing, and I saw that under the sun the race is not to the swift nor the battle to the strong nor bread to the wise nor riches to the learned nor favour to the skillful, but time and chance in all. 12 Man knoweth not his own end, but as fishes are taken with the hook and as birds are caught with the snare, so men are taken in the evil time when it shall suddenly come upon them.

13 This wisdom also I have seen under the sun, and *it seemed to me* to be very great: 14 a little city and few men in it, there came against it a great king and invested it and built bulwarks round about it, and the siege was perfect. 15 Now there was found in it a man poor and wise, and he delivered the city by his wisdom, and no man afterward remembered

deinceps recordatus est hominis illius pauperis. 16 Et dicebam ego meliorem esse sapientiam fortitudine, quomodo ergo sapientia pauperis contempta est et verba eius non sunt audita? 17 Verba sapientium audiuntur in silentio, plus quam clamor principis inter stultos. 18 Melior est sapientia quam arma bellica, et qui in uno peccaverit multa bona perdet.

Caput 10

Muscae morientes perdunt suavitatem unguenti. Pretiosior est sapientia et gloria parva et ad tempus stultitia. 2 Cor sapientis in dextera eius, et cor stulti in sinistra illius. 3 Sed et in via stultus ambulans, cum ipse insipiens sit, omnes stultos aestimat. 4 Si spiritus potestatem habentis ascenderit super te, locum tuum ne dimiseris, quia curatio cessare faciet peccata maxima.

5 Est malum quod vidi sub sole, quasi per errorem egrediens a facie principis: 6 positum stultum in dignitate sublimi, et divites sedere deorsum. 7 Vidi servos in equis et

that poor man. 16 And I said that wisdom is better than strength, how then is the wisdom of the poor man slighted and his words not heard? 17 The words of the wise are heard in silence, more than the cry of a prince among fools. 18 Better is wisdom than weapons of war, and he that shall offend in one shall lose many good things.

Chapter 10

Observations on wisdom and folly, ambition and detraction.

Dying flies spoil the sweetness of the ointment. Wisdom and glory is more precious than a small and shortlived folly. 2 The heart of a wise man is in his right hand, and the heart of a fool is in his left hand. 3 Yea and the fool when he walketh in the way, whereas he himself is a fool, esteemeth all men fools. 4 If the spirit of him that hath power ascend upon thee, leave not thy place, because care will make the greatest sins to cease.

5 There is an evil that I have seen under the sun, as it were by an error proceeding from the face of the prince: 6 a fool set in high dignity, and the rich sitting beneath. 7 I have seen

principes ambulantes quasi servos super terram. 8 Qui fodit foveam incidet in eam, et qui dissipat sepem, mordebit eum coluber. 9 Qui transfert lapides adfligetur in eis, et qui scindit ligna vulnerabitur ab eis.

10 Si retunsum fuerit ferrum et hoc non ut prius sed hebetatum erit, multo labore exacuetur, et post industriam sequetur sapientia. 11 Si mordeat serpens in silentio, nihil eo minus habet qui occulte detrahit. 12 Verba oris sapientis gratia, et labia insipientis praecipitabunt eum. 13 Initium verborum eius stultitia, et novissimum oris illius error pessimus. 14 Stultus verba multiplicat. Ignorat homo quid ante se fuerit, et quod post se futurum est, quis illi poterit indicare? 15 Labor stultorum adfliget eos qui nesciunt in urbem pergere.

16 Vae tibi, terra, cuius rex est puer et cuius principes mane comedunt. 17 Beata terra cuius rex nobilis est et cuius principes vescuntur in tempore suo ad reficiendum et non ad luxuriam. 18 In pigritiis humiliabitur contignatio, et in infirmitate manuum perstillabit domus. 19 In risu faciunt panem ac vinum ut epulentur viventes, et pecuniae oboediunt omnia.

20 In cogitatione tua regi ne detrahas, et in secreto cubiculi tui ne maledixeris diviti, quia et aves caeli portabunt vocem tuam, et qui habet pinnas adnuntiabit sententiam.

servants upon horses and princes walking on the ground as servants. 8 He that diggeth a pit shall fall into it, and he that breaketh a hedge, a serpent shall bite him. 9 He that removeth stones shall be hurt by them, and he that cutteth trees shall be wounded by them.

10 If the iron be blunt and be not as before but be made blunt, with much labour it shall be sharpened, and after industry shall follow wisdom. 11 If a serpent bite in silence, *he is nothing better* that backbiteth secretly. 12 The words of the mouth of a wise man are grace, *but* the lips of a fool shall throw him down headlong. 13 The beginning of his words is folly, and the end of his talk is a *mischievous* error. 14 A fool multiplieth words. A man cannot tell what hath been before him, and what shall be after him, who can tell him? 15 The labour of fools shall afflict them that know not how to go to the city.

16 Woe to thee, O land, *when thy* king is a child and *when* the princes eat in the morning. 17 Blessed is the land whose king is noble and whose princes eat in due season for refreshment and not for riotousness. 18 By slothfulness a building shall be brought down, and through the weakness of hands the house shall drop through. 19 For laughter they make bread and wine that the living may feast, and all things obey money.

20 Detract not the king, *no, not* in thy thought, and speak not evil of the rich man in thy private chamber, because even the birds of the air will carry thy voice, and he that hath wings will tell *what thou hast said.*

Caput 11

Mitte panem tuum super transeuntes aquas, quia post multa tempora invenies illum. 2 Da partem septem necnon et octo, quia ignoras quid futurum sit mali super terram. 3 Si repletae fuerint nubes, imbrem super terram effundent. Si ceciderit lignum ad austrum aut ad aquilonem, in quocumque loco ceciderit, ibi erit. 4 Qui observat ventum non seminat, et qui considerat nubes numquam metet. 5 Quomodo ignoras quae sit via spiritus et qua ratione conpingantur ossa in ventre praegnatis, sic nescis opera Dei qui fabricator est omnium. 6 Mane semina sementem tuam, et vespere ne cesset manus tua, quia nescis quid magis oriatur, hoc an illud, et si utrumque simul, melius erit.

7 Dulce lumen, et delectabile est oculis videre solem. 8 Si annis multis vixerit homo et in omnibus his laetatus fuerit, meminisse debet tenebrosi temporis et dierum multorum qui cum venerint vanitatis arguentur praeterita. 9 Laetare, ergo, iuvenis, in adulescentia tua, et in bono sit cor tuum in diebus iuventutis tuae, et ambula in viis cordis tui et in intuitu oculorum tuorum, et scito quod pro omnibus his ad-

Chapter 11

Exhortation to works of mercy while we have time, to diligence in good and to the remembrance of death and judgment.

Cast thy bread upon the running waters, for after a long time thou shalt find it *again*. 2 Give a portion to seven and also to eight, for thou knowest not what evil shall be upon the earth. 3 If the clouds be full, they will pour out rain upon the earth. If the tree fall to the south or to the north, in what place soever it shall fall, there shall it be. 4 He that observeth the wind *shall* not sow, and he that considereth the clouds shall never reap. 5 As thou knowest not what is the way of the spirit nor how the bones are joined together in the womb of her that is with child, so thou knowest not the works of God who is the maker of all. 6 In the morning sow thy seed, and in the evening let not thy hand cease, for thou knowest not which may rather spring up, this or that, and if both together, it shall be the better.

7 The light is sweet, and it is delightful for the eyes to see the sun. 8 If a man live many years and have rejoiced in them all, he must remember the darksome time and the many days which when they shall come the things past shall be accused of vanity. 9 Rejoice therefore, O young man, in thy youth, and let thy heart be in that which is good in the days of thy youth, and walk in the ways of thy heart and in the

ducet te Deus in iudicium. 10 Aufer iram a corde tuo, et amove malitiam a carne tua, adulescentia enim et voluptas vana sunt.

Caput 12

Memento creatoris tui in diebus iuventutis tuae, antequam veniat tempus adflictionis et adpropinquent anni de quibus dicas, "Non mihi placent," 2 antequam tenebrescat sol et lumen et luna et stellae et revertantur nubes post pluviam, 3 quando commovebuntur custodes domus et nutabunt viri fortissimi et otiosae erunt molentes in minuto numero et tenebrescent videntes per foramina. 4 Et claudent ostia in platea in humilitate vocis molentis, et consurgent ad vocem volucris, et obsurdescent omnes filiae carminis. 5 Excelsa quoque timebunt, et formidabunt in via. Florebit amigdalum; inpinguabitur lucusta, et dissipabitur capparis, quoniam ibit homo in domum aeternitatis suae, et circumi-

sight of thy eyes, and know that for all these God will bring thee into judgment. 10 Remove anger from thy heart, and put away evil from thy flesh, for youth and pleasure are vain.

Chapter 12

The Creator is to be remembered in the days of our youth.
All worldly things are vain. We should fear God and keep his
commandments.

Remember thy creator in the days of thy youth, before the time of affliction come and the years draw nigh of which thou *shalt* say, "They please me not," 2 before the sun and the light and the moon and the stars be darkened and the clouds return after the rain, 3 when the keepers of the house shall tremble and the strong men shall stagger and the grinders shall be idle in a small number and they that look through the holes shall be darkened. 4 And they shall shut the doors in the street when the grinder's voice shall be low, and they shall rise up at the voice of the bird, and all the daughters of music shall grow deaf. 5 And they shall fear high things, and they shall be afraid in the way. The almond tree shall flourish; the locust shall be made fat, and the caper tree shall be destroyed, because man shall go into the house of his eternity, and the mourners shall go round about in the street

bunt in platea plangentes 6 antequam rumpatur funis argenteus et recurrat vitta aurea et conteratur hydria super fontem et confringatur rota super cisternam 7 et revertatur pulvis in terram suam unde erat et spiritus redeat ad Deum qui dedit illum.

8 "Vanitas vanitatum," dixit Ecclesiastes, "et omnia vanitas!" 9 Cumque esset sapientissimus Ecclesiastes, docuit populum et enarravit quae fecerat, et investigans conposuit parabolas multas. 10 Quaesivit verba utilia et conscripsit sermones rectissimos ac veritate plenos. 11 Verba sapientium sicut stimuli et quasi clavi in altum defixi quae per magistrorum consilium data sunt a pastore uno. 12 His amplius, fili mi, ne requiras. Faciendi plures libros nullus est finis, frequensque meditatio carnis adflictio est.

13 Finem loquendi omnes pariter audiamus. Deum time, et mandata eius observa, hoc est enim omnis homo, 14 et cuncta quae fiunt adducet Deus in iudicium pro omni errato, sive bonum sive malum sit.

6 before the silver cord be broken and the golden fillet shrink back and the pitcher be crushed at the fountain and the wheel be broken upon the cistern 7 and the dust return into its earth from whence it was and the spirit return to God who gave it.

8 "Vanity of vanities," said Ecclesiastes, "and all things are vanity!" 9 And whereas Ecclesiastes was very wise, he taught the people and declared the things that he had done, and seeking out he set forth many parables. 10 He sought profitable words and wrote words most right and full of truth. 11 The words of the wise are as goads and as nails deeply fastened in, which by the counsel of masters are given from one shepherd. 12 More than these, my son, require not. Of making many books there is no end, and much study is an affliction of the flesh.

13 Let us all hear together the conclusion of the discourse. Fear God, and keep his commandments, for this is all man, 14 and all things that are done God will bring into judgment for every error, whether it be good or evil.

CANTICLE OF CANTICLES

Caput 1

Osculetur me osculo oris sui! Quia meliora sunt ubera tua vino, 2 fragrantia unguentis optimis. Oleum effusum nomen tuum; ideo adulescentulae dilexerunt te. 3 Trahe me; post te curremus in odorem unguentorum tuorum. Introduxit me rex in cellaria sua. Exultabimus et laetabimur in te, memores uberum tuorum super vinum. Recti diligunt te.

4 Nigra sum sed formonsa, filiae Hierusalem, sicut tabernacula Cedar, sicut pelles Salomonis. 5 Nolite me considerare quod fusca sim, quia decoloravit me sol. Filii matris meae pugnaverunt contra me. Posuerunt me custodem in vineis; vineam meam non custodivi.

6 Indica mihi, quem diligit anima mea, ubi pascas, ubi cubes in meridie, ne vagari incipiam post greges sodalium tuorum.

7 Si ignoras te, O pulcherrima inter mulieres, egredere, et abi post vestigia gregum, et pasce hedos tuos iuxta tabernacula pastorum. 8 Equitatui meo in curribus Pharaonis adsimilavi te, amica mea. 9 Pulchrae sunt genae tuae sicut turtu-

Chapter 1

The spouse aspires to an union with Christ. Their mutual love for one another.

Let him kiss me with the kiss of his mouth! For thy breasts are better than wine, 2 smelling sweet of the best ointments. Thy name is as oil poured out; therefore young maidens have loved thee. 3 Draw me; we will run after thee to the odour of thy ointments. The king hath brought me into his storerooms. We will be glad and rejoice in thee, remembering thy breasts more than wine. The righteous love thee.

4 I am black but beautiful, O ye daughters of Jerusalem, as the tents of Kedar, as the curtains of Solomon. 5 Do not consider me that I am brown, because the sun hath altered my colour. The sons of my mother have fought against me. They have made me the keeper in the vineyards; my vineyard I have not kept.

6 Shew me, O thou whom my soul loveth, where thou feedest, where thou liest in the midday, lest I begin to wander after the flocks of thy companions.

7 If thou know not thyself, O fairest among women, go forth, and follow after the steps of the flocks, and feed thy kids beside the tents of the shepherds. 8 To my company of horsemen in Pharaoh's chariots have I likened thee, O my love. 9 Thy cheeks are beautiful as the turtledove's, thy

ris, collum tuum sicut monilia. 10 Murenulas aureas faciemus tibi, vermiculatas argento. 11 Dum esset rex in accubitu suo, nardus mea dedit odorem suum.

12 Fasciculus murrae dilectus meus mihi; inter ubera mea commorabitur. 13 Botrus cypri dilectus meus mihi, in vineis Engaddi. 14 Ecce: tu pulchra es, amica mea; ecce: tu pulchra; oculi tui columbarum.

15 Ecce: tu pulcher es, dilecte mi, et decorus. Lectulus noster floridus. 16 Tigna domorum nostrarum cedrina, laquearia nostra cypressina.

Caput 2

Ego flos campi et lilium convallium. 2 Sicut lilium inter spinas, sic amica mea inter filias. 3 Sicut malus inter ligna silvarum, sic dilectus meus inter filios. Sub umbra illius quem desideraveram sedi, et fructus eius dulcis gutturi meo. 4 Introduxit me in cellam vinariam; ordinavit in me caritatem. 5 Fulcite me floribus; stipate me malis, quia amore langueo. 6 Leva eius sub capite meo, et dextera illius amplexabitur me.

7 Adiuro vos, filiae Hierusalem, per capreas cervosque camporum, ne suscitetis neque evigilare faciatis dilectam quoadusque ipsa velit. 8 Vox dilecti mei, ecce: iste venit

neck as jewels. 10 We will make thee chains of gold, inlaid with silver. 11 While the king was at his repose, my spikenard sent forth the odour thereof.

12 A bundle of myrrh is my beloved to me; he shall abide between my breasts. 13 A cluster of cypress my love is to me, in the vineyards of En-gedi. 14 Behold: thou art fair, O my love; behold: thou art fair; thy eyes are as those of doves.

15 Behold: thou art fair, my beloved, and comely. Our bed is flourishing. 16 The beams of our houses are of cedar, our rafters of cypress trees.

Chapter 2

Christ caresses his spouse. He invites her to him.

I am the flower of the field and the lily of the valleys. 2 As the lily among thorns, so is my love among the daughters. 3 As the apple tree among the trees of the woods, so is my beloved among the sons. I sat down under his shadow whom I desired, and his fruit was sweet to my palate. 4 He brought me into the cellar of wine; he set in order charity in me. 5 Stay me up with flowers; compass me about with apples, because I languish with love. 6 His left hand is under my head, and his right hand shall embrace me.

7 I adjure you, O ye daughters of Jerusalem, by the roes and the harts of the fields, that you stir not up nor make the beloved to awake till she please. 8 The voice of my beloved,

saliens in montibus, transiliens colles. 9 Similis est dilectus meus capreae hinuloque cervorum. En: ipse stat post parietem nostrum, respiciens per fenestras, prospiciens per cancellos. 10 En: dilectus meus loquitur mihi, "Surge; propera, amica mea, columba mea, formonsa mea, et veni, 11 iam enim hiemps transiit; imber abiit et recessit. 12 Flores apparuerunt in terra nostra. Tempus putationis advenit. Vox turturis audita est in terra nostra. 13 Ficus protulit grossos suos. Vineae florentes dederunt odorem suum. Surge, amica mea, speciosa mea, et veni. 14 Columba mea in foraminibus petrae, in caverna maceriae, ostende mihi faciem tuam; sonet vox tua in auribus meis, vox enim tua dulcis et facies tua decora. 15 Capite nobis vulpes parvulas quae demoliuntur vineas, nam vinea nostra floruit. 16 Dilectus meus mihi et ego illi qui pascitur inter lilia 17 donec adspiret dies et inclinentur umbrae. Revertere; similis esto, dilecte mi, capreae hinuloque cervorum super montes Bether."

Caput 3

In lectulo meo per noctes quaesivi quem diligit anima mea; quaesivi illum et non inveni. 2 Surgam et circuibo civitatem; per vicos et plateas quaeram quem diligit anima mea.

behold: he cometh leaping upon the mountains, skipping over the hills. 9 My beloved is like a roe *or* a young hart. Behold: he standeth behind our wall, looking through the windows, looking through the lattices. 10 Behold: my beloved speaketh to me, "Arise; make haste, my love, my dove, my beautiful one, and come, 11 for winter is now past; the rain is over and gone. 12 The flowers have appeared in our land. The time of pruning is come. The voice of the turtle is heard in our land. 13 The fig tree hath put forth her green figs. The vines in flower yield their sweet smell. Arise, my love, my beautiful one, and come. 14 My dove in the clefts of the rock, in the hollow places of the wall, shew me thy face; let thy voice sound in my ears, for thy voice is sweet and thy face comely. 15 Catch us the little foxes that destroy the vines, for our vineyard hath flourished. 16 My beloved to me and I to him who feedeth among the lilies 17 till the day break and the shadows retire. Return; be like, my beloved, to a roe *or* to a young hart upon the mountains of Bether."

Chapter 3

The spouse seeks Christ. The glory of his humanity.

In my bed by night I sought him whom my soul loveth; I sought him and found him not. 2 I will rise and will go about the city; in the streets and the broad ways I will seek him

whom my soul loveth. I sought him, and I found him not. 3 The watchmen who keep the city found me, "Have you seen him whom my soul loveth?" 4 When I had a little passed by them, I found him whom my soul loveth. I held him, and I will not let him go till I bring him into my mother's house and into the chamber of her that bore me.

5 I adjure you, O daughters of Jerusalem, by the roes and the harts of the fields that you stir not up nor awake my beloved till she please. 6 Who is she that goeth up by the desert as a pillar of smoke of aromatical spices, of myrrh and frankincense and of all the powders of the perfumer? 7 Behold: threescore valiant ones of the most valiant of Israel surround the bed of Solomon, 8 all holding swords and most expert in war, every man's sword upon his thigh, because of fears in the night. 9 King Solomon hath made him a litter of the wood of Lebanon; 10 the pillars thereof he made of silver, the seat of gold, the going up of purple; the midst he covered with charity for the daughters of Jerusalem.

11 Go forth, ye daughters of Zion, and see King Solomon in the diadem wherewith his mother crowned him in the day of his *espousals* and in the day of the joy of his heart.

Caput 4

Quam pulchra es, amica mea; quam pulchra es! Oculi tui columbarum, absque eo quod intrinsecus latet. Capilli tui sicut greges caprarum quae ascenderunt de Monte Galaad. 2 Dentes tui sicut greges tonsarum quae ascenderunt de lavacro, omnes gemellis fetibus, et sterilis non est inter eas. 3 Sicut vitta coccinea labia tua et eloquium tuum dulce. Sicut fragmen mali punici ita genae tuae, absque eo quod intrinsecus latet. 4 Sicut turris David collum tuum, quae aedificata est cum propugnaculis. Mille clypei pendent ex ea, omnis armatura fortium. 5 Duo ubera tua sicut duo hinuli capreae gemelli qui pascuntur in liliis.

6 Donec adspiret dies et inclinentur umbrae vadam ad montem murrae et ad collem turis. 7 Tota pulchra es, amica mea, et macula non est in te. 8 Veni de Libano, sponsa mea; veni de Libano; veni; coronaberis de capite Amana, de vertice Sanir et Hermon, de cubilibus leonum, de montibus pardorum. 9 Vulnerasti cor meum, soror mea, sponsa; vulnerasti cor meum in uno oculorum tuorum et in uno crine colli tui.

10 Quam pulchrae sunt mammae tuae, soror mea, sponsa! Pulchriora ubera tua vino, et odor unguentorum tuorum

Chapter 4

Christ sets forth the graces of his spouse and declares his love for her.

How beautiful art thou, my love; how beautiful art thou! Thy eyes are doves' eyes, besides what is hid within. Thy hair is as flocks of goats which come up from Mount Gilead. 2 Thy teeth as flocks of sheep that are shorn which come up from the washing, all with twins, and there is none barren among them. 3 Thy lips are as a scarlet lace and thy speech sweet. Thy cheeks are as a piece of a pomegranate, besides that which lieth hid within. 4 Thy neck is as the tower of David, which is built with bulwarks. A thousand bucklers hang upon it, all the armour of valiant men. 5 Thy two breasts like two young roes that are twins which feed among the lilies.

6 Till the day break and the shadows retire I will go to the mountain of myrrh and to the hill of frankincense. 7 Thou art all fair, O my love, and there is not a spot in thee. 8 Come from Lebanon, my spouse; come from Lebanon; come; thou shalt be crowned from the top of Amana, from the top of Senir and Hermon, from the dens of the lions, from the mountains of the leopards. 9 Thou hast wounded my heart, my sister, my spouse; thou hast wounded my heart with one of thy eyes and with one hair of thy neck.

10 How beautiful are thy breasts, my sister, my spouse! Thy breasts are more beautiful than wine, and the sweet

super omnia aromata. 11 Favus distillans labia tua, sponsa; mel et lac sub lingua tua, et odor vestimentorum tuorum sicut odor turis.

12 Hortus conclusus soror mea, sponsa, hortus conclusus, fons signatus. 13 Emissiones tuae paradisus malorum punicorum cum pomorum fructibus. Cypri cum nardo, 14 nardus et crocus, fistula et cinnamomum cum universis lignis Libani, murra et aloe cum omnibus primis unguentis, 15 fons hortorum, puteus aquarum viventium quae fluunt impetu de Libano. 16 Surge, aquilo, et veni, auster; perfla hortum meum, et fluant aromata illius!

Caput 5

Veniat dilectus meus in hortum suum et comedat fructum pomorum suorum. Veni in hortum meum, soror mea, sponsa; messui murram meam cum aromatibus meis; comedi favum cum melle meo. Bibi vinum meum cum lacte meo. Comedite, amici, et bibite, et inebriamini, carissimi!

smell of thy ointments above all aromatical spices. 11 Thy lips, my spouse, are as a dropping honeycomb; honey and milk are under thy tongue, and the smell of thy garments as the smell of frankincense.

12 My sister, my spouse, is a garden enclosed, a garden enclosed, a fountain sealed up. 13 Thy plants are a paradise of pomegranates with the fruits of the orchard. Cypress with spikenard, 14 spikenard and saffron, sweet cane and cinnamon with all the trees of Lebanon, myrrh and aloes with all the chief perfumes, 15 the fountain of gardens, the well of living waters which run with a strong stream from Lebanon. 16 Arise, O north wind, and come, O south wind; blow through my garden, and let the aromatical spices thereof flow!

Chapter 5

Christ calls his spouse. She languishes with love and describes him by his graces.

Let my beloved come into his garden and eat the fruit of his apple trees. I am come into my garden, O my sister, my spouse; I have gathered my myrrh with my aromatical spices; I have eaten the honeycomb with my honey. I have drunk my wine with my milk. Eat, O friends, and drink, and be inebriated, my dearly beloved!

2 Ego dormio, et cor meum vigilat. Vox dilecti mei pulsantis: "Aperi mihi, soror mea, amica mea, columba mea, inmaculata mea, quia caput meum plenum est rore, et cincinni mei guttis noctium. 3 Expoliavi me tunica mea; quomodo induar illa? Lavi pedes meos, quomodo inquinabo illos?"

4 Dilectus meus misit manum suam per foramen, et venter meus intremuit ad tactum eius. 5 Surrexi ut aperirem dilecto meo; manus meae stillaverunt murram, et digiti mei pleni murra probatissima. 6 Pessulum ostii mei aperui dilecto meo, at ille declinaverat atque transierat. Anima mea liquefacta est ut locutus est. Quaesivi et non inveni illum. Vocavi, et non respondit mihi.

7 Invenerunt me custodes qui circumeunt civitatem; percusserunt me, et vulneraverunt me. Tulerunt pallium meum mihi custodes murorum. 8 Adiuro vos, filiae Hierusalem, si inveneritis dilectum meum, ut nuntietis ei quia amore langueo.

9 Qualis est dilectus tuus ex dilecto, O pulcherrima mulierum? Qualis est dilectus tuus ex dilecto quia sic adiurasti nos?

10 Dilectus meus candidus et rubicundus, electus ex milibus. 11 Caput eius aurum optimum, comae eius sicut elatae palmarum, nigrae quasi corvus. 12 Oculi eius sicut columbae super rivulos aquarum quae lacte sunt lotae et resident iuxta fluenta plenissima. 13 Genae illius sicut areolae aromatum consitae a pigmentariis. Labia eius lilia distillantia murram primam. 14 Manus illius tornatiles, aureae, plenae hyacinthis. Venter eius eburneus distinctus sapphyris. 15 Crura illius columnae marmoreae quae fundatae sunt super bases aureas, species eius ut Libani, electus ut cedri, 16 guttur illius

2 I sleep, and my heart watcheth. The voice of my beloved knocking: "Open to me, my sister, my love, my dove, my undefiled, for my head is full of dew, and my locks of the drops of the nights. 3 I have put off my garment; how shall I put it on? I have washed my feet; how shall I defile them?"

4 My beloved put his hand through the key hole, and my bowels were moved at his touch. 5 I arose up to open to my beloved; my hands *dropped with* myrrh, and my fingers were full of the choicest myrrh. 6 I opened the bolt of my door to my beloved, but he had turned aside and was gone. My soul melted when he spoke. I sought him and found him not. I called, and he did not answer me.

7 The keepers that go about the city found me; they struck me and wounded me. The keepers of the walls took away my veil from me. 8 I adjure you, O daughters of Jerusalem, if you find my beloved, that you tell him that I languish with love.

9 What manner of one is thy beloved of the beloved, O thou most beautiful among women? What manner of one is thy beloved of the beloved that thou hast so adjured us?

10 My beloved is white and ruddy, chosen out of thousands. 11 His head is as the finest gold, his locks as branches of palm trees, black as a raven. 12 His eyes as doves upon brooks of waters which are washed with milk and sit beside the plentiful streams. 13 His cheeks are as beds of aromatical spices set by the perfumers. His lips are as lilies dropping choice myrrh. 14 His hands are turned *and as* of gold, full of hyacinths. His belly as of ivory set with sapphires. 15 His legs as pillars of marble that are set upon bases of gold, his form as of Lebanon, excellent as the cedars, 16 his throat most

suavissimum, et totus desiderabilis. Talis est dilectus meus, et iste est amicus meus, filiae Hierusalem.

17 Quo abiit dilectus tuus, O pulcherrima mulierum? Quo declinavit dilectus tuus, et quaeremus eum tecum?

Caput 6

Dilectus meus descendit in hortum suum, ad areolam aromatum, ut pascatur in hortis et lilia colligat. 2 Ego dilecto meo et dilectus meus mihi qui pascitur inter lilia. 3 Pulchra es, amica mea, suavis et decora sicut Hierusalem, terribilis ut castrorum acies ordinata. 4 Averte oculos tuos a me, quia ipsi me avolare fecerunt. Capilli tui sicut grex caprarum quae apparuerunt de Galaad. 5 Dentes tui sicut grex ovium quae ascenderunt de lavacro, omnes gemellis fetibus, et sterilis non est in eis. 6 Sicut cortex mali punici, sic genae tuae, absque occultis tuis.

7 Sexaginta sunt reginae et octoginta concubinae et adulescentularum non est numerus, 8 una est columba mea, perfecta mea; una est matris suae, electa genetrici suae. Vide-

sweet, and he is all lovely. Such is my beloved, and he is my friend, O ye daughters of Jerusalem.

17 Whither is thy beloved gone, O thou most beautiful among women? Whither is thy beloved turned aside, and we will seek him with thee?

Chapter 6

The spouse of Christ is but one. She is fair and terrible.

My beloved is gone down into his garden, to the bed of aromatical spices, to feed in the gardens and to gather lilies. 2 I to my beloved and my beloved to me who feedeth among the lilies. 3 Thou art beautiful, O my love, sweet and comely as Jerusalem, terrible as an army set in array. 4 Turn away thy eyes from me, for they have made me flee away. Thy hair is as a flock of goats that appear from Gilead. 5 Thy teeth as a flock of sheep which come up from the washing, all with twins, and there is none barren among them. 6 Thy cheeks are as the bark of a pomegranate, beside what is hidden within thee.

7 There are threescore queens and fourscore concubines and young maidens without number. 8 One is my dove; my perfect one *is but one;* she is the only one of her mother, the chosen of her that bore her. The daughters saw her and de-

runt illam filiae et beatissimam praedicaverunt, reginae et concubinae, et laudaverunt eam.

9 Quae est ista quae progreditur quasi aurora consurgens, pulchra ut luna, electa ut sol, terribilis ut castrorum acies ordinata? 10 Descendi in hortum nucum ut viderem poma convallium et inspicerem si floruisset vinea et germinassent mala punica. 11 Nescivi anima mea conturbavit me propter quadrigas Aminadab.

12 Revertere; revertere, Sulamitis; revertere; revertere ut intueamur te!

Caput 7

Quid videbis in Sulamiten nisi choros castrorum? Quam pulchri sunt gressus tui in calciamentis, filia principis! Iuncturae feminum tuorum sicut monilia quae fabricata sunt manu artificis. 2 Umbilicus tuus crater tornatilis numquam indigens poculis. Venter tuus sicut acervus tritici vallatus liliis. 3 Duo ubera tua sicut duo hinuli gemelli capreae. 4 Collum tuum sicut turris eburnea. Oculi tui sicut piscinae in Esebon quae sunt in porta filiae multitudinis. Nasus tuus

clared her most blessed, the queens and concubines, and they praised her.

9 Who is she that cometh forth as the morning rising, fair as the moon, *bright* as the sun, terrible as an *army* set in array? 10 I went down into the garden of nuts to see the fruits of the valleys and to look if the vineyard had flourished and the pomegranates budded. 11 I knew not my soul troubled me for the chariots of Aminadab.

12 Return; return, O Shulammitess; return; return that we may behold thee!

Chapter 7

A further description of the graces of the church, the spouse of Christ.

What shalt thou see in the Shulamitess but the companies of camps? How beautiful are thy steps in shoes, O prince's daughter! The joints of thy thighs are like jewels that are made by the hand of a skillful workman. 2 Thy navel is like a round bowl never wanting cups. Thy belly is like a heap of wheat set about with lilies. 3 Thy two breasts are like two young roes that are twins. 4 Thy neck as a tower of ivory. Thy eyes like the fishpools in Heshbon which are in the gate of the daughter of the multitude. Thy nose is as the tower of

sicut turris Libani quae respicit contra Damascum. 5 Caput tuum ut Carmelus, et comae capitis tui sicut purpura regis vincta canalibus.

6 Quam pulchra es et quam decora, carissima, in deliciis! 7 Statura tua adsimilata est palmae, et ubera tua botris. 8 Dixi, "Ascendam in palmam et adprehendam fructus eius, et erunt ubera tua sicut botri vineae, et odor oris tui sicut malorum. 9 Guttur tuum sicut vinum optimum, dignum dilecto meo ad potandum labiisque et dentibus illius ruminandum."

10 Ego dilecto meo, et ad me conversio eius. 11 Veni, dilecte mi; egrediamur in agrum; commoremur in villis. 12 Mane surgamus ad vineas; videamus si floruit vinea, si flores fructus parturiunt. Si floruerunt mala punica, ibi dabo tibi ubera mea. 13 Mandragorae dederunt odorem. In portis nostris omnia poma; nova et vetera, dilecte, mi servavi tibi.

Caput 8

Quis mihi det te fratrem meum, sugentem ubera matris meae, ut inveniam te foris et deosculer te, et iam me nemo despiciat? 2 Adprehendam te et ducam in domum matris

Lebanon that looketh toward Damascus. 5 Thy head is like Carmel, and the hairs of thy head as the purple of the king bound in the channels.

6 How beautiful art thou and how comely, my dearest, in delights! 7 Thy stature is like to a palm tree, and thy breasts to clusters of grapes. 8 I said, "I will go up into the palm tree and will take hold of the fruit thereof, and thy breasts shall be as the clusters of the vine, and the odour of thy mouth like apples. 9 Thy throat like the best wine, worthy for my beloved to drink and for his lips and his teeth to ruminate."

10 I to my beloved, and his turning is towards me. 11 Come, my beloved; let us go forth into the field; let us abide in the villages. 12 Let us get up early to the vineyards; let us see if the vineyard flourish, if the flowers be ready to bring forth fruits. If the pomegranates flourish, there will I give thee my breasts. 13 The mandrakes *give* a smell. In our gates are all fruits; the new and the old, my beloved, I have kept for thee.

Chapter 8

The love of the church to Christ. His love to her.

W ho shall give thee to me *for* my brother, sucking the breasts of my mother, that I may find thee without and kiss thee, and now no man may despise me? 2 I will take hold of

meae. Ibi me docebis, et dabo tibi poculum ex vino condito et mustum malorum granatorum meorum. 3 Leva eius sub capite meo, et dextera illius amplexabitur me.

4 Adiuro vos, filiae Hierusalem, ne suscitetis neque evigilare faciatis dilectam donec ipsa velit. 5 Quae est ista quae ascendit de deserto, deliciis affluens, innixa super dilectum suum? Sub arbore malo suscitavi te; ibi corrupta est mater tua; ibi violata est genetrix tua.

6 Pone me ut signaculum super cor tuum, ut signaculum super brachium tuum, quia fortis est ut mors dilectio, dura sicut inferus aemulatio; lampades eius lampades ignis atque flammarum. 7 Aquae multae non possunt extinguere caritatem, nec flumina obruent illam. Si dederit homo omnem substantiam domus suae pro dilectione, quasi nihil despiciet eum.

8 Soror nostra parva et ubera non habet. Quid faciemus sorori nostrae in die quando adloquenda est? 9 Si murus est, aedificemus super eum propugnacula argentea; si ostium est, conpingamus illud tabulis cedrinis.

10 Ego murus, et ubera mea sicut turris ex quo facta sum coram eo quasi pacem repperiens.

11 Vinea fuit pacifico in ea quae habet populos; tradidit eam custodibus; vir adfert pro fructu eius mille argenteos. 12 Vinea mea coram me est. Mille tui pacifici et ducenti his qui custodiunt fructus eius.

13 Quae habitas in hortis, amici auscultant; fac me audire vocem tuam. 14 Fuge, dilecte mi, et adsimilare capreae hinuloque cervorum super montes aromatum.

thee and bring thee into my mother's house. There thou shalt teach me, and I will give thee a cup of spiced wine and new wine of my pomegranates. 3 His left hand under my head, and his right hand shall embrace me.

4 I adjure you, O daughters of Jerusalem, that you stir not up nor awake my love till she please. 5 Who is this that cometh up from the desert, flowing with delights, leaning upon her beloved? Under the apple tree I raised thee up; there thy mother was corrupted; there she was defloured that bore thee.

6 Put me as a seal upon thy heart, as a seal upon thy arm, for love is strong as death, jealousy as hard as hell; the lamps thereof are fire and flames. 7 Many waters cannot quench charity, neither *can* the floods *drown* it. If a man should give all the substance of his house for love, he shall despise it as nothing.

8 Our sister is little and hath no breasts. What shall we do to our sister in the day when she is to be spoken to? 9 If she be a wall, let us build upon it bulwarks of silver; if she be a door, let us join it together with boards or cedar.

10 I am a wall, and my breasts are as a tower since I am become in his presence as one finding peace.

11 The peaceable had a vineyard in that which hath people; he let out the same to keepers; *every* man bringeth for the fruit thereof a thousand pieces of silver. 12 My vineyard is before me. A thousand are *for thee, the peaceable,* and two hundred for them that keep the fruit thereof.

13 Thou that dwellest in the gardens, the friends hearken; make me hear thy voice. 14 Flee away, O my beloved, and be like to the roe and to the young hart upon the mountains of aromatical spices.

WISDOM

Caput 1

Diligite iustitiam, qui iudicatis terram. Sentite de Domino in bonitate, et in simplicitate cordis quaerite illum, 2 quoniam invenitur ab his qui non temptant illum, apparet autem eis qui fidem habent in illum. 3 Perversae enim cogitationes separant a Deo, probata autem virtus corripit insipientes. 4 Quoniam in malivolam animam non intrabit sapientia nec habitabit in corpore subdito peccatis. 5 Sanctus enim spiritus disciplinae effugiet fictum et auferet se a cogitationibus quae sunt sine intellectu, et corripietur a superveniente iniquitate. 6 Benignus est enim spiritus sapientiae et non liberabit maledicum a labiis suis, quoniam renum illius testis est Deus, et cordis eius scrutator est verus et linguae illius auditor. 7 Quoniam spiritus Domini replevit orbem terrarum, et hoc quod continet omnia scientiam habet vocis. 8 Propter hoc qui loquitur iniqua non potest latere, nec praeteriet illum corripiens iudicium. 9 In cogitationibus enim impii interrogatio erit sermonum autem illius auditio

Chapter 1

An exhortation to seek God sincerely, who cannot be deceived and desireth not our death.

Love justice, you that are the judges of the earth. Think of the Lord in goodness, and seek him in simplicity of heart, 2 for he is found by them that tempt him not, and he sheweth himself to them that have faith in him. 3 For perverse thoughts separate from God, and his power when it is tried reproveth the unwise. 4 For wisdom will not enter into a malicious soul nor dwell in a body subject to sins. 5 For the Holy Spirit of discipline will flee from the deceitful and will withdraw himself from thoughts that are without understanding, and he shall *not abide when* iniquity cometh in. 6 For the spirit of wisdom is benevolent and will not acquit the evil speaker from his lips, for God is witness of his reins, and he is a true searcher of his heart and a hearer of his tongue. 7 For the spirit of the Lord hath filled the whole world, and that which containeth all things hath knowledge of the voice. 8 Therefore he that speaketh unjust things cannot be hid, neither shall the chastising judgment pass him by. 9 For inquisition shall be made into the thoughts of the ungodly

ad Deum veniet ad correptionem iniquitatum illius. 10 Quoniam auris zeli audit omnia et tumultus murmurationum non abscondetur.

11 Custodite ergo vos a murmuratione, quae nihil prodest, et a detractione parcite linguae, quoniam sermo obscurus in vacuum non ibit os autem quod mentitur occidit animam. 12 Nolite zelare mortem in errore vitae vestrae, neque adquiratis perditionem in operibus manuum vestrarum, 13 quoniam Deus mortem non fecit, nec laetatur in perditione vivorum. 14 Creavit enim ut essent omnia, et sanabiles fecit nationes orbis terrarum, et non est in illis medicamentum exterminii nec inferorum regnum in terra. 15 Iustitia enim perpetua est et inmortalis, 16 impii autem manibus et verbis arcessierunt illam et aestimantes illam amicam defluxerunt et sponsiones posuerunt ad illam quoniam digni sunt qui sint ex parte illius.

Caput 2

Dixerunt enim, apud se cogitantes non recte, "Exiguum et cum taedio est tempus vitae nostrae, et non est refrigerium in fine hominis, et non est qui agnitus sit reversus ab

and the hearing of his words shall come to God to the chastising of his iniquities. 10 For the ear of jealousy heareth all things and the tumult of murmuring shall not be hid.

11 Keep yourselves therefore from murmuring, which profiteth nothing, and refrain your tongue from detraction, for an obscure speech shall not go for nought and the mouth that belieth killeth the soul. 12 Seek not death in the error of your life, neither procure ye destruction by the works of your hands, 13 for God made not death, neither hath he pleasure in the destruction of the living. 14 For he created all things that they might be, and he made the nations of the earth for health, and there is no poison of destruction in them nor kingdom of hell upon the earth. 15 For justice is perpetual and immortal, 16 but the wicked with *works* and words have called it to them and esteeming it a friend have fallen away and have made *a covenant* with it because they are worthy to be of the part thereof.

Chapter 2

The vain reasonings of the wicked. Their persecuting the just, especially the Son of God.

For they have said, reasoning with themselves, *but* not right, "The time of our life is short and tedious, and in the end of a man there is no remedy, and no man hath been

inferis. 2 Quia ex nihilo nati sumus, et post hoc erimus tamquam non fuerimus, quoniam fumus afflatus est in naribus nostris, et sermo scintilla ad commovendum cor nostrum, 3 qua extincta, cinis erit corpus nostrum, et spiritus diffundetur tamquam mollis aer, et transiet vita nostra tamquam vestigium nubis et sicut nebula dissolvetur quae fugata est a radiis solis et a calore illius adgravata. 4 Et nomen nostrum oblivionem accipiet per tempus, et nemo memoriam habebit operum nostrorum. 5 Umbrae enim transitus est tempus nostrum, et non est reversio finis nostri, quoniam consignata est, et nemo revertitur.

6 "Venite, ergo, et fruamur bonis quae sunt, et utamur creaturam tamquam in iuventute celeriter. 7 Vino pretioso et unguentis nos impleamus, et non praetereat nos flos temporis. 8 Coronemus nos rosis antequam marcescant; nullum pratum sit quod non pertranseat luxuria nostra. 9 Nemo nostrum exors sit luxuriae nostrae; ubique relinquamus signa laetitiae, quoniam haec est pars nostra et haec est sors. 10 Opprimamus pauperem iustum et non parcamus viduae nec veterani revereamur canos multi temporis. 11 Sit autem fortitudo nostra lex iustitiae, quod infirmum est enim inutile invenitur.

12 "Circumveniamus ergo iustum, quoniam inutilis est nobis et contrarius est operibus nostris et inproperat nobis peccata legis et diffamat in nos peccata disciplinae nostrae. 13 Promittit scientiam Dei se habere et filium Dei se nominat. 14 Factus est nobis in traductionem cogitationum nostrarum. 15 Gravis est nobis etiam ad videndum, quoniam dissimilis est aliis vita illius, et inmutatae sunt viae eius. 16 Tamquam nugaces aestimati sumus ab illo, et abstinet se a

known to have returned from hell. 2 For we are born of nothing, and after this we shall be as if we had not been, for the breath in our nostrils is smoke, and speech a spark to move our heart, 3 which being put out, our body shall be ashes, and our spirit shall be poured abroad as soft air, and our life shall pass away as the trace of a cloud and shall be dispersed as a mist which is driven away by the beams of the sun and overpowered with the heat thereof. 4 And our name in time shall be forgotten, and no man shall have any remembrance of our works. 5 For our time is as the passing of a shadow, and there is no going back of our end, for it is fast sealed, and no man returneth.

6 "Come therefore, and let us enjoy the good things that are present, and let us speedily use the creatures as in youth. 7 Let us fill ourselves with costly wine and ointments, and let not the flower of the time pass by us. 8 Let us crown ourselves with roses before they be withered; let *no meadow escape our riot.* 9 Let none of us *go without his part* in luxury; let us everywhere leave tokens of joy, for this is our portion and this our lot. 10 Let us oppress the poor just man and not spare the widow nor honour the ancient grey hairs of the aged. 11 But let our strength be the law of justice, for that which is feeble is found to be nothing worth.

12 "Let us therefore *lie in wait for* the just, because he is *not for our turn* and he is contrary to our doings and upbraideth us with transgressions of the law and divulgeth against us the sins of our way of life. 13 He boasteth that he hath the knowledge of God and calleth himself the son of God. 14 He is become *a censurer* of our thoughts. 15 He is grievous unto us even to behold, for his life is not like other men's, and his ways are very different. 16 We are esteemed by him as tri-

viis nostris tamquam ab inmunditiis, et praefert novissima iustorum et gloriatur patrem Deum se habere. 17 Videamus ergo si sermones illius veri sunt, et temptemus quae ventura sunt illi, et sciemus quae erunt novissima illius, 18 si enim est verus filius Dei, suscipiet illum et liberabit eum de manibus contrariorum. 19 Contumelia et tormento interrogemus eum ut sciamus reverentiam illius et probemus patientiam ipsius. 20 Morte turpissima condemnemus illum, erit enim ei respectus ex sermonibus illius."

21 Haec cogitaverunt et erraverunt, excaecavit enim illos malitia eorum. 22 Et nescierunt sacramenta Dei neque mercedem speraverunt iustitiae nec iudicaverunt honorem animarum sanctarum, 23 quoniam Deus creavit hominem inexterminabilem, et ad imaginem suae similitudinis fecit illum, 24 invidia autem diaboli mors introivit in orbem terrarum, 25 imitantur autem illum qui sunt ex parte illius.

Caput 3

Iustorum autem animae in manu Dei sunt, et non tanget illos tormentum mortis. 2 Visi sunt in oculis insipientium mori, et aestimata est adflictio exitus illorum 3 et quod

flers, and he abstaineth from our ways as from filthiness, and he preferreth the latter end of the just and glorieth that he hath God for his father. 17 Let us see then if his words be true, and let us prove what shall happen to him, and we shall know what his end shall be, 18 for if he be the true son of God, he will defend him and will deliver him from the hands of his enemies. 19 Let us examine him by outrages and tortures that we may know his meekness and try his patience. 20 Let us condemn him to a most shameful death, for there shall be respect had unto him by his words."

21 These things they thought and *were deceived,* for their own malice blinded them. 22 And they knew not the secrets of God nor hoped for the wages of justice nor esteemed the honour of holy souls, 23 for God created man incorruptible, and to the image of his own likeness he made him, 24 but by the envy of the devil death came into the world, 25 and they follow him that are of his side.

Chapter 3

The happiness of the just and the unhappiness of the wicked.

But the souls of the just are in the hand of God, and the torment of death shall not touch them. 2 In the sight of the unwise they seemed to die, and their departure was taken for misery 3 and *their going away from us for utter* destruction,

a nobis est iter exterminium, illi autem sunt in pace. 4 Et si coram hominibus tormenta passi sunt, spes illorum inmortalitate plena est. 5 In paucis vexati, in multis bene disponentur, quoniam Deus tentavit illos et invenit illos dignos se. 6 Tamquam aurum in fornace probavit illos, et quasi holocausti hostiam accepit illos, et in tempore erit respectus illorum. 7 Fulgebunt iusti et tamquam scintillae in harundineto discurrent. 8 Iudicabunt nationes et dominabuntur populis, et regnabit Dominus illorum in perpetuum. 9 Qui confidunt in illum intellegent veritatem, et fideles in dilectione adquiescent illi, quoniam donum et pax est electis illius.

10 Impii autem secundum quae cogitaverunt correptionem habebunt, qui neglexerunt iustum et a Domino recesserunt. 11 Sapientiam enim et disciplinam qui abicit infelix est, et vacua est spes illorum et labores sine fructu et inutilia opera eorum. 12 Mulieres eorum insensatae sunt et nequissimi filii eorum. 13 Maledicta creatura illorum, quoniam felix sterilis et incoinquinata quae non scivit torum in delicto—habebit fructum in respectione animarum sanctarum —14 et spado qui non operatus est per manus suas iniquitatem nec cogitavit adversus Deum nequissima, dabitur enim illi fidei donum electum et sors in templo Dei acceptissima.

15 Bonorum enim laborum gloriosus est fructus, et quae non concidat radix sapientiae. 16 Filii autem adulterorum in consummatione erunt, et ab iniquo toro semen exterminabitur. 17 Et si quidem longae vitae erunt, in nihilum conputa-

but they are in peace. 4 And though in the sight of men they suffered torments, their hope is full of immortality. 5 Afflicted in few things, in many they shall be well rewarded, because God hath tried them and found them worthy of himself. 6 As gold in the furnace he hath proved them, and as a victim of a holocaust he hath received them, and in time there shall be respect had to them. 7 The just shall shine and shall run to and fro like sparks among the reeds. 8 They shall judge nations and rule over people, and their Lord shall reign for ever. 9 They that trust in him shall understand the truth, and they that are faithful in love shall rest in him, for *grace* and peace is to his elect.

10 But the wicked shall be punished according to their own devices, who have neglected the just and have revolted from the Lord. 11 For he that rejecteth wisdom and discipline is unhappy, and their hope is vain and their labours without fruit and their works unprofitable. 12 Their wives are foolish and their children wicked. 13 Their offspring is cursed, for happy is the barren and the undefiled that hath not known bed in sin—she shall have fruit in the visitation of holy souls—14 and the eunuch that hath not wrought iniquity with his hands nor thought wicked things against God, for the precious gift of faith shall be given to him and a most acceptable lot in the temple of God.

15 For the fruit of good labours is glorious, and the root of wisdom never faileth. 16 But the children of adulterers shall *not come to perfection,* and the seed of the unlawful bed shall be rooted out. 17 And if they live long, they shall be nothing

buntur, et sine honore erit novissima senectus illorum. 18 Et si celerius defuncti fuerint, non habebunt spem nec in die agnitionis adlocutionem, 19 nationis enim iniquae dirae sunt consummationes.

Caput 4

O quam pulchra est casta generatio cum claritate! Inmortalis est enim memoria illius, quoniam et apud Deum nota est et apud homines. 2 Cum praesens est, imitantur illam, et desiderant eam cum se eduxerit, et in perpetuum coronata triumphat, incoinquinatorum certaminum praemium vincens. 3 Multigena autem impiorum multitudo non erit utilis, et spuria vitulamina non dabunt radices altas nec stabile firmamentum conlocabunt. 4 Et si in ramis in tempore germinaverint, infirmiter posita, a vento commovebuntur, et a nimietate ventorum eradicabuntur. 5 Confringentur enim rami inconsummati, et fructus illorum inutiles et acerbi ad manducandum et ad nihilum apti. 6 Ex iniquis enim somnis filii qui nascuntur testes sunt nequitiae adversus parentes in interrogatione sua.

regarded, and their last old age shall be without honour. 18 And if they die quickly, they shall have no hope nor speech of comfort in the day of *trial,* 19 for dreadful are the ends of a wicked race.

Chapter 4

The difference between the chaste and the adulterous generations and between the death of the just and the wicked.

O how beautiful is the chaste generation with glory! For the memory thereof is immortal, because it is known both with God and with men. 2 When it is present, they imitate it, and they desire it when it hath withdrawn itself, and it triumpheth crowned for ever, winning the reward of undefiled conflicts. 3 But the *multiplied brood of the wicked shall not thrive,* and bastard slips shall not take deep root nor *any* fast foundation. 4 And if they flourish in branches for a time, *yet standing not fast,* they shall be shaken with the wind, and through the force of winds they shall be rooted out. 5 For the branches not being perfect shall be broken, and their fruits shall be unprofitable and sour to eat and fit for nothing. 6 For the children that are born of unlawful *beds* are witnesses of wickedness against their parents in their trial.

7 Iustus autem, si morte praeoccupatus fuerit, in refrigerio erit. 8 Senectus enim venerabilis est non diuturna neque numero annorum conputata, cani sunt autem sensus hominis, 9 et aetas senectutis vita inmaculata. 10 Placens Deo factus dilectus, et vivens inter peccatores translatus est. 11 Raptus est ne malitia mutaret intellectum illius aut ne fictio deciperet animam illius. 12 Fascinatio enim nugacitatis obscurat bona, et inconstantia concupiscentiae transvertit sensum sine malitia. 13 Consummatus in brevi, explevit tempora multa, 14 placita enim erat Deo anima illius. Propter hoc properavit educere illum de medio iniquitatum, populi autem videntes et non intellegentes, nec ponentes in praecordiis talia, 15 quoniam gratia Dei et misericordia est in sanctos illius et respectus in electos illius.

16 Condemnat autem iustus mortuus vivos impios et iuventus celerius consummata, longam vitam iniusti, 17 videbunt enim finem sapientis et non intellegent quid cogitaverit de illo Deus et quare munierit illum Dominus. 18 Videbunt et contemnent eum, illos autem Dominus inridebit. 19 Et erunt post haec decidentes sine honore et in contumelia inter mortuos in perpetuum, quoniam disrumpet illos inflatos sine voce et commovebit illos a fundamentis, et usque ad supremum desolabuntur. Et erunt gementes, et memoria illorum periet. 20 Venient in cogitatione peccatorum suorum timidi, et traducent illos ex adverso iniquitates ipsorum.

7 But the just man, if he be prevented with death, shall be in rest. 8 For venerable old age is not that of long time nor counted by the number of years, but the understanding of a man is grey hairs, 9 and a spotless life is old age. 10 He pleased God and was beloved, and living among sinners he was translated. 11 He was taken away lest wickedness should alter his understanding or deceit beguile his soul. 12 For the bewitching of vanity obscureth good things, and the wandering of concupiscence overturneth the innocent mind. 13 Being made perfect in a short space, he fulfilled a long time, 14 for his soul pleased God. Therefore he hastened to bring him out of the midst of iniquities, but the people see this and understand not, nor lay up such things in their hearts, 15 that the grace of God and his mercy is with his saints and that he hath respect to his chosen.

16 But the just that is dead condemneth the wicked that are living and youth soon ended, the long life of the unjust, 17 for they shall see the end of the wise man and shall not understand what God hath designed for him and why the Lord hath set him in safety. 18 They shall see him and shall despise him, but the Lord shall laugh them to scorn. 19 And they shall fall after this without honour and be a reproach among the dead for ever, for he shall burst them puffed up and speechless and shall shake them from the foundations, and they shall be utterly laid waste. *They* shall be in sorrow, and their memory shall perish. 20 They shall come with fear at the thought of their sins, and their iniquities shall *stand against them to* convict them.

Caput 5

Tunc stabunt iusti in magna constantia adversus eos qui se angustaverunt et qui abstulerunt labores illorum. 2 Videntes turbabuntur timore horribili et mirabuntur in subitatione insperatae salutis. 3 Dicentes intra se, paenitentiam agentes et per angustiam spiritus gementes, "Hi sunt quos habuimus aliquando in risu et in similitudine inproperii! 4 Nos insensati vitam illorum aestimabamus insaniam et finem illorum sine honore. 5 Ecce quomodo conputati sunt inter filios Dei et inter sanctos sors illorum est. 6 Ergo erravimus a via veritatis, et iustitiae lumen non luxit nobis, et sol intelligentiae non est ortus nobis. 7 Lassati sumus in via iniquitatis et perditionis et ambulavimus vias difficiles, viam autem Domini ignoravimus. 8 Quid nobis profuit superbia? Aut quid divitiarum iactatio contulit nobis? 9 Transierunt omnia illa tamquam umbra et tamquam nuntius percurrens 10 et tamquam navis quae pertransit fluctuantem aquam cuius cum praeterierit non est vestigium invenire neque semitam carinae illius in fluctibus, 11 aut tamquam avis quae transvolat in aere cuius nullum invenitur argumentum itineris illius, sed tantum sonitus alarum verberans levem ventum

Chapter 5

The fruitless repentance of the wicked in another world.
The reward of the just.

Then shall the just stand with great constancy against those that have afflicted them and taken away their labours. 2 These seeing it shall be troubled with terrible fear and shall be amazed at the suddenness of their unexpected salvation. 3 Saying within themselves, repenting and groaning for anguish of spirit, "These are they whom we had some time in derision and for a parable of reproach! 4 We fools esteemed their life madness and their end without honour. 5 Behold how they are numbered among the children of God and their lot is among the saints. 6 Therefore we have erred from the way of truth, and the light of justice hath not shined unto us, and the sun of understanding hath not risen upon us. 7 We wearied ourselves in the way of iniquity and destruction and have walked through hard ways, but the way of the Lord we have not known. 8 What hath pride profited us? Or what *advantage* hath the boasting of riches brought us? 9 All those things are passed away like a shadow and like a post that runneth on 10 and as a ship that passeth through the waves whereof when it is gone by the trace cannot be found nor the path of its keel in the waters, 11 or as *when* a bird flieth through the air of *the* passage of which no mark can be found, but only the sound of the wings beating the

et scindens per vim itineris aerem; commotis alis transvolavit, et post hoc nullum signum invenitur itineris illius, 12 aut tamquam sagitta emissa in locum destinatum, divisus aer continuo in se reclusus est ut ignoretur transitus illius. 13 Sic et nos nati continuo desivimus esse et virtutis quidem signum nullum valuimus ostendere in malignitate autem nostra consumpti sumus!"

14 Talia dixerunt in inferno hi qui peccaverunt, 15 quoniam spes impii tamquam lanugo est quae a vento tollitur et tamquam spuma gracilis quae a procella dispergitur et tamquam fumus qui a vento diffusus est et tamquam memoria hospitis unius diei praetereuntis. 16 Iusti autem in perpetuum vivent, et apud Dominum est merces eorum et cogitatio illorum apud Altissimum. 17 Ideo accipient regnum decoris et diadema speciei de manu Domini, quoniam dextera sua teget eos et brachio sancto suo defendet illos. 18 Accipiet armaturam zelus illius, et armabit creaturam ad ultionem inimicorum. 19 Induet pro torace iustitiam et accipiet pro galea iudicium certum. 20 Sumet scutum inexpugnabile aequitatem, 21 acuet autem duram iram in lanceam, et pugnabit cum illo orbis terrarum contra insensatos. 22 Ibunt directe emissiones fulgorum, et tamquam a bene curvato arcu nubium exterminabuntur et ad certum locum insilient. 23 Et a petrosa ira plenae mittentur grandines, et scandescet in illos aqua maris, et flumina concurrent duriter. 24 Contra illos stabit spiritus virtutis et tamquam turbo venti dividet illos, et ad heremiam perducet omnem terram iniquitas illorum, et malignitas evertet sedes potentium.

light *air* and parting *it* by the force of her flight; she moved her wings and hath flown through, and there is no mark found afterwards of her way, 12 or as when an arrow is shot at a mark, the divided air presently cometh together again so that the passage thereof is not known. 13 So we also being born forthwith ceased to be and have been able to shew no mark of virtue but are consumed in our wickedness!"

14 Such things as these the sinners said in hell, 15 for the hope of the wicked is as dust which is blown away with the wind and as a thin froth which is dispersed by the storm and a smoke that is scattered abroad by the wind and as the remembrance of a guest of one day that passeth by. 16 But the just shall live for evermore, and their reward is with the Lord and the care of them with the Most High. 17 Therefore shall they receive a kingdom of glory and a crown of beauty at the hand of the Lord, for with his right hand he will cover them and with his holy arm he will defend them. 18 And his zeal will take armour, and he will arm the creature for the revenge of his enemies. 19 He will put on justice as a breastplate and will take true judgment instead of a helmet. 20 He will take equity for an invincible shield, 21 and he will sharpen his severe wrath for a spear, and the whole world shall fight with him against the unwise. 22 Then shafts of lightning shall go directly *from the clouds; as* from a *bow* well bent they shall be shot out and shall fly to the mark. 23 And thick hail shall be cast upon them from the *stone-casting* wrath; the water of the sea shall rage against them, and the rivers shall run together in a terrible manner. 24 A mighty wind shall stand up against them and as a whirlwind shall divide them, and their iniquity shall bring all the earth to a desert, and wickedness shall overthrow the thrones of the mighty.

Caput 6

Melior est sapientia quam vires, et vir prudens quam fortis. 2 Audite ergo, reges, et intellegite. Discite, iudices finium terrae. 3 Praebete aures, vos qui continetis multitudines et placetis vobis in turbis nationum, 4 quoniam data est a Domino potestas vobis et virtus ab Altissimo, qui interrogabit opera vestra et cogitationes scrutabitur 5 quoniam cum essetis ministri regni illius, non recte iudicastis neque custodistis legem iustitiae neque secundum voluntatem Dei ambulastis. 6 Horrende et cito apparebit vobis, quoniam iudicium durissimum in his qui praesunt fiet. 7 Exiguo enim, conceditur misericordia, potentes autem potenter tormenta patientur. 8 Non enim subtrahet personam cuiusquam Deus, nec verebitur magnitudinem cuiusquam, quoniam pusillum et magnum ipse fecit, et aequaliter cura est illi de omnibus. 9 Fortioribus autem fortior instat cruciatio.

10 Ad vos ergo, reges, sunt hi sermones mei, ut discatis sapientiam et non excidatis. 11 Qui enim custodierint iusta iuste iustificabuntur, et qui didicerint ista invenient quid respondeant. 12 Concupiscite ergo sermones meos, et diligite illos, et habebitis disciplinam. 13 Clara est et quae num-

Chapter 6

An address to princes to seek after wisdom. She is easily
found by those that seek her.

Wisdom is better than strength, and a wise man is better than a strong man. 2 Hear therefore, ye kings, and understand. Learn, ye that are judges of the ends of the earth.
3 Give ear, you that rule the people and that please yourselves in multitudes of nations, 4 for power is given you by
the Lord and strength by the Most High, who will examine
your works and search out your thoughts 5 because being
ministers of his kingdom, you have not judged rightly nor
kept the law of justice nor walked according to the will of
God. 6 Horribly and speedily will he appear to you, for a
most severe judgment shall be for them that bear rule. 7 For
to him that is little, mercy is granted, but the mighty shall
be mightily tormented. 8 For God will not except any man's
person, neither will he stand in awe of any man's greatness,
for he made the little and the great, and he hath equally care
of all. 9 But a greater punishment is ready for the more
mighty.

10 To you, therefore, O kings, are these my words, that
you may learn wisdom and not fall from it. 11 For they that
have kept just things justly shall be justified, and they that
have learned these things shall find what to answer. 12 Covet
ye therefore my words, and love them, and you shall have
instruction. 13 Wisdom is glorious and never fadeth away

quam marcescit sapientia et facile videtur ab his qui diligunt eam et invenitur ab his qui quaerunt illam. 14 Praeoccupat qui se concupiscunt ut illis se prior ostendat. 15 Qui de luce vigilaverit ad illam non laborabit, adsidentem enim illam foribus suis inveniet. 16 Cogitare ergo de illa sensus est consummatus, et qui vigilaverit propter illam cito erit securus. 17 Quoniam dignos se ipsa circuit quaerens, et in viis ostendit se illis hilariter et in omni providentia occurrit illis. 18 Initium enim illius verissima est disciplinae concupiscentia, 19 cura ergo disciplinae dilectio est, et dilectio custoditio legum illius est, custoditio autem legum consummatio incorruptionis est, 20 incorruptio autem facit esse proximum Deo. 21 Concupiscentia itaque sapientiae deducit ad regnum perpetuum.

22 Si ergo delectamini sedibus et sceptris, O reges populi, diligite sapientiam ut in perpetuum regnetis. 23 Diligite lumen sapientiae, omnes qui praeestis populis. 24 Quid est autem sapientia et quemadmodum facta sit referam, et non abscondam a vobis sacramenta Dei sed ab initio nativitatis investigabo et ponam in lucem scientiam illius et non praeteribo veritatem, 25 neque cum invidia tabescente iter habebo, quoniam talis homo non erit particeps sapientiae. 26 Multitudo autem sapientium sanitas est orbis terrarum, et rex sapiens populi stabilimentum est. 27 Ergo accipite disciplinam per sermones meos, et proderit vobis.

and is easily seen by them that love her and is found by them that seek her. 14 She preventeth them that covet her so that she first sheweth herself unto them. 15 He that awaketh early *to seek* her shall not labour, for he shall find her sitting at his door. 16 To think therefore upon her is perfect understanding, and he that watcheth for her shall quickly be secure. 17 For she goeth about seeking *such as* are worthy of her, and she sheweth herself to them cheerfully in the ways and meeteth them with all providence. 18 For the beginning of her is the most true desire of discipline, 19 and the care of discipline is love, and love is the keeping of her laws, and the keeping of her laws is the *firm foundation* of incorruption, 20 and incorruption bringeth near to God. 21 Therefore the desire of wisdom bringeth to the everlasting kingdom.

22 If then your delight be in thrones and sceptres, O ye kings of the people, love wisdom that you may reign for ever. 23 Love the light of wisdom, all ye that bear rule over peoples. 24 Now what wisdom is and what was her origin I will declare, and I will not hide from you the mysteries of God but will seek her out from the beginning of her birth and bring the knowledge of her to light and will not pass over the truth, 25 neither will I go with consuming envy, for such a man shall not be partaker of wisdom. 26 Now the multitude of the wise is the welfare of the whole world, and a wise king is the upholding of the people. 27 Receive therefore instruction by my words, and it shall be profitable to you.

Caput 7

Sum quidem et ego mortalis homo, similis omnibus, et ex genere terreno illius qui prior finctus est, et in ventre matris figuratus sum caro. 2 Decem mensuum tempore coagulatus in sanguine ex semine hominis et delectamento somni conveniente. 3 Et ego natus accepi communem aerem et in similiter factam decidi terram, et primam vocem, similem omnibus, emisi plorans. 4 In involumentis nutritus sum et curis magnis. 5 Nemo enim ex regibus aliud habuit nativitatis initium. 6 Unus ergo introitus est omnibus ad vitam et similis exitus. 7 Propter hoc optavi, et datus est mihi sensus, et invocavi, et venit in me spiritus sapientiae, 8 et praeposui illam regnis et sedibus et divitias nihil esse duxi in conparatione illius. 9 Nec conparavi illi lapidem pretiosum, quoniam omne aurum in conparatione illius harena est exigua, et tamquam lutum aestimabitur argentum in conspectu illius. 10 Super salutem et speciem dilexi illam et proposui pro luce habere illam, quoniam inextinguibile est lumen illius. 11 Venerunt autem mihi omnia bona pariter cum illa et innumerabilis honestas per manus illius, 12 et laetatus sum in omnibus, quoniam antecedebat me ista sapientia, et ignorabam quoniam horum omnium mater est, 13 quam sine fictione

Chapter 7

The excellence of wisdom. How she is to be found.

I myself also am a mortal man, like all *others,* and of the race of him that was first made *of the earth,* and in the womb of my mother I was fashioned to be flesh. 2 In the time of ten months I was compacted in blood of the seed of man and the pleasure of sleep concurring. 3 And being born I drew in the common air and fell upon the earth that is made alike, and the first voice which I uttered was crying, *as all others do.* 4 I was nursed in swaddling clothes and with great cares. 5 For none of the kings had any other beginning of birth. 6 *For* all men have one entrance into life and the like going out. 7 *Wherefore* I wished, and understanding was given me, and I called *upon God,* and the spirit of wisdom came upon me, 8 and I preferred her before kingdoms and thrones and esteemed riches nothing in comparison of her. 9 Neither did I compare unto her any precious stone, for all gold in comparison of her is as a little sand, and silver in respect to her shall be counted as clay. 10 I loved her above health and beauty and chose to have her instead of light, for her light cannot be put out. 11 Now all good things came to me together with her and innumerable riches through her hands, 12 and I rejoiced in all these, for this wisdom went before me, and I knew not that she was the mother of them all, 13 which I have learned without guile and communicate

didici et sine invidia communico, et honestatem illius non abscondo. 14 Infinitus enim thesaurus est hominibus quod qui usi sunt participes facti sunt amicitiae Dei, propter disciplinae dona commendati.

15 Mihi autem dedit Deus dicere ex sententia et praesumere digna horum quae mihi dantur, quoniam ipse sapientiae dux est et sapientium emendator. 16 In manu enim illius et nos et sermones nostri et omnis sapientia et operum scientia et disciplina. 17 Ipse enim mihi dedit horum quae sunt scientiam veram, ut sciam dispositionem orbis terrarum et virtutes elementorum, 18 initium et consummationem et medietatem temporum, vicissitudinum permutationes et consummationes temporum, 19 anni cursus et stellarum dispositiones, 20 naturas animalium et iras bestiarum, vim ventorum et cogitationes hominum, differentias virgultorum et virtutes radicum. 21 Et quaecumque sunt absconsa et inprovisa didici, omnium enim artifex docuit me, sapientia. 22 Est enim in illa spiritus intellectus, sanctus, unicus, multiplex, subtilis, mobilis, dissertus, incoinquinatus, certus, suavis, amans bonum, acutus, qui nihil vetat, benefaciens, 23 humanus, benignus, stabilis, certus, securus, omnem habens virtutem, omnia prospiciens et qui capiat omnes spiritus intellegibiles, mundos, subtiles.

24 Omnibus enim mobilibus mobilior est sapientia adtingit autem ubique propter suam munditiam. 25 Vapor est enim virtutis Dei et emanatio quaedam est claritatis omnipotentis Dei sincera, et ideo nihil inquinatum in illa incurrit. 26 Candor est enim lucis aeternae et speculum sine macula Dei maiestatis et imago bonitatis illius. 27 Et, cum sit una, omnia potest, et permanens in se omnia innovat et per

without envy, and her riches I hide not. 14 For she is an infinite treasure to men which they that use become the friends of God, being commended for the gift of discipline.

15 And God hath given to me to speak as I would and to conceive thoughts worthy of those things that are given me, because he is the guide of wisdom and the director of the wise. 16 For in his hand are both we and our words and all wisdom and the knowledge and skill of works. 17 For he hath given me the true knowledge of the things that are, to know the disposition of the whole world and the virtues of the elements, 18 the beginning and ending and midst of the times, the alterations of their courses and the *changes* of seasons, 19 the revolutions of the year and the dispositions of the stars, 20 the natures of living creatures and rage of wild beasts, the force of winds and reasonings of men, the diversities of plants and the virtues of roots. 21 And all such things as are hid and not foreseen I have learned, for wisdom, which is the worker of all things, taught me. 22 For in her is the spirit of understanding, holy, one, manifold, subtile, eloquent, active, undefiled, sure, sweet, loving that which is good, quick, which nothing hindereth, beneficent, 23 gentle, kind, steadfast, assured, secure, having all power, overseeing all things and containing all spirits intelligible, pure, subtile.

24 For wisdom is more active than all active things and reacheth everywhere by reason of her purity. 25 For she is a vapour of the power of God and a certain pure emanation of the glory of the almighty God, and therefore no defiled thing cometh into her. 26 For she is the brightness of eternal light and the unspotted mirror of God's majesty and the image of his goodness. 27 And, being *but* one, she can do all things, and remaining in herself the same. She reneweth all

nationes in animas sanctas se transfert. Amicos Dei et prophetas constituit. 28 Neminem enim diligit Deus nisi eum qui cum sapientia inhabitat. 29 Est enim haec speciosior sole et super omnem stellarum dispositionem. Luci conparata invenitur prior, 30 illi enim succedit nox, sapientiam autem non vincit malitia.

Caput 8

Adtingit ergo a fine usque ad finem fortiter et disponit omnia suaviter. 2 Hanc amavi et exquisivi a iuventute mea et quaesivi sponsam mihi adsumere, et amator factus sum formae illius. 3 Generositatem illius glorificat contubernium habens Dei, sed et omnium Dominus dilexit illam, 4 doctrix est enim disciplinae Dei et electrix operum illius.

5 Et si divitiae appetuntur in vita, quid sapientiae locupletius, quae omnia operatur? 6 Si autem sensus operatur, quis horum quae sunt magis quam illa est artifex? 7 Et si iustitiam quis diligit, labores huius magnas habent virtutes, sobrietatem enim et prudentiam docet et iustitiam et virtutem, quibus utilius nihil est in vita hominibus. 8 Et si multitudinem

things and through nations conveyeth herself into holy souls she maketh the friends of God and prophets. 28 For God loveth none but him that dwelleth with wisdom. 29 For she is more beautiful than the sun and above all the order of the stars. Being compared with the light she is found before it, 30 for after this cometh night, but no evil can overcome wisdom.

Chapter 8

Further praises of wisdom and her fruits.

She reacheth therefore from end to end mightily and ordereth all things sweetly. 2 Her have I loved and have sought her out from my youth and have desired to take her for my spouse, and I became a lover of her beauty. 3 She glorifieth her nobility by being conversant with God, yea and the Lord of all things hath loved her, 4 for it is she that teacheth the knowledge of God and is the chooser of his works.

5 And if riches be desired in life, what is richer than wisdom, which maketh all things? 6 And if sense do work, who is a more artful worker than she of those things that are? 7 And if a man love justice, her labours have great virtues, for she teacheth temperance and prudence and justice and fortitude, *which are such things as men can have nothing* more profitable in life. 8 And if a man desire much knowledge, she

scientiae desiderat quis, scit praeterita et de futuris aestimat; scit versutias sermonum et dissolutiones argumentorum; signa et monstra scit antequam fiant et eventus temporum et saeculorum. 9 Proposui ergo hanc adducere mihi ad convivendum, sciens quoniam communicabit mecum de bonis et erit adlocutio cogitationis et taedii mei. 10 Habebo propter hanc claritatem ad turbas et honorem apud seniores, iuvenis, 11 et acutus inveniar in iudicio et in conspectu potentium admirabilis ero, et facies principum mirabuntur me. 12 Tacentem me sustinebunt, et loquentem me respicient, et sermocinante plura manus ori suo inponent. 13 Praeterea habebo per hanc inmortalitatem et memoriam aeternam his qui post me futuri sunt relinquam.

14 Disponam populos, et nationes mihi erunt subiectae. 15 Timebunt me audientes reges horrendi. In multitudine videbor bonus et in bello fortis. 16 Intrans in domum meam, conquiescam cum illa, non enim habet amaritudinem conversatio illius nec taedium convictus ipsius, sed laetitiam et gaudium.

17 Haec cogitans apud me et commemorans in corde meo, quoniam inmortalitas est in cognatione sapientiae 18 et in amicitia illius delectatio bona et in operibus manuum illius honestas sine defectione et in certamine loquellae illius

knoweth things past and judgeth of things to come; she knoweth the subtilties of speeches and the solutions of arguments; she knoweth signs and wonders before they be done and the events of times and ages. 9 I purposed therefore to take her to me to live with me, knowing that she will communicate to me of her good things and will be a comfort in my cares and grief. 10 For her sake I shall have glory among the multitude and honour with the ancients, though I be young, 11 and I shall be found of a quick conceit in judgment and shall be admired in the sight of the mighty, and the faces of princes shall wonder at me. 12 They shall wait for me when I hold my peace, and they shall look upon me when I speak, and if I talk much they shall lay their hands on their mouths. 13 Moreover by the means of her I shall have immortality and shall leave behind me an everlasting memory to them that come after me.

14 I shall set the people in order, and nations shall be subject to me. 15 Terrible kings hearing shall be afraid of me. Among the multitude I shall be found good and valiant in war. 16 When I go into my house, I shall repose myself with her, for her conversation hath no bitterness nor her company any tediousness, but joy and gladness.

17 Thinking these things with myself and pondering them in my heart, that *to be allied to* wisdom is immortality 18 and that there is great delight in her friendship and inexhaustible riches in the works of her hands and in the exercise of

sapientia et praeclaritas in communicatione sermonum ipsius, circuibam quaerens ut mihi illam adsumerem. 19 Puer autem eram ingeniosus et sortitus sum animam bonam. 20 Et cum essem magis bonus, veni ad corpus incoinquinatum. 21 Et ut scivi quoniam aliter non possem esse continens nisi Deus det—et hoc ipsum erat sapientia, scire cuius esset hoc donum—adii Dominum et deprecatus sum illum et dixi ex totis praecordiis meis:

Caput 9

"Deus patrum meorum et Domine misericordiae, qui fecisti omnia verbo tuo 2 et sapientia tua constituisti hominem ut dominetur creaturae quae a te facta est, 3 ut disponat orbem terrarum in aequitate et iustitia et in directione cordis iudicium iudicet, 4 da mihi sedium tuarum adsistricem sapientiam, et noli me reprobare a pueris tuis. 5 Quoniam ego servus tuus et filius ancillae tuae sum, homo infirmus et exigui temporis et minor ad intellectum iudicii et legum. 6 Et si quis erit consummatus inter filios hominum, si afuerit ab illo sapientia tua, in nihilum conputabitur.

conference with her wisdom and glory in the communication of her words, I went about seeking that I might take her to myself. 19 And I was a witty child and had received a good soul. 20 And whereas I was more good, I came to a body undefiled. 21 And as I knew that I could not otherwise be continent except God gave it—and this also was *a point of wisdom*, to know whose gift it was—I went to the Lord and besought him and said with my whole heart:

Chapter 9

Solomon's prayer for wisdom.

"God of my fathers and Lord of mercy, who hast made all things with thy word 2 and by thy wisdom hast appointed man that he should have dominion over the creature that was made by thee, 3 that he should order the world according to equity and justice and execute justice with an upright heart, 4 give me wisdom that sitteth by thy throne, and cast me not off from among thy children. 5 For I am thy servant and the son of thy handmaid, a weak man and of short time and *falling short of* the understanding of judgment and laws. 6 *For* if one be perfect among the children of men, *yet* if thy wisdom be not with him, he shall be nothing regarded.

7 "Tu me elegisti regem populo tuo et iudicem filiorum tuorum et filiarum 8 et dixisti me aedificare templum in monte sancto tuo et in civitate habitationis tuae aram, similitudinem tabernaculi sancti tui quod praeparasti ab initio. 9 Et tecum sapientia tua, quae novit opera tua, quae et adfuit tunc cum orbem terrarum faceres et sciebat quid placitum esset oculis tuis et quid directum in praeceptis tuis, 10 mitte illam de sanctis caelis tuis et a sede magnitudinis tuae ut mecum sit et mecum laboret, ut sciam quid acceptum sit apud te, 11 scit enim illa omnia et intellegit, et deducet me in operibus meis sobrie et custodiet me in sua potentia.

12 "Et erunt accepta opera mea, et disponam populum tuum iuste et ero dignus sedium patris mei. 13 Quis enim hominum poterit scire consilium Dei? Aut quis poterit cogitare quid velit Deus? 14 Cogitationes enim mortalium timidae et incertae providentiae nostrae. 15 Corpus enim quod corrumpitur adgravat animam, et deprimit terrena inhabitatio sensum multa cogitantem. 16 Et difficile aestimamus quae in terra sunt, et quae in prospectu sunt invenimus cum labore. Quae in caelis sunt autem, quis investigabit? 17 Sensum autem tuum quis sciet, nisi tu dederis sapientiam et miseris sanctum spiritum tuum de altissimis, 18 et sic correctae sint semitae eorum qui in terris sunt, et quae tibi placent didicerint homines? 19 Nam per sapientiam sanati sunt, quicumque placuerunt tibi, Domine, a principio."

7 "Thou hast chosen me to be king of thy people and a judge of thy sons and daughters 8 and hast commanded me to build a temple on thy holy mount and an altar in the city of thy dwelling place, a resemblance of thy holy tabernacle which thou hast prepared from the beginning. 9 And thy wisdom with thee, which knoweth thy works, which then also was present when thou madest the world and knew what was agreeable to thy eyes and what was right in thy commandments, 10 send her out of thy holy heaven and from the throne of thy majesty that she may be with me and may labour with me, that I may know what is acceptable with thee, 11 for she knoweth and understandeth all things, and shall lead me soberly in my works and shall preserve me by her power.

12 "So shall my works be acceptable, and I shall govern thy people justly and shall be worthy of the throne of my father. 13 For who among men is he that can know the counsel of God? Or who can think what the will of God is? 14 For the thoughts of mortal men are fearful and our counsels uncertain. 15 For the corruptible body is a load upon the soul, and the earthly habitation presseth down the mind that museth upon many things. 16 And hardly do we guess aright at things that are upon earth, and with labour do we find the things that are before us. But the things that are in heaven, who shall search out? 17 And who shall know thy thought, except thou give wisdom and send thy holy spirit from above, 18 and so the ways of them that are upon earth may be corrected, and men may learn the things that please thee? 19 For by wisdom they were healed, whosoever have pleased thee, O Lord, from the beginning."

Caput 10

Haec illum qui primus finctus est a Deo, patre orbis terrarum, cum solus esset creatus custodivit, 2 et eduxit illum a delicto suo et dedit illi virtutem continendi omnia. 3 Ab hac ut recessit iniustus in ira sua, per iram homicidii fraterni deperiit. 4 Propter quem cum aqua deleret terram, iterum sanavit sapientia, per contemptibile lignum iustum gubernans. 5 Haec et in consensu nequitiae cum se nationes contulissent, scivit iustum et servavit sine querella Deo et in filii misericordia fortem custodivit. 6 Haec iustum a pereuntibus impiis liberavit fugientem descendente igne in Pentapoli, 7 quibus in testimonium nequitiae fumigabunda constat deserta terra, et incerto tempore fructus habentes arbores, et incredibilis animae memoria stans figmentum salis. 8 Sapientiam enim praetereuntes non tantum in hoc lapsi sunt, ut ignorarent bona, sed et insipientiae suae reliquerunt hominibus memoriam, ut in his quae peccaverunt nec latere potuissent.

Chapter 10

What wisdom did for Adam, Noah, Abraham, Lot, Jacob,
Joseph and the people of Israel.

She preserved him that was first formed by God, the father of the world, when he was created alone, 2 and she
brought him out of his sin and gave him power to govern all
things. 3 *But* when the unjust went away from her in his anger, he perished by the fury *wherewith he murdered his brother.*
4 For whose cause when water destroyed the earth, wisdom
healed it again, directing *the course of* the just by contemptible wood. 5 Moreover when the nations had conspired together to consent to wickedness, she knew the just and preserved him without blame to God and kept him strong
against the compassion for his son. 6 She delivered the just
man who fled from the wicked that were perishing when the
fire came down upon Pentapolis, 7 whose land for a testimony of their wickedness is desolate and smoketh to this
day, and the trees bear fruits *that ripen not,* and a standing *pillar* of salt is a monument of an incredulous soul. 8 For regarding not wisdom they did not only slip in this, that they
were ignorant of good things, but they left also unto men a
memorial of their folly, so that in the things in which they
sinned they could not *so much as* lie hid.

9 Sapientia autem hos qui se observant a doloribus liberavit. 10 Haec profugum irae fratris iustum deduxit per vias rectas et ostendit illi regnum Dei et dedit illi scientiam sanctorum, honestavit illum in laboribus et conplevit labores illius. 11 In fraude circumvenientium illum, adfuit illi et honestum illum fecit. 12 Custodivit illum ab inimicis, et a seductoribus tutavit eum et certamen forte dedit illi ut vinceret et sciret quoniam omnium potentior est sapientia. 13 Haec venditum iustum non dereliquit sed a peccatoribus liberavit illum. Descenditque cum illo in foveam. 14 Et in vinculis non dereliquit illum donec adferret illi sceptrum regni et potentiam adversus eos qui eum deprimebant et mendaces ostendit qui maculaverunt ipsum et dedit illi claritatem aeternam. 15 Haec populum iustum et semen sine querella liberavit a nationibus quae illum conprimebant.

16 Intravit in animam servi Dei et stetit contra reges horrendos in portentis et signis. 17 Et reddidit iustis mercedem laborum suorum et deduxit illos in via mirabili, et fuit illis in velamento diei et in luce stellarum nocte, 18 et transtulit illos per Mare Rubrum et transvexit illos per aquam nimiam. 19 Inimicos autem illorum demersit in mare, et ab altitudine inferorum eduxit illos. Ideo iusti tulerunt spolia impiorum. 20 Et decantaverunt, Domine, nomen sanctum tuum, et victricem manum tuam laudaverunt pariter, 21 quoniam sapientia aperuit os mutorum et linguas infantium fecit dissertas.

9 But wisdom hath delivered from sorrow them that attend upon her. 10 She conducted the just when he fled from his brother's wrath through the right ways and shewed him the kingdom of God and gave him the knowledge of the holy things, made him honourable in his labours and accomplished his labours. 11 In the deceit of them that overreached him, she stood by him and made him honourable. 12 She kept him safe from his enemies, and she defended him from seducers and gave him a strong conflict that he might overcome and know that wisdom is mightier than all. 13 She forsook not the just when he was sold but delivered him from sinners. *She* went down with him into the pit. 14 And in bands she left him not till she brought him the sceptre of the kingdom and power against those that oppressed him and shewed them to be liars that had *accused* him and gave him everlasting glory. 15 She delivered the just people and blameless seed from the nations that oppressed them.

16 She entered into the soul of the servant of God and stood against dreadful kings in wonders and signs. 17 And she rendered to the just the wages of their labours and conducted them in a wonderful way, and she was to them for a covert by day and for the light of stars by night, 18 and she brought them through the Red Sea and carried them over through a great water. 19 But their enemies she drowned in the sea, and from the depth of hell she brought them out. Therefore the just took the spoils of the wicked. 20 And they sung to thy holy name, O Lord, and they praised with one accord thy victorious hand, 21 for wisdom opened the mouth of the dumb and made the tongues of infants eloquent.

Caput 11

Direxit opera illorum in manibus prophetae sancti. 2 Iter fecerunt per deserta quae non inhabitabantur, et in locis desertis fixerunt casas. 3 Steterunt contra hostes et de inimicis se vindicaverunt. 4 Sitierunt, et invocaverunt te, et data est illis de petra altissima aqua, et requies sitis de lapide duro. 5 Per quae enim poenas passi sunt inimici illorum a defectione potus sui et in eis cum abundarent filii Israhel laetati sunt, 6 per haec cum illis deessent bene cum illis actum est. 7 Nam pro fonte quidem sempiterni fluminis humanum sanguinem dedisti iniustis. 8 Qui cum minuerentur in traductione infantum occisorum, dedisti illis abundantem aquam insperate, 9 ostendens per sitim quae tunc fuit quemadmodum tuos exaltares et adversarios illorum necares. 10 Cum enim temptati sunt et quidem cum misericordia disciplinam accipientes, scierunt quemadmodum cum ira iudicati impii tormenta paterentur. 11 Hos quidem tamquam pater monens probasti, illos autem tamquam durus rex interrogans condemnasti. 12 Absentes enim et praesentes similiter torquebantur. 13 Duplex enim illos acceperat tae-

Chapter 11

Other benefits of wisdom to the people of God.

She prospered their works in the hands of the holy prophet. 2 They went through wildernesses that were not inhabited, and in desert places they pitched their tents. 3 They stood against their enemies and revenged themselves of their adversaries. 4 They were thirsty, and they called upon thee, and water was given them out of the high rock, and a refreshment of their thirst out of the hard stone. 5 For by what things their enemies were punished when their drink failed them while the children of Israel abounded therewith and rejoiced, 6 by the same things they in their need were benefited. 7 For instead of a fountain of an ever running river thou gavest human blood to the unjust. 8 And whilst they were diminished for a manifest reproof of their murdering the infants, thou gavest to thine abundant water unlooked for, 9 shewing by the thirst that was then how thou didst exalt thine and didst kill their adversaries. 10 For when they were tried and *chastised* with mercy, they knew how the wicked were judged with wrath and tormented. 11 For thou didst admonish and try them as a father, but the others as a severe king thou didst examine and condemn. 12 For *whether* absent *or* present, they were tormented alike. 13 For a double

dium et gemitus cum memoria praeteritorum. 14 Cum enim audirent per sua tormenta bene secum agi commemorati sunt Dominum, admirantes in finem exitus. 15 Quem enim in expositione prava olim proiectum deriserunt, in finem eventus mirati sunt, non similiter iustis sitientes.

16 Pro cogitationibus autem insensatis iniquitatis illorum, quod quidam errantes colebant mutos serpentes et bestias supervacuas, inmisisti illis multitudinem mutorum animalium in vindictam 17 ut scirent quia per quae peccat quis per haec et torquetur, 18 non enim inpossibilis erat omnipotens manus tua, quae creavit orbem terrarum ex materia invisa, inmittere illis multitudinem ursorum aut audaces leones 19 aut novi generis, ira plenas, ignotas bestias, aut vaporem ignium spirantes aut odorem fumi proferentes aut horrendas ab oculis scintillas emittentes 20 quarum non solum laesura poterat illos exterminare, sed et aspectus per timorem occidere. 21 Sed et sine his uno spiritu occidi poterant, persecutionem passi ab ipsis factis suis et dispersi per spiritum virtutis tuae, sed omnia in mensura et numero et pondere disposuisti. 22 Multum enim valere tibi soli supererat semper, et virtuti brachii tui quis resistet? 23 Quoniam tamquam momentum staterae sic ante te est orbis terrarum et tamquam gutta roris antelucani quae descendit in terram.

24 Sed misereris omnium quoniam omnia potes et dissimulas peccata hominum propter paenitentiam. 25 Diligis enim omnia quae sunt et nihil odisti horum quae fecisti, nec

affliction came upon them and a groaning for the remembrance of things past. 14 For when they heard that by their punishments *the others were benefited* they remembered the Lord, wondering at the end of what was come to pass. 15 For whom they scorned before, when he was thrown out *at the time of his being wickedly exposed* to perish, him they admired in the end when they saw the event, *their thirsting being unlike to that of* the just.

10 But for the foolish devices of their iniquity, because some being deceived worshipped dumb serpents and worthless beasts, thou didst send upon them a multitude of dumb beasts for vengeance 17 that they might know that by what things a man sinneth by the same also he is tormented, 18 for thy almighty hand, which made the world of matter *without form,* was not unable to send upon them a multitude of bears or fierce lions 19 or unknown beasts of a new kind, full of rage, either breathing out a fiery vapour or sending forth a *stinking smoke* or shooting horrible sparks out of their eyes 20 whereof not only the hurt might be able to destroy them, but also the *very* sight might kill them through fear. 21 Yea and without these they might have been slain with one blast, persecuted by their own deeds and scattered by the breath of thy power, but thou hast ordered all things in measure and number and weight. 22 For great power always belonged to thee alone, and who shall resist the strength of thy arm? 23 For the whole world before thee is as the least *grain* of the balance and as a drop of the morning dew that falleth down upon the earth.

24 But thou hast mercy upon all because thou canst do all things and overlookest the sins of men for the sake of repentance. 25 For thou lovest all things that are and hatest none

enim odiens aliquid constituisti aut fecisti. 26 Quomodo autem posset aliquid permanere, nisi tu voluisses? Aut quod a te vocatum non esset conservaretur? 27 Parcis autem omnibus quoniam tua sunt, Domine, qui animas amas.

Caput 12

O quam bonus et suavis est, Domine, spiritus tuus in omnibus! 2 Ideoque hos qui exerrant partibus corripis et de quibus peccant admones et adloqueris, ut relicta malitia credant in te, Domine. 3 Illos enim antiquos inhabitatores sanctae tuae terrae quos exhorruisti, 4 quoniam odibilia tibi opera faciebant per medicamina et sacrificia iniusta 5 et filiorum suorum necatores sine misericordia et comestores viscerum hominum et devoratores sanguinis a medio sacramento tuo, 6 et auctores parentes animarum inauxiliatarum voluisti perdere per manus parentum nostrorum 7 ut dignam

of the things which thou hast made, for thou didst not appoint or make any thing hating it. 26 And how could any thing endure, if thou wouldst not? Or be preserved, if not called by thee? 27 But thou sparest all because they are thine, O Lord, who lovest souls.

Chapter 12

God's wisdom and mercy in his proceedings with the Canaanites.

O how good and sweet is thy spirit, O Lord, in all things! 2 And therefore thou chastisest them that err by *little and little* and admonishest them and speakest to them concerning the things wherein they offend, that leaving their wickedness they may believe in thee, O Lord. 3 For those ancient inhabitants of thy holy land whom thou didst abhor, 4 because they did works hateful to thee by their sorceries and wicked sacrifices 5 and those merciless murderers of their own children and eaters of men's bowels and devourers of blood from the midst of thy consecration, 6 and those parents *sacrificing with their own hands* helpless souls it was thy will to destroy by the hands of our parents 7 that the land

perciperent peregrinationem puerorum Dei quae tibi omnium carior est terra.

8 Sed et his tamquam hominibus pepercisti et misisti antecessores exercitus tui, vespas, ut illos paulatim exterminarent. 9 Non quia inpotens eras in bello subicere impios iustis aut bestiis saevis aut verbo duro simul exterminare, 10 sed partibus iudicans dabas locum paenitentiae, non ignorans quoniam nequa est natio illorum et naturalis malitia ipsorum et quoniam non poterat mutari cogitatio illorum in perpetuum. 11 Semen enim erat maledictum ab initio, nec timens aliquem veniam dabas peccatis illorum.

12 Quis enim dicet tibi, "Quid fecisti?" Aut quis stabit contra iudicium tuum? Aut quis in conspectu tuo veniet vindex iniquorum hominum? Aut quis tibi inputabit si nationes perierint quas tu fecisti? 13 Non enim est alius Deus quam tu, cuius cura est de omnibus, ut ostendas quoniam non iniuste iudicas iudicium. 14 Neque rex neque tyrannus in conspectu tuo inquirent de his quos perdidisti. 15 Cum sis ergo iustus, iuste omnia disponis, ipsum quoque qui non debet puniri condemnas exterum aestimas a tua virtute. 16 Virtus enim tua iustitiae initium est, et ob hoc quod omnium Dominus es omnibus te parcere facis. 17 Virtutem enim ostendis tu qui non crederis esse in virtute consummatus, et horum qui te nesciunt audaciam traducis. 18 Tu autem dominator virtutis cum tranquillitate iudicas et cum magna reverentia disponis nos, subest enim tibi cum voles posse.

which of all is most dear to thee might receive a worthy colony of the children of God.

8 Yet even those thou sparedst as men and didst send wasps, forerunners of thy host, to destroy them by little and little. 9 Not that thou wast unable to bring the wicked under the just by war or by cruel beasts or with one rough word to destroy them at once, 10 but executing thy judgments by degrees thou gavest them place of repentance, not being ignorant that *they were a wicked generation* and their malice natural and that their thought could never be changed. 11 For it was a cursed seed from the beginning, neither didst thou for fear of any one give pardon to their sins.

12 For who shall say to thee, "What hast thou done?" Or who shall withstand thy judgment? Or who shall come before thee to be a revenger of wicked men? Or who shall accuse thee if the nations perish which thou hast made? 13 For there is no other God but thou, who hast care of all, that thou shouldst shew that thou dost not give judgment unjustly. 14 Neither shall king nor tyrant in thy sight inquire about them whom thou hast destroyed. 15 For so much then as thou art just, thou orderest all things justly, *thinking* it not agreeable to thy power to condemn him who deserveth not to be punished. 16 For thy power is the beginning of justice, and because thou art Lord of all thou makest thyself gracious to all. 17 For thou shewest thy power *when men will not believe thee* to be absolute in power, and thou convincest the boldness of them that know thee not. 18 But thou being master of power judgest with tranquillity and with great favour disposest of us, for thy power is at hand when thou wilt.

19 Docuisti autem populum tuum per talia opera quoniam oportet iustum esse et humanum et bonae spei fecisti filios tuos quoniam iudicans das locum in peccatis paenitentiae. 20 Si enim inimicos servorum tuorum et debitos morti cum tanta cruciasti adtentione, dans tempus et locum per quae possent mutari a malitia, 21 cum quanta diligentia iudicasti filios tuos quorum parentibus iuramenta et conventiones dedisti bonarum promissionum? 22 Cum ergo nobis disciplinam das, inimicos nostros multipliciter flagellas ut bonitatem tuam cogitemus iudicantes et cum de nobis iudicatur speremus misericordiam tuam. 23 Unde et illis qui in vita sua insensate et iniuste vixerunt per haec quae coluerunt dedisti summa tormenta. 24 Etenim in erroris via diutius erraverunt, deos aestimantes haec quae in animalibus sunt supervacua, infantum insensatorum more viventes. 25 Propter hoc tamquam pueris insensatis iudicium in derisum dedisti. 26 Qui autem ludibriis et increpationibus non correcti sunt dignum Dei iudicium experti sunt. 27 In quibus enim patientes indignabantur per haec quos putabant deos, in ipsis cum exterminarentur videntes illum quem olim negabant se nosse Deum verum agnoverunt, propter quod et finis condemnationis illis veniet.

19 But thou hast taught thy people by such works that they must be just and humane and hast made thy children to be of a good hope because in judging thou givest place for repentance for sins. 20 For if thou didst punish the enemies of thy servants and that deserved to die with so great deliberation, giving them time and place whereby they might be changed from their wickedness, 21 with what circumspection hast thou judged thy own children to whose parents thou hast sworn and made covenants of good promises? 22 Therefore whereas thou chastisest us, thou scourgest our enemies very many ways to the end that when we judge we may think on thy goodness and when we are judged we may hope for thy mercy. 23 Wherefore thou hast also greatly tormented them who in their life have lived foolishly and unjustly by the same things which they worshipped. 24 For they went astray for a long time in the *ways* of error, holding those things for gods which are the most worthless among beasts, living after the manner of children without understanding. 25 Therefore thou hast sent a judgment upon them as senseless children to mock them. 26 But they that were not amended by mockeries and reprehensions experienced the worthy judgment of God. 27 For *seeing with indignation that they suffered* by those *very* things which they took for gods, when they were destroyed by the same they acknowledged him the true God whom in time past they denied that they knew, for which cause the end also of their condemnation *came* upon them.

Caput 13

Vani sunt autem omnes homines in quibus non subest scientia Dei et de his quae videntur bona non potuerunt intellegere eum qui est, neque operibus adtendentes agnoverunt quis esset artifex 2 sed aut ignem aut spiritum aut citatum aerem aut gyrum stellarum aut nimiam aquam aut solem et lunam rectores orbis terrarum deos putaverunt, 3 quorum si specie, delectati, deos putaverunt, sciant quanto his dominator eorum speciosior est, speciei enim generator haec omnia constituit. 4 Aut si virtutem et opera eorum mirati sunt, intellegant ab ipsis quoniam qui haec constituit fortior est illis, 5 a magnitudine enim speciei et creaturae cognoscibiliter poterit horum creator videri.

6 Sed tamen adhuc in his minor est querella, et hii enim fortassis errant, Deum quaerentes et volentes invenire. 7 Etenim cum in operibus illius conversentur inquirunt, et persuasum habent quoniam bona sunt quae videntur. 8 Iterum autem nec his debet ignosci, 9 si enim tantum potuerunt scire ut possent aestimare saeculum, quomodo huius

Chapter 13

Idolaters are inexcusable, and those most of all that worship
for gods the works of the hands of men.

But all men are vain in whom there is not the knowledge
of God and who by these *good things* that are seen could not
understand him that is, neither by attending to the works
have acknowledged who was the workman 2 but have imagined either the fire or the wind or the swift air or the circle
of the stars or the great water or the sun and moon to be the
gods that rule the world, 3 with whose beauty if they, being
delighted, took them to be gods, let them know how much
the Lord of them is more beautiful than they, for the first
author of beauty made all those things. 4 Or if they admired
their power and their effects, let them understand by them
that he that made them is mightier than they, 5 for by the
greatness of the beauty and of the creature the creator of
them may be seen so as to be known thereby.

6 But yet *as to these they are less to be blamed,* for *they* perhaps err, seeking God and desirous to find him. 7 For being
conversant among his works they search, and they are per-
suaded that the things are good which are seen. 8 But then
again they are not to be pardoned, 9 for if they were able to
know so much as to make a judgment of the world, how did

Dominum non facilius invenerunt? 10 Infelices autem sunt, et inter mortuos spes illorum est qui appellaverunt deos opera manuum hominum, aurum et argentum, artis inventionem et similitudines animalium aut lapidem inutilem, opus manus antiquae. 11 Aut si quis artifex, faber, de silva lignum rectum secaverit et huius docte eradat omnem corticem et arte sua usus diligenter fabricet vas utile in conversatione vitae 12 reliquias autem eius operis ad praeparationem escae abutatur 13 et reliquum horum quod ad nullos usus facit, lignum curvum et verticibus plenum, sculpat diligenter per vacuitatem suam et per scientiam artis suae figuret illud et adsimilet illud imagini hominis 14 aut alicui ex animalibus illud conparet, perliniens rubrica et rubicundum faciens fuco colorem illius et omnem maculam quae in illo est perliniens 15 et faciat ei dignam habitationem et in pariete ponens illud et confirmans ferro, 16 ne forte cadat prospiciens illi, sciens quoniam non potest se adiuvare, imago enim est et opus est illi adiutorium, 17 et de substantia sua et filiis suis et nuptiis, votum faciens, inquirit; non erubescit loqui cum illo qui sine anima est, 18 et pro sanitate quidem infirmum deprecatur et pro vita mortuum rogat et in adiutorium inutilem invocat, 19 et pro itinere petit ab hoc qui ambulare non potest, et de adquirendo et de operando et de omnium rerum eventu petit ab eo qui in omnibus est inutilis.

they not more easily find out the Lord thereof? 10 But un-happy are they, and their hope is among the dead who have called gods the works of the hands of men, gold and silver, the inventions of art and the resemblances of beasts or an unprofitable stone, the work of an ancient hand. 11 Or if an artist, a carpenter, hath cut down a tree *proper for his use* in the wood and skillfully taken off all the bark thereof and with his art diligently formeth a vessel profitable for the common uses of life 12 and useth the chips of his work to dress his meat 13 and *taking* what was left thereof which is good for nothing, being a crooked piece of wood and full of knots, carveth it diligently *when he hath nothing else to do* and by the skill of his art fashioneth it and maketh it like the im-age of a man 14 or *the resemblance of* some beast, laying it over with vermilion and painting it red and covering every spot that is in it 15 and maketh a convenient dwelling place for it and setting it in a wall and fastening it with iron, 16 provid-ing for it lest it should fall, knowing that it is unable to help itself, for it is an image and hath need of help, 17 and then *maketh prayer* to it, *inquiring* concerning his substance and his children or his marriage, *and* he is not ashamed to speak to that which hath no life, 18 and for health he maketh sup-plication to the weak and for life prayeth to that which is dead and for help calleth upon that which is unprofitable, 19 and for a *good* journey he petitioneth him that cannot walk, and for getting and for working and for the event of all things he asketh him that is unable to do any thing.

Caput 14

Iterum alius, navigare cogitans et per feros fluctus incipiens iter facere, ligno portante se fragilius lignum invocat. 2 Illud enim cupiditas adquirendi excogitavit, et artifex sapientia fabricavit sua. 3 Tua autem, pater, gubernat providentia, quoniam dedisti et in mari viam et inter fluctus semitam firmissimam, 4 ostendens quoniam potes ex omnibus salvare, etiam si sine arte aliquis adeat mare. 5 Sed ut non esset vacua sapientiae tuae opera, propter hoc etiam et exiguo ligno credunt homines animas suas et transeuntes mare per ratem liberati sunt. 6 Sed et ab initio cum perirent superbi gigantes, spes orbis terrarum ad ratem confugiens remisit saeculo semen nativitatis quae manu tua erat gubernata. 7 Benedictum est enim lignum per quod fit iustitia. 8 Per manus autem quod fit idolum maledictum, et ipsum et qui fecit illud, quia ille quidem operatus est, illud autem cum esset fragile deus cognominatus est.

9 Similiter autem odio sunt Deo impius et impietas eius, 10 etenim quod factum est cum illo qui fecit tormenta patietur. 11 Propter hoc et in idolis Nationum non erit respectus quoniam creaturae Dei in odium factae sunt et in temptationem animis hominum et in muscipulum pedibus insipientium. 12 Initium enim fornicationis est exquisitio idolorum, et adinventio illorum corruptio vitae est. 13 Neque

Chapter 14

The beginning of worshipping idols and the effects thereof.

Again another, designing to sail and beginning to make his voyage through the raging waves, calleth upon a piece of wood more frail than the wood that carrieth him. 2 For this the desire of gain devised, and the workman built it by his skill. 3 But thy providence, O Father, governeth it, for thou hast made a way even in the sea and a most sure path among the waves, 4 shewing that thou art able to save out of all things, yea though a man went to sea without art. 5 But that the works of thy wisdom might not be idle, therefore men also trust their lives even to a little wood and passing over the sea by ship are saved. 6 *And* from the beginning also when the proud giants perished, the hope of the world fleeing to a vessel which was governed by thy hand left to the world seed of generation. 7 For blessed is the wood by which justice cometh. 8 But the idol that is made by hands is cursed, as well it as he that made it, he because *he* made it, and it *because* being frail it is called a god.

9 But to God the wicked and his wickedness are hateful alike, 10 for that which is made together with him that made it shall suffer torments. 11 Therefore there shall be no respect had even to the idols of the Gentiles because the creatures of God are turned to an abomination and a temptation to the souls of men and a snare to the feet of the unwise. 12 For the beginning of fornication is the devising of idols, and the invention of them is the corruption of life. 13 For

enim erant ab initio, neque erunt in perpetuum. 14 Supervacuitas enim hominum haec advenit in orbem terrarum, et ideo brevis illorum finis inventus est.

15 Acerbo enim luctu dolens pater cito sibi filii rapti fecit imaginem et illum, qui tunc homo mortuus fuerat nunc tamquam deum colere coepit et constituit inter servos suos sacra et sacrificia. 16 Deinde interveniente tempore, convalescente iniqua consuetudine, hic error tamquam lex custodita est, et tyrannorum imperio colebantur figmenta. 17 Et hos quos in palam honorare non poterant homines propter quod longe essent, e longinquo figura illorum adlata evidentem imaginem regis quem honorare volebant fecerunt, ut illum qui aberat tamquam praesentem colerent sua sollicitudine. 18 Provexit autem ad horum culturam et hos qui ignorabant artificis eximia diligentia, 19 ille enim volens placere illi qui se adsumpsit elaboravit arte sua ut similitudinem in melius figuraret. 20 Multitudo autem hominum, abducta per speciem operis, eum qui ante modicum tamquam homo honoratus fuerat nunc deum existimaverunt. 21 Et haec fuit vitae humanae deceptio, quoniam aut adfectui aut regibus deservientes homines incommunicabile nomen lapidibus et lignis inposuerunt.

22 Et non sufficerat errasse eos circa Dei scientiam, sed et in magno viventes inscientiae bello, tot et tam magna mala pacem appellant, 23 aut enim filios suos sacrificantes aut obscura sacrificia facientes aut insaniae plenas vigilias habentes, 24 neque vitam neque nuptias mundas iam custodiunt, sed alius alium per invidiam occidit aut adulterans contristat, 25 et omnia commixta sunt, sanguis, homicidium,

neither were they from the beginning, neither shall they be for ever. 14 For *by the vanity of men they* came into the world, and therefore *they shall be found to come shortly to an end.*

15 For a father being afflicted with bitter grief made to himself the image of his son who was quickly taken away, and him who then had died *as* a man he began now to worship as a god and appointed him rites and sacrifices among his servants. 16 Then in process of time, wicked custom prevailing, this error was kept as a law, and statues were worshipped by the commandment of tyrants. 17 And those whom men could not honour in presence because they dwelt far off, they brought their resemblance from afar and made an express image of the king whom they had a mind to honour, that by *this* their diligence they might honour as present him that was absent. 18 And to worshipping of these the singular diligence also of the artificer helped to set forward the ignorant, 19 for he being willing to please him that employed him laboured with all his art to make the resemblance in the best manner. 20 And the multitude of men, carried away by the beauty of the work, took him now for a god that a little before was *but* honoured as a man. 21 And this was the occasion of deceiving human life, for men serving either their affection or their kings gave the incommunicable name to stones and wood.

22 And it was not enough for them to err about the knowledge of God, but whereas they lived in a great war of ignorance, they call so many and so great evils peace, 23 for either they sacrifice their own children or use hidden sacrifices or keep watches full of madness, 24 so that now they neither keep life nor marriage undefiled, but one killeth another through envy or grieveth him by adultery, 25 and all things are mingled together, blood, murder, theft and dissimula-

furtum et fictio, corruptio et infidelitas, turbatio et periurium, tumultus bonorum, 26 Dei inmemoratio, animarum inquinatio, nativitatis inmutatio, nuptiarum inconstantia, inordinatio moechiae et inpudicitia.

27 Infandorum enim idolorum cultura omnis mali causa est et initium et finis. 28 Aut enim dum laetantur insaniunt, aut certe vaticinantur falsa, aut vivunt iniuste aut periurant cito. 29 Dum enim confidunt in idolis quae sunt sine anima, male iurantes, noceri se non sperant. 30 Utraque ergo illis evenient digne: quoniam male senserunt de Deo, adtendentes idolis, et iniuste iuraverunt, in dolo contemnentes iustitiam. 31 Non enim iuratorum est virtus, sed peccantium poena perambulat semper in iniustorum praevaricationem.

Caput 15

Tu autem, Deus noster, suavis et verus es, patiens et in misericordia disponens omnia. 2 Etenim si peccaverimus, tui sumus, scientes magnitudinem tuam, et si non peccaverimus, scimus quoniam apud te sumus conputati. 3 Nosse

tion, corruption and unfaithfulness, *tumults* and perjury, disquieting of the good, 26 forgetfulness of God, defiling of souls, changing of nature, disorder in marriage and the irregularity of adultery and uncleanness.

27 For the worship of abominable idols is the cause and the beginning and end of all evil. 28 For either they are mad when they are merry, *or* they prophesy lies, or they live unjustly or easily forswear themselves. 29 For whilst they trust in idols which are without life, though they swear amiss, they *look* not to be hurt. 30 *But for both these things they shall be justly punished:* because they have thought not well of God, giving heed to idols, and have sworn unjustly, in guile despising justice. 31 For it is not the power of them by whom they swear, but the *just vengeance* of sinners always *punisheth* the transgression of the unjust.

Chapter 15

The servants of God praise him who hath delivered them from idolatry, condemning both the makers and the worshippers of idols.

But thou, our God, art gracious and true, patient and ordering all things in mercy. 2 For if we sin, we are thine, knowing thy greatness, and if we sin not, we know that we are counted with thee. 3 For to know thee is perfect justice, and

enim te consummata iustitia est, et scire iustitiam et virtutem tuam radix est inmortalitatis. 4 Non enim in errorem induxit nos hominum malae artis excogitatio, nec umbra picturae, labor sine fructu, effigies sculpta per varios colores 5 cuius aspectus insensato dat concupiscentiam, et diligit mortuae imaginis effigiem sine anima. 6 Malorum amatores digni qui spem in talibus habeant, et qui faciunt illos et qui diligunt et qui colunt. 7 Sed et figulus mollem terram premens, laboriose fingit ad usus nostros unumquodque vas, et de eodem luto fingit quae munda sunt in usum vasa et similiter quae his sunt contraria, horum autem vasorum qui sit usus iudex est figulus. 8 Et cum labore vano deum de eodem fingit luto, ille qui paulo ante de terra factus fuerat et post pusillum se ducit unde acceptus est repetitus debitum animae quem habebat. 9 Sed est illi cura non quia laboraturus est nec quoniam brevis illi vita est, sed concertatur aurificibus et argentariis, sed et aerarios imitatur et gloriam praefert quoniam res supervacuas fingit, 10 cinis est enim cor eius et terra supervacua spes illius et luto vilior vita illius 11 quoniam ignoravit qui se finxit et qui inspiravit illi animam quae operatur et qui insuflavit ei spiritum vitalem. 12 Sed et aestimaverunt ludum esse vitam nostram et conversationem vitae conpositam ad lucrum et oportere undecumque, etiam ex malo, adquirere, 13 hic enim super omnes scit se delinquere, qui ex terrae materia fragilia vasa et sculptilia fingit.

14 Omnes enim insipientes et infelices supra modum animae superbi sunt inimici populi tui et imperantes illi, 15 quoniam omnia idola nationum aestimaverunt deos quibus

to know thy justice and thy power is the root of immortality. 4 For the invention of mischievous men hath not deceived us, nor the shadow of a picture, a fruitless labour, a graven figure with divers colours 5 the sight whereof *enticeth the fool to lust after it,* and he loveth the lifeless figure of a dead image. 6 The lovers of evil things deserve to have *no better things to trust in,* both they that make them and they that love them and they that worship them. 7 The potter also tempering soft earth, with labour fashioneth every vessel for our service, and of the same clay he maketh *both vessels that are for clean uses and likewise such as serve to* the contrary, but what is the use of these vessels the potter is the judge. 8 And of the same clay by a vain labour he maketh a god, he who a little before was made of earth *himself* and a little after returneth *to the same* out of which he was taken *when his life which was lent him shall be called for again.* 9 But his care is not that he shall labour nor that his life is short, but he striveth with the goldsmiths and silversmiths, and he endeavoureth to do like the workers in brass and counteth it a glory to make vain things, 10 for his heart is ashes and his hope vain earth and his life more base than clay 11 forasmuch as he knew not his maker and him that inspired into him the soul that worketh and that breathed into him a living spirit. 12 Yea and they have counted our life a pastime and the business of life to be gain and that we must be getting every way, even out of evil, 13 for that man knoweth that he offendeth above all *others,* who of earthly matter maketh brittle vessels and graven gods.

14 *But* all the enemies of thy people *that hold them in subjection* are foolish and unhappy and proud beyond *measure,* 15 for they have esteemed all the idols of the heathens for

neque oculorum usus est ad videndum neque nares ad perci-
piendum spiritum neque aures ad audiendum nec digiti manuum ad tractandum, sed et pedes eorum, pigri ad ambulan-
dum. 16 Homo enim fecit illos, et qui spiritum mutuatus est
is finxit illos. Nemo enim sibi similem homo poterit deum
fingere. 17 Cum sit enim mortalis mortuum fingit manibus
iniquis. Melior est enim ipse his quos colit quia ipse quidem
vixit, cum esset mortalis, illi autem numquam. 18 Sed et animalia miserrima colunt, insensata enim conparata his illis
sunt deteriora. 19 Sed nec aspectu aliquis ex his animalibus
bona potest conspicere, effugerunt autem Dei laudem et
benedictionem eius.

Caput 16

Propter haec et per his similia passi sunt digne tormenta
et per multitudinem bestiarum exterminati sunt. 2 Pro quibus tormentis, bene disposuisti populum tuum quibus dedisti concupiscentiam delectamenti sui, novum saporem,
escam parans eis ortygometram, 3 ut illi quidem concupis-
centes escam propter ea quae illis ostensa et missa sunt

gods which neither have the use of eyes to see nor noses to draw breath nor ears to hear nor fingers of hands to handle, and as for their feet, they are slow to walk. 16 For man made them, and he that borroweth his own breath fashioned them. For no man can make a god like to himself. 17 For being mortal himself he formeth a dead thing with his wicked hands. For he is better than they whom he worshippeth because he indeed hath lived, though he were mortal, but they never. 18 Moreover they worship also the vilest creatures, *but* things without sense compared to these are worse than they. 19 Yea neither by sight can any man see good of these beasts, but they have fled from the praise of God and from his blessing.

Chapter 16

God's different dealings with the Egyptians and with his own people.

For these things and by the like things to these they were worthily punished and were destroyed by a multitude of beasts. 2 Instead of which punishment, *dealing* well with thy people thou gavest *them* their desire of delicious food, of a new taste, preparing for them quails for their meat, 3 to the end that they indeed desiring food by means of those things that were shewn and sent among them might *loathe* even

etiam a necessaria concupiscentia averterentur. Hi autem in brevi inopes facti novam gustaverunt escam. 4 Oportebat enim illis quidem sine excusatione supervenire interitum exercentibus tyrannidem, his autem tantum ostendere quemadmodum inimici illorum exterminabantur. 5 Etenim cum supervenit illis saeva bestiarum ira, morsibus perversarum colubrarum exterminabantur. 6 Sed non in perpetuum permansit ira tua, sed ad correptionem in brevi turbati sunt, signum habentes salutis ad commemorationem mandati legis tuae. 7 Qui enim conversus est non per hoc quod videbat sanabatur, sed per te, omnium salvatorem.

8 In hoc autem ostendisti inimicis nostris quia tu es qui liberas ab omni malo. 9 Illos enim lucustarum et muscarum occiderunt morsus, et non est inventa sanitas animae illorum quia digni erant ab huiusmodi exterminari. 10 Filios autem tuos nec draconum venenatorum vicerunt dentes, misericordia enim tua adveniens sanabat illos. 11 In memoria enim sermonum tuorum examinabantur et velociter salvabantur ne in altam incidentes oblivionem non possent tuo uti adiutorio. 12 Etenim neque herba neque malagma sanavit illos, sed tuus, Domine, sermo, qui sanat omnia. 13 Tu es enim, Domine, qui vitae et mortis habes potestatem et deducis ad portas mortis et reducis.

14 Homo autem occidit quidem per malitiam, et cum exierit spiritus, non revertetur, nec revocabit animam quae recepta est, 15 sed tuam manum effugere inpossibile est. 16 Negantes enim nosse te impii per fortitudinem brachii tui

that which was necessary to satisfy their desire. But these after suffering want for a short time tasted a new meat. 4 For it was requisite that *inevitable* destruction should come upon them that exercised tyranny, but to these it should only be shewn how their enemies were destroyed. 5 For when the fierce rage of beasts came upon these, they were destroyed with the bitings of crooked serpents. 6 But thy wrath endured not for ever, but they were troubled for a short time for their correction, having a sign of salvation to put them in remembrance of the commandment of thy law. 7 For he that turned to it was not healed by that which he saw, but by thee, the saviour of all.

8 And in this thou didst shew to our enemies that thou art he who deliverest from all evil. 9 For the bitings of locusts and of flies killed them, and there was found no remedy for their life because they were worthy to be destroyed by such things. 10 But not even the teeth of venomous serpents overcame thy children, for thy mercy came and healed them. 11 For they were examined for the remembrance of thy words and were quickly healed lest falling into deep forgetfulness they might not be able to use thy help. 12 For it was neither herb nor mollifying plaster that healed them, but thy word, O Lord, which healeth all things. 13 For it is thou, O Lord, that hast power of life and death and leadest down to the gates of death and bringest back again.

14 A man indeed killeth through malice, and when the spirit is gone forth, it shall not return, neither shall he call back the soul that is received, 15 but it is impossible to escape thy hand. 16 For the wicked that denied to know thee were scourged by the strength of thy arm, being persecuted

flagellati sunt, novis aquis et grandinibus et pluviis persecutionem passi et per ignem consumpti. 17 Quod enim mirabile erat, in aqua, quae omnia extinguit, plus ignis valebat,
vindex est enim orbis iustorum. 18 Quodam enim tempore,
mansuetabatur ignis ne conburerentur quae ad impios missa
erant animalia sed ut ipsi videntes scirent quoniam Dei iudicio patiuntur persecutionem. 19 Et quodam tempore in aqua,
super virtutem, ignis ardebat undique ut iniquae terrae nationem exterminaret. 20 Pro quibus angelorum esca nutristi
populum tuum et paratum panem e caelo praestitisti illis
sine labore, omne delectamentum in se habentem et omnis
saporis suavitatem. 21 Substantia enim tua dulcedinem tuam
quam in filios habes ostendebat, et serviens uniuscuiusque voluntati ad quod quisque volebat convertebatur. 22 Nix
autem et glacies sustinebant vim ignis et non tabescebant,
ut scirent quoniam fructus inimicorum exterminabat ignis
ardens in grandine et pluvia coruscans. 23 Hoc autem iterum
ut nutrirentur iusti etiam suae virtutis oblitus est, 24 creatura enim tibi, Factori, deserviens excandescit in tormentum adversus iniustos et lenior fit ad benefaciendum pro his
qui in te confidunt. 25 Propter hoc et tunc in omnia transfi-
gurata omnium nutrici gratiae tuae deserviebant ad voluntatem horum qui a te desiderabant 26 ut scirent filii tui, quos
dilexisti, Domine, quoniam non nativitatis fructus pascunt
homines, sed sermo tuus hos qui in te crediderint conservat,
27 quod enim ab igni non poterat exterminari, statim ab exi-

by strange waters and hail and rain and consumed by fire. 17 *And,* which was wonderful, in water, which extinguisheth all things, the fire had more force, for the world fighteth for the just. 18 For at one time, the fire was mitigated that the beasts which were sent against the wicked might not be burned but that they might see and perceive that they were persecuted by the judgment of God. 19 And at another time the fire, above its own power, burned in the midst of water to destroy the *fruits* of a wicked land. 20 Instead of which things thou didst feed thy people with the food of angels and gavest them bread from heaven prepared without labour, having in it all that is delicious and the sweetness of every taste. 21 For thy sustenance shewed thy sweetness *to* thy children, and serving every man's will it was turned to what every man liked. 22 But snow and ice endured the force of fire and melted not, that they might know that fire burning in the hail and flashing in the rain destroyed the fruits of the enemies. 23 But this same again that the just might be nourished did even forget its own strength, 24 for the creature serving thee, the Creator, is made fierce against the unjust for their punishment and abateth its strength for the benefit of them that trust in thee. 25 Therefore even then *it was* transformed into all things and *was* obedient to thy grace that nourisheth all according to the will of them that desired it of thee 26 that thy children, O Lord, whom thou lovedst, might know that it is not the growing of fruits that nourisheth men, but thy word preserveth them that believe in thee, 27 for that which could not be destroyed by

guo radio solis calefactum tabescebat, 28 ut notum omnibus esset quoniam oportet praevenire solem ad benedictionem tuam et ad orientem lucis tibi adorare. 29 Ingrati enim fides tamquam hibernalis glacies tabescet et disperiet tamquam aqua supervacua.

Caput 17

Magna enim sunt iudicia tua, Domine, et inenarrabilia verba tua. Propter hoc indisciplinatae animae erraverunt. 2 Dum enim persuasum habent iniqui posse dominari nationi sanctae, vinculis tenebrarum et longae noctis conpediti, inclusi sub tectis, fugitivi perpetuae providentiae iacuerunt. 3 Et dum putant se latere in obscuris peccatis, tenebroso oblivionis velamento dispersi sunt, paventes horrende et cum admiratione nimia perturbati. 4 Neque enim quae continebat illos spelunca sine timore custodiebat, quoniam sonitus descendens perturbabat illos, et personae tristes illis apparentes pavorem illis praestabant. 5 Et ignis quidem nulla vis poterat illis lumen praebere, nec siderum limpidae flammae inluminare poterant illam noctem horrendam. 6 Apparebat autem illis subitaneus ignis, timore

fire, being warmed with a little sunbeam presently melted away, 28 that it might be known to all that we ought to prevent the sun to bless thee and adore thee at the dawning of the light. 29 For the *hope* of the unthankful shall melt away as the winter's ice and shall run off as unprofitable water.

Chapter 17

The Egyptian darkness.

For thy judgments, O Lord, are great, and thy words cannot be expressed. Therefore undisciplined souls have erred. 2 For while the wicked thought to be able to have dominion over the holy nation, they *themselves* being fettered with the bonds of darkness and a long night, shut up in their houses, lay *there* exiled from the eternal providence. 3 And while they thought to lie hid in their obscure sins, they were scattered under a dark veil of forgetfulness, being horribly afraid and troubled with exceeding great astonishment. 4 For neither did the den that held them keep them from fear, for noises coming down troubled them, and sad visions appearing to them affrighted them. 5 And no power of fire could give them light, neither could the bright flames of the stars enlighten that horrible night. 6 But there appeared to them

plenus, et timore percussi illius quae non videbatur faciei aestimabant deteriora esse quae videbantur. 7 Et magicae artis adpositi erant derisus, et sapientiae gloriae correptio cum contumelia. 8 Illi enim qui promittebant timores et perturbationes expellere se ab anima languente hi cum derisu pleni timore languebant. 9 Nam et si nihil illos ex monstris perturbabat, transitu animalium et serpentium sibilatione commoti, tremebundi peribant et aerem quem nulla ratione quis effugere posset negantes se videre.

10 Cum sit enim timida nequitia, dat testimonium condemnata, semper enim praesumit saeva conturbata conscientia. 11 Nihil enim est timor nisi praesumptionis adiutorium proditio cogitationis auxiliorum. 12 Et dum ab intro minor est expectatio, maiorem conputat inscientiam eius causae de qua tormentum praestat.

13 Illi autem qui inpotentem vere noctem et ab infimis et ab altissimis inferis supervenientem eundem somnum dormientes 14 aliquando monstrorum exagitabantur timore, aliquando animae deficiebant traductione, subitaneus enim illis et insperatus timor supervenerat. 15 Deinde si quisquam ex illis decidisset, custodiebatur in carcere sine ferro reclusus. 16 Si enim rusticus quis erat aut pastor aut agri laborum operarius praeoccupatus esset, ineffugibilem sustinebat necessitatem. 17 Una enim catena tenebrarum omnes erant conligati. Sive spiritus sibilans aut inter spissos arborum ramos avium sonus suavis aut vis aquae decurrentis nimium 18 aut sonus validus praecipitatarum petrarum aut ludentium animalium cursus invisus aut mugientium valida bes-

a sudden fire, very dreadful, and being struck with the fear of that face which was not seen they thought the things which they saw to be worse. 7 And *the delusions* of their magic art *were put down,* and their boasting of wisdom *was reproachfully rebuked.* 8 For they who promised to drive away fears and troubles from a sick soul were sick *themselves of a fear worthy to be laughed at.* 9 For though no terrible thing disturbed them, yet being scared with the passing by of beasts and hissing of serpents, they died for fear and denying that they saw the air which *could* by no means *be avoided.*

10 For whereas wickedness is fearful, it beareth witness of its condemnation, for a troubled conscience always forecasteth grievous things. 11 For fear is nothing else but a *yielding up* of the succours from thought. 12 And while there is less expectation from within, the greater doth it count the ignorance of that cause which bringeth the torment.

13 But they that during that night *in which nothing could be done* and which came upon them from the lowest and deepest hell slept the same sleep 14 were sometimes molested with the fear of monsters, sometimes fainted away, their soul failing them, for a sudden and unlooked for fear was come upon them. 15 Moreover if any of them had fallen down, he was kept shut up in prison without irons. 16 For if any one were a husbandman or a shepherd or a labourer in the field *and* was suddenly overtaken, he endured a necessity from which he could not fly. 17 For they were all bound together with one chain of darkness. Whether it were a whistling wind or the melodious voice of birds among the *spreading* branches of trees or a *fall* of water running down *with violence* 18 or the mighty noise of stones tumbling down or the running that could not be seen of beasts playing together

tiarum vox aut resonans de altissimis montibus echo, deficientes faciebant illos prae timore. 19 Omnis enim orbis terrarum limpido inluminabatur lumine, et non inpeditis operibus continebatur, 20 solis autem illis superposita erat gravis nox, imago tenebrarum quae superventura illis. Erat ipsi ergo sibi erant graviores tenebris.

Caput 18

Sanctis autem tuis maxima erat lux, et horum quidem vocem audiebant sed figuram non videbant. Et quia non et ipsi per eadem passi erant magnificabant te. 2 Et qui ante laesi erant quoniam non laedebantur gratias agebant et ut esset differentia donum petebant. 3 Propter quod ignis ardentem columnam ducem habuerunt ignotae viae, et solem sine laesura boni hospitii praestitisti.

4 Digni quidem illi carere luce et pati carcerem tenebrarum, qui inclusos custodiebant filios tuos per quos incipie-

or the *roaring* voice of *wild* beasts or a rebounding echo from the highest mountains, these things made them to swoon for fear. 19 For the whole world was enlightened with a clear light, and none were hindered in their labours, 20 but over them only was spread a heavy night, an image of that darkness which was to come upon them. But they were to themselves more grievous than the darkness.

Chapter 18

The slaughter of the firstborn in Egypt. The efficacy of Aaron's intercession in the sedition on occasion of Korah.

But thy saints had a very great light, and they heard their voice indeed but did not see their shape. And because they also did not suffer *the* same things they glorified thee. 2 And they that before had been wronged gave thanks because they were not hurt *now* and asked *this* gift that there might be a difference. 3 Therefore they received a burning pillar of fire for a guide of the way which they knew not, and thou gavest them a harmless sun of a good entertainment.

4 *The others* indeed were worthy to be deprived of light and imprisoned in darkness, who kept thy children shut up by whom the pure light of the law *was* to be given to the

bat incorruptum legis lumen saeculo dari. 5 Cum cogitarent iustorum occidere infantes, et uno exposito filio et liberato in traductionem illorum, multitudinem filiorum abstulisti et pariter illos perdidisti in aquam validam. 6 Illa enim nox ante cognita est a patribus nostris ut vere scientes quibus iuramentis crediderunt animaequiores essent. 7 Suscepta est autem a populo tuo sanitas quidem iustorum iniustorum autem exterminatio. 8 Sicut enim laesisti adversarios, sic et nos provocans magnificasti. 9 Absconse enim sacrificabant iusti pueri bonorum, et iustitiae legem in concordia disposuerunt similiter et bona et mala recepturos iustos, patrum iam decantantes laudes.

10 Resonabat autem inconveniens inimicorum vox, et flebilis audiebatur planctus ploratorum infantium. 11 Simili autem poena servus cum domino adflictus, et popularis homo regi similia passus. 12 Similiter ergo omnes uno nomine mortis mortuos habebant innumerabiles. Nec enim ad sepeliendum vivi sufficiebant, quoniam uno momento quae erat praeclarior natio illorum exterminata est. 13 De omnibus enim non credentes propter veneficia, tunc vero primum cum fuit exterminium primogenitorum spoponderunt populum Dei esse. 14 Cum enim quietum silentium contineret omnia et nox in suo cursu medium iter haberet, 15 omnipotens sermo tuus de caelo a regalibus sedibus durus debellator in mediam exterminii terram prosilivit, 16 gladius acutus insimulatum imperium tuum portans, et stans replevit omnia morte et usque ad caelum adtingebat stans in

world. 5 *And* whereas they thought to kill the babes of the just, *one* child being cast forth and saved to reprove them, thou tookest away a multitude of their children and destroyedst them all together in a mighty water. 6 For that night was known before by our fathers that assuredly knowing what oaths they had trusted to they might be of better courage. 7 So thy people received the salvation of the just and destruction of the unjust. 8 For as thou didst punish the adversaries, so thou didst also encourage and glorify us. 9 For the just children of good men were offering sacrifice secretly, and they unanimously ordered a law of justice that the just should receive both good and evil alike, singing now the praises of the fathers.

10 But *on the other side* there sounded an ill according cry of the enemies, and a lamentable mourning was heard for the children that were bewailed. 11 And the servant suffered the same punishment as the master, and a common man suffered in like manner as the king. 12 So all alike had innumerable dead with one kind of death. *Neither* were the living sufficient to bury them, for in one moment the noblest offspring of them was destroyed. 13 For *whereas they would not believe any thing before* by reason of the *enchantments,* then first upon the destruction of the firstborn they acknowledged the people to be of God. 14 For while all things were in quiet silence and the night was in the midst of her course, 15 thy almighty word leapt down from heaven from thy royal throne as a fierce conqueror into the midst of the land of destruction, 16 with a sharp sword carrying thy unfeigned commandment, and he stood and filled all things with death

terra. 17 Tum continuo visus somniorum malorum turbaverunt illos, et timores supervenerunt insperati. 18 Et alius alibi proiectus, semivivus, propter quam moriebatur causam demonstrabat mortis. 19 Visiones enim quae illos turbaverunt haec praemonebant ne inscii quare mala patiebantur perirent.

20 Tetigit autem tunc et iustos temptatio mortis, et commotio in heremo facta est multitudinis, sed non diu permansit ira tua. 21 Properans enim homo sine querella deprecari pro populis, proferens servitutis suae scutum, orationem, et per incensum deprecationem allegans restitit irae et finem inposuit necessitati, ostendens quoniam tuus est famulus. 22 Vicit autem turbas, non in virtute corporis nec armaturae potentia, sed verbo illum qui se vexabat subiecit, iuramenta parentum et testamentum commemorans. 23 Cum enim iam acervatim cecidissent super alterutrum mortui interstetit et amputavit impetum et divisit illam quae ad vivos ducebat viam. 24 In veste enim poderis quam habebat totus erat orbis terrarum, et parentum magnalia in quattuor ordinibus lapidum erant sculpta, et magnificentia tua in diademate capitis illius erat scripta. 25 His autem cessit qui exterminabat et haec extimuit, erat enim sola temptatio irae sufficiens.

and standing on the earth reached even to heaven. 17 Then suddenly visions of evil dreams troubled them, and fears unlooked for came upon them. 18 And one thrown here, another there, half dead, shewed the cause of his death. 19 For the visions that troubled them foreshewed these things lest they should perish and not know why they suffered these evils.

20 But *the just also were afterwards touched by an assault* of death, and there was a disturbance of the multitude in the wilderness, but thy wrath did not long continue. 21 For a blameless man made haste to pray for the people, bringing forth the shield of his ministry, prayer, and by incense making supplication withstood the wrath and put an end to the calamity, shewing that he was thy servant. 22 And he overcame the disturbance, not by strength of body nor with force of arms, but with a word he subdued him that *punished them,* alleging the oaths and covenant made with the fathers. 23 For when they were now fallen down dead by heaps one upon another he stood between and stayed the assault and cut off the way to the living. 24 For in the priestly robe which he wore was the whole world, and in the four rows of the stones the glory of the fathers was graven, and thy majesty was written upon the diadem of his head. 25 And to these the destroyer gave place and was afraid of them, for the proof only of wrath was enough.

Caput 19

Impiis autem, usque in novissimum sine misericordia ira supervenit, praesciebat enim et futura illorum, 2 quoniam ipsi cum permisissent ut se educerent et cum magna sollicitudine praemisissent illos, consequebantur illos paenitentia acti. 3 Adhuc enim inter manus habentes luctum et deplorantes ad monumenta mortuorum aliam sibi adsumpserunt cogitationem inscientiae et quos rogantes proiecerant hos tamquam fugitivos persequebantur. 4 Ducebat enim illos ad hunc finem digna necessitas, et horum quae acciderant memorationem amittebant ut quae deerant tormentis repleret punitio 5 et populus quidem tuus mirabiliter transiret, illi autem novam mortem invenirent.

6 Omnis enim creatura ad suum genus ab initio refigurabatur, deserviens tuis praeceptis, ut pueri tui custodirentur inlaesi. 7 Nam nubis castra eorum adumbrabat, et ex aqua quae ante erat, terra arida apparuit, et in Mari Rubro via sine inpedimento, et campus germinans de profundo nimio 8 per quem omnis natio transivit quae tegebatur tua manu,

Chapter 19

Why God shewed no mercy to the Egyptians. His favour to
the Israelites. All creatures obey God's orders for the service of the good and the punishment of the wicked.

But as to the wicked, even to the end there came upon
them wrath without mercy, for he knew before also what
they would do, 2 for when they had given them leave to depart and had sent them away with great care, they repented
and pursued after them. 3 For *whilst they were yet mourning*
and lamenting at the graves of the dead they took up another foolish device and pursued them as fugitives whom
they had *pressed to be gone.* 4 For a necessity of which they
were worthy brought them to this end, and they lost the remembrance of those things which had happened that their
punishment might fill up what was wanting to their torments 5 and that thy people *might* wonderfully pass through,
but they might find a new death.

6 For every creature according to its kind was fashioned
again as from the beginning, obeying thy commandments,
that thy children might be kept without hurt. 7 For a cloud
overshadowed their camp, and *where water* was before, dry
land appeared, and in the Red Sea a way without hindrance,
and out of the great deep a springing field 8 through which
all the nation passed which was protected with thy hand,

videntes tua mirabilia et monstra. 9 Tamquam equi enim depaverunt, et tamquam agni exultaverunt, magnificantes te, Domine, qui liberasti illos. 10 Memores enim erant adhuc eorum quae in incolatu illorum facta fuerant, quemadmodum pro natione animalium eduxit terra muscas et pro piscibus eructavit fluvius multitudinem ranarum. 11 Novissime autem viderunt novam creaturam avium cum adducti concupiscentia postulaverunt escas epulationis. 12 In adlocutione enim desiderii ascendit illis de mari ortygometra et vexationes peccatoribus supervenerunt, non sine illis quae ante facta erant argumentis per vim fulminum, iuste enim patiebantur secundum suas nequitias.

13 Etenim detestabiliorem inhospitalitatem instituerunt, alii quidem ignotos non recipiebant advenas, alii autem bonos hospites in servitutem redigebant. 14 Et non solum haec, sed et alius quidam respectus erat illorum, quoniam inviti recipiebant extraneos. 15 Qui autem cum laetitia receperunt hos qui eisdem usi erant iustitiis saevissimis adflixerunt doloribus. 16 Percussi sunt autem caecitate sicut illi in foribus iusti cum subitaneis cooperti essent tenebris, unusquisque ostii sui transitum quaerebat. 17 In se enim elementa dum convertuntur sicut in organo qualitatis sonus inmutatur, et omnia suum sonum custodiunt, unde aestimari ex ipso visu certo potest. 18 Agrestia enim in aquatica convertebantur, et quaecumque erant natantia in terram transiebant. 19 Ignis in aqua valebat supra suam virtutem, et aqua extinguentis naturae obliviscebatur.

seeing thy miracles and wonders. 9 For they fed on their food like horses, and they skipped like lambs, praising thee, O Lord, who hadst delivered them. 10 For they were yet mindful of those things which had been done in the time of their sojourning, how the ground brought forth flies instead of cattle and how the river cast up a multitude of frogs instead of fishes. 11 And at length they saw a new generation of birds when being led by their appetite they asked for *delicate meats.* 12 For to satisfy their desire the quail came up to them from the sea and punishments came upon the sinners, not without foregoing signs by the force of thunders, for they suffered justly according to their own wickedness.

13 For they exercised a more detestable inhospitality *than any; others* indeed received not strangers unknown to them, but *these* brought their guests into bondage *that had deserved well of them.* 14 And not only so, but *in another respect also they were worse,* for *the others* against their will received the strangers. 15 But these *grievously* afflicted them whom they had received with joy and who lived under the same laws. 16 But they were struck with blindness as those *others* were at the doors of the just man when they were covered with sudden darkness, *and* every one sought the passage of his own door. 17 For while the elements are changed in themselves as in an instrument the sound of the quality is changed, yet all keep their sound, *which* may clearly be perceived by the very sight. 18 For the things of the land were turned into things of the water, and the things before swam in the water passed upon the land. 19 The fire had power in water above its own virtue, and the water forgot its quenching nature.

20 Flammae e contrario corruptibilium animalium non vexaverunt carnes coambulantium, nec dissolvebant illam quae facile dissolvebatur sicut glacies bonam escam. In omnibus enim, Domine, magnificasti populum tuum et honorasti et non despexisti in omni tempore et in omni loco adsistens eis.

20 On the other side the flames wasted not the flesh of corruptible animals walking therein, neither did they melt that good food which was *apt to melt* as ice. For in all things thou didst magnify thy people, O Lord, and didst honour them and didst not despise them but didst assist them at all times and in every place.

ECCLESIASTICUS

Prologus

Multorum nobis et magnorum per legem et prophetas aliosque qui secuti sunt illos sapientia demonstrata est, in quibus oportet laudare Israhel doctrinae et sapientiae causa, quia non solum ipsos loquentes necesse est peritos, sed etiam extraneos posse et dicentes et scribentes doctissimos fieri.

[2] Avus meus Iesus postquam se amplius dedit ad diligentiam lectionis legis et prophetarum et aliorum librorum qui nobis a parentibus nostris traditi sunt voluit et ipse scribere aliquid horum quae ad doctrinam et sapientiam pertinent ut desiderantes discere et illorum periti facti magis magisque adtendant animo et confirmentur ad legitimam vitam. [3] Hortor itaque venire vos cum benevolentia et adtentiore studio lectionem facere et veniam habere in illis in quibus videmur sequentes imaginem sapientiae deficere in verborum conpositione, nam deficiunt et verba Hebraica quando translata fuerint ad alteram linguam. [4] Non solum autem haec, sed et ipsa lex et prophetae ceteraque aliorum librorum non parvam habent differentiam quando inter se dicuntur, nam in octavo et tricesimo anno temporibus

Prologue by the author's grandson

The knowledge of many and great things hath been shewed us by the law and the prophets and others that have followed them, for which things Israel is to be commended for doctrine and wisdom, because not only they that speak must needs be skilful, but strangers also both speaking and writing may by their means become most learned.

[2] My grandfather Jesus after he had much given himself to a diligent reading of the law and the prophets and other books that were delivered to us from our fathers had a mind also to write *something* himself pertaining to doctrine and wisdom that such as are desirous to learn and are made knowing in these things may be more and more attentive in mind and be strengthened to live according to the law. [3] I entreat you therefore to come with benevolence and to read with attention and to pardon us for those things wherein we may seem while we follow the image of wisdom to come short in the composition of words, for the Hebrew words *have not the same force in them* when translated into another tongue. [4] And not only these, but the law also itself and the prophets and the rest of the *books* have no small difference when they are spoken in their own language, for in the eight

Ptolomei Euergetis regis postquam perveni in Aegyptum et cum multum temporis ibi fuissem, inveni ibi libros relictos non parvae neque contemnendae doctrinae. [5] Itaque bonum et necessarium putavi et ipse aliquam addere diligentiam et laborem interpretandi istum librum, et multa vigilia adtuli doctrinam in spatio temporis ad illa quae ad finem ducunt librum dare et illis qui volunt animum intendere quemadmodum oporteat instituere mores, qui secundum legem Domini proposuerunt vitam agere.

Caput 1

Omnis sapientia a Deo Domino est et cum illo fuit semper et est ante aevum. 2 Harenam maris et pluviae guttas et dies saeculi quis dinumeravit? Altitudinem caeli et latitudinem terrae et profundum abyssi quis mensus est? 3 Sapientiam Dei praecedentem omnia quis investigavit? 4 Prior omnium creata est sapientia, et intellectus prudentiae ab aevo. 5 Fons sapientiae verbum Dei in excelsis, et ingressus illius mandata aeterna.

and thirtieth year coming into Egypt when Ptolemy Euergetes was king and *continuing* there a long time, I found there books left of no small not contemptible learning. [5] Therefore *I* thought it good and necessary *for me* to bestow some diligence and labour to interpret this book, and with much watching *and study* in some space of time I *brought the book to an end and set it forth for the service of them* that are willing to apply their mind *and to learn* how they ought to conduct themselves, who purpose to lead their life according to the law of the Lord.

Chapter 1

All wisdom is from God and is given to them that fear and love God.

All wisdom is from the Lord God and hath been always with him and is before all time. 2 Who hath numbered the sand of the sea and the drops of rain and the days of the world? Who hath measured the height of heaven and the breadth of the earth and the depth of the abyss? 3 Who hath searched out the wisdom of God that goeth before all things? 4 Wisdom hath been created before all things, and the understanding of prudence from everlasting. 5 The word of God on high is the fountain of wisdom, and her ways are everlasting commandments.

6 Radix sapientiae cui revelata est, et astutias illius quis agnovit? 7 Disciplina sapientiae cui revelata est et manifestata? Et multiplicationem ingressus illius quis intellexit? 8 Unus est Altissimus Creator Omnipotens et rex potens et metuendus nimis, sedens super thronum illius et dominans Deus. 9 Ipse creavit illam in Spiritu Sancto et vidit et dinumeravit et mensus est. 10 Et effudit illam super omnia opera sua et super omnem carnem secundum datum suum et praebuit illam diligentibus se.

11 Timor Domini gloria et gloriatio et laetitia et corona exultationis. 12 Timor Domini delectabit cor et dabit laetitiam et gaudium in longitudine dierum. 13 Timenti Dominum bene erit in extremis, et in die defunctionis suae benedicetur. 14 Dilectio Dei honorabilis sapientia, 15 quibus autem apparuerit in visu diligunt eam in visione et in agnitione magnalium suorum. 16 Initium sapientiae timor Domini et cum fidelibus in vulva concreatus est. Cum electis feminis graditur et cum iustis et fidelibus agnoscitur. 17 Timor Domini scientiae religiositas. 18 Religiositas custodiet et iustificabit cor; iucunditatem atque gaudium dabit. 19 Timenti Dominum bene erit, et in diebus consummationis illius benedicetur.

20 Plenitudo sapientiae timere Deum, et plenitudo a fructibus illius. 21 Omnem domum illius implebit a generationibus et receptacula a thesauris illius. 22 Corona sapientiae timor Domini, replens pacem et salutis fructum. 23 Et vidit et

6 To whom hath the root of wisdom been revealed, and who hath known her wise counsels? 7 To whom hath the discipline of wisdom been revealed and made manifest? And who hath understood the multiplicity of her steps? 8 There is one Most High Creator Almighty and a powerful king and greatly to be feared, who sitteth upon his throne and is the God of dominion. 9 He created her in the Holy Ghost and saw her and numbered her and measured her. 10 And he poured her out upon all his works and upon all flesh according to his gift and hath given her to them that love him.

11 The fear of the Lord is honour and glory and gladness and a crown of joy. 12 The fear of the Lord shall delight the heart and shall give joy and gladness *and* length of days. 13 With him that feareth the Lord it shall go well in the latter end, and in the day of his death he shall be blessed. 14 The love of God is honourable wisdom, 15 and they to whom she shall *shew herself* love her by the sight and by the knowledge of her great works. 16 The fear of the Lord is the beginning of wisdom and was created with the faithful in the womb. It walketh with chosen women and is known with the just and faithful. 17 The fear of the Lord is the religiousness of knowledge. 18 Religiousness shall keep and justify the heart; it shall give joy and gladness. 19 It shall go well with him that feareth the Lord, and in the days of his end he shall be blessed.

20 To fear God is the fulness of wisdom, and fulness is from the fruits thereof. 21 She shall fill all her house with her *increase* and the storehouses with her treasures. 22 The fear of the Lord is a crown of wisdom, filling up peace and the fruit of salvation. 23 And it hath seen and numbered her, but

dinumeravit eam, utraque autem sunt dona Dei. 24 Scientiam et intellectum prudentiae sapientia conpartietur et gloriam tenentium se exaltat.

25 Radix sapientiae est timere Dominum, rami enim illius longevi. 26 In thesauris sapientiae intellectus et scientiae religiositas, execratio autem peccatoribus sapientia. 27 Timor Domini expellit peccatum, 28 nam qui sine timore est non poterit iustificari, iracundia enim animositatis illius subversio illius est. 29 Usque in tempus sustinebit patiens, et postea redditio iucunditatis. 30 Bonus sensus usque in tempus abscondebit verba illius, et labia multorum enarrabunt sensum illius. 31 In thesauris sapientiae significatio disciplinae, 32 execratio autem peccatori cultura Dei.

33 Fili, concupiscens sapientiam, conserva iustitiam, et Deus praebebit illam tibi, 34 sapientia enim et disciplina timor Domini, et quod beneplacitum est illi 35 fides et mansuetudo, et adimplebit thesauros illius. 36 Non sis incredibilis timori Domini, et ne accesseris ad illum duplici corde. 37 Ne fueris hypocrita in conspectu hominum, et non scandalizeris labiis tuis. 38 Adtende in illis ne forte cadas et adducas animae tuae inhonorationem 39 et revelet Deus absconsa tua et in medio synagogae elidat te 40 quoniam accessisti maligne ad Dominum et cor tuum plenum est dolo et fallacia.

both are the gifts of God. 24 Wisdom shall distribute knowledge and understanding of prudence and exalteth the glory of them that hold her.

25 The root of wisdom is to fear the Lord, *and* the branches thereof are longlived. 26 In the treasures of wisdom is understanding and religiousness of knowledge, but to sinners wisdom is an abomination. 27 The fear of the Lord driveth out sin, 28 for he that is without fear cannot be justified, for the wrath of his high spirits is his ruin. 29 A patient man shall bear for a time, and afterwards joy shall be restored to him. 30 A good understanding will hide his words for a time, and the lips of many shall declare his wisdom. 31 In the treasures of wisdom is the signification of discipline, 32 but the worship of God is an abomination to a sinner.

33 Son, *if thou desire* wisdom, keep justice, and God will give her to thee, 34 for the fear of the Lord is wisdom and discipline, and that which is agreeable to him 35 is faith and meekness, and he will fill up his treasures. 36 Be not incredulous to the fear of the Lord, and come not to him with a double heart. 37 Be not a hypocrite in the sight of men, and *let not thy lips be a stumbling block to thee.* 38 Watch over them lest thou fall and bring dishonour upon thy soul 39 and God discover thy secrets and cast thee down in the midst of the congregation 40 because thou camest to the Lord wickedly and thy heart is full of guile and deceit.

Caput 2

Fili, accedens servituti Dei, sta in iustitia et timore, et praepara animam tuam ad temptationem. 2 Deprime cor tuum, et sustine. Inclina aurem tuam, et excipe verba intellectus, et ne festines in tempore obductionis. 3 Sustine sustentationes Dei. Coniungere Deo, et sustine, ut crescat in novissimo vita tua. 4 Omne quod tibi adplicitum fuerit accipe, et in dolore sustine, et in humilitate tua habe patientiam, 5 quoniam in igne probatur aurum et argentum, homines vero receptibiles in camino humiliationis. 6 Crede Deo, et recuperabit te, et dirige viam tuam, et spera in illum. Serva timorem illius, et in illo veteresce.

7 Metuentes Dominum, sustinete misericordiam eius, et non deflectatis ab illo ne cadatis. 8 Qui timetis Dominum, credite illi, et non evacuabitur merces vestra. 9 Qui timetis Dominum, sperate in illum, et in oblectatione veniet vobis misericordia. 10 Qui timetis Dominum, diligite illum, et inluminabuntur corda vestra.

Chapter 2

God's servants must look for temptations and must arm themselves with patience and confidence in God.

Son, when thou comest to the service of God, stand in justice and in fear, and prepare thy soul for temptation. 2 Humble thy heart, and endure. Incline thy ear, and receive the words of understanding, and make not haste in the time of *clouds*. 3 *Wait on God with patience.* Join thyself to God, and endure, that thy life may be increased in the latter end. 4 Take all that shall be brought upon thee, and in thy sorrow endure, and in thy humiliation keep patience, 5 for gold and silver are tried in the fire, but acceptable men in the furnace of humiliation. 6 Believe God, and he will recover thee, and direct thy way, and trust in him. Keep his fear, and grow old therein.

7 Ye that fear the Lord, wait for his mercy, and go not aside from him lest ye fall. 8 Ye that fear the Lord, believe him, and your reward shall not be made void. 9 Ye that fear the Lord, hope in him, and mercy shall come to you for your delight. 10 Ye that fear the Lord, love him, and your hearts shall be enlightened.

11 Respicite, filii, nationes hominum, et scitote quia nullus speravit in Dominum et confusus est, 12 quis enim permansit in mandatis eius et derelictus est? Aut quis invocavit illum, et despexit illum? 13 Quoniam pius et misericors est Deus et remittet in die tribulationis peccata, et protector est omnibus exquirentibus se in veritate.

14 Vae duplici corde et labiis scelestis et manibus malefacientibus et peccatori terram ingredienti duabus viis. 15 Vae dissolutis corde, qui non credunt Deo, et ideo non protegentur ab eo. 16 Vae his qui perdiderunt sustinentiam et qui dereliquerunt vias rectas et deverterunt in vias pravas. 17 Et quid facient cum inspicere coeperit Dominus? 18 Qui timent Dominum non erunt incredibiles verbo illius, et qui diligunt illum conservabunt viam illius. 19 Qui timent Dominum inquirent quae beneplacita sunt illi, et qui diligunt eum replebuntur lege ipsius. 20 Qui timent Dominum parabunt corda sua et in conspectu illius sanctificabunt animas suas. 21 Qui timent Dominum custodiunt mandata illius et patientiam habebunt usque ad inspectionem illius, 22 dicentes, "Si paenitentiam non egerimus, incidemus in Domini manus et non in manus hominum," 23 secundum enim magnitudinem illius, sic et misericordia ipsius cum ipso est.

11 My children, behold the generations of men, and know ye that no one hath hoped in the Lord and hath been confounded, 12 for who hath continued in his commandment and hath been forsaken? Or who hath called upon him, and he despised him? 13 For God is compassionate and merciful and will forgive sins in the day of tribulation, and he is a protector to all that seek him in truth.

14 Woe to them that are of a double heart and to wicked lips and to the hands that do evil and to the sinner that goeth on the earth two ways. 15 Woe to them that are fainthearted, who believe not God, and therefore they shall not be protected by him. 16 Woe to them that have lost patience and that have forsaken the right ways and have gone aside into crooked ways. 17 And what will they do when the Lord shall begin to examine? 18 They that fear the Lord will not be incredulous to his word, and they that love him will keep his way. 19 They that fear the Lord will seek after the things that are well pleasing to him, and they that love him shall be filled with his law. 20 They that fear the Lord will prepare their hearts and in his sight will sanctify their souls. 21 They that fear the Lord keep his commandments and will have patience even until his visitation, 22 saying, "If we do not penance, we shall fall into the hands of the Lord and not into the hands of men," 23 for according to his greatness, so also is his mercy with him.

Caput 3

Filii sapientiae ecclesia iustorum, et natio illorum obaudientia et dilectio. 2 Iudicium patris audite, filii, et sic facite ut salvi sitis, 3 Deus enim honoravit patrem in filiis et iudicium matris exquirens firmavit in filios.

4 Qui diligit Deum exorabit pro peccatis et continebit se ab illis et in oratione dierum exaudietur. 5 Et sicut qui thesaurizat ita et qui honorificat matrem suam. 6 Qui honorat patrem suum iucundabitur in filiis, et in die orationis suae exaudietur. 7 Qui honorat patrem suum vita vivet longiore, et qui obaudit patrem refrigerabit matri. 8 Qui timet Dominum honorat parentes et quasi dominis serviet his qui se generaverunt.

9 In opere et sermone et omni patientia honora patrem tuum 10 ut superveniat tibi benedictio ab eo et benedictio illius in novissimo maneat. 11 Benedictio patris firmat domos filiorum, maledictio autem matris eradicat fundamenta. 12 Ne glorieris in contumelia patris tui, non est enim tibi glo-

Chapter 3

Lessons concerning the honour of parents and humility and avoiding curiosity.

The sons of wisdom are the church of the just, and their generation obedience and love. 2 Children, hear the judgment of your father, and so do that you may be saved, 3 for God hath made the father honourable to the children and seeking the judgment of the mothers hath confirmed it upon the children.

4 He that loveth God shall obtain pardon for his sins by prayer and shall refrain himself from them and shall be heard in the prayer of days. 5 And he that honoureth his mother is as one that layeth up a treasure. 6 He that honoureth his father shall have joy in his own children, and in the day of his prayer he shall be heard. 7 He that honoureth his father shall *enjoy* a long life, and he that obeyeth the father shall be a comfort to his mother. 8 He that feareth the Lord honoureth his parents and will serve them as his masters that brought him into the world.

9 Honour thy father in work and word and all patience 10 that a blessing may come upon thee from him and his blessing may remain in the latter end. 11 The father's blessing establisheth the houses of the children, but the mother's curse rooteth up the foundation. 12 Glory not in the dishon-

ria eius confusio, 13 gloria enim hominis ex honore patris sui, et dedecus filii pater sine honore.

14 Fili, suscipe senectam patris tui, et ne contristes eum in vita illius, 15 et si defecerit sensu, veniam da, et ne spernas eum in tua virtute, elemosyna enim patris non erit in oblivione, 16 nam pro peccato matris restituetur tibi bonum. 17 Et in iustitia aedificabitur tibi, et in die tribulationis commemorabitur tui, et sicut in sereno glacies solventur tua peccata.

18 Quam malae famae est qui relinquit patrem! Et est maledictus a Deo qui exasperat matrem. 19 Fili, in mansuetudine opera tua perfice, et super hominum gloriam diligeris. 20 Quanto magnus es, humilia te in omnibus, et coram Deo invenies gratiam, 21 quoniam magna potentia Dei solius, et ab humilibus honoratur. 22 Altiora te ne scrutaveris, et fortiora te ne exquisieris, sed quae praecepit tibi Deus, illa cogita semper, et in pluribus operibus eius ne fueris curiosus, 23 non est enim tibi necessarium ea quae abscondita sunt videre oculis tuis. 24 In supervacuis rebus noli scrutari multipliciter, et in pluribus operibus eius non eris curiosus, 25 plurima enim super sensum hominum ostensa sunt tibi, 26 multos quoque subplantavit suspicio illorum et in vanitate detinuit sensus illorum.

27 Cor durum male habebit in novissimo, et qui amat periculum in illo peribit. 28 Cor ingrediens duas vias non habe-

our of thy father, for his shame is no glory to thee, 13 for the glory of a man is from the honour of his father, and a father without honour is the disgrace of the son.

14 Son, support the old age of thy father, and grieve him not in his life, 15 and if his understanding fail, have patience with him, and despise him not when thou art in thy strength, for the relieving of the father shall not be forgotten, 16 for good shall be repaid to thee for the sin of thy mother. 17 And in justice thou shalt be built up, and in the day of affliction thou shalt be remembered, and thy sins shall melt away as the ice in the fair warm weather.

18 Of what an evil fame is he that forsaketh his father! And he is cursed of God that angereth his mother. 19 My son, do thy works in meekness, and thou shalt be beloved above the glory of men. 20 The greater thou art, the more humble thyself in all things, and thou shalt find grace before God, 21 for great is the power of God alone, and he is honoured by the humble. 22 Seek not the things that are too high for thee, and search not into things above thy ability, but the things that God hath commanded thee, think on them always, and in many of his works be not curious, 23 for it is not necessary for thee to see with thy eyes those things that are hid. 24 In unnecessary matters be not over curious, and in many of his works thou shalt not be inquisitive, 25 for many things are shewn to thee above the understanding of men, 26 and the suspicion of them hath deceived many and hath detained their minds in vanity.

27 A hard heart shall fare evil at the last, and he that loveth danger shall perish in it. 28 A heart that goeth two ways shall

bit successus, et pravus corde in illis scandalizabitur. 29 Cor nequam gravabitur doloribus, et peccator adiciet ad peccandum. 30 Synagogae superborum non erit sanitas, frutex enim peccati radicabitur in illis et non intellegetur. 31 Cor sapientis intellegitur in sapientia, et auris bona audiet cum omni concupiscentia sapientiam. 32 Sapiens cor et intellegibile abstinebit se a peccatis et in operibus iustitiae successus habebit.

33 Ignem ardentem extinguit aqua, et elemosyna resistit peccatis. 34 Et Deus conspector est eius qui reddit gratiam; meminit eius in posterum, et in tempore casus sui inveniet firmamentum.

Caput 4

Fili, elemosynam pauperis ne fraudes, et oculos tuos ne transvertas a paupere. 2 Animam esurientem ne despexeris, et non exasperes pauperem in inopia sua. 3 Cor inopis ne adflixeris, et non protrahas datum angustianti. 4 Rogationem contribulati ne abicias, et non avertas faciem tuam ab

not have success, and the perverse of heart shall be scandalized therein. 29 A wicked heart shall be laden with sorrows, and the sinner will add *sin to* sin. 30 The congregation of the proud shall not be healed, for the plant of wickedness shall take root in them, and it shall not be perceived. 31 The heart of the wise is understood in wisdom, and a good ear will hear wisdom with all desire. 32 A wise heart and which hath understanding will abstain from sins and in the works of justice shall have success.

33 Water quencheth a flaming fire, and alms resisteth sins. 34 And God provideth for him that sheweth favour; he remembereth him afterwards, and in the time of his fall he shall find a sure stay.

Chapter 4

An exhortation to works of mercy and to the love of wisdom.

Son, defraud not the poor of alms, and turn not away thy eyes from the poor. 2 Despise not the hungry soul, and provoke not the poor in his want. 3 Afflict not the heart of the needy, and defer not to give to him that is in distress. 4 Reject not the petition of the afflicted, and turn not away thy

egeno. 5 Ab inope ne avertas oculos tuos propter iram, et non relinquas quaerentibus tibi retro maledicere, 6 maledicentis enim te in amaritudine animae exaudietur precatio illius, exaudiet autem eum qui fecit illum.

7 Congregationi pauperum affabilem te facito, et presbytero humilia animam tuam, et magnato humilia caput tuum. 8 Declina pauperi sine tristitia aurem tuam, et redde debitum tuum, et responde illi pacifica in mansuetudine. 9 Libera eum qui iniuriam patitur de manu superbi, et non acedieris in anima tua. 10 In iudicando esto pupillis misericors ut pater et pro viro matri illorum. 11 Et eris velut filius Altissimi obaudiens, et miserebitur tui magis quam mater.

12 Sapientia filiis suis vitam inspirat et suscipit exquirentes se et praeibit in via iustitiae. 13 Et qui illam diligit diligit vitam, et qui vigilaverint ad illam conplectebuntur placorem eius. 14 Qui tenuerint illam vitam hereditabunt, et quo introibit benedicet Deus. 15 Qui serviunt ei obsequentes erunt sancto, et eos qui diligunt illam diligit Deus. 16 Qui audit illam iudicat gentes, et qui intuetur illam permanebit confidens. 17 Si crediderit ei, hereditabit illam, et erunt in confirmatione creaturae illius, 18 quoniam in temptatione ambulat cum eo et in primis eligit eum. 19 Timorem et metum et probationem inducet super illum, et cruciabit illum in tribulatione doctrinae suae donec temptet illum in cogitationibus

face from the needy. 5 Turn not away thy eyes from the poor for *fear of* anger, and leave not to them that ask of thee to curse thee behind thy back, 6 for the prayer of him that curseth thee in the bitterness of his soul shall be heard, *for* he that made him will hear him.

7 Make thyself affable to the congregation of the poor, and humble thy soul to the ancient, and bow thy head to a great man. 8 Bow down thy ear cheerfully to the poor, and pay what thou owest, and answer him peaceable words with mildness. 9 Deliver him that suffereth wrong out of the hand of the proud, and be not fainthearted in thy soul. 10 In judging be merciful to the fatherless as a father and as a husband to their mother. 11 And thou shalt be as the obedient son of the Most High, and he will have mercy on thee more than a mother.

12 Wisdom inspireth life into her children and protecteth them that seek after her and will go before them in the way of justice. 13 And he that loveth her loveth life, and they that watch for her shall embrace her sweetness. 14 They that hold her fast shall inherit life, and whithersoever she entereth God will give a blessing. 15 They that serve her shall be servants to the holy one, and God loveth them that love her. 16 He that hearkeneth to her shall judge nations, and he that looketh upon her shall remain secure. 17 If he trust to her, he shall inherit her, and *his generation* shall be in assurance, 18 for she walketh with him in temptation and at the first she chooseth him. 19 She will bring upon him fear and dread and trial, and she will scourge him with the affliction of her discipline till she try him by her *laws* and trust his

illius et credat animae illius. 20 Et firmabit illum et iter adducet directum ad illum et laetificabit illum 21 et denudabit absconsa sua illi et thesaurizabit super illum scientiam et intellectum iustitiae. 22 Si autem oberraverit, derelinquet eum et tradet illum in manus inimici sui.

23 Fili, conserva tempus, et devita a malo, 24 pro anima tua non confundaris dicere verum, 25 est enim confusio adducens peccatum, et est confusio adducens gloriam et gratiam. 26 Ne accipias faciem adversus faciem tuam, nec adversus animam tuam mendacium. 27 Non reverearis proximum tuum in casum suum, 28 nec retineas verbum in tempus salutis. Non abscondas sapientiam tuam in decore eius, 29 in lingua enim dignoscitur sapientia, et sensus et scientia et doctrina in verbo sensati, et firmamentum in operibus iustitiae. 30 Non contradicas verbo veritatis ullo modo, et de mendacio ineruditionis tuae confundere. 31 Non confundaris confiteri peccata tua, et ne subicias te omni homini pro peccato. 32 Noli resistere contra faciem potentis, nec coneris contra ictum fluvii. 33 Pro iustitia agoniare pro anima tua, et usque ad mortem certa pro iustitia, et Deus expugnabit pro te inimicos tuos. 34 Noli citatus esse in lingua tua et inutilis et remissus in operibus tuis. 35 Noli esse sicut leo in domo tua, evertens domesticos tuos et opprimens subiectos tibi. 36 Non sit porrecta manus tua ad accipiendum et ad dandum collecta.

soul. 20 Then she will strengthen him and make a straight way to him and give him joy 21 and will disclose her secrets to him and will heap upon him treasures of knowledge and understanding of justice. 22 But if he go astray, she will forsake him and deliver him into the hands of his enemy.

23 Son, observe the time, and fly from evil, 24 for thy soul be not ashamed to say the truth, 25 for there is a shame that bringeth sin, and there is a shame that bringeth glory and grace. 26 Accept no person against thy own person, nor against thy soul a lie. 27 Reverence not thy neighbour in his fall, 28 and refrain not to speak in the time of salvation. Hide not thy wisdom in her beauty, 29 for by the tongue wisdom is discerned, and understanding and knowledge and learning by the word of the wise, and steadfastness in the works of justice. 30 In nowise speak against the *truth, but* be ashamed of the lie of thy ignorance. 31 Be not ashamed to confess thy sins, *but* submit not thyself to every man for sin. 32 Resist not against the face of the mighty, and do not strive against the stream of the river. 33 Strive for justice for thy soul, and even unto death fight for justice, and God will overthrow thy enemies for thee. 34 Be not hasty in thy tongue and slack and remiss in thy works. 35 Be not as a lion in thy house, terrifying them of thy household and oppressing them that are under thee. 36 Let not thy hand be stretched out to receive and shut *when thou shouldst* give.

Caput 5

Noli adtendere ad possessiones iniquas, et ne dixeris, "Est mihi sufficiens vita," nihil enim proderit in tempore vindictae et obductionis. 2 Non sequaris in fortitudine tua concupiscentiam cordis tui, 3 et ne dixeris, "Quomodo potui!" aut "Quis me subiciet propter facta mea?" Deus enim vindicans vindicabit. 4 Ne dixeris, "Peccavi, et quid accidit mihi triste?" Altissimus enim est patiens redditor. 5 De propitiato peccato noli esse sine metu, neque adicias peccatum super peccatum, 6 et ne dicas, "Miseratio Domini magna est; multitudinis peccatorum meorum miserebitur," 7 misericordia enim et ira ab illo cito proximant et in peccatores respicit ira illius.

8 Non tardes converti ad Dominum, et ne differas de die in diem, 9 subito enim veniet ira illius, et in tempore vindictae disperdet te. 10 Noli anxius esse in divitiis iniustis, non enim proderunt tibi in die obductionis et vindictae. 11 Non ventiles te in omnem ventum, et non eas in omnem viam, sic enim omnis peccator probatur duplici lingua.

Chapter 5

We must not presume of our wealth or strength nor of the mercy of God to go on in sin. We must be steadfast in virtue and truth.

Set not thy heart upon unjust possessions, and say not, "I have enough to live on," for it shall be of no service in the time of vengeance and darkness. 2 Follow not in thy strength the *desires* of thy heart, 3 and say not, "How mighty am I! And who shall bring me under for my deeds?" for God will surely take revenge. 4 Say not, "I have sinned, and what harm hath befallen me?" for the Most High is a patient rewarder. 5 Be not without fear about sin forgiven, and add not sin upon sin, 6 and say not, "The mercy of the Lord is great; he will have mercy on the multitude of my sins," 7 for mercy and wrath quickly come from him and his wrath looketh upon sinners.

8 Delay not to be converted to the Lord, and defer it not from day to day, 9 for his wrath shall come on a sudden, and in the time of vengeance he will destroy thee. 10 Be not anxious for goods unjustly gotten, for they shall not profit thee in the day of calamity and revenge. 11 Winnow not with every wind, and go not into every way, for so is every sinner proved by a double tongue.

12 Esto firmus in via Domini et in veritate sensus tui et scientia, et prosequatur te verbum pacis et iustitiae. 13 Esto mansuetus ad audiendum verbum ut intellegas et cum sapientia fers responsum verum. 14 Si est tibi intellectus, responde proximo, sin autem, sit manus tua super os tuum ne capiaris in verbo indisciplinato et confundaris.

15 Honor et gloria in sermone sensati, lingua vero inprudentis subversio est ipsius. 16 Non appelleris susurro, et lingua tua ne capiaris et confundaris, 17 super furem enim est confusio et paenitentia et denotatio pessima super bilinguem, susurratori autem odium et inimicitia et contumelia. 18 Iustifica pusillo et magno similiter.

Caput 6

Noli fieri pro amico inimicus proximo, inproperium enim et contumeliam malus hereditabit et omnis peccator invidus et bilinguis. 2 Non te extollas in cogitatione animae tuae velut taurus ne forte elidatur virtus tua per stultitiam 3 et folia tua comedat et fructus tuos perdat et relinquaris velut lignum aridum in heremo, 4 anima enim nequa disperdet qui se habet et in gaudium inimicis dat illum et deducet

12 Be steadfast in the way of the Lord and in the truth of thy judgment and in knowledge, and let the word of peace and justice keep with thee. 13 Be meek to hear the word that thou mayst understand and return a true answer with wisdom. 14 If thou have understanding, answer thy neighbour, but if not, let thy hand be upon thy mouth lest thou be surprised in an unskillful word and be confounded.

15 Honour and glory is in the word of the wise, but the tongue of the fool is his ruin. 16 Be not called a whisperer, and be not taken in thy tongue and confounded, 17 for confusion and repentance is upon a thief and an evil mark of disgrace upon the double tongued, but to the whisperer hatred and enmity and reproach. 18 Justify alike the small and the great.

Chapter 6

Of true and false friends and of the fruits of wisdom.

Instead of a friend become not an enemy to thy neighbour, for an evil man shall inherit reproach and shame; *so* shall every sinner that is envious and double tongued. 2 Extol not thyself in the thoughts of thy soul like a bull *lest* thy strength be quashed by folly 3 and it eat up thy leaves and destroy thy fruit and thou be left as a dry tree in the wilderness, 4 for a wicked soul shall destroy him that hath it and maketh

in sortem impiorum. 5 Verbum dulce multiplicat amicos et mitigat inimicos, et lingua eucharis in bono homine abundat. 6 Multi pacifici sint tibi, et consilarius tibi sit unus de mille.

7 Si possides amicum, in temptatione posside eum, et non facile credas illi, 8 est enim amicus secundum tempus suum, et non permanebit in die tribulationis, 9 et est amicus qui convertitur ad inimicitiam, et est amicus qui odium et rixam et convicia denudabit, 10 est autem amicus socius mensae, et non permanebit in die necessitatis. 11 Amicus, si permanserit fixus, erit tibi quasi coaequalis et in domesticis tuis fiducialiter aget. 12 Si humiliaverit se contra te et a facie tua absconderit se, unianimem habebis amicitiam bonam.

13 Ab inimicis tuis separare, et ab amicis tuis adtende. 14 Amicus fidelis protectio fortis, qui autem invenit illum invenit thesaurum. 15 Amico fideli nulla est conparatio, et non est digna ponderatio auri et argenti contra bonitatem fidei illius. 16 Amicus fidelis medicamentum vitae et inmortalitatis, et qui metuunt Dominum invenient illum. 17 Qui timet Deum aeque habebit amicitiam bonam quoniam secundum illum erit amicus illius.

18 Fili, a iuventute tua excipe doctrinam, et usque ad canos invenies sapientiam. 19 Quasi is qui arat et seminat accede ad illam, et sustine bonos fructus illius, 20 in opere enim ipsius exiguum laborabis et cito edes de generationibus illius.

21 Quam aspera est nimium sapientia indoctis hominibus,

him to be a joy to his enemies and shall lead him into the lot of the wicked. 5 A sweet word multiplieth friends and appeaseth enemies, and a gracious tongue in a good man aboundeth. 6 *Be in peace with many, but* let one of a thousand be thy counsellor.

7 If thou wouldst get a friend, try him before thou takest him, and do not credit him easily, 8 for there is a friend for his own occasion, and he will not abide in the day of thy trouble, 9 and there is a friend that turneth to enmity, and there is a friend that will disclose hatred and strife and reproaches, 10 and there is a friend a companion at the table, and he will not abide in the day of distress. 11 A friend, if he continue steadfast, shall be to thee as thyself and shall act with confidence among them of thy household. 12 If he humble himself before thee and hide himself from thy face, thou shalt have unanimous friendship for good.

13 Separate thyself from thy enemies, and take heed of thy friends. 14 A faithful friend is a strong defence, and he that hath found him hath found a treasure. 15 Nothing can be compared to a faithful friend, and no weight of gold and silver is able to countervail the goodness of his fidelity. 16 A faithful friend is the medicine of life and immortality, and they that fear the Lord shall find him. 17 He that feareth God shall likewise have good friendship because according to him shall his friend be.

18 My son, from thy youth up receive instruction, and even to thy grey hairs thou shalt find wisdom. 19 Come to her as one that plougheth and soweth, and wait for her good fruits, 20 for in working about her thou shalt labour a little and shalt quickly eat of her fruits.

21 How very unpleasant is wisdom to the unlearned, and

et non permanebit in illa excors. 22 Quasi lapidis virtus probatio erit in illis, et non demorabuntur proicere illam, 23 sapientia enim doctrinae secundum nomen est eius, et non multis est manifesta, quibus autem agnita est permanet usque ad conspectum Dei.

24 Audi, fili, et accipe consilium intellectus, et ne abicias consilium meum. 25 Inice pedem tuum in conpedes illius et in torques eius tuum collum. 26 Subice umerum tuum, et porta illam, et ne acedieris vinculis eius. 27 In omni animo tuo accede ad illam, et in omni virtute tua serva vias eius. 28 Investiga illam, et manifestabitur tibi, et continens factus, ne derelinqueris eam, 29 in novissimis enim invenies requiem in ea, et convertetur tibi in oblectationem. 30 Et erunt tibi conpedes eius in protectionem fortitudinis et bases virtutis, et torques illius in stolam gloriae, 31 decor enim vitae est in illa, et vincula illius alligatura salutaris. 32 Stolam gloriae indues eam, et coronam gratulationis superpones tibi.

33 Fili, si adtenderis mihi, disces, et si adcommodaveris animum tuum, sapiens eris. 34 Si inclinaveris aurem tuam, excipies doctrinam, et si dilexeris audire, sapiens eris. 35 In multitudine presbyterorum prudentium sta, et sapientiae illorum ex corde coniungere ut omnem narrationem Dei possis audire et proverbia laudis non effugiant te. 36 Et si videris sensatum, evigila ad illum, et gradus ostiorum illius exterat pes tuus. 37 Cogitatum tuum habe in praeceptis Dei, et in mandatis illius maxime adsiduus esto, et ipse dabit cor tibi, et concupiscentia sapientiae dabitur tibi.

the unwise will not continue with her. 22 She shall be to them as a *mighty stone of trial,* and they will cast her from them before it be long, 23 for the wisdom of doctrine is according to her name, and she is not manifest unto many, but with them to whom she is known she continueth even to the sight of God.

24 Give ear, my son, and take wise counsel, and cast not away my advice. 25 Put thy feet into her fetters and thy neck into her chains. 26 Bow down thy shoulder, and bear her, and be not grieved with her bands. 27 Come to her with all thy mind, and keep her ways with all thy power. 28 Search for her, and she shall be made known to thee, and when thou hast gotten her, let her not go, 29 for in the latter end thou shalt find rest in her, and she shall be turned to thy joy. 30 Then shall her fetters be a strong defence for thee and a firm foundation, and her chain a robe of glory, 31 for in her is the beauty of life, and her bands are a healthful binding. 32 Thou shalt put her on as a robe of glory, and thou shalt set her upon thee as a crown of joy.

33 My son, if thou wilt attend to me, thou shalt learn, and if thou wilt apply thy mind, thou shalt be wise. 34 If thou wilt incline thy ear, thou shalt receive instruction, and if thou love to hear, thou shalt be wise. 35 Stand in the multitude of ancients that are wise, and join thyself from thy heart to their wisdom that thou mayst hear every discourse of God and the sayings of praise may not escape thee. 36 And if thou see a man of understanding, *go* to him *early in the morning,* and let thy foot wear the steps of his doors. 37 Let thy thoughts be upon the precepts of God, and *meditate continually* on his commandments, and he will give thee a heart, and the desire of wisdom shall be given to thee.

Caput 7

Noli facere mala, et non te adprehendent. 2 Discede ab iniquo, et deficient mala abs te. 3 Fili, non semines mala in sulcis iustitiae, et non metes ea in septuplum. 4 Noli quaerere a Domino ducatum, neque a rege cathedram honoris. 5 Non te iustifices ante Deum, quoniam agnitor cordis ipse est, et penes regem noli velle videri sapiens. 6 Noli quaerere fieri iudex, nisi si valeas virtute inrumpere iniquitates, ne forte extimescas faciem potentis et ponas scandalum in aequitate tua. 7 Non pecces in multitudinem civitatis, nec te inmittas in populum, 8 neque alliges duplicia peccata, nec enim in uno eris inmunis. 9 Noli esse pusillanimis in animo tuo; 10 exorare et facere elemosynam non despicias.

11 Ne dicas, "In multitudine munerum meorum respiciet Deus, et offerente me Deo altissimo suscipiet munera mea." 12 Non inrideas hominem in amaritudine animae, est enim qui humiliat et exaltat: circumspector Deus. 13 Noli arare mendacium adversus fratrem tuum, neque amico similiter facias. 14 Noli velle mentiri omne mendacium, adsiduitas enim illius non bona. 15 Noli verbosus esse in multitudine presbyterorum, et non iteres verbum in tua oratione. 16 Non oderis laboriosa opera et rusticationem ab Altissimo crea-

Chapter 7

Religious and moral duties.

Do no evils, and *no evils* shall lay hold of thee. 2 Depart from the unjust, and evils shall depart from thee. 3 My son, sow not evils in the furrows of *injustice,* and thou shalt not reap them sevenfold. 4 Seek not of the Lord a pre-eminence, nor of the king the seat of honour. 5 Justify not thyself before God, for he knoweth the heart, and desire not to appear wise before the king. 6 Seek not to be made a judge, unless thou have strength enough to extirpate iniquities, lest thou fear the person of the powerful and lay a stumbling block for thy integrity. 7 Offend not against the multitude of a city, neither cast thyself in upon the people, 8 nor bind sin to sin, for even in one thou shalt not be unpunished. 9 Be not fainthearted in thy mind; 10 neglect not to pray and to give alms.

11 Say not, "God will have respect to the multitude of my gifts, and when I offer to the most high God he will accept my offerings." 12 Laugh no man to scorn in the bitterness of his soul, for there is one that humbleth and exalteth: God who seeth all. 13 Devise not a lie against thy brother, neither do the like against thy friend. 14 Be not willing to make any manner of lie, for the custom thereof is not good. 15 Be not full of words in a multitude of ancients, and repeat not the word in thy prayer. 16 Hate not laborious works nor hus-

tam. 17 Non te reputes in multitudine indisciplinatorum. 18 Memento irae, quoniam non tardabit. 19 Humilia valde spiritum tuum, quoniam vindicta carnis impii ignis et vermes.

20 Noli praevaricari in amicum pecuniam differentem, neque fratrem carissimum auro spreveris. 21 Noli discedere a muliere sensata et bona quam sortitus es in timore Domini, gratia enim verecundiae illius super aurum. 22 Non laedas servum operantem in veritate, neque mercennarium dantem animam suam. 23 Servus sensatus sit tibi dilectus quasi anima tua. Non defraudes illum libertate, neque inopem derelinquas illum.

24 Pecora tibi sunt? Adtende illis, et si sunt utilia, perseverent apud te. 25 Filii tibi sunt? Erudi illos, et curva illos a pueritia illorum. 26 Filiae tibi sunt? Serva corpus illarum, et non ostendas hilarem faciem tuam ad illas. 27 Trade filiam, et grande opus feceris, et homini sensato da illam. 28 Mulier si est tibi secundum animam tuam, non proicias illam, et odibili non credas te. In toto corde tuo 29 honora patrem tuum, et gemitus matris tuae ne obliviscaris. 30 Memento quoniam nisi per illos natus non fuisses, et retribue illis quomodo et illi tibi.

31 In tota anima tua time Dominum, et sacerdotes illius sanctifica. 32 In omni virtute tua dilige eum qui te fecit, et ministros eius non derelinquas. 33 Honora Deum ex tota anima tua, et honorifica sacerdotes, et propurga te cum brachiis. 34 Da illis partem sicut mandatum est tibi primitiarum et purgationis, et de neglegentia tua purga te cum paucis. 35 Datum brachiorum tuorum et sacrificium sanctificationis

bandry ordained by the Most High. 17 Number not thyself among the multitude of the disorderly. 18 Remember wrath, for it will not tarry long. 19 Humble thy spirit very much, for the vengeance on the flesh of the ungodly is fire and worms.

20 Do not transgress against thy friend deferring money, nor despise thy dear brother for the sake of gold. 21 Depart not from a wise and good wife whom thou hast gotten in the fear of the Lord, for the grace of her modesty is above gold. 22 Hurt not the servant that worketh faithfully, nor the hired man that giveth thee his life. 23 Let a wise servant be dear to thee as thy own soul. Defraud him not of liberty, nor leave him needy.

24 Hast thou cattle? Have an eye to them, and if they be for thy profit, keep them with thee. 25 Hast thou children? Instruct them, and bow *down their neck* from their childhood. 26 Hast thou daughters? Have a care of their body, and shew not thy countenance gay towards them. 27 Marry thy daughter *well,* and thou shalt do a great work, and give her to a wise man. 28 If thou hast a wife according to thy soul, cast her not off, and to her that is hateful trust not thyself. With thy whole heart 29 honour thy father, and forget not the groanings of thy mother. 30 Remember that thou hadst not been born but through them, and make a return to them as they have done for thee.

31 With all thy soul fear the Lord, and reverence his priests. 32 With all thy strength love him that made thee, and forsake not his ministers. 33 Honour God with all thy soul, and give honour to the priests, and purify thyself with thy arms. 34 Give them their portion as it is commanded thee of the firstfruits and of purifications, and for thy negligences purify thyself with a few. 35 Offer to the Lord the gift

offeres Domino et initia sanctorum, 36 et pauperi porrige manum tuam ut perficiatur propitiatio et benedictio tua. 37 Gratia dati in conspectu omnis viventis, et mortuo non prohibeas gratiam.

38 Non desis plorantibus in consolatione, et cum lugentibus ambula. 39 Non te pigeat visitare infirmum, ex his enim in dilectione firmaberis. 40 In omnibus operibus tuis memorare novissima tua, et in aeternum non peccabis.

Caput 8

Non litiges cum homine potente ne forte incidas in manus illius. 2 Non contendas cum viro locuplete ne forte contra consistat litem tibi, 3 multos enim perdidit aurum atque argentum et usque cor regum extendit et convertit. 4 Non litiges cum homine linguato, et non strues in igne illius ligna. 5 Non communices homini indocto ne male de progenie tua loquatur. 6 Ne despicias hominem avertentem se a peccato, neque inproperes ei. Memento quoniam omnes sumus in correptionem.

of thy shoulders and the sacrifice of sanctification and the firstfruits of the holy things, 36 and stretch out thy hand to the poor that thy expiation and thy blessing may be perfected. 37 *A gift hath grace* in the sight of all the living, and restrain not grace from the dead.

38 Be not wanting in comforting them that weep, and walk with them that mourn. 39 Be not slow to visit the sick, for by these things thou shalt be confirmed in love. 40 In all thy works remember thy last end, and thou shalt never sin.

Chapter 8

Other lessons of wisdom and virtue.

S trive not with a powerful man *lest* thou fall into his hands. 2 Contend not with a rich man lest he bring an action against thee, 3 for gold and silver hath destroyed many and hath reached even to the heart of kings and perverted them. 4 Strive not with a man that is full of tongue, and heap not wood upon his fire. 5 Communicate not with an ignorant man lest he speak ill of thy family. 6 Despise not a man that turneth away from sin, nor reproach him therewith. Remember that we are all worthy of reproof.

7 Ne spernas hominem in sua senecta, etenim ex nobis senescunt. 8 Noli de mortuo inimico tuo gaudere, sciens quoniam omnes morimur et in gaudium nolumus venire. 9 Ne despicias narrationem presbyterorum sapientium, et in proverbiis illorum conversare, 10 ab ipsis enim disces sapientiam et doctrinam intellectus et servire magnatis sine querella. 11 Non te praetereat narratio seniorum, ipsi enim didicerunt a patribus suis, 12 quoniam ab ipsis disces intellectum et in tempore necessitatis dare responsum.

13 Non incendas carbones peccatorum arguens eos, et ne incendaris flamma ignis peccatorum illorum. 14 Ne contra faciem stes contumeliosi ne sedeat quasi insidiator ori tuo. 15 Noli fenerare homini fortiori te, quod si feneraveris, tamquam perditum habe. 16 Non spondeas super virtutem tuam, quod si spoponderis, quasi restituens cogita. 17 Non iudices contra iudicem, quoniam secundum quod iustum est iudicat. 18 Cum audace non eas in via, ne forte gravet mala sua in te, ipse enim secundum voluntatem suam vadit, et simul cum stultitia illius peries. 19 Cum iracundo non facias rixam, et cum audace non eas in desertum, quoniam quasi nihil est ante illum sanguis, et ubi non est adiutorium elidet te. 20 Cum fatuis ne consilium habeas, non enim poterunt diligere nisi quae ipsis placent. 21 Coram extraneo ne facias consilium, nescis enim quid pariet. 22 Non omni homini cor tuum manifestes ne forte inferat tibi gratiam falsam et convicietur tibi.

7 Despise not a man in his old age, for we also shall become old. 8 Rejoice not at the death of thy enemy, knowing that we all die and are not willing *that others should rejoice at our death.* 9 Despise not the discourse of them that are ancient and wise, *but* acquaint thyself with their proverbs, 10 for of them thou shalt learn wisdom and instruction of understanding and to serve great men without blame. 11 Let not the discourse of the ancients escape thee, for they have learned of their fathers, 12 for of them thou shalt learn understanding and to give an answer in time of need.

13 Kindle not the coals of sinners by rebuking them *lest* thou be burnt with the flame of the fire of their sins. 14 Stand not against the face of an injurious person lest he sit as a spy *to entrap thee in thy words.* 15 Lend not to a man that is mightier than thyself, and if thou lendest, count it as lost. 16 Be not surety above thy power, and if thou be surety, think as if thou wert to pay it. 17 Judge not against a judge, for he judgeth according to that which is just. 18 Go not on the way with a bold man, *lest* he burden thee with his evils, for he goeth according to his own will, and thou shalt perish together with his folly. 19 Quarrel not with a passionate man, and go not into the desert with a bold man, for blood is as nothing in his sight, and where there is no help he will overthrow thee. 20 Advise not with fools, for they cannot love but such things as please them. 21 Before a stranger do no matter of counsel, for thou knowest not what he will bring forth. 22 Open not thy heart to every man *lest* he repay thee with an *evil turn* and speak reproachfully to thee.

Caput 9

Non zeles mulierem sinus tui ne ostendat super te malitiam doctrinae nequam. ² Non des mulieri potestatem animae tuae ne ingrediatur in virtute tua et confundaris. ³ Ne respicias mulierem multivolam ne forte incidas in laqueos illius. ⁴ Cum saltatrice ne adsiduus sis, nec audias illam ne forte pereas in efficacia illius. ⁵ Virginem ne conspicias ne forte scandalizeris in decore illius. ⁶ Non des fornicariis animam tuam in nullo ne perdas te et hereditatem tuam.

⁷ Noli circumspicere in vicis civitatis, nec oberraveris in plateis illius. ⁸ Averte faciem tuam a muliere compta, et non circumspicias speciem alienam, ⁹ propter speciem mulieris multi perierunt, et ex hoc concupiscentia quasi ignis exardescit. ¹⁰ Omnis mulier quae est fornicaria quasi stercus in via conculcabitur. ¹¹ Speciem mulieris alienae multi admirati reprobi facti sunt, conloquium enim illius quasi ignis exardescit. ¹² Cum aliena muliere ne sedeas omnino, nec accum-

Chapter 9

Cautions with regard to women and dangerous conversations.

Be not jealous over the wife of thy bosom lest she shew in thy regard the malice of a wicked lesson. 2 Give not the power of thy soul to a woman lest she enter upon thy strength and thou be confounded. 3 Look not upon a woman that hath a mind for many lest thou fall into her snares. 4 Use not much the company of her that is a dancer, and hearken not to her *lest* thou perish by *the force of her charms*. 5 Gaze not upon a maiden *lest* her beauty be a stumbling block to thee. 6 Give not thy soul to harlots in any point lest thou destroy thyself and thy inheritance.

7 Look not round about thee in the ways of the city, nor wander up and down in the streets thereof. 8 Turn away thy face from a woman dressed up, and gaze not about upon another's beauty, 9 for many have perished by the beauty of a woman, and hereby lust is enkindled as a fire. 10 Every woman that is a harlot shall be trodden upon as dung in the way. 11 Many by admiring the beauty of another man's wife have become reprobate, for her conversation burneth as fire. 12 Sit not at all with another man's wife, nor repose upon

bas cum ea super cubitum, 13 et non alterceris cum ea in vino, ne forte declinet cor tuum in illa et sanguine tuo labaris in perditionem.

14 Ne derelinquas amicum antiquum, novus enim non erit similis illi. 15 Vinum novum amicus novus: veterascet, et cum suavitate bibes illud. 16 Non zeles gloriam et opes peccatoris, non enim scis quae futura sit illius subversio. 17 Non placeat tibi iniuria iniustorum, sciens quoniam usque ad inferos non placebit impius. 18 Longe abesto ab homine potestatem habente occidendi, et non suspicaberis timorem mortis. 19 Et si accesseris ad illum, noli aliquid committere ne forte auferat vitam tuam. 20 Communionem mortis scito, quoniam in medium laqueorum ingredieris et super dolentium arma ambulabis.

21 Secundum virtutem tuam cave te a proximo tuo, et cum sapientibus et prudentibus tracta. 22 Viri iusti sint tibi convivae, et in timore Dei sit gloriatio tibi. 23 Et in sensu sit tibi cogitatus Dei et omnis enarratio tua in praeceptis Altissimi. 24 In manus artificum opera laudabuntur, et princeps populi in sapientia sermonis sui, in sensu vero seniorum verbum. 25 Terribilis est in civitate sua homo linguosus, et temerarius in verbo suo odibilis erit.

the bed with her, 13 and strive not with her over wine, lest thy heart decline towards her and by thy blood thou fall into destruction.

14 Forsake not an old friend, for the new will not be like to him. 15 A new friend is as new wine: it shall grow old, and thou shalt drink it with pleasure. 16 Envy not the glory and riches of a sinner, for thou knowest not what his ruin shall be. 17 Be not pleased with the wrong done by the unjust, knowing that even to hell the wicked shall not please. 18 Keep thee far from the man that hath power to kill, *so* thou shalt not suspect the fear of death. 19 And if thou come to him, commit no fault *lest* he take away thy life. 20 Know it to be a communication with death, for thou art going in the midst of snares and walking upon the arms of them that are grieved.

21 According to thy power beware of thy neighbour, and treat with the wise and prudent. 22 Let just men be thy guests, and let thy glory be in the fear of God. 23 And let the thought of God be in thy mind and all thy discourse on the commandments of the Highest. 24 Works shall be praised for the *hand* of the artificers, and the prince of the people for the wisdom of his speech, but the word of the ancients for the sense. 25 A man full of tongue is terrible in his city, and he that is rash in his word shall be hateful.

Caput 10

Iudex sapiens iudicabit populum suum, et principatus sensati stabilis erit. 2 Secundum iudicem populi, sic et ministri eius, et qualis rector est civitatis, tales et inhabitantes in ea. 3 Rex insipiens perdet populum suum, et civitates inhabitabuntur per sensum prudentium. 4 In manu Dei potestas terrae, et utilem rectorem in tempus suscitabit super illam. 5 In manu Dei prosperitas hominis, et super faciem scribae inponet honorem suum.

6 Omnis iniuriae proximi ne memineris, et nihil agas in operibus iniuriae. 7 Odibilis coram Deo et hominibus superbia, et execrabilis omnis iniquitas gentium. 8 Regnum a gente in gentem transfertur propter iniustitias et iniurias et contumelias et diversos dolos, 9 avaro autem nihil est scelestius.

Quid superbit terra et cinis? 10 Nihil est iniquius quam amare pecuniam, hic enim et animam suam venalem habet quoniam in vita sua proiecit intima sua. 11 Omnis potentatus brevis vita. Languor prolixior gravat medicum. 12 Brevem languorem praecidit medicus; sic et rex hodie est, et

Chapter 10

The virtues and vices of men in power, the great evil of pride.

A wise judge shall judge his people, and the government of a prudent man shall be steady. 2 As the judge of the people *is himself,* so also are his ministers, and what manner of man the ruler of a city is, such also are they that dwell therein. 3 An unwise king shall be the ruin of his people, and cities shall be inhabited through the *prudence of the rulers.* 4 The power of the earth is in the hand of God, and *in his* time he will raise up a profitable ruler over it. 5 The prosperity of man is in the hand of God, and upon the person of the scribe he shall lay his honour.

6 Remember not any injury done thee by thy neighbour, and do thou nothing by deeds of injury. 7 Pride is hateful before God and men, and all iniquity of nations is execrable. 8 A kingdom is translated from one people to another because of injustices and wrongs and injuries and divers deceits, 9 but nothing is more wicked than the covetous man.

Why is earth and ashes proud? 10 There is not a more wicked thing than to love money, for *such a one* setteth even his own soul to sale because while he liveth he hath cast away his bowels. 11 All power is of short life. A long sickness is troublesome to the physician. 12 The physician cutteth off a short sickness; so also a king is today, and tomorrow he

cras morietur, 13 cum enim morietur homo, hereditabit serpentes et bestias et vermes.

14 Initium superbiae hominis apostatare a Deo 15 quoniam ab eo qui fecit illum recessit cor eius, quoniam initium peccati omnis superbia: qui tenuerit illam adimplebitur maledictis, et subvertet eum in finem. 16 Propterea exhonoravit Dominus conventus malorum et destruxit eos usque in finem. 17 Sedes ducum superborum destruxit Deus et sedere fecit mites pro illis. 18 Radices gentium superbarum arefecit Deus et plantavit humiles ex ipsis gentibus. 19 Terras Gentium evertit Dominus et perdidit eas usque ad fundamentum. 20 Arefecit ex ipsis et disperdidit illos et cessare fecit memoriam eorum a terra. 21 Perdidit Deus memoriam superborum et reliquit memoriam humilium sensu. 22 Non est creata hominibus superbia, neque iracundia nationi mulierum.

23 Semen hominum honorabitur hoc quod timet Deum, semen autem hoc exhonorabitur quod praeterit mandata Domini. 24 In medio fratrum rector illorum in honore, et qui timent Dominum erunt in oculis illius. 25 Gloria divitum, honoratorum et pauperum timor Dei est. 26 Non despicere hominem iustum pauperem, et non magnificare virum peccatorem divitem. 27 Magnus et iudex et potens est in honore, et non est maior illo qui timet Deum.

28 Servo sensato liberi servient, et vir prudens et disciplinatus non murmurabit correptus, et inscius non honorabi-

shall die, 13 for when a man shall die, he shall inherit serpents and beasts and worms.

14 The beginning of the pride of man is to fall off from God 15 because his heart is departed from him that made him, for pride is the beginning of all sin: he that holdeth it shall be filled with maledictions, and it shall ruin him in the end. 16 Therefore hath the Lord disgraced the assemblies of the wicked and hath utterly destroyed them. 17 God hath overturned the thrones of proud princes and hath set up the meek in their stead. 18 God hath made the roots of proud nations to wither and hath planted the humble of these nations. 19 The Lord hath overthrown the lands of the Gentiles and hath destroyed them even to the foundation. 20 He hath made some of them to wither away and hath destroyed them and hath made the memory of them to cease from the earth. 21 God hath abolished the memory of the proud and hath preserved the memory of them that are humble in mind. 22 Pride was not made for men, nor wrath for the race of women.

23 That seed of men shall be honoured which feareth God, but that seed shall be dishonoured which transgresseth the commandments of the Lord. 24 In the midst of brethren their chief is honourable; *so* shall they that fear the Lord be in his eyes. 25 The fear of God is the glory of the rich *and* of the honourable and of the poor. 26 Despise not a just man that is poor, and do not magnify a sinful man that is rich. 27 The great man and the judge and the mighty is in honour, and there is none greater than he that feareth God.

28 They that are free shall serve a servant that is wise, and a man that is prudent and well instructed will not murmur when he is reproved, and he that is ignorant shall not be

tur. 29 Noli te extollere in faciendo opere tuo, et noli cunctari in tempore angustiae. 30 Melior est qui operatur et abundat in omnibus quam qui gloriatur et eget panem.

31 Fili, in mansuetudine serva animam tuam, et da illi honorem secundum meritum suum. 32 Peccantem in animam suam quis iustificabit? Et quis honorificabit exhonorantem animam suam? 33 Pauper gloriatur per disciplinam et timorem suum, et est homo qui honorificatur propter substantiam suam. 34 Qui autem gloriatur in paupertate, quanto magis in substantia? Et qui gloriatur in substantia, paupertatem vereatur.

Caput 11

Sapientia humiliati exaltabit caput illius et in medio magnatorum consedere illum faciet. 2 Non laudes virum in specie sua, neque spernas hominem in visu suo. 3 Brevis in volatilibus est apis, et initium dulcoris habet fructus illius. 4 In vestitu ne glorieris umquam, nec in die honoris tui extollaris, quoniam mirabilia opera Altissimi solius, et gloriosa et absconsa et invisa opera illius. 5 Multi tyranni sederunt in throno, et insuspicabilis portavit diadema. 6 Multi potentes

honoured. 29 Extol not thyself in doing thy work, and linger not in the time of distress. 30 Better is he that laboureth and aboundeth in all things than he that boasteth himself and wanteth bread.

31 My son, keep thy soul in meekness, and give it honour according to its desert. 32 Who will justify him that sinneth against his own soul? And who will honour him that dishonoureth his own soul? 33 The poor man is glorified by his discipline and fear, and there is a man that is honoured for his wealth. 34 But he that is glorified in poverty, how much more in wealth? And he that is glorified in wealth, let him fear poverty.

Chapter 11

Lessons of humility and moderation in all things.

The wisdom of the humble shall exalt his head and shall make him sit in the midst of great men. 2 Praise not a man for his beauty, neither despise a man for his look. 3 The bee is small among flying things, *but* her fruit hath the chiefest sweetness. 4 Glory not in apparel at any time, and be not exalted in the day of thy honour, for the works of the Highest only are wonderful, and his works are glorious and secret and hidden. 5 Many tyrants have sat on the throne, and he whom no man would think on hath worn the crown. 6 Many

pressi sunt valide, et gloriosi traditi sunt in manus alterorum.

7 Priusquam interroges ne vituperes quemquam, et cum interrogaveris corripe iuste. 8 Priusquam audias ne respondeas verbum, et in medio seniorum ne adicias loqui. 9 De re ea quae te non molestat ne certeris, et in iudicio peccantium ne consistas. 10 Fili, ne in multis sint actus tui, et si dives fueris, non eris inmunis a delicto, si enim secutus fueris non adprehendes, et non effugies si praecucurreris.

11 Est homo laborans et festinans et dolens impius et tanto magis non abundabit. 12 Est homo marcidus egens recuperatione, plus deficiens virtute et abundans paupertate, 13 et oculus Dei respexit illum in bono et erexit illum ab humilitate ipsius et exaltavit caput eius, et mirati sunt in illo multi et honoraverunt Deum.

14 Bona et mala, vita et mors, paupertas et honestas a Deo sunt. 15 Sapientia et disciplina et scientia legis apud Deum. Dilectio et viae bonorum apud ipsum. 16 Error et tenebrae peccatoribus concreata sunt, qui autem exultant in malis consenescunt in malo. 17 Datio Dei permanet iustis, et profectus illius successus habebit in aeternum.

18 Est qui locupletatur parce agendo, et haec pars mercedis illius, 19 in eo quod dicit, "Inveni requiem mihi, et nunc manducabo de bonis meis solus," 20 et nescit quod tempus praetereat et mors appropinquet et relinquat omnia aliis et morietur. 21 Sta in testamento tuo, et in illo conloquere, et

mighty men have been greatly brought down, and the glorious have been delivered into the hand of others.

7 Before thou inquire blame no man, and when thou hast inquired reprove justly. 8 Before thou hear answer not a word, and interrupt not *others* in the midst of *their discourse.* 9 Strive not in a matter which doth not concern thee, and sit not in judgment with sinners. 10 My son, meddle not with many matters, and if thou be rich, thou shalt not be free from sin, for if thou pursue after thou shalt not overtake, and if thou run before thou shalt not escape.

11 There is an ungodly man that laboureth and maketh haste and is in sorrow and is so much the more in want. 12 *Again,* there is an inactive man that wanteth help, is very weak in ability and full of poverty, 13 *yet* the eye of God hath looked upon him for good and hath lifted him up from his low estate and hath exalted his head, and many have wondered at him and have glorified God.

14 Good things and evil, life and death, poverty and riches are from God. 15 Wisdom and discipline and the knowledge of the law are with God. Love and the ways of good things are with him. 16 Error and darkness are created with sinners, and they that glory in evil things grow old in evil. 17 The gift of God abideth with the just, and his advancement shall have success for ever.

18 There is one that is enriched by living sparingly, and this is the portion of his reward, 19 in that he saith, "I have found me rest, and now I will eat of my goods alone," 20 and he knoweth not what time *shall pass* and that death approacheth and that he must leave all to others and shall die. 21 Be steadfast in thy covenant, and be conversant therein,

in opere mandatorum tuorum veteresce. 22 Ne manseris in operibus peccatorum, fide autem in Deo, et mane in loco tuo, 23 facile est enim in oculis Dei subito honestare pauperem. 24 Benedictio Dei in mercedem iusti festinat, et in hora veloci processus illius fructificat.

25 Ne dicas, "Quid est mihi opus, et quae erunt mihi ex hoc bona?" 26 Ne dicas, "Sufficiens mihi sum, et quid ex hoc pessimabor?"

27 In die bonorum ne inmemor sis malorum, et in die malorum ne inmemor sis bonorum, 28 quoniam facile coram Deo in die obitus retribuere unicuique secundum vias suas. 29 Malitia horae oblivionem facit luxuriae magnae, et in fine hominis denudatio operum illius. 30 Ante mortem ne laudes hominem quemquam, quoniam in filiis suis agnoscitur vir. 31 Non omnem hominem inducas in domum tuam, multae enim insidiae sunt dolosi, 32 sicut enim eructant praecordia foetentium et sicut perdix inducitur in caveam et ut caprea in laqueum, sic et cor superborum et sicut prospectator videns casum proximi sui, 33 bona enim in mala convertens insidiatur, et in electis inponet maculam.

34 Ab scintilla una augetur ignis, et ab uno doloso augetur sanguis, homo vero peccator sanguini insidiatur. 35 Adtende tibi a pestifero, fabricat enim mala, ne forte inducat super te subsannationem in perpetuum. 36 Admitte ad te alienigenam, et subvertet te in turbore et abalienabit te a tuis propriis.

and grow old in the work of thy commandments. 22 Abide not in the works of sinners, but trust in God, and stay in thy place, 23 for it is easy in the eyes of God on a sudden to make the poor man rich. 24 The blessing of God maketh haste to reward the just, and in a swift hour his blessing beareth fruit.

25 Say not, "What need I, and what good shall I have by this?" 26 Say not, "I am sufficient for myself, and what shall I be made worse by this?"

27 In the day of good things be not unmindful of evils, and in the day of evils be not unmindful of good things, 28 for it is easy before God in the day of death to reward every one according to his ways. 29 The affliction of an hour maketh one forget great delights, and in the end of a man is the disclosing of his works. 30 Praise not any man before death, for a man is known by his children. 31 Bring not every man into thy house, for many are the snares of the deceitful, 32 for as corrupted bowels send forth stinking breath and as the partridge is brought into the cage and as the roe into the snare, so also is the heart of the proud and as a spy that looketh on the fall of his neighbour, 33 for he lieth in wait and turneth good into evil, and on the elect he will lay a blot.

34 Of one spark *cometh* a great fire, and of one deceitful man much *blood,* and a sinful man lieth in wait for blood. 35 Take heed to thyself of a mischievous man, for he worketh evils, *lest* he bring upon thee reproach for ever. 36 Receive a stranger in, and he shall overthrow thee with a whirlwind and shall turn thee out of thy own.

Caput 12

Si benefeceris, scito cui feceris, et erit gratia in bonis tuis multa. 2 Benefac iusto, et invenies retributionem magnam, et si non ab ipso, certe a Domino, 3 non est enim ei bene qui adsiduus est in malis et elemosynam non danti, quoniam et Altissimus odio habet peccatores et misertus est paenitentibus. 4 Da misericordi, et ne suscipias peccatorem. Et impiis et peccatoribus reddet vindictam custodiens eos in die vindictae. 5 Da bono, et non receperis peccatorem. 6 Benefac humili, et non dederis impio: prohibe panes illi dare ne in ipsis potentior te sit, 7 nam duplicia mala invenies in omnibus bonis quaecumque feceris illi, quoniam et Altissimus odio habet peccatores et impiis reddet vindictam. 8 Non agnoscetur in bonis amicus, et non abscondetur in malis inimicus. 9 In bonis viri, inimici illius in tristitia, et in malitia illius amicus agnitus est.

10 Non credas inimico tuo in aeternum, sicut enim aeramentum eruginat nequitia illius. 11 Et si humiliatus vadat curvus, adice animum tuum et custodi te ab illo. 12 Non statuas illum penes te, nec sedeat ad dexteram tuam ne forte conversus in locum tuum inquirat cathedram tuam, et in novissimo cognoscas verba mea et in sermonibus meis stimuleris.

Chapter 12

We are to be liberal to the just and not to trust the wicked.

If thou do good, know to whom thou dost it, and there shall be much thanks for thy good deeds. 2 Do good to the just, and thou shalt find great recompense, and if not of him, assuredly of the Lord, 3 for there is no good for him that is always occupied in evil and that giveth no alms, for the Highest *hateth* sinners and hath mercy on the penitent. 4 Give to the merciful, and uphold not the sinner. *God* will repay vengeance to the ungodly and to sinners and keep them against the day of vengeance. 5 Give to the good, and receive not a sinner. 6 Do good to the humble, and give not to the ungodly: *hold back thy bread, and give it not* to him lest thereby he overmaster thee, 7 for thou shalt receive twice as much evil for all the good thou shalt have done to him, for the Highest also hateth sinners and will repay vengeance to the ungodly. 8 A friend shall not be known in prosperity, and an enemy shall not be hidden in adversity. 9 In the prosperity of a man, his enemies are grieved, and a friend is known in his adversity.

10 Never trust thy enemy, for as a brass pot his wickedness rusteth. 11 Though he humble himself and go crouching, yet take good heed and beware of him. 12 Set him not by thee, neither let him sit on thy right hand *lest* he turn into thy place and seek to take thy seat, and at the last thou *acknowledge* my words and be pricked with my sayings.

13 Quis miserebitur incantatori a serpente percusso et omnibus qui adpropiant bestiis? Sic et qui comitatur cum viro iniquo et obvolutus est in peccatis eius. 14 Una hora tecum permanebit, si autem declinaveris, non subportabit. 15 In labiis suis indulcat inimicus, et in corde suo insidiatur ut subvertat te in foveam. 16 In oculis suis lacrimatur inimicus, et si invenerit tempus non satiabitur sanguine. 17 Et si incurrerint tibi mala, invenies eum illic priorem. 18 In oculis suis lacrimatur inimicus, et quasi adiuvans suffodiet plantas tuas. 19 Caput suum movebit et plaudebit manu et multa susurrans commutabit vultum suum.

Caput 13

Qui tetigerit picem inquinabitur ab illa, et qui communicaverit superbo induet superbiam. 2 Pondus super se tollet qui honestiori se communicat. Et ditiori te ne socius fueris. 3 Quid communicabit caccabus ad ollam, quando enim se conliserint confringetur? 4 Dives iniuste egit, et fremebit, pauper autem laesus tacebit. 5 Si largitus fueris, adsumet te,

13 Who will pity an enchanter struck by a serpent or any that come near wild beasts? So is it with him that keepeth company with a wicked man and is involved in his sins. 14 For an hour he will abide with thee, but if thou begin to decline, he will not endure it. 15 An enemy speaketh sweetly with his lips, *but* in his heart he lieth in wait to throw thee into a pit. 16 An enemy weepeth with his eyes, *but* if he find an opportunity he will not be satisfied with blood, 17 and if evils come upon thee, thou shalt find him there first. 18 An enemy hath tears in his eyes, and while he pretendeth to help thee will undermine thy feet. 19 He will shake his head and clap his hands and whisper much and change his countenance.

Chapter 13

Cautions in the choice of company.

He that toucheth pitch shall be defiled with it, and he that hath fellowship with the proud shall put on pride. 2 He shall take a burden upon him that hath fellowship with one more honourable than himself. And have no fellowship with one that is richer than thyself.

3 What agreement shall the earthen pot have with the kettle, for if they knock one against the other, it shall be broken? 4 The rich man hath done wrong, and *yet* he will fume, but the poor is wronged and *must* hold his peace. 5 If thou give, he will make use of thee, and if thou have noth-

et si non habueris, derelinquet te. 6 Si habes, convivet tecum et evacuabit te, et ipse non dolebit super te. 7 Si necessarius illi fueris subplantabit te et subridens spem dabit. Narrans tibi bona et dicet, "Quid opus est tibi?" 8 Et confundet te in cibis suis donec te exinaniat bis et ter, et in novissimo deridebit te, et postea videns derelinquet te et caput suum movebit ad te.

9 Humiliare Deo, et expecta manus eius. 10 Adtende ne seductus in stultitiam humilieris. 11 Noli esse humilis in sapientia tua ne humiliatus in stultitiam seducaris. 12 Advocatus a potentiore, discede, ex hoc enim magis te advocabit. 13 Ne inprobus sis ne inpingaris, et ne longe sis ab eo ne eas in oblivionem. 14 Ne retineas ex aequo loqui cum illo, nec credas multis verbis illius, ex multa enim loquella temptabit te et subridens interrogabit te de absconditis tuis. 15 Inmitis animus illius conservabit verba tua, et non parcet de malitia et de vinculis. 16 Cave tibi, et adtende diligenter auditui tuo, quoniam cum subversione tua ambulas. 17 Audiens vero illa, quasi in somnis vide, et vigilabis.

18 Omni vita tua dilige Deum, et invoca eum in salute tua. 19 Omne animal diligit similem sibi, sic et omnis homo proximum sibi. 20 Omnis caro ad similem sibi coniungetur, et omnis homo simili sui sociabitur. 21 Si communicabit lupus agno aliquando, sic peccator iusto. 22 Quae communicatio sancto homini ad canem, aut quae pars diviti ad pauperem? 23 Venatio leonis onager in heremo, sic et pascua sunt divitum pauperes. 24 Et sicut abominatio est superbo humi-

ing, he will forsake thee. 6 If thou have *any thing,* he will live with thee and will make thee bare, and he will not be sorry for thee. 7 If he have need of thee he will deceive thee and smiling upon thee will put thee in hope. He will speak thee fair and will say, "What wantest thou?" 8 And he will shame thee by his meats till he have drawn thee dry twice or thrice, and at last he will laugh at thee, and afterward when he seeth thee he will forsake thee and shake his head at thee.

9 Humble thyself to God, and wait for his hands. 10 Beware that thou be not deceived into folly and be humbled. 11 Be not lowly in thy wisdom lest being humbled thou be deceived into folly. 12 If thou be invited by one that is mightier, withdraw thyself, for so he will invite thee the more. 13 Be not troublesome to him lest thou be put back, and keep not far from him lest thou be forgotten. 14 Affect not to speak with him as an equal, and believe not his many words, for by much talk he will sift thee and smiling will examine thee concerning thy secrets. 15 His cruel mind will lay up thy words, and he will not spare *to do thee hurt and to cast thee into prison.* 16 Take heed to thyself, and attend diligently to what thou hearest, for thou walkest *in danger of* thy ruin. 17 When thou hearest those things, see as it were in sleep, and thou shalt awake.

18 Love God all thy life, and call upon him for thy salvation. 19 Every beast loveth its like, so also every man him that is nearest to himself. 20 All flesh shall consort with the like to itself, and every man shall associate himself to his like. 21 If the wolf shall at any time have fellowship with the lamb, so the sinner with the just. 22 What fellowship hath a holy man with a dog, or what part hath the rich with the poor? 23 The wild ass is the lion's prey in the desert, so also the poor are devoured by the rich. 24 And as humility is an

litas, sic et execratio divitis pauper. 25 Dives commotus, confirmatur ab amicis suis, humilis autem cum ceciderit, expelletur et a notis. 26 Diviti decepto, multi recuperatores; locutus est superba, et iustificaverunt illum. 27 Humilis deceptus est, et insuper arguitur; locutus est sensate et non est datus ei locus. 28 Dives locutus est, et omnes tacuerunt, et verbum illius usque ad nubes perducent. 29 Pauper locutus est, et dicunt, "Quis est hic?" Et si offenderit, subvertent illum. 30 Bona est substantia cui non est peccatum in conscientia, et nequissima paupertas in ore impii.

31 Cor hominis inmutat faciem illius, sive in bona sive in mala. 32 Vestigium cordis boni et faciem bonam difficile invenies et cum labore.

Caput 14

Beatus vir qui non est lapsus verbo ex ore suo et non est stimulatus in tristitia delicti. 2 Felix qui non habuit animi sui tristitiam et non excidit ab spe sua. 3 Viro cupido et tenaci sine ratione est substantia, et homini livido ad quid

abomination to the proud, so also the rich man abhorreth the poor. 25 When a rich man is shaken, he is kept up by his friends, but when a poor man is fallen down, he *is* thrust away even by his acquaintance. 26 When a rich man hath been deceived, he hath many helpers; he hath spoken proud things, and they have justified him. 27 The poor man was deceived, and he is rebuked also; he hath spoken wisely and could have no place. 28 The rich man spoke, and all held their peace, and what he said they extol even to the clouds. 29 The poor man spoke, and they say, "Who is this?" And if he stumble, they will overthrow him. 30 Riches are good to him that hath no sin in his conscience, and poverty is very wicked in the mouth of the ungodly.

31 The heart of a man changeth his countenance, either for good or for evil. 32 The token of a good heart and a good countenance thou shalt hardly find and with labour.

Chapter 14

The evil of avarice. Works of mercy are recommended and the love of wisdom.

Blessed is the man that hath not slipped by a word out of his mouth and is not pricked with the remorse of sin. 2 Happy is he that hath had no sadness of his mind and who is not fallen from his hope. 3 Riches are *not comely* for a covetous man and a niggard, and what should an envious man

aurum? 4 Qui acervat ex animo suo iniuste aliis congregat, et in bonis illius alius luxuriabitur. 5 Qui sibi nequa est, cui alii bonus erit? Et non iucundabitur in bonis suis. 6 Qui sibi invidet nihil est illo nequius, et haec redditio est malitiae illius, 7 et si bene fecerit, ignoranter et non volens facit, et in novissimo manifestat malitiam suam. 8 Nequa est oculus lividi, et avertens faciem suam et despiciens animam suam. 9 Insatiabilis oculus cupidi in parte iniquitatis; non satiabitur donec consummat, arefaciens, animam suam. 10 Oculus malus ad mala, et non satiabitur pane sed indigens et in tristitia erit super mensam suam.

11 Fili, si habes, benefac tecum, et Deo dignas oblationes offer. 12 Memor esto quoniam mors non tardat et testamentum inferorum quia demonstratum est tibi, testamentum enim huius mundi morte morietur. 13 Ante mortem benefac amico tuo et secundum vires tuas, exporrigens da pauperi. 14 Non defrauderis a die bono, et particula boni doni non te praetereat. 15 Nonne aliis relinques dolores et labores tuos in divisione sortis? 16 Da, et accipe, et iustifica animam tuam. 17 Ante obitum tuum operare iustitiam, quoniam non est apud inferos invenire cibum.

18 Omnis caro sicut faenum veterascet et sicut folium fructificans in arbore viridi. 19 Alia generantur, et alia deiciuntur; sic generatio carnis et sanguinis: alia finitur, et alia nascitur. 20 Omne opus corruptibile in fine deficiet, et qui

do with gold? 4 He that gathereth together by wronging his own soul gathereth for others, and another will *squander away his goods in rioting.* 5 He that is evil to himself, to *whom* will he be good? And he shall not take pleasure in his goods. 6 There is none worse than he that envieth himself, and this is the reward of his wickedness, 7 and if he do good, he doth it ignorantly and unwillingly and at the last he discovereth his wickedness. 8 The eye of the envious is wicked, and he turneth away his face and despiseth his own soul. 9 The eye of the covetous man is insatiable in his portion of iniquity; he will not be satisfied till he consume his own soul, drying it up. 10 An evil eye is towards evil things, and he shall not have his fill of bread but shall be needy and pensive at his own table.

11 My son, if thou have *any thing,* do good to thyself, and offer to God worthy offerings. 12 Remember that death is not slow and that the covenant of hell hath been shewn to thee, for the covenant of this world shall surely die. 13 Do good to thy friend before thou die and according to thy ability, stretching out thy hand give to the poor. 14 Defraud not thyself of the good day, and let not the part of a good gift overpass thee. 15 Shalt thou not leave to others to divide by lot thy sorrows and labours? 16 Give, and take, and justify thy soul. 17 Before thy death work justice, for in hell there is no finding food.

18 All flesh shall fade as grass and as the leaf that springeth out on a green tree. 19 Some grow, and some fall off; so is the generation of flesh and blood: one cometh to an end, and another is born. 20 Every work that is corruptible shall

illud operatur ibit cum ipso, 21 et omne opus electum iustificabitur, et qui operatur illud honorabitur in illo.

22 Beatus vir qui in sapientia morabitur et qui in iustitia sua meditabitur et in sensu cogitabit circumspectionem Dei. 23 Qui excogitat vias illius in suo corde et in absconsis illius intellegens, vadens post illam quasi vestigator et in viis illius consistens, 24 qui respicit per fenestras illius et in ianuas illius audiens, 25 qui requiescit iuxta domum illius et in parietibus illius figens palum statuet casulam suam ad manus illius, et requiescent in casula eius bona per aevum, 26 statuet filios suos sub tegimen illius et sub ramis illius morabitur. 27 Protegetur sub tegmine illius a fervore et in gloria eius requiescet.

Caput 15

Qui timet Deum faciet bona, et qui continens est iustitiae adprehendet illam, 2 et obviabit illi quasi mater honorificata et quasi mulier a virginitate suscipiet illum. 3 Cibabit illum pane vitae et intellectus et aqua sapientiae salutaris

fail in the end, and the worker thereof shall go with it, 21 and every excellent work shall be justified, and the worker thereof shall be honoured therein.

22 Blessed is the man that shall continue in wisdom and that shall meditate in his justice and in his mind shall think of the *all seeing eye of* God. 23 He that considereth her ways in his heart and hath understanding in her secrets, who goeth after her as one that traceth and stayeth in her ways, 24 he who looketh in at her windows and hearkeneth at her door, 25 he that lodgeth near her house and fastening a pin in her walls shall set up his tent nigh unto her, *where* good things shall rest in his lodging for ever, 26 he shall set his children under her shelter and shall lodge under her branches. 27 He shall be protected under her covering from the heat and shall rest in her glory.

Chapter 15

Wisdom embraceth them that fear God. God is not the author of sin.

He that feareth God will do good, and he that possesseth justice shall lay hold on her, 2 and she will meet him as an honourable mother and will receive him as a wife *married of a virgin*. 3 With the bread of life and understanding she shall feed him and give him the water of wholesome wisdom

potabit illum, et firmabitur in illo, et non flectetur, 4 et continebit illum, et non confundetur, et exaltabit illum apud proximos suos. 5 Et in medio ecclesiae aperiet os illius et adimplebit illum spiritu sapientiae et intellectus et stolam gloriae vestiet illum. 6 Iucunditatem et exultationem thesaurizabit super illum et nomine aeterno hereditabit illum. 7 Homines stulti non adprehendent illam, et homines sensati obviabunt illi. Homines stulti non videbunt illam, longe enim abest a superbia et dolo. 8 Viri mendaces non erunt illius memores, et viri veraces invenientur in illa et successum habebunt usque ad inspectionem Dei.

9 Non est speciosa laus in ore peccatoris, 10 quoniam a Deo profecta est sapientia, sapientiae enim Dei adstabit laus et in ore fideli abundabit, et Dominator dabit eam illi. 11 Non dixeris, "Per Deum abest," quae odit enim ne feceris. 12 Non dicas, "Ille me inplanavit," non enim necessarii sunt illi homines impii. 13 Omne execramentum erroris odit Dominus, et non erit amabile timentibus illum.

14 Deus ab initio constituit hominem et reliquit illum in manu consilii sui. 15 Adiecit mandata et praecepta sua. 16 Si volueris mandata servare, conservabunt te, et in perpetuum fidem placitam facere. 17 Adposuit tibi aquam et ignem: ad quod voles porrige manum tuam. 18 Ante hominem vita et mors, bonum et malum: quod placuerit ei dabitur illi, 19 quoniam multa sapientia Dei et fortis in potentia, videns omnes sine intermissione. 20 Oculi Domini ad timentes eum, et

to drink, and she shall be made strong in him, and he shall not be moved, 4 and she shall hold him fast, and he shall not be confounded, and she shall exalt him among his neighbours. 5 And in the midst of the church she shall open his mouth and shall fill him with the spirit of wisdom and understanding and shall clothe him with a robe of glory. 6 She shall heap upon him a treasure of joy and gladness and shall cause him to inherit an everlasting name. 7 But foolish men shall not obtain her, and wise men shall meet her. Foolish men shall not see her, for she is far from pride and deceit. 8 Lying men shall not be mindful of her, *but* men that speak truth shall be found with her and shall advance even till they come to the sight of God.

9 Praise is not seemly in the mouth of a sinner, 10 for wisdom came forth from God, for praise shall be with the wisdom of God and shall abound in a faithful mouth, and the sovereign Lord will give praise unto it. 11 Say not, "It is through God that she is not with me," for do not thou the things that he hateth. 12 Say not, "He hath caused me to err," for he hath no need of wicked men. 13 The Lord hateth all abomination of error, and they that fear him shall not love it.

14 God made man from the beginning and left him in the hand of his own counsel. 15 He added his commandments and precepts. 16 If thou wilt keep the commandments and perform acceptable fidelity for ever, they shall preserve thee. 17 He hath set water and fire before thee: stretch forth thy hand to which thou wilt. 18 Before man is life and death, good and evil: that which he shall choose shall be given him, 19 for the wisdom of God is great and he is strong in power, seeing all men without ceasing. 20 The eyes of the Lord are

ipse agnoscit omnem operam hominis. 21 Nemini mandavit impie agere, et nemini dedit spatium peccandi, 22 non enim concupiscit multitudinem filiorum infidelium et inutilium.

Caput 16

Ne iucunderis in filiis impiis, si multiplicentur; nec oblecteris super ipsos, si non est timor Dei in illis. 2 Non credas vitae illorum, et ne respexeris in labores illorum, 3 melior est enim unus timens Deum quam mille filii impii. 4 Et utile mori sine filiis quam relinquere filios impios.

5 Ab uno sensato inhabitabitur patria, et tribus impiorum deseretur. 6 Multa talia vidit oculus meus, et fortiora horum audivit auris mea. 7 In synagoga peccantium exardebit ignis, et in gente incredibili exardescet ira. 8 Non exoraverunt pro peccatis suis antiqui gigantes, qui destructi sunt confidentes suae virtuti, 9 et non pepercit peregrinationi Loth et execratus est illos prae superbia verbi illorum. 10 Non misertus est illis, gentem totam perdens et extollentes se in suis peccatis.

towards them that fear him, and he knoweth all the work of man. 21 He hath commanded no man to do wickedly, and he hath given no man license to sin, 22 for he desireth not a multitude of faithless and unprofitable children.

Chapter 16

It is better to have none than many wicked children. Of the justice and mercy of God. His ways are unsearchable.

Rejoice not in ungodly children, if they be multiplied, neither be delighted in them, if the fear of God be not with them. 2 Trust not to their life, and respect not their labours, 3 for better is one that feareth God than a thousand ungodly children. 4 And it is better to die without children than to leave ungodly children.

5 By one that is wise a country shall be inhabited; *the* tribe of the ungodly shall become desolate. 6 Many such things hath my eyes seen, and greater things than these my ear hath heard. 7 In the congregation of sinners a fire shall be kindled, and in an unbelieving nation wrath shall flame out. 8 The ancient giants did not obtain pardon for their sins, who were destroyed trusting to their own strength, 9 and he spared not the place where Lot sojourned *but* abhorred them for the pride of their word. 10 He had not pity on them, destroying the whole nation *that extolled* themselves in their sins.

11 Et sicut sescenta milia peditum qui congregati sunt in duritia cordis sui, et si unus fuisset cervicatus, mirum si fuisset inmunis, 12 misericordia enim et ira est cum illo, potens exoratio et effundens iram. 13 Secundum misericordiam suam, sic correptio illius hominem secundum opera sua iudicat. 14 Non effugiet in rapina peccator, et non retardabit sufferentia misericordiam facientis. 15 Omnis misericordia faciet locum unicuique secundum meritum operum suorum et secundum intellectum peregrinationis ipsius.

16 Non dicas, "A Deo abscondar, et ex summo quis mei memorabitur? 17 In populo magno non agnoscar, quae est enim anima mea in tam inmensa creatura?" 18 Ecce: caelum et caeli caelorum, abyssus et universa terra et quae in eis sunt in conspectu illius commovebuntur. 19 Montes simul et colles et fundamenta terrae, et cum conspexerit illa Deus tremore concutientur. 20 Et in omnibus his insensatum est cor, et omne cor intellegetur. 21 Et vias illius quis intellegit, et procella, quam nec oculus videbit hominis? 22 Nam plurima opera illius sunt in absconsis, sed opera iustitiae eius quis enuntiabit, aut quis sustinebit? Longe enim est testamentum a quibusdam, et interrogatio omnium in consummatione est.

23 Qui minoratur corde cogitat inania, et vir inprudens et errans cogitat stulta. 24 Audi me, fili, et disce disciplinam sensus, et in verbis meis adtende in corde tuo, 25 et dicam in aequitate disciplinam et scrutabor enarrare sapientiam, et in verbis meis adtende in corde tuo, et dico in aequitate

11 *So did he with* the six hundred thousand footmen who were gathered together in the hardness of their heart, and if one had been stiffnecked, it is a wonder if he had *escaped* unpunished, 12 for mercy and wrath are with him. *He is mighty to forgive and to pour out* indignation. 13 According as his mercy is, so his correction judgeth a man according to his works. 14 The sinner shall not escape in *his rapines,* and the patience of him that sheweth mercy shall not be put off. 15 All mercy shall make a place for every man according to the merit of his works and according to the wisdom of his sojournment.

16 Say not, "I shall be hidden from God, and who shall remember me from on high? 17 In *such a multitude* I shall not be known, for what is my soul in such an immense creation?" 18 Behold: the heaven and the heavens of heavens, the deep and all the earth and the things that are in them shall be moved in his sight. 19 The mountains also and the hills and the foundations of the earth, *when* God shall look upon them they shall be shaken with trembling. 20 And in all these things the heart is senseless, and every heart is understood by him. 21 And his ways who shall understand, and the storm, which no eye of man shall see? 22 For many of his works are hidden, but the works of his justice who shall declare, or who shall endure? For the testament is far from some, and the examination of all is in the end.

23 He that *wanteth understanding* thinketh vain things, and the foolish and erring man thinketh foolish things. 24 Hearken to me, my son, and learn the discipline of understanding, and attend to my words in thy heart, 25 and I will shew forth *good* doctrine in equity and will seek to declare wisdom, and attend to my words in thy heart, *whilst* with

spiritus virtutes quas posuit Deus in opera sua ab initio et in veritate enuntio scientiam eius.

26 In iudicio Dei opera ipsius ab initio, et ab institutione ipsorum distinxit partes illorum et initia ipsorum in gentibus suis. 27 Ornavit in aeternum opera illorum; nec esurierunt nec laboraverunt, et non destiterunt ab operibus suis; 28 unusquisque proximum sibi non angustiabit usque in aevum. 29 Non incredibilis sis verbo illius. 30 Post haec Deus in terram respexit et implevit illam bonis suis. 31 Anima omnis vitalis denudavit ante faciem ipsius, et in ipsam iterum reversio illorum.

Caput 17

Deus creavit de terra hominem et secundum imaginem suam fecit illum. 2 Et iterum convertit illum in ipsam et secundum se vestivit illum virtutem. 3 Numerum dierum et tempus dedit illi et dedit illi potestatem eorum quae sunt super terram. 4 Posuit timorem illius super omnem carnem, et dominatus est bestiarum et volatilium. 5 Creavit ex ipso adiutorium similem sibi; consilium et linguam et oculos et aures et cor dedit illis excogitandi, et disciplinam intellectus

equity of spirit I tell thee the virtues that God hath put upon his works from the beginning and I shew forth in truth his knowledge.

26 The works of God are done in judgment from the beginning, and from the making of them he distinguished their parts and their beginnings in their generations. 27 He beautified their works for ever; they have neither hungered nor laboured, and they have not ceased from their works, 28 *nor* shall any of them straiten his neighbour at any time. 29 Be not thou incredulous to his word. 30 After this God looked upon the earth and filled it with his goods. 31 The soul of every living thing hath shewn forth before the face thereof, and into it they return again.

Chapter 17

The creation and favour of God to man. An exhortation to turn to God.

God created man of the earth and made him after his own image. 2 And he turned him into it again and clothed him with strength according to himself. 3 He gave him the number of his days and time and gave him power over *all* things that are upon the earth. 4 He put the fear of him upon all flesh, and he had dominion over beasts and fowls. 5 He created of him a helpmate like to himself; he gave them counsel and a tongue and eyes and ears and a heart to devise,

replevit illos. 6 Creavit illis scientiam spiritus; sensum implevit cor illorum et mala et bona ostendit illis. 7 Posuit oculum ipsorum super corda illorum ostendere illis magnalia operum suorum 8 ut nomen sanctificationis conlaudent et gloriari in mirabilibus illius, ut magnalia enarrent operum eius. 9 Addidit illis disciplinam, et legem vitae hereditavit illos. 10 Testamentum aeternum constituit cum illis, et iustitiam et iudicia sua ostendit illis. 11 Et magnalia honoris eius vidit oculus illorum, et honorem vocis audierunt aures illorum, et dixit illis, "Adtendite ab omni iniquo." 12 Et mandavit illis unicuique de proximo. 13 Viae illorum coram ipso sunt semper; non sunt absconsae ab oculis ipsius.

14 In unamquamque gentem praeposuit rectorem, 15 et pars Dei Israhel facta est manifesta. 16 Et omnia opera illorum velut sol in conspectu Dei, et oculi eius sine intermissione inspicientes in viis eorum. 17 Non sunt absconsa testamenta per iniquitatem eorum, et omnes iniquitates eorum in conspectu Dei. 18 Elemosyna viri quasi signaculum cum ipso et gratiam hominis quasi pupillam conservabit, 19 et postea resurget et retribuet illis retributionem, unicuique in caput illorum, et convertet in interiores partes terrae. 20 Paenitentibus autem dedit viam iustitiae, et confirmavit deficientes sustinere et destinavit illis sortem veritatis.

21 Convertere ad Dominum, et relinque peccata tua. 22 Precare ante faciem Domini, et minue offendicula. 23 Revertere ad Dominum, et avertere ab iniustitia tua, et

and he filled them with the knowledge of understanding. 6 He created in them the science of the spirit; he filled their heart with wisdom and shewed them both good and evil. 7 He set his eye upon their hearts to shew them the greatness of his works 8 that they might praise the name which he hath sanctified and glory in his wondrous acts, that they might declare the glorious things of his works. 9 Moreover he gave them *instructions* and the law of life *for an inheritance.* 10 He made an everlasting covenant with them, and he shewed them his justice and judgments. 11 And their eye saw the majesty of his *glory,* and their ears heard his *glorious* voice, and he said to them, "Beware of all iniquity." 12 And he gave to every one of them commandment concerning his neighbour. 13 Their ways are always before him; they are not hidden from his eyes.

14 Over every nation he set a ruler, 15 and Israel was made the manifest portion of God. 16 And all their works are as the sun in the sight of God, and his eyes are continually upon their ways. 17 Their covenants were not hid by their iniquity, and all their iniquities are in the sight of God. 18 The alms of a man is as a signet with him and shall preserve the grace of a man as the apple of the eye, 19 and afterward he shall rise up and shall render them their reward, to every one upon their own head, and shall turn them down into the bowels of the earth. 20 But to the penitent he hath given the way of justice, and he hath strengthened them that were fainting in patience and hath appointed to them the lot of truth.

21 Turn to the Lord, and forsake thy sins. 22 Make thy prayer before the face of the Lord, and offend less. 23 Return to the Lord, and turn away from thy injustice, and greatly

nimis odito execrationem. 24 Et cognosce iustitias et iudicia Dei, et sta in sorte propositionis et orationis altissimi Dei. 25 In partes vade saeculi sancti cum vivis et dantibus confessionem Deo. 26 Non demoreris in errore impiorum; ante mortem confitere. A mortuo quasi nihil perit confessio. 27 Confiteberis vivens; vivus et sanus confiteberis et laudabis Deum et gloriaberis in miserationibus illius.

28 Quam magna misericordia Domini et propitiatio illius convertentibus ad se! 29 Nec enim omnia possunt esse in hominibus, quoniam non est inmortalis filius hominis, et in vanitate malitiae placuerunt. 30 Quid lucidius sole, et hic deficiet, aut quid nequius quam quod excogitavit caro et sanguis, et hoc arguetur? 31 Virtutem altitudinis caeli ipse conspicit, et omnes homines terra et cinis.

Caput 18

Qui vivit in aeternum creavit omnia simul. Deus solus iustificabitur, et manet invictus rex in aeternum. 2 Quis sufficit enarrare opera illius? 3 Quis enim investigabit magnalia

hate abomination. 24 And know the justices and judgments of God, and stand firm in the lot set before thee and in prayer to the most high God. 25 Go to the side of the holy age with them that live and give praise to God. 26 Tarry not in the error of the ungodly; give glory before death. Praise perisheth from the dead as nothing. 27 Give thanks whilst thou art living; whilst thou art alive and in health thou shalt give thanks and shalt praise God and shalt glory in his mercies.

28 How great is the mercy of the Lord and his forgiveness to them that turn to him! 29 For all things cannot be in men, because the son of man is not immortal, and they are delighted with the vanity of evil. 30 What is brighter than the sun, *yet* it shall be eclipsed, or what is more wicked than that which flesh and blood hath invented, and this shall be reproved? 31 He beholdeth the power of the height of heaven, and all men are earth and ashes.

Chapter 18

God's works are wonderful. We must serve him and not our lusts.

He that liveth for ever created all things together. God only shall be justified, and he remaineth an invincible king for ever. 2 Who is able to declare his works? 3 For who shall

eius? 4 Virtutem autem magnitudinis eius quis enuntiabit? Aut quis adiciet enarrare misericordiam eius? 5 Non est minuere neque adicere, nec est invenire magnalia Dei. 6 Cum consummaverit homo, tunc incipiet, et cum quieverit operabitur.

7 Quid est homo, et quae est gratia illius, et quid est bonum, aut quid nequam illius? 8 Numerus dierum hominum ut multum centum anni. Quasi guttae aquae maris deputati sunt, et sicut calculus harenae; sic exigui anni in die aevi. 9 Propter hoc patiens est Deus in illis et effundit super eos misericordiam suam. 10 Vidit praesumptionem cordis illorum quoniam mala est et cognovit subversionem illorum quoniam nequa est. 11 Ideo adimplevit propitiationem suam in illis et ostendit illis viam aequitatis.

12 Miseratio hominis circa proximum suum, misericordia autem Dei super omnem carnem. 13 Qui misericordiam habet, docet et erudit quasi pastor gregem suum. 14 Miseretur excipientis doctrinam miserationis et qui festinat in iudiciis eius.

15 Fili, in bonis non des querellam, et in omni dato non des tristitiam verbi mali. 16 Nonne ardorem refrigerabit ros? Sic et verbum melius quam datus. 17 Nonne, ecce, verbum super datum bonum? Sed utraque cum homine iustificato. 18 Stultus acriter inproperabit, et datus indisciplinati tabescere facit oculos.

search out his glorious acts? 4 And who shall shew forth the power of his majesty? Or who shall *be able* to declare his mercy? 5 Nothing may be taken away nor added, neither is it possible to find out the glorious works of God. 6 When a man hath done, then shall he begin, and when he leaveth off he shall *be at a loss.*

7 What is man, and what is his grace, and what is his good, or what is his evil? 8 The number of the days of men at the most are a hundred years. As *a drop* of water of the sea are they esteemed, and as a pebble of the sand; so are a few years compared to eternity. 9 Therefore God is patient in them and poureth forth his mercy upon them. 10 He hath seen the presumption of their heart that it is wicked and hath known their end that it is evil. 11 Therefore hath he filled up his mercy in their favour and hath shewn them the way of justice.

12 The compassion of man is toward his neighbour, but the mercy of God is upon all flesh. 13 He hath mercy *and* teacheth and correcteth as a shepherd doth his flock. 14 He hath mercy on him that receiveth the discipline of mercy and that maketh haste in his judgments.

15 My son, in thy good deeds make no complaint, and when thou givest any thing add not grief by an evil word. 16 Shall not the dew assuage the heat? So also the good word is better than the gift. 17 Lo: is not a word better than a gift? But both are with a justified man. 18 A fool will upbraid bitterly, and a gift of one ill taught consumeth the eyes.

19 Ante iudicium para iustitiam tibi, et antequam loquaris disce. 20 Ante languorem adhibe medicinam, et ante iudicium interroga te ipsum, et in conspectu Dei invenies propitiationem. 21 Ante languorem humilia te, et in tempore infirmitatis ostende conversationem tuam. 22 Non inpediaris orari semper, et non verearis usque ad mortem iustificari, quoniam merces Dei manet in aeternum. 23 Ante orationem praepara animam tuam, et noli esse quasi homo qui temptat Deum. 24 Memento irae in die consummationis et tempus retributionis in conversatione faciei. 25 Memento paupertatis in tempore abundantiae et necessitatum paupertatis in die divitiarum. 26 A mane usque ad vesperam inmutabitur tempus, et haec omnia citata in oculis Dei.

27 Homo sapiens in omnibus metuet et in diebus delictorum adtendet ab inertia. 28 Omnis astutus agnoscit sapientiam et invenienti eam dabit confessionem. 29 Sensati in verbis et ipsi sapienter egerunt et intellexerunt veritatem et iustitiam et impluerunt proverbia et iudicia.

30 Post concupiscentias tuas non eas, et a voluntate tua avertere. 31 Si praestes animae tuae concupiscentias eius, faciet te in gaudium inimicis. 32 Ne oblecteris in turbis, nec in modicis, assidua est enim commissio illorum. 33 Ne fueris mediocris in contentione ex fenore et est tibi nihil in sacculo, eris enim invidus tuae vitae.

19 Before judgment prepare thee justice, and learn before thou speak. 20 Before sickness take a medicine, and before judgment examine thyself, and thou shalt find mercy in the sight of God. 21 Humble thyself before thou art sick, and in the time of sickness shew thy conversation. 22 Let nothing hinder thee from praying always, and be not afraid to be justified even to death, for the reward of God continueth for ever. 23 Before prayer prepare thy soul, and be not as a man that tempteth God. 24 Remember the wrath *that shall be* at the last day and the time of repaying when he shall turn away his face. 25 Remember poverty in the time of abundance and the necessities of poverty in the day of riches. 26 From the morning until the evening the time shall be changed, and all these are swift in the eyes of God.

27 A wise man will fear in every thing and in the days of sins will beware of sloth. 28 Every man of understanding knoweth wisdom and will give praise to him that findeth her. 29 They that were of good understanding in words have also done wisely themselves and have understood truth and justice and have poured forth proverbs and judgments.

30 Go not after thy lusts, *but* turn away from thy own will. 31 If thou give to thy soul her desires, she will make thee a joy to *thy* enemies. 32 Take no pleasure in riotous assemblies, be they ever so small, for their concertation is continual. 33 Make not thyself poor *by borrowing to contribute to feasts when* thou hast nothing in thy purse, for thou shalt be an enemy to thy own life.

Caput 19

Operarius ebriacus non locupletabitur, et qui spernit modica paulatim decidet. 2 Vinum et mulieres apostatare faciunt sapientes et arguent sensatos, 3 et qui se iungit fornicariis erit nequa. Putredo et vermes hereditabunt illum, et extolletur in exemplum maius, et tolletur de numero anima eius. 4 Qui credit cito levis corde est et minorabitur, et qui delinquit in animam suam insuper habebitur. 5 Qui gaudet iniquitati denotabitur, et qui odit correptionem minuetur vita, et qui odit loquacitatem extinguit malitiam. 6 Qui peccat in animam suam paenitebit, et qui iucundatur in malitia denotabitur.

7 Ne iteres verbum nequam et durum, et non minoraberis. 8 Amico et inimico noli enarrare sensum tuum, et si est tibi delictum, noli denudare, 9 audiet enim te et custodiet te, et quasi defendens peccatum odiet te, et sic aderit tibi semper. 10 Audisti verbum adversus proximum tuum? Conmoriatur in te, fidens quoniam non te disrumpet. 11 A facie verbi parturit fatuus, tamquam gemitus partus infantis.

Chapter 19

Admonition against sundry vices.

A workman that is a drunkard shall not be rich, and he that contemneth small things shall fall by little and little. 2 Wine and women make wise men fall off and shall rebuke the prudent, 3 and he that joineth himself to harlots will be wicked. Rottenness and worms shall inherit him, and he shall be lifted up for a greater example, and his soul shall be taken away out of the number. 4 He that is hasty to give credit is light of heart and shall be lessened, and he that sinneth against his own soul *shall be despised.* 5 He that rejoiceth in iniquity shall be censured, and he that hateth chastisement shall have less life, and he that hateth babbling extinguisheth evil. 6 He that sinneth against his own soul shall repent, and he that is delighted with wickedness shall be condemned.

7 Rehearse not again a wicked and harsh word, and thou shalt not fare the worse. 8 Tell not thy mind to friend or foe, and if there be a sin with thee, disclose it not, 9 for he will hearken to thee and will watch thee, and as it were defending thy sin he will hate thee, and so will he be with thee always. 10 Hast thou heard a word against thy neighbour? Let it die within thee, trusting that it will not burst thee. 11 At the hearing of a word the fool is in travail, as a *woman* groan-

12 Sagitta infixa femori carnis, sic verbum in corde stulti. 13 Corripe amicum ne forte non intellexerit et dicat, "Non feci," aut si fecerit ne iterum addat facere. 14 Corripe proximum ne forte non dixerit, et si dixerit ne forte iteret. 15 Corripe amicum, saepe enim fit commissio. 16 Et non omni verbo credas.

Est qui labitur lingua sed non ex animo, 17 quis est enim qui non deliquerit in lingua sua? Corripe proximum antequam commineris. 18 Et da locum timori Altissimi, quia omnis sapientia timor Dei et in illa timere Deum et in omni sapientia dispositio legis. 19 Et non est sapientia nequitiae disciplina, et non est cogitatus peccatorum prudentia. 20 Est nequitia, et in ipsa execratio, et est insipiens, qui minuitur sapientia.

21 Melior est homo qui minuitur sapientia et deficiens sensu in timore quam qui abundat sensu et transgreditur legem Altissimi. 22 Est sollertia certa, et ipsa iniqua. 23 Et est qui emittit verbum certum enarrans veritatem. Est qui nequiter humiliat se, et interiora eius plena sunt dolo. 24 Et est iustus qui se nimium submittit a multa humilitate, et est iustus qui inclinat faciem suam et fingit se non videre quod ignoratum est. 25 Et si ab inbecillitate virium vetetur peccare, si invenerit tempus malefaciendi, malefaciet.

ing in the bringing forth a child. 12 As an arrow that sticketh in a *man's* thigh, so is a word in the heart of a fool. 13 Reprove a friend lest he may not have understood and say, "I did it not," or if he did it that he may do it no more. 14 Reprove thy neighbour, *for it may be* he hath not said it, and if he hath said it that he may not say it again. 15 Admonish thy friend, for there is often a fault committed. 16 And believe not every word.

There is one that slippeth with the tongue but not from his heart, 17 for who is there that hath not offended with his tongue? Admonish thy neighbour before thou threaten him. 18 And give place to the fear of the Most High, for the fear of God is all wisdom and therein is to fear God and the disposition of the law is in all wisdom. 19 *But* the learning of wickedness is not wisdom, and the device of sinners is not prudence. 20 There is a *subtle* wickedness, and *the same is detestable,* and there is a man that is foolish, wanting in wisdom.

21 Better is a man that hath less wisdom and wanteth understanding with the fear *of God* than he that aboundeth in understanding and transgresseth the law of the Most High. 22 There is an *exquisite* subtilty, and the same is unjust. 23 And there is one that uttereth an exact word telling the truth. There is one that humbleth himself wickedly, and his interior is full of deceit. 24 And there is *one* that submitteth himself exceedingly with a great lowliness, and there is *one* that casteth down his countenance and maketh as if he did not see that which is unknown. 25 And if he be hindered from sinning for want of power, if he shall find opportunity to do evil, he will do it.

26 Ex visu cognoscitur vir, et ab occursu faciei cognoscitur sensatus. 27 Amictus corporis et risus dentium et ingressus hominis enuntiant de illo. 28 Est correptio mendax in ira contumeliosi, et est iudicium quod non probatur esse bonum, et est tacens, et ipse est prudens.

Caput 20

Quam bonum est arguere quam irasci et confitentem in oratione non prohibere! 2 Concupiscentia spadonis devirginabit iuvenem; 3 sic qui facit per vim iudicium iniquum. 4 Quam bonum est correptum manifestare paenitentiam! Sic enim effugies voluntarium peccatum.

5 Est tacens qui invenitur sapiens, et est odibilis qui procax est ad loquendum. 6 Est tacens non habens sensum loquellae, et est tacens, sciens tempus apti temporis. 7 Homo sapiens tacebit usque ad tempus, lascivus autem et inprudens non servabunt tempus. 8 Qui multis utitur verbis laedet

26 A man is known by his look, and a wise man when thou meetest him is known by his countenance. 27 The attire of the body and the laughter of the teeth and the gait of the man shew what he is. 28 There is a lying rebuke in the anger of an injurious man, and there is a judgment that is not allowed to be good, and there is one that holdeth his peace, and he is wise.

Chapter 20

Rules with regard to correction, discretion and avoiding lies.

How much better is it to reprove than to be angry and not to hinder him that confesseth in prayer! 2 The lust of an eunuch shall deflower a young maiden; 3 so is he that by violence executeth unjust judgment. 4 How good is it when thou art reproved to shew repentance! For so thou shalt escape wilful sin.

5 There is one that holdeth his peace that is found wise, and there is another that is hateful that is bold in speech. 6 There is one that holdeth his peace because he knoweth not what to say, and there is another that holdeth his peace, knowing the *proper time.* 7 A wise man will hold his peace till *he see* opportunity, but a babbler and a fool will regard no time. 8 He that useth many words shall hurt his own soul,

animam suam, et qui potestatem sibi adsumit iniuste odietur. 9 Est processio in malis viro indisciplinato, et est inventio in detrimentum. 10 Est datus qui non sit utilis, et est datus cuius retributio duplex. 11 Est propter gloriam minoratio, et est qui ab humilitate levabit caput. 12 Est qui multa redimat modico pretio et restituens ea septuplum.

13 Sapiens in verbis se ipsum amabilem faciet, gratiae autem fatuorum effundentur. 14 Datus insipientis non erit utilis tibi, oculi enim illius septimplices sunt. 15 Exigua dabit et multa inproperabit, et apertio oris illius inflammatio est. 16 Hodie fenerat quis, et cras expetit: odibilis est homo huiusmodi. 17 Fatuo non erit amicus, et non erit gratia bonis illius, 18 qui enim edunt panem illius falsae linguae sunt. Quotiens et quanti inridebunt eum! 19 Neque enim quod habendum erat directo sensu distribuit, similiter et quod non erat habendum.

20 Lapsus falsae linguae quasi qui pavimento cadens, sic casus malorum festinanter venient. 21 Homo acharis quasi fabula vana: in ore indisciplinatorum adsidua erit. 22 Ex ore fatui reprobabitur parabola, non enim dicit illam in tempore suo.

23 Est qui vetatur peccare prae inopia, et in requie sua stimulabitur. 24 Est qui perdet animam suam prae confusione, et ab inprudenti persona perdet eam, personae autem ac-

and he that taketh authority to himself unjustly shall be hated. 9 There is success in evil things to a man without discipline, and there is a finding that turneth to loss. 10 There is a gift that is not profitable, and there is a gift the recompense of which is double. 11 There is an abasement because of glory, and there is one that shall lift up his head from a low estate. 12 There is that buyeth much for a small price and restoreth the same sevenfold.

13 A man wise in words shall make himself beloved, but the graces of fools shall be poured out. 14 The gift of the fool shall do thee no good, for his eyes are sevenfold. 15 He will give a few things and upbraid much, and the opening of his mouth is the kindling of a fire. 16 Today a man lendeth, and tomorrow he asketh it again: such a man as this is hateful. 17 A fool shall have no friend, and there shall be no thanks for his good deeds, 18 for they that eat his bread are of a false tongue. How often and how many will laugh him to scorn! 19 For he doth not distribute with right understanding that which was to be had, in like manner also that which was not to be had.

20 The slipping of a false tongue is as one that falleth on the pavement; so the *fall* of the wicked shall come speedily. 21 A man without grace is as a vain fable: it shall be continually in the mouth of the unwise. 22 A parable coming out of a fool's mouth shall be rejected, for he doth not speak it in due season.

23 There is that is hindered from sinning through want, and in his rest he shall be pricked. 24 There is that will destroy his own soul through shamefacedness, and by occasion of an unwise person he will destroy it, and by respect of

ceptione perdet se. 25 Est qui prae confusione promittit amico et lucratus est eum inimicum gratis.

26 Obprobrium nequa in homine mendacium, et in ore indisciplinatorum adsidue erit. 27 Potior fur quam adsiduitas viri mendacis, perditionem autem ambo hereditabunt. 28 Mores hominum mendacium sine honore, et confusio illorum cum ipsis sine intermissione. 29 Sapiens in verbis producet se ipsum, et homo prudens placebit magnatis. 30 Qui operatur terram suam inaltabit acervum fructuum, et qui operatur iustitiam ipse exaltabitur, qui vero placet magnatis effugiet iniquitatem.

31 Xenia et dona excaecant oculos iudicum et quasi mutus in ore avertit correptiones eorum. 32 Sapientia absconsa et thesaurus invisus, quae utilitas in utrisque? 33 Melior est qui celat insipientiam suam quam homo qui abscondit sapientiam suam.

Caput 21

Fili, peccasti? Non adicias iterum, sed et de pristinis deprecare ut tibi dimittantur. 2 Quasi a facie colubri fuge peccata, et si accesseris ad illa, suscipient te. 3 Dentes leonis

person he will destroy himself. 25 There is that for bashfulness promiseth to his friend and maketh him his enemy for nothing.

26 A lie is a foul blot in a man, and *yet* it will be continually in the mouth of men without discipline. 27 A thief is better than *a man that is always lying,* but both of them shall inherit destruction. 28 The manners of lying men are without honour, and their confusion is with them without ceasing. 29 A wise man shall advance himself with his words, and a prudent man shall please the great ones. 30 He that tilleth his land shall make a high heap of corn, and he that worketh justice shall be exalted, and he that pleaseth great men shall escape iniquity.

31 Presents and gifts blind the eyes of judges and *make them* dumb in the mouth *so that they cannot correct.* 32 Wisdom that is hid and treasure that is not seen, what profit is there in them both? 33 Better is he that hideth his folly than the man that hideth his wisdom.

Chapter 21

Cautions against sin in general and some sins in particular.

My son, hast thou sinned? Do so no more, but for thy former sins also pray that they may be forgiven thee. 2 Flee from sins as from the face of a serpent, *for* if thou comest near them, they will take hold of thee. 3 The teeth thereof

dentes eius, interficientes animas hominum. 4 Quasi romphea bis acuta omnis iniquitas: plagae illius non est sanitas.

5 Cataplectatio et iniuriae adnullabunt substantiam, et
domus quae nimis locuples est adnullabitur superbia; sic
substantia superbiae eradicabitur. 6 Deprecatio pauperis ex
ore usque ad aures eius veniet, et iudicium festinato adve-
niet illi. 7 Qui odit correptionem vestigium est peccatoris,
et qui timet Deum convertet ad cor suum. 8 Notus a longe
potens lingua audaci, et sensatus scit labi se ab ipso. 9 Qui
aedificat domum suam inpendiis alienis quasi qui colligat
lapides suos in hieme. 10 Stuppa collecta synagoga peccantium, et consummatio illorum flamma ignis. 11 Via peccantium conplanata lapidibus, et in fine illorum inferi et
tenebrae et poenae. 12 Qui custodit iustitiam continebit
sensum eius.

13 Consummatio timoris Dei sapientia et sensus. 14 Non
erudietur qui non est sapiens in bono. 15 Est autem sapientia
quae abundat in malo, et non est sensus ubi est amaritudo.
16 Scientia sapientis tamquam inundatio abundabit, et consilium illius sicut fons vitae permanet. 17 Cor fatui quasi vas
confractum, et omnem sapientiam non tenebit. 18 Verbum
sapiens quodcumque audierit scius laudabit et ad se adiciet.
Audivit luxuriosus, et displicebit illi, et proiciet illud post
dorsum suum. 19 Narratio fatui quasi sarcina in via, nam in

are the teeth of a lion, killing the souls of men. 4 All iniquity is like a two-edged sword: there is no remedy for the wound thereof.

5 *Injuries* and wrongs will waste riches, and the house that is very rich shall be brought to nothing by pride; so the substance of the proud shall be rooted out. 6 The prayer out of the mouth of the poor shall reach the ears *of God,* and judgment shall come for him speedily. 7 He that hateth to be reproved walketh in the trace of a sinner, and he that feareth God will turn to his own heart. 8 He that is mighty by a bold tongue is known afar off, but a wise man knoweth to slip by him. 9 He that buildeth his house at other men's charges is as he that gathereth *himself* stones *to build* in the winter. 10 The congregation of sinners is like tow heaped together, and the end of them is a flame of fire. 11 The way of sinners is made plain with stones, and in their end is hell and darkness and pains. 12 He that keepeth justice shall get the understanding thereof.

13 The perfection of the fear of God is wisdom and understanding. 14 He that is not wise in good will not be taught. 15 But there is a wisdom that aboundeth in evil, and there is no understanding where there is bitterness. 16 The knowledge of a wise man shall abound like a flood, and his counsel continueth like a fountain of life. 17 The heart of a fool is like a broken vessel, and no wisdom at all shall it hold. 18 A man of sense will praise every wise word he shall hear and will apply it to himself. The luxurious man hath heard it, and it shall displease him, and he will cast it behind his back. 19 The talking of a fool is like a burden in the way, *but* in the lips of

labiis sensati invenietur gratia. 20 Os prudentis quaeritur in ecclesia, et verba illius cogitabunt in cordibus suis. 21 Tamquam domus exterminata sic fatuo sapientia, et scientia insensati inenarrabilia verba. 22 Conpedes in pedibus stulto doctrina et quasi vincula manuum supra manum dexteram. 23 Fatuus in risu exaltat vocem suam, vir autem sapiens vix tacite ridebit. 24 Ornamentum aureum prudenti doctrina et quasi brachiale in brachio dextro. 25 Pes fatui facilis in domum proximi, et homo peritus confundetur a persona potentis. 26 Stultus a fenestra respiciet in domum, vir autem eruditus foris stabit. 27 Stultitia hominis audire per ostium, et prudens gravabitur contumelia. 28 Labia inprudentium stulta narrabunt, verba autem prudentium statera ponderabuntur. 29 In ore fatuorum cor illorum, et in corde sapientium os illorum.

30 Dum maledicit impius diabolum, maledicit ipse animam suam. 31 Susurro coinquinabit animam suam et in omnibus odietur, et qui cum eo manserit odiosus erit. Tacitus et sensatus honorabitur.

the wise grace shall be found. 20 The mouth of the prudent is sought after in the church, and they will think upon his words in their hearts. 21 As a house that is destroyed so is wisdom to a fool, and the knowledge of the unwise is as words without sense. 22 Doctrine to a fool is as fetters on the feet and like manacles on the right hand. 23 A fool lifteth up his voice in laughter, but a wise man will scarce laugh low to himself. 24 Learning to the prudent is as an ornament of gold and like a bracelet upon his right arm. 25 The foot of a fool is soon in his neighbour's house, *but* a man of experience will be abashed at the person of the mighty. 26 A fool will peep through the window into the house, but he that is well taught will stand without. 27 It is the folly of a man to hearken at the door, and a wise man will be grieved with the disgrace. 28 The lips of the unwise will be telling foolish things, but the words of the wise shall be weighed in a balance. 29 The heart of fools is in their mouth, and the mouth of wise men is in their heart.

30 While the ungodly curseth the devil, he curseth his own soul. 31 The talebearer shall defile his own soul and shall be hated by all, and he that shall abide with him shall be hateful. The silent and wise man shall be honoured.

Caput 22

In lapide luteo lapidatus est piger, et omnes loquentur super aspernationem illius. 2 De stercore boum lapidatus est piger, et omnis qui tetigerit eum excutiet manus.

3 Confusio patris est de filio indisciplinato, filia autem in deminoratione fiet. 4 Filia prudens hereditas viro suo, nam quae confundit in contumeliam fit genitoris. 5 Patrem et virum confundit audax et ab impiis non minorabitur ab utrisque autem inhonorabitur.

6 Musica in luctu inportuna narratio; flagella et doctrina in omni tempore sapientia. 7 Qui docet fatuum quasi qui conglutinet testam. 8 Qui narrat verbum non audienti quasi qui excitat dormientem de gravi somno, 9 cum dormiente loquitur qui enarrat stulto sapientiam et in fine narrationis dicit, "Quis est hic?"

10 Super mortuum plora, defecit enim lux eius, et super fatuum plora, deficit enim sensus. 11 Modicum plora supra mortuum, quoniam requievit, 12 nequissimi enim nequissima vita super mortem fatui. 13 Luctus mortui septem dies, fatui autem et impii omnes dies vitae illorum. 14 Cum stulto

Chapter 22

Wise sayings on divers subjects.

The sluggard is pelted with a dirty stone, and all men will speak of his disgrace. 2 The sluggard is pelted with the dung of oxen, and every one that toucheth him will shake his hands.

3 A son ill taught is the confusion of the father, and a foolish daughter shall be to his loss. 4 A wise daughter *shall bring* an inheritance to her husband, *but* she that confoundeth becometh a disgrace to her father. 5 She that is bold shameth both her father and husband and will not be inferior to the ungodly and shall be disgraced by them both.

6 A tale out of time is like music in mourning, but the stripes and instruction of wisdom are never out of time. 7 He that teacheth a fool is like one that glueth a potsherd together. 8 He that telleth a word to him that heareth not is like one that waketh a man out of a deep sleep: 9 he speaketh with one that is asleep, who uttereth wisdom to a fool and in the end of the discourse he saith, "Who is this?"

10 Weep for the dead, for his light hath failed, and weep for the fool, for his understanding faileth. 11 Weep but a little for the dead, for he is at rest, 12 for the wicked life of a wicked fool is worse than death. 13 The mourning for the dead is seven days, but for a fool and an ungodly man all the days of their life. 14 Talk not much with a fool, and go not

non multum loquaris, et cum insensato ne abieris. 15 Serva te ab illo ut non molestiam habeas, et non coinquinaberis peccato illius. 16 Deflecte ab illo, et invenies requiem et non acediaberis in stultitiam illius.

17 Super plumbum quid gravabitur? Et quod illi aliud nomen quam fatuus? 18 Harenam et salem et massam ferri facilius est portare quam hominem inprudentem et fatuum et impium. 19 Loramentum ligneum conligatum in fundamento aedificii non dissolvetur; sic et cor confirmatum in cogitatione consilii. 20 Cogitatus sensati in omni tempore vel metu non pravabitur. 21 Sicut pali in excelsis et cementa sine inpensa posita contra faciem venti non permanebunt, 22 sic et cor timidum in cogitatione stulti contra impetum timoris non resistet. 23 Sicut cor trepidum in cogitatione fatui omni tempore non metuebit, sic et qui in praeceptis Dei permanet semper.

24 Pungens oculum deducit lacrimas, et qui pungit cor profert sensum. 25 Mittens lapidem in volatilia deiciet illa; sic et qui conviciatur amico dissolvit amicitiam. 26 Ad amicum et si produxeris gladium, non desperes, est enim regressus. Ad amicum 27 si aperueris os triste, non timeas, est enim concordatio, excepto convicio et inproperio et superbia et mysterii revelatione et plaga dolosa; in his omnibus effugiet amicus. 28 Fidem posside cum amico in paupertate illius ut et in bonis illius laeteris. 29 In tempore tribulationis illius permane illi fidelis ut et in hereditate illius coheres sis. 30 Ante ignem camini vapor et fumus ignis inaltatur, sic et

with him that hath no sense. 15 Keep thyself from him that thou mayst not have trouble, and thou shalt not be defiled with his sin. 16 Turn away from him, and thou shalt find rest and shalt not be wearied out with his folly.

17 What is heavier than lead? And what other name hath he but fool? 18 Sand and salt and a mass of iron is easier to bear than a man without sense that is both foolish and wicked. 19 A frame of wood bound together in the foundation of a building shall not be loosed, so neither shall the heart that is established by advised counsel. 20 The thought of him that is wise at all times shall not be depraved *by* fear. 21 As pales set in high places and plasterings made without cost will not stand against the face of the wind, 22 so also a fearful heart in the imagination of a fool shall not resist against the violence of fear. 23 As a fearful heart in the thought of a fool at all times will not fear, so neither shall he that continueth always in the commandments of God.

24 He that pricketh the eye bringeth out tears, and he that pricketh the heart bringeth forth *resentment*. 25 He that flingeth a stone at birds shall drive them away; so he that upbraideth his friend breaketh friendship. 26 Although thou hast drawn a sword at a friend, despair not, for there *may be* a returning. To a friend 27 if thou hast opened a sad mouth, fear not, for there *may be* a reconciliation, except upbraiding and reproach and pride and disclosing of secrets *or* a treacherous wound, *for* in all these cases a friend will flee away. 28 Keep fidelity with a friend in his poverty that in his prosperity also thou mayst rejoice. 29 In the time of his trouble continue faithful to him that thou mayst also be heir with him in his inheritance. 30 As the vapour of a chimney and the smoke of the fire goeth up before the fire, so also injurious

ante sanguinem maledicta et contumeliae et minae. 31 Amicum salutare non confundar, a facie illius non me abscondam, et si mala mihi evenerint per illum, sustinebo. 32 Omnis qui audiet cavebit se ab eo. 33 Quis dabit ori meo custodiam et supra labia mea signaculum certum uti ne cadam ab ipsis et lingua mea perdat me?

Caput 23

Domine, pater et dominator vitae meae, ne relinquas me in consilio eorum, nec sinas me cadere in illis. 2 Quis superponet in cogitatu meo flagella et in corde meo doctrinam sapientiae ut ignorationibus eorum non parcant mihi et non pareant delicta illorum 3 et ne adincrescant ignorantiae meae et multiplicentur delicta mea et peccata mea abundent et incidam in conspectu adversariorum meorum et gaudeat inimicus meus? 4 Domine, pater et Deus vitae meae, ne derelinquas me in cogitatu illorum. 5 Extollentiam oculorum meorum ne dederis mihi, et omne desiderium averte a me. 6 Aufer a me ventris concupiscentias, et concubitus concupiscentiae ne adprehendant me, et animae inreverenti et infrunitae ne tradas me.

words and reproaches and threats before blood. 31 I will not be ashamed to salute a friend, neither will I hide myself from his face, and if any evil happen to me by him, I will bear it. 32 But every one that shall hear it will beware of him. 33 Who will set a guard before my mouth and a sure seal upon my lips that I fall not by them and that my tongue destroy me not?

Chapter 23

A prayer for grace to flee sin. Cautions against profane swearing and other vices.

O Lord, father and sovereign ruler of my life, leave me not to their counsel, nor suffer me to fall by them. 2 Who will set scourges over my thoughts and the discipline of wisdom over my heart that they spare me not in their ignorances and that their sins may not appear 3 *lest* my ignorance increase and my offences be multiplied and my sins abound and I fall before my adversaries and my enemy rejoice *over me?* 4 O Lord, father and God of my life, leave me not to their devices. 5 Give me not haughtiness of my eyes, and turn away from me all coveting. 6 Take from me the greediness of the belly, and let not the *lusts of the flesh* take hold of me, and give me not over to a shameless and foolish mind.

7 Doctrinam oris audite, filii, et qui custodierit illam non periet in labiis suis, nec scandalizabitur in operibus nequissimis. 8 In vanitate sua adprehenditur peccator, et superbus et maledicus scandalizabitur in illis. 9 Iurationi non adsuescat os tuum, multi enim casus in illa. 10 Nominatio vero Dei non sit adsidua in ore tuo, et nominibus sanctorum non admiscearis, quoniam non eris inmunis ab eis, 11 sicut enim servus interrogatus adsidue a livore non minuitur, sic omnis iurans et nominans in toto a peccato non purgabitur. 12 Vir multum iurans implebitur iniquitate, et non discedet a domo illius plaga. 13 Et si frustraverit, delictum ipsius super ipsum erit, et si dissimulaverit, delinquit dupliciter, 14 et si in vacuum iuraverit, non iustificabitur, replebitur enim retributione domus illius.

15 Est et alia loquella contraria morti: non inveniatur in hereditate Iacob, 16 etenim a misericordibus omnia haec auferentur et in delictis non volutabunt. 17 Indisciplinatae loquellae non adsuescat os tuum, est enim in illa verbum peccati. 18 Memento patris et matris tuae, in medio enim magnatorum consistis, 19 ne forte obliviscatur te Deus in conspectu illorum et adsiduitate tua infatuatus inproperium patiaris et maluisses non nasci et diem nativitatis tuae maledicas. 20 Homo adsuetus in verbis inproperii in omnibus diebus suis non erudietur.

21 Duo genera abundant in peccatis, et tertium adducit iram et perditionem. 22 Anima calida quasi ignis ardens non extinguetur donec aliquid gluttiat. 23 Et homo nequam in

7 Hear, O ye children, the discipline of the mouth, and he that will keep it shall not perish by his lips, nor be brought to fall into most wicked works. 8 A sinner is caught in his own vanity, and the proud and the evil speakers shall fall thereby. 9 Let not thy mouth be accustomed to swearing, for in it there are many falls. 10 And let not the naming of God be usual in thy mouth, and meddle not with the names of saints, for thou shalt not escape free from them, 11 for as a slave daily put to the question is never without a blue mark, so every one that sweareth and nameth shall not be wholly pure from sin. 12 A man that sweareth much shall be filled with iniquity, and a scourge shall not depart from his house. 13 And if he make it void, his sin shall be upon him, and if he dissemble it, he offendeth double, 14 and if he swear in vain, he shall not be justified, for his house shall be filled with his punishment.

15 There is also another speech opposite to death: let it not be found in the inheritance of Jacob, 16 for from the merciful all these things shall be taken away and they shall not wallow in sins. 17 Let not thy mouth be accustomed to indiscreet speech, for therein is the word of sin. 18 Remember thy father and thy mother, for thou sittest is the midst of great men, 19 lest God forget thee in their sight and thou by thy daily custom be infatuated and suffer reproach and wish that thou hadst not been born and curse the day of thy nativity. 20 The man that is accustomed to opprobrious words will never be corrected all the days of his life.

21 Two sorts of men multiply sins, and the third bringeth wrath and destruction. 22 A hot soul *is* a burning fire; it will never be quenched till it devour some thing. 23 And a man

ore carnis suae non desinet donec incendat ignem. 24 Homini fornicario omnis panis dulcis; non fatigabitur transgrediens usque ad finem. 25 Omnis homo qui transgreditur lectum suum, contemnens in animam suam et dicens, "Quis me videt? 26 Tenebrae circumdant me, et parietes cooperiunt me, et nemo circumspicit me. Quem vereor? Delictorum meorum non memorabitur Altissimus," 27 et non intellegit quoniam omnia videt oculus illius, quoniam expellit a se timorem Dei huiusmodi hominis timor et oculi hominum timentes illum, 28 et non cognovit quoniam oculi Domini multo plus lucidiores super solem, circumspicientes omnes vias hominum et profundum abyssi et hominum corda intuentes, in absconsas partes, 29 Domino enim Deo antequam crearentur omnia sunt agnita, sic et post perfectum respicit omnia, 30 hic in plateis civitatis vindicabitur, et quasi pullus equinus fugabitur, et ubi non speravit adprehendetur. 31 Et erit dedecus omnibus eo quod non intellexerit timorem Domini. 32 Sic et mulier omnis relinquens virum suum et statuens hereditatem ex alieno matrimonio, 33 primo enim in lege Altissimi incredibilis fuit, et secundo in virum suum deliquit; tertio in adulterio fornicata est et ex alio viro filios statuit sibi. 34 Haec in ecclesiam adducetur, et in filios eius respicietur. 35 Non tradent filii eius radices, et rami eius non dabunt fructum. 36 Derelinquet in maledictum memoriam illius, et dedecus illius non delebitur. 37 Et agnoscent qui

that is wicked in the mouth of his flesh will not leave off till he hath kindled a fire. 24 To a man that is a fornicator all bread is sweet; he will not be weary of sinning unto the end. 25 Every man that passeth beyond his own bed, despising his own soul and saying, "Who seeth me? 26 Darkness compasseth me about, and the walls cover me, and no man seeth me. Whom do I fear? The Most High will not remember my sins," 27 and he understandeth not that his eye seeth all things, for such a man's fear driveth from him the fear of God and the eyes of men fearing him, 28 and he knoweth not that the eyes of the Lord are far brighter than the sun, beholding round about all the ways of men and the bottom of the deep and looking into the hearts of men, into the *most* hidden parts, 29 for all things were known to the Lord God before they were created, so also after they were perfected he beholdeth all things, 30 this man shall be punished in the streets of the city, and he shall be chased as a colt, and where he suspected not he shall be taken. 31 And he shall be in disgrace with all men because he understood not the fear of the Lord. 32 So every woman also that leaveth her husband and *bringeth in an heir by another,* 33 for first she hath been unfaithful to the law of the Most High, and secondly she hath offended against her husband; thirdly she hath fornicated in adultery and hath gotten her children of another man. 34 This woman shall be brought into the assembly, and inquisition shall be made of her children. 35 Her children shall not take root, and her branches shall bring forth no fruit. 36 She shall leave her memory to be cursed, and her infamy shall not be blotted out. 37 And they that remain shall know that

derelicti sunt quoniam nihil melius quam timor Dei et nihil dulcius quam respicere in mandatis Domini.

38 Gloria magna est sequi Dominum, longitudo enim dierum adsumetur ab eo.

Caput 24

Sapientia laudabit animam suam et in Deo honorabitur et in medio populi sui gloriabitur 2 et in ecclesiis Altissimi aperiet os suum et in conspectu virtutis illius gloriabitur, 3 et in medio populi sui exaltabitur et in plenitudine sancta admirabitur. 4 Et in multitudine electorum habebit laudem, et inter benedictos benedicetur, dicens, 5 "Ego ex ore Altissimi prodivi, primogenita ante omnem creaturam. 6 Ego in caelis feci ut oriretur lumen indeficiens, et sicut nebula texi omnem terram. 7 Ego in altissimis habitavi, et thronus meus in columna nubis. 8 Gyrum caeli circuivi sola et in profundum abyssi penetravi et in fluctibus maris ambulavi 9 et in omni terra steti et in omni populo, 10 et in omni gente primatum

there is nothing better than the fear of God and that there is nothing sweeter than to have regard to the commandments of the Lord.

38 It is great glory to follow the Lord, for length of days shall be received from him.

Chapter 24

Wisdom praiseth herself, her origin, her dwelling, her dignity and her fruits.

Wisdom shall praise her own self and shall be honoured in God and shall glory in the midst of her people 2 and shall open her mouth in the churches of the Most High and shall glorify herself in the sight of his power, 3 and in the midst of her own people she shall be exalted and shall be admired in the holy assembly. 4 And in the multitude of the elect she shall have praise, and among the blessed she shall be blessed, saying, 5 "I came out of the mouth of the Most High, the firstborn before all creatures. 6 I made that in the heavens there should rise light that never faileth, and as a cloud I covered all the earth. 7 I dwelt in the highest places, and my throne is in a pillar of a cloud. 8 I alone have compassed the circuit of heaven and have penetrated into the bottom of the deep and have walked in the waves of the sea 9 and have stood in all the earth and in every people, 10 and in every na-

habui. 11 Et omnium excellentium et humilium corda virtute calcavi, et in his omnibus requiem quaesivi, et in hereditate Domini morabor.

12 "Tunc praecepit et dixit mihi creator omnium, et qui creavit me requievit in tabernaculo meo, 13 et dixit mihi, 'In Iacob inhabita, et in Israhel hereditare, et in electis meis ede radices.' 14 Ab initio et ante saecula creata sum, et usque ad futurum saeculum non desinam, et in habitatione sancta coram ipso ministravi. 15 Et sic in Sion firmata sum, et in civitate sanctificata similiter requievi, et in Hierusalem potestas mea. 16 Et radicavi in populo honorificato, et in parte Dei mei hereditas illius, et in plenitudine sanctorum detentio mea. 17 Quasi cedrus exaltata sum in Libano et quasi cypressus in Monte Sion. 18 Quasi palma exaltata sum in Cades et quasi plantatio rosae in Hiericho; 19 quasi oliva speciosa in campis et quasi platanus exaltata sum iuxta aquam in plateis. 20 Sicut cinnamomum et balsamum aromatizans odorem dedi. Quasi murra electa dedi suavitatem odoris, 21 et quasi storax et galbanus et onyx et gutta et quasi libanus non incisus vaporavi habitationem meam, et quasi balsamum non mixtum odor meus. 22 Ego quasi terebinthus extendi ramos meos, et rami mei honoris et gratiae. 23 Ego quasi vitis fructificavi suavitatem odoris, et flores mei fructus honoris et honestatis.

24 "Ego mater pulchrae dilectionis et timoris et agnitionis et sanctae spei. 25 In me gratia omnis viae et veritatis. In me omnis spes vitae et virtutis. 26 Transite ad me, omnes qui

tion I have had the chief rule. 11 And by my power I have trodden under my feet the hearts of all the high and low, and in all these I sought rest, and I shall abide in the inheritance of the Lord.

12 "Then the creator of all things commanded and said to me, and he that made me rested in my tabernacle, 13 and he said to me, 'Let thy dwelling be in Jacob and thy inheritance in Israel, and take root in my elect.' 14 From the beginning and before the world was I created, and unto the world to come I shall not cease to be, and in the holy dwelling place I have ministered before him. 15 And so was I established in Zion, and in the holy city likewise I rested, and my power was in Jerusalem. 16 And I took root in an honourable people, and in the portion of my God his inheritance, and my abode is in the full assembly of saints. 17 I was exalted like a cedar in Lebanon and as a cypress tree on Mount Zion. 18 I was exalted like a palm tree in Kadesh and as a rose plant in Jericho; 19 as a fair olive tree in the plains and as a plane tree by the water in the streets was I exalted. 20 I gave a sweet smell like cinnamon and aromatical balm. I yielded a sweet odour like the best myrrh, 21 and I perfumed my dwelling as storax and galbanum and onyx and aloes and as the frankincense not cut, and my odour is as the *purest* balm. 22 I have stretched out my branches as the turpentine tree, and my branches are of honour and grace. 23 As the vine I have brought forth a pleasant odour, and my flowers are the fruit of honour and riches.

24 "I am the mother of fair love and of fear and of knowledge and of holy hope. 25 In me is all grace of the way and of the truth. In me is all hope of life and of virtue. 26 Come over to me, all ye that desire me, and be filled with my

concupiscitis me, et a generationibus meis implemini, 27 spiritus enim meus super melle dulcis, et hereditas mea super mel et favum. 28 Memoria mea in generationes saeculorum. 29 Qui edunt me adhuc esurient, et qui bibunt me adhuc sitient. 30 Qui audit me non confundetur, et qui operantur in me non peccabunt. 31 Qui elucidant me vitam aeternam habebunt."

32 Haec omnia liber vitae et testamentum Altissimi et agnitio veritatis. 33 Legem mandavit Moses in praeceptis iustitiarum et hereditatem domui Iacob et Israhel promissiones. 34 Posuit David, puero suo, excitare regem ex ipso fortissimum et in throno honoris sedentem in sempiternum, 35 qui implet quasi Phison sapientiam et sicut Tigris in diebus novorum, 36 qui adimplet quasi Eufrates sensum, qui multiplicat quasi Iordanis in tempore messis, 37 qui mittit disciplinam sicut lucem et adsistens quasi Geon in die vindemiae, 38 qui perficit primus scire ipsam, et infirmior non investigabit eam, 39 a mari enim abundavit cogitatio eius et consilium illius ab abysso magna.

40 "Ego, sapientia, effudi flumina. 41 Ego, quasi tramis aquae inmensae de fluvio, ego, quasi fluvius Dioryx et sicut aquaeductus, exivi a paradiso. 42 Dixi, 'Rigabo meum hortum plantationum, et inebriabo pratus mei fructum.' 43 Et ecce: facta est mihi tramis abundans, et fluvius meus propinquavit ad mare, 44 quoniam doctrinam quasi antelucanum inlumino omnibus, et enarrabo illam usque in longinquo. 45 Penetrabo omnes inferiores partes terrae et inspiciam omnes dormientes et inluminabo omnes sperantes in Domino. 46 Adhuc doctrinam quasi prophetiam effundam et

fruits, 27 for my spirit is sweet above honey, and my inheritance above honey and the honeycomb. 28 My memory is unto everlasting generations. 29 They that eat me shall yet hunger, and they that drink me shall yet thirst. 30 He that hearkeneth to me shall not be confounded, and they that work by me shall not sin. 31 They that explain me shall have life everlasting."

32 All these things are the book of life and the covenant of the Most High and the knowledge of truth. 33 Moses commanded a law in the precepts of justices and an inheritance to the house of Jacob and the promises to Israel. 34 He appointed to David, his servant, to raise up of him a most mighty king and sitting on the throne of glory for ever, 35 who filleth up wisdom as the Pishon and as the Tigris in the days of the new fruits, 36 who maketh understanding to abound as the Euphrates, who multiplieth it as the Jordan in the time of harvest, 37 who sendeth knowledge as the light and riseth up as Gihon in the time of the vintage, 38 who first hath perfect knowledge of her, and a weaker shall not search her out, 39 for her thoughts are more vast than the sea and her counsels more deep than the great ocean.

40 "I, wisdom, have poured out rivers. 41 I, like a brook out of a river of a mighty water, I, like a channel of a river and like an aqueduct, came out of paradise. 42 I said, 'I will water my garden of plants, and I will water abundantly the fruits of my meadow.' 43 And behold: my brook became a great river, and my river came near to a sea, 44 for I make doctrine to shine forth to all as the morning light, and I will declare it afar off. 45 I will penetrate to all the lower parts of the earth and will behold all that sleep and will enlighten all that hope in the Lord. 46 I will yet pour out doctrine as

relinquam illam quaerentibus sapientiam et non desinam in progenies illorum usque in aevum sanctum. 47 Videte quoniam non soli mihi laboravi, sed omnibus exquirentibus veritatem."

Caput 25

In tribus placitum est spiritui meo quae sunt probata coram Deo et hominibus: 2 concordia fratrum et amor proximorum et vir et mulier bene sibi consentientes. 3 Tres species odivit anima mea, et adgravor valde animae illorum: 4 pauperem superbum, et divitem mendacem, senem fatuum et insensatum.

5 Quae in iuventute tua non congregasti, quomodo invenies in senectute tua? 6 Quam speciosum canitiei iudicium et presbyteris cognoscere consilium! 7 Quam speciosa veteranis sapientia et gloriosis intellectus et consilium! 8 Corona senum multa peritia, et gloria illorum timor Dei.

9 Novem insuspicabilia cordis magnificavi, et decimum dicam in lingua hominibus. 10 Homo qui iucundatur in filiis vivens et videns subversionem inimicorum suorum. 11 Beatus qui inhabitat cum muliere sensata et qui lingua sua non

prophecy and will leave it to them that seek wisdom and will not cease *to instruct* their offspring even to the holy age. 47 See ye that I have not laboured for myself only, but for all that seek out the truth."

Chapter 25

Documents of wisdom on several subjects.

With three things my spirit is pleased which are approved before God and men: 2 the concord of brethren and the love of neighbours and man and wife that agree well together. 3 Three sorts my soul hateth, and I am greatly grieved at their life: 4 a poor man that is proud, *a* rich man that is a liar, an old man that is a fool and doting.

5 The things that thou hast not gathered in thy youth, how shalt thou find them in thy old age? 6 O how comely is judgment for a grey head and for ancients to know counsel! 7 O how comely is wisdom for the aged and understanding and counsel to men of honour! 8 Much experience is the crown of old men, and the fear of God is their glory.

9 Nine things that are not to be imagined by the heart have I magnified, and the tenth I will utter to men with my tongue. 10 A man that hath joy of his children *and* he that liveth and seeth the fall of his enemies. 11 Blessed is he that dwelleth with a wise woman and that hath not slipped with

est lapsus et qui non servivit indignis se. 12 Beatus qui invenit amicum verum et qui enarrat iustitiam auri audienti. 13 Quam magnus qui invenit sapientiam et scientiam! Sed non est super timentem Dominum. 14 Timor Dei super omnia se superposuit. 15 Beatus homo cui donatum est habere timorem Dei: qui tenet illum, cui adsimilabitur? 16 Timor Dei initium dilectionis eius, fidei autem initium adglutinandum est ei.

17 Omnis plaga tristitia cordis est, et omnis malitia nequitia mulieris. 18 Et omnem plagam et non plagam videbit cordis, 19 et omnem nequitiam et non nequitiam mulieris, 20 et omnem obductum et non obductum odientium, 21 et omnem vindictam et non vindictam inimicorum.

22 Non est caput nequius super caput colubri, 23 et non est ira super iram mulieris. Commorari leoni et draconi placebit quam habitare cum muliere nequa. 24 Nequitia mulieris inmutat faciem eius, et obcaecat vultum suum tamquam ursus et quasi saccum ostendit. In medio proximorum eius 25 ingemuit vir eius, et audiens suspiravit modicum. 26 Brevis omnis malitia super malitiam mulieris: sors peccatorum cadat super illam. 27 Sicut ascensus harenosus in pedibus veterani, sic mulier linguata homini quieto. 28 Ne respicias in mulieris speciem, et non concupiscas mulierem in specie. 29 Mulieris ira et inreverentia et confusio magna. 30 Mulier, si primatum habeat, contraria est viro suo. 31 Cor humile et facies tristis et plaga cordis mulier nequa. 32 Manus debiles et genua dissoluta, mulier quae non beatificat virum suum.

his tongue and that hath not served such as are unworthy of him. 12 Blessed is he that findeth a true friend and that declareth justice to an ear that heareth. 13 How great is he that findeth wisdom and knowledge! But there is none above him that feareth the Lord. 14 The fear of God hath set itself above all things. 15 Blessed is the man to whom it is given to have the fear of God: he that holdeth it, to whom shall he be likened? 16 The fear of God is the beginning of his love, and the beginning of faith is to be fast joined unto it.

17 The sadness of the heart is every plague, and the wickedness of a woman is all evil. 18 And *a man will choose any plague but* the plague of the heart, 19 and any wickedness but the wickedness of a woman, 20 and any affliction but the affliction from them that hate him, 21 and any revenge but the revenge of enemies.

22 There is no head worse than the head of a serpent, 23 and there is no anger above the anger of a woman. It will be more agreeable to abide with a lion and a dragon than to dwell with a wicked woman. 24 The wickedness of a woman changeth her face, and she darkeneth her countenance as a bear and sheweth it like sackcloth. In the midst of her neighbours 25 her husband groaned, and hearing he sighed a little. 26 All malice is short to the malice of a woman: let the lot of sinners fall upon her. 27 As the climbing of a sandy way is to the feet of the aged, so is a wife full of tongue to a quiet man. 28 Look not upon a woman's beauty, and desire not a woman for beauty. 29 A woman's anger and impudence and confusion is great. 30 A woman, if she have superiority, is contrary to her husband. 31 A wicked woman *abateth the courage and maketh a heavy countenance and a wounded heart.* 32 Feeble hands and disjointed knees, a woman that doth not make

33 A muliere initium factum est peccati, et per illam omnes morimur. 34 Non des aquae tuae exitum, nec modicum, nec mulieri nequam veniam prodeundi. 35 Si non ambulaverit ad manum tuam, confundet te in conspectu inimicorum. 36 A carnibus tuis abscide illam ne semper te abutatur.

Caput 26

Mulieris bonae beatus vir, numerus enim annorum illius duplex. 2 Mulier fortis oblectat virum suum et annos vitae illius in pace implebit. 3 Pars bona mulier bona; in parte bona timentium Deum dabitur viro pro factis bonis. 4 Divitis autem et pauperis cor bonum in omni tempore vultus illorum hilaris.

5 A tribus timuit cor meum, et in quarto facies mea metuit: 6 delatura civitatis et collectio populi 7 calumniam mendacem. Super mortem omnia gravia.

8 Dolor cordis et luctus mulier zelotypa. 9 In muliere zelotypa flagellum linguae omnibus communicans. 10 Sicut boum iugum quod movetur, ita et mulier nequam. Qui tenet illam quasi qui adprehendat scorpionem. 11 Mulier ebriosa

her husband happy. 33 From the woman came the beginning of sin, and by her we all die. 34 Give no issue to thy water, no, not a little, nor to a wicked woman liberty to *gad abroad.* 35 If she walk not at thy hand, she will confound thee in the sight of thy enemies. 36 Cut her off from thy flesh lest she always abuse thee.

Chapter 26

Of good and bad women.

Happy is the husband of a good wife, for the number of his years is double. 2 A virtuous woman rejoiceth her husband and shall fulfill the years of his life in peace. 3 A good wife is a good portion; she shall be given in the *portion* of them that fear God to a man for his good deeds. 4 *Rich or poor, if his heart* is good, his countenance shall be cheerful at all times.

5 Of three things my heart hath been afraid, and at the fourth my face hath trembled: 6 the accusation of a city and the gathering together of the people 7 *and* a false calumny. All are more grievous than death.

8 A jealous woman is the grief and mourning of the heart. 9 With a jealous woman is a scourge of the tongue which communicateth with all. 10 As a yoke of oxen that is moved *to and fro,* so also is a wicked woman. He that hath hold of her is as he that taketh hold of a scorpion. 11 A drunken

ira magna, et contumelia et turpitudo illius non contegetur. 12 Fornicatio mulieris in extollentia oculorum et in palpebris illius agnoscetur. 13 In filia non avertente se firma custodiam ne inventa occasione utatur se. 14 Ab omni inreverentia oculorum eius cave, et ne mireris si te neglexerit. 15 Sicut viator sitiens ad fontem os aperiet et ab omni aqua proxima bibet et contra omnem palum sedebit et contra omnem sagittam aperiet faretram donec deficiat.

16 Gratia mulieris sedulae delectabit virum suum et ossa illius inpinguabit. 17 Disciplina illius datus Dei. 18 Mulier sensata et tacita non est inmutatio eruditae animae. 19 Gratia super gratiam mulier sancta et pudorata, 20 omnis autem ponderatio non est digna continentis animae. 21 Sicut sol oriens mundo in altissimis Dei, sic mulieris bonae species in ornamentum domus eius, 22 lucerna splendens super candelabrum sanctum et species faciei super aetatem stabilem, 23 columnae aureae super bases argenteas et pedes firmi super plantas stabilis mulieris, 24 fundamenta aeterna super petram solidam et mandata Dei in corde mulieris sanctae.

25 In duobus contristatum est cor meum, et in tertio iracundia mihi advenit: 26 vir bellator deficiens per inopiam et vir sensatus contemptus 27 et qui transgreditur a iustitia ad peccatum. Deus paravit eum ad rompheam.

28 Duae species difficiles et periculosae mihi apparuerunt: difficile exuitur negotians a neglegentia, et non iustificabitur caupo a peccatis labiorum.

woman is a great wrath, and her reproach and shame shall not be hid. 12 The fornication of a woman shall be known by the haughtiness of her eyes and by her eyelids. 13 On a daughter that turneth not away herself set a strict watch lest finding an opportunity she abuse herself. 14 Take heed of the impudence of her eyes, and wonder not if she slight thee.

15 She will open her mouth as a thirsty traveller to the fountain and will drink of every water near her and will sit down by every hedge and open her quiver against every arrow until she fail.

16 The grace of a diligent woman shall delight her husband and shall fat his bones. 17 Her discipline is the gift of God. 18 *Such is* a wise and silent woman, *and* there is *nothing so much worth as a well* instructed soul. 19 A holy and shamefaced woman is grace upon grace, 20 and no price is worthy of a continent soul. 21 As the sun when it riseth to the world in the high places of God, so is the beauty of a good wife for the ornament of her house. 22 *As* the lamp shining upon the holy candlestick, *so* is the beauty of the face *in a ripe* age. 23 *As* golden pillars upon bases of silver, *so* are the firm feet upon the soles of a steady woman. 24 *As* everlasting foundations upon a solid rock, *so* the commandments of God in the heart of a holy woman.

25 At two things my heart is grieved, and the third bringeth anger upon me: 26 a man of war fainting through poverty and a man of sense despised 27 and he that passeth over from justice to sin. God hath prepared such an one for the sword.

28 Two sorts of callings have appeared to me hard and dangerous: a merchant is hardly free from negligence, and a huckster shall not be justified from the sins of the lips.

Caput 27

Propter inopiam multi deliquerunt, et qui quaerit locupletari avertit oculum suum. 2 Sicut in medio conpaginis lapidum palus figitur, sic et inter medium venditionis et emptionis angustabitur peccatum. 3 Conteretur cum delinquente delictum. 4 Si non in timore Domini tenueris te instanter, cito subvertetur domus tua. 5 Sicut in percussura cribri remanebit pulvis, sic aporia hominis in cogitatu illius.

6 Vasa figuli probat fornax, et homines iustos temptatio tribulationis. 7 Sicut rusticatio de ligno ostendit fructum illius, sic verbum ex cogitatu hominis cordis. 8 Ante sermonem non conlaudes virum, haec enim temptatio est hominum. 9 Si sequaris iustitiam, adprehendes illam et indues quasi poderem honoris, et inhabitabis cum ea, et proteget te in sempiternum, et in die agnitionis invenies firmamentum.

10 Volatilia ad sibi similia conveniunt, et veritas ad eos qui operantur illam revertetur. 11 Leo venationi insidiatur semper; sic peccata operantibus iniquitates. 12 Homo sanctus in sapientia manet sicut sol, nam stultus sicut luna inmutatur. 13 In medio insensatorum serva verbum tempori, in medio autem cogitantium adsiduus esto.

Chapter 27

Dangers of sin from several heads. The fear of God is the best preservative. He that diggeth a pit shall fall into it.

Through poverty many have sinned, and he that seeketh to be enriched turneth away his eye. 2 As a stake sticketh fast in the midst of the joining of stones, so also in the midst of selling and buying sin shall *stick fast.* 3 Sin shall be destroyed with the sinner. 4 Unless thou hold thyself diligently in the fear of the Lord, thy house shall quickly be overthrown. 5 As when one sifteth with a sieve the dust will remain, so will the perplexity of a man in his thoughts.

6 The furnace trieth the potter's vessels, and the trial of affliction just men. 7 As the *dressing* of a tree sheweth the fruit thereof, so a word out of the thought of the heart of man. 8 Praise not a man before he speaketh, for this is the trial of men. 9 If thou followest justice, thou shalt obtain her and shalt put her on as a long robe of honour, and thou shalt dwell with her, and she shall protect thee for ever, and in the day of acknowledgment thou shalt find a strong foundation.

10 Birds resort unto their like; *so* truth will return to them that practise her. 11 The lion always lieth in wait for prey; so do sins for them that work iniquities. 12 A holy man continueth in wisdom as the sun, *but* a fool is changed as the moon. 13 In the midst of the unwise keep in the word till its time, but be continually among men that think.

14 Narratio peccantium odiosa, et risus illorum in deliciis peccati. 15 Loquella multum iurans horripilationem capiti statuet, et inreverentia ipsius obturatio aurium. 16 Effusio sanguinis in rixa superborum, et maledictio illorum auditus gravis. 17 Qui denudat arcana amici perdit fidem et non inveniet amicum ad animum suum.

18 Dilige proximum, et coniungere fide cum illo. 19 Quod si denudaveris absconsa illius, non persequeris post eum, 20 sicut enim homo qui perdit amicum suum, sic et qui perdit amicitiam proximi sui. 21 Et sicut qui dimittit avem de manu sua, sic reliquisti proximum tuum, et non eum capies. 22 Non illum sequaris, quoniam longe abest, effugit enim quasi caprea de laqueo quoniam vulnerata est anima eius. 23 Ultra eum non poteris conligare. Et maledicti est concordatio, 24 denudare autem amici mysteria desperatio est animae infelicis.

25 Annuens oculo fabricat iniqua, et nemo eum abiciet. 26 In conspectu oculorum tuorum condulcabit os suum et super sermones tuos admirabitur, novissime autem pervertet os suum, et in verbis tuis dabit scandalum. 27 Multa audivi et non coaequavi ei, et Dominus odiet illum.

28 Qui in altum mittit lapidem, super caput eius cadet, et plaga dolosa dolosi dividet vulnera. 29 Qui foveam fodit in illam incidet, et qui statuit lapidem proximo offendet in eo, et qui laqueum alii ponit peribit in illo. 30 Facienti nequissimum consilium super ipsum devolvetur, et non agnoscet unde adveniat illi. 31 Inlusio et inproperium superborum,

14 The discourse of sinners is hateful, and their laughter is at the pleasures of sin. 15 The speech that sweareth much shall make the hair of the head stand upright, and its irreverence shall make one stop his ears. 16 In the quarrels of the proud is the shedding of blood, and their cursing is a grievous hearing. 17 He that discloseth the secret of a friend loseth his credit and shall *never* find a friend to his mind.

18 Love thy neighbour, and be joined to him with fidelity. 19 But if thou discover his secrets, follow no more after him, 20 for as a man that destroyeth his friend, so also is he that destroyeth the friendship of his neighbour. 21 And as one that letteth a bird go out of his hand, so hast thou *let* thy neighbour *go,* and thou shalt not get him again. 22 Follow after him no more, for he is gone afar off; *he* is fled as a roe *escaped* out of the snare because his soul is wounded. 23 Thou canst no more bind him up. And of a curse there is reconciliation, 24 but to disclose the secrets of a friend *leaveth no hope to* an unhappy soul.

25 He that winketh with the eye forgeth wicked things, and no man will cast him off. 26 In the sight of thy eyes he will sweeten his mouth and will admire thy words, but at the last he will writhe his mouth, and on thy words he will lay a stumbling block. 27 I have *hated* many things, *but not like him,* and the Lord *himself* will hate him.

28 If one cast a stone on high, it will fall upon his own head, and the deceitful stroke will *wound* the deceitful. 29 He that diggeth a pit shall fall into it, and he that setteth a stone for his neighbour shall stumble upon it, and he that layeth a snare for another shall perish in it. 30 A mischievous counsel shall be rolled back upon the author, and he shall not know from whence it cometh to him. 31 Mockery and reproach are

et vindicta sicut leo insidiabitur illi. 32 Laqueo peribunt qui oblectantur casu iustorum, dolor autem consumet illos antequam moriantur. 33 Ira et furor utraque execrabilia sunt, et vir peccator continens erit illorum.

Caput 28

Qui vindicari vult a Domino inveniet vindictam, et peccata illius servans servabit. 2 Relinque proximo tuo nocenti te, et tunc deprecanti tibi peccata solventur. 3 Homo homini reservat iram, et a Deo quaerit medellam? 4 In hominem similem sibi non habet misericordiam, et de peccatis suis deprecatur? 5 Ipse cum caro sit reservat iram, et propitiationem petit a Deo? Quis exorabit pro delictis illius? 6 Memento novissimorum, et desine inimicari, 7 tabitudo enim et mors inminet in mandatis eius. 8 Memorare timorem Dei, et non irascaris proximo. 9 Memorare testamenti Altissimi, et despice ignorantiam proximi. 10 Abstine te a lite, et minues peccata, 11 homo enim iracundus incendit litem, et vir peccator

of the proud, and vengeance as a lion shall lie in wait for him. 32 They shall perish in a snare that are delighted with the fall of the just, and sorrow shall consume them before they die. 33 Anger and fury are both of them abominable, and the sinful man shall be subject to them.

Chapter 28

Lessons against revenge and quarrels. The evils of the tongue.

He that seeketh to revenge himself shall find vengeance from the Lord, and he will surely keep his sins in remembrance. 2 Forgive thy neighbour *if he hath hurt* thee, and then shall thy sins be forgiven to thee when thou prayest. 3 Man to man reserveth anger, and doth he seek remedy of God? 4 He hath no mercy on a man like himself, and doth he entreat for his own sins? 5 *He that* is *but* flesh nourisheth anger, and doth he ask forgiveness of God? Who shall obtain pardon for his sins? 6 Remember thy last things, and let enmity cease, 7 for corruption and death hang over in his commandments. 8 Remember the fear of God, and be not angry with thy neighbour. 9 Remember the covenant of the Most High, and overlook the ignorance of thy neighbour. 10 Refrain from strife, and thou shalt diminish thy sins, 11 for a passionate man kindleth strife, and a sinful man will trouble his

turbabit amicos et in medium pacem habentium inmittet inimicitiam, 12 secundum enim ligna silvae, sic ignis exardescit, et secundum virtutem hominis, sic iracundia illius erit, et secundum substantiam suam exaltabit iram suam. 13 Certamen festinatum incendit ignem, et lis festinans effundit sanguinem, et lingua testificans adducit mortem. 14 Si sufflaveris in scintillam, quasi ignis exardebit, et si expueris super illam, extinguetur: utraque ex ore proficiscuntur.

15 Susurro et bilinguis maledictus, multos enim turbavit pacem habentes. 16 Lingua tertia multos commovit et dispersit illos a gente in gentem. 17 Civitates muratas divitum destruxit et domos magnatorum effodit. 18 Virtutes populorum concidit et gentes fortes dissolvit. 19 Lingua tertia mulieres viratas eiecit et privavit illas laboribus suis. 20 Qui respicit illam non habebit requiem, nec habebit amicum in quo requiescat. 21 Flagelli plaga livorem facit, plaga autem linguae comminuet ossa. 22 Multi ceciderunt in ore gladii, sed non sic quasi qui interierunt per linguam suam. 23 Beatus qui tectus est a lingua nequa, qui in iracundiam illius non transivit et qui non adtraxit iugum eius et in vinculis illius non est ligatus, 24 iugum enim illius iugum ferreum est et vinculum illius vinculum aereum est. 25 Mors illius mors nequissima, et utilis potius infernus quam illa. 26 Perseverantia illius non permanebit, sed obtinebit vias iniustorum, et in flamma sua non conburet iustos. 27 Qui derelinquunt Deum incident in illam, et exardebit in illis et non extinguetur, et inmittetur in illos quasi leo, et quasi pardus laedebit illos.

friends and bring in *debate* in the midst of them that are at peace, 12 for as the wood of the forest is, so the fire burneth, and as a man's strength is, so shall his anger be, and according to his riches he shall increase his anger. 13 A hasty contention kindleth a fire, and a hasty quarrel sheddeth blood, and a tongue that beareth witness bringeth death. 14 If thou blow *the* spark, it shall burn as a fire, and if thou spit upon it, it shall be quenched: both come out of the mouth.

15 The whisperer and the double tongued is accursed, for he hath troubled many that were at peace. 16 The tongue of a third person hath disquieted many and scattered them from nation to nation. 17 It hath destroyed the strong cities of the rich and hath overthrown the houses of great men. 18 It hath cut in pieces the forces of people and undone strong nations. 19 The tongue of a third person hath cast out valiant women and deprived them of their labours. 20 He that *hearkeneth to* it shall *never* have rest, neither shall he have a friend in whom he may repose. 21 The stroke of a whip maketh a blue mark, but the stroke of the tongue will break the bones. 22 Many have fallen by the edge of the sword, but not so many as have perished by their own tongue. 23 Blessed is he that is defended from a wicked tongue, that hath not passed into the wrath thereof and that hath not drawn the yoke thereof and hath not been bound in its bands, 24 for its yoke is a yoke of iron and its bands are bands of brass. 25 The death thereof is a most evil death, and hell is preferable to it. 26 Its continuance shall not be for a long time, but it shall possess the ways of the unjust, and the just shall not be burnt with its flame. 27 They that forsake God shall fall into it, and it shall burn in them and shall not be quenched, and it shall be sent upon them as a lion, and as a leopard it shall tear

28 Sepi aures tuas spinis, et noli audire linguam nequam, et ori tuo facito ostia et seras. 29 Aurum tuum et argentum tuum constitue, et verbis tuis facito stateram et frenos ori tuo rectos, 30 et adtende ne forte labaris in lingua et cadas in conspectu inimicorum insidiantium tibi et sit casus tuus insanabilis in mortem.

Caput 29

Qui facit misericordiam fenerat proximo suo, et qui praevalet manu mandata servat. 2 Fenera proximo tuo in tempore necessitatis illius, et iterum redde proximo in tempore suo. 3 Confirma verbum, et fideliter age cum illo, et in omni tempore invenies quod tibi necessarium est. 4 Multi quasi inventionem aestimaverunt fenus et praestiterunt molestiam his qui se adiuvaverunt. 5 Donec accipiant osculantur manus dantis, et in promissionibus humiliant vocem suam, 6 et in tempore redditionis, postulabit tempus et loquetur verba taedii et murmurationum et tempus causabitur. 7 Si autem potuerit reddere, adversabitur; solidi vix reddet dimidium et conputabit illud quasi inventionem. 8 Sin autem, fraudabit illum pecunia sua et possidebit illum ini-

them. 28 Hedge in thy ears with thorns. *Hear* not a wicked tongue, and make doors and bars to thy mouth. 29 *Melt down thy gold and silver,* and make a balance for thy words and a just bridle for thy mouth, 30 and take heed *lest* thou slip with thy tongue and fall in the sight of thy enemies who lie in wait for thee and thy fall be incurable unto death.

Chapter 29

Of charity in lending money and justice in repaying. Of alms and of being surety.

He that sheweth mercy lendeth to his neighbour, and he that is stronger in hand keepeth the commandments. 2 Lend to thy neighbour in the time of his need, and pay thou thy neighbour again in due time. 3 Keep thy word, and deal faithfully with him, and thou shalt always find that which is necessary for thee. 4 Many have looked upon a thing lent as a thing found and have given trouble to them that helped them. 5 Till they receive they kiss the hands of the lender, and in promises they humble their voice, 6 *but* when they should repay, they will ask time and will return tedious and murmuring words and will complain of the time. 7 And if he be able to pay, he will stand off; he will scarce pay one *half* and will count it as if he had found it. 8 But if not, he will defraud him of his money and he shall get him for an enemy

micum gratis, 9 et convicia et maledicta reddet illi et pro honore et beneficio reddet illi contumeliam.

10 Multi, non causa nequitiae, non feneraverunt, sed fraudari gratis timuerunt. 11 Verumtamen super humilem animo fortior esto, et pro elemosyna non trahas illum. 12 Propter mandatum adsume pauperem, et propter inopiam eius ne dimittas illum vacuum. 13 Perde pecuniam pro fratre et amico, et non abscondas illam sub lapide in perditionem. 14 Pone thesaurum tuum in praeceptis Altissimi, et proderit tibi magis quam aurum. 15 Conclude elemosynam in corde pauperis, et haec pro te exorabit ab omni malo. 16 Super scutum potentis et super lanceam, 17 adversus inimicum tuum pugnabit.

18 Vir bonus fidem facit proximo suo, et qui perdiderit confusionem derelinquet sibi. 19 Gratiam fideiussoris ne obliviscaris, dedit enim pro te animam suam. 20 Repromissorem fugit peccator et inmundus. 21 Bona repromissoris sibi adscribit peccator, et ingratus sensu derelinquet liberantem se. 22 Vir repromittit de proximo suo, et cum perdiderit reverentiam, relinquetur ab eo. 23 Repromissio nequissima multos perdidit dirigentes et commovit illos quasi fluctus maris. 24 Viros potentes gyrans migrare fecit, et vagati sunt in gentibus alienis. 25 Peccator transgrediens mandatum Domini incidet in promissionem nequa, et qui conatur multa agere incidet in iudicium.

26 Recupera proximum secundum virtutem tuam, et adtende tibi ne incidas. 27 Initium vitae hominis aqua et panis

without cause, 9 and he will pay him with reproaches and curses and instead of honour and good turn will repay him injuries.

10 Many have *refused to lend,* not out of wickedness, but they were afraid to be defrauded without cause. 11 But yet towards the poor be thou more hearty, and *delay not to shew him mercy.* 12 Help the poor because of the commandment, and send him not away empty handed because of his poverty. 13 Lose thy money for thy brother and thy friend, and hide it not under a stone to be lost. 14 Place thy treasure in the commandments of the Most High, and it shall bring thee more profit than gold. 15 Shut up alms in the heart of the poor, and it shall obtain help for thee against all evil. 16 Better than the shield of the mighty and better than the spear, 17 it shall fight for thee against thy enemy.

18 A good man is surety for his neighbour, and he that hath lost shame will leave him to himself. 19 Forget not the kindness of thy surety, for he hath given his life for thee. 20 The sinner and the unclean fleeth from his surety. 21 A sinner attributeth to himself the goods of his surety, and he that is of an unthankful mind will leave him that delivered him. 22 A man is surety for his neighbour, and when he hath lost all shame, he shall forsake him. 23 Evil suretyship hath undone many of good estate and hath tossed them as a wave of the sea. 24 It hath made powerful men to go *from place to place round about,* and they have wandered in strange countries. 25 A sinner that transgresseth the commandment of the Lord shall fall into an evil suretyship, and he that undertaketh many things shall fall into judgment.

26 Recover thy neighbour according to thy power, and take heed to thyself that thou fall not. 27 The chief thing for

et vestimentum et domus protegens turpitudinem. 28 Melior est victus pauperis sub tegimen asserum quam epulae splendidae in peregre sine domicilio. 29 Minimum pro magno placeat tibi, et inproperium peregrinationis non audies. 30 Vita nequa hospitandi de domo in domum, et ubi hospitabitur non fiducialiter aget nec aperiet os. 31 Hospitabit et pascet et potabit ingratos et ad haec amara audiet: 32 "Transi, hospes, et orna mensam, et quae in manu habes ciba ceteros. 33 Exi a facie honoris amicorum meorum, necessitudine domus meae, hospitio mihi factus est frater." 34 Gravia haec homini habenti sensum, correptio domus et inproperium feneratoris.

Caput 30

Qui diligit filium suum adsiduat illi flagella ut laetetur in novissimo suo et non palpet proximorum ostia. 2 Qui docet filium suum laudabitur in illo et in medio domesticorum in illo gloriabitur. 3 Qui docet filium suum in zelum mittit ini-

man's life is water and bread and clothing and a house to cover shame. 28 Better is the poor man's fare under a roof of boards than sumptuous cheer abroad *in another man's* house. 29 Be contented with little instead of much, and thou shalt not hear the reproach of going abroad. 30 It is a miserable life to go as a guest from house to house, *for* where a man is a stranger he shall not deal confidently nor open his mouth. 31 He shall entertain and feed and give drink to the unthankful and moreover he shall hear bitter words: 32 "Go, stranger, and furnish the table, and give others to eat what thou hast in thy hand. 33 Give place to the honourable presence of my friends, *for I want* my house, my brother being to be lodged with me." 34 These things are grievous to a man of understanding, the upbraiding of houseroom and the reproaching of the lender.

Chapter 30

Of correction of children. Health is better than wealth. Excessive grief is hurtful.

He that loveth his son frequently chastiseth him that he may rejoice in his latter end and not grope after the doors of his neighbours. 2 He that instructeth his son shall be praised in him and shall glory in him in the midst of them of his household. 3 He that teacheth his son maketh his enemy

micum, et in medio amicorum gloriabitur in illo. 4 Mortuus est pater illius, et quasi non est mortuus, similem enim reliquit sibi post se. 5 In vita ipsius vidit et laetatus est in illo; in obitu illius non est contristatus, nec confusus est coram inimicis, 6 reliquit enim defensorem domus contra inimicos et amicis reddentem gratiam, 7 pro animabus filiorum conligabit vulnera sua, et super omnem vocem turbabuntur viscera eius.

8 Equus indomitus evadit durus, et filius remissus evadet praeceps. 9 Lacta filium, et paventem te faciet. Lude cum eo, et contristabit te. 10 Non conrideas illi ne doleas et in novissimo obstupescent dentes tui. 11 Non des illi potestatem in iuventute, et ne despicias cogitatus illius. 12 Curva cervicem eius in iuventute, et tunde latera illius dum infans est ne forte induret et non credat tibi et erit tibi dolor animae. 13 Doce filium tuum, et operare in illum ne in turpitudinem illius offendas.

14 Melior est pauper sanus et fortis viribus quam dives inbecillis et flagellatus malitia. 15 Salus animae in sanctitate iustitiae melior est omni auro et argento, et corpus validum quam census inmensus. 16 Non est census super censum salutis corporis, et non est oblectatio super cordis gaudium. 17 Melior est mors quam vita amara, et requies aeterna quam languor perseverans.

18 Bona absconsa in ore cluso quasi adpositiones epularum circumpositae sepulchro. 19 Quid proderit libatio idolo? Nec enim manducabit nec odorabitur. 20 Sic qui effugatur

jealous, and in the midst of his friends he shall glory in him. 4 His father is dead, and he is as if he were not dead, for he hath left one behind him that is like himself. 5 While he lived he saw and rejoiced in him, *and* when he died he was not sorrowful, neither was he confounded before his enemies, 6 for he left behind him a defender of his house against his enemies and one that will requite kindness to his friends, 7 for the souls of his sons he shall bind up his wounds, and at every cry his bowels shall be troubled.

8 A horse not broken becometh stubborn, and a child left to himself will become headstrong. 9 *Give* thy son *his way,* and he shall make thee afraid. Play with him, and he shall make thee sorrowful. 10 Laugh not with him lest thou have sorrow and at the last thy teeth be set on edge. 11 Give him not liberty in his youth, and wink not at his devices. 12 Bow down his neck while he is young, and beat his sides while he is a child *lest* he grow stubborn and regard thee not and *so* be a sorrow of heart to thee. 13 Instruct thy son, and labour about him lest his lewd behaviour be an offence to thee.

14 Better is a poor man who is sound and strong of constitution than a rich man who is weak and afflicted with evils. 15 Health of the soul in holiness of justice is better than all gold and silver, and a sound body than immense revenues. 16 There is no riches above the riches of the health of the body, and there is no pleasure above the joy of the heart. 17 Better is death than a bitter life, and everlasting rest than continual sickness.

18 Good things that are hidden in a mouth that is shut are as masses of meat set about a grave. 19 What good shall an offering do to an idol? For it *can* neither eat nor smell. 20 So

a Domino, portans mercedes iniquitatis, 21 videns oculis et ingemescens sicut spado conplectens virginem et suspirans.

22 Tristitiam non des animae tuae, et non adfligas temet ipsum in consilio tuo. 23 Iucunditas cordis, haec est vita hominis et thesaurus sine defectione sanctitatis, et exultatio viri est longevitas. 24 Miserere animae tuae, placens Deo, et contine, et congrega cor tuum in sanctitate eius, et tristitiam longe expelle a te, 25 multos enim occidit tristitia et non est utilitas in illa. 26 Zelus et iracundia minuit dies, et ante tempus senectam adducet cogitatus. 27 Splendidum cor bonum in epulis, epulae enim illius diligenter fiunt.

Caput 31

Vigilia honestatis tabefaciet carnes, et cogitatus illius auferet somnum. 2 Cogitatus praescientiae avertit sensum, et infirmitas gravis sobriam facit animam. 3 Laboravit dives in congregatione substantiae, et in requie sua replebitur bonis suis. 4 Laboravit pauper in diminutione victus, et in fine inops fit. 5 Qui aurum diligit non iustificabitur, et qui inse-

is he that is persecuted by the Lord, bearing the reward of his iniquity. 21 He seeth with his eyes and groaneth as an eunuch embracing a virgin and sighing.

22 Give not up *thy soul to sadness,* and afflict not thyself in thy own counsel. 23 The joyfulness of the heart *is* the life of a man and a never failing treasure of holiness, and the joy of a man is length of life. 24 Have pity on thy own soul, pleasing God, and contain thyself; *gather* up thy heart in his holiness, and drive away sadness far from thee, 25 for sadness hath killed many and there is no profit in it. 26 Envy and anger shorten a man's days, and pensiveness will bring old age before the time. 27 *A cheerful and good heart is always feasting,* for his banquets are prepared with diligence.

Chapter 31

Of the desire of riches and of moderation in eating and drinking.

Watching for riches *consumeth* the flesh, and the thought thereof driveth away sleep. 2 The thinking beforehand turneth away the understanding, and a grievous sickness maketh the soul sober. 3 The rich man hath laboured in gathering riches together, and when he resteth he shall be filled with his goods. 4 The poor man hath laboured in his low way of life, and in the end he is still poor. 5 He that loveth gold shall not be justified, and he that followeth after corruption shall

quitur consumptionem replebitur ex ea. 6 Multi dati sunt in auri casus, et facta est in specie ipsius perditio illorum. 7 Lignum offensionis est aurum sacrificantium. Vae illis qui sectantur illud, et omnis inprudens deperiet in illo. 8 Beatus dives qui inventus est sine macula et qui post aurum non abiit nec speravit in pecunia et thesauris. 9 Quis est hic? Et laudabimus eum, fecit enim mirabilia in vita sua. 10 Qui probatus est in illo et perfectus est, erit illi gloria aeterna, qui potuit transgredi et non est transgressus et facere mala et non fecit. 11 Ideo stabilita sunt bona illius in Domino, et elemosynas illius enarrabit omnis ecclesia sanctorum.

12 Supra mensam magnam sedisti? Non aperias super illam faucem tuam prior. 13 Non dicas sic: "Multa sunt quae super illam sunt." 14 Memento quoniam malus est oculus nequa. 15 Nequius oculo quid creatum est? Ideo ab omni facie sua lacrimabitur cum viderit. 16 Ne extendas manum tuam prior et invidia contaminatus obrubescas. 17 Ne conprimaris in convivio. 18 Intellege quae sunt proximi tui ex te ipso. 19 Utere quasi homo frugi his quae tibi adponuntur ne cum manducas multum odio habearis. 20 Cessa prior, causa disciplinae, et noli nimius esse ne forte offendas. 21 Et si in medio multorum sedisti, prior illis non extendas manum tuam, nec prior poscas bibere. 22 Quam sufficiens est homini erudito vinum exiguum, et in dormiendo non laborabis ab illo, et non senties dolorem.

be filled with it. 6 Many have been brought to fall for gold, and the beauty thereof hath been their ruin. 7 Gold is a stumbling block to them that sacrifice to it. Woe to them that eagerly follow after it, and every fool shall perish by it. 8 Blessed is the rich man that is found without blemish and that hath not gone after gold nor put his trust in money nor in treasures. 9 Who is he? And we will praise him, for he hath done wonderful things in his life. 10 Who hath been tried thereby and made perfect, he shall have glory everlasting, he that could have transgressed and hath not transgressed and could do evil things and hath not done them. 11 Therefore are his goods established in the Lord, and all the church of the saints shall declare his alms.

12 Art thou set at a great table? Be not the first to open thy mouth upon it. 13 Say *not,* "There are many things which are upon it." 14 Remember that a wicked eye is evil. 15 What is created more wicked than an eye? Therefore shall it weep over all the face when it shall see. 16 Stretch not out thy hand first *lest* being disgraced with envy thou be *put to confusion.* 17 Be not hasty in a feast. 18 Judge *of the disposition* of thy neighbour by thyself. 19 Use as a frugal man the things that are set before thee lest *if* thou eatest much thou be hated. 20 Leave off first, for manners' sake, and exceed not *lest* thou offend. 21 And if thou sittest among many, reach not thy hand out *first of all,* and be not the first to ask for drink. 22 How sufficient is a little wine for a man well taught, and in sleeping thou shalt not be uneasy with it, and thou shalt feel no pain.

23 Vigilia et cholera et tortura viro infrunito. 24 Somnus sanitatis in homine parco; dormiet usque mane, et anima illius cum ipso delectabitur. 25 Et si coactus fueris in edendo multum, surge e medio, et vome, et refrigerabit te, et non adduces corpori tuo infirmitatem.

26 Audi me, fili, et ne spernas me, et in novissimo invenies mea verba. 27 In omnibus operibus tuis esto velox, et omnis infirmitas non occurret tibi. 28 Splendidum in panibus benedicent labia multorum, et testimonium veritatis illius fidele. 29 In nequissimo pane murmurabit civitas, et testimonium nequitiae illius verum est.

30 Diligentes in vino noli provocare, multos enim exterminavit vinum. 31 Ignis probat ferrum durum; sic vinum corda superborum arguet in ebrietate potatum. 32 Aequa vita hominibus vinum in sobrietate. Si bibas illud moderate eris sobrius. 33 Quae vita est ei quae minuitur vino? 34 Quid defraudat vitam? Mors. 35 Vinum in iucunditate creatum est et non in ebrietate ab initio. 36 Exultatio animae et cordis vinum moderate potatum. 37 Sanitas est animae et corpori sobrius potus. 38 Vinum multum potatum inritationem et iram et ruinas multas facit. 39 Amaritudo animae vinum multum potatum. 40 Ebrietatis animositas inprudentis offensio, minorans virtutem et faciens vulnera. 41 In convivio vini non arguas proximum, et non despicias eum in iucunditate illius. 42 Verba inproperii non dicas illi, et non premas illum in repetendo.

23 Watching and choler and gripes are with an intemperate man. 24 *Sound and wholesome* sleep with a moderate man; he shall sleep till morning, and his soul shall be delighted with him. 25 And if thou hast been forced to eat much, arise, *go out,* and vomit, and it shall refresh thee, and thou shalt not bring sickness upon thy body.

26 Hear me, my son, and despise me not, and in the end thou shalt find my words. 27 In all thy works be quick, and no infirmity shall come to thee. 28 The lips of many shall bless him that is liberal of his bread, and the testimony of his truth is faithful. 29 Against him that is niggardly of his bread the city will murmur, and the testimony of his niggardliness is true.

30 Challenge not them that love wine, for wine hath destroyed very many. 31 Fire trieth hard iron; so wine drunk to excess shall rebuke the hearts of the proud. 32 Wine taken with sobriety is equal life to men. If thou drink it moderately, thou shalt be sober. 33 What is his life *who* is diminished with wine? 34 What taketh away life? Death. 35 Wine was created from the beginning to make men joyful and not to make them drunk. 36 Wine drunken with moderation is the joy of the soul and the heart. 37 Sober drinking is health to soul and body. 38 Wine drunken with excess raiseth quarrels and wrath and many ruins. 39 Wine drunken with excess is bitterness of the soul. 40 The heat of drunkenness is the stumblingblock of the fool, lessening strength and causing wounds. 41 Rebuke not thy neighbour in a banquet of wine, and despise him not in his mirth. 42 Speak not to him words of reproach, and press him not in demanding again.

Caput 32

Rectorem te posuerunt? Noli extolli; esto in illis quasi unus ex ipsis. 2 Curam illorum habe, et sic conside, et omni cura tua explicita, recumbe 3 ut laeteris propter illos et ornamentum gratiae accipias coronam et dignationem consequaris conrogationis.

4 Loquere, maior natu, decet enim te 5 primum verbum diligenti scientia et non inpedias musicam. 6 Ubi auditus non est, non effundas sermonem, et inportune noli extolli in sapientia tua. 7 Gemmula carbunculi in ornamento auri et conparatio musicorum in convivio vini. 8 Sicut in fabricatione auri signum est zmaragdi, sic numerus musicorum in iucundo et moderato vino. 9 Audi tacens, et pro reverentia accedet tibi bona gratia.

10 Adulescens, loquere in tua causa vix. 11 Si bis interrogatus fueris, habeat caput responsum tuum. 12 In multis esto quasi inscius, et audi tacens simul et quaerens. 13 In medio magnatorum non praesumas, et ubi sunt senes, non multum loquaris. 14 Ante grandinem praeibit coruscatio, et ante verecundiam praeibit gratia, et pro reverentia accedet tibi

Chapter 32

Lessons for superiors and inferiors. Advantages of fearing
God and doing nothing without counsel.

Have they made thee ruler? Be not lifted up; be among
them as one of them. 2 Have care of them, and so sit down,
and when thou hast acquitted thyself of all thy charge, *take
thy place* 3 that thou mayst rejoice for them and receive a
crown as an ornament of grace and get the honour of the
contribution.

4 Speak, thou that art elder, for it becometh thee 5 to
speak the first word with careful knowledge and hinder not
music. 6 Where there is no hearing, pour not out words, and
be not lifted up out season with thy wisdom. 7 *A concert of
music in a banquet of wine is as a carbuncle set in gold.* 8 As a signet of an emerald in a work of gold, so is the melody of music with pleasant and moderate wine. 9 Hear in silence, and
for thy reverence good grace shall come to thee.

10 Young man, scarcely speak in thy own cause. 11 If thou
be asked twice, let thy answer be short. 12 In many things be
as if thou wert ignorant, and hear in silence and withal seeking. 13 In the company of great men take not upon thee, and
when the ancients are present, speak not much. 14 Before a
storm goeth lightning, and before shamefacedness goeth fa-

bona gratia. 15 Et hora surgendi non te trices, praecurre autem prior in domum tuam, et illic avocare, et illic lude. 16 Et age conceptiones tuas, et non in delictis et verbo superbo. 17 Et super his omnibus benedicito Dominum qui fecit te et inebriantem te ab omnibus bonis suis.

18 Qui timet Dominum excipiet doctrinam eius, et qui vigilaverint ad illum invenient benedictionem. 19 Qui quaerit legem replebitur ab ea, et qui insidiose agit scandalizabitur in ea. 20 Qui timent Dominum invenient iudicium iustum et iustitias quasi lucem accendent. 21 Peccator homo devitabit correptionem et secundum voluntatem suam inveniet conparationem. 22 Vir consilii non disperdet intellegentiam; alienus et superbus non pertimescet timorem. 23 Etiam postquam fecit cum eo sine consilio, et suis insectationibus arguetur. 24 Fili, sine consilio nihil facias, et post factum non paeniteberis. 25 In via ruinae non eas, et non offendes in lapides; ne credas te viae laboriosae ne ponas animae tuae scandalum. 26 Et a filiis tuis cave, et a domesticis tuis adtende. 27 In omni opere tuo crede ex fide animae tuae, haec est enim conservatio mandatorum. 28 Qui credit Deo adtendit mandatis, et qui confidit in illo non minorabitur.

vour, and for thy reverence good grace shall come to thee. 15 And at the time of rising be not slack, but be first to run home to thy house, and there withdraw thyself, and there take thy pastime. 16 And do what thou hast a mind, *but* not in sin or proud speech. 17 And for all these things bless the Lord that made thee and that replenisheth thee with all his good things.

18 He that feareth the Lord will receive his discipline, and they that will seek him early shall find a blessing. 19 He that seeketh the law shall be filled with it, and he that dealeth deceitfully shall meet with a stumbling block therein. 20 They that fear the Lord shall find just judgment and shall kindle justice as a light. 21 A sinful man will flee reproof and will find an excuse according to his will. 22 A man of counsel will not *neglect* understanding; a strange and proud man will not dread fear. 23 Even after he hath done with fear without counsel, he shall be controlled *by* the things of his own seeking. 24 My son, do thou nothing without counsel, and thou shalt not repent when thou hast done. 25 Go not in the way of ruin, and thou shalt not stumble against the stones; trust not thyself to a rugged way lest thou set a stumbling block to thy soul. 26 And beware of thy own children, and take heed of them of thy household. 27 In every work of thine regard thy soul in faith, for this is the keeping of the commandments. 28 He that believeth God taketh heed to the commandments, and he that trusteth in him shall *fare never the worse.*

Caput 33

Timenti Dominum non occurrent mala, sed in temptatione Deus illum conservabit et liberabit a malis. 2 Sapiens non odit mandata et iustitias, et non inlidetur quasi in procella navis. 3 Homo sensatus credit legi Dei, et lex illi fidelis. 4 Qui interrogationem manifestat parabit verbum, et sic deprecatus exaudietur et conservabit disciplinam, et tunc respondebit.

5 Praecordia fatui quasi rota carri, et quasi axis versatilis cogitatus illius. 6 Equus admissarius sicut amicus subsannator: sub omni suprasedenti hinnit.

7 Quare dies diem superat et iterum lux lucem et annus annum a sole? 8 A Domini scientia separati sunt, facto sole et praeceptum custodiente. 9 Et inmutavit tempora et dies festos ipsorum, et in illis dies festos celebraverunt ad horam. 10 Ex ipsis exaltavit et magnificavit Deus, et ex ipsis posuit in numerum dierum. Et homines omnes de solo et ex terra unde creatus est Adam. 11 In multitudine disciplinae

Chapter 33

The fear of God is the best security. Times and men are in the hands of God. Take care of thyself as long as thou livest, and look to thy servants.

No evils shall happen to him that feareth the Lord, but in temptation God will keep him and deliver him from evils. 2 A wise man hateth not the commandments and justices, and he shall not be dashed in pieces as a ship in a storm. 3 A man of understanding is faithful to the law of God, and the law is faithful to him. 4 He that cleareth up a question shall prepare what to say, and so having prayed he shall be heard and shall keep discipline, and then he shall answer.

5 The heart of a fool is as a wheel of a cart, and his thoughts are like a rolling axletree. 6 A friend that is a mocker is like a stallion horse: he neigheth under every one that sitteth upon him.

7 Why doth one day excel another and one light another and one year another year *when all come* of the sun? 8 By the knowledge of the Lord they were distinguished, the sun being made and keeping his commandment. 9 And he *ordered* the seasons and holidays of them, and in them they celebrated festivals at an hour. 10 Some of them God made high and great *days,* and some of them he put in the number of ordinary days. And all men are from the ground and out of the earth from whence Adam was created. 11 With much

Domini separavit eos et inmutavit vias eorum. 12 Ex ipsis benedixit et exaltavit, et ex ipsis sanctificavit et ad se adplicavit, et ex ipsis maledixit et humiliavit et convertit illos a separatione ipsorum. 13 Quasi lutum figuli in manu ipsius plasmare illud et disponere—14 omnes viae eius secundum dispositionem eius—sic homo in manu illius qui se fecit, et reddet illi secundum iudicium suum. 15 Contra malum bonum est et contra mortem vita; sic et contra virum iustum peccator. Et sic intuere in omnia opera Altissimi, duo contra duo, et unum contra unum.

16 Et ego novissimus vigilavi et quasi qui colligit acinos post vindemiatores. 17 In benedictione Dei et ipse speravi, et quasi qui vindemiat replevi torcular. 18 Respicite quoniam non soli mihi laboravi sed omnibus exquirentibus disciplinam. 19 Audite me, magnati et omnes populi, et, rectores ecclesiae, auribus percipite. 20 Filio et mulieri, fratri et amico non des potestatem super te in vita tua, et non dederis alii possessionem tuam ne forte paeniteat te et depreceris pro illis. 21 Dum adhuc superes et adspiras non inmutabit te omnis caro, 22 melius est enim ut filii tui te rogent quam te respicere in manus filiorum tuorum. 23 In omnibus operibus tuis praecellens esto. 24 Ne dederis maculam in gloriam tuam. In die consummationis dierum vitae tuae et in tempore exitus tui distribue hereditatem tuam.

25 Cibaria et virga et onus asino, panis et disciplina et opus servo. 26 Operatur in disciplina et quaerit requiescere; laxa manus illi, et quaerit libertatem. 27 Iugum et lorum curvant collum durum, et servum inclinant operationes adsiduae. 28 Servo malivolo tortura et conpedes; mitte illum in

knowledge *the Lord* hath divided them and diversified their ways. 12 Some of them hath he blessed and exalted, and some of them hath he sanctified and set near himself, and some of them hath he cursed and brought low and turned them from their station. 13 As the potter's clay is in his hand to fashion and order it—14 all his ways are according to his ordering—so man is in the hand of him that made him, and he will render to him according to his judgment. 15 Good is set against evil and life against death; so also is the sinner against a just man. And so look upon all the works of the Most High, two *and* two, and one against another.

16 And I awaked last *of all* and as one that *gathereth* after the grapegatherers. 17 In the blessing of God I also have hoped, and as one that gathereth grapes have I filled the winepress. 18 See that I have not laboured for myself only but for all that seek discipline. 19 Hear me, ye great men and all ye people, and hearken with your ears, ye rulers of the church. 20 Give not to son *or* wife, brother *or* friend power over thee while thou livest, and give not thy estate to another *lest* thou repent and thou entreat for the same. 21 As long as thou livest and hast breath in thee *let no man* change thee, 22 for it is better that thy children should ask of thee than that thou look toward the hands of thy children. 23 In all thy works keep the pre-eminence. 24 *Let no stain sully* thy glory. In the time when thou shalt end the days of thy life and in the time of thy decease distribute thy inheritance.

25 Fodder and a wand and a burden are for an ass, bread and correction and work for a slave. 26 He worketh under correction and seeketh to rest; let his hands be idle, and he seeketh liberty. 27 The yoke and the thong bend a stiff neck, and continual labours bow a slave. 28 Torture and fetters are

operationem ne vacet, 29 multam enim malitiam docuit otio-
sitas. 30 In opera constitue eum, sic enim condecet illum.
Et si non obaudierit, curva illum conpedibus, et non ampli-
fices super omnem carnem, verum sine iudicio nihil facias
grave. 31 Si est tibi servus fidelis, sit tibi quasi anima tua,
quasi fratrem sic eum tracta, quoniam in sanguine animae
parasti eum. 32 Si laeseris illum iniuste, in fugam convertetur; 33 si extollens discesserit, quem quaeras et in qua via
quaeras illum nescis.

Caput 34

Vana spes et mendacium insensato viro, et somnia extol-
lunt inprudentes. 2 Quasi qui adprehendit umbram et persequitur ventum sic et qui adtendit ad visa mendacia. 3 Secundum hoc visio somniorum ante faciem hominis similitudo
hominis.

4 Ab inmundo quid mundabitur? Et a mendace quid verum dicetur? 5 Divinatio erroris et auguria mendacia et somnia malefacientium vanitas est, 6 et sicut parturientis cor
tuum phantasias patitur. Nisi ab Altissimo fuerit emissa visi-

for a malicious slave; send him to work that he be not idle, 29 for idleness hath taught much evil. 30 Set him to work, for so it is fit for him. And if he be not obedient, bring him down with fetters, *but* be not excessive towards *any one, and* do no grievous thing without judgment. 31 If thou have a faithful servant, let him be to thee as thy own soul, treat him as a brother because in the blood of thy soul thou hast gotten him. 32 If thou hurt him unjustly, he will run away, 33 *and* if he rise up and depart, thou knowest not whom to ask and in what way to seek him.

Chapter 34

The vanity of dreams. The advantage of experience and of the fear of God.

The hopes of a man that is void of understanding are vain and deceitful, and dreams lift up fools. 2 The man that giveth heed to lying visions is like to him that catcheth at a shadow and followeth after the wind. 3 *The vision of dreams is the resemblance of one thing to another as when* a man's likeness *is* before the face of a man.

4 What can be made clean by the unclean? And what truth can come from that which is false? 5 Deceitful divinations and lying omens and the dreams of evildoers are vanity, 6 and *the heart fancieth* as that of a woman in travail. Except it be a vision sent forth from the Most High, set not thy heart

tatio, ne dederis in illis cor tuum, 7 multos enim errare fecerunt somnia et exciderunt sperantes in illis.

8 Sine mendacio consummabitur verbum legis, et sapientia in ore fidelis conplanabitur. 9 Qui non temptatus est quid
scit? Vir in multis expertus cogitabit multa, et qui multa didicit enarrabit intellectum. 10 Qui non est expertus pauca
recognoscit, qui autem in multis factus est multiplicat malitiam. 11 Qui temptatus non est, qualia scit? Et qui inplanatus
est abundabit nequitia.

12 Multa vidi errando et plurimas verborum consuetudi-
nes. 13 Aliquotiens usque ad mortem periclitatus sum horum
causa, et liberatus sum gratia Dei. 14 Spiritus timentium
Deum quaeritur et in respectu illius benedicetur, 15 spes
enim illorum in salvantem illos, et oculi Dei in diligentes se.
16 Qui timet Dominum nihil trepidabit et non pavebit quoniam ipse est spes eius. 17 Timentis Dominum beata est
anima eius 18 Ad quem respicit, et quis est fortitudo eius?
19 Oculi Domini super timentes eum. Protector potentiae,
firmamentum virtutis, tegimen ardoris et umbraculum me-
ridiani 20 servatio offensionis et adiutorium casus, exaltans
animam et inluminans oculos dans sanitatem et vitam et
benedictionem.

21 Immolantis ex iniquo oblatio est maculata, et non sunt
beneplacitae subsannationes iniustorum. 22 Dominus solus
sustinentibus se in via veritatis et iustitiae. 23 Dona iniquorum non probat Altissimus, nec respicit in oblationes

upon them, 7 for dreams have deceived many and they have failed that put their trust in them.

8 The word of the law shall be fulfilled without a lie, and wisdom shall be made plain in the mouth of the faithful. 9 What doth he know that hath not been tried? A man that hath much experience shall think of many things, and he that hath learned many things shall shew forth understanding. 10 He that hath no experience knoweth little, and he that hath been experienced in many things multiplieth *prudence.* 11 He that hath not been tried, what manner of things doth he know? He that hath been *surprised* shall abound with *subtlety.*

12 I have seen many things by travelling and many customs of things. 13 Sometimes I have been in danger of death for these things, and I have been delivered by the grace of God. 14 The spirit of those that fear God is sought after and by his regard shall be blessed, 15 for their hope is on him that saveth them, and the eyes of God are upon them that love him. 16 He that feareth the Lord shall tremble at nothing and shall not be afraid for he is his hope. 17 The soul of him that feareth the Lord is blessed. 18 To whom doth he look, and who in his strength? 19 The eyes of the Lord are upon them that fear him. He is their powerful protector and strong stay, a defence from the heat and a cover from the sun at noon, 20 a preservation from stumbling and a help from falling. He raiseth up the soul and enlighteneth the eyes and giveth health and life and blessing.

21 The offering of him that sacrificeth of a thing wrongfully gotten is stained, and the mockeries of the unjust are not acceptable. 22 The Lord is only for them that wait upon him in the way of truth and justice. 23 The Most High approveth not the gifts of the wicked, neither hath he respect

iniquorum, nec in multitudine sacrificiorum eorum propitiabitur peccatis. 24 Qui offert sacrificium ex substantia pauperum quasi qui victimat filium in conspectu patris sui. 25 Panis egentium vita pauperum est; qui defraudat illum homo sanguinis. 26 Qui aufert in sudore panem quasi qui occidit proximum suum. 27 Qui effundit sanguinem et qui fraudem facit mercennario fratres sunt. 28 Unus aedificans et unus destruens, quid prodest illis nisi labor? 29 Unus orans et unus maledicens, cuius vocem exaudiet Deus? 30 Qui baptizatur a mortuo, et iterum tangit illum, quid proficit lavatio illius? 31 Sic homo qui ieiunat in peccatis suis et iterum eadem faciens, quid proficit humiliando se? Orationem illius quis exaudiet?

Caput 35

Qui conservat legem multiplicat oblationem. 2 Sacrificium salutare adtendere mandatis et discedere ab omni iniquitate. 3 Beneplacito est Domino recedere ab iniquitate, et deprecatio pro peccatis recedere ab iniustitia.

to the oblations of the unjust, nor will he be pacified for sins by the multitude of their sacrifices. 24 He that offereth sacrifice of the goods of the poor is as one that sacrificeth the son in the presence of his father. 25 The bread of the needy is the life of the poor; he that defraudeth *them thereof* is a man of blood. 26 He that taketh away the bread gotten by sweat is like him that killeth his neighbour. 27 He that sheddeth blood and he that defraudeth the labourer *of his hire* are brothers. 28 When one buildeth up and another pulleth down, what profit have they but the labour? 29 When one prayeth and another curseth, whose voice will God hear? 30 He that washeth *himself after touching* the dead, *if* he toucheth him again, what doth his washing avail? 31 So a man that fasteth for his sins and doth the same again, what doth his humbling himself profit him? Who will hear his prayer?

Chapter 35

What sacrifices are pleasing to God.

He that keepeth the law multiplieth offerings. 2 It is a wholesome sacrifice to take heed to the commandments and to depart from all iniquity. 3 *And to depart from injustice is to offer a propitiatory sacrifice for injustices* and a begging of pardon for sins. 4 *He shall return thanks that offereth fine flour, and he that doth mercy offereth sacrifice.* 5 *To depart from iniquity*

6 Non apparebis ante conspectum Domini vacuus, 7 haec enim omnia propter mandatum Dei fiunt. 8 Oblatio iusti inpinguat altare et odor suavitatis est in conspectu Altissimi. 9 Sacrificium iusti acceptum est, et memoriam eius non obliviscetur Dominus. 10 Bono animo gloriam redde Deo, et non minuas primitias manuum tuarum. 11 In omni dato hilarem fac vultum tuum, et in exultatione sanctifica decimas tuas. 12 Da Altissimo secundum datum eius, et in bono oculo ad inventionem fac manuum tuarum, 13 quoniam Dominus retribuens est et septies tantum reddet tibi. 14 Noli offerre munera prava, non enim suscipiet illa. 15 Et noli inspicere sacrificium iniustum, quoniam Dominus iudex est, et non est apud illum gloria personae.

16 Non accipiet Dominus personam in pauperem, et precationem laesi exaudiet. 17 Non despiciet preces pupilli, nec viduam si effundat loquellam gemitus. 18 Nonne lacrimae viduae ad maxillam descendunt et exclamatio eius super deducentem eas? 19 A maxilla enim ascendunt usque ad caelum, et Dominus exauditor non delectabitur in illis. 20 Qui adorat Deum in oblectatione suscipietur, et precatio illius usque ad nubes propinquabit. 21 Oratio humiliantis se nubes penetrabit, et donec propinquet non consolabitur, et non discedet donec aspiciat Altissimus.

is that which pleaseth the Lord, and to depart from injustice is an intreating for sins.

6 Thou shalt not appear empty in the sight of the Lord, 7 for all these things are to be done because of the commandment of God. 8 The oblation of the just maketh the altar fat and is an odour of sweetness in the sight of the Most High. 9 The sacrifice of the just is acceptable, and the Lord will not forget the memorial thereof. 10 Give glory to God with a good heart, and diminish not the firstfruits of thy hands. 11 In every gift *shew a* cheerful countenance, and sanctify thy tithes with joy. 12 Give to the Most High according to what he hath given to thee, and with a good eye do according to the ability of thy hands, 13 for the Lord maketh recompense and will give thee seven times as much. 14 Do not offer wicked gifts, for *such* he will not receive. 15 And look not upon an unjust sacrifice, for the Lord is judge, and there is not with him respect of person.

16 The Lord will not accept *any* person against a poor man, and he will hear the prayer of him that is wronged. 17 He will not despise the prayers of the fatherless, nor the widow *when* she poureth out her complaint. 18 Do not the widow's tears run down the cheek and her cry against him that causeth them to fall? 19 For from the cheek they go up even to heaven, and the Lord that heareth will not be delighted with them. 20 He that adoreth God with joy shall be accepted, and his prayer shall approach even to the clouds. 21 The prayer of him that humbleth himself shall pierce the clouds, and till it come nigh he will not be comforted, and he will not depart till the Most High behold.

22 Et Dominus non longinquabit sed iudicabit iustos et faciet iudicium, et Fortissimus non habebit in illis patientiam ut contribulet dorsum ipsorum, 23 et Gentibus reddet vindictam donec tollat plenitudinem superborum et sceptra iniquorum contribulet, 24 donec reddat hominibus secundum actus suos et secundum opera Adae et secundum praesumptionem illius, 25 donec iudicet iudicium plebis suae, et oblectabit iustos misericordia sua. 26 Speciosa misericordia Dei in tempore tribulationis, quasi nubes pluviae in tempore siccitatis.

Caput 36

Miserere nostri, Deus omnium, et respice nos, et ostende nobis lucem miserationum tuarum, 2 et inmitte timorem tuum super gentes quae non exquisierunt te ut cognoscant quia non est Deus nisi tu et enarrent magnalia tua. 3 Adleva manum tuam super gentes alienas ut videant potentiam tuam, 4 sicut enim in conspectu eorum sanctificatus es

22 And the Lord will not be *slack* but will judge for the just and will do judgment, and the Almighty will not have patience with them that he may crush their back, 23 and he will repay vengeance to the Gentiles till he have taken away the multitude of the proud and broken the sceptres of the unjust, 24 till he have rendered to men according to their deeds and according to the works of Adam and according to his presumption, 25 till he have judged the cause of his people, and he shall delight the just with his mercy. 26 The mercy of God is beautiful in the time of affliction, as a cloud of rain in the time of drought.

Chapter 36

A prayer for the church of God. Of a good heart and a good wife.

Have mercy upon us, O God of all, and behold us, and shew us the light of thy mercies, 2 and send thy fear upon the nations that have not sought after thee that they may know that there is no God beside thee and that they may shew forth thy wonders. 3 Lift up thy hand over the strange nations that they may see thy power, 4 for as thou hast been

in nobis sic in conspectu nostro magnificaberis in illis 5 ut cognoscant te sicut et nos agnovimus, quoniam non est Deus praeter te, Domine. 6 Innova signa, et inmuta mirabilia. 7 Glorifica manum et brachium dextrum. 8 Excita furorem, et effunde iram. 9 Extolle adversarium, et adflige inimicum. 10 Festina tempus, et memento finis ut enarrent mirabilia tua. 11 In ira flammae devoretur qui salvatur, et qui pessimant plebem tuam inveniant perditionem. 12 Contere caput principum inimicorum dicentium, "Non est alius praeter nos." 13 Congrega omnes tribus Iacob, et cognoscant quia non est Deus nisi tu ut enarrent magnalia tua, et hereditabis eos sicut ab initio. 14 Miserere plebi tuae super quam invocatum est nomen tuum et Israhel quem coaequasti primogenito tuo. 15 Miserere civitati sanctificationis tuae, Hierusalem, civitati requiei tuae. 16 Reple Sion inenarrabilibus verbis tuis et gloria tua populum tuum. 17 Da testimonium his qui ab initio creaturae tuae sunt, et suscita praedicationes quas locuti sunt in nomine tuo prophetae priores. 18 Da mercedem sustinentibus te ut prophetae tui fideles inveniantur, et exaudi orationes servorum tuorum 19 secundum benedictionem Aaron de populo tuo, et dirige nos in viam iustitiae, et sciant omnes qui inhabitant terram quia tu es Deus, conspector saeculorum.

20 Omnem escam manducabit venter, et est cibus cibo melior. 21 Fauces contingunt cibum ferae et cor sensatum verba mendacia. 22 Cor pravum dabit tristitiam, et homo peritus resistet illi. 23 Omnem masculum excipiet mulier,

sanctified in us in their sight so thou shalt be magnified among them in our presence 5 that they may know thee as we also have known thee, that there is no God beside thee, O Lord. 6 Renew thy signs, and work new miracles. 7 Glorify thy hand and thy right arm. 8 Raise up indignation, and pour out wrath. 9 Take away the adversary, and crush the enemy. 10 Hasten the time, and remember the end that they may declare thy wonderful works. 11 Let him that escapeth be consumed by the rage of the fire, and let them perish that oppress thy people. 12 Crush the head of the princes of the enemies that say, "There is no other beside us." 13 Gather together all the tribes of Jacob *that they may* know that there is no God besides thee *and* may declare thy great works, and thou shalt inherit them as from the beginning. 14 Have mercy on thy people upon whom thy name is invoked and upon Israel whom thou hast *raised up to be* thy firstborn. 15 Have mercy on Jerusalem, the city which thou hast sanctified, the city of thy rest. 16 Fill Zion with thy unspeakable words and thy people with thy glory. 17 Give testimony to them that are thy creatures from the beginning, and raise up the prophecies which the former prophets spoke in thy name. 18 Reward them that patiently wait for thee that thy prophets may be found faithful, and hear the prayers of thy servants 19 according to the blessing of Aaron over thy people, and direct us into the way of justice, and let all know that dwell upon the earth that thou art God, the beholder of *all* ages.

20 The belly will devour all meat, *yet* one is better than another. 21 The *palate tasteth* venison and the wise heart false speeches. 22 A perverse heart will cause grief, and a man of experience will resist it. 23 A woman will receive every man,

et est filia melior filiae. 24 Species mulieris exhilarat faciem viri sui, et super omnem concupiscentiam hominis superducit desiderium. 25 Si est lingua curationis, est et mitigationis et misericordiae: non est vir illius secundum filios hominum. 26 Qui possidet mulierem bonam inchoat possessionem; adiutorium secundum illum est et columna ut requies. 27 Ubi non est sepis diripietur possessio, et ubi non est mulier gemescit egens. 28 Quis credit ei qui non habet nidum et deflectens ubicumque obscuraverit quasi succinctus latro exiliens de civitate in civitatem?

Caput 37

Omnis amicus dicet, "Et ego amicitiam copulavi," sed est amicus solo nomine amicus. Nonne tristitia inest usque ad mortem? 2 Sodalis autem et amicus ad inimicitiam convertentur. 3 O praesumptio nequissima, unde creata es cooperire aridam malitia et dolositate illius? 4 Sodalis amico coniucundatur in oblectationibus et in tempore tribulationis adversarius erit. 5 Sodalis amico condolet causa ventris, et

yet one daughter is better than another. 24 The beauty of a woman cheereth the countenance of her husband, and *a man desireth nothing more.* 25 If she have a tongue *that can cure and likewise mitigate and shew* mercy, her husband is not *like other men.* 26 He that possesseth a good wife beginneth a possession; she is a help like to himself and a pillar of rest. 27 Where there is no hedge the possession shall be spoiled, and where there is no wife he mourneth that is in want. 28 Who *will* trust him that hath no nest and that lodgeth wheresoever *the night taketh him* as a robber well appointed that skippeth from city to city?

Chapter 37

Of the choice of friends and counsellors.

Every friend will say, "I also *am his friend,*" but there is a friend that is only a friend in name. Is not this a grief even to death? 2 But a companion and a friend shall be turned to an enemy. 3 O wicked presumption, whence camest thou to cover the earth with *thy* malice and deceitfulness? 4 There is a companion who rejoiceth with his friend in his joys but in the time of trouble he will be against him. 5 There is a companion who condoleth with his friend for his belly's sake,

contra hostem accipiet scutum. 6 Non obliviscaris amici tui in animo tuo, et non inmemor sis illius in opibus tuis. 7 Noli consiliari cum eo qui tibi insidiatur, et a zelantibus te absconde consilium.

8 Omnis consiliarius prodit consilium, sed est consiliarius in semet ipso. 9 A consiliario serva animam tuam. Prius scito quae sit illius necessitas, et ipse enim animo suo cogitabit, 10 ne forte mittat sudem in terram et dicat tibi, 11 "Bona est via tua," et stet e contrario videre quid tibi eveniat.

12 Cum viro inreligioso tracta de sanctitate, et cum iniusto de iustitia, et cum muliere de ea quae aemulatur, cum timido de bello, cum negotiatore de traiecticio, cum emptore de venditione, cum viro livido de gratiis agendis, 13 cum impio de pietate, cum inhonesto de honestate, cum operario agri de omni opere, 14 cum operario annuali de consummatione anni, cum servo pigro de multa operatione. Non adtendas his in omni consilio. 15 Sed cum viro sancto adsiduus esto, quemcumque cognoveris observantem timorem Dei, 16 cuius anima est secundum animam tuam; et qui cum titubaveris in tenebris condolebit tibi. 17 Et cor boni consilii statue tecum, non est enim tibi aliud pluris illo. 18 Anima viri sancti enuntiat aliquando vera, quam septem circumspectores sedentes in excelso ad speculandum.

and he will take up a shield against the enemy. 6 Forget not thy friend in thy mind, and be not unmindful of him in thy riches. 7 Consult not with him that layeth a snare for thee, and hide thy counsel from them that envy thee.

8 Every counsellor giveth out counsel, but there is one that is a counsellor for himself. 9 Beware of a counsellor. *And* know before what need he hath, for he will devise to his own mind, 10 lest he thrust a stake into the ground and say to thee, 11 "Thy way is good," and then stand on the other side to see what shall befall thee.

12 Treat not with a man without religion concerning holiness, nor with an unjust man concerning justice, nor with a woman touching her of whom she is jealous, *nor* with a coward concerning war, *nor* with a merchant about traffic, *nor* with a buyer of selling, *nor* with an envious man of giving thanks, 13 *nor* with the ungodly of piety, *nor* with the dishonest of honesty, *nor* with the field labourer of every work, 14 *nor* with him that worketh by the year of the finishing of the year, *nor* with an idle servant of much business. Give no heed to these in any matter of counsel. 15 But be continually with a holy man, whomsoever thou shalt know to observe the fear of God, 16 whose soul is according to thy own soul, and who, when thou shalt stumble in the dark, will be sorry for thee. 17 And establish within thyself a heart of good counsel, for there is no other thing of more worth to thee than it. 18 The soul of a holy man discovereth sometimes true things, more than seven watchmen that sit in a high piece to watch.

19 Et in his omnibus deprecare Altissimum ut dirigat in veritate viam tuam. 20 Ante omnia opera verbum verax praecedat te et ante omnem actum consilium stabile. 21 Verbum nequa inmutabit cor, ex quo quattuor partes oriuntur: bonum et malum, vita et mors, et dominatrix illorum est adsidua lingua. Est vir astutus multorum eruditor et animae suae inutilis est. 22 Vir peritus multos erudivit et animae suae suavis est. 23 Qui sofistice loquitur odibilis est; in omni re defraudabitur, 24 non est data illi a Domino gratia, omni enim sapientia defraudatus est. 25 Est sapiens animae suae sapiens, et fructus sensus illius laudabilis. 26 Vir sapiens plebem suam erudit, et fructus sensus eius fideles sunt. 27 Vir sapiens implebitur benedictionibus, et videntes illum laudabunt. 28 Vita viri in numero dierum, dies autem Israhel innumerabiles sunt. 29 Sapiens in populo hereditabit honorem, et nomen illius erit vivens in aeternum.

30 Fili, in vita tua tempta animam tuam, et si fuerit nequam, non des illi potestatem, 31 non enim omnia omnibus expediunt, et non omni animae omne genus placet. 32 Noli avidus esse in omni epulatione, et non te effundas super omnem escam, 33 in multis enim escis erit infirmitas, et aviditas adpropinquabit usque ad choleram. 34 Propter aplestiam multi obierunt, qui autem abstinens est adiciet vitam.

19 *But above* all these things pray to the Most High that he may direct thy way in truth. 20 *In* all thy works let the true word go before thee and steady counsel before every action. 21 A wicked word shall change the heart, out of which four *manner of things* arise: good and evil, life and death, and the tongue is continually the ruler of them. There is a man that is subtle and a teacher of many and *yet* is unprofitable to his own soul. 22 A skillful man hath taught many and is sweet to his own soul. 23 He that speaketh sophistically is hateful; he shall be destitute of every thing. 24 Grace is not given him from the Lord, for he is deprived of all wisdom. 25 There is a wise man that is wise to his own soul, and the fruit of his understanding is commendable. 26 A wise man instructeth his own people, and the fruits of his understanding are faithful. 27 A wise man shall be filled with blessings, and they that see shall praise him. 28 The life of a man is in the number of his days, but the days of Israel are innumerable. 29 A wise man shall inherit honour among his people, and his name shall live for ever.

30 My son, prove thy soul in thy life, and if it be wicked, give it no power, 31 for all things are not expedient for all, and every kind pleaseth not every soul. 32 Be not greedy in any feasting, and pour not out thyself upon any meat, 33 for in many meats there will be sickness, and greediness will turn to choler. 34 By surfeiting many have perished, but he that is temperate shall prolong life.

Caput 38

Honora medicum propter necessitatem, etenim illum creavit Altissimus, 2 a Deo est enim omnis medella, et a rege accipiet dationem. 3 Disciplina medici exaltabit caput illius, et in conspectu magnatorum conlaudabitur. 4 Altissimus creavit de terra medicinam, et vir prudens non abhorrebit illi. 5 Nonne a ligno indulcata est amara aqua? 6 Ad agnitionem hominum virtus illorum, et dedit hominibus scientiam Altissimus honorari in mirabilibus suis. 7 In his curans mitigabit dolorem, et unguentarius faciet pigmenta suavitatis et unctiones conficiet sanitatis, et non consummabuntur opera eius, 8 pax enim Dei super faciem terrae.

9 Fili, in tua infirmitate non despicias te ipsum, sed ora Dominum, et ipse curabit te. 10 Averte a delicto, et dirige manus, et ab omni delicto munda cor tuum. 11 Da suavitatem et memoriam similaginis, et inpingua oblationem, et da locum medico, 12 etenim illum Dominus creavit, et non dis-

Chapter 38

Of physicians and medicines. What is to be done in sickness
and how we are to mourn for the dead. Of the employments
of labourers and artificers.

Honour the physician for the need *thou hast of him,* for
the Most High hath created him, 2 for all healing is from
God, and he shall receive gifts of the king. 3 The skill of the
physician shall lift up his head, and in the sight of great men
he shall be praised. 4 The Most High hath created medicines
out of the earth, and a wise man will not abhor them. 5 Was
not bitter water made sweet with wood? 6 The virtue of
these things is come to the knowledge of men, and the Most
High hath given knowledge to men that he may be honoured in his wonders. 7 By these he shall cure and shall allay
their pains, and *of these* the apothecary shall make sweet
confections and shall make up ointments of health, and of
his works there shall be no end, 8 for the peace of God is
over all the face of the earth.

9 My son, in thy sickness *neglect* not thyself, but pray to
the Lord, and he shall heal thee. 10 Turn away from sin, and
order thy hands aright, and cleanse thy heart from all offence. 11 Give a sweet savour and a memorial of fine flour,
and make a fat offering, and *then* give place to the physician,
12 for the Lord created him, and let him not depart from

cedat a te, quoniam opera eius sunt necessaria, 13 est enim tempus quando in manus eorum incurras. 14 Ipsi vero Dominum deprecabuntur ut dirigat requiem eorum et sanitatem, propter conversationem illorum. 15 Qui delinquit in conspectu eius qui fecit eum incidet in manus medici.

16 Fili, in mortuum produc lacrimas, et quasi dira passus incipe plorare, et secundum iudicium contege corpus illius, et non despicias sepulturam illius. 17 Propter delaturam autem amare fer luctum illius uno die, et consolare propter tristitiam. 18 Et fac luctum secundum meritum eius uno die vel duobus propter dectractionem, 19 a tristitia enim festinat mors, et cooperit virtutem, et tristitia cordis flectit cervicem. 20 In abductione permanet tristitia, et substantia inopis secundum cor eius. 21 Non dederis in tristitia cor tuum, sed repelle eam a te, et memento novissimorum. 22 Noli oblivisci, neque enim est conversio et huic nihil proderis et te ipsum pessimabis.

23 Memor esto iudicii mei, sic enim erit et tuum: mihi heri et tibi hodie. 24 In requie mortui, requiescere fac memoriam eius, et consolare illum in exitu spiritus sui. 25 Sapientia scribae in tempore vacuitatis, et qui minoratur actu sapientiam percipiet. 26 Qua sapientia replebitur qui tenet aratrum et qui gloriatur in iaculo stimulo, boves agit et conversatur in operibus eorum et narratio eius in filiis taurorum? 27 Cor suum dabit ad versandos sulcos, et vigilia eius

thee, for his works are necessary, 13 for there is a time when thou *must* fall into their hands. 14 And they shall beseech the Lord that he would *prosper what they give for* ease and remedy, for their conversation. 15 He that sinneth in the sight of his maker shall fall into the hands of the physician.

16 My son, shed tears over the dead, and begin to lament as if thou hadst suffered some great harm, and according to judgment cover his body, and neglect not his burial. 17 And for *fear of* being ill spoken of weep bitterly for a day, and *then* comfort thyself *in* thy sadness. 18 And make mourning *for him* according to his merit for a day or two for *fear of* detraction, 19 for of sadness cometh death, and it overwhelmeth the strength, and the sorrow of the heart boweth down the neck. 20 In withdrawing aside sorrow remaineth, and the substance of the poor is according to his heart. 21 Give not up thy heart to sadness, but drive it from thee, and remember the latter end. 22 Forget it not, for there is no returning, and thou shalt do him no good and shalt hurt thyself.

23 Remember my judgment, for thine also shall be so: yesterday for me and today for thee. 24 When the dead is at rest, let his remembrance rest, and comfort him in the departing of his spirit. 25 The wisdom of a scribe *cometh* by his time of leisure, and he that is less in action shall receive wisdom. 26 With what wisdom shall he be furnished that holdeth the plough and that glorieth in the goad, that driveth the oxen therewith and is occupied in their labours and his *whole* talk is about the offspring of bulls? 27 He shall give his mind to

in sagina vaccarum. 28 Sic omnis faber et architectus qui noctem tamquam diem transigit, qui sculpit signacula sculptilia et adsiduitas eius variat picturam, cor suum dabit in similitudinem picturae et vigilia sua perficiet opus. 29 Sic faber ferrarius sedens iuxta incudem et considerans opus ferri. Vapor ignis uret carnes eius, et in calore fornacis concertatur. 30 Vox mallei innovat aurem eius, et contra similitudinem vasi oculus eius. 31 Cor suum dabit in consummationem operum et vigilia sua ornabit in perfectionem. 32 Sic figulus sedens ad opus suum, convertens pedibus suis rotam, qui in sollicitudine positus est semper propter opus suum et in numero est omnis operatio eius. 33 In brachio suo formabit lutum et ante pedes suos curvabit virtutem suam. 34 Cor suum dabit ut consummet linitionem et vigilia sua mundabit fornacem. 35 Omnes hi in manibus suis speraverunt, et unusquisque in arte sua sapiens est. 36 Sine his omnibus non aedificatur civitas. 37 Et non inhabitabunt nec inambulabunt, et in ecclesiam non transilient. 38 Super sellam iudicis non sedebunt, et testamentum iudicii non intellegent, neque palam facient disciplinam et iudicium, et in parabolis non invenientur, 39 sed creaturam aevi confirmabunt, et deprecatio illorum in operatione artis, adcommodantes animam suam et conquirentes in lege Altissimi.

turn up furrows, and his care is to give the kine fodder. 28 So every craftsman and workmaster that laboureth night and day, he who maketh graven seals and *by* his continual diligence varieth the figure, he shall give his mind to the resemblance of the picture and by his watching shall finish the work. 29 So doth the smith sitting by the anvil and considering the iron work. The vapour of the fire wasteth his flesh, and he fighteth with the heat of the furnace. 30 The noise of the hammer *is always in his ears,* and his eye is upon the pattern of the vessel *he maketh.* 31 He setteth his mind to finish his work and his watching *to* polish them to perfection. 32 So doth the potter sitting at his work, turning the wheel about with his feet, who is always carefully set to his work and *maketh all his work by* number. 33 He fashioneth the clay with his arm and boweth down his strength before his feet. 34 He shall give his mind to finish the glazing and his watching *to* make clean the furnace. 35 All these trust to their hands, and every one is wise in his own art. 36 Without these a city is not built. 37 And they shall not dwell nor walk about therein, and they shall not go up into the assembly. 38 Upon the judge's seat they shall not sit, and the ordinance of judgment they shall not understand, neither shall they declare discipline and judgment, and they shall not be found where parables are spoken, 39 but they shall strengthen the *state* of the world, and their prayer shall be in the work of their craft, applying their soul and searching in the law of the Most High.

Caput 39

Sapientiam omnium antiquorum exquiret sapiens et in prophetis vacabit. 2 Narrationem virorum nominatorum conservabit et in versutias parabolarum simul introibit. 3 Occulta proverbiorum exquiret et in absconditis parabo- larum conversabitur. 4 In medio magnatorum ministrabit et in conspectu praesidis apparebit. 5 In terram alienarum gentium pertransiet, bona enim et mala in hominibus temptabit. 6 Cor suum tradet ad vigilandum diluculo ad Dominum qui fecit illum, et in conspectu Altissimi depreca- bitur. 7 Aperiet os suum in oratione et pro delictis suis de- precabitur, 8 si enim Dominus magnus voluerit, spiritu in- tellegentiae replebit illum, 9 et ipse tamquam imbres mittet eloquia sapientiae suae, et in oratione confitebitur Domino. 10 Et ipse diriget consilium eius et disciplinam, et in abscon- ditis suis consiliabitur. 11 Ipse palam faciet disciplinam doc- trinae suae et in lege testamenti Domini gloriabitur. 12 Conlaudabunt multi sapientiam eius, et usque in saecu- lum non delebitur. 13 Non recedet memoria eius, et nomen eius requiretur a generatione in generationem. 14 Sapien- tiam eius enarrabunt gentes, et laudem eius enuntiabit ec- clesia. 15 Si inmanserit, nomen derelinquet plus quam mille, et si requieverit, proderit illi.

Chapter 39

The exercises of the wise man. The Lord is to be glorified for his works.

The wise man will seek out the wisdom of all the ancients and will be occupied in the prophets. 2 He will keep the sayings of renowned men and will enter withal into the subtilties of parables. 3 He will search out the hidden meanings of proverbs and will be conversant in the secrets of parables. 4 He shall serve among great men and appear before the governor. 5 He shall pass into strange countries, for he shall try good and evil among men. 6 He will give his heart to *resort* early to the Lord that made him, and he will pray in the sight of the Most High. 7 He will open his mouth in prayer and will make supplication for his sins, 8 for if it shall please the great Lord, he will fill him with the spirit of understanding, 9 and he will pour forth the words of his wisdom as showers, and in his prayer he will confess to the Lord. 10 And he shall direct his counsel and his knowledge, and in his secrets shall he meditate. 11 He shall shew forth the discipline he hath learned and shall glory in the law of the covenant of the Lord. 12 Many shall praise his wisdom, and it shall never be forgotten. 13 The memory of him shall not depart away, and his name shall be in request from generation to generation. 14 Nations shall declare his wisdom, and the church shall shew forth his praise. 15 If he continue, he shall leave a name above a thousand, and if he rest, it shall be to his advantage.

16 Adhuc consiliabor ut enarrem, ut furore enim repletus sum. 17 In voce dicit, "Obaudite me, divini fructus, et quasi rosa plantata super rivos aquarum fructificate. 18 Quasi libanus odorem suavitatis habete. 19 Florete flores quasi lilium, et date odorem, et frondete in gratiam, et conlaudate canticum, et benedicite Dominum in operibus suis. 20 Date nomini eius magnificentiam, et confitemini illi in voce labiorum vestrorum et in canticis labiorum et cinyris, et sic dicetis in confessione, 21 'Opera Domini universa bona valde. 22 In verbo eius stetit aqua sicut congeries, et in sermone oris eius sicut exceptoria aquarum, 23 quoniam in praecepto ipsius placor fit, et non est minoratio in salute illius. 24 Opera omnis carnis coram illo, et non est quicquam absconditum ab oculis eius. 25 A saeculo usque in saeculum respicit, et nihil est mirabile in conspectu eius. 26 Non est dicere, "Quid est hoc?" aut "Quid est illud?" omnia enim in tempore suo quaerentur. 27 Benedictio illius quasi fluvius inundavit. 28 Et quomodo cataclysmus aridam inebriavit, sic ira ipsius gentes quae non exquisierunt eum hereditabit. 29 Quomodo convertit aquas in siccitatem et siccata est terra et viae illius viis illorum directae sunt, sic peccatoribus offensiones in ira eius. 30 Bona bonis creata sunt ab initio, sic nequissimis, bona et mala.'"

31 Initium necessariae rei vitae hominum aqua, ignis et ferrum, sal, lac et panis similagineus et mel et botrus uvae et oleum et vestimentum. 32 Haec omnia sanctis in bona. Sic et impiis et peccatoribus: in mala convertentur.

33 Sunt spiritus qui ad vindictam creati sunt, et in furore

16 I will yet meditate that I may declare, for I am filled as with a holy transport. 17 By a voice he saith, "Hear me, ye divine offspring, and bud forth as the rose planted by the brooks of waters. 18 Give ye a sweet odour as frankincense. 19 Send forth flowers as the lily, and yield a smell, and bring forth leaves in grace, and praise with canticles, and bless the Lord in his works. 20 Magnify his name, and give glory to him with the voice of your lips and with the canticles of your mouths and with harps, and in praising him you shall say in this manner, 21 'All the works of the Lord are exceeding good. 22 At his word the waters stood as a heap, and at the words of his mouth the receptacles of waters, 23 for at his commandment favour is shewn, and there is no diminishing of his salvation. 24 The works of all flesh are before him, and there is nothing hid from his eyes. 25 He seeth from eternity to eternity, and there is nothing wonderful before him. 26 There is no saying, "What is this," or, "What is that?" for all things shall be sought in their time. 27 His blessing hath overflowed like a river. 28 And as a flood hath watered the earth, so shall his wrath inherit the nations that have not sought after him. 29 Even as he turned the waters into a dry land and the earth was made dry and his ways were made plain for their journey, so to sinners they are stumbling blocks in his wrath. 30 Good things were created for the good from the beginning, so for the wicked, good and evil things.'"

31 The *principal things* necessary for the life of men are water, fire and iron, salt, milk and bread of flour and honey and the cluster of the grape and oil and clothing. 32 All these things shall be for good to the holy. So to the sinners and the ungodly: they shall be turned into evil.

33 There are spirits that are created for vengeance, and in

suo confirmaverunt tormenta sua. 34 In tempore consummationis effundent virtutem, et furorem eius qui fecit illos placabunt. 35 Ignis, grando, famis et mors, omnia haec ad vindictam creata sunt, 36 bestiarum dentes et scorpii et serpentes et romphea vindicans in exterminium impios. 37 In mandatis eius epulabuntur, et super terram in necessitatem praeparabuntur, et in temporibus suis non praeterient verbum. 38 Propterea ab initio confirmatus sum, et consiliatus sum et cogitavi et scripta dimisi. 39 Omnia opera Domini bona, et omne opus hora sua subministrabit. 40 Non est dicere, "Hoc illo nequius est," omnia enim in tempore suo conprobabuntur. 41 Et nunc in omni corde et ore conlaudate, et benedicite nomen Domini.

Caput 40

Occupatio magna creata est omnibus hominibus, et iugum grave super filios Adam, a die exitus de ventre matris eorum usque in diem sepulturae in matrem omnium, 2 cogitationes eorum et timores cordis, adinventio expectationis

their fury they *lay on grievous* torments. 34 In the time of destruction they shall pour out their force, and they shall appease the wrath of him that made them. 35 Fire, hail, famine and death, all these were created for vengeance, 36 the teeth of beasts and scorpions and serpents and the sword taking vengeance upon the ungodly unto destruction. 37 In his commandments they shall feast, and they shall be ready upon earth when need is, and when their time is come they shall not transgress his word. 38 Therefore from the beginning I was resolved, and I have meditated and thought *on these things* and left them in writing. 39 All the works of the Lord are good, and he will furnish every work in due time. 40 It is not to be said, "This is worse than that," for all shall be well approved in their time. 41 Now *therefore* with the whole heart and mouth praise ye him, and bless the name of the Lord.

Chapter 40

The miseries of the life of man are relieved by the grace of God and his fear.

Great labour is created for all men, and a heavy yoke is upon the children of Adam, from the day of their coming out of their mother's womb until the day of their burial into the mother of all, 2 their thoughts and fears of the heart,

et dies finitionis, 3 a residente super sedem gloriosam usque ad humiliatum in terra et cinere, 4 ab eo qui utitur hyacintho et portat coronam usque ad eum qui operitur lino crudo, furor, zelus, tumultus, fluctuatio et timor mortis, iracundia perseverans et contentio, 5 et in tempore refectionis in cubile, somnus noctis inmutat scientiam eius. 6 Modicum tamquam nihil in requie et ab eo in somnis quasi in die respectus. 7 Conturbatus est in visu cordis sui tamquam qui evaserit in die belli. In tempore salutis suae exsurrexit et admirans ad nullum timorem. 8 Cum omni carne, ab homine usque ad pecus, et super peccatores septuplum. 9 Ad haec mors, sanguis, contentio et romphea, oppressiones, famis et contritio et flagella, 10 super iniquos creata sunt haec omnia, et propter illos factus est cataclysmus.

11 Omnia quae de terra sunt in terram convertentur, et aquae omnes in mare revertentur. 12 Omne munus et iniquitas delebitur, et fides in saeculum stabit. 13 Substantiae iniustorum sicut fluvius siccabuntur et sicut tonitruum magnum in pluvia personabunt. 14 In aperiendo manus suas laetabitur; sic praevaricatores in consummatione tabescent. 15 Nepotes impiorum non multiplicabunt ramos et radices inmundae super cacumen petrae sonant. 16 Viriditas super omnem aquam et ad oram fluminis ante omnem faenum evelletur. 17 Gratia sicut paradisus in benedictionibus,

their imagination of things to come and the day of their end, 3 from him that sitteth on a glorious throne unto him that is humbled in earth and ashes, 4 from him that weareth purple and beareth the crown even to him that is covered with rough linen, wrath, envy, trouble, unquietness and the fear of death, continual anger and strife, 5 and in the time of rest upon his bed, the sleep of the night changeth his knowledge. 6 A little *and* as nothing *is his* rest and afterward in sleep as in the day of keeping watch. 7 He is troubled in the vision of his heart as if he had escaped in the day of battle. In the time of his safety he rose up and wondereth that there is no fear. 8 *Such things happen to* all flesh, from man even to beast, and upon sinners are sevenfold more. 9 Moreover death *and* bloodshed, strife and sword, oppressions, famine and affliction and scourges, 10 all these things are created for the wicked, and for their sakes came the flood.

11 All things that are of the earth shall return to the earth again, and all waters shall return to the sea. 12 All bribery and injustice shall blotted out, and fidelity shall stand for ever. 13 The riches of the unjust shall be dried up like a river and shall pass away with a noise like a great thunder in rain. 14 While he openeth his hands he shall rejoice, *but* transgressors shall pine away in the end. 15 The offspring of the ungodly shall not bring forth many branches and make a noise as unclean roots upon the top of a rock. 16 The *weed growing* over every water and at the bank of the river shall be pulled up before all grass. 17 Grace is like a paradise in blessings,

et misericordia in saeculo permanet. 18 Vita sibi sufficientis operarii condulcabitur, et in ea invenies thesaurum. 19 Filii et aedificatio civitatis confirmabit nomen, et super haec mulier inmaculata conputatur. 20 Vinum et musica laetificant cor, et super utraque dilectio sapientiae. 21 Tibiae et psalterium suavem faciunt melodiam, et super utraque lingua suavis. 22 Gratiam et speciem desiderabit oculus tuus, et super haec virides sationes. 23 Amicus et sodalis in tempore convenientes, et super utrosque mulier cum viro. 24 Fratres in adiutorium in tempore tribulationis, et super eos misericordia liberabit. 25 Aurum et argentum est constitutio pedum, et super utrumque consilium beneplacitum. 26 Facultates et virtutes exaltant cor, et super haec timor Domini. 27 Non est in timore Domini minoratio, et non est in eo inquirere adiutorium. 28 Timor Domini sicut paradisus benedictionis, et super omnem gloriam operuerunt illum.

29 Fili, in tempore vitae tuae ne indigeas, melius est enim mori quam indigere. 30 Vir respiciens in mensam alienam non est vita eius in cogitatione victus, alit enim animam suam cibis alienis. 31 Vir autem disciplinatus et eruditus custodiet se. 32 In ore inprudentis condulcabitur inopia, et in ventre eius ignis ardebit.

and mercy remaineth for ever. 18 The life of a labourer that is *content with what he hath* shall be sweet, and in it thou shalt find a treasure. 19 Children and the building of a city shall establish a name, but a blameless wife shall be counted above them both. 20 Wine and music rejoice the heart, *but* the love of wisdom is above them both. 21 The flute and the psaltery make a sweet melody, *but* a pleasant tongue is above them both. 22 Thy eye desireth favour and beauty, *but* more than these green sown fields. 23 A friend and companion meeting together in season, *but* above them both is a wife with her husband. 24 Brethren are a help in the time of trouble, *but* mercy shall deliver more than they. 25 Gold and silver *make the feet stand sure, but* wise counsel is above them both. 26 Riches and strength lift up the heart, *but* above these is the fear of the Lord. 27 There is no want in the fear of the Lord, and it needeth not to seek for help. 28 The fear of the Lord is like a paradise of blessing, and they have covered it above all glory.

29 My son, in thy lifetime be not indigent, for it is better to die than to want. 30 The life of him that looketh toward another man's table is not to be counted a life, for he feedeth his soul with another man's meat. 31 But a man well instructed and taught will look to himself. 32 *Begging* will be sweet in the mouth of the unwise, *but* in his belly there shall burn a fire.

Caput 41

O mors, quam amara est memoria tua homini pacem habenti in substantiis suis, 2 viro quieto et cuius viae directae sunt in omnibus et adhuc valenti accipere cibum! 3 O mors, bonum est iudicium tuum homini indigenti et qui minoratur viribus, 4 defecto aetate et cui de omnibus cura est et incredibili qui perdit patientiam! 5 Noli metuere iudicium mortis. Memento quae ante te fuerunt et quae superventura sunt tibi: hoc iudicium a Domino omni carni. 6 Et quid superveniet tibi in beneplacita Altissimi, sive decem sive centum sive mille anni? 7 Non est enim in inferno accusatio vitae.

8 Filii abominationum fiunt filii peccatorum et qui conversantur secus domos impiorum. 9 Filiorum peccatorum periet hereditas, et cum semine illorum adsiduitas obprobrii. 10 De patre impio queruntur filii quoniam propter illum sunt in obprobrio. 11 Vae vobis, viri impii, qui dereliquistis legem Domini altissimi. 12 Et si nati fueritis, in maledictione nascemini, et si mortui fueritis, in maledictione erit pars vestra. 13 Omnia quae de terra sunt in terram

Chapter 41

Of the remembrance of death, of an evil and of a good
name, of what things we ought to be ashamed.

O death, how bitter is the remembrance of thee to a man
that hath peace in his possessions, 2 to a man that is at rest
and whose ways are prosperous in all things and that is yet
able to take meat! 3 O death, thy sentence is welcome to the
man that is in need and to him whose strength faileth, 4 who
is in a decrepit age and that is in care about all things and to
the distrustful that loseth patience! 5 Fear not the sentence
of death. Remember what things have been before thee and
what shall come after thee: this sentence is from the Lord
upon all flesh. 6 And what shall come upon thee by the good
pleasure of the Most High, whether ten or a hundred or
a thousand years? 7 For *among the dead* there is no accusing
of life.

8 The children of sinners become children of abominations and they that converse near the houses of the ungodly.
9 The inheritance of the children of sinners shall perish, and
with their posterity shall be a perpetual reproach. 10 The
children will complain of an ungodly father because for his
sake they are in reproach. 11 Woe to you, ungodly men, who
have forsaken the law of the most high Lord. 12 And if you
be born, you shall be born in malediction, and if you die, in
malediction shall be your portion. 13 All things that are of

convertentur; sic impii a maledicto in perditionem. 14 Luctus hominum in corpore ipsorum, nomen autem impiorum delebitur.

15 Curam habe de bono nomine, hoc enim magis permanebit tibi quam mille thesauri pretiosi et magni. 16 Bonae vitae numerus dierum, bonum autem nomen permanebit in aevo. 17 Disciplinam in pace conservate, filii, sapientia enim abscondita et thesaurus invisus, quae utilitas in utrisque?

18 Melior est homo qui abscondit stultitiam suam quam homo qui abscondit sapientiam suam. 19 Verumtamen reveremini in his quae procedunt de ore meo, 20 non est enim bonum omnem reverentiam observare, et non omnia omnibus beneplacent in fide. 21 Erubescite a patre et a matre de fornicatione et a praesidente et a potente de mendacio, 22 a principe et a iudice de delicto, a synagoga et plebe de iniquitate, 23 a socio et amico de iniustitia et a loco in quo habitas, 24 de furto de veritate Dei et testamento, de discubitu in panibus et ab offuscatione dati et accepti, 25 a salutantibus de silentio, a respectu mulieris fornicariae et ab aversione vultus cognati—26 ne avertas faciem a proximo tuo—et ab auferendo partem et non restituendo. 27 Ne respicias mulierem alieni viri, et ne scruteris ancillam eius, neque steteris ad lectum eius. 28 Ab amicis de sermonibus inproperii, et cum dederis ne inproperes.

the earth shall return into the earth; so the ungodly shall from malediction to destruction. 14 The mourning of men is about their body, but the name of the ungodly shall be blotted out.

15 Take care of a good name, for this shall continue with thee more than a thousand treasures precious and great. 16 A good life hath its number of days, but a good name shall continue for ever. 17 My children, keep discipline in peace, for wisdom that is hid and a treasure that is not seen, what profit is there in them both?

18 Better is the man that hideth his folly than the man that hideth his wisdom. 19 Wherefore have a shame of these things I am now going to speak of, 20 for it is not good to keep all shamefacedness, and all things do not please all men in opinion. 21 Be ashamed of fornication before father and mother and of a lie before a governor and a man in power, 22 of an offence before a prince and a judge, of iniquity before a congregation and a people, 23 of injustice before a companion and friend and *in regard to* the place where thou dwellest 24 of theft and of the truth of God and the covenant, of leaning *with thy elbow over* meat and of deceit in giving and taking, 25 of silence before them that salute thee, of looking upon a harlot and of turning away thy face from thy kinsman—26 turn not away thy face from thy neighbour—and of taking away a portion and not restoring. 27 Gaze not upon another man's wife, and be not inquisitive after his handmaid, and approach not her bed. 28 *Be ashamed* of upbraiding speeches before friends, and after thou hast given upbraid not.

Caput 42

Non duplices sermonem auditus, de revelatione sermonis absconditi, et eris vere sine confusione et invenies gratiam in conspectu omnium hominum. Ne pro his omnibus confundaris, et ne accipias personam ut delinquas: 2 de lege Altissimi et testamento et de iudicio iustificare impium, 3 de verbo sociorum et viatorum et de datione hereditatis amicorum, 4 de aequalitate staterae et ponderum, de adquisitione multorum et paucorum, 5 de corruptione emptionis et negotiatorum et de multa disciplina filiorum et servo pessimo latus sanguinare.

6 Super mulierem nequam bonum est signum. 7 Ubi manus multae sunt, clude et quodcumque trades numera et adpende, datum vero et acceptum omne describe. 8 De disciplina insensati et fatui et de senioribus qui iudicantur ab adulescentibus, et eris eruditus in omnibus et probabilis in conspectu omnium vivorum.

9 Filia patris abscondita est vigilia, et sollicitudo eius aufert somnum ne forte in adulescentia sua adulta efficia-

Chapter 42

Of what things we ought not to be ashamed. Cautions with regard to women. The works and greatness of God.

Repeat not the word which thou hast heard, *and disclose not* the thing that is secret; *so* shalt thou be truly without confusion and shall find favour before all men. Be not ashamed of any of these things, and accept no person to sin thereby: 2 of the law of the Most High and of his covenant and of judgment to justify the ungodly, 3 of the affair of companions and travellers and of the gift of the inheritance of friends, 4 of exactness of balance and weights, of getting much *or* little, 5 of the corruption of buying and of merchants and of much correction of children and to make the side of a wicked slave to bleed.

6 *Sure keeping* is good over a wicked wife. 7 Where there are many hands, shut up and *deliver all things in number and weight,* and put all in writing that thou givest out *or* receivest in. 8 *Be not ashamed to inform* the unwise and foolish and the aged that are judged by young men, and thou shalt be well instructed in all things and well approved in the sight of all men living.

9 *The father waketh for the daughter when no man knoweth,* and the care for her taketh away his sleep when she is young *lest she pass away the flower of her age and when she is married*

tur et commorata cum viro odibilis fiat, 10 nequando poll-
uatur in virginitate sua et in paternis suis gravida inveniatur, ne forte cum viro commorata transgrediatur aut certe
sterilis efficiatur. 11 Super filiam luxuriosam confirma custodiam nequando faciat te in obprobrium venire inimicis a
detractatione in civitate et obiectione plebis et confundat
te in multitudine populi.

12 Omni homini noli intendere in specie, et in medio mulierum noli commorari, 13 de vestimentis enim procedit tinea et a muliere iniquitas viri, 14 melior est enim iniquitas
viri quam benefaciens mulier et mulier confundens in obprobrium.

15 Memor ero igitur operum Domini, et quae vidi adnuntiabo. In sermonibus Domini opera eius. 16 Sol inluminans
per omnia respexit, et gloria Domini plenum est opus eius.
17 Nonne Dominus fecit sanctos enarrare omnia mirabilia
sua quae confirmavit Dominus Omnipotens stabiliri in gloria sua? 18 Abyssum et cor hominum investigavit et in astutia illorum excogitavit, 19 cognovit enim Dominus omnem
scientiam et inspexit in signum aevi, adnuntians quae praeterierunt et quae superventura sunt revelans vestigia occul-
torum. 20 Non praeterit illum omnis cogitatus, et non abscondit se ab eo ullus sermo. 21 Magnalia sapientiae suae
decoravit, qui est ante saeculum et usque in saeculum, neque adiectum est, 22 neque minuitur, et non eget alicuius
consilio. 23 Quam desiderabilia omnia opera eius, et tamquam scintilla quae est considerare! 24 Omnia haec vivunt et
manent in saeculum, et in omni necessitate omnia obau-

lest she should be hateful, 10 in her virginity, *lest* she should be corrupted and be found with child in her father's house, *and having a husband lest she should misbehave herself* or at the least become barren. 11 Keep a sure watch over a shameless daughter lest at any time she make thee become a laughing-stock to thy enemies *and a byword* in the city and a reproach among the people and she make thee ashamed before all the *multitude.*

12 Behold not everybody's beauty, and tarry not among women, 13 for from garments cometh a moth and from a woman the iniquity of a man, 14 for better is the iniquity of a man than a woman doing a good turn and a woman *bringing shame and* reproach.

15 I will now remember the works of the Lord, and I will declare the things I have seen. By the words of the Lord are his works. 16 The sun giving light hath looked upon all things, and full of the glory of the Lord is his work. 17 Hath not the Lord made the saints to declare all his wonderful works which the Lord Almighty hath firmly settled to be established for his glory? 18 He hath searched out the deep and the heart of men and considered their crafty devices, 19 for the Lord knoweth all knowledge and hath beheld the *signs of the world.* He declareth the things that are past and the things that are to come and revealeth the traces of hidden things. 20 No thought escapeth him, and no word *can hide* itself from him. 21 He hath beautified the glorious works of his wisdom, and he is from eternity to eternity, and *to him nothing may be added,* 22 nor *can he be* diminished, and he hath no need of any counsellor. 23 O how desirable are all his works, and *what we can know is but* as a spark! 24 All these things live and remain for ever, and for every use all things

diunt ei. 25 Omnia duplicia, unum contra unum, et non fecit quicquam deesse. 26 Uniuscuiusque confirmavit bona. Et quis satiabitur videns gloriam eius?

Caput 43

Altitudinis firmamentum pulchritudo eius est, species caeli in visione gloriae, 2 sol in aspectu adnuntians in exitu, vas admirabile, opus Excelsi. 3 In meridiano exurit terram, et in conspectu ardoris eius quis poterit sustinere? Fornacem custodiens in operibus ardoris 4 tripliciter sol exurens montes, radios igneos exsuflans et refulgens radiis suis obcaecat oculos. 5 Magnus Dominus qui fecit illum, et in sermonibus eius festinavit iter.

6 Et luna in omnibus in tempore suo ostensio temporis et signum aevi. 7 A luna signum diei festi, luminare quod minuitur in consummatione. 8 Mensis secundum nomen eius est, crescens mirabiliter in consummatione, 9 vas castrorum in excelsis, in firmamento caeli resplendens gloriose.

10 Species caeli gloria stellarum; mundum inluminans in

obey him. 25 All things are double, one against another, and he hath made nothing defective. 26 He hath established the good things of every one. And who shall be filled with beholding his glory?

Chapter 43

The works of God are exceedingly glorious and wonderful.
No man is able sufficiently to praise him.

The firmament on high is his beauty, the beauty of heaven with its glorious shew, 2 the sun when he appeareth shewing forth at his rising, an admirable instrument, the work of the Most High. 3 At noon he burneth the earth, and who can abide *his burning heat?* As one keeping a furnace in the works of heat 4 the sun three times as much burneth the mountains, breathing out fiery vapours, and shining with his beams he blindeth the eyes. 5 Great is the Lord that made him, and at his words he hath hastened his course.

6 And the moon in all in her season is for a declaration of times and a sign of *the world.* 7 From the moon is the sign of the festival day, a light that decreaseth in her perfection. 8 The month is called after her name, increasing wonderfully in her perfection, 9 being an instrument of the armies on high, shining gloriously in the firmament of heaven.

10 The glory of the stars is the beauty of heaven; the Lord

excelsis Dominus. 11 In verbis sancti stabunt ad iudicium et non deficient in vigiliis suis.

12 Vide arcum, et benedic eum qui fecit illum. Valde speciosus est in splendore suo. 13 Gyravit caelum in circuitu gloriae suae; manus Excelsi aperuerunt illum.

14 Imperio suo adceleravit nivem et adcelerat coruscationes emittere iudicii sui. 15 Propterea aperti sunt thesauri, et evolaverunt nebulae sicut aves. 16 In magnitudine sua posuit nubes, et confracti sunt lapides grandinis. 17 In conspectu eius commovebuntur montes, et in voluntate eius adspirabit notus. 18 Vox tonitrui eius verberabit terram; tempestas aquilonis et congregatio spiritus. 19 Et sicut avis deponens ad sedendum aspargit nivem, et sicut lucusta demergens descensus eius. 20 Pulchritudinem candoris eius admirabitur oculus, et super imbrem eius expavescet cor. 21 Gelum sicut salem effundet super terram, et dum gelaverit fiet tamquam cacumina tribuli.

22 Frigidus ventus aquilo flavit, et gelavit cristallus ab aqua. Super omnem congregationem aquarum requiescet et sicut lorica induet se aquis. 23 Et devorabit montes et exuret desertum et extinguet viridem sicut ignem. 24 Medicina omnium in festinationem nebulae, et ros obvians ab ardore venienti humilem efficiet eum.

25 In sermone eius siluit ventus, et cogitatione sua placavit abyssum, et plantavit in illa Dominus insulas. 26 Qui navigant mare enarrent pericula eius, et audientes auribus

enlighteneth the world on high. 11 By the words of the holy one they shall stand in judgment and shall *never* fail in their watches.

12 Look upon the rainbow, and bless him that made it. It is very beautiful in its brightness. 13 It encompasseth the heaven about with the circle of its glory; the hands of the Most High have displayed it.

14 By his commandment he *maketh the snow to fall apace* and sendeth forth swiftly the lightnings of his judgment. 15 Through this are the treasures opened, and the clouds fly out like birds. 16 By his greatness he hath fixed the clouds, and the hailstones are broken. 17 At his sight shall the mountains be shaken, and at his will the south wind shall blow. 18 The noise of his thunder shall strike the earth; *so doth* the northern storm and the *whirlwind.* 19 And as the birds lighting *upon the earth* he scattereth snow, and the falling thereof is as the coming down of locusts. 20 The eye admireth at the beauty of the whiteness thereof, and the heart is astonished at the shower thereof. 21 He shall pour frost as salt upon the earth, and when it freezeth it shall become like the tops of thistles.

22 The cold north wind *bloweth,* and the water *is congealed* into crystal. Upon every gathering together of waters it shall rest and shall clothe the waters as a breastplate. 23 And it shall devour the mountains and burn the wilderness and consume *all that* is green as *with* fire. 24 A present remedy of all is the speedy coming of a cloud, and a dew that meeteth it by the heat that cometh shall overpower it.

25 At his word the wind is still, and with his thought he appeaseth the deep, and the Lord hath planted islands therein. 26 Let them that sail on the sea tell the dangers thereof, and when we hear with our ears we shall admire.

nostris admirabimur. 27 Illic praeclara et mirabilia opera, varia genera bestiarum et omnium pecorum et creatura beluarum. 28 Propter ipsum confirmatus est itineris finis, et in sermone eius conposita sunt omnia.

29 Multa dicemus et deficiemus in verbis, consummatio autem sermonum: "Ipse est in omnibus." 30 Gloriantes ad quid valebimus? Ipse enim Omnipotens super omnia opera sua. 31 Terribilis Dominus et magnus vehementer, et mirabilis potentia ipsius. 32 Glorificantes Dominum quantumcumque potueritis, supervalebit adhuc, et admirabilis magnificentia eius. 33 Benedicentes Dominum, exaltate illum quantum potestis, maior est enim omni laude. 34 Exaltantes eum replemini virtute; ne laboretis, non enim comprehendetis.

35 Quis videbit eum et enarrabit? Et quis magnificabit eum sicut est ab initio? 36 Multa abscondita sunt maiora horum, pauca enim vidimus operum eius. 37 Omnia autem Dominus fecit, et pie agentibus dedit sapientiam.

Caput 44

Laudemus viros gloriosos et parentes nostros in generatione sua. 2 Multam gloriam fecit Dominus magnificentia sua a saeculo. 3 Dominantes in potestatibus suis, homines

27 There are great and wonderful works, a variety of beasts and of all living things and the *monstrous creatures* of *whales*. 28 Through him is established the end of their journey, and by his word all things are regulated.

29 We shall say much and yet shall want words, but the sum of our words is, "He is *all.*" 30 What shall we be able to do to glorify him? For the Almighty himself is above all his works. 31 The Lord is terrible and exceeding great, and his power is admirable. 32 *Glorify* the Lord as much as ever you can, *for* he will yet far exceed, and his magnificence is wonderful. 33 Blessing the Lord, exalt him as much as you can, for he is above all praise. 34 When you exalt him *put forth all your strength, and* be not weary, for you *can never go far enough.*

35 Who shall see him and declare him? And who shall magnify him as he is from the beginning? 36 There are many things hidden *from us* that are greater than these, for we have seen but a few of his works. 37 But the Lord hath made all things, and to the godly he hath given wisdom.

Chapter 44

The praises of the holy fathers, in particular of Enoch,
Noah, Abraham, Isaac and Jacob.

Let us *now* praise men of renown and our fathers in their generation. 2 The Lord hath wrought great glory through his magnificence from the beginning. 3 *Such as have borne rule* in

magni virtute, et prudentia sua praediti, nuntiantes in prophetis dignitatem prophetarum 4 et imperantes in praesenti populo et virtute prudentiae populis sanctissima verba, 5 in peritia sua requirentes modos musicos et narrantes carmina scripturarum, 6 homines divites in virtute, pulchritudinis studium habentes, pacificantes in domibus suis, 7 omnes isti in generationibus gentis suae gloriam adepti sunt et in diebus suis habentur in laudibus. 8 Qui de illis nati sunt reliquerunt nomen narrandi laudes eorum, 9 et sunt quorum non est memoria: perierunt quasi qui non fuerint et nati sunt quasi non nati et filii ipsorum cum illis. 10 Sed illi viri misericordiae sunt quorum pietates non defuerunt. 11 Cum semine ipsorum permanent bona. 12 Hereditas sancta nepotes illorum, et in testamentis stetit semen eorum. 13 Et filii ipsorum propter illos usque in aeternum manet; semen eorum et gloria eorum non derelinquetur. 14 Corpora ipsorum in pace sepulta sunt, et nomen eorum vivit in generationem et generationem. 15 Sapientiam ipsorum narrent populi et laudem eorum nuntiet ecclesia.

16 Enoch placuit Deo et translatus est in paradisum ut det gentibus paenitentiam. 17 Noe inventus est perfectus, iustus, et in tempore iracundiae factus est reconciliatio. 18 Ideo dimissum est reliquum terrae cum factum est diluvium. 19 Testamenta saeculi posita sunt apud illum ne deleri possit diluvio omnis caro.

20 Abraham magnus pater multitudinis gentium, et non est inventus similis illi in gloria qui conservavit legem

their dominions, men of great power, and endued with their wisdom, shewing forth in the prophets the dignity of prophets 4 and ruling over the present people and by the strength of wisdom *instructing* the people *in* most holy words, 5 *such as* by their skill sought out musical tunes and published canticles of the scriptures, 6 rich men in virtue, studying beautifulness, living at peace in their houses, 7 all these have gained glory in their generations and were praised in their days. 8 They that were born of them have left a name behind them that their praises might be related, 9 and there are some of whom there is no memorial *who* are perished as if they had never been and are born as if they had never been born and their children with them. 10 But these were men of mercy whose godly deeds have not failed. 11 Good things continue with their seed. 12 Their posterity are a holy inheritance, and their seed hath stood in the covenants. 13 And their children for their sakes remain for ever; their seed and their glory shall not be forsaken. 14 Their bodies are buried in peace, and their name liveth unto generation and generation. 15 Let the people shew forth their wisdom and the church declare their praise.

16 Enoch pleased God and was translated into paradise that he may give repentance to the nations. 17 Noah was found perfect, just, and in the time of wrath he was made a reconciliation. 18 Therefore was there a remnant left to the earth when the flood came. 19 The covenants of the world were made with him that all flesh should no more be destroyed with the flood.

20 Abraham was the great father of a multitude of nations, and there was not found the like to him in glory who kept the law of the Most High and was in covenant

Excelsi et fuit in testamento cum illo. 21 In carne eius stare fecit testamentum, et in temptatione inventus est fidelis. 22 Ideo iureiurando dedit illi gloriam in gente sua crescere illum quasi terrae cumulum 23 et ut stellas exaltare semen eius et hereditare illos a mari usque ad mare et a flumine usque ad terminos terrae.

24 Et in Isaac eodem fecit modo propter Abraham, patrem ipsius. 25 Benedictionem omnium gentium dedit illi Dominus et testamentum confirmavit super caput Iacob. 26 Agnovit eum in benedictionibus suis et dedit illi hereditatem et divisit ei partem in tribubus duodecim. 27 Et conservavit illi homines misericordiae invenientes gratiam in oculis omnis carnis.

Caput 45

Dilectus Deo et hominibus Moses, cuius memoria in benedictione est. 2 Similem illum fecit in gloria sanctorum et magnificavit eum in timore inimicorum et in verbis suis monstra placavit. 3 Glorificavit illum in conspectu regum et iussit illi coram populo suo et ostendit illi gloriam suam. 4 In fide et lenitate ipsius sanctum fecit illum et elegit illum de omni carne, 5 audivit enim eum et vocem ipsius et induxit illum in nubem. 6 Et dedit illi coram praecepta et legem

with him. 21 In his flesh he established the covenant, and in temptation he was found faithful. 22 Therefore by an oath he gave him glory in his posterity that he should increase as the dust of the earth 23 and that he would exalt his seed as the stars and they should inherit from sea to sea and from the river to the ends of the earth.

24 And he did in like manner with Isaac for the sake of Abraham, his father. 25 The Lord gave him the blessing of all nations and confirmed his covenant upon the head of Jacob. 26 He acknowledged him in his blessings and gave him an inheritance and divided him his portion in twelve tribes. 27 And he preserved for him men of mercy that found grace in the eyes of all flesh.

Chapter 45

The praises of Moses, of Aaron and of Phinehas.

Moses was beloved of God and men, whose memory is in benediction. 2 He made him like the saints in glory and magnified him in the fear of his enemies and with his words he made prodigies to cease. 3 He glorified him in the sight of kings and gave him *commandments* in the sight of his people and shewed him his glory. 4 He sanctified him in his faith and meekness and chose him out of all flesh, 5 for he heard him and his voice and brought him into a cloud. 6 And he

vitae et disciplinae docere Iacob testamentum suum et iudicia sua Israhel.

7 Excelsum fecit Aaron, fratrem eius, et similem sibi de tribu Levi. 8 Statuit ei testamentum aeternum et dedit illi sacerdotium gentis et beatificavit illum in gloria. 9 Et circumcinxit illum zonam et induit illum stolam gloriae et coronavit illum in vasis virtutis. 10 Circumpedes et femoralia et umeralem posuit ei, et cinxit illum tintinabulis aureis plurimis in gyro 11 dare sonitum in successu suo auditum facere sonitum in templo in memoriam filiis gentis suae. 12 Stola sancta auro et hyacintho et purpura, opus textile viri sapientis iudicio et veritate praediti, 13 torto cocco opus artificis gemmis pretiosis figuratis in ligatura auri et opere lapidarii sculptilis in memoriam, secundum numerum tribuum Israhel, 14 coronam auream supra mitram eius expressam signo sanctitatis et gloria honoris, opus virtutis et desideria oculorum ornata. 15 Sic pulchra ante ipsum non fuerunt talia usque ad originem. 16 Non indutus est illa alienigena aliquis, sed tantum filii ipsius soli et nepotes eius per omne tempus. 17 Sacrificia ipsius consumpta sunt igni cotidie. 18 Conplevit Moses manus eius et unxit illum oleo sancto. 19 Factum est illi in testamentum aeternum et semini eius sicut dies caeli fungi sacerdotio et habere laudem et glorificare populum suum in nomine suo. 20 Ipsum elegit ab omni vivente offerre sacrificium Deo, incensum et bonum odorem, in memoriam placare pro populo suo. 21 Et dedit illi in praeceptis suis po-

gave him commandments before his face and a law of life and instruction that he might teach Jacob his covenant and Israel his judgments.

7 He exalted Aaron, his brother, and like to himself of the tribe of Levi. 8 He made an everlasting covenant with him and gave him the priesthood of the nation and made him blessed in glory. 9 And he girded him about with a *glorious* girdle and clothed him with a robe of glory and crowned him with *majestic* attire. 10 He put upon him a garment to the feet and breeches and an ephod, and he compassed him with many little bells of gold all round about 11 that as he went *there might be a sound and a noise made that might be* heard in the temple for a memorial to the children of his people. 12 *He gave him* a holy robe of gold and blue and purple, a woven work of a wise man endued with judgment and truth, 13 of twisted scarlet the work of an artist with precious stones cut *and set* in gold and graven by the work of a lapidary for a memorial, according to the number of the tribes of Israel, 14 and a crown of gold upon his mitre *wherein was engraved Holiness, an ornament* of honour, a work of power and *delightful to the eyes for its beauty.* 15 Before him there were none so beautiful even from the beginning. 16 No stranger was ever clothed with them, but only his children alone and his grandchildren for ever. 17 His sacrifices were consumed with fire every day. 18 Moses filled his hands and anointed him with holy oil. 19 This was made to him for an everlasting testament and to his seed as the days of heaven to execute the office of the priesthood and to have praise and to glorify his people in his name. 20 He chose him out of all men living to offer sacrifice to God, incense and a good savour, for a memorial to make reconciliation for his people. 21 And he

testatem, in testamentis iudiciorum, docere Iacob testimonia et in lege sua lucem dare Israhel. 22 Quia contra illum steterunt alieni, et propter invidiam circumdederunt illum in deserto homines qui erant cum Dathan et Abiron et congregatio Chore in iracundiam. 23 Vidit Dominus Deus, et non placuit illi, et consumpti sunt in impetu iracundiae. 24 Fecit illis monstra et consumpsit eos in flamma ignis. 25 Et addidit Aaron gloriam et dedit illi hereditatem et primitias fructuum terrae divisit illi. 26 Panem ipsis in primis paravit in satietatem, nam et sacrificia Domini edent, quae dedit ipsi et semini eius. 27 Ceterum in terra gentes non hereditabit, et pars non est illi in gente, ipse enim pars eius est et hereditas.

28 Finees, filius Eleazari, tertius in gloria est, in imitando eum in timore Domini. 29 Et stare in reverentia gentis, in bonitate et alacritate animae suae placuit Deo pro Israhel. 30 Ideo statuit ad illum testamentum pacis principem sanctorum et gentis suae ut sit illi et semini eius sacerdotii dignitas in aeternum 31 et testamentum David, regi, filio Iesse de tribu Iuda, hereditas ipsi et semini eius, ut daret sapientiam in cor nostrum iudicare gentem suam in iustitia, ne abolerentur bona ipsorum, et gloriam eorum in gentem ipsorum aeternam fecit.

gave him power in his commandments, in the covenants of his judgments, that he should teach Jacob his testimonies and give light to Israel in his law. 22 *And* strangers stood up against him, and through envy the men that were with Dathan and Abiram compassed him about in the wilderness and the congregation of Korah in their wrath. 23 The Lord God saw, and it pleased him not, and they were consumed in his wrathful indignation. 24 He wrought wonders upon them and consumed them with a flame of fire. 25 And he added glory to Aaron and gave him an inheritance and divided unto him the firstfruits of the increase of the earth. 26 He prepared them bread in the first place unto fulness, for the sacrifices also of the Lord they shall eat, which he gave to him and to his seed. 27 But he shall not inherit *among* the people in the land, and he hath no portion among the people, for he himself is his portion and inheritance.

28 Phinehas, the son of Eleazar, is the third in glory, by imitating him in the fear of the Lord. 29 And *he stood up in the shameful fall* of the people; in the goodness and readiness of his soul he appeased God for Israel. 30 Therefore he made to him a covenant of peace to be the prince of the sanctuary and of his people that the dignity of priesthood should be to him and to his seed for ever 31 and a covenant to David, the king, the son of Jesse of the tribe of Judah, an inheritance to him and to his seed, that he might give wisdom into our heart to judge his people in justice, that their good things might not be abolished, and he made their glory in their nation everlasting.

Caput 46

Fortis in bello Iesus Nave, successor Mosi in prophetis, qui fuit magnus secundum nomen suum, 2 maximus in salutem electorum Dei, expugnare insurgentes hostes, ut consequeretur hereditatem Israhel. 3 Quam gloriam adeptus est in tollendo manus suas et iactando contra civitates rompheas! 4 Quis ante illum sic restitit? Nam hostes ipse Dominus perduxit. 5 Aut non in iracundia eius inpeditus est sol et una dies facta est quasi duo? 6 Invocavit Altissimum Potentem in obpugnando inimicos undique, et audivit illum magnus et sanctus Deus in saxis grandinis virtutis valde fortis. 7 Impetum fecit contra gentem hostilem, et in descensu perdidit contrarios 8 ut cognoscant gentes potentiam eius, quia contra Deum pugnare non est facile.

Et secutus est a tergo potentis, 9 et in diebus Mosi misericordiam fecit, ipse et Chaleb, filius Iepphonne, stare contra hostem et prohibere gentem a peccatis et sedare murmur malitiae. 10 Et ipsi duo constituti a periculo liberati sunt a numero sescentorum milium peditum inducere illos in hereditatem, in terram quae manat lac et mel. 11 Et dedit Dominus ipsi Chaleb fortitudinem, et usque ad senectutem

Chapter 46

The praise of Joshua, of Caleb and of Samuel.

Valiant in war was Jesus, the son of Nave, who was successor of Moses among the prophets, who was great according to his name, 2 very great for the saving the elect of God, to overthrow the enemies that rose up against them, that he might get the inheritance for Israel. 3 How great glory did he gain when he lifted up his hands and stretched out swords against the cities! 4 Who before him hath so resisted? For the Lord himself brought the enemies. 5 Was not the sun stopped in his anger and one day made as two? 6 He called upon the Most High Sovereign when the enemies assaulted him on every side, and the great and holy God heard him by hailstones of exceeding great force. 7 He made a violent assault against the nation of his enemies, and in the descent he destroyed the adversaries 8 that the nations might know his power, that it is not easy to fight against God.

And he followed the mighty one, 9 and in the days of Moses he did a work of mercy, he and Caleb, the son of Jephunneh, in standing against the enemy and withholding the people from sins and *appeasing* the wicked murmuring. 10 And they two being appointed were delivered out of the danger from among the number of six hundred thousand men on foot to bring them into their inheritance, into the land that floweth with milk and honey. 11 And the Lord gave strength *also* to Caleb, and his strength continued even to

permansit illi virtus ut ascenderet in excelsum terrae locum, et semen ipsius obtinuit hereditatem 12 ut viderent omnes filii Israhel quod bonum est obsequi sancto Deo.

13 Et iudices, singuli suo nomine quorum non est corruptum cor, qui non aversi sunt a Domino 14 ut sit memoria illorum in benedictione et ossa eorum pullulent de loco suo 15 et nomen eorum permaneat in aeternum, permanens ad filios illorum sanctorum virorum gloria.

16 Dilectus a Domino, Deo suo, Samuhel, propheta Domini, renovavit imperium et unxit principes in gente sua. 17 In lege Domini iudicavit congregationem, et vidit Deus Iacob, et in fide sua probatus est propheta. 18 Et cognitus est in verbis suis fidelis quia vidit Deum lucis 19 et invocavit Dominum Omnipotentem in obpugnando hostes circumstantes undique in oblatione agni inviolati. 20 Et intonuit e caelo Dominus et in sonitu magno auditam fecit vocem suam. 21 Et conteruit principes Tyriorum et omnes duces Philisthim. 22 Et ante tempus finis vitae suae et saeculi testimonium praebuit in conspectu Domini et christi: pecunias et usque ad calciamenta ab omni carne non accepit, et non accusavit illum homo. 23 Et post hoc dormivit, et notum fecit regi et ostendit illi finem vitae suae, et exaltavit vocem eius de terra in prophetia delere impietatem gentis.

his old age so that he went up to the high places of the land, and his seed obtained it for an inheritance 12 that all the children of Israel might see that it is good to obey the holy God.

13 *Then all* the judges, every one *by* name whose heart was not corrupted, who turned not away from the Lord 14 that their memory might be blessed and their bones spring up out of their place 15 and their name continue for ever, the glory of the holy men remaining unto their children.

16 Samuel, the prophet of the Lord, the beloved of the Lord, his God, established a new government and anointed princes over his people. 17 By the law of the Lord he judged the congregation, and the God of Jacob beheld, and by his fidelity he was proved a prophet. 18 And he was known to be faithful in his words because he saw the God of light 19 and called upon *the name of* the Lord Almighty in fighting against the enemies who beset him on every side when he offered a lamb without blemish. 20 And the Lord thundered from heaven and with a great noise made his voice to be heard. 21 And he crushed the princes of the Tyrians and all the lords of the Philistines. 22 And before the time of the end of his life *in* the world he *protested* before the Lord and his anointed: money *or any thing else,* even to a shoe, he had not taken of *any man,* and no man did accuse him. 23 And after this he slept, and he made known to the king and shewed him the end of his life, and he lifted up his voice from the earth in prophecy to blot out the wickedness of the nation.

Caput 47

Post haec surrexit Nathan, propheta, in diebus David. 2 Et quasi adeps separatus a carne, sic David a filiis Israhel. 3 Cum leonibus lusit quasi cum agnis, et in ursis similiter fecit sicut cum agnis ovium in iuventute sua. 4 Numquid non occidit gigantem et extulit obprobrium de gente? 5 In tollendo manum in saxo fundae deiecit exultationem Goliae, 6 nam invocavit Dominum Omnipotentem, et dedit in dexteram eius tollere hominem fortem in bello et exaltare cornum gentis suae. 7 Sic in decem milibus glorificavit illum et laudavit eum in benedictionibus Domini in offerendo illi coronam gloriae, 8 conteruit enim inimicos undique et extirpavit Philisthim, contrarios, usque in hodiernum diem: conteruit cornum ipsorum usque in aeternum. 9 In omni opere dedit confessionem Sancto et Excelso in verbo gloriae. 10 De omni corde suo laudavit Dominum et dilexit Deum qui fecit illum, et dedit illi contra inimicos potentiam. 11 Et stare fecit cantores contra altarium et in sono eorum dulces fecit modos. 12 Et dedit in celebrationibus decus et ornavit tempora usque ad consummationem vitae ut laudarent sanctum no-

Chapter 47

The praise of Nathan, of David and of Solomon. Of his fall
and punishment.

Then Nathan, the prophet, arose in the days of David.
2 And as the fat taken away from the flesh, so was David
chosen from among the children of Israel. 3 He played with
lions as with lambs, and with bears he did in like manner as
with the lambs of the flock in his youth. 4 Did not he kill the
giant and take away reproach from his people? 5 In lifting up
his hand with the stone in the sling he beat down the boasting of Goliath, 6 for he called upon the Lord the Almighty,
and he gave strength in his right hand to take away the
mighty warrior and to set up the horn of his nation. 7 So in
ten thousand did he glorify him and praised him in the blessings of the Lord in offering to him a crown of glory, 8 for he
destroyed the enemies on every side and extirpated the Philistines, the adversaries, unto this day: he broke their horn
for ever. 9 In all his works he gave thanks to the holy one and
to the Most High with words of glory. 10 With his whole
heart he praised the Lord and loved God that made him,
and he gave him power against his enemies. 11 And he set
singers before the altar and by their *voices* he made sweet
melody. 12 And to the festivals he added beauty and set in order the *solemn* times even to the end of his life that they

men Domini et amplificarent mane Dei sanctitatem. 13 Dominus purgavit peccata ipsius et exaltavit in aeternum cornum ipsius et dedit illi testamentum regni et sedem gloriae in Israhel.

14 Post ipsum surrexit filius sensatus, et propter illum deiecit omnem potentiam inimicorum. 15 Salomon imperavit in diebus pacis, cui subiecit Deus omnes hostes ut conderet domum in nomine suo et pararet sanctitatem in sempiternum. Quemadmodum eruditus es in iuventute tua! 16 Et impletus es quasi flumen sapientia, et terram retexit anima tua. 17 Et replesti in conparationibus enigmata; ad insulas longe divulgatum est nomen tuum, et dilectus es in pace tua. 18 In cantilenis et proverbiis et conparationibus et interpretationibus miratae sunt terrae 19 et in nomine Domini Dei, cui est cognomen Deus Israhel. 20 Collegisti quasi auricalcum aurum et ut plumbum conplesti argentum, 21 et reclinasti femora tua mulieribus; potestatem habuisti in tuo corpore. 22 Dedisti maculam in gloria tua et profanasti semen tuum inducere iracundiam ad liberos tuos et incitari stultitiam tuam 23 ut faceres imperium bipertitum et ex Efraim imperare imperium durum. 24 Deus autem non derelinquet misericordiam suam, et non corrumpet nec delebit opera sua, neque perdet ab stirpe nepotes electi sui, et semen eius qui diligit Dominum non corrumpet. 25 Dedit autem reliquum Iacob et David de ipsa stirpe. 26 Et finem habuit Salomon cum patribus suis. 27 Et reliquit post se de semine suo gentis stultitiam, 28 et inminutum a prudentia Roboam qui

should praise the holy name of the Lord and magnify the holiness of God in the morning. 13 The Lord took away his sins and exalted his horn for ever and he gave him a covenant of the kingdom and a throne of glory in Israel.

14 After him arose up a wise son, and for his sake he cast down all the power of the enemies. 15 Solomon reigned in days of peace, and God brought all his enemies under him that he might build a house in his name and prepare a sanctuary for ever. O how wise wast thou in thy youth! 16 And thou wast filled as a river with wisdom, and thy soul covered the earth. 17 And thou didst multiply riddles in parables; thy name went abroad to the islands far off, and thou wast beloved in thy peace. 18 The countries wondered at *thee for thy* canticles and proverbs and parables and interpretations 19 and at the name of the Lord God, whose surname is God of Israel. 20 Thou didst gather gold as copper and didst multiply silver as lead, 21 and thou didst bow *thyself* to women, and *by thy body thou wast brought under subjection.* 22 Thou hast stained thy glory and defiled thy seed so as to bring wrath upon thy children and to have thy folly kindled 23 that thou shouldst make the kingdom to be divided and out of Ephraim a *rebellious* kingdom to rule. 24 But God will not leave off his mercy, and he will not destroy nor abolish his own works, neither will he cut up by the roots the offspring of his elect, and he will not utterly take away the seed of him that loveth the Lord. 25 *Wherefore* he gave a remnant to Jacob and to David of the same stock. 26 And Solomon had an end with his fathers. 27 And he left behind him of his seed the folly of the nation, 28 even Rehoboam that had little wis-

avertit gentem consilio suo 29 et Hieroboam, filium Nabath, qui peccare fecit Israhel et dedit Efraim viam peccandi, et plurima redundaverunt peccata ipsorum. 30 Valde averterunt illos a terra sua. 31 Et quaesivit omnes nequitias usque dum perveniret ad illos defensio et ab omnibus peccatis liberavit eos.

Caput 48

Et surrexit Helias, propheta, quasi ignis, et verbum ipsius quasi facula ardebat. 2 Qui induxit in illos famem, et irritantes illum invidia sua pauci facti sunt, non poterant enim sustinere praecepta Domini. 3 Verbo Domini continuit caelum, et deiecit de caelo ignem ter. 4 Sic amplificatus est Helias in mirabilibus suis. Et quis potest similiter sic gloriari tibi, 5 qui sustulisti mortuum ab inferis de sorte mortis in verbo Domini Dei, 6 qui deiecisti reges ad perniciem et confregisti facile potentiam ipsorum et gloriosos de lecto suo, 7 qui audis in Sina iudicium et in Coreb iudicia defensionis, 8 qui unguis reges ad paenitentiam et prophetas facis successores post te, 9 qui receptus es in turbine ignis, in curru equorum

dom who turned away the people through his counsel 29 and Jeroboam, the son of Nebat, who caused Israel to sin and shewed Ephraim the way of sin, and their sins were multiplied exceedingly. 30 They removed them far away from their land. 31 And they sought out all iniquities till vengeance came upon them and *put an end to* all *their* sins.

Chapter 48

The praise of Elijah, of Elisha, of Hezekiah and of Isaiah.

And Elijah, the prophet, stood up, as a fire, and his word burnt like a torch. 2 He brought a famine upon them, and they that provoked him in their envy were reduced to a small number, for they could not endure the commandments of the Lord. 3 By the word of the Lord he shut up the heaven, and he brought down fire from heaven thrice. 4 Thus was Elijah magnified in his wondrous works. And who can glory like to thee, 5 who raisedst up a dead man from below from the lot of death by the word of the Lord God, 6 who broughtest down kings to destruction and brokest easily their po`wer in pieces and the glorious from their bed, 7 who hearest judgment in Sinai and in Horeb the judgments of vengeance, 8 who anointest kings to penance and makest prophets successors after thee, 9 who wast taken up in a whirlwind

igneorum, 10 qui scriptus es in iudiciis temporum lenire iracundiam Domini, conciliare cor patris ad filium et restituere
tribus Iacob? 11 Beati sunt qui te viderunt et in amicitia tua
decorati sunt, 12 nam nos vita vivimus tantum, post mortem
autem non erit tale nomen nostrum.

13 Helias quidem in turbine tectus est, et in Heliseo
conpletus est spiritus eius. In diebus suis non pertimuit
principem, et potentia nemo vicit illum. 14 Nec superavit illum verbum aliquod, et mortuum prophetavit corpus eius.
15 In vita sua fecit monstra, et in morte mirabilia operatus
est. 16 In omnibus istis non paenituit populus, et non recesserunt a peccatis suis usque dum eiecti sunt de terra sua et
dispersi sunt in omnem terram. 17 Et relicta est gens per-
pauca et princeps in domo David. 18 Quidam ipsorum fecerunt quod placeret Deo, alii autem multa commiserunt peccata. 19 Ezechias munivit civitatem suam et induxit in
medium ipsius aquam, et fodit ferro rupem et aedificavit ad
aquam puteum. 20 In diebus ipsius ascendit Sennacherim et
misit Rapsacen et sustulit manum suam contra illos, et extulit manum suam in Sion et superbus factus est potentia sua.

21 Tunc mota sunt corda et manus ipsorum, et doluerunt
quasi parturientes mulieres. 22 Et invocaverunt Dominum
misericordem et expandentes manus suas extulerunt ad caelum, et sanctus Dominus Deus audivit cito vocem ipsorum.
23 Non est commemoratus peccatorum illorum, neque dedit
illos inimicis suis, sed purgavit illos in manu Esaiae, sancti
prophetae. 24 Subiecit castra Assyriorum, et conteruit illos

of fire, in a chariot of fiery horses, 10 who art registered in the judgments of times to appease the wrath of the Lord, to reconcile the heart of the father to the son and to restore the tribes of Jacob? 11 Blessed are they that saw thee and were honoured with thy friendship, 12 for we live only in our life, but after death our name shall not be such.

13 Elijah was indeed covered with the whirlwind, and his spirit was filled up in Elisha. In his days he feared not the prince, and no man was more powerful than he. 14 *No word could* overcome him, and after death his body prophesied. 15 In his life he did great wonders, and in death he wrought miracles. 16 For all this the people repented not, neither did they depart from their sins till they were cast out of their land and were scattered through all the earth. 17 And there was left but a small people and a prince in the house of David. 18 Some of these did that which pleased God, but others committed many sins. 19 Hezekiah fortified his city and brought in water into the midst thereof, and he digged a rock with iron and made a well for water. 20 In his days Sennacherib came up and sent Rabshakeh and lifted up his hand against them, and he stretched out his hand against Zion and became proud through his power.

21 Then their hearts and hands trembled, and they were in pain as women in travail. 22 And they called upon the Lord who is merciful and spreading their hands they lifted them up to heaven, and the holy Lord God quickly heard their voice. 23 He was not mindful of their sins, neither did he deliver them up to their enemies, but he purified them by the hand of Isaiah, the holy prophet. 24 He overthrew the army

angelus Domini. 25 Nam fecit Ezechias quod placuit Deo et fortiter ivit in via David, patris sui, quam mandavit illi Esaias, propheta magnus et fidelis in conspectu Dei. 26 In diebus ipsius retro rediit sol, et addidit regi vitam. 27 Spiritu magno vidit ultima et consolatus est lugentes in Sion. Usque in sempiternum 28 ostendit futura et abscondita antequam evenirent.

Caput 49

Memoria Iosiae in conpositionem odoris facti opus pigmentarii. 2 In omni ore quasi mel indulcabitur eius memoria et ut musica in convivio vini. 3 Ipse est directus divinitus in paenitentiam gentis, et tulit abominationes impietatis. 4 Et gubernavit ad Dominum cor ipsius, et in diebus peccatorum corroboravit pietatem.

of the Assyrians, and the angel of the Lord destroyed them. 25 For Hezekiah did that which pleased God and walked valiantly in the way of David, his father, which Isaiah, the great prophet and faithful in the sight of God, had commanded him. 26 In his days the sun went backward, and he lengthened the king's life. 27 With a great spirit he saw the things that are to come to pass at last and comforted the mourners in Zion. 28 He shewed what should come to pass for ever and secret things before they came.

Chapter 49

The praise of Josiah, of Jeremiah, Ezekiel and the twelve
prophets. Also of Zerubbabel, Jeshua, the son of Jozadak,
Nehemiah, Enoch, Joseph, Seth, Shem and Adam.

The memory of Josiah is like the composition of a sweet smell made by the art of a perfumer. 2 His remembrance shall be sweet as honey in every mouth and as music at a banquet of wine. 3 He was directed by God unto the repentance of the nation, and he took away the abominations of wickedness. 4 And he directed his heart towards the Lord, and in the days of sinners he strengthened godliness.

5 Praeter David et Ezechiam et Iosiam, omnes peccatum commiserunt, 6 nam reliquerunt legem Altissimi reges Iudae et contempserunt timorem Dei. 7 Dederunt enim regnum suum aliis et gloriam suam alienae genti. 8 Incenderunt electam sanctitatis civitatem et desertas fecerunt vias ipsius in manu Hieremiae, 9 nam male tractaverunt illum qui a ventre matris consecratus est propheta evertere et eruere et perdere et iterum aedificare et renovare.

10 Ezechihel qui vidit conspectum gloriae quam ostendit illi in curru cherubin, 11 nam commemoratus est inimicorum in imbri benefacere illis qui ostenderunt rectas vias.

12 Et duodecim prophetarum ossa pullulent de loco suo, nam conroboraverunt Iacob et redimerunt se in fide virtutis.

13 Quomodo amplificemus Zorobabel? Nam et ipse quasi signum in dextera manu. 14 Sic et Iesum, filium Iosedec, qui in diebus suis aedificaverunt domum et exaltaverunt templum sanctum Domino paratum in gloria sempiterna. 15 Et Neemia in memoria multi temporis, qui erexit nobis muros eversos et stare fecit portas et seras, qui erexit domos nostras. 16 Nemo natus est in terra qualis Enoch, nam et ipse receptus est a terra, 17 neque ut Ioseph, qui natus est homo princeps fratrum, firmamentum gentis, rector fratrum, stabilimentum populi. 18 Et ossa ipsius visitata sunt, et post mortem prophetaverunt. 19 Seth et Sem apud homines gloriam adepti sunt, et super omnem animam in origine Adam.

5 Except David and Hezekiah and Josiah, all committed sin, 6 for the kings of Judah forsook the law of the Most High and despised the fear of God. 7 *So* they gave their kingdom to others and their glory to a strange nation. 8 They burnt the chosen city of holiness and made the streets thereof desolate *according to the prediction* of Jeremiah, 9 for they treated him evil who was consecrated a prophet from his mother's womb to overthrow and pluck up and destroy and to build again and renew.

10 It was Ezekiel that saw the glorious vision which *was shewn* him upon the chariot of cherubims, 11 for he made mention of the enemies *under the figure of rain and of doing* good to them that shewed right ways.

12 And may the bones of the twelve prophets spring up out of their place, for they strengthened Jacob and redeemed themselves by strong faith.

13 How shall we magnify Zerubbabel? For he was as a signet on the right hand. 14 In like manner Jeshua, the son of Jozadak, who in their days built the house and set up a holy temple to the Lord prepared for everlasting glory. 15 And let Nehemiah be a long time remembered, who raised up for us our walls that were cast down and set up the gates and the bars, who rebuilt our houses. 16 No man was born upon earth like Enoch, for he also was taken up from the earth, 17 nor as Joseph, who was a man born prince of his brethren, the support of his family, the ruler of his brethren, the stay of the people. 18 And his bones were visited, and after death they prophesied. 19 Seth and Shem obtained glory among men, and above every soul Adam in the beginning.

Caput 50

Simon, Onii filius, sacerdos magnus, qui in vita sua suffulsit domum et in diebus suis corroboravit templum, 2 templi etiam altitudo ab ipso fundata est, duplex aedificatio et excelsi parietes templi. 3 In diebus ipsius emanaverunt putei aquarum, et quasi mare adimpleti sunt supra modum. 4 Qui curavit gentem suam et liberavit illam a perditione. 5 Qui praevaluit amplificare civitatem qui adeptus est gloriam in conversatione gentis et ingressum domus et atrii amplificavit. 6 Quasi stella matutina in medio nebulae et quasi luna plena in diebus suis lucet. 7 Et quasi sol refulgens sic ille effulsit in templo Dei, 8 quasi arcus effulgens inter nebulas gloriae et quasi flos rosarum in diebus veris et quasi lilia quae sunt in transitu aquae et quasi tus redolens in diebus aestatis, 9 quasi ignis effulgens et tus ardens in igni, 10 quasi vas auri solidum ornatum omni lapide pretioso, 11 quasi oliva pullulans et cypressus in altitudinem se tollens in accipiendo ipsum stolam gloriae et vestiri eum in consummationem virtutis.

12 In ascensu altarii sancti gloriam dedit sanctitatis amictum, 13 in accipiendo autem partes de manu sacerdotum et ipse stans iuxta aram. Circa illum corona fratrum, et quasi

Chapter 50

The praises of Simon, the high priest. The conclusion.

Simon, the high priest, the son of Onias, who in his life propped up the house and in his days fortified the temple, 2 by him also the height of the temple was founded, the double building and the high walls of the temple. 3 In his days the wells of water flowed out, and they were filled as the sea above measure. 4 He took care of his nation and delivered it from destruction. 5 He prevailed to enlarge the city and obtained glory in his conversation with the people and enlarged the entrance of the house and the court. 6 He shone in his days as the morning star in the midst of a cloud and as the moon at the full. 7 And as the sun when it shineth so did he shine in the temple of God 8 *and* as the rainbow giving light in the *bright* clouds and as the flower of roses in the days of the spring and as the lilies that are on the brink of the water and as the sweet smelling frankincense in the time of summer, 9 as a bright fire and frankincense burning in the fire, 10 as a massy vessel of gold adorned with every precious stone, 11 as an olive tree budding forth and a cypress tree rearing itself on high when he put on the robe of glory and was clothed with the perfection of power.

12 When he went up to the holy altar he honoured the vesture of holiness. 13 And when he took the portions out of the hands of the priests he *himself* stood by the altar. *And* about him was the ring of his brethren, and as the cedar

plantatio cedri in Monte Libano, 14 sic circa illum steterunt quasi rami palmae et omnes filii Aaron in gloria sua. 15 Oblatio autem Domini in manibus ipsorum coram omni synagoga Israhel et consummationem fungens in ara amplificare oblationem excelsi regis 16 porrexit manum suam in libatione et libavit de sanguine uvae. 17 Effudit in fundamento altarii odorem divinum excelso principi.

18 Tunc exclamaverunt filii Aaron; in tubis productilibus sonaverunt et auditam fecerunt magnam vocem in memoriam coram Deo. 19 Tunc omnis populus simul properaverunt et ceciderunt in faciem super terram adorare Dominum, Deum suum, et dare preces Deo Omnipotenti, Excelso. 20 Et amplificaverunt psallentes in vocibus suis, et in magna domo auctus est sonus suavitatis plenus. 21 Et rogavit populus Dominum, Excelsum, in prece usque dum perfectus est honor Domini et munus suum perfecerunt. 22 Tunc descendens extulit manus suas in omnem congregationem filiorum Israhel dare gloriam Deo a labiis suis et in nomine ipsius gloriari, 23 et iteravit orationem suam, volens ostendere virtutem Dei:

24 "Et nunc orate Deum omnium, qui magna fecit in omni terra, qui auxit dies nostros a ventre matris nostrae et fecit nobiscum secundum suam misericordiam. 25 Det nobis iucunditatem cordis et fieri pacem in diebus nostris in Israhel per dies sempiternos, 26 credere Israhel nobiscum esse misericordiam Dei ut liberet nos in diebus suis."

27 Duas gentes odit anima mea, tertia autem non est gens

planted in Mount Lebanon 14 *and as* branches of palm trees *they* stood round about him and all the sons of Aaron in their glory. 15 And the oblation of the Lord was in their hands before all the congregation of Israel and finishing his service on the altar to honour the offering of the most high king 16 he stretched forth his hand to make a libation and offered of the blood of the grape. 17 He poured out at the foot of the altar a divine odour to the most high prince.

18 Then the sons of Aaron shouted; they sounded with beaten trumpets and made a great noise to be heard for a remembrance before God. 19 Then all the people together made haste and fell down to the earth upon their faces to adore the Lord, their God, and to pray to the Almighty God, the Most High. 20 And the singers lifted up their voices, and in the great house the sound of sweet melody was increased. 21 And the people in prayer besought the Lord, the Most High, until the worship of the Lord was perfected and they had finished their office. 22 Then coming down he lifted up his hands over all the congregation of the children of Israel to give glory to God with his lips and to glory in his name, 23 and he repeated his prayer, willing to shew the power of God:

24 "And now pray ye to the God of all, who hath done great things in all the earth, who hath increased our days from our mother's womb and hath done with us according to his mercy. 25 May he grant us joyfulness of heart and that there be peace in our days in Israel for ever, 26 that Israel may believe that the mercy of God is with us to deliver us in his days."

27 There are two nations which my soul abhorreth, and

quam oderim: 28 qui sedent in Monte Seir et Philisthim et stultus populus qui habitat in Sicimis. 29 Doctrinam sapientiae et disciplinae scripsit in codice isto Iesus, filius Sirach Hierosolymita, qui renovavit sapientiam de corde suo. 30 Beatus qui in istis versatur bonis, et qui ponit illa in corde suo sapiens erit semper, 31 si enim haec fecerit ad omnia valebit quia lux Dei vestigium eius est.

Caput 51

Oratio Iesu, filii Sirach.

Confitebor tibi Domine, Rex, et conlaudabo te, Deum, salvatorem meum. 2 Confitebor nomini tuo, quoniam adiutor et protector factus es mihi 3 et liberasti corpus meum a perditione, a laqueo linguae iniquae et a labiis operantium mendacium, et in conspectu adstantium factus es mihi adiutor. 4 Et liberasti me secundum multitudinem misericordiae nominis tui a rugientibus, praeparatis ad escam, 5 de manibus quaerentium animam meam et de portis tribulationum quae circumdederunt me, 6 a pressura flammae

the third is no nation which I hate: 28 they that sit on Mount Seir and the Philistines and the foolish people that dwell in Shechem. 29 Jesus, the son of Sirach of Jerusalem, hath written in this book the doctrine of wisdom and instruction, who renewed wisdom from his heart. 30 Blessed is he that is conversant in these good things, and he that layeth them up in his heart shall be wise always, 31 for if he do them he shall be strong to do all things because the light of God guideth his steps.

Chapter 51

A prayer of praise and thanksgiving.

A prayer of Jesus, the son of Sirach.

I will give glory to thee, O Lord, O King, and I will praise thee, O God, my Saviour. 2 I will give glory to thy name, for thou hast been a helper and protector to me 3 and hast preserved my body from destruction, from the snare of an unjust tongue and from the lips of them that forge lies, and in the sight of them that stood by thou hast been my helper. 4 And thou hast delivered me according to the multitude of the mercy of thy name from them that did roar, prepared to devour, 5 out of the hands of them that sought my life and from the gates of afflictions which compassed me about, 6 from the oppression of the flame which surrounded me,

quae circumdedit me, et in medio ignis non sum aestuatus, 7 de altitudine ventris inferi et a lingua coinquinata et a verbo mendacii, a rege iniquo et a lingua iniusta. 8 Laudabit usque ad mortem anima mea Dominum. 9 Et vita mea adpropinquans erat in inferno deorsum. 10 Circumdederunt me undique, et non erat qui adiuvaret. Respiciens eram ad adiutorium hominum, et non erat. 11 Memoratus sum misericordiae tuae, Domine, et operationis tuae quae a saeculo sunt, 12 quoniam eruis sustinentes te, Domine, et liberas eos de manibus gentium. 13 Exaltasti super terram habitationem meam, et pro morte defluenti deprecatus sum. 14 Invocavi Dominum, patrem Domini mei, ut non derelinquat me in die tribulationis meae et in tempore superborum sine adiutorio. 15 Laudabo nomen tuum adsidue et conlaudabo illud in confessione, et exaudita est oratio mea. 16 Et liberasti me de perditione et eripuisti me de tempore iniquo. 17 Propterea confitebor et laudem dicam tibi et benedicam nomen Domini.

18 Cum adhuc iunior essem, priusquam oberrarem quaesivi sapientiam palam in oratione mea. 19 Ante templum postulabam pro illa, et usque in novissimis inquiram eam, et floriet tamquam praecox uva. 20 Laetatum est cor meum in ea; ambulavit pes meus iter rectum. A iuventute mea investigabam eam. 21 Inclinavi modice aurem meam et excepi illam. 22 Multam inveni in me ipso sapientiam, et multum profeci in ea. 23 Danti mihi sapientiam dabo gloriam, 24 consiliatus sum enim ut facerem illam. Zelatus sum bonum et non confundar. 25 Conluctata est anima mea in illa,

and in the midst of the fire I was not burnt, 7 from the depth of the belly of hell and from an unclean tongue and from lying words, from an unjust king and from a slanderous tongue. 8 My soul shall praise the Lord even to death.

9 And my life was drawing near to hell beneath. 10 They compassed me on every side, and there was no one that would help me. I looked for the succour of men, and there was none. 11 I remembered thy mercy, O Lord, and thy works which are from the beginning of the world, 12 how thou deliverest them that wait for thee, O Lord, and savest them out of the hands of the nations.

13 Thou hast exalted my dwelling place upon the earth, and I have prayed for death to pass away. 14 I called upon the Lord, the father of my Lord, that he would not leave me in the day of my trouble and in the time of the proud without help. 15 I will praise thy name continually and will praise it with thanksgiving, and my prayer was heard. 16 And thou hast saved me from destruction and hast delivered me from the evil time. 17 Therefore I will give thanks and praise thee and bless the name of the Lord.

18 When I was yet young, before I wandered about I sought for wisdom openly in my prayer. 19 I prayed for her before the temple, and unto the very end I will seek after her, and she *flourished* as a grape soon ripe. 20 My heart delighted in her; my foot walked in the right way. From my youth up I sought after her. 21 I bowed down my ear a little and received her. 22 I found much wisdom in myself, and I profited much therein. 23 To him that giveth me wisdom will I give glory, 24 for I have determined to follow her. I have had a zeal for good and shall not be confounded. 25 My soul hath wrestled for her, and in doing it I have been

et in faciendo eam confirmatus sum. 26 Manus meas extendi in altum, et insipientiam eius luxi. 27 Animam meam direxi ad illam, et in agnitione inveni eam. 28 Possedi cum ipsa cor ab initio; propter hoc non derelinquar. 29 Venter meus conturbatus est quaerendo illam; propterea possidebo bonam possessionem. 30 Dedit mihi Dominus linguam mercedem meam, et in ipsa laudabo eum.

31 Adpropiate ad me, indocti, et congregate vos in domum disciplinae. 32 Quid adhuc retardatis? Et quid dicitis in his? Animae vestrae sitiunt vehementer. 33 Aperui os meum et locutus sum. Conparate vobis sine argento, 34 et collum vestrum subicite iugo, et suscipiat anima vestra disciplinam, in proximo est enim invenire eam. 35 Videte oculis vestris quoniam modicum laboravi et inveni mihi multam requiem. 36 Adsumite disciplinam in multo numero argenti, et copiosum aurum possidete in ea. 37 Laetetur anima vestra in misericordia eius, et non confundemini in laude ipsius. 38 Operamini opus vestrum ante tempus, et dabit vobis mercedem vestram in tempore suo.

confirmed. 26 I stretched forth my hands on high, and I bewailed my ignorance of her. 27 I directed my soul to her, and in knowledge I found her. 28 I possessed my heart with her from the beginning; therefore I shall not be forsaken. 29 My entrails were troubled in seeking her; therefore shall I possess a good possession. 30 The Lord hath given me a tongue for my reward, and with it I will praise him.

31 Draw near to me, ye unlearned, and gather yourselves together into the house of discipline. 32 Why are ye slow? And what do you say of these things? Your souls are exceeding thirsty. 33 I have opened my mouth and have spoken. Buy her for yourselves without silver, 34 and submit your neck to the yoke, and let your soul receive discipline, for she is near at hand to be found. 35 Behold with your eyes how I have laboured a little and have found much rest to myself. 36 Receive ye discipline as a great sum of money, and possess abundance of gold by her. 37 Let your soul rejoice in his mercy, and you shall not be confounded in his praise. 38 Work your work before the time, and he will give you your reward in his time.

Note on the Text

This edition is meant to present a Latin text close to what the Douay-Rheims translators saw. Therefore the readings in this edition are not necessarily preferred in the sense that they are thought to be "original"; instead, they represent the Latin Bible as it was read by many from the eighth through the sixteenth century. Furthermore, in the service of economy, sources for the text are cited according to a hierarchy and consequently the lists of sources following the lemmas and alternate readings are not necessarily comprehensive. If a reading appears in Weber's text or apparatus, no other sources are cited; if it is not in Weber but is in Quentin, only the sources cited by Quentin are reproduced. The complete list of sources for the Latin text, in their hierarchical order, is Weber, the Sixto-Clementine edition, Weber's apparatus, Quentin, his apparatus, the Vetus Latina edition of Pierre Sabatier (1682–1742), the *Glossa Ordinaria* attributed (wrongly) to Walafrid Strabo in the Patrologia Latina, and the database of the Beuroner Vetus Latina-Institut.

When no source can be found for what seems to be the correct Latin, a reconstruction is proposed in the Notes to the Text but the Weber text is generally printed in the edition. Trivial differences between the Weber and Sixto-Clementine editions in word order and orthography, alternative spellings and inflections of proper names, and synco-

pation of verbs have not been noted, nor have many differences that do not affect translation, such as the omission or inclusion of forms of *esse,* variant forms of personal pronouns, conjunctions treated by the Douay-Rheims translators as synonymous, and the omission or inclusion of certain pronouns or possessive adjectives.

Whenever it has been necessary to stray from Weber's text (about one thousand times in the first volume), the departures are recorded in the Notes to the Text. These notes by no means constitute a true *apparatus criticus,* but they enable interested readers to see both the deviations from Weber (whose text is preferable for people wanting to get as close as possible to the earliest versions of the many Latin texts which, combined, form the Vulgate Bible) and significant differences among the Weber, Sixto-Clementine, and Douay-Rheims texts.

When the translation reflects a reading closer to Weber's than to the Sixto-Clementine edition, the Sixto-Clementine variation is printed in the Notes to the Text. Less frequently, there are two readings that would translate the same way but that differ sufficiently to warrant noting, as at Gen 19:6, where Weber reads "umbraculum tegminis" while the Sixto-Clementine version has "umbra culminis."

Often the punctuation of the Douay-Rheims edition reflects an understanding of the Latin different from that of the Weber, Sixto-Clementine, or both editions. The Weber edition has no punctuation marks in most books; rather, the editors inserted line breaks to mark new clauses or sentences, a punctuation style known as *per cola et commata,* which is meant to assist readers without inserting anachronistic markings. These line breaks have been represented in

the notes by slashes (/). In general, differences in punctuation among this edition, the Sixto-Clementine Bible, and Weber's edition have been cited only when they demonstrate considerably different understandings of the Latin. Often Weber's presentation is too equivocal to shed light on his understanding; in these cases, his edition is not cited.

While the Douay-Rheims translation belongs to a tradition of exceptionally literal renderings of the Latin Bible, Challoner's revision contains some divergences from the Latin. Any English that does not square with the text *en face* is italicized, and where possible, Challoner's source has been indicated in the Notes to the Text. When Challoner's source is given, it is not necessarily quoted word for word in the lemma; indeed, the Septuagint is cited as a source, yet almost no Greek is quoted in the notes. Whenever there can be doubt of a source based on a slight difference between its reading and Challoner's, the difference has been recorded following the lemma, either in parentheses or in brackets when containing explanatory material that is not a quotation from the source. Sources for the English text are cited in a hierarchical fashion similar to that of the Latin, in the following order: Douay-Rheims, Sixto-Clementine, King James, Septuagint, Hebrew text; this means that if an English reading is found in the King James Version that may also be in the Septuagint, only the King James Version is cited. Also, if Challoner's translation seems to approximate a source that is cited, the distance between source and translation is indicated by a question mark following the siglum.

Words cited from biblical sources are in italics in the notes, and the sigla and any comments are in roman type. Lemmas precede colons; other readings follow them. Occa-

sionally Challoner indicated that he was adding words to his revision that did not appear in the Latin text; he did this by italicizing the relevant words, much as the authors of the King James Version printed occasional words in roman as opposed to black-letter type to indicate an addition. Brack- eted explanations or underlinings draw attention to these typographical variations in the Notes to the Text where nec- essary.

Notes to the Text

*D-R = Latin text that seems to give rise to the D-R translation but that is not represented in S-C, Weber, or in any of the manuscripts cited in those editions.

D-R = *The Holie Bible: Faithfully Translated into English out of the Authentical Latin* (The English Colleges of Douay and Rheims, OT 1609–10, NT 1582)

D-Rn = marginalia in D-R

D-R/C = *The Holy Bible: Translated from the Latin Vulgat* (Challoner's 1750 revision, Dublin?)

Heb = Hebrew sources for the text

KJV = *The Holy Bible, Conteyning the Old Testament, and the New: Newly Translated out of the Originall tongues: & with the former Translations diligently compared and reuised: by his Maiesties speciall Comandement Apppointed to be read in Churches* (London: Robert Barker, Printer to the Kings most Excellent Maiestie, 1611, rpr. Thomas Nelson Publishers, 1990)

KJVn = marginalia in KJV

PG = J.-P. Migne, ed., *Patrologiae Graecae* (Paris, 1857–1866)

PL = J.-P. Migne, ed., *Patrologia Latina* (Paris, 1844–1864)

Quentin = *Biblia sacra iuxta Vulgatam versionem* (Typis Polyglottis Vaticanis, 1926–[1995])

S = A. Rahlfs, ed., R. Hanhart, rev., *Septuaginta,* 2nd ed. (Deutsche Bibelgesellschaft, 2006)

S-C = *Biblia Sacra: Vulgatae Editionis Sixti V Pont. Max. iussu recognita et Clementis VIII auctoritate edita* (Vatican City: Marietti, 1959)

Sabatier: P. Sabatier, *Bibliorum Sacrorum Latinae versiones antiquae, seu Vetus Italica.* 3 vols. (Rheims: Apud Reginaldum Florentain, Regis Typographicum & Bibliopolam, sub signo Bibliorum aureorum, 1743–1749)

Smyth = H. W. Smyth, ed., G. M. Messing, rev., *Greek Grammar* (Cambridge, MA: Harvard University Press, 1956)

Weber = R. Weber, ed., *Biblia Sacra Vulgata,* 5th ed. (Deutsche Bibelgesellschaft, 2007); in the Psalms this siglum refers to Weber's Psalmi Iuxta LXX

Weber Iuxta Hebr. = Psalmi Iuxta Hebr. in R. Weber, ed., *Biblia Sacra Vulgata,* 5th ed. (Deutsche Bibelgesellschaft, 2007)

The use of sigla from Weber and Quentin's critical apparatus is indicated in brackets following the sigla; Weber's practice of adding a full stop after certain entries to indicate that a citation is limited to the sources referenced has not been followed.

Other abbreviations follow those found in H. J. Frede, *Kirchenschriftsteller: Verzeichnis und Sigel* (Freiburg: Verlag Herder, 1995), and R. Gryson, *Altlateinische Handschriften.* 2 vols. (Freiburg: Verlag Herder, 1999).

JOB

1:5	*per singulos: pro singulis* S-C
<1:5	*blessed* D-R: alternatively, *cursed*>
<1:9	*And* S?: *To whom* D-R>

1:11   *faciem*: *facie tua* Weber; *benedixerit tibi*: *benedixerit* *D-R

<1:11   *and see if . . . not* D-R/C: *vnlesse* D-R; *to thy face* KJV: *in the face* D-R>

<1:14   *and* KJV: *which* D-R>

1:18   *Adhuc loquebatur*: *loquebatur* Weber

<1:19   *fell upon* KJV: *falling oppressed* D-R>

1:20   *vestimenta sua*: *tunicam suam* Weber

1:21   *et Dominus* Gryson 132Z/160E/161Z (Caspari, *Das Buch Hiob*, p. 510), Frede AU Ps 32 en 2 s 2.12.36 (p. 263), AU s 15A.6 (p. 208.201), AU s 22A.2 (p. 304.54), CY mort 10 (Hartel 1868, p. 302.12), QU bar 2.10.10 (p. 483.34, sigla AV), PL 40.704, PL 51.750C: *Dominus* S-C, Weber; *abstulit; sicut Domino placuit ita factum est*: *abstulit* Weber

1:22   *Iob labiis suis*: *Iob* Weber

2:3   *ac timens*: *timens* Weber

<2:8   *took* KJV: *with* D-R; *and* D-R/C: omitted in D-R>

2:8   *deradebat*: *radebat* S-C

2:10   *stultis mulieribus*: *stultis* Weber; *Dei*: *Domini* Weber

2:12   *levassent*: *elevassent* S-C

3:4   *inlustretur*: *inlustret* Weber

3:24   *quasi*: *tamquam* S-C

4:2   *accipias*: *accipies* S-C; *possit*: *poterit* S-C

4:6   *Ubi est timor*: *timor* Weber

4:7   *periit*: *perierit* Weber; *sunt*: *sint* Weber

5:5   *ebibent*: *bibent* S-C

5:6   *orietur*: *oritur* S-C

<5:6   *doth* S-C: *shal* D-R>

5:15   *egenum a*: *a* Weber

5:17   *Deo*: *Domino* Weber

5:22   *bestias*: *bestiam* Weber

5:26   *tritici in*: *in* Weber

6:12   *aerea*: *aenea* S-C

6:25   *arguere me*: *arguere* Weber

<7:2   *as* D-R/C: *& as* D-R>

<7:4   *lie down to* KJV (without *to*): omitted in D-R>

7:4   *dicam*: *dico* Weber

<7:7   *but* D-R/C: *a* D-R>

<7:11   *I* KJV: *I also* D-R>

<7:14   *terrify me* KJV: *shake me with horrour* D-R>

<7:15   *so that* KJV: *For the which thing* D-R; *rather* D-R/C: omitted in D-R>

7:17   *quid: quia* Weber; *ponis: apponis* S-C

<7:17   *upon* KJV: *toward* D-R>

7:19   *parcis: parces* Weber

<7:19   *wilt* KJV: *doth* D-R>

7:21   *tollis: tolles* Weber; *aufers: auferes* Weber

8:2   *sermonis* VCΣDS [Weber's sigla]: *sermones* S-C, Weber

<8:2   *words of thy mouth be like a strong wind* KJV (*be like* in roman type in KJV): *spirit of the word of thy mouth be multiplied* D-R>

8:3   *aut: et* Weber

8:7   *ut si: ut* Weber; *novissima* PL 26.635D: *et novissima* S-C, Weber

8:11   *virere: vivere* Weber; *crescere: crescet* Weber

8:16   *ortu: horto* Weber; *egredietur: egreditur* Weber

9:11   *videbo eum: videbo* Weber; *intellegam: intellegam eum* Weber

9:12   *Cur ita: cur* Weber

<9:14   *what* D-R/C: *How great* D-R; *have words* D-R/C: *speake in my wordes* D-R>

9:14   *qui: ut* S-C

<9:16   *if* KJV: *when* D-R>

9:20   *ostendero: ostendere* Weber

9:24   *manus: manu* Weber

<9:24   *hand* KJV: *handes* D-R>

<9:27   *If* KJV: *When* D-R>

<9:30   *never so* KJV: *as most* D-R>

10:3   *me et: et* Weber

<10:4   *thou* KJV: *thou also* D-R>

10:11   *Ossibus: et ossibus* Weber

10:19   *non: qui non* Weber

<10:21   *no more* D-R/C: *not* D-R>

10:22   *sed: et* Weber; *inhabitat: inhabitans* Weber

11:6   *ab eo: a Deo* Weber

11:9   *terra: terrae* Weber

<11:14   *let* KJV: omitted in D-R>

11:15   *tum: tunc* S-C

<11:16 *only* D-R/C: omitted in D-R>

11:16 *praeterierint: praeterierunt* S-C

<12:3 *you* S?: *you, neither am I inferiour to you* D-R>

12:6 *manus: manibus* Weber

<12:7 *But ask now* KJV: *For aske* D-R>

<12:12 *length of days* KJV: *long time* D-R>

12:14 *Si incluserit: et si incluserit* Weber

12:21 *eos: et eos* Weber

12:23 *perdit: perdet* Weber; *restituit: restituet* Weber

13:1 *haec: et* Weber

13:6 *correptiones meas: correptionem meam* S-C

<13:6 *reproof* S-C: *correptions* D-R>

13:22 *Voca: et voca* Weber; *respondebo: ego respondebo* S-C

14:1 *repletur: repletus* Weber

14:2 *qui quasi: quasi* Weber

14:5 *et numerus* PL 51.709A: *numerus* S-C, Weber; *praeteriri: praeterire*
       Weber

14:13 *et abscondas: ut abscondas* Weber

14:14 *vivet: vivat* S-C

14:15 *Vocabis me: vocabis* Weber

14:16 *parces: parce* S-C

<14:16 *spare* S-C: *thou wilt spare* D-R>

14:18 *defluit: defluet* Weber

14:19 *homines: hominem* S-C

<14:19 *man* KJV: *and men* D-R [at beginning of clause]>

14:20 *pertransiret: transiret* S-C

15:3 *aequalis tibi: aequalis tui* Weber

<15:7 *or* KJV: *and* D-R>

15:13 *ore tuo: ore* Weber

15:16 *aquam: aquas* Weber

<15:17 *and* KJV: omitted in D-R>

15:19 *transivit: transibit* Weber

15:21 *ille semper: ille* Weber

15:22 *tenebris ad lucem: tenebris* Weber

15:31 *credet: credat* Weber

15:32 *arescent: arescet* Weber

<16:3 *no* S: *an* DR>

16:6   *labia mea*: *labia* Weber

16:8   *nihili*: *nihilum* S-C

16:11   *et exprobrantes*: *exprobrantes* Weber

<16:13   *so* D-R/C: omitted in D-R; *to be* D-R/C: *as it were* D-R>

16:13   *me sibi*: *sibi* Weber

16:16   *carnem meam*: *cornu meum* Weber

16:21   *amici*: *mei amici* Weber

17:3   *Libera me*: *Libera me, Domine* S-C; *pone me*: *pone* Weber

<17:3   *O Lord* S-C: omitted in D-R>

17:4   *et propterea*: *propterea* S-C

<17:4   *therefore* S-C: *and therfore* D-R>

17:7   *nihili*: *nihilum* S-C

<17:9   *he that hath clean hands shall be stronger and stronger* KJV: *with cleane handes shal adde strength* D-R>

17:13   *et in*: *in* Weber

<19:4   *if* D-R/C: *although* D-R>

19:24   *celte*: *certe* Weber

19:25   *vivat*: *vivit* S-C; *novissimo die*: *novissimo* Weber; *sim*: *sum* S-C

19:26   *Deum*: *Deum meum* S-C

<19:26   *my* S-C: omitted in D-R>

<20:2   *various . . . in me* D-R/C: *my diuerse* D-R>

<20:9   *eyes* D-R/C: *eye* D-R; *no more* KJV: *not* D-R>

20:16   *et occidet*: *occidet* Weber

20:20   *cupierat*: *concupierat* S-C

20:22   *super*: *in* Weber

<20:23   *God* KJV (in roman type in KJV and italics in D-R/C): *he* D-R>

21:2   *agite*: *agetis* Weber

21:3   *ut et*: *et* S-C

<21:3   *and I* S-C: *that I also* D-R>

21:10   *abortivit*: *abortit* Weber

<21:11   *and play* D-R/C: *with pastimes* D-R>

21:14   *scientiam* CΛ^LX$\Pi^F\Phi^P$HD$\Psi^D\Omega$ [Quentin's sigla]: *et scientiam* D-R>

21:15   *Quis*: *quid* Weber

<21:21   *what befalleth* D-R/C: *concerning* D-R>

21:30   *servatur*: *servabitur* Weber; *ducetur*: *ducitur* Weber

<22:7   *thou* D-R/C: *and . . . thou* D-R>

22:11   *oppressurum iri*: *oppressurum* Weber

22:12 *An non: an* Weber; *verticem: vertices* Weber

<22:13 *What* KJVn: *For what* D-R>

22:17 *posset: possit* Weber

22:29 *oculos suos: oculos* S-C

22:30 *autem in: autem* Weber

<23:2 more grievous than KJV (*heauier* for *more grievous*): *aggrauated vpon* D-R>

23:9 *agam: agat* Weber

23:13 *voluerit: voluit* S-C; *fecit: facit* Weber

23:14 *Cumque* S*Ware* [Quentin's sigla]: *Cum* S-C, Weber

24:5 *Vigilantes: vigilantesque* Weber

24:6 *oppresserunt: oppresserint* Weber

<24:8 who are wet with KJV: *Whom . . . doe wash* D-R>

24:13 *lumini: luminis* Weber

24:14 *interficit: inter fecit* Clementine edition of 1598

<24:20 no more KJV: *not* D-R>

24:21 *et quae: quae* S-C

<24:21 that S-C: *and her that* D-R>

<25:6 less KJV: *more* D-R>

26:2 *inbecilli: inbecillis* S-C

26:4 *spiramentum: spiramen tuum* Weber

26:6 *infernus: inferus* Weber

26:7 *nihilum: nihili* Weber

<26:8 and fall D-R/C: omitted in D-R>

27:10 *in omni: omni* S-C

27:19 *Aperiet: aperit* Weber

27:20 *Adprehendet: adprehendit* Weber

<27:22 willingly KJV? (*faine*): *fleing* D-R>

28:4 *hominis: hominum* Weber

28:7 *est eam: est* Weber

<28:17 crystal KJV: *glasse* D-R; any D-R/C: omitted in D-R>

28:19 *topazius: topazium* Weber

28:20 *venit: veniet* Weber

28:25 *in mensura: mensura* Weber

<28:25 by KJV: *in a* D-R>

29:12 *eo quod: quod* Weber

29:14 *vestivi: vestivit* Weber

<30:5   *and* D-R/C: omitted in D-R>

30:9   *eis: eis in* S-C

30:12   *calamitates: calamitatis* Weber

30:15   *nihili: nihilum* S-C

30:18   *succinxerunt: sic cinxerunt* Weber

30:23   *trades: tradas* Weber

30:28   *clamavi: clamabam* S-C

31:7   *si manibus: in manibus* Weber

31:10   *alterius: alteri* Weber

<31:13   *or* KJV: *and* D-R>

31:13   *ancilla mea: ancillae meae* Weber

<31:15   *that made* KJV: *make* D-R; *womb make* KJV: *wombe that made* D-R; *and the same* D-R/C: omitted in D-R>

31:15   *formavit me: formavit* Weber

31:27   *laetatum: lactatum* Weber

<31:30   *by wishing a curse to* KJV: *that cursing I wished* D-R>

32:4   *se essent: essent* S-C

32:6   *dimisso: demisso* S-C

32:10   *sapientiam: scientiam* Weber

32:15   *nec: non* Weber

<33:2   *now* KJV: omitted in D-R>

33:8   *verborum tuorum: verborum* Weber

33:9   *ego et: ego* Weber

33:16   *disciplina: disciplinam* Weber

<33:16   *what they are to learn* D-R/C: *discipline* D-R>

33:22   *Adpropinquavit: adpropinquabit* Weber

33:23   *unus: unum* Weber

33:24   *ut: et* Weber

<33:27   *what* D-R/C: *as* D-R>

<33:28   *that it may live and* D-R/C: *but liuing* D-R>

33:31   *loquar: loquor* S-C

<34:1   *And Elihu continued his discourse and said* D-R/C: *Eliu therfore pronouncing, spake these wordes also* D-R>

34:11   *restituet eis: restituet* Weber

34:17   *sanari: sanare* Weber

<34:22   *where* KJV: *that* D-R>

34:24   *multos et: multos* Weber

34:29 *gentes: gentem* Weber
<34:29 *whether it regard* KJV (*it be done* for *it regard*): *both vpon* D-R; *or* KJV:
        and vpon D-R>
<34:31 *of* D-R/C: *to* D-R; *in thy turn* D-R/C: *also* D-R>
34:31 *prohibebo: prohibeo* Weber
34:36 *ab homine: in hominibus* Weber
<35:1 *Moreover* KJV: *Therfore . . . againe* D-R>
<35:8 *may* [both times] KJV (in roman type); *shal* D-R>
<36:1 *proceeded and said* KJV: *adding speake these wordes* D-R>
36:7 *auferet: aufert* Weber
36:9 *fuerint: fuerunt* S-C
<36:16 *set thee at large* D-R/C: *saue thee most largely* D-R>
36:16 *habentis: habente* S-C
36:23 *quis potest: quis* Weber
<37:1 *attentiuely* KJV: *his speach in* D-R>
37:9 *egredietur: egreditur* Weber
<37:9 *north* KJV, D-Rn?: *Arcturus* D-R>
37:14 *miracula: mirabilia* S-C
37:21 *cogetur: cogitur* Weber
38:6 *demisit: dimisit* Weber
<38:10 *bars* KJV: *barre* D-R>
38:18 *latitudinem: latitudines* Weber
<38:24 *and* D-R/C (in italics): *is* D-R>
<38:25 *or* KJV: *and* D-R>
<38:34 *that* KJV: *&* D-R>
38:37 *enarrabit: enarravit* Weber
<38:37 *can* [both times] KJV: *shal* D-R; *or* KJV: *and* D-R>
<38:41 *food* S: *her meate* D-R>
39:4 *earum et: earum* Weber
39:12 *ei quoniam: illi quod* S-C
39:13 *strutionis: strutionum* Weber
39:14 *calefacies: calefacis* Weber
39:15 *bestia: bestiae* Weber; *conterat: conterant* Weber
39:18 *equum: equitem* Weber
<39:22 *turneth . . . his back* KJV: *yealdeth* D-R>
39:25 *dicit: dicet* Weber
<39:25 *Ha, ha* KJV: *Vah* D-R>

39:27 *Numquid: aut* Weber

40:6 *in furore: furore* Weber

40:11 *umbilico: umbilicis* Weber

40:12 *Constringit: Stringit* S-C

40:16 *in locis: locis* Weber

40:18 *et habet: habet* Weber

<40:20 *or* KJV: *and* D-R; *canst* D-R/C: *shalt* D-R>

<40:21 *Canst* KJV: *Shalt* D-R>

40:21 *aut: et* Weber

41:4 *revelabit: revelavit* Weber

<41:4 *can* [both times] KJV: *shal* Weber; *Or* KJV: *and* D-R>

<41:5 *can* KJV: *shal* D-R>

41:6 *conpactum: et conpactum* Weber

<41:7 *can come* KJV: *entereth* D-R>

41:8 *adherebit: adherebunt* Weber

<41:8 *They stick one* KJV: *One shal sticke* D-R>

41:13 *praecedit: praecedet* Weber

41:15 *quasi: tamquam* S-C

<41:19 *are to him like* S?: *to him are turned into* D-R>

41:21 *et sternet: sternet* Weber

41:22 *et ponet: ponet* Weber

42:4 *Interrogabo te: interrogabo* Weber; *responde: ostende* Weber

<42:10 *gave Job twice as much as he had before* KJV: *added al thinges whatsoeuer had bene Iobes, duble* D-R>

<42:11 *bemoaned* KJV: *wagged the head vpon* D-R>

41:11 *Deus* D* [Quentin's siglum]: *Dominus* S-C, Weber

<42:12 *latter end* KJV: *last daies* D-R>

42:14 *Cornustibii* PL 76.774B, Frede LATH 35 p. 362.159: *Cornu stibii* S-C, Weber

Psalms

<1:3 *running* D-R/C: *streames of* D-R>

1:5 *concilio: consilio* Weber

2:1 *Quare: psalmus david / Quare* Weber

2:2 *eius: eius / diapsalma* Weber

2:9   *ferrea et: ferrea* Weber

2:11   *cum: in* Weber

3:3   *eius: eius / diapsalma* Weber

3:5   *suo: suo / diapsalma* Weber

3:6   *et exsurrexi: exsurrexi* Weber; *suscepit: suscipiet* Weber

<4:2   *upon him* D-R/C: omitted in D-R>

4:3   *mendacium: mendacium / diapsalma* Weber

4:5   *conpungimini: conpungimini / diapsalma* Weber

4:6   *ostendit: ostendet* Weber

4:8   *et vini: vini* S-C

<4:8   *their* S-C: *and* D-R>

5:5   *Deus* *D-R: *deus* S-C, Weber

5:9   *tuo viam meam: meo viam tuam* Weber

<5:12   *But* KJV: *And* D-R>

5:13   *voluntatis tuae: voluntatis* Weber

6:4   *Sed: et* Weber

6:5   *et eripe: eripe* Weber

6:7   *lacrimis: in lacrimis* Weber

7:6   *deducat: deducat / diapsalma* Weber

7:7   *et exaltare: exaltare* Weber

7:10   *Consumetur: consummetur* Weber; *qui scrutaris* Frede A-SS Cetheus
         10 (185D); *scrutans* S-C, *et scrutans* Weber

<7:10   *The searcher . . . is* S-C (*is* in italics in D-R/C): *which searchest . . . ô*
         D-R>

7:11   *Domino: Deo* Weber

7:12   *fortis: et fortis* Weber

7:15   *concepit: et concepit* Weber

7:16   *incidit: incidet* Weber

8:3   *lactantium: lactentium* S-C

9:7   *civitates eorum: civitates* Weber

<9:8   *but* KJV: *and* D-R>

<9:12   *ways* S: *studies* D-R>

9:17   *Cognoscetur: cognoscitur* Weber; *peccator: peccator / canticum diapsal-*
         matis Weber

9:21   *ut sciant: sciant* Weber

<9:21   *but* KJV (in italics in D-R/C): omitted in D-R>

9:21   *Psalmus 10 secundum Hebraeos* (*sec.* for *secundum* S-C): *diapsalma* Weber

10:1–18   (*secundum Hebraeos* / *according to the Hebrews*) S-C, D-R: 9:22(1)– 39(18) Weber; these verses will be referenced here as 10.1:1–18, to distinguish them from the next Psalm, which will be referenced as 10:1–8

<10.1:6 *and shall be* KJV (in roman type in KJV and italics in D-R/C): omitted in D-R>

10.1:14   *eris*: *eras* Weber

<10:2   *Get thee away from hence to* D-R/C: *Passe ouer vnto* D-R>

10:2   *montem*: *montes* Weber

<11:2   *Truths* D-R/C: *because verities* D-R>

<11:3   *and with a double heart* KJV (*and* in roman type in KJV and italics in D-R/C): *in hart and hart* D-R>

11:4   *dolosa et*: *dolosa* Weber

<11:7   *purged* D-R/C: *tryed* D-R>

11:8   *et in*: *in* S-C

12:4   *et exaudi*: *exaudi* Weber

<12:5   *when* KJV: *if* D-R>

<13:1   *ways* S: *studies* D-R>

13:6   *Dominus in*: *Deus in* Weber

<13:6   *but* D-R/C: *because* D-R>

14:5   *innocentes*: *innocentem* S-C

15:2   *Deus*: *Dominus* Weber

15:3   *omnes*: *mihi omnes* Weber

<15:4   *for blood offerings* D-R/C (*offerings* is in KJV, italicized in D-R/C): *of bloud* D-R>

15:7   *increpaverunt*: *increpuerunt* S-C

15:10   *nec*: *non* Weber; *Delectationes*: *delectatio* Weber

<15:10   *Thou hast*: verse 11 starts here D-R/C, S-C>

<16:1   *which proceedeth not from* KJV (*that goeth not out of; which proceedeth* is in italics in D-R/C): *not in* D-R>

16:3   *meum et*: *meum* Weber

<16:7   *Shew forth thy wonderful mercies* KJV (*marueilous louing kindnesse* for *wonderful mercies*): *Make thy mercies meruelous* D-R>

16:8   *protege*: *proteges* Weber

16:9   *circumdederunt*: *circumdederunt super me* Weber

16:10 *superbiam: superbia* Weber

<16:10 *proudly* KJV: *pride* D-R>

<16:13 *Disappoint: preuent* D-R>

17:1 *qui: quae* Weber

<17:3 *my* D-R/C: *and my* D-R>

<17:6 *and* D-R/C: omitted in D-R>

17:7 *In tribulatione: cum tribularer* Weber; *et exaudivit: exaudivit* Weber; *introivit: introibit* Weber

17:8 *Commota: et commota* Weber; *fundamenta: et fundamenta* Weber

17:13 *nubes: nubes eius* Weber

17:15 *sagittas suas: sagittas* Weber; *Fulgora: et fulgora* Weber

17:17 *me et: me* Weber

17:18 *Eripuit: eripiet* Weber; *confirmati: confortati* S-C

17:20 *fecit: faciet* Weber

17.24 *me ab: ab* Weber

<17:28 *but* KJV: *and* D-R>

17:29 *inlumina: inluminas* Weber

17:31 *eum: se* S-C

17:32 *Deus* [both times]: *deus* Weber; *Aut: et* Weber

17:33 *praecinxit: praecingit* Weber

17:35 *docet: doces* Weber; *ad: in* Weber; *ut arcum: arcum* Weber

<17:38 *are consumed* KJV (*were* for *are*): *faile* D-R>

17:40 *bellum et: bellum* Weber

17:41 *disperdisti: disperdidisti* S-C

<17:42 *but* [both times] KJV: *neither* D-R>

17:44 *Eripies: eripe* Weber

<17:46 *faded away* KJV: *inueterated* D-R>

17:48 *das: dat* Weber; *subdis: subdidit* Weber; *inimicis meis: gentibus* Weber

<17:51 *giving great deliverance* KJV: *Magnifying the saluations* D-R>

18:6 *viam: viam suam* Weber

18:7 *caeli: caelo* S-C

<18:13 *O Lord* D-R/C: omitted in D-R>

19:4 *fiat: fiat / diapsalma* Weber

<19:10 continuation of verse 9 D-R/C, after KJV?>

20:3 *cordis: animae* Weber; *eum: eum / diapsalma* Weber

<20:3 *withholden from* KJV: *defrauded* Weber>

20:7   *benedictionem*: *in benedictionem* S-C
<20:10   *anger* KJV: *countenance* D-R>
20:13   *reliquis*: *reliquiis* Weber
21:1   *susceptione*: *adsumptione* Weber
<21:1   *protection* S: *enterprise* D-R>
21:2   *respice in*: *respice* Weber
21:4   *laus*: *Laus* Weber
21:8   *labiis et*: *labiis* Weber
21:15   *universa*: *omnia* S-C
21:16   *pulverem*: *limum* Weber
21:20   *tuum a me*: *tuum* Weber
21:21   *framea, Deus*: *framea* Weber
<21:21   *my* KJV: *and myne* D-R>
21:23   *media ecclesia*: *medio ecclesiae* S-C
21:24   *glorificate*: *magnificate* Weber
21:29   *Domini*: *Dei* Weber
21:32   *caeli iustitiam*: *iustitiam* Weber
22:1   *regit*: *reget* Weber
<22:2   *pasture* KJV: *pasture there* D-R>
22:6   *subsequetur*: *subsequitur* Weber
23:3   *ascendet*: *ascendit* Weber
23:5   *salvatore*: *salutari* S-C
23:6   *Iacob*: *Iacob / diapsalma* Weber
23:10   *Gloriae*: *gloriae / diapsalma* Weber
24:1   *In finem. Psalmus*: *psalmus* Weber
24:4   *doce*: *edoce* S-C
24:5   *veritate tua*: *veritatem tuam* Weber
24:6   *quae*: *quia* Weber
<24:6   *bowels* KJVn *of compassion* D-R/C: *commiserations* D-R; *the begin-ning of the world* D-R [for this translation, see the gloss at PL 113.877D: *Id est, ab initio saeculi sunt*]: literally, *everlasting*>
24:11   *propitiaberis*: *et propitiaberis* Weber
24:12   *statuit*: *statuet* Weber
25:1   *In finem. Psalmus*: *psalmus* Weber
25:9   *impiis, Deus*: *impiis* Weber
26:1   *Psalmus David*: *david* Weber
26:2   *inimici*: *et inimici* Weber

26:4 *omnes dies: omnibus diebus* S-C; *voluptatem: voluntatem* S C

26:5 *tabernaculo suo: tabernaculo* Weber

26:6 *iubilationis* L cum Ro [Quentin's sigla]: *vociferationis* S-C, Weber

26:7 *clamavi ad te: clamavi* Weber

26:8 *te facies: facies* Weber

<26:8 *still* D-R/C: omitted in D-R>

26:9 *salvator: salutaris* S-C

26:11 *semita recta: semitam rectam* S-C

27:1 *Psalmus ipsi: huic* Weber

<27:1 *if* KJV (in italics in D-R/C): *at any time* D-R; *I become* KJV: *and I shal be* D-R>

27:2 *Exaudi, Domine: exaudi* Weber

27:3 *trahas: tradas* Weber; *perdas: perdideris* Weber; *in: sunt in* Weber

<27:5 *the operations* KJV: *in the workes* D-R>

27:9 *Salvam fac plebem tuam, Domine: Salvum fac populum tuum, Domine* S-C, *salvam fac plebem tuam* Weber

28:9 *omnis dicet: omnes dicent* S-C

28:10 *Dominus virtutem:* verse 11 begins here S-C, Weber

29:8 *tuam a me: tuam* Weber

30:1 *David pro extasi: david* Weber

30:6 *commendo: commendabo* Weber

30:16 *de manibus* Sabatier: *de manu* S-C, Weber

30:21 *abdito: abscondito* S-C; *tabernaculo tuo: tabernaculo* Weber

<30:22 *shewn his wonderful mercy* KJV (*maruellous kindnesse* for *wonderful mercy*): *made his mercie merueilous* D-R>

30:24 *veritatem requiret: veritates requirit* Weber; *retribuet: retribuit* Weber

31:1 *Ipsi: huic* Weber

31:2 *inputavit: inputabit* Weber

31:4 *spina: mihi spina / diapsalma* Weber

31:5 *mei: mei / diapsalma* Weber

31:7 *circumdantibus me: circumdantibus me / diapsalma* Weber

32:1 *laudatio: collaudatio* S-C

<32:2 *the instrument* KJV: omitted in D-R>

32:3 *ei in: in* Weber

<32:16 *great army* KJV (*multitude of an hoste*): *much powre* D-R; *his own great strength* KJV: *the multitude of his strength* D-R>

32:18 *eum et in eis: eum* Weber

33:1   *Abimelech*: *Achimelech* S-C

<33:1   *Ahimelech* S-C: *Abimelech* D-R; *who* KJV: *and he* D-R>

33:8   *Inmittet*: *vallabit* Weber

<33:8   *encamp* KJV: *put in him selfe* D-R>

33:13   *diligit*: *cupit* Weber

33:15   *Deverte*: *diverte* Weber

33:16   *preces*: *precem* Weber

33:17   *facies autem*: *Vultus autem* S-C, *facies* Weber

33:18   *eos et*: *et* Weber

<33:20   *but* KJV: *and* D-R>

33:20   *liberabit eos Dominus*: *liberavit eos* Weber

34:1   *Ipsi*: *huic* Weber; *inpugnantes*: *expugnantes* Weber

34:8   *conprehendat*: *adprehendat* S-C; *laqueum cadat in ipsum*: *laqueo cadat in ipso* Weber

34:9   *Domino et*: *Domino* Weber

34:10   *tibi*: *tui* Weber

<34:12   *to the depriving me* KJVn (without *me*): *sterilitie* D-R>

34:13   *sinum meum*: *sinu meo* S-C

<34:14   *an own* D-R/C: *our* D-R>

<34:15   *But* KJV: *And* D-R>

<34:17   *upon me* D-R/C: omitted in D-R>

<35:1   *God* D-R/C: *our Lord* D-R>

35:1   *ipsi David*: *david* Weber

35:9   *voluptatis*: *voluntatis* Weber

35:10   *et in*: *in* Weber

36:1   *Psalmus ipsi*: *psalmus* Weber

<36:2   *green* KJV: *blossomes of* D-R>

<36:5   *Commit* KJV: *Reuele* D-R>

<36:10   *for* KJV: *And* D-R>

36:13   *quia prospicit quoniam*: *quoniam prospicit quod* S-C

36:14   *decipiant*: *deiciant* S-C

<36:14   *cast down* S-C: *deceiue* D-R>

36:20   *mox ut*: *mox* Weber; *deficient*: *defecerunt* Weber

36:25   *etenim*: *et* Weber; *panes*: *panem* S-C

36:38   *peribunt*: *interibunt* S-C

<37:3   *thy hand hath been strong* D-R/C: *thou hast fastened thy hand* D-R>

37:4   *in carne mea*: *carni meae* Weber

<37:4   *because* [both times] KJV: *at the face of* D-R>

37:5   *meum et: meum* Weber

<37:6   *because* D-R: literally, *at the presence of*>

37:7   *ad: in* S-C

<37:11   *itself* D-R/C: *and the same* D-R>

37:16   *exaudies me: exaudies* Weber

37:20   *vivunt et confirmati: vivent et firmati* Weber

37:22   *Non: Ne* S-C

37:23   *Domine, Deus: Domine* Weber

38:1   *Ipsi Idithun: idithun* Weber

38:6   *vivens: vivens / diapsalma* Weber

<38:12   *Thou hast:* verse begins here D-R/C, after KJV; *any* D-R/C: *euerie*
          D-R>

38:12   *homo: homo / diapsalma* Weber

38:13   *sum: ego sum* S-C

39:1   *Ipsi David: david* Weber

<39:7   *pierced* D-R/C: *perfited* [i.e., *perfected*] D-R>

39:10   *tuam in: in* Weber

<39:12   *tender mercies* KJV: *commiserations* D-R>

<39:17   *such as* KJV: *them that* D-R>

40:1   *ipsi David: david* Weber

40:7   *vana: vane* Weber; *in:* verse 8 begins here S-C, Weber

40:14   *et: et usque* S-C

41:1   *Intellectus: in intellectum* Weber

41:3   *parebo: apparebo* S-C

41:4   *panes: panis* Weber

41:5   *locum: loco* Weber

41:6   *quoniam adhuc: quoniam* Weber

41:7   *et Deus: Deus* Weber

41:8   *abyssum: ad abyssum* Weber

41:10   *Et quare: quare* Weber

41:11   *me inimici mei: me* Weber

41:12   *Deum: Deo* Weber

42:2   *Et quare: quare* Weber

42:5   *Quare:* verse 5 begins here S-C, Weber

42:6   no new verse number S-C, Weber

43:2   *et in: in* Weber

43:3   *disperdit*: *disperdidit* S-C

43:4   *faciei tuae*: *vultus tui* S-C

<43:6   **push down** KJV: *turne out* D-R, with note *As an oxe vvith his horne casteth a smal thing into the vvind*>

<43:8   *but* KJV: *for* D-R>

43:9   *saeculum*: *saeculum / diapsalma* Weber

43:10   *egredieris, Deus*: *egredieris* Weber

<43:11   **made us turn our back to** KJV (without *our* or *to*): *turned vs backe behind* D-R>

<43:13   **reckoning** D-R/C: *multitude* D-R; **exchange** D-R/C: *exchanges* D-R>

43:13   *eorum*: *nostris* Weber

<43:19   **neither** D-Rn: *and* D-R>

43:22   *omni*: *tota* S-C

43:23   *dormis*: *obdormis* S-C

<43:24   *and* KJV (in roman type in KJV): omitted in D-R>

43:26   *Exurge, Domine*: *exurge* Weber

44:5   *intende*: *et intende* Weber

44:6   *corda*: *corde* Weber

<44:9   **stacte** S: *Aloes* [i.e., *resin*] D-R; **perfume** D-R/C: *from* D-R>

44:12   *Dominus, Deus*: *dominus* Weber

44:13   *omnes divites*: *divites* Weber

<44:13   *yea* KJV (*euen*; in italics in D-R/C): omitted in D-R>

44:18   *Memores erunt*: *memor ero* Weber

45:1   *Filiis*: *pro filiis* Weber; *arcanis* PL 53.389A: *arcanis*. *Psalmus* S-C, Weber [without punctuation or capitalization]

45:4   *Sonaverunt*: *Sonuerunt* S-C; *eius*: *eius / diapsalma* Weber

45:7   *et inclinata*: *inclinata* Weber

45:8   *Iacob*: *Iacob / diapsalma* Weber

45:10   *igni*: *in igne* Weber

45:11   *et exaltabor*: *exaltabor* Weber

46:1   *Core* *D-R: *Core*. *Psalmus* S-C, Weber [without punctuation or capitalization]

46:5   *dilexit*: *dilexit / diapsalma* Weber

46:6   *et Dominus*: *Dominus* Weber

46:9   *Regnabit*: *regnavit* Weber; *sedet*: *sedit* Weber

46:10   *dii*: *Dei* Weber

47:1   *Psalmus cantici*: *canticum psalmi* Weber

47:3   *Mons: montes* Weber

47:4   *cognoscetur: cognoscitur* Weber

47:5   *reges terrae: reges* Weber

47:9   *aeternum: aeternum / diapsalma* Weber

47:12   *et exultent: exultent* Weber; *Iudae: Iudaeae* Weber

48:3   *simul in: in* Weber

<48:8   *can* KJV: *doth* D-R; *nor* KJV: omitted in D-R>

48:9   *laborabit: laboravit* Weber

48:14   *conplacebunt: conplacebunt / diapsalma* Weber

48:15   *veterescet: veterascet* S-C

48:16   *me: me / diapsalma* Weber

48:18   *eo: eo pone* Weber

<48:19   *and* KJV: omitted in D-R>

48:20   *et usque: usque* Weber

<49:1   *thereof* KJV: omitted in D-R>

<49:3   *shall come* D-R/C (in italics): omitted in D-R>

49:6   *est: est / diapsalma* Weber

49:7   *loquar: loquar tibi* Weber

49:15   *eruam: et eruam* Weber; *honorificabis me: honorificabis me / diapsalma* Weber

<49:17   *seeing* KJV: *but* D-R>

<49:18   *hast been a partaker* KJV: *didst put thy portion* D-R>

<49:21   *but* KJV (in roman type in KJV and italics in D-R/C): omitted in D-R>

49:22   *haec: nunc haec* Weber

49:23   *quo: quod* Weber

50:2   *quando cum Bethsabee peccavit* Frede PROL Ps Inq 78.22 [without capitalization]: *quando intravit ad Bethsabee* S-C, Weber [without capitalization]

<50:3   *tender* KJV: omitted in D-R>

50:10   *et exaltabunt: exaltabunt* Weber

<50:14   *perfect* D-R/C: *principal* D-R>

50:16   *et exultabit: exultabit* Weber

50:19   *despicies: spernet* Weber

50:20   *ut: et* Weber

51:2   *adnuntiavit: nuntiavit* S-C; *Saul: saul et dixit* Weber; *domum: domo* Weber

51:3   *gloriaris*: *gloriatur* Weber; *es*: *es in* S-C, *est* Weber

<51:5   *and* KJV (in roman type in KJV and italics in D-R/C): omitted in D-R>

51:5   *aequitatem*: *aequitatem / diapsalma* Weber

51:6   *linguam dolosam*: *lingua dolosa* S-C

<51:6   *O* S-C: omitted in D-R>

51:7   *tuo et*: *et* Weber; *viventium*: *viventium / diapsalma* Weber

52:1   *Maeleth*: *melech* Weber

52:3   *super*: *in* Weber

<52:5   *they eat* KJV: *food of* D-R>

52:6   *trepidaverunt*: *trepidabunt* Weber; *fuit*: *erat* S-C

52:7   *Cum converterit*: *dum convertit* Weber

53:5   *oculos suos* A. M. Amelli. 1912. *Liber Psalmorum iuxta Antiquissimam Latinam Versionem: Nunc ex Casiensi Cod. 557.* Fredricus Pustet: Rome, p. 38, Frede AR Ps 53 p. 76.2–15, PL 53.400B, PL 70.383B: *conspectum suum* S-C, *conspectum suum / diapsalma* Weber; *et non*: *non* Weber

53:6   *et Dominus*: *Dominus* Weber

53:7   *Averte*: *avertet* Weber; *et in*: *in* Weber

53:8   *tibi et*: *tibi* Weber

<53:8   *God* D-R/C: *Lord* D-R>

54:4   *iniquitates*: *iniquitatem* Weber

54:6   *venerunt*: *venit* Weber; *contexit me tenebra*: *contexerunt me tenebrae* S-C

54:8   *solitudine*: *solitudine / diapsalma* Weber

54:9   *et*: *et a* Weber

54:10   *et divide* Q*l cum Ro [Quentin's sigla]: *divide* S-C, Weber

54:11   *iniquitas*: *et iniquitas* Weber

54:13   *inimicus meus*: *inimicus* Weber

<54:20 *the Eternal* D-Rn (*Eternal God*): *he which is before the worldes* D-R>

54:20   *saecula*: *saecula / diapsalma* Weber

54:24   *doli*: *dolosi* Weber

<55:1   *removed at a distance from the sanctuary* D-R/C: *made far from the Sainctes* D-R; *or pillar* D-R/C (in italics): omitted in D-R>

55:6   *cogitationes*: *consilia* Weber

<55:8   *thy* KJV (in roman type in KJV): omitted in D-R>

<55:13 my KJV?: and my D-R>
<56:1 from KJV: from the face of D-R>
56:1 speluncam: spelunca Weber
56:4 conculcantes me: conculcantes me / diapsalma Weber
<56:5 whose KJV: their D-R>
<56:6 above all KJV: vpon al D-R>
56:7 eam: eam / diapsalma Weber
56:10 et psalmum: psalmum Weber
<56:10 I KJV: and I D-R>
57:3 iniustitiam: iniustitias S-C
<57:5 that KJV (in roman type in KJV): and D-R>
<57:9 shall not see KJV?: haue not seene D-R>
<57:10 could know KJV (can feel): did vnderstand D-R>
57:10 sic: sicut Weber; eos: vos Weber
58:2 Deus meus: Deus Weber; protege Weber Iuxta Hebr.. libera S-C, Weber
<58:5 my steps D-R/C (in italics): omitted in D-R>
58:6 iniquitatem: iniquitatem / diapsalma Weber
<58:8 say they KJV (in roman type in KJV and italics in D-R/C): omitted in D-R; us D-R/C (in italics): omitted in D-R>
<58:9 But KJV: And D-R>
58:10 tu susceptor meus es PL 53.406C, I. Hilberg. 1912. Sancti Eusebii Hieronymi Epistulae. 2nd ed. vol. 2. Vienna: 1996. 106.33.14–15 (susceptor meus es tu): Deus susceptor meus es S-C, Weber (without es)
58:11 misericordia tua PL 53.406C, Frede AU Ps 58 s 1.19.1 p. 743 siglum κ (i.e. Sinai, S. Catharina), ORA Ps H 58 p. 135: misericordia eius S-C, voluntas eius Weber
<58:11 his S-C: thy D-R>
<58:13 for KJV (in roman type in KJV and italics in D-R/C): omitted in D-R; and KJV (in roman type in KJV): omitted in D-R>
58:14 dominabitur Iacob et: dominatur Iacob Weber; terrae: terrae / diapsalma Weber
<58:16 murmur KJV (grudge): murmur also D-R>
59:1 Pro his: his Weber; ipsi David: david Weber
59:2 Mesopotamiam Syriae: syriam mesopotamiam Weber; Sobal: syriam soba Weber; Idumaeam in Valle: vallem Weber

59:4   *turbasti*: *conturbasti* Weber

59:6   *arcus*: *arcus / diapsalma* Weber

59:13   *quia*: *et* Weber

60:5   *tuarum*: *tuarum / diapsalma* Weber

<60:7   *generation* KJVn: *the day of generation* D-R>

<61:4   *you were thrusting down* D-R/C (in italics): *vpon* D-R; *tottering* KJV: *shaken* D-R>

<61:5   *but* KJV: *and* D-R>

61:5   *maledicebant*: *maledicebant / diapsalma* Weber

62:1   *Iudaeae*: *Idumeae* S-C

<62:1   *Edom* S-C: *Iuda* D-R>

<62:5   *all my life long* D-R/C (*all* in italics): *in my life* D-R>

62:5   *et in*: *in* Weber

62:6   *labiis*: *labia* Weber

62:7   *meditabor*: *meditabar* Weber

62:12   *Laudabitur omnis*: *laudabuntur omnes* S-C; *iurat*: *iurant* S-C

<62:12 *they* S-C: omitted in D-R>

<63:2   *to thee* D-R/C: omitted in D-R>

<63:5   *are resolute in wickedness* D-R/C: *haue confirmed to themselues a wicked worde* D-R>

63:7   *ad*: *et* Weber

64:1   *Ezechielis populo transmigrationis*: *aggei de verbo peregrinationis* Weber; *quando incipiebant proficisci*: *cum inciperent exire* S-C

64:3   *orationem meam*: *orationem* Weber

<64:5   *to thee* KJV (in roman type): omitted in D-R>

64:9   *inhabitant*: *habitant* S-C

<64:9   *uttermost* KJV: omitted in D-R>

65:4   *adoret*: *adorent* Weber; *psallat*: *psallant* Weber; *dicat*: *dicant* Weber; *tuo*: *tuo / diapsalma* Weber

65:7   *ipsis*: *ipsis / diapsalma* Weber

65:15   *incensu*: *incenso* S-C; *hircis*: *hircis / diapsalma* Weber

<65:16 *and* KJV (in roman type): omitted in D-R>

65:18   *exaudiet*: *exaudiat* Weber

65:19   *Deus et*: *Deus* Weber

66:1   *cantici David*: *cantici* Weber

66:2   *et misereatur nostri*: *et misereatur nostri / diapsalma* Weber

66:5   *dirigis: diriges / diapsalma* Weber

67:1   *Ipsi David: david* Weber

67:4   *et exultent: exultent* Weber; *Dei et: Dei* Weber

67:5   *Exultate: et exultate* Weber

<67:5   *But the wicked* D-R/C (in italics): *they* D-R>

67:8   *pertransieris: pertransires* S-C; *deserto: deserto / diapsalma* Weber

67:9   *Sina* Sabatier: *Sinai* S-C, Weber

67:11 *habitabunt: habitant* Weber

<67:13 *the beauty of the house shall divide* D-R/C: *to the beautie of the house, to diuide* D-R, literally, *for the beauty of the house divides*>

67:15 *caelestis: Caelestis* Weber

<67:18 *attended by ten thousands* D-R/C: *ten thousand folde* D-R>

<67:19 *for those also that do not believe, the dwelling of the Lord God* D-R/C: *for euen those that doe not belieue, our Lord God to inhabite* D-R, literally *even those not believing that the Lord God dwells*>

67:19 *Dominum Deum: Dominum / Deus* Weber

67:20 *nostrorum: nostrorum / diapsalma* Weber

67:23 *profundum: profundis* Weber

67:25 *tui: tuos* S-C

67:27 *Deum, Dominum: Deo* ¶ *Domino* S-C

67:29 *virtutem tuam: virtuti tuae* S-C; *es in: es* Weber

67:30 *adferent: offerent* Weber

<67:32 *soon* KJV: omitted in D-R>

67:33 *Domino: Domino / diapsalma* Weber

<67:36 *is he who* KJV (*is* in roman type): *he* D-R>

<68:3   *sure standing* D-R: literally, *substance*>

68:3   *altitudinem: altitudines* Weber

68:13 *loquebantur: exercebantur* Weber

68:15 *libera me: liberer* Weber

<68:17 *tender* KJV: omitted in D-R>

68:17 *ad me* Weber Iuxta Hebr.: *in me* S-C, *me* Weber

68:20 *meam et: meam* Weber

<68:21 *looked for* KJV (*for* in roman type in KJV): *expected* D-R; *but* KJV: *and* D-R>

68:28 *iustitiam tuam: iustitia tua* Weber

68:31 *cantico, et: cantico* Weber

68:36   *Iuda: Iudaeae* Weber

68:37   *possidebit: possidebunt* Weber

69:1   *Psalmus David: david* Weber; *quod: eo quod* Weber; *fecit: fecerit* S-C,
        me fecit Weber

69:5   *Dominus: Deus* Weber

<69:5   *such as* KJV: *them . . . which* D-R>

70:4   *et de: de* Weber

<70:6   *Of thee shall I continually sing* D-R/C: *In thee is my singing alwaies*
        D-R>

<70:7   *but* KJV: *and* D-R>

70:9   *Non: ne* S-C; *deficiet: defecerit* S-C

<70:10   *against* KJV: *to* D-R>

70:12   *adiutorium: auxilium* Weber

<70:12   *make haste* KJV: *haue respect to* D-R>

70:15   *salutem tuam: salutare tuum* S-C

70:16   *potentias: potentiam* Weber

70:17   *ex: a* S-C

70:22   *sanctus: Sanctus* Weber

71:1   *In: Psalmus in* S-C

<71:1   *A psalm* S-C: omitted in D-R>

71:5   *in generatione et generationem: generationes generationum* Weber

71:11   *reges terrae: reges* Weber

71:12   *liberabit: liberavit* Weber

<71:15   *for* D-R/C: *and* D-R>

71:15   *orabunt: adorabunt* S-C

71:16   *Et erit: erit* Weber

71:17   *magnificabunt: beatificabunt* Weber

71:18   *Dominus: Dominus Deus* Weber

<72:4   *stripes* D-R/C: *plague* D-R>

<72:5   *like other* KJV (*other* in roman type in KJV and italics in D-R/C):
        with D-R>

72:7   *Prodiit: prodiet* Weber

72:8   *nequitiam: in nequitia* Weber

<72:13   *in vain* KJV: *without cause* D-R>

72:14   *matutinis: matutino* Weber

<72:15   *generation* KJV: *nation* D-R>

72:16 *Existimabam ut cognoscerem: et existimabam cognoscere* Weber
72:17 *Dei et: Dei* Weber
<72:25 *do I desire* D-R/C; *would I* D-R>
<72:26 *For thee* D-R/C (in italics): omitted in D-R>
72:27 *omnem qui fornicatur: omnes qui fornicantur* S-C
<72:27 *them* S-C: omitted in D-R>
<73:2 *which* KJV (in roman type in KJV and italics in D-R/C): omitted in D-R>
<73:3 *see what* D-R/C (*see* in italics): *how great* D-R>
<73:5 *both* D-R/C: *as* D-R; *and* D-R/C: omitted in D-R>
<73:6 *at once* KJV: *together* D-R>
73:12 *saecula: saeculum* Weber; *salutem: salutes* Weber
73:15 *fontes: fontem* Weber
<73:17 *were formed by thee* D-R/C: *thou hast formed them* D-R>
73:19 *animas confitentes tibi, et: animam confitentem tibi* Weber
73:22 *quae: qui* Weber
<73:22 *thy* S: *those thy* D-R; *with which* D-R/C *the foolish man hath reproached thee* KJV: *that are from the foolish man* D-R>
74:4 *eius: eius / diapsalma* Weber
74:5 *facere: agere* Weber
74:9 *verumtamen: verum* Weber
<74:11 *but* KJV (in roman type): *and* D-R>
75:1 *Assyrios: assyrium* Weber
75:4 *gladium: et gladium* Weber; *bellum: bellum / diapsalma* Weber
75:5 *Inluminas: Illuminans* S-C; *de: a* S-C
75:6 *manibus: in manibus* S-C
75:9 *tremuit: timuit* Weber
75:10 *terrae: terrae / diapsalma* Weber
75:12 *adfertis: adferent* Weber
75:13 *spiritum: spiritus* Weber
76:2 *mihi: me* Weber
<76:2 *gave ear* KJV: *attended* D-R>
<76:3 *lifted up to* D-R/C (*lifted up* in italics): *before* D-R>
76:4 *et exercitatus: exercitatus* Weber; *meus: meus / diapsalma* Weber
76:7 *et exercitabar: exercitabar* Weber; *scobebam: scopabam* *D-R
76:8 *Aut: et* Weber

76:9   *abscidet*: *abscindet* S-C

76:10 *suas*: *suas / diapsalma* Weber

76:14 *Quis Deus*: *quis deus* Weber

76:16 *Ioseph*: *Ioseph / diapsalma* Weber

77:1   *populus*: *popule* S-C

77:2   *parabolis*: *parabola* Weber; *eloquar*: *loquar* S-C

77:7   *opera*: *operum* S-C

77:8   *non est* Frede AU Ps 77.8.39 p. 1073: *et non est* S-C, Weber

<77:8   and *whose* KJV: *their* D-R>

77:9   *arcum*: *arcus* Weber

77:12 *eorum*: *eorum quae* Weber

77:13 *et statuit*: *statuit* Weber; *in utre*: *utrem* Weber

<77:16 *He* KJV: *And he* D-R>

77:17 *iram*: *ira* Weber

77:20 *potest*: *poterit* S-C

<77:21 *was angry* KJV (*wroth* for *angry*): *made delay* D-R>

<77:23–24 *had* [first three times] KJV: omitted in D-R; *had given* KJV: *gaue*
           D-R>

<77:29 *So* KJV: *And* D-R>

77:31 *super*: *in* Weber

77:32 *mirabilibus*: *in mirabilibus* S-C

<77:32 *for* KJV: *in* D-R>

77:34 *ad eum*: *ad Deum* Weber

77:38 *perdet*: *disperdet* S-C; *abundavit ut averteret*: *abundabit ut avertat*
        Weber; *accendit*: *accendet* Weber

<77:40 *and* KJV: omitted in D-R>

77:40 *iram*: *ira* Weber

77:41 *sanctum*: *Sanctum* Weber

<77:43 *how* KJV: *As* D-R>

77:45 *coenomyiam*: *cynomiam* Weber

<77:45 *divers sorts of flies which* KJV: *a swarme of flies, and it* D-R; *frogs which*
         KJV: *the frogge, and it* D-R>

77:47 *vineas*: *vineam* Weber

<77:49 *And* D-R/C: omitted in D-R>

77:49 *inmissiones*: *inmissionem* Weber

77:50 *animabus*: *animarum* Weber

77:51 *primogenitum*: *primitivum* Weber; *omnis laboris*: *laborum* Weber

<77:56 *Yet* KJV: *And* D-R>

77:58 *In iram*: *et in ira* Weber

<77:59 *as it were* D-R/C (in italics): omitted in D-R>

77:64 *plorabantur*: *plorabuntur* Weber

<77:64 *did not mourn* KJV (*made no lamentation*): *were not wept for* D-R>

<77:65 *and* KJV (in roman type): omitted in D-R>

77:68 *sed*: *et* Weber

<77:70 *following the ewes great with young* KJV: *after the ewes with yong* D-R, literally *ewes* would be omitted>

78:3 *ipsorum*: *eorum* S-C

78:4 *circum nos*: *in circuitu nostro* S-C

78:9 *et propter*: *propter* Weber

<78:10 *say* KJV: *say perhaps* D-R; *let him* KJV: omitted in D-R; *by the revenging* KJV (*by* in roman type in KJV and italics in D-R/C): *the reuenge of* D-R>

<78:12 *the* D-R/C: *their* D-R>

79:2 *tamquam*: *velut* S-C; *ovem*: *oves* Weber

79:3 *Beniamin*: *et Beniamin* Weber

79:10 *plantasti*: *et plantasti* Weber

79:12 *flumen*: *Flumen* Weber

<79:13 *so that* KJV: *and* D-R>

<79:16 *the same* D-R/C: *it* D-R>

79:16 *filium hominis*: *filium* Weber

80:1 *Psalmus ipsi Asaph*: *asaph* Weber

80:4 *vestrae*: *nostrae* Weber

80:5 *in Israhel*: *Israhel* Weber; *Deo*: *Dei* Weber

80:7 *Devertit*: *Divertit* S-C

<80:7 *had* D-R/C: omitted in D-R>

<80:8 *Waters* KJV: *water* D-R>

80:8 *Contradictionis*: *Contradictionis / diapsalma* Weber

80:9 *audieris*: *audias* Weber

<80:12 *But* KJV: *And* D-R>

<80:13 *So* KJV: *And* D-R>

<80:15 *soon* KJV *for nothing, perhaps* D-R>

80:16 *saeculo*: *saecula* S-C

81:1 *deos*: *Deus* Weber; *deiudicat*: *diiudicat* S-C

<81:2 *unjustly* KJV: *iniquitie* D-R>

81:2   *sumitis: sumitis / diapsalma* Weber

81:3   *egeno et pupillo: egenum et pupillum* Weber

82:3   *sonaverunt: sonuerunt* S-C

<82:5   *so that they be not a* KJV *(from being a): out of the* Weber>

<82:8   *Philistines* D-Rn: *foreners* D-R>

<82:9   *joined* KJV: *come* D-R>

82:9   *Loth: Loth / diapsalma* Weber

<82:11   *who* KJV *(which;* italicized in D-R/C): *they* D-R; *and* D-R/C: *they*
         D-R>

82:14   *et sicut: sicut* Weber

82:15   *et sicut: sicut* Weber

83:3   *deficit: defecit* Weber; *exultavit: exultaverunt* S-C

83:5   *tua, Domine: tua* Weber; *te: te / diapsalma* Weber

83:6   *cuius: cui* Weber

<83:6   *to ascend by steps* D-Rn: *ascension* D-R>

83:8   *benedictionem: benedictiones* Weber; *legis dator: legislator* S-C

83:9   *Iacob: Iacob / diapsalma* Weber

83:13   *vir: homo* S-C

84:3   *iniquitatem: iniquitates* Weber; *eorum: eorum / diapsalma* Weber

84:5   *salutaris noster: salutum nostrarum* Weber

85:3   *clamavi: clamabo* Weber

85:6   *deprecationis: orationis* Weber

<85:14   *before their eyes* D-R/C: *in their sight* D-R>

85:17   *bono: bonum* S-C, *Deum* *D-R

<85:17   *Shew me a token for good* KJV: *Make with me a signe vnto God* D-R>

86:3   *Dei: Dei / diapsalma* Weber

86:4   *scientium: scientibus* Weber

86:6   *scripturis: scriptura* Weber; *ea: ea / diapsalma* Weber

87:2   *in die: die* Weber

87:4   *inferno: in inferno* Weber

87:8   *super me: super me / diapsalma* Weber

87:11   *tibi: tibi / diapsalma* Weber

<87:14   *But* KJV: *And* D-R>

87:18   *Circuierunt: Circumdederunt* S-C

<88:5   *settle* KJV *(stablish): prepare* D-R>

88:5   *tuam: tuam / diapsalma* Weber

<88:7 *can be compared* KJV: *shal be equal* D-R; *or* D-R/C *who* KJV (in roman type): omitted in D-R>

88:7 *Domino: Deo* Weber

88:8 *terribilis: horrendus* Weber

88:10 *potestatis: potestati* S-C

88:20 *et exaltavi: exaltavi* Weber

88:21 *oleo: in oleo* Weber; *linui: unxi* S-C

88:22 *confirmabit: confortabit* S-C

<88:23 *have power* D-R/C: *adde* D-R>

88:23 *eum· ei* S-C.

88:31 *Si autem: si* Weber

88:34 *auferam* Weber Iuxta Hebr.: *dispergam* S-C, Weber

<88:34 *suffer my truth to fail* KJV: *hurt in my truth* D-R>

<88:36 *I will not lie* D-Rn: *if I lie* D-R>

88:38 *fidelis: fidelis / diapsalma* Weber

<88:39 *been angry with* KJV (*wroth* for *angry*): *differed* D-R>

88:41 *firmamentum: firmamenta* Weber

88:45 *ab emundatione, et: a mundatione* Weber

<88:45 *made his purification to cease* KJV (*glory* for *purification*): *destroied him from emundation* D-R>

88:46 *confusione: confusione / diapsalma* Weber

88:49 *inferi: inferi / diapsalma* Weber

89:1 *a: in* Weber; *in generationem: et generatione* Weber

89:2 *aut: et* Weber; *usque: et usque* S-C

<89:2 *and* S-C: *euen* D-R>

<89:8 *before* KJV *thy eyes* D-R/C: *in thy sight* D-R; *life* D-R/C: *age* D-R>

89:9 *et in: in* Weber; *meditabuntur: meditabantur* Weber

89:12 *eruditos: conpeditos* Weber

89:13 *deprecare* Sabatier: *deprecabilis* S-C, Weber

89:14 *omnibus: in omnibus* Weber

89:16 *Respice: et respice* Weber

<90:1 *Jacob* D-R/C: *heauen* D-R>

90:3 *liberavit: liberabit* Weber

90:4 *In scapulis: scapulis* S-C; *te: tibi* S-C

90:10 *accedet: accedent* Weber; *malum: mala* Weber

90:11 *mandavit: mandabit* Weber

<90:12 *lest* KJV: *lest perhaps* D-R>

90:14 *speravit*: *speravit et* Weber

90:15 *glorificabo*: *clarificabo* Weber

<91:11 *But* KJV: *And* D-R>

91:12 *inimicis meis, et*: *inimicos meos, et in* S-C

<91:12 *of the downfall* D-R/C (in italics): omitted in D-R>

91:13 *ut cedrus*: *sicut cedrus* S-C

<91:13 *grow up* KJV: *be multiplied* D-R>

91:14 *domus Dei*: *Dei* Weber

92:1 *cantici ipsi*: *cantici* Weber; *fundata*: *inhabitata* Weber; *Decorem*: *decore*
Weber; *fortitudinem*: *fortitudine* Weber

<92:1 *in the way* D-R/C (in italics): omitted in D-R>

92:3 *elevaverunt* [third time]: *elevabunt* Weber

93:1 *ipsi David*: *david* Weber

<93:1 *to whom revenge belongeth* KJV (*vengeance* for *revenge*): *of reuenges*
D-R>

93:8 *insipientes*: *qui insipientes estis* Weber

93:15 *corde*: *corde / diapsalma* Weber

93:17 *habitasset*: *habitavit* Weber

93:20 *adherit*: *aderit* Weber; *laborem*: *dolorem* Weber

<93:22 *But* KJV: *And* D-R>

93:22 *adiutorium*: *adiutorem* Weber

94:1 *cantici ipsi*: *cantici* Weber

94:4 *fines*: *sunt omnes fines* S-C

<94:4 *all* S-C: omitted in D-R>

94:7 *est Dominus*: *est* Weber

94:10 *Semper hi*: *semper* Weber

94:11 *intrabunt*: *introibunt* S-C

95:1 *ipsi*: *huic* Weber

95:2 *et benedicite*: *benedicite* Weber; *de die in diem*: *diem de die* Weber

95:4 *nimis*: *valde* Weber

95:5 *Dominus autem*: *at vero Dominus* Weber

<95:10 *The* S: *that our* D-R>

95:10 *orbem terrae*: *orbem* Weber; *movebitur*: *commovebitur* S-C

<96:1 *the same* D-R/C: *this* D-R>

96:1 *est ei* PL 113.1006B: *est* S-C, Weber

<96:2 *establishment* KJV n: *correction* D-R>
96:4 *Adluxerunt: Illuxerunt* S-C
96:5 *terra: terrae* Weber
96:7 *et qui: qui* Weber
96:8 *Iudae: Iudaeae* Weber
96:9 *altissimus: Altissimus* Weber; *exaltatus: superexaltatus* Weber
96:10 *Dominus animas: animas* Weber
97:1 *ipsi David: david* Weber
97:3 *veritatem suam: veritatis suae* S-C
97:4 *Deo: Domino* Weber
<97:4 *rejoice* D-R/C: *and reioyce* D-R>
<97:6 *our* D-R/C (in italics): omitted in D-R>
98:1 *ipsi David: david* Weber
98:2 *super: est super* Weber
99:2 *Deo: Domino* Weber
<99:4 *and* D-R/C: omitted in D-R>
100:1 *Ipsi David: david* Weber
<100:4 *and* D-R/C: omitted in D-R>
100:4 *declinantem: declinante* Weber; *malignum: maligno* Weber
100:6 *sedeant: sederent* Weber
<100:6 *were* S: *are* D-R>
100:7 *habitabit: habitabat* Weber
101:1 *coram Domino: in conspectu Domini* S-C
101:4 *gremium: cremium* S-C
101:5 *Percussus sum: percussum est* Weber
101:10 *manducavi et poculum: manducabam et potum* S-C
101:16 *tuum, Domine: Domini* Weber
101:17 *aedificavit: aedificabit* Weber
101:21 *gemitus: gemitum* Weber; *solvat: solveret* S-C
101:22 *adnuntient: adnuntiet* Weber
101:27 *veterescent: veterascent* S-C
<101:29 *continue* KJV: *inhabite* D-R>
<102:1 *let* D-R/C: omitted in D-R; *praise* KJV (*blesse;* in roman type in KJV and italics in D-R/C): omitted in D-R>
<102:2 *never forget* D-R/C: *forget not* D-R; *he hath done for thee* D-R/C: *his retributions* D-R>

102:10   *iniquitates: iniustitias* Weber

<102:15   *Man's* D-R/C: *man, his* D-R>

102:16   *pertransibit: pertransivit* Weber

<102:18   *such as* KJV: *them that* D-R>

102:20   *omnes angeli: angeli* Weber; *ad audiendam: qui timent* *D-R

<102:20   *hearkening* KJV: *that feare* D-R, literally *to hear*; *orders* D-R/C: *wordes* D-R>

103:3   *aquis: in aquis* Weber

<103:3   *clouds thy chariot* KJV: *cloude for thee to ascend on* D-R>

<103:4   *bases* KJVn: *stabilitie* D-R>

103:12   *voces: vocem* Weber

<103:13   *thy* D-R/C: *his* D-R>

103:15   *laetificet: laetificat* Weber; *confirmet: confirmat* Weber

<103:17   *highest* D-R/C: *leader* D-R>

<103:21   *after their prey* KJV: *to rauen* D-R; *seeking* D-R/C: *to seeke* D-R>

<103:25   *So is* KJV (in roman type in KJV and italics in D-R/C): omitted in D-R; *which stretcheth wide its arms* D-R/C: *and very large* D-R; *and* KJV: *with* D-R>

103:25   *spatiosum* Sabatier: *spatiosum manibus* S-C, Weber

<103:28   *What thou givest* KJV: *Thou geuing* D-R>

<103:33   *as long as I live* KJV: *in my life* D-R; *while I have my being* KJV: *as long as I am* D-R>

<103:35   *be consumed* KJV: *faile* D-R>

<104:10   *the same* KJV: *it* D-R>

104:12   *brevi, paucissimi et incolae: breves / paucissimos et incolas* Weber

<104:12   *but* KJV: omitted in D-R; *yea* KJV (in italics in D-R/C): omitted in D-R>

104:16   *et omne: omne* Weber

<104:17   *who* KJV (in roman type in KJV and italics in D-R/C): omitted in D-R>

104:18   *animam: anima* Weber

104:25   *et: ut* Weber

<104:27   *He gave them power to shew* D-R/C: *he did put in them the wordes of* D-R>

104:30   *Edidit: dedit* Weber; *penetralibus: penetrabilibus* Weber

104:31   *coenomyia: cynomia* Weber

<104:31   *divers sorts of flies* KJV: *caenomyia* D-R, *a svvarme of flies* D-Rn>
<104:32   *gave them hail for rain* KJV: *made theyr raynes haile* D-R>
<104:33   *trees* KJV: *wood* D-R>
104:37   *cum: in* Weber
104:40   *pane: panem* Weber
<105:2   *Who shall set forth* KJV (*who* in roman type): *shal make . . . to be heard* D-R>
105:5   *ut: et* Weber
<105:7   *mercies* KJV: *mercie* D-R; *even* KJV (in roman type): omitted in D-R>
105:12   *verbis: in verbis* Weber
105:13   *et non: non* Weber
105:15   *animas: anima* Weber
105:20   *similitudinem: similitudine* Weber
105:25   *murmuraverunt: murmurabant* Weber
105:32   *eum ad Aquas: ad aquam* Weber
105:38   *infecta: interfecta* Weber
<105:40   *exceedingly angry* D-R/C: *wrath with furie* D-R>
105:41   *oderant: oderunt* S-C
105:44   *audivit: audiret* Weber
106:2   *et de: de* Weber
106:3   *ab: et ab* Weber
<106:10   *such as* KJV: *Them that* D-R>
<106:25   *the word* D-R/C: omitted in D-R>
106:32   *Et exaltent: exaltent* Weber
<106:35   *dry land* KJV: *land without water* D-R>
<106:38   *suffered not to decrease* KJV: *lessened not* D-R>
<106:41   *a flock of* KJV (in italics in D-R/C): omitted in D-R>
106:43   *intelleget: intellegent* Weber
107:1   *psalmi ipsi: psalmi* Weber
107:3   *Exurge, gloria mea! Exurge: exurge* Weber
107:8   *Exaltabo: exaltabor* Weber
108:3   *circuierunt: circumdederunt* S-C
<108:4   *Instead of making me a return of love* D-R/C: *For that they should loue me* D-R; *gave myself to prayer* KJV (*giue my selfe unto prayer*; in roman type): *prayed* D-R>

108:10   *et eiciantur*: *eiciantur* Weber

<108:13   *posterity be cut off* KJV: *children come to destruction* D-R>

<108:21   *But* KJV: *And* D-R>

108:22   *turbatum*: *conturbatum* S-C

108:23   *et excussus*: *excussus* Weber

108:25   *et moverunt*: *moverunt* Weber

108:27   *et tu*: *tu* Weber

109:6   *cadavera*: *ruinas* S-C

110:1   *Alleluia*: *alleluia reversionis aggei et zacchariae* Weber

<112:3   *of the same* KJV: omitted in D-R>

112:4   *et super*: *super* Weber

113:4   *et colles*: *colles* Weber

<113:8   *Here the Hebrews begin Psalm CXV* D-R/C: omitted in D-R; D-R/C numbers 113:9–26 as 1–18, after S-C>

113:9–26 these verses numbered 1–18 S-C

<113:13–15 *speak, see, hear, feel, walk* KJV (*handle* for *feel*): *shal . . . speake, shal . . . see, shal . . . heare, shal . . . handle, shal . . . walke* D-R>

113:14   *odorabuntur*: *odorabunt* S-C

<113:21   *both* KJV (in roman type): omitted in D-R; *and* KJV: *with* D-R>

<113:22   *blessings* D-R/C: omitted in D-R>

113:23   *vos a*: *vos* Weber

114:2   *invocabo*: *invocabo te* Weber

114:3   *et pericula*: *pericula* Weber

115:1–10 these verses numbered 10–19 S-C, Weber

<115:1–10 these verses numbered 10–19 D-R/C, 1–10 D-R>

115:8   *nomen*: *in nomine* Weber

116:2   *saeculum*: *aeternum* S-C

<117:5   *and enlarged me* D-R/C: *in largenes* D-R>

117:10   *ultus* Weber Iuxta Hebr.: *quia ultus* S-C, Weber

117:11   *ultus* Weber Iuxta Hebr.: *quia ultus* S-C, Weber

117:12   *ultus* Sabatier: *quia ultus* S-C, Weber

117:14   *laudatio*: *laus* S-C

117:23   *et*: *hoc* Weber

117:25   *me fac*: *fac* Weber; *bene prosperare*: *prosperare* Weber

117:26   *venit*: *venturus est* Weber

117:27   *cornu*: *cornua* Weber

118:2	*exquirunt*: *exquirent* Wcbcr
118:4	*custodiri*: *custodire* Weber
118:9	*corrigit*: *corriget* Weber
118:10	*non*: *ne* S-C
<118:10	let me not stray KJV (*wander* for *stray*): *repel me not* D-R>
<118:17	*bountifully* KJV: omitted in D-R>
<118:28	*heaviness* KJV: *tediousnes* D-R>
118:29	*et de*: *et* Weber
118:35	*semitam*: *semita* Weber
<118:42	So KJV: *And* D-R; *them that reproach me in any thing* KJV n: *a word to them that vpbrayde me* D-R>
<118:44	So KJV: *And* D-R>
118:46	*de*: *in* Weber
118:48	*mandata tua*: *mandata* Weber
118:53	*prae*: *pro* S-C
118:55	*in nocte*: *nocte* S-C
118:57	*Domine*: *Dominus* Weber
118:59	*converti*: *avertisti* Weber
<118:61	*but* KJV (in roman type): *and* D-R>
118:64	*Misericordia tua, Domine*: *misericordia Domini* Weber
118:69	*corde*: *corde meo* Weber
118:75	*et in*: *et* Weber
<118:77	*tender* KJV: omitted in D-R>
118:78	*iniuste* Weber Iuxta Hebr. (*inique*): *iniuste iniquitatem* S-C, Weber
118:81	*et in*: *in* Weber
118:84	*servi tui*: *servo tuo* Weber
<118:95	*but* KJV (in italics in D-R/C): omitted in D-R>
118:96	*Omnis consummationis*: *Omni consummationi* Weber
118:97	*tuam, Domine*: *tuam* Weber
118:114	*Adiutor*: *adiutor meus* Weber; *et in*: *in* Weber
<118:116	let me not be confounded in KJV (*ashamed of* for *confounded in*): *confound me not of* D-R>
118:118	*iudiciis*: *iustitiis* Weber
118:125	*ut*: *et* Weber
118:126	*Domine*: *Domino* Weber
118:134	*ut*: *et* Weber

<118:141 *but* KJV (*yet*; in italics in D-R/C): omitted in D-R>
118:146 *te: ad te* S-C; *ut: et* Weber
<118:147 *the dawning of the day* KJV (*morning* for *day*): *in maturitie* D-R>
118:147 *quia in: in* Weber
118:148 *ad te diluculo: diluculum* Weber
<118:148 *the morning* D-R/C: *early* D-R>
118:149 *et secundum: secundum* Weber
118:150 *iniquitati: iniquitate* Weber
118:156 *iudicium tuum: iudicia tua* Weber
<118:157 *but* KJV (*yet*; in italics in D-R/C): omitted in D-R>
<118:159 *Behold* D-R/C: *See that* D-R>
118:160 *in: et in* Weber
118:167 *dilexit: dilexi* Weber
<118:173 *with me* D-R/C: omitted in D-R>
119:2 *et a: a* Weber
119:3 *aut: et* Weber
119:5 *habitantibus: habitationibus* Weber
119:7 *oderant: oderunt* S-C
121:1 *graduum: graduum huic david* Weber
<121:3 *which is compact together* KJV: *whose participation is together in it self* D-R>
121:4 *illuc: illic* Weber
122:1 *caelis: caelo* Weber
123:1 *graduum: graduum huic david* Weber
<124:2 *so* KJV: *and* D-R>
124:3 *Dominus virgam: virgam* Weber
125:1 *Dominus: Dominum* Weber
125:6 *mittentes: portantes* Weber
125:7 no new verse S-C, Weber; *cum: in* Weber
<126:1 *labour* KJV: *haue laboured* D-R>
126:1 *vigilat: vigilavit* Weber; *custodit eam: custodit* Weber
126:2 *surgite: surgere* Weber
126:5 *implevit: implebit* Weber; *confundetur cum loquetur: confundentur cum loquentur* Weber
127:3 *novellae: novella* Weber
<127:3 *olive plants* KJV: *young plantes of oliuetrees* D-R>

127:5   *te*: *tibi* S-C
127:6   *pacem*: *pax* Weber
<127:6   *and* KJV (in roman type in KJV and italics in D-R/C): omitted
         in D-R>
128:3   *fabricaverunt*: *fabricabantur* Weber
128:4   *concidet*: *concidit* S-C
129:3   *observabis*: *observaveris* S-C
<129:4   *merciful* D-R/C *forgiveness* KJV: *propiciation* D-R>
129:4   *et propter*: *propter* Weber
130:2   *ablactatus est*: *ablactatum* Weber
<131:2   *how* KJV: *As* D-R>
<131:3   *wherein I lie* D-R/C: *of my couch* D-R>
<131:4   *or* KJV (in roman type): *and* D-R>
131:7   *tabernaculum*: *tabernacula* Weber
<131:8   *which thou hast sanctified* D-R/C: *of thy sanctification* D-R>
131:9   *induantur*: *induentur* Weber; *iustitia*: *iustitiam* S-C; *exultent*: *ex-
         ultabunt* Weber
131:11   *frustrabit*: *frustrabitur* S-C; *eam*: *eum* Weber
131:17   *Illuc*: *illic* Weber
<132:1   *together in unity* KJV: *in one* D-R>
<132:2   *precious* KJV: omitted in D-R>
132:2   *oram*: *ora* Weber
132:3   *Montem*: *montes* Weber
133:2   *Domino*: *Dominum* S-C
134:6   *quaecumque*: *quae* Weber; *in terra*: *et in terra* Weber
134:9   *Emisit*: *et misit* S-C
<134:16–17 *but they speak not, but they see not, but they hear not, neither* KJV:
         and shal not speake, and shal not see, and shal not heare, for neither
         D-R>
134:18   *confidunt*: *sperant* Weber
<135:12 *stretched out* KJV: *loftie* D-R>
135:14   *eduxit*: *duxit* Weber
135:16   *per desertum*: *in deserto* Weber
136:1   *Psalmus David*: *david* Weber
<136:3   *said* KJV (*saying*): omitted in D-R>
136:6   *praeposuero*: *proposuero* S-C

136:7	*in die*: *diem* Weber
137:3	*multiplicabis*: *multiplicabis me* Weber; *virtutem*: *virtute* Weber
<137:4	*earth* D-R/C: *earth ô Lord* D-R>
137:7	*et super*: *super* Weber
137:8	*pro*: *propter* Weber
138:1	verse 2 begins here S-C, Weber
138:2	*surrectionem*: *resurrectionem* S-C
<138:6	*high* KJV: *made great* D-R>
138:6	*et non*: *non* Weber
<138:7	*Or* KJV: *and* D-R>
138:8	*in infernum*: *ad infernum* Weber
138:11	*mea in*: *in* Weber
<138:12	*But* D-R/C: *For* D-R; *The darkness thereof and the light thereof are alike to thee* KJV (*to thee* in roman type in KJV and italics in D-R/C): *as the darkenes therof, so also the light therof* D-R>
138:16	*Dies*: *die* Weber
138:17	*confortatus est*: *confirmati sunt* Weber
138:19	*viri*: *et viri* Weber
138:20	*dicitis*: *dices* Weber
138:22	*inimici*: *et inimici* S-C
<138:22	*and* S-C: omitted in D-R>
139:4	*linguas suas*: *linguam suam* Weber; *eorum*: *eorum / diapsalma* Weber
<139:4	*a* KJV: *that of a* Weber>
139:5	*et ab*: *ab* Weber
139:9	*Non*: *Ne* S-C; *tradas me*: *tradas* Weber; *a desiderio*: *desiderio* Weber; *exaltentur*: *exaltentur / diapsalma* Weber
<139:9	*lest they* KJV (*lest* in roman type): *lest they perhaps* D-R>
139:11	*ignem*: *igne* Weber
139:14	*et habitabunt*: *habitabunt* Weber
<140:6	*falling upon* D-R/C: *ioyned to* D-R>
<140:8	*But* KJV: *for* D-R>
141:3	*deprecationem*: *orationem* S-C; *et tribulationem*: *tribulationem* Weber
<141:4	*then* KJV: *and* D-R>
141:5	*requirat*: *requirit* Weber
142:1	*Absalom filius eius*: *filius* Weber

142:2   *iudicium: iudicio* Weber

142:6   *tibi: tibi / diapsalma* Weber

<142:7   *lest I be* KJV: *and I shal be* D-R>

142:10   *viam rectam* several Old Latin sources, including PL 86.695A,
         698C, 840D, 1213D, 1324A: *terram rectam* S-C, *terra recta*
         Weber

<142:10 *land* S-C: *way* D-R>

<142:12 *cut off* KJV: *destroy* D-R>

143:1   *Psalmus David: david* Weber; *et digitos: digitos* Weber

143:2   *subdit: subdis* Weber

<143:6   *Send forth* KJV (*Cast* for *Send*): *Lighten* D-R>

<143:9   *and an instrument* KJV (*and* in roman type in KJV and italics in
         D-R/C): omitted in D-R>

143:10   *redimisti: redimit* Weber; *tuum: suum* Weber

143:11   *erue: eripe* Weber; *alienorum: alienigenarum* Weber

143:12   *novellae plantationes: novella plantationis* Weber

143:14   *crassi: crassae* S-C

<143:15 *but* KJV (*yea*; in italics in D-R/C): omitted in D-R>

144:1   *ipsi David: david* Weber

<144:9   *tender* KJV: omitted in D-R>

144:10   *benedicant: confiteantur* Weber

144:13   *generationem: progenie* Weber

144:15   *Domine, et: et* Weber

<144:20 *but* KJV: *and* D-R>

145:3   *in quibus: quibus* Weber

<145:5   *whose* KJV: *his* D-R>

145:8   *adlisos: elisos* S-C

145:9   *vias: viam* Weber

146:1   *Alleluia: alleluia aggei et zacchariae* Weber

<146:4   *telleth the number* KJV: *numbereth the multitude* D-R>

146:4   *vocat: vocans* Weber

146:9   *qui: et* Weber

147:1–9 these verses numbered 12–20 S-C, Weber, D-R/C

147:6   *suum: suam* S-C

147:9   *eis. ¶ Alleluia: eis* Weber

148:4   *aquae quae super caelos sunt* IWSKΦ [Weber's sigla]: *aquae omnes
         quae super caelos sunt* S-C, *aqua quae super caelum est* Weber

148:6   *saeculum et: aeternum et* S-C
148:14   *exaltavit: exaltabit* Weber; *sibi.* ¶ *Alleluia: sibi* Weber
149:4   *salutem: salute* Weber
149:9   *eius.* ¶ *Alleluia: eius* Weber
<150:5   *high* KJV: *wel* D-R>
150:6   *Dominum!* ¶ *Alleluia: Dominum* Weber

PROVERBS

1:6   *sapientium: sapientum* S-C
1:7   *sapientiae: scientiae* Weber
1:9   *torques aurea* PG 93.1180A: *torques* S-C, Weber
1:10   *adquiescas eis: adquiescas* Weber
1:18   *ipsi quoque: ipsique* Weber
1:22   *cupiunt: cupient* S-C
1:23   *vobis verba: verba* Weber
1:26   *id quod: quod* Weber
<1:30   *but* D-R/C: *&* D-R>
<1:33   *without fear of evils* D-R/C: *feare of euils being taken away* D-R>
2:2   *noscendam: cognoscendam* S-C
2:11   *et prudentia: prudentia* Weber
2:12   *de: a* S-C; *et ab: ab* Weber
2:18   *inferos: impios* Weber
3:7   *Deum: Dominum* Weber
3:9   *tuarum da ei: tuarum* Weber
3:10   *torcularia tua: torcularia* Weber
3:14   *auro primo et purissimo* Y [Quentin's siglum]: *auri primi et purissimi*
         S-C, *auro primo* Weber
3:16   *et in: in* Weber
3:28   *et cras: cras* S-C
4:6   *servabit: conservabit* S-C
4:11   *monstrabo: monstravi* Weber; *ducam: duxi* Weber
4:14   *in semitis: semitis* Weber
4:15   *nec: ne* Weber
<4:15   *not* KJV: *neither* D-R>
4:16   *capitur* Cs [Quentin's sigla]: *rapitur* S-C, Weber

<4:16 *their sleep is taken away unless they have made some to fall* KJV: *they take no sleepe vnlesse they supplant* D-R>

4:27 *neque*: et Weber; *malo, vias enim quae a dextris sunt novit Dominus, perversae vero sunt quae a sinistris sunt. Ipse autem rectos faciet cursus tuos, initera autem tua in pace producet*: *malo* Weber

5:1 *adtende*: *adtende ad* S-C

5:2 *conservent. Ne adtendas fallaciae mulieris*: *conservent* Weber

5:3 *distillans*: *stillans* Weber

5:6 *ambulant*: *ambulat* Weber

5:7 *fili mi*: *fili* Weber

<5:10 *lest* KJV: *lest perhaps* D-R>

5:11 *carnes tuas*: *carnes* Weber

5:19 *omni*: *in omni* S-C

5:20 *sinu*: *in sinu* S-C

5:23 *et in*: *et* Weber

6:3 *manum*: *manu* Weber

6:5 *manu aucupis*: *insidiis aucupis* Weber

6:8 *parat*: *parat in* S-C

<6:8 *her food* KJV: *for to eate* D-R>

6:9 *dormies*: *dormis* Weber

6:11 *armatus. Si vero impiger fueris, veniet ut fons messis tua, et egestas longe fugiet a te*: *armatus* Weber

6:14 *et in*: *et* S-C

<6:15 *such a one* D-R/C: *him* D-R>

<6:27 *and* KJV: *that* D-R>

6:28 *ut non conburantur*: *et non conburentur* Weber

<6:28 *and* KJV: *that* D-R>

6:30 *culpa*: *culpae* Weber

<6:30 *so* D-Rn: omitted in D-R>

7:1 *tibi. Fili*: *tibi* Weber

7:8 *per plateas* Φ [Weber's siglum]: *per plateam* S-C, *in platea* Weber; *propter*: *prope* S-C

<7:8 *street* S-C: *streates* D-R>

<7:11 *still* D-R/C: *on her feete* D-R>

7:14 *vovi*: *debui* Weber

7:16 *lectum*: *lectulum* S-C

<7:17 *perfumed* KJV: *sprinkled* D-R>

7:17 *aloe* ΦΩ^SJ [Quentin's sigla]: *et aloe* S-C, Weber

7:18 *et fruamur cupitis amplexibus donec inlucescat dies*: *donec inlucescat dies et fruamur cupitis amplexibus* Weber

7:20 *est*: *est in* S-C

7:24 *fili mi*: *fili* Weber; *verba*: *verbis* S-C

<7:26 *the* D-R/C: *al* D-R>

<7:27 *way* KJV: *wayes* D-R>

7:27 *in interiora*: *interiora* Weber

<8:2 *top of the highest places by* KJV: *high & loftie toppes ouer* D-R>

8:2 *super*: *supra* S-C

<8:13 *every* D-R/C: *omitted in* D-R>

8:14 *est prudentia*: *prudentia* Weber

8:19 *est enim*: *est* Weber

<8:20 *way* KJV: *wayes* D-R>

8:22 *in initio*: *initium* Weber

8:23 *ordinata*: *ordita* Weber

8:24 *Nondum*: *necdum* Weber

8:34 *me et*: *me* Weber

<8:35 *have* D-R/C: *draw* D-R>

<9:4 *Whosoever* KJV (without *ever*): *If any* D-R>

9:9 *sapienti occasionem*: *sapienti* Weber

9:12 *si autem*: *si* Weber

9:15 *per viam*: *viam* Weber

9:16 *Qui*: *quis* Weber

9:18 *Parabolae Salomonis*: 10:1 starts here Weber

10:2 *Nil*: *non* Weber

<10:4 *industrious* KJV (*diligent*): *strong* D-R>

10:4 *parat. Qui nititur mendaciis, hic pascit ventos, idem autem ipse sequitur aves volantes*: *parat* Weber

10:6 *Benedictio Domini*: *benedictio* Weber; *iniquitas*: *iniquitatem* Weber

10:8 *suscipiet*: *suscipit* S-C

<10:8 *receiveth* S-C: *shal receiue* D-R>

10:10 *et stultus*: *stultus* Weber

10:11 *operit*: *operiet* Weber

10:13 *invenitur*: *invenietur* Weber

10:16 *fructus autem*: *fructus* Weber

10:20 *cor autem*: *cor* Weber

10:22 *eis*: *ei* Weber

<10:25 *so* KJV: omitted in D-R>

10:30 *in terram*: *super terram* S-C

<10:32 *uttereth* KJV (*speaketh*): omitted in D-R>

11:13 *celat amici* Ω arels [Quentin's sigla]: *animi celat amici* S-C, *animi celat* Weber

11:17 *Benefacit animae suae vir misericors, qui autem crudelis est et propinquos abicit*: *Benefacit etiam propinquis suis vir misericors* *D-R; *et*: *etiam* S-C

11:28 *confidit*: *confidet* Weber

12:2 *confidit*: *confidit in* S-C

12:5 *fraudulenta*: *fraudulentia* Weber

12:11 *saturabitur*: *satiabitur* S-C; *est. Qui suavis est in vini demorationibus in suis munitionibus relinquit contumeliam*: *est* Weber

12:23 *provocat*: *provocabit* Weber

12:25 *illum*: *illud* Weber

<12:25 *but* KJV: *&* D-R>

<12:27 *but* KJV: *and* D-R; *just* D-Rn: omitted in D-R>

13:2 *oris sui*: *oris* Weber; *saturabitur*: *satiabitur* S-C

13:5 *impius autem*: *impius* Weber

13:6 *peccatorem*: *peccato* Weber

13:10 *cuncta*: *omnia cum* S-C

<13:11 *got* KJV (in roman type) *in haste* D-R/C: *hastened* D-R>

13:13 *versabitur. Animae dolosae errant in peccatis, iusti autem misericordes sunt et miserantur*: *versabitur* Weber, *autem* omitted *D-R

13:17 *legatus autem*: *legatus* Weber

<13:19 *that is* KJV?: *if it be* D-R>

13:21 *persequitur*: *persequetur* Weber

13:22 *relinquit*: *relinquet* Weber

<13:23 *but* KJV: *and* D-R>

13:23 *aliis*: *alii* Weber

13:24 *virgae*: *virgae suae* Weber

<13:25 *is never to be filled* D-R/C: *vnsatiable* D-R>

14:1 *aedificat*: *aedificavit* Weber; *instructam*: *extructam* S-C

<14:1 *but* KJV: omitted in D-R>

14:3 *labia autem*: *labia* Weber

14:5   *mentietur: mentitur* S-C; *profert autem: profert* Weber

14:6   *invenit: inveniet* Weber

14:7   *nescit: nescito* Weber

14:9   *Stultus: stultis* Weber; *et inter: inter* Weber

<14:9   *but* KJV: *and* D-R>

14:11   *tabernacula: tabernacula vero* S-C

<14:11   *but* S-C: omitted in D-R>

14:15   *suos: suos.* ¶ *Filio doloso nihil erit boni;* ¶ *servo autem sapienti prosperi erunt actus, et dirigetur via eius* S-C

<14:15   No good shall come to the deceitful son, but the wise servant shall prosper in his dealings, and his way shall be made straight S-C: omitted in D-R>

14:16   *a malo: malum* Weber

14:18   *Possibebunt parvuli: Possidebit parvulus* *D-R

14:21   *pauperi: pauperis* S-C; *erit: erit.* ¶ *Qui credit in Domino misericordiam diligit* S-C

<14:22   *but* KJV: omitted in D-R>

14:23   *plurima ibi: plurima* Weber

14:27   *declinet: declinent* S-C

<14:30   *but* KJV (in italics in D-R/C): omitted in D-R>

<14:31   *oppresseth* KJV: *doth calumniate* D-R>

14:33   *quosque: quoque* Weber

14:34   *miseros autem: miseros* Weber

15:1   *sermo: sermo autem* *D-R

<15:2   *but* KJV (in italics in D-R/C): omitted in D-R>

15:4   *quae autem: quae* Weber

15:5   *fiet.* ¶ *In abundanti iustitia virtus maxima est, cogitationes autem impiorum eradicabuntur: fiet* Weber

15:6   *conturbatio: conturbatur* Weber

15:9   *diligitur: diligetur* Weber

15:10   *viam vitae: viam* Weber

<15:13   *but by* KJV: *in* D-R>

15:14   *pascitur: pascetur* Weber

<15:16   *without content* D-R/C: *and vnsatiable* D-R>

15:17   *vocari: vocare* Weber

<15:20   *but* KJV: *and* D-R>

<15:24 *for* KJV (*to*): omitted in D-R>
15:25 *faciet: facit* Weber
15:26 *pulcherrimus firmabitur ab eo: pulcherrimus* Weber
<15:27 *greedy of gain* KJV: *pursueth auarice* D-R>
15:27 *vivet.* **Per misericordiam et fidem purgantur peccata, per timorem autem Domini declinat omnis a malo: vivet** Weber
15:32 *qui autem: qui* Weber
16:1 *animam: animum* Weber; *Domini: Dei* Weber
16:2 *hominis: hominum* Weber
16:5 *non est: non erit* Weber; *innocens.* **Initium viae bonae facere iustitiam, accepta est autem apud Deum magis quam immolare hostias: innocens** Weber
16:9 *disponit: disponet* Weber
<16:9 *the Lord must* D-R/C: *it perteyneth to our Lord to* D-R>
16:24 *sanitas: et sanitas* Weber
<16:24 *and* KJV: omitted in D-R>
16:25 *novissima: novissimum* Weber; *ducunt: ducit* Weber
16:31 *quae in: in* Weber
16:33 *sinum: sinu* Weber
<16:33 *disposed* KJV: *ordered* D-R>
17:5 *ruina: in ruina* Weber
17:8 *vertit: verterit* Weber
<17:9 *again* D-R/C: *in other word* D-R>
17:12 *sibi in: in* S-C
<17:12 *in* S-C: *to himselfe in* D-R>
17:15 *Qui: et qui* Weber; *Deum: Dominum* Weber
17:16 *stultum: stulto* S-C; *possit?* **Qui altam facit domum suam quaerit ruinam, et qui evitat discere incidet in mala: possit** Weber
<17:16 *seeing* KJV: *wheras* D-R>
17:19 *discordias: discordiam* Weber
17:28 *reputabitur: putabitur* Weber
18:6 *inmiscunt: miscent* S-C
18:8 *ventris.* ¶ **Pigrum deicit timor, animae autem effeminatorum esurient: ventris** Weber
18:13 *respondet: respondit* Weber
18:17 *investigabit: investigavit* Weber

18:22   *mulierem bonam*: *mulierem* Weber; *Domino*: *Domino.* ¶ *Qui expellit mulierem bonam expellit bonum;* ¶ *qui autem tenet adulteram stultus est et impius* S-C

<18:22   *He that driveth away a good wife driveth away a good thing, but he that keepeth an adulteress is foolish and wicked.* S-C: omitted in D-R>

18:24   *amicalis*: *amabilis* S-C

19:1   *quam dives*: *quam* Weber; *labia sua et*: *labia* Weber

19:2   *offendet*: *offendit* Weber

19:6   *tribuenti*: *tribuentis* S-C

19:12   *ita et hilaritas*: *ita hilaritas* Weber

<19:12   *his* KJV: *so also his* D-R>

19:14   *parentibus*: *patribus* Weber

19:16   *viam suam*: *vias suas* Weber

19:23   *pessima*: *pessimi* Weber

<19:23   *being visited with evil* KJV: *the visitation most noysome* D-R>

<19:24   *will* KJV: *doth* D-R>

19:25   *sin*: *si* S-C

20:2   *ita et*: *ita* Weber

<20:3   *to separate* KJV: *that separateth* D-R>

<20:10   *Diverse weights and diverse measures* KJV: *Weight and weight, measure and measure* D-R>

20:11   *et*: *et si* Weber

20:15   *vas autem*: *et vas* S-C

<20:17   *but* KJV: *and* D-R>

<20:21   *gotten hastily* KJV: *wherunto haste is made* D-R>

20:23   *Dominum*: *Deum* Weber

<20:23   *Diverse weights* KJV: *Weight and weight* D-R>

20:25   *homini*: *hominis* Weber; *retractare*: *tractare* Weber

20:26   *curvat*: *incurvat* S-C

<20:26   *bringeth over them the wheel* KJV: *bendeth ouer them a triumphant arch* D-R>

21:3   *placet*: *placent* Weber

21:4   *est*: *et* Weber

<21:5   *always bring forth* D-R/C: *are alwayes in* D-R>

21:6   *et excors est*: *est* Weber

21:12   *a malo*: *in malum* Weber

21:14   *extinguit*: *extinguet* Weber

21:21 *vitam: vitam et* Weber

21:28 *loquetur: loquitur* Weber

21:31 *tribuit: tribuet* Weber

<22:1 *and* KJV (in roman type): omitted in D-R>

22:5 *custos autem: custos* Weber

22:9 *pauperi. Victoriam et honorem acquiret qui dat munera, animam autem aufert accipientium: pauperi* Weber, *pauperi. Victoriam et honorem acquiret qui dat munera, qui autem accipit animam aufert datoris* *D-R

<22:9 *maketh* D-R/C: *geueth* D-R>

<22:18 *if* KJV: *when* D-R>

22:21 *illis qui miserunt: illi qui misit* Weber

22:23 *confinxerint: confinxerunt* S-C

23:1 *posita: adposita* S-C

<23:2 *it be so that* D-R/C: *notwithstanding* D-R>

23:5 *volabunt: avolabunt* Weber

23:11 *fortis: Fortis* Weber

<23:21 *club together* D-R/C: *pay shottes* D-R>

<23:24 *greatly* KJV: *with gladnes* D-R>

23:28 *interficiet: interficit* Weber

<23:29 *Who falls into* D-R/C: *to whom* D-R; *redness of* KJV: *bloud sheeding* D-R>

23:30 *morantur: commorantur* S-C

24:5 *fortis: et fortis* Weber

24:8 *mala facere: malefacere* Weber

24:14 *novissimis spem: novissimis* Weber

24:24 *dicunt: dicit* Weber; *eis: ei* Weber; *eos: eum* Weber

<24:24 *shall be cursed by the people* S: *peoples shal curse them* D-R>

24:25 *arguunt eum: arguunt* Weber

<24:31 *it was all filled with nettles* D-R/C: *nettels had filled it wholy* D-R>

24:31 *et operuerant: operuerant* Weber

24:34 *veniet tibi: veniet* Weber; *egestas: egestas tua* Weber

25:1 *Hae: haec* Weber

25:9 *non: ne* S-C

25:10 *cesset. Gratia et amicitia liberant; quas tibi serva ne exprobrabilis fias: cesset* Weber

<25:10 *lest* KJV: *lest perhaps* D-R; *a man; keep these* D-R/C: *which kepe* D-R>

<25:11 *To speak* S: *he that speaketh* D-R>

<25:12 *so* KJV (in roman type): omitted in D-R>

<25:13 *for he refresheth his soul* KJV: *maketh his soule to rest* D-R>

<25:14 *when no rain followeth* D-R/C: *and no rayne folowing* D-R; *so* S: omitted in D-R>

<25:16 *lest* KJV: *lest perhaps* D-R>

25:16 *saturatus: satiatus* S-C

25:19 *lassus: lapsus* Weber

<25:19 *To trust* D-R/C: *he that hopeth* D-R>

25:20 *qui: et qui* Weber

25:20 *pessimo. Sicut tinea vestimento et vermis ligno, ita tristitia viri nocet cordi: pessimo* Weber

<25:20 *so* KJV: omitted in D-R; *by* [both times] D-R/C: omitted in D-R>

25:21 *si sitierit: et si sitierit* Weber

25:22 *prunas: prunam* Weber

<25:23 *so* KJV: *&* D-R>

<25:25 *so* KJV: *and* D-R>

25:27 *opprimetur a: opprimitur* Weber

26:1 *nix: nix in* S-C; *pluvia: pluviae* S-C

26:3 *in dorso: dorso* Weber

<26:12 *There shall be more hope of a fool* KJV (*there is* for *There shall be*): *the foole shal haue hope rather* D-R>

26:12 *stultus: insipiens* S-C

26:13 *Leo est in via et leaena: leaena in via leo* Weber

26:15 *manum sub ascella sua: manus sub ascellas suas* Weber; *eam: eas* Weber

26:17 *inpatiens et: et inpatiens* Weber

<26:17 *in anger* KJVn? (*is enraged*): *impatient* D-R>

26:18 *in: et* Weber

26:19 *sic: ita* S-C

26:20 *conquiescunt: conquiescent* S-C

<26:20 *shall* S-C: omitted in D-R>

26:21 *prunas: prunam* Weber

<26:22 *but* S: *and* D-R>

<26:23 *are like ... adorned* KJV (*are like* in roman type; *covered* for *adorned*): *As if thou wouldest adorne* D-R>

27:7 *et anima: anima* Weber; *et amarum: etiam amarum* S-C

27:8 *relinquit*: *derelinquit* S-C

<27:9 *perfumes* KJV: *diuers odours* D-R>

27:11 *possis*: *possim* Weber

27:13 *aufer ei*: *auferto* Weber

27:17 *acuitur*: *exacuitur* S-C

<27:17 *so* KJV: *and* D-R>

27:20 *numquam*: *non* Weber; *replentur*: *implentur* S-C

27:21 *laudantis. Cor iniqui inquirit mala, cor autem rectum inquirit scientiam*: *laudantis* Weber

<27:22 *sodden barley* D-R/C: *ptisane* [i.e., *husked barley*] D-R >

27:24 *generationem et generationem*: *generatione generationum* Weber

27:26 *agri*: *ad agri* Weber

<27:26 *for* S-C: omitted in D-R>

27:27 *et in*: *in* Weber

28:5 *requirunt*: *inquirunt* S-C

28:6 *dives*: *dives in* S-C

28:7 *qui autem*: *qui* Weber

28:9 *aures suas*: *aurem suam* Weber

28:10 *bona eius*: *bona* Weber

28:12 *gloria est*: *gloria* Weber

28:13 *qui autem*: *qui* Weber

<28:16 *shall prolong his days* KJV (*his* in roman type): *his dayes shal be made long* D-R>

28:17 *sustinet*: *sustentet* Weber

<28:17 *will stay* D-R/C: *abideth* D-R>

28:18 *graditur*: *ingreditur* Weber

<28:18 *is perverse in his* KJV (*in his* in roman type): *goeth peruerse* D-R>

28:19 *saturabitur*: *satiabitur* S-C; *qui autem*: *qui* Weber

28:21 *facit bene*: *benefacit* S-C

<28:21 *such a* S: *this* D-R>

28:22 *superveniet*: *superveniat* Weber

<28:24 *or* KJV: *and* D-R>

28:24 *et a*: *et* Weber; *esse*: *est* Weber

28:25 *sanabitur*: *saginabitur* Weber

28:26 *salvus erit* Frede PS-AU spe 38 p. 467.8, PL 86.1179A: *ipse salvabitur* S-C, *iste salvabitur* Weber

29:1   *ei superveniet*: *superveniet* Weber; *sequetur*: *sequitur* Weber

<29:1   shall suddenly be destroyed KJV: *soden destruction shal come vpon him*
        D-R>

<29:7   *void* D-R/C: *ignorant* D-R>

29:8   *sapientes vero*: *sapientes* Weber

29:10   *iusti autem*: *iusti* Weber

29:12   *habet*: *habebit* Weber

29:13   *obviam fuerunt*: *obviaverunt* S-C

29:15   *tribuit*: *tribuet* Weber; *confundit*: *confundet* Weber

<29:16 *but* KJV: *and* D-R>

29:18   *qui vero*: *qui* Weber

<29:19 will [first time] KJV: *can* D-R; will not KJV: *contemneth to* D-R>

29:20   *Stultitia*: *stulti* Weber

29:22   *peccandum*: *peccata* Weber

29:24   *partitur*: *participat* S-C

29:27   *via. Verbum custodiens filius extra perditionem erit*: *via* Weber

30:4   *in manibus*: *manibus* Weber

<30:6   lest S: *and so* D-R>

30:9   *saturatus*: *satiatus* S-C; *aut*: *et* Weber

<30:10 lest KJV: *lest perhaps* D-R>

30:15   *quartum* Frede AN scrip 2.9 p. 122: *quartum quod* S-C, Weber

30:17   *eum corvi*: *corvi* Weber

30:19   *adulescentia*: *adulescentula* Weber

30:20   *est et*: *est* Weber

30:25   *qui praeparat*: *quae praeparant* Weber

30:26   *quae*: *qui* S-C

<30:27 yet KJV: *and* D-R>

30:27   *turmas suas*: *turmas* Weber

<30:30 who KJV (*which*): omitted in D-R>

30:31   *et rex* s [Quentin's siglum]: *nec est rex* S-C, Weber

30:32   *Est*: *et* Weber; *elatus*: *elevatus* S-C

30:33   *emungit*: *emungitur* Weber

31:3   *divitias*: *vias* Weber

31:5   *et ne*: *ne* Weber; *bibant et obliviscantur*: *bibat et obliviscatur* Weber;
        mutent: *mutet* Weber

<31:5   lest KJV: *lest perhaps* Weber>

31:7   *et obliviscantur*: *ut obliviscantur* Weber; *doloris sui*: *doloris* Weber

1124

31:10–28, 31 Each verse begins with a letter of the Hebrew alphabet (in Latin) in Weber in the following (alphabetical) order: *Aleph, Beth, Gimel, Deleth, He, Vav, Zai, Heth, Teth, Ioth, Caph, Lameth, Mem, Nun, Samech, Ain, Phe, Sade, Coph, Res, Sin, Thav.* Letters omitted in S-C

31:14 *portans*: *portat* Weber

31:18 *Gustavit et vidit*: *gustavit* Weber

31:22 *Stragulam*: *Stragulatam* S-C

31:27 *Consideravit*: *considerat* Weber; *comedit*: *comedet* Weber

ECCLESIASTES

1:2   *et omnia*: *omnia* Weber

1:3   *quo*: *quod* Weber

<1:3   *that* S-C: *wherby* D-R; *taketh* KJV: *laboreth* D-R>

<1:4   *One* KJV (in roman type in KJV and italics in D-R/C): omitted in D-R; *another* KJV (in roman type in KJV and italics in D-R/C): omitted in D-R>

1:6   *in circuitu*: *circuitu* Weber; *regreditur*: *revertitur* S-C

1:7   *in mare*: *mare* Weber

<1:7   *yet* KJV: *and* D-R>

1:9   *fiendum*: *faciendum* S-C

<1:15   *hard to be* D-R/C: *hardly* D-R>

1:16   *didici*: *didicit* Weber

1:18   *addit et*: *addat et* Weber

2:3   *quod*: *quo* S-C

<2:4   *made me great* KJV: *haue magnified my* D-R>

2:4   *domos et*: *domos* Weber

2:5   *pomaria*: *pomeria* Weber

2:6   *et extruxi*: *extruxi* Weber

<2:6   *therewith* KJV: omitted in D-R>

2:8   *cantrices*: *cantatrices* S-C

<2:9   *My* KJV: omitted in D-R>

2:10   *cor meum*: *cor* Weber; *paraveram*: *praeparaveram* S-C

2:13   *tenebris*: *a tenebris* S-C

<2:14   *they were to die both alike* D-R/C: *there was one death of both* D-R>

2:15   *stulti* ΧΣΛΘ [Quentin's sigla]: *et stulti* S-C, Weber

<2:15   *applied myself more to the study of* D-R/C: *bestowed greater labour for*
        D-R>
2:16   *obruent: operient* S-C; *similiter et: similiter ut* S-C
2:18   *qua: quae* Weber
2:23   *hoc nonne: haec non* Weber
2:25   *vorabit: devorabit* S-C
3:5   *a conplexibus: ab amplexibus* S-C
3:17   *omnis: omni* Weber
3:19   *condicio: conditio* S-C
3:20   *revertuntur: revertentur* Weber
<4:8   *but* KJV (*alone*): omitted in D-R>
4:10   *ruerit: ceciderit* S-C; *sublevantem se: sublevantem* Weber
4:12   *resistunt: resistent* Weber
<4:12   *shall* KJV: omitted in D-R>
4:13   *praevidere: providere* Weber
4:14   *de: et de* Weber
4:15   *consurget: consurgit* Weber
4:17   *Dei, et adpropinqua ut audias: Dei* Weber; *faciant: faciunt* S-C
5:2   *invenietur: invenitur* Weber
5:4   *conplere: reddere* S-C
5:5   *faciat: facias* S-C; *contra sermones tuos: super sermone tuo* Weber
<5:5   *lest* KJV (*wherefore*): *lest perhaps* D-R>
<5:8   *moreover* KJV: *and besides* D-R; *there is the king that reigneth over all*
        the land subject to him D-R/C: *the king of al the earth reigneth ouer*
        his seruant D-R>
5:9   *fructum: fructus* Weber
5:10   *comedant: comedunt* S-C
5:17   *quo: quod* Weber; *numerum: numero* S-C
<5:17   *all* KJV: *the number of* D-R>
6:3   *centum liberos: centum* Weber
<6:3   *attain to a great* D-R/C: *haue manie dayes of* D-R>
6:7   *implebitur: impletur* Weber
6:11   *multam* ΣT [Weber's sigla]: *multamque* S-C, *multa* Weber
<7:1   *all* KJV: *the number of* D-R>
7:1   *quo: quod* S-C
<7:3   *all* D-R/C: *al men* D-R>

<7:13   *excel in this* KJV?: *haue this much more* D-R>
<7:15   *any just complaint* D-R/C: *iust complants* D-R>
<7:18   *before* KJV: *not in* D-R>
 7:20   *confortavit: confortabit* Weber
<7:25   *It is* D-R/C (in italics): *and* D-R>
<7:27   *and* KJV (in roman type): omitted in D-R>
 7:28   *dixit: dicit* Weber
<7:28   *weighing one thing after* KJV n: *one thing and* D-R>
 8:1   *commutabit: commutavit* Weber
 8:7   *ventura: futura* S-C
 8:8   *dicione: potestate* S-C
<8:9   *one* KJV: omitted in D-R; *another* KJV: *man* D-R>
 8:10   *adhuc viverent: adviverent* Weber
<8:12   *from thence* D-R/C: omitted in D-R>
<8:13   *But* KJV: omitted in D R>
 8:13   *Domini: Dei* Weber
 8:14   *mala: multa* Weber
 8:15   *vitae suae: vitae* Weber
<8:16   *for* KJV *there are some* D-R/C: *There is a man* D-R>
 9:2   *futuro: futurum* S-C
<9:4   *or* D-R/C: *and* D-R; *hopeth* KJV?: *can haue confidence* D-R>
 9:4   *vivens: vivus* S-C
 9:6   *invidiae: invidia* Weber
<9:6   *any* KJV: omitted in D-R>
 9:9   *quo: quod* Weber
 9:11   *alio: ad aliud* S-C
 9:12   *in tempore: tempore* Weber
<9:13   *it seemed to me* KJV (*seemed* in roman type): *haue proved it* D-R>
 9:15   *est in: in* Weber; *et liberavit: liberavit* Weber
 10:1   *et ad: ad* Weber
 10:10   *erit: fuerit* S-C; *exacuetur: exacuatur* Weber; *sequetur: sequitur* Weber
<10:11   *he is nothing better* KJV: *nothing lesse then it hath he* D-R>
<10:12   *but* KJV: *and* D-R>
<10:13   *mischievous* KJV: *most wicked* D-R>
 10:14   *quod: quid* S-C; *post se: post* Weber; *est: sit* Weber
<10:16   *when thy* KJV: *whose* D-R; *when the* KJV: *whose* D-R>

10:19 *risu: risum* S-C; *oboediunt: oboedient* Weber

<10:20 *no, not* KJV: omitted in D-R; *what thou hast said* D-R/C: *the sentence*
   D-R>

10:20 *et aves caeli portabunt: avis caeli portabit* Weber

<11:1 *again* D-R/C: omitted in D-R>

<11:4 *shall not sow* KJV: *soweth not* D-R>

11:5 *praegnatis: praegnantis* S-C

11:6 *sementem tuam: semen tuum* S-C

<12:1 *shalt* KJV: *maist* D-R>

12:3 *nutabunt: nutabuntur* Weber; *in minuto: inminuto* Weber

12:5 *amigdalum: amygdalus* S-C

12:6 *funis: funiculus* S-C

12:8 *et omnia: omnia* Weber

12:9 *fecerat: fecerit* Weber

12:11 *consilium: concilium* Weber

12:14 *sit: illud sit* S-C

CANTICLE OF CANTICLES

1:2 *fragrantia: fraglantia* Weber

1:3 *curremus in odorem unguentorum tuorum: curremus* Weber

1:6 *post: per* Weber

1:7 *pulcherrima: pulchra* Weber

2:3 *malus: malum* Weber; *quem: quam* Weber

<2:9 *or* KJV: *and* D-R>

2:9 *respiciens: despiciens* Weber

2:10 *En: et* Weber; *mea, columba mea: mea* Weber

2:12 *terra nostra: terra* Weber

2:13 *florentes: florent* Weber; *odorem suum: odorem* Weber

2:15 *vulpes: vulpes vulpes* Weber

2:17 *hinuloque: aut hinulo* Weber

<2:17 *or* KJV: *and* D-R>

3:3 *diligit: dilexit* Weber

3:11 *desponsationis: disponsionis* Weber

<3:11 *espousals* KJV: *despousing* D-R>

4:8 *sponsa mea: sponsa* Weber

5:1 *et bibite: bibite* Weber

5:5   *murram, et*: *murra* Weber

<5:5   *dropped with* KJV (*with* in roman type): *have distilled* D-R>

5:6   *ostii mei*: *ostii* Weber

5:7   *et vulneraverunt*: *vulneraverunt* Weber

<5:14   *and as* D-R/C: omitted in D-R>

6:1   *aromatum*: *aromatis* Weber

6:6   *sic genae*: *genae* Weber

<6:8   *is but one* KJV (*but* in roman type in KJV and italics in D-R/C): omitted in D-R>

6:9   *ut castrorum*: *ut* Weber

<6:9   *bright* KJV? (*clear*): *elect* D-R; *army* KJV (in roman type): *armie of a campe* D-R>

6:10   *in*: *ad* Weber; *convallium et*: *convallis* / *ut* Weber

7:1   *Iuncturae*: *iunctura* Weber

7:8   *palmam et*: *palmam* Weber

7:9   *illius*: *illius ad* S-C

<7:13   *give* KJV: *haue geuen* D-R>

<8:1   *for* KJV (*as*): omitted in D-R>

8:1   *deosculer te*: *deosculer* Weber

8:4   *neque*: *et* Weber

8:5   *innixa*: *et nixa* Weber

8:6   *inferus*: *infernus* S-C

8:7   *possunt* C [Quentin's siglum]: *potuerunt* S-C, *poterunt* Weber; *despiciet*: *despicient* Weber; *eum*: *eam* S-C

<8:7   *can the floods drown* KJV: *shal flouds ouerwhelme* D-R>

8:11   *pacifico*: *Pacifico* S-C, Weber

<8:11   *every* KJV: *a* D-R>

8:12   *pacifici*: *Pacifici* S-C, *Pacifice* Weber

<8:12   *for thee, the peaceable* S-C: *thy peacemakers* D-R>

WISDOM

1:4   *intrabit*: *introibit* S-C

1:5   *corripietur a*: *corripietur* Weber

<1:5   *not abide when iniquity cometh* KJV (*vnrighteousnesse* for *iniquity*): *chastened of iniquitie oncoming* D-R>

1:6   *maledicum*: *maledictum* Weber

1:9   *Deum*: *Dominum* Weber
1:11   *sermo obscurus*: *responsum obscurum* Weber
1:14   *sanabiles fecit*: *sanabiles* Weber
1:15   *perpetua est et inmortalis*: *inmortalis est* Weber
1:16   *sponsiones*: *sponsionem* Weber; *sint*: *sunt* Weber
<1:16   *works* KJV: *handes* D-R; *a covenant* KJV: *couenances* D-R>
<2:1   *but* KJV (in italics in D-R/C): omitted in D-R>
2:2   *afflatus*: *flatus* S-C; *scintilla*: *scintillae* Weber
2:3   *qua*: *quia* Weber; *corpus nostrum*: *corpus* Weber; *transiet*: *transibit* S-C
2:5   *revertitur*: *revertetur* Weber
<2:8   *no meadow escape our riot* D-R/C: *there be no medow, which our riote shal not passe through* D-R>
2:9   *Nemo nostrum exors sit luxuriae nostrae*; *ubique*: *ubique* Weber
<2:9   *go without his part* KJV: *be exempted from* D-R>
2:11   *iustitiae*: *iniustitiae* Weber
<2:12   *lie in wait for* KJV: *circumuent* D-R; *not for our turn* KJV: *vnprofitable to vs* D-R>
<2:14   *a censurer* D-R/C: *vnto us to the defaming* D-R>
2:17   *veri sunt*: *veri sint* S-C
2:18   *manibus*: *manu* Weber
<2:21   *were deceived* KJV: *haue erred* D-R>
<3:3   *their going away from us for utter* KJV: *that which with vs is the way, is* D-R>
3:3   *exterminium*: *exterminii* Weber
3:5   *In paucis*: *et in paucis* Weber
3:6   *holocausti*: *holocausta* Weber
3:7   *iusti et*: *et* Weber
3:9   *donum*: *requies* *D-R
<3:9   *grace* KJV: *rest* D-R>
3:11   *inutilia*: *inhabitabilia* Weber; *eorum*: *illorum sunt* Weber
3:13   *sterilis et*: *sterilis* Weber; *non scivit*: *nescivit* S-C; *animarum sanctarum*: *animarum* Weber
3:14   *Dei*: *Domini* Weber
3:16   *in consummatione* ΑΛΜΦ [Weber's sigla]: *in inconsummatione* S-C, *inconsummati* Weber
<3:16   *not come to perfection* KJV: *be in consummation* D-R>
<3:18   *trial* KJV: *acknowledging* D-R>

4:1 *O quam pulchra est casta: melior est* Weber; *Inmortalis: inmortalitas*
  Weber; *memoria: in memoria* Weber

4:2 *eduxerit: duxerit* Weber

<4:3 multiplied *brood of the wicked shall not thrive* KJV: *the multitnde* [sic]
  of the impious, that hath manie children shal not be profitable D-R;
  any KJV: *lay* D-R>

<4:4 yet standing not fast KJV: *being weakly set* D-R>

4:5 *enim rami: rami* Weber; *inutiles: inutilis* Weber

4:6 *somnis: omnes* Weber

<4:6 beds KJV; *sleepes* D-R>

4:8 *hominis: hominibus* Weber

4:11 *ne fictio deciperet: fictio decipiat* Weber

4:15 *est in: in* Weber

4:18 *et: enim et* Weber; *contemnent eum: contemnent* Weber

<4:19 They D-R/C: *and* D-R>

4:19 *periet: peribit* S-C

<4:20 stand against them to D-R/C: *on the contrarie* D-R>

5:1 *angustaverunt: angustiaverunt* S-C

5:3 *Dicentes intra: dicent inter* Weber; *per angustiam: prae angustia* S-C;
  risu: derisum S-C

5:5 *Ecce quomodo: quomodo* Weber

5:6 *sol intelligentiae: sol* Weber

<5:8 advantage KJV (good): *commoditie* D-R>

5:8 *iactatio: iactantia* S-C

5:11 *aut tamquam: aut* Weber; *aere cuius: aere* Weber; *itineris illius: itineris*
  S-C; *sonitus: sonitus est* Weber

<5:11 when a bird KJV: *a bird, that* D-R; *the* S-C: *her* D-R; light air KJV:
  light wind D-R; *it* D-R/C: *the ayre* D-R>

5:12 *sagitta emissa: sagittae emissae* Weber

5:14 *in inferno hi qui: et* Weber

5:17 *sancto suo: suo* Weber

5:20 *inexpugnabile: inexpugnabilem* Weber

5:22 *directe: directae* Weber

<5:22 from the clouds; as KJV: *& as* D-R; bow KJV: *bow of the clouds* D-R>

<5:23 stone-casting S: *rocked* D-R>

5:24 *turbo: turbedo* Weber; *heremiam: heremum* S-C; *iniquitas illorum: ini-*
  quitatis Weber

6:1   *prudens*: *prudens magis* Weber

6:6   *in his*: *his* S-C

6:8   *Deus*: *Dominus* Weber; *verebitur*: *reverebitur* Weber; *de*: *pro* Weber

6:12   *et diligite* Ω^{SJ} ag [Quentin's sigla]: *diligite* S-C, Weber

6:13   *marcescit*: *marcescat* Weber; *invenitur*: *invenietur* Weber

<6:15   *to seek* KJV (*Whoso seeketh*): *to* D-R>

<6:17   *such as* KJV: *them that* D-R>

6:19   *custoditio legum*: *custodia legum* S-C

<6:19   *firm foundation* S?: *consummation* D-R>

6:21   *deducit*: *deducet* Weber

6:22   *sceptris, o*: *stemmatibus* Weber

6:23   verse omitted Weber

6:25   *talis homo*: *ista* Weber

7:1   *terreno*: *terreni* S-C; *finctus*: *factus* S-C

<7:1   *others* D-R/C (in italics): omitted in D-R; *race of him that was first made of the earth* S-C: *earthlie kinred of him, that was made first* D-R>

7:3   *et primam*: *primam* Weber

<7:3   *as all others do* KJV: *like to al men* D-R>

<7:6   *For* KJV: *therfore* D-R>

<7:7   *Wherefore* KJV: *For this cause* D-R; *upon God* KJV (in roman type): omitted in D-R>

7:12   *me ista*: *ista* Weber

7:14   *quod*: *quo* S-C

7:15   *dedit*: *det* Weber; *quae mihi*: *quae* Weber; *ipse*: *ipse et* Weber

7:16   *scientia et*: *scientiae* Weber

7:18   *vicissitudinum permutationes et consummationes temporum* MΦ [Weber's sigla], S-C (*commutationes* for *consummationes*): *et meditationem omnium morum mutationes et divisiones temporum* Weber

<7:18   *changes* S-C: *consummations* D-R>

7:20   *virgultorum*: *arborum* Weber

7:22   *intellectus*: *intellegentiae* S-C; *qui*: *quem* S-C; *benefaciens*: *benefacere* Weber

7:23   *benignus, stabilis*: *stabilis* Weber; *intellegibiles, mundos, subtiles*: *intellegibilis, mundus, subtilis* S-C

7:24   *ubique*: *ubique et capit* Weber

<7:27   *but* KJV: omitted in D-R>

8:1   *ergo*: *enim* Weber

8:3   *Generositatem illius*: *generositatem* Weber

8:5   *sapientiae*: *sapientia* S-C

8:7   *prudentiam*: *sapientiam* Weber

<8:7 *which are such things as men can have nothing* KJV: *then the which nothing is* D-R>

8:11 *et acutus*: *acutus* Weber

8:13 *Praeterea*: *propterea* Weber

8:14 *subiectae*: *subditae* S-C

8:17 *cognatione*: *cogitatione* Weber

<8:17 *to be allied to* KJV: *in the kindred of* D-R>

8:21 *possem*: *possum* Weber; *sapientia* YΦZ²ΓᴹΨᴰΩarelvs [Quentin's sigla]: *sapientiae* S-C, Weber

<8:21 *a point of* KJV: omitted in D-R>

9:1   *patrum meorum*: *parentum* Weber; *misericordiae*: *misericordiae tuae* Weber

9:2   *dominetur*: *dominaretur* S-C

<9:5 *falling short of* D-R/C: *lesse to* D-R>

9:6   *Et*: *Nam et* S-C; *si afuerit*: *et afuerit* *D-R

<9:6 *For* S-C: *And* D-R; *yet* KJV: *and* D-R>

9:8   *et dixisti me*: *dixisti* Weber; *aram*: *altare* S-C

9:9   *sapientia tua*: *sapientia* Weber

9:10 *a*: *mitte illam a* Weber; *ut sciam*: *et sciam* Weber

9:13 *Deus*: *Dominus* Weber

9:16 *investigabit*: *investigavit* Weber

9:17 *sciet*: *scivit* Weber

9:18 *sint*: *sunt* Weber; *didicerint*: *didicerunt* Weber

9:19 *Nam*: *et* Weber; *sunt, quicumque placuerunt tibi, Domine, a principio*: *sunt* Weber

10:1 *finctus*: *formatus* S-C; *est a Deo*: *est* Weber; *patre* Q²Y [Quentin's sigla]: *pater* S-C, *patrem* Weber

<10:3 *But* KJV: omitted in D-R; *wherewith he murdered his brother* KJV: *of brothers manslaughter* D-R>

10:3 *fraterni*: *fraternitatis* Weber

<10:4 *the course of* KJV: omitted in D-R>

10:5 *servavit*: *conservavit* S-C

10:6 *descendente igne*: *descendentem ignem* Weber

10:7 *quibus: cuius* Weber

<10:7 *that ripen not* KJV (*that neuer come to ripenesse*): *at vncertain season*
   D-R; *pillar* D-R: literally, *formation*>

<10:8 *so much as* KJV: *neither* D-R>

10:11 *illi et: et* Weber

10:12 *et sciret: ut sciret* Weber

10:13 *Descenditque: Descendit* Weber

<10:13 *She* KJV: *and she* D-R>

<10:14 *accused* KJV: *spotted* D-R>

10:15 *conprimebant: deprimebant* S-C

10:16 *Dei: Domini* Weber

10:17 *nocte: per noctem* S-C

10:18 *et transulit* $X\Phi Z^2\Psi^D\Omega q$(ut vid.)arels [Quentin's sigla]: *Transtulit*
   S-C, Weber (without capitalization); *per Mare: mare* Weber

11:2 *inhabitabantur: habitabantur* S-C; *desertis: secretis* Weber

11:5 *illorum a defectione potus sui et in eis cum abundarent filii Israhel laetati
   sunt: illorum* Weber

11:6 *deessent: deesset* Weber

11:8 *cum minuerentur: comminuerentur* Weber

<11:10 *chastised with mercy* KJV: *in deede with mercie taking discipline* D-R>

<11:12 *whether* KJV: *the* D-R; *or* KJV: *and the* D-R>

<11:14 *the others were benefited* KJV: *it went wel with them* D-R>

11:14 *Dominum, admirantes in finem exitus: Dominum* Weber

11:15 *prava olim* Z* [Quentin's siglum]: *prava* S-C, Weber; *sitientes: faciens*
   Weber

<11:15 *at the time of his being wickedly exposed* D-R/C: *in that wicked laying
   out* D-R; *their thirsting being unlike to that of* D-R/C: *not thirsting in
   like maner to* D-R>

11:16 *iniquitatis: iniquitates* Weber

<11:18 *without form* KJV: *inuisible* D-R>

11:19 *ignotas: et ignotas* Weber; *ignium: igneum* Weber

<11:19 *stinking smoke* D-R/C: *sauour of smoke* D-R>

<11:20 *very* D-R/C: omitted in D-R>

11:21 *in mensura: mensura* Weber

11:22 *supererat: superat* Weber

<11:23 *grain* KJV: *weight* D-R>

11:25 *constituisti aut fecisti: constituisti* Weber

12:1   *O quam bonus et suavis est, Domine, spiritus tuus: bonus enim spiritus tuus est* Weber

12:2   *Ideoque: propter quod* Weber; *admones et: admonens* Weber

<12:2   *little and little* KJV: *partes* D-R>

12:3   *Illos: et illos* Weber; *quos exhorruisti: odiens* Weber

12:5   *filiorum suorum: filiorum* Weber; *et devoratores: devorationem et* Weber

<12:6   *sacrificing with their own hands* KJV (*that killed* for *sacrificing*): *authors of* D-R>

12:10   *nequa: nequam* S-C

<12:10   *they were a wicked generation* KJV (*naughtie* for *wicked*): *the nation of them is wicked* D-R>

12:12   *conspectu tuo: conspectum tuum* Weber

12:13   *Non: nec* Weber; *iudicas iudicium: iudicasti* Weber

<12:15   *thinking* KJV: *thou also estemest* D-R>

<12:17   *when men will not believe thee* KJV (without *thee*): *which art not thought* D-R>

12:17   *horum qui te nesciunt: hos qui* Weber

12:18   *voles: volueris* S-C

12:19   *iudicans das: das* Weber

12:20   *adtentione: adtentione et liberasti* Weber; *possent: possint* Weber

12:22   *misericordiam tuam: misericordiam* Weber

<12:24   *ways* KJV: *way* D-R>

12:26   *et increpationibus: increpationis* Weber; *correcti: correpti* Weber

12:27   *In quibus enim: in his enim quae patiebantur moleste ferebant / in quibus* Weber; *illis veniet: eorum venit super illos* S-C

<12:27   *seeing with indignation that they suffered* D-R/C: *in what thinges they suffering tooke indignation* D-R; *very* D-R/C: omitted in D-R; *came* S-C: *shal come* D-R>

13:1   *in quibus: quibus* Weber; *bona: bonis* *D-R

13:3   *quanto his: quanto* Weber

13:4   *constituit: fecit* S-C

<13:6   *yet as to these they are less to be blamed* KJV: *notwithstanding there is yet in these lesse complainte* D-R; *they* KJV: *they also* D-R>

13:6   *fortassis: fortasse* S-C

13:10   *et similitudines: similitudines* Weber

<13:11   *a tree proper for his use* D-R/C: *streight timber* D-R>

13:11   *secaverit: secuerit* S-C

13:12   *reliquias: reliquiis* S-C

<13:13   *taking* KJV: *maketh* D-R; *when he hath nothing else to do* KJV (*had* for *hath*): *in the holownes therof* D-R>

<13:14   *the resemblance of* D-R/C: *compareth it to* D-R>

13:14   *rubrica: lubrica* Weber

13:15   *et in: in* Weber; *illud et: illud* Weber

13:16   *adiutorium: adiutorio* Weber

13:17   *nuptiis: de nuptiis* S-C

<13:17   *maketh prayer* KJV: *making a vow* D-R; *inquiring* D-R/C: *he seeketh* D-R; *and* KJV: omitted in D-R>

<13:19   *good* KJV: omitted in D-R>

14:4   *potes: potens es* S-C; *salvare: sanare* Weber; *arte: rate* Weber; *adeat mare: adeat* Weber

14:5   *esset: essent* S-C; *etiam et: etiam* Weber

14:6   *Sed et: sed* Weber

<14:6   *And* S?: *But* D-R>

14:8   *fit idolum: fit* Weber; *deus: Deus* Weber

<14:8   *he* KJV: *he in deede* D-R; *because* KJV: omitted in D-R>

14:11   *in idolis: idolis* Weber; *animis: animabus* S-C; *muscipulum: muscipulam* S-C

14:13   *Neque enim: neque* Weber

14:14   *haec advenit: venit* Weber

<14:14   *by the vanity of men they* KJV: *this vanitie of men* D-R; *they shall be found to come shortly to an end* KJV (without *be found to*): *there is found a short end of them* D-R>

14:15   *fecit imaginem et: faciens imaginem* Weber; *tunc: tunc quasi* S-C

<14:15   *as* S-C: omitted in D-R>

14:17   *Et hos: hos* Weber; *quod: hoc quod* S-C

<14:17   *this* KJV: omitted in D-R>

14:20   *hominum, abducta: adducta* Weber; *modicum* Z* [Quentin's siglum]: *tempus* S-C, Weber

<14:20   *but* KJV: omitted in D-R>

14:25   *corruptio et: corruptio* Weber

<14:25   *tumults* KJV: *truble* D-R>

14:26   *Dei: Domini* Weber; *inordinatio moechiae: moechiae* Weber; *inpudicitia: inpudicitiae* S-C

14:28 *aut certe: aut* Weber
<14:28 *or* KJV: *or certes* D-R>
14:29 *noceri: renoceri* Weber
<14:29 *look* KJV: *hope* D-R>
14:30 *Utraque: Utraque mala* *D-R
<14:30 *But for both these things they shall be justly punished* KJV: *Two euil thinges therfor shal happen to them worthely* D-R>
14:31 *iuratorum: iurantium* Weber
<14:31 *just vengeance* KJV: *punishment* D-R; *punisheth* KJV: *goeth . . . through* D-R>
15:1 *et in: et* Weber
<15:5 *enticeth the fool to lust after it* KJV: *geueth concupiscence to the sensles* D-R>
15:6 *habeant: habent* Weber
<15:6 *no better things* D-R/C *to trust in* KJV: *their hope in such thinges* D-R>
<15:7 *both vessels that are for clean uses and likewise such as serve to* KJV: *the vessels, that are cleane to vse, and in like maner them, that are* D-R>
15:7 *qui: quis* S-C
15:8 *vano: vanum* Weber; *quem: quam* S-C
<15:8 *himself* KJV: omitted in D-R; *to the same* KJV: omitted in D-R; *when his life which was lent him shall be called for again* KJV: *being exacted of the debte of the life which he had* D-R>
15:10 *est enim: est* Weber
15:11 *ei spiritum: spiritum* Weber
15:12 *Sed et: sed* Weber; *ludum: lusum* S-C
<15:13 *others* KJV: *men* D-R>
<15:14 *But* S?: *For* D-R; *that hold them in subjection* KJV: *and rule ouer them* D-R; *measure* D-R/C: *measure of the soule* D-R>
15:15 *usus: visus* Weber
15:18 *insensata: insensate* Weber; *illis: aliis* Weber
<15:18 *but* D-R/C: *for* D-R>
15:19 *effugerunt: effugit* Weber
16:1 *haec et: hoc* Weber
<16:2 *dealing* KJV: *thou didst . . . dispose* D-R; *them* KJV: *to whom* D-R>
<16:3 *loathe* KJV: *be turned away . . . from* D-R; *that which was necessary to satisfy their* D-R/C: *necessarie* D-R>
<16:4 *inevitable* S: *without excuse* D-R>

16:5   *perversarum colubrarum*: *perversorum colubrorum* S-C
16:6   *Sed non*: *non* Weber
16:8   *In*: *et in* Weber
16:11 *et velociter*: *et* Weber
16:13 *es enim, Domine, qui*: *enim* Weber
16:14 *malitiam*: *malitiam animam suam* Weber; *exierit*: *exibit* Weber
16:16 *consumpti*: *consummati* Weber
<16:17 *And* D-R/C: *For* D-R>
16:19 *super*: *supra* S-C; *ardebat*: *exardescebat* S-C; *undique ut*: *ut* Weber
<16:19 *fruits* KJV: *nation* D-R>
16:20 *e*: *de* S-C
<16:21 *to* KJV (*vnto*): *which thou hast toward* D-R>
16:21 *serviens*: *deserviens* S-C; *quisque*: *quis* Weber
16:23 *Hoc*: *hic* S-C
16:24 *excandescit*: *exardescit* S-C
16:25 *deserviebant*: *deserviebat* S-C; *desiderabant*: *desiderati sunt* Weber
<16:25 *it was* S-C: omitted in D-R; *was obedient* S-C: *they serued* D-R>
16:28 *orientem*: *ortum* S-C; *tibi*: *te* S-C
16:29 *fides*: *spes* S-C; *tabescet*: *tabescit* Weber
<16:29 *hope* S-C: *faith* D-R>
17:1   *tua, Domine*: *tua* Weber
<17:2   *themselves* D-R/C (in italics): omitted in D-R; *there* KJV (bracketed
        in KJV and in italics in D-R/C); omitted in D-R>
17:4   *tristes illis*: *tristes* Weber
17:6   *percussi*: *perculsi* S-C
<17:7   *the delusions of their magic art were put down* KJV: *there were added
        derisions of the magical art* D-R; *their boasting of wisdom was re-
        proachfully rebuked* KJV (*their vaunting in wisedome was reprooued
        with disgrace*): *contumelious rebuke of the glorie of their wisdom*
        D-R>
17:8   *et perturbationes*: *turbationes* Weber
<17:8   *were sick themselves of a fear worthy to be laughed at* KJV: *with derision
        languished ful of feare* D-R>
<17:9   *could ... be avoided* KJV: *any man could avoyde* D-R>
<17:11 *yielding up* D-R/C: *bewraying* D-R>
17:12 *intro*: *intus* S-C; *conputat*: *putat* Weber; *inscientiam* [earliest printed
        Clementine editions had *in scientiam*]: *scientiam* Weber

<17:13 *in which nothing could be done* KJVn (*in which they could do nothing*):
in deede impotent D-R>

17:15 *quisquam: quicumque* Weber

<17:16 *and* D-R/C: omitted in D-R>

17:17 *arborum ramos: ramos* Weber

<17:17 *spreading* KJV: *thicke* D-R; *fall* KJV: *force* D-R; *with violence* KJV:
exceedingly D-R>

17:18 *praecipitatarum: praecipitarum* Weber; *faciebant: faciebat* Weber

<17:18 *roaring* KJV: *mightie* D-R; *wild* KJV: *roaring* D-R>

17:19 *inluminabatur: luminabatur* Weber

18:1 *per eadem: eadem* S-C; *magnificabant te: magnificabant* Weber

<18:1 *the* S-C: *by the* D-R>

<18:2 *now* KJV (in roman type): omitted in D-R; *this* D-R/C: *a* D-R>

18:3 *ignis: igni* Weber

<18:4 *The others* D-R/C: *They* D-R; *was* KJV. *began* D-R>

<18:5 *And* KJV: omitted in D-R; *one* KJV: *and one* D-R>

18:6 *enim nox: nox* Weber; *patribus: parentibus* Weber

18:8 *sic et: sic* Weber

18:9 *et bona: bona* Weber; *recepturos: percepturos* Weber; *patrum: patri*
Weber

<18:10 *on the other side* KJV: omitted in D-R>

<18:12 *Neither* KJV: *For neitheir* D-R>

18:13 *tunc vero primum: tunc* Weber; *esse: se esse* Weber

<18:13 *whereas they would not believe any thing* KJV *before* D-R/C: *concerning
al thinges being incredulous* D-R; *enchantments* KJV: *inchantments,
but* D-R>

18:17 *Tum: Tunc* S-C

18:18 *demonstrabat mortis: demonstrabat* Weber

<18:20 *the just also were afterwards touched by an assault* D-R/C: *then there
touched the iust also a tentation* D-R>

18:20 *ira tua: ira* Weber

18:21 *deprecari pro populis: propugnavit* Weber

18:22 *non in: non* Weber; *armaturae potentia: armatura potentiae* Weber;
illum qui se vexabat: vexatorem Weber

<18:22 *punished them* KJV (without *them*): *vexed him* D-R>

18:24 *scripta: sculpta* S-C

18:25 *His autem: haec autem his* Weber

19:2   *permisissent: reversi essent* Weber; *educerent: ducerent* Weber
19:3   *luctum: luctus* Weber; *proiecerant: proiecerunt* Weber
<19:3   *whilst they were yet mourning* KJV: *hauing as yet moorning betwen their*
         hands D-R; *they had pressed to be gone* KJV (*entreated* for *pressed*): *by*
         intreating they had cast forth D-R
19:4   *memorationem: commemorationem* S-C; *quae deerant: eam quae deerat*
         Weber; *repleret punitio: replerent punitionem* Weber
<19:5   *might* KJV: *certes might* D-R>
19:7   *adumbrabat: obumbrabat* S-C; *in: ex* Weber
<19:7   *where water* KJV: *out of the water which* D-R>
19:8   *tua mirabilia et: mirabilia* Weber
19:9   *depaverunt escam: depaverunt* Weber
19:11   *adducti: abducti* Weber; *escas: escam* Weber
<19:11   *delicate meats* KJV: *meates of deliciousnes* D-R>
19:12   *fulminum: fluminum* Weber
19:13   *redigebant: accipiebant* Weber
<19:13   *than any; others* D-R/C (*than any* in italics): *some* D-R; *these* KJV:
         other some D-R; *guests . . . that had deserved well of them* KJV (*friends*
         for *guests*): *good strangers* D-R>
19:14   *haec: hoc* Weber; *quidam: quis* Weber; *erat: erit* Weber
<19:14   *in another respect also they were worse* D-R/C: *in deede there was an*
         other respect also of them D-R; *the others* D-R/C: *they* D-R>
<19:15   *grievously* KJV: *with most cruel sorowes* D-R>
<19:16   *others* D-R/C: omitted in D-R; *and* D-R/C: omitted in D-R>
<19:17   *which* KJV: *wherfore* D-R>
19:17   *aestimari: est aestimare et* Weber; *visu certo potest: certo visu* Weber
19:20   *dissolvebatur: dissolvitur* Weber
<19:20   *apt to melt* KJV: *easely dissolued euen* D-R>

ECCLESIASTICUS

Prologue 1   *sapientia demonstrata est: sapientiam demonstratam* Weber;
              necesse est: necesse S-C
Prologue 2   *voluit: volui* Weber
<Prologue 2   *something* KJV: *some of those thinges* D-R>

Prologue 3   *deficere: et deficere* Weber; *et verba* ΙΙ^HΙ˙Ω^Mrels [Quentin's
    sigla]: *verba*: S-C, Weber
<Prologue 3   *have not the same force in them* KJV: *also fayle* D-R>
Prologue 4   *aliorum librorum: librorum* Weber; *fuissem, inveni ibi: fecissem,
    inveni* Weber
<Prologue 4   *books* KJV: *other bookes* D-R; *continuing* KJV: *when I had bene*
    D-R>
Prologue 5   *ad illa quae ad finem ducunt librum dare et illis: ut illa quae docent
    homines discerent* *D-R, *ad illa quae ad finem ducunt librum istum
    dare et illis* S-C; *intendere* ΤΤ^HS* [Quenti's sigla]; *intendere et discere*
    S-C, Weber; *proposuerunt: proposuerint* S-C
<Prologue 5   *I . . . for me* KJV: *myself also* D-R; *and study* S: omitted in
    D-R; *brought the book to an end and set it forth for the service of them*
    KJV: *brought forth this doctrin in space of time, that men may lerne
    those thinges which teach them* D-R; *and to learn* S-C: omitted in
    D-R>
  1:2   *mensus: dimensus* S-C
  1:8   *et rex: rex* Weber
  1:9   *illam in: illam* Weber
  1:12   *in longitudine: et longitudinem* S-C
<1:12   *and* S-C: *in* D-R>
<1:15   *shew herself* D-R/C: *appeare in vision* D-R>
  1:16   *Cum: et cum* Weber; *feminis graditur: seminis creditur* Weber
  1:19   *Dominum: Deum* Weber
  1:20   *timere: est timere* S-C
<1:21   *increase* KJV: *generations* D-R>
  1:22   *replens: repollens* Weber
  1:24   *exaltat: inaltat* Weber
  1:25   *rami enim: et rami* S-C
<1:25   *and* S-C: *for* D-R>
  1:27   *Domini: Dei* Weber
  1:30   *abscondebit: abscondet* S-C
  1:31–32   omitted in Weber
  1:33   *Fili, concupiscens: concupiscens* Weber
<1:33   *if thou desire* KJV: *coueting* D-R>
  1:36   *Non: Ne* S-C

<1:37   *let not thy lips be a stumbling block to thee* D-R/C: *be not scandalized in thy lippes* D-R>

2:1   *servituti: ad servitutem* S-C

2:2   *Inclina aurem tuam: declina aurem* Weber; *excipe: suscipe* S-C; *tempore: tempus* Weber

<2:2   *clouds* D-R/C: *obduction* D-R>

<2:3   *Wait on God with patience* D-R/C: *Susteyne the sustentations of God* D-R>

2:6   *veteresce: veterasce* S-C

2:7   *Dominum: Deum* Weber

2:8   *Dominum: Deum* Weber

2:9   *Dominum: Deum* Weber

2:10   *Dominum: Deum* Weber

2:11   *quia nullus: quis* Weber

2:12   *quis enim permansit: permansit* Weber; *Aut: et* Weber

2:13   *est Deus: Deus* Weber; *remittet in die: remittit in tempore* Weber; *peccata, et protector est: peccata* Weber

2:15   *et ideo: ideo* Weber

2:16   *et qui: qui* Weber; *deverterunt: diverterunt* S-C

2:17   *facient: facietis* Weber; *Dominus: Deus* Weber

2:20   *parabunt: praeparabunt* S-C

2:22   *Domini: Dei* Weber

2:23   *ipso est: ipso* Weber

3:1   *obaudientia: oboedientia* S-C

3:2   *filii: filii dilecti* Weber

3:3   *exquirens firmavit: exquirens* Weber

3:4   *illis et: illis* Weber

3:6   *patrem suum: patrem* Weber; *filiis, et in die orationis suae exaudietur: filiis* Weber

<3:7   *enjoy* D-R/C: *liue* D-R>

3:7   *obaudit patrem: oboedit patri* S-C; *matri: matrem* S-C

3:8   *Dominum: Deum* Weber; *his: in his* Weber; *generaverunt: genuerunt* S-C

3:10   *ab eo: a Deo* Weber; *maneat: manet* Weber

3:12   *eius: sed* Weber

3:13   *filii: filiis* Weber

3:14   *ne: non* S-C

3:17   *in iustitia: iniustitia* Weber; *et in die: in die* Weber; *et sicut: sicut*
       Weber

3:18   *relinquit: derelinquit* S-C

3:22   *scrutaveris: quaesieris* S-C; *exquisieris: scrutatus fueris* S-C

3:25   *hominum: hominis* Weber

3:26   *quoque subplantavit: enim inplanavit* Weber

3:28   *pravus corde: pravicordius* Weber

3:29   *doloribus: in doloribus* S-C

<3:29   *sin to* KJV: *to commit* D-R >

3:30   *erit: est* Weber; *radicabitur: eradicabitur* Weber

3:31   *sapientis: sapiens* Weber

3:34   *conspector: prospector* S-C; *est eius qui: qui* Weber; *eius in: in* Weber; *sui*
       inveniet: tui invenies Weber

4:1   *fraudes: defraudes* S-C

4:5   *oculos tuos: oculos* Weber

<4:5   *fear of* D-R/C: omitted in D-R>

4:6   *te: tibi* S-C; *amaritudine animae: amaritudine* Weber; *precatio: depre-*
       catio S-C

<4:6   *for* D-R/C: *and* D-R>

4:8   *pauperi sine tristitia: pauperi* Weber; *responde illi: responde* Weber

4:9   *acedieris* Sabatier's translation of S: *acide feras* S-C, Weber

4:11   *eris: eris tu* S-C; *obaudiens: oboediens* S-C

4:12   *inspirat: inspiravit* Weber; *exquirentes: inquirentes* S-C; *via: viam*
       Weber

4:13   *conplectebuntur: conplectentur* S-C

4:14   *benedicet: benedicit* Weber

4:17   *illius: illorum* Weber

<4:17   *his generation* KJV: *her creatures* D-R>

4:19   *probationem: adprobationem* Weber

<4:19   *laws* KJV: *cogitations* D-R>

4:20   *iter: iterum* Weber; *illum et laetificabit illum: illum* Weber

4:21   *denudabit: denudat* Weber; *illi et thesaurizabit: et thesaurizat* Weber

4:24   *non: ne* S-C

4:27   *Non: Ne* S-C; *casum suum: casu suo* S-C

4:28   *tempus: tempore* S-C

4:29   *dignoscitur: agnoscitur* Weber; *verbo sensati: verbis veritatis* Weber

4:30   *verbo veritatis: veritati* Weber

<4:30   *truth, but* KJV: *word of truth . . . and* D-R>

4:31   *omni homini: homini* Weber

<4:31   *but* D-R/C: *and* D-R>

4:33   *agoniare: agonizare* S-C

4:36   *dandum: reddendum* Weber

<4:36   *when thou shouldst* KJV: *to* D-R>

5:2   *Non: Ne* S-C; *sequaris in fortitudine tua: sequaris* Weber; *cordis tui: cordis* Weber

<5:2   *desires* KJV *(wayes): concupiscence* D-R>

5:5   *propitiato peccato: propitiatu peccatorum* Weber

5:6   *Domini: Dei* Weber

5:7   *ab illo cito proximant: a Deo cito proximant* *D-R, *ab illo* Weber

5:8   *Dominum: Deum* Weber

5:9   *veniet: venit* Weber

5:10   *non: nihil* Weber

5:11   *omnem viam: omni via* Weber; *enim omnis: enim* Weber; *duplici: in duplici* S-C

5:12   *Domini: Dei* Weber

5:13   *verbum: verbum Dei* S-C, according to appartuses of Weber and Quentin, but not according to Marietti edition (or D-R)

5:15   *lingua vero: lingua* Weber; *est ipsius: ipsius* Weber

5:16   *susurro: susurrio* Weber; *tua ne: tua* Weber

5:18   *pusillo et magno: pusillum et magnum* S-C

<6:1   *so shall* KJV: *and* D-R>

<6:2   *lest* S: *lest perhaps* D-R>

6:3   *comedat: comedet* Weber; *perdat et relinquaris: perdet et relinqueris* Weber

6:4   *inimicis: inimici* Weber; *deducet: deducit* Weber

<6:6   *Be in peace with many, but* KJV *(neuerthelesse* for *but): Let there be manie at peace with thee, and* D-R>

6:6   *consiliarius tibi sit: consiliarii tibi sint* Weber

6:7   *non: ne* S-C

6:9   *convertitur: egreditur* Weber

6:10   *permanebit: permanet* Weber

6:12   *absconderit: abscondet* Weber
6:16   *invenient: inveniunt* Weber
6:21   *permanebit: permanet* Weber
<6:22   *she shall be to them as a mighty stone of trial* KJV: *As the vertue of a stone she shal be a probation in them* D-R>
6:22   *illam: illum* Weber
6:23   *agnita: cognita* S-C
6:27   *serva: conserva* S-C
6:28   *derelinqueris: derelinquas* S-C
6:30   *conpedes eius: conpedes* Weber
6:31   *alligatura: netura* Weber
6:33   *animum tuum: animam tuam* Weber
6:34   *Si: et si* Weber
6:35   *te: a te* S-C
<6:36   *go to him early in the morning* D-R/C: *watch after him* D-R>
6:37   *tuum habe: habe* Weber
<6:37   *meditate continually* KJV: *most of al be dayly conuersant* D-R>
<7:1   *no evils shall* KJV (*harme* for *evils*): *they shal not* D-R>
7:3   *Fili, non: non* Weber; *iustitiae* Q cum Brev. goth. [Quentin's sigla]: *iniustitiae* S-C, *iniuriae* Weber
<7:3   *injustice* S-C: *justice* D-R>
7:4   *a Domino: ab homine* Weber
7:6   *nisi si: nisi* S-C; *aequitate: agilitate* Weber
7:9   *animo tuo: anima tua* Weber
7:10   *non: ne* S-C
7:11   *offerente: offerentem* Weber
7:13   *arare: amare* Weber
7:14   *non: non est* S-C
7:20   *pecuniam differentem: pecunia differenti* Weber
7:21   *Domini: Dei* Weber
7:23   *sensatus sit tibi: sensatus* Weber
<7:24   *down their neck* KJV: *them* D-R>
<7:27   *well* D-R/C (in italics): omitted in D-R>
7:28   *corde tuo: corde* Weber
7:30   *natus non: non* Weber
7:31   *Dominum: Deum* Weber

7:32   *virtute tua*: *virtute* Weber; *non*: *ne* S-C

7:34   *illis*: *illi* Weber; *tua purga*: *purga* Weber

7:35   *offeres Domino et*: *offers* Weber

7:37   *dati*: *datus* Weber

<7:37   *A gift hath grace* KJV: *The grace of a gift is* D-R>

7:38   *consolatione*: *conrogatione* Weber

<8:1   *lest* KJV: *lest perhaps* D-R>

8:2   *consistat*: *te constituat* S-C

8:3   *multos enim*: *multos* Weber; *usque*: *usque ad* S-C

8:4   *igne*: *ignem* S-C

8:6   *correptionem*: *correptione* S-C

8:7   *senecta*: *senectute* S-C

8:8   *mortuo inimico tuo*: *mortuo* Weber

<8:8   *that others should rejoice at our death* D-R (*therat* for *at our death*): literally, *to become a source of joy*>

<8:9   *but* KJV: *and* D-R>

8:10   *disces sapientiam et*: *disces* Weber

8:11   *ipsi*: *et ipsi* Weber

8:12   *dare responsum*: *responsum* Weber

8:13   *peccatorum arguens*: *peccatoris arguens* Weber; *et ne*: *ne* Weber

<8:13   *lest thou be* KJV: *and be not* D-R>

<8:14   *to entrap thee in thy words* KJV: *in wayte for thy mouth* D-R>

8:15   *fenerare*: *fenerari* S-C; *tamquam*: *quasi* S-C

8:17   *iustum*: *dignum* Weber

<8:18   *lest* KJV: *lest perhaps* D-R>

8:19   *facias*: *facies* S-C [first three editions, but later corrected]; *et cum*: *cum* Weber

8:20   *ne*: *non* S-C

8:22   *gratiam falsam*: *gratiam* Weber

<8:22   *lest* KJV: *lest perhaps* D-R; *evil turn* KJV (*shrewd* for *evil*): *false kindnes* D-R>

9:1   *ostendat*: *ostendas* Weber

9:2   *virtute tua*: *virtutem tuam* S-C

9:4   *saltatrice*: *psaltrice* Weber

<9:4   *lest* KJV: *lest perhaps* D-R; *the force of her charms* D-R/C: *her efficacie* D-R>

<9:5   *lest* KJV (*that . . . not*): *lest perhaps* D-R>
9:6   *Non: Ne* S-C; *nullo: ullo* S-C
9:7   *circumspicere: conspicere* Weber
9:8   *non: ne* S-C
9:10   *conculcabitur: conculcatur* Weber
9:12   *Cum aliena: cum aliena muliere non accumbas super cubitum / cum aliena*
        Weber
9:13   *illa: illam* S-C
9:15   *veterascet: veterescat* Weber
‹9:18 *so* KJV: *and* D-R›
<9:19 *lest* KJV: *lest perhaps* D-R>
9:21   *proximo tuo: proximo* Weber
9:23   *cogitatus Dei: cogitatus* Weber; *enarratio: narratio* Weber
9:24   *manus: manu* S-C; *laudabuntur: laudabitur* Weber
<9:24 *hand* S-C: *handes* D-R>
10:1   *iudicabit: vindicabit* Weber
<10:2 *is himself* KJV: omitted in D-R>
10:2   *inhabitantes in ea: inhabitantes* Weber
10:3   *prudentium: potentium* S-C
<10:3 *prudence of the rulers* KJV (*them which are in authoritie* for *rulers*):
        vnderstanding of the prudent D-R>
10:4   *terrae: terrae / et exclamabilis omnis iniquitas gentium* Weber
<10:4 *in his time* KJV (*due* for *his*): *for a time* D-R>
10:5   *prosperitas: potestas* Weber
10:7   *Deo: Deo est* S-C
<10:10 *such a one* KJV: *he* D-R>
10:11 *vita. Languor prolixior gravat medicum: via* Weber
10:13 *morietur: moritur* Weber
10:15 *omnis: omnis est* S-C; *eum: eos* Weber
10:23 *Deum: Dominum* Weber; *exhonorabitur: exhonorabitur hominum*
        Weber
<10:24 *so* KJV: *and* D-R>
10:24 *Dominum: Deum* Weber
<10:25 *and* KJV: omitted in D-R>
10:26 *Non: Noli* S-C; *non: noli* S-C
10:27 *et iudex: est iudex* Weber

10:28 *prudens et: prudens* Weber

10:30 *panem: pane* S-C

10:34 *Qui autem: qui* Weber

<11:3 *but* KJV: *and* D-R>

11:6 *pressi: oppressi* S-C

11:8 *seniorum* ΑϹΣΛΣΜΦ [Weber's sigla]: *sermonum* S-C, Weber

<11:8 *others* D-R/C: omitted in D-R; *their discourse* S-C: *ancients* D-R>

11:11 *Est homo: est* Weber; *abundabit: abundat* Weber

<11:12 *Again* KJV: omitted in D-R>

<11:13 *yet* KJV: *and* D-R>

11:14 *mors: mors / et* Weber

11:15–16 both verses omitted in Weber

11:17 *habebit: habebunt* Weber

11:18 *haec: haec est* S-C

11:20 *praetereat: praeteriet* S-C; *et mors appropinquet et relinquat: et relinquet* Weber; *aliis et morietur: aliis* Weber

<11:20 *shall pass* S-C: *passeth* D-R>

11:21 *veteresce: veterasce* S-C

11:22 *fide: confide* S-C

11:23 *subito honestare: de subito honestari* Weber

11:24 *hora: honore* Weber

11:26 *mihi sum: sum* Weber

11:28 *facile: facile est* S-C

11:32 *foetentium et: fetantium* Weber; *prospectator: prospector* S-C

<11:34 *cometh* D-R/C: *is increased* D-R; *blood* D-R/C: *is increased* D-R>

11:35 *tibi: te* Weber

<11:35 *lest* KJV: *lest perhaps* D-R>

11:36 *turbore: turbine* S-C

12:3 *enim ei: ei* Weber; *est in: est* Weber; *elemosynam: elemosynas* S-C

<12:3 *hateth* KJV: *both hateth* D-R>

<12:4 *God* D-R/C: *& ... he* D-R>

12:6 *dare: dari* S-C

<12:6 *hold back thy bread, and give it not to him* KJV: *prohibite to geue him bread* D-R>

12:7 *bonis quaecumque feceris illi: bonis* Weber

12:12 *tuam: tuam / ne conversus stet in loco tuo* Weber; *cognoscas: agnoscas* S-C

<12:12 *lest* KJV: *lest perhaps* D-R; *acknowledge* S-C; *know* D-R>

12:13 *Sic et* C [Weber's siglum]: *et sic* S-C, *et* Weber

<12:15 *but* KJV: *and* D-R>

<12:16 *but* KJV: *and* D-R>

12:17 *Et si: si* Weber

12:19 *plaudebit: plaudet* S-C

13:1 *induet: inducet* Weber

13:2 *tollet: tollit* Weber; *honestiori se: honestiori* Weber

13:3 *enim se: enim* Weber

13:4 *fremehit: fremet* S-C

<13:4 *yet* KJV: omitted in D-R; *must* KJV: *wil* D-R>

<13:6 *any thing* KJV: omitted in D-R>

13:8 *deridebit te, et: derideat te* Weber

13:9 omitted in Weber

13:13 *ne longe sis ab eo: longe abesto* Weber

13:14 *nec: ne* Weber

<13:15 *to do thee hurt and to cast thee into prison* KJV: *for malice, and for bandes* D-R>

<13:16 *in danger of* KJV (*peril* for *danger*): *with* D-R>

13:19 *similem: simile* S-C

13:20 *coniungetur: coniungitur* Weber

13:22 *pars: pax bona* Weber

13:23 *sic et: sic* Weber

13:24 *sic et: sic* Weber

13:25 *amicis suis: amicis* Weber; *expelletur: expellitur* Weber

<13:25 *is* D-R/C: *shal be* D-R>

13:29 *subvertent: subvertunt* Weber

<14:3 *not comely* KJV: *without reason* D-R>

<14:4 *another will squander away his goods in rioting* KJV (*spend his goods riotously*): *in his goodes an other wil keepe riote* D-R>

<14:5 *whom* KJV: *what other man* D-R>

14:8 *faciem suam: faciem* Weber

14:9 *consummat: consummet* Weber

14:10 *sed indigens et: et* Weber

<14:11 *any thing* D-R/C: omitted in D-R>

14:11 *dignas: bonas* Weber

14:18 *veterascet: veterescit* Weber

14:19 *generantur: generat* Weber; *deiciuntur: deicit* Weber

14:22 *morabitur: sua morietur* Weber

<14:22 *all-seeing eye of* D-R/C: *prouidence* D-R>

14:23 *absconsis illius: absconditis suis* S-C; *vestigator: investigator* S-C

14:24 *illius et: et* Weber; *ianuas: ianuis* S-C

<14:25 *where* D-R/C: *and* D-R>

14:25 *requiescent: requiescunt* Weber

14:26 *tegimen: tegmine* S-C

14:27 *sub tegmine: in subtegmine* Weber

15:1 *bona: illud* Weber

<15:2 *married of a virgin* KJV: *from virginitie* D-R>

15:3 *pane: panem* Weber

15:4 *exaltabit: inaltabit* Weber

15:5 *et adimplebit: adimplebit* Weber; *stolam: stola* S-C

<15:8 *but* D-R/C: *and* D-R>

15:8 *invenientur: inveniuntur* Weber

15:13 *Dominus: Deus* Weber

15:16 *mandata servare: mandata* Weber

15:17 *voles: volueris* S-C

15:20 *Domini: Dei* Weber

16:1 *Ne: et ne* Weber; *nec: non* Weber; *in illis: cum illis* Weber

16:4 *utile: utile est* S-C

16:5 *et tribus impiorum: tribus impiorium* S-C, *et a tribus impiis* Weber

<16:5 *the* S-C: *and the* D-R>

16:7 *exardescet: exardescit* Weber

16:8 *antiqui gigantes, qui destructi sunt: antiquis gigantibus / qui destruxerunt* Weber

16:9 *Loth: illorum* Weber

<16:9 *but* KJV: *and* D-R>

16:10 *exollentes: extollentem* S-C

<16:10 *that extolled* D-R/C: *and extolling* D-R>

<16:11 *So did he with* D-R/C: *And as* D-R; *escaped* KJV: *bene* D-R>

<16:12 *He is mighty to forgive and to pour out* KJV: *Mightie exoration, & powring out* D-R>

16:13 *opera sua: operam suam* Weber

16:14 *rapina: rapinam* Weber

<16:14 *his rapines* KJV (*spoiles* for *rapines*): *robberie* D-R>
<16:17 *such a multitude* KJV? (*so many people*): *a great people* D-R>
16:19 *et cum*: *cum* S-C
<16:19 *when* S-C: *& when* D-R>
16:20 *Et in omnibus his insensatum est cor, et*: *et* Weber
16:21 *procella*: *procellam* S-C
16:22 *sed opera iustitiae eius*: *opera iustitiae* Weber
<16:23 *wanteth understanding* KJV: *is lesse of hart* D-R>
16:24 *corde tuo*: *corde* Weber
16:25 *et dicam*: *edicam* Weber
<16:25 *good* D-R/C: omitted in D-R; *whilst* D-R/C: *and* D-R>
<16:28 *nor shall any of them* D-R/C: *Euerie one shal not* D-R>
16:28 *angustiabit*: *angustiavit* Weber; *aevum*: *aeternum* S-C
16:29 *incredibilis sis*: *incredibiles* Weber
16:31 *denudavit*: *denuntiavit* S-C; *in ipsam*: *ipsa* Weber
17:2 *virtutem*: *virtute* S-C
<17:3 *all* D-R/C: *those* D-R>
17:5 *similem*: *simile* S-C; *sibi*: *ipsi* Weber; *et aures*: *aures* Weber; *disciplinam*:
      disciplina S-C
17:6 *sensum*: *sensu* S-C
17:8 *ut* [both times]: *et* Weber
<17:9 *instructions* D-R/C: *discipline* D-R; *for an inheritance* KJV: *made them
      inherite* D-R>
17:10 *et iustitiam et*: *et* Weber
<17:11 *glory* KJV: *honour* D-R; *his glorious* KJV: *the honour of his* D-R>
17:16 *Et omnia*: *omnia* Weber
17:18 *signaculum*: *sacculum* Weber
17:20 *confirmavit*: *conrogavit* Weber
17:21 *Dominum*: *Deum* Weber
17:22 *faciem Domini*: *faciem* Weber; *offendicula*: *offendiculum* Weber
17:23 *Revertere*: *refer te* Weber; *iniustitia tua*: *iniustitia* Weber
17:25 *confessionem Deo*: *confessionem* Weber
17:26 *ante mortem confitere. A*: *a* Weber; *perit confessio*: *perit* Weber
17:28 *Domini*: *Dei* Weber
<17:30 *yet* KJV: *&* D-R>
17:30 *quam quod excogitavit*: *excogitabit* Weber; *arguetur*: *arguitur* Weber

18:4   *Aut: et* Weber
<18:4   *be able* D-R/C: *adde* D-R>
18:6   *incipiet: incipit* Weber; *operabitur: aporiabitur* S-C
<18:6   *be at a loss* S-C: *worke* D-R>
18:7   *Quid est: quid* Weber; *quae est: quae* Weber; *quid est: quid* Weber
18:8   *ut multum: multum* Weber; *guttae: gutta* S-C; *maris deputati sunt: a*
        mare Weber
<18:8   *a drop* S-C: *droppes* D-R>
18:9   *effundit: effudit* Weber
18:13   *docet et: et docet* Weber
<18:13 *and* KJV: omitted in D-R>
18:14   *Miseretur excipientis: misereatur excipiens* Weber; *festinat: festinant*
        Weber
18:15   *in omni: omni* Weber
18:16   *datus: datum* S-C
18:17   *Sed: et* Weber
18:18   *acriter: achariter* Weber
18:21   *infirmitatis: infirmitatum* Weber
18:22   *orari: operari* Weber; *non verearis: ne verearis* S-C, *non veteris* Weber
<18:24 *that shall be* KJV: omitted in D-R>
18:24   *faciei: facies* Weber
18:25   *necessitatum: necessitatem* Weber
18:26   *inmutabitur: mutatur* Weber
18:28   *agnoscit: agnovit* Weber
18:29   *impluerunt* S-C according to Quentin and Weber: *impleverunt* S-C
        [1959 edition], *inploraverunt* Weber
18:30   *Post: de continentia animae / Post* Weber
<18:30 *but* KJV: *and* D-R>
18:31   *concupiscentias: concupiscentiam* Weber; *inimicis: inimicis tuis* S-C
<18:31 *thy* S-C: *the* D-R>
18:32   *assidua: ad duas* Weber
<18:33 *by borrowing to contribute to feasts when* KJV? (*by banquetting vpon*
        borrowing, when): *in contention of borowing, and* D-R>
18:33   *et: et non* Weber
19:1   *ebriacus: ebriosus* S-C
19:4   *corde est et: corde* Weber
<19:4   *he . . . shall be despised* D-R/C: *he shal more ouer be counted one* D-R>

19:5 *iniquitati: iniquitate* S-C; *minuetur: comminuetur* Weber

19:6 *paenitebit: paenitebitur* Weber; *in malitia: malitia* Weber

19:8 *enarrare: narrare* S-C

19:10 *proximum tuum: proximum* Weber

<19:11 *woman* KJV: omitted in D-R>

<19:12 *man's thigh* KJV: *thigh of flesh* D-R>

<19:14 *for it may be* KJV (without *for*): *lest perhaps* D-R>

19:17 *in lingua: lingua* Weber

<19:19 But D-R/C: *And* D-R>

19:20 *et in: et* Weber

<19:20 *subtle* D-R/C: omitted in D-R; *the same is detestable* D-R/C: *in it execration* D-R>

19:21 *minuitur: deficit* Weber

<19:21 *of God* KJV (in italics in D-R/C): omitted in D-R>

<19:22 *exquisite* KJV: *assured* D-R>

19:24 *est iustus* [both times]: *est* S-C; *faciem suam: faciem* Weber; *se non: non* Weber

<19:24 *one* [first time] S-C: *a iust man* D-R; *one* [second time] S-C: *a iust one* D-R>

19:28 *iudicium: indicium* Weber

20:2 *devirginabit: devirginavit* Weber; *iuvenem: iuvenculam* S-C

20:3 *iniquum: inique* Weber

20:5 verse 4 continues until *et* Weber

20:6 *Est: est autem* Weber; *apti temporis: aptum* S-C

<20:6 *proper time* S-C: *time of fitte opportunitie* D-R>

<20:7 *he see opportunity* KJV: *a time* D-R>

20:8 *laedet: laedit* Weber; *adsumit: sumit* S-C

20:10 *datus qui non sit utilis: datum quod non est utile* S-C; *datus cuius: datum cuius* S-C

20:11 *levabit: levavit* Weber

20:12 *ea: ea in* S-C

20:13 *faciet* A [Weber's siglum]: *facit* S-C, Weber

20:16 *fenerat: feneratur* S-C; *odibilis est: et odibilis* Weber

20:18 *falsae: falsi* Weber

20:20 *qui: qui in* S-C; *sic: nam et sic* Weber; *venient: veniet* S-C

<20:20 *fall* S-C: *falles* D-R>

20:23 *prae: ab* Weber

20:24 *perdet animam*: *perdit animam* Weber

<20:26 *yet* KJV: omitted in D-R>

20:27 *Potior fur*: *potius furem* Weber

<20:27 *a man that is always lying* KJV (*accustomed to lie* for *always lying*): *the continual custome of a lying man* D-R>

20:29 *Sapiens*: *verbum parabolarum / Sapiens* Weber

20:30 *fructuum*: *frugum* S-C

<20:31 *make them dumb in the mouth so that they cannot correct* D-R/C: *as one dumbe in the mouth turneth away their chastisementes* D-R>

20:33 *Melior est qui celat*: *melius in hominibus qui abscondent* Weber; *homo qui abscondit*: *qui abscondunt* Weber

21:1 *dimittantur*: *remittatur* Weber

<21:2 *for* KJV: *and* D-R>

21:5 *Cataplectatio*: *obiurgatio* S-C, *iurgium* *D-R; *et domus quae nimis loculex est adnullabitur superbia; sic*: *sic* Weber

<21:5 *Injuries* D-R/C: *Brawling* D-R>

<21:6 *ears of God* KJV: *his ears* D-R>

21:7 *convertet*: *convertetur* S-C

21:9 *domum suam*: *domum* Weber; *colligat*: *colligit* S-C

<21:9 *himself stones to build* D-R/C (*to build* in italics): *his stones* D-R>

21:11 *poenae*: *poena* Weber

21:15 *sapientia*: *insipientia* Weber; *ubi est*: *ubi abundat* Weber

<21:19 *but* D-R/C: *for* D-R>

21:23 *exaltat*: *inaltat* Weber

<21:25 *but* KJV: *&* D-R>

21:27 *audire*: *auscultare* S-C

21:29 *In ore*: *et in ore* Weber

21:31 *Susurro*: *susurrio* Weber; *qui cum eo*: *qui* Weber

22:3 *filia*: *in filia* Weber

<22:4 *shall bring* KJV: *is* D-R; *but* KJV: *for* D-R>

22:7 *conglutinet*: *conglutinat* S-C

22:8 *audienti*: *adtendenti* Weber

22:9 *cum dormiente loquitur qui enarrat stulto sapientiam et in fine narrationis*: *qui enumerat stulto et in fine* Weber

22:10 *deficit*: *defecit* Weber

22:14 *non*: *ne* S-C

22:15   *peccato: in inpactu* Weber
22:16   *stultitiam: stultitia* S-C
22:17   *plumbum quid: plumbum* Weber
22:18   *portare: ferre* S-C
22:19   *in fundamento: fundamento* Weber
22:20   *vel metu non pravabitur: metu non depravabitur* S-C
<22:20 *by* S-C: *yea by* D-R>
22:21   *sine: in* Weber
22:22   *resistet: resistit* Weber
22:23   *Sicut: sic et* Weber; *motuobit: motuet* S-C
22:24   *deducit: deducens* Weber; *profert: proferet* Weber
<22:24 *resentment* D-R/C: *feeling* D-R>
<22:26 *may be* KJV: *is* D-R>
22:27   *aperueris: aperuerit* Weber
<22:27 *may be* KJV: *is* D-R; *or* KJV: *and* D-R; *for* KJV: omitted in D-R>
22:28   *amico: proximo* Weber
22:31   *confundar: confundaris / et* Weber; *sustinebo: sustineo* Weber
22:33   *uti ne: ut non* S-C
23:1   *ne: non* Weber; *relinquas: derelinquas* S-C; *in consilio eorum, nec: ne*
        Weber
23:2   *superponet: superponet in me* Weber; *pareant: appareant* Weber
23:3   *et ne: et* Weber; *meorum et: et* Weber; *gaudeat: gaudeat super me* S-C
<23:3   *lest . . . increase* KJV: *and . . . increase not* D-R; *over me* S-C: omitted in
        D-R>
<23:6   *lusts of the flesh* KJV: *concupiscences of copulation* D-R>
23:7   *Doctrinam: doctrina oris / Doctrinam* Weber; *in labiis suis: labiis* S-C
23:8   *adprehenditur: adprehendetur* Weber; *illis: illo* Weber
23:9   *multi: multus* Weber
23:11   *minuitur: minuetur* Weber
23:13   *delinquit: delinquet* Weber
23:16   *volutabunt: volutabuntur* S-C
23:17   *Indisciplinatae loquellae: indisciplinose* Weber
23:19   *te Deus: te* Weber
<23:22 *is* D-R/C: *as* D-R>
23:24   *fatigabitur: cessabit* Weber; *usque ad finem: a lecto suo* Weber
23:27   *intellegit: intelleget* Weber

23:28　*lucidiores: lucidiores sunt* S-C; *absconsas: absconditas* S-C
<23:28　*most* KJV: omitted in D-R>
23:30　*et quasi: quasi* Weber
23:31　*eo quod: quod* Weber; *Domini: Dei* Weber
<23:32　*bringeth in an heir by another* KJV: *getteth inheritance by mariage of an other* D-R>
23:33　*et secundo: secundo* S-C; *in virum suum deliquit: virum suum dereliquit* Weber
23:36　*Derelinquet: derelinquent* Weber
23:37　*melius: melius est* Weber
23:38　*Gloria: et gloria* Weber
24:1　*Sapientia: sapientiae laus / Sapientia* Weber
24:3　*et in medio populi sui: in medio populo* Weber
24:7　*altissimis: altis* Weber
24:8　*in profundum: profundum* S-C; *penetravi et: penetravi* S-C
24:13　*ede: mitte* S-C
24:14　*et ante saecula: ante saeculum* Weber
24:18　*Quasi palma: et quasi palma* Weber
24:20　*balsamum: aspaltum* Weber
24:21　*onyx* Frede AN glo B [sigla RPV] (*onix*), PL 85.166A (*onix*), Frede ANT-M 1011 p. 61 (*honix*): *ungula* S-C, Weber
<24:21　*purest* D-R/C: *non mingled* D-R>
24:25　*viae: vitae* Weber
24:27　*melle: mel* S-C
24:28　*generationes: generatione* Weber
24:32　*vitae et: vitae* Weber
24:33　*promissiones: promissionis* Weber
24:34　*et in: in* Weber
24:38　*investigabit: investigavit* Weber
24:39　*illius ab: illius* Weber
24:41　*fluvius Dioryx: fluvii dioryx* S-C, *fluvius Doryx* Weber; *a: de* S-C
24:42　*pratus: prati* S-C
24:43　*facta: factus* S-C; *tramis: trames* S-C; *propinquavit: adpropinquavit* S-C
24:44　*in longinquo: ad longinquum* S-C
24:45　*omnes inferiores: inferiores* Weber; *omnes sperantes: sperantes* Weber; *Domino: Deo* Weber

<24:46 *to instruct* D-R/C: *vnto* D-R>
25:2   *bene sibi: sibi* Weber
25:4   *et divitem: divitem* S-C; *senem: et senem* Weber
<25:4   *a* S-C: *& a* D-R>
25:5   *Quae in: in* Weber; *quomodo: et quomodo* Weber; *invenies: invenies eam* Weber
25:6   *canitiei: canitiae* Weber
<25:10 *and* KJV: omitted in D-R>
25:10 *inimicorum suorum: inimicorum* Weber
25:11 *inhabitati habitat* S-C; *lingua. in lingua* Weber
25:13 *Dominum: Deum* Weber
25:14 *omnia se: omnia* Weber
25:15 *homo cui: cui* Weber
25:17 *mulieris: mulieris est* Weber
<25:18 *a man will choose any plague but* D-R/C: *he wil see al plague, and not* D-R>
25:23 *mulieris: inimici* Weber
25:24 *obcaecat: obcaecabit* Weber
25:25 *ingemuit vir eius, et: et* Weber; *suspiravit: suspirabit* Weber
25:26 *Brevis omnis: brevis* Weber
25:27 *Sicut ascensus: ascensus* Weber
25:31 *cordis: mortis* Weber
<25:31 *A wicked woman abateth the courage and maketh a heavy countenance and a wounded heart* KJV: *An humbled hart, and heauie countenance, and plague of hart, is a wicked woman* D-R>
25:34 *nequam: nequa* Weber
<25:34 *gad abroad* KJV: *goe forth* D-R>
25:35 *confundet: et confundet* Weber
25:36 *abscide: abscinde* S-C
26:1 *illius: illorum* Weber
26:3 *parte bona: parte* S-C
<26:3 *portion* S-C: *good portion* D-R>
<26:4 *Rich or poor, if his heart* KJV: *And the hart of rich and poore* D-R>
26:6 *delatura: delaturam* S-C; *collectio: collectionem* S-C
26:7 *calumniam: et calumniam* Weber
<26:7 *and* KJV: omitted in D-R>
26:9 *zelotypa: infideli* Weber

<26:10 *to and fro* KJV: omitted in D-R>

26:10 *mulier*: *mulierem* Weber; *adprehendat*: *apprehendit* S-C

26:11 *contegetur*: *tegetur* S-C

26:14 *oculorum eius*: *oculis* Weber

26:17 *datus Dei*: *Datum Dei est* S-C

<26:18 *Such is* D-R/C (in italics): omitted in D-R; *and there is nothing so much worth as a well* KJV (*and* in italics in D-R/C): *there is no exchange for a* D-R>

<26:22 *As* KJV: omitted in D-R; *so is* KJV: *&* D-R; *in a ripe* KJV: *vpon stayed* D-R>

<26:23 *As* KJV: omitted in D-R; *so are* KJV: *and* D-R>

<26:24 *As* D-R/C: omitted in D-R; *so* D-R/C: *and* D-R>

26:28 *labiorum*: *labiae* Weber

27:2 *Sicut*: *si* Weber; *angustabitur*: *angustiabitur* S-C; *peccatum*: *peccatis* Weber

<27:2 *stick fast* KJV (*close* for *fast*): *be straytened* D-R>

27:3 *Conteretur cum delinquente*: *conteretur* Weber

27:4 *tenueris te*: *tenueris* Weber

27:5 *Sicut in percussura*: *si in pertusura* Weber; *pulvis*: *stercus* Weber

<27:7 *dressing* KJV: *husbandrie* D-R>

27:7 *ex cogitatu*: *excogitatum* Weber

27:8 *conlaudes*: *laudes* S-C

<27:10 *so* KJV: *and* D-R>

<27:12 *but* KJV: *for* D-R>

27:12 *inmutatur*: *mutatur* S-C

27:14 *in deliciis*: *delictis* Weber

27:17 *perdit*: *perdet* Weber

<27:17 *never* KJV: *not* D-R>

27:20 *sic et*: *sic* Weber

27:21 *reliquisti*: *dereliquisti* S-C

<27:21 *let . . . go* KJV: *leaft* D-R>

<27:22 *he* KJV: *for he* D-R; *escaped* KJV: omitted in D-R>

27:22 *est anima eius*: *est* Weber

27:23 *Ultra eum non poteris conligare*: *conligare* Weber

<27:24 *leaveth no hope to* D-R/C: *is the desperation of* D-R>

27:24 *est animae infelicis*: *est* Weber

27:26 *condulcabit os suum*: *condulcabit os tuum* Weber
27:27 *audivi*: *odivi* S-C
<27:27 *hated* S-C: *heard* D-R; *but not like him* KJV: *& haue not esteemed them
    equal to him* D-R; *himself* D-R/C (in italics): omitted in D-R>
27:28 *plaga dolosa*: *plaga* Weber
<27:28 *wound* D-R/C: *diuide the woundes of* D-R>
27:29 *Qui* CQΘZ*TΩ^M [Quentin's sigla]: *Et qui* S-C, Weber (without
    capitalization in Weber); *incidet*: *decidet* Weber; *alii ponit*: *alio*
    Weber
27:30 *nequissimum consilium*: *nequissimum* Weber
27:33 *execrabilia sunt*: *execrabilia* Weber
28:1 *Domino*: *Deo* Weber
<28:2 *if he hath hurt* KJV: *hurting* D-R>
28:3 *reservat*: *servat* Weber
28:4 *In*: *et in* Weber
28:5 *cum*: *dum* Weber
<28:5 *He that is but* KJV: *Himself whereas he is* D-R>
28:7 *inminet*: *inminent* S-C; *mandatis eius*: *mandatis* Weber
28:9 *testamenti*: *testamentum* S-C
28:11 *medium*: *medio* S-C; *inmittet*: *inmittit* Weber
<28:11 *debate* KJV: *enmitie* D-R>
28:12 *sic iracundia*: *iracundia* Weber
28:14 *sufflaveris in scintillam*: *sufflaveris* Weber
<28:14 *the* KJV: *vpon a* D-R>
28:15 *Susurro*: *susurrio* Weber; *turbavit*: *turbabit* S-C
28:16 *a*: *de* S-C
28:19 *viratas*: *viritas* Weber
<28:20 *hearkeneth to it shall never* KJV: *regardeth it, shal not* D-R>
28:20 *habebit amicum in quo requiescat*: *habitabit cum requie* Weber
28:23 *iracundiam*: *iracundia* Weber
28:25 *infernus*: *inferus* Weber
28:27 *derelinquunt*: *relinquunt* S-C; *laedebit*: *laedet* S-C
<28:28 *Hear* S?: *and heare* D-R>
28:29 *Aurum tuum et argentum tuum*: *aurum tuum et argentum* Weber,
    Argentum tuum *D-R; *consitue* Frede HIL Ps 140.5 p. 792.13: *confla*
    S-C, Weber

<28:29 *Melt down thy gold and silver* S-C: *Lay together thy siluer* D-R>
<28:30 *lest* KJV: *lest perhaps* D-R>
29:1 *Qui*: *de fenore* / *Qui* Weber; *fenerat*: *feneratur* S-C; *proximo suo*: *proximum* Weber
29:2 *Fenera*: *Fenerare* S-C; *proximo tuo*: *proximum tibi* Weber
29:4 *adiuvaverunt*: *adiuverunt* S-C
29:5 *manus*: *manum* Weber
<29:6 *but* KJV: *and* D-R>
29:6 *taedii*: *acediae* Weber
29:7 *adversabitur; solidi*: *aversatus solide* Weber
<29:7 *half* D-R (*halfe of the whole*): more likely, *half a solidus* [type of coin]>
29:8 *fraudabit*: *fraudavit* Weber
29:10 *feneraverunt*: *fenerati sunt* S-C
<29:10 *refused to lend* KJV: *not lent* D-R>
<29:11 *delay not to shew him mercy* KJV: *for almes differre him not* D-R>
29:13 *pro fratre et amico*: *propter fratrem et amicum tuum* S-C
29:16 = 29:16–18 S-C, 29:18 Weber [Weber has no 16 or 17]; all verses after 17 are numbered 1 higher in S-C and Weber. The texts of S-C and Weber do not differ here.
29:18 *proximo*: *pro proximo* S-C
29:22 *relinquetur*: *derelinquetur* S-C
<29:24 *It hath made powerful men to go from place to place round about* D-R/C: *Whurling round about, it hath made mightie men to remoue* D-R>
29:25 *mandatum*: *mandata* Weber
29:27 *vitae hominis*: *vitae* Weber
29:28 *Melior est*: *melior* Weber; *tegimen*: *tegmine* S-C
<29:28 *in another man's* KJV: *without a* D-R>
29:29 *Minimum pro magno*: *super minimum et magnum* Weber
<29:30 *for* KJV: *and* D-R>
29:31 *Hospitabit*: *hospitabitur* S-C
<29:33 *for I want* KJV (*haue neede of* for *want*): *for the necessitie of* D-R>
30:1 *Qui*: *de filiis* / *Qui* Weber; *suo et non palpet proximorum ostia*: *suo* Weber
<30:5 *and* KJV: omitted in D-R>
30:6 *contra inimicos et*: *et* Weber
30:8 *evadet*: *evadit* Weber

<30:9   *Give thy son his way* D-R/C: *Pamper thy sonne* D-R>
<30:12   *lest* KJC: *lest perhaps* D-R; *so* KJV: omitted in D-R>
30:15   *melior est: et melior* Weber
30:16   *oblectatio: oblectamentum* S-C
30:18   *absconsa: abscondita* S-C
30:19   *manducabit: manducat* Weber
<30:19   *can* KJV: *shal* D-R>
30:20   *portans: et portans* Weber
<30:22   *thy soul to sadness* S: *heuines to thy soule* D-R>
<30:23   *is* KJV: *this is* D-R>
30:24   *et congrega: congrega* S-C; *expelle: repelle* S-C
<30:24   *gather up* S-C: *and comfort* D-R>
30:26   *minuit: minuunt* S-C; *adducet: adducit* Weber
30:27   *cor: cor et* S-C; *epulis: epulis est* S-C
<30:27   *A cheerful and good heart* KJV: *A magnifical hart* D-R; *is always feast-
ing* D-R/C: *is good in bankettes* D-R>
31:1   *tabefaciet: tabefacit* Weber
<31:1   *consumeth* KJV: *shal pine* D-R>
31:2   *praescientiae: praesentiae* Weber
31:3   *bonis suis: bonorum suorum* Weber
31:6   *specie: facie* Weber
31:10   *Qui: quis* Weber; *erit illi: et erit illi in* Weber; *et facere: facere* S-C
31:11   *Domino: Deo* Weber; *enarrabit omnis: enarrabit* Weber
31:12   *Supra: de continentia / Supra* Weber
31:13   *sic: "Multa: simulata* Weber; *illam: illa* Weber
<31:13   *not* KJV: *not this* D-R>
31:14   *malus est: malum* Weber
31:16   *obrubescas: erubescas* S-C
<31:16   *lest* KJV: *and* D-R; *put to confusion* D-R/C: *ashamed* D-R>
31:17   *Ne: nec* Weber
31:18   *quae sunt proximi: proximi* Weber
<31:18   *of the disposition of thy neighbour: what thy neighbours thinges are*
D-R>
31:19   *his quae: quae* Weber; *ne: et non* Weber
<31:19   *if* D-R/C: *when* D-R>
<31:20   *lest* KJV: *lest . . . perhaps* D-R>

31:21   *non*: *ne* S-C
<31:21   *first of all* KJV: *before them* D-R>
31:23   *et cholera*: *cholera* S-C
<31:24   *Sound and wholesome sleep* D-R/C: *sleepe of health* D-R>
31:24   *mane*: *in mane* Weber
<31:25   *go out* KJV (*forth* for *out*): *from the middes* D-R>
31:25   *et vome*: *evome* S-C; *infirmitatem*: *infirmitates* Weber
31:32   *Aequa vita hominibus vinum in sobrietate*: *Aequavit in vita vinum hominibus* Weber
31:33   *Quae vita est ei*: *quae est vita* Weber
<31:33   *who* D-R/C: *that* D-R>
31:35   *iucunditate*: *iucunditatem* S-C; *est et*: *est* Weber; *ebrietate*: *ebrietatem* S-C
31:37   *animae et corpori sobrius potus*: *et corpori et animae* Weber
<32:2   *take thy place* KJV: *repose* D-R>
32:5   *scientia*: *scientiam* Weber; *musicam*: *musica* Weber
32:6   *non est*: *est* Weber
<32:7   *A concert of music in a banquet of wine is as a carbuncle set in gold* KJV: *A litle pearle of the carbuncle in an ornament of gold, and the comparison of musicians in a banket of wine* D-R>
32:14   *et ante verecundiam praeibit gratia, et*: *et* Weber
<32:16   *but* KJV: *and* D-R>
32:18   *Dominum*: *Deum* Weber
32:20   *lucem*: *lumen* S-C
32:21   *devitabit*: *vitabit* S-C
32:22   *disperdet intellegentiam*: *disperiet intellegentia* Weber; *pertimescet*: *pertimescit* Weber
<32:22   *neglect* S: *destroy* D-R>
<32:23   *by* D-R/C: *euen by* D-R>
32:24   *paeniteberis*: *paenitebis* S-C
32:25   *ne credas*: *nec credas* S-C
32:27   *opere tuo*: *opere* Weber; *haec*: *hoc* S-C
32:28   *confidit*: *confident* Weber; *minorabitur*: *minorabuntur* Weber
<32:28   *fare never the worse* KJV: *not be lessened* D-R>
33:1   *conservabit*: *conservat* Weber
33:2   *inlidetur*: *inludetur* Weber

33:6 *admissarius sicut: emissarius, sic et* S-C

33:7 *iterum lux: lux* *D-R

<33:7 *when all come* KJV: omitted in D-R>

<33:9 *ordered* D-R/C: *changed* D-R>

<33:10 *days* KJV: omitted in D-R>

33:11 *Domini: Dominus* S-C

<33:11 *the Lord* S-C: *of our Lord he* D-R>

33:12 *Ex: et ex* Weber

33:13 *manu: manus* Weber

33:14 *et reddet illi: reddet illis* Weber

33:15 *duo contra duo* Ψ^{D2}Ωarels [Quentin's sigla]: *duo et duo* S-C; *duo duo* Weber; *et unum: unum* Weber

<33:15 *and* S-C: *against* D-R>

33:16 *vigilavi: evigilavi* S-C

<33:16 *of all* KJV: omitted in D-R; *gathereth* KJV: *gathereth bearies* D-R>

33:19 *magnati: magnates* S-C

33:20 *et non dederis alii: non dederis alio* Weber

<33:20 *or* [both times] D-R/C: omitted in D-R; *lest* KJV: *lest perhaps* D-R>

<33:21 *let no man* D-R/C: *al flesh shal not* D-R>

33:24 *gloriam tuam: gloria tua* S-C

<33:24 *Let no stain sully* D-R/C: *Geue no staine to* D R>

33:28 *operationem: operatione* Weber

33:30 *illum: illi* Weber; *Et si* Ω^S [Quentin's siglum, without capitalization]: *quod si* S-C, Weber; *curva: grava* Weber

<33:30 *but* KJV: *and* D-R; *any one, and* KJV (without *one*): *al flesh: but* D-R>

33:31 *servus fidelis: servus* Weber; *parasti: conparasti* S-C

33:32 *iniuste, in fugam convertetur: iniuste* Weber

33:33 *si: et si* S-C, *et* Weber [*et* is omitted in Weber's sigla ΣT]; *quem quaeras: quem quaeres* Weber

<33:33 *and* S-C: omitted in D-R>

34:3 *Secundum* T²Ωg [Quentin's sigla]: *Hoc secundum* S-C, Weber [without capitalization]

<34:3 *The vision of dreams is the resemblance of one thing to another as when* KJV (without *as when*): *According to this is the vision of dreams: as* D-R; *is* D-R/C: omitted in D-R>

34:6 *phantasias: fantasiam* Weber

<34:6   *the heart fancieth* KJV: *thy hart suffereth phantasies* D-R>

34:8   *verbum legis: verbum* Weber

34:9   *cogitabit: cogitavit* Weber

34:10   *multiplicat: multiplicabit* Weber

<34:10   *prudence* KJV: *wickednes* D-R>

34:11   omitted in Weber

<34:11   *surprised* D-R/C: *deceiued* D-R; *subtlety* D-R/C: *wickednes* D-R>

34:14   *quaeritur: quaeretur* Weber; *benedicetur: benedicentur* Weber

34:20   *servatio* cf. G [i.e., Septuagint; Quentin's siglum]: *deprecatio* S-C, *et precatio* Weber; *et vitam: vitam* Weber

34:21   *Immolantis: immolans* Weber

34:23   *nec respicit in oblationes: in oblationibus* Weber

34:25   *pauperum: pauperis* Weber; *sanguinis: sanguinis est* S-C

<34:25   *them thereof* KJV (*him* for *them*): *it* D-R>

34:27   *mercennario fratres sunt: mercedem mercennario* Weber

<34:27   *of his hire* KJV: omitted in D-R>

<34:30   *washeth himself after touching* KJV: *is washed from* D-R; *if he* KJV: *and* D-R>

34:30   *lavatio: lavatione* Weber

35:1   *oblationem: orationem* Weber

35:2   *salutare: salutare est* S-C

35:3   *Beneplacito est Domino recedere ab iniquitate, et* ΣΠ^HALQΘ^{AM}Γw [Quentin's sigla]: *et propitiationem litare sacrificii super iniustitias /* *et* S-C, *et* Weber; *deprecatio pro peccatis: deprecatio* Weber

<35:3   *And to depart from injustice is to offer a propitiatory sacrifice for injustices* S-C: *To depart from iniquitie is a thing that pleaseth our Lord wel* D-R>

35:4–5   *Retribuet gratiam qui offert similaginem, et qui facit misericordiam offert sacrificium. Beneplacitum est Domino recedere ab iniquitate, et deprecatio pro peccatis recedere ab iniustitia* S-C

<35:4–5   *He shall return thanks that offereth fine flour, and he that doth mercy offereth sacrifice. To depart from iniquity is that which pleaseth the Lord, and to depart from injustice is an intreating for sins.* S-C: omitted in D-R>

35:6–26   these verses numbered two lower in D-R

35:6   *Domini: Dei* Weber

35:7   *Dei: Domini* Weber

<35:11 *shew a* KJV: *make thy* D-R>

35:12 *fac: facito* S-C

<35:14 *such* KJV: *them* D-R>

<35:16 *any* KJV: omitted in D-R>

35:16 *precationem: deprecationem* S-C

<35:17 *when* KJV: *if* D-R>

35:18 *lacrimae viduae: lacrima* Weber; *descendunt et exclamatio eius super deducentem eas: descendit / et exclamatio* Weber

35:19 *enim ascendunt usque ad caelum: ascendit* Weber; *non delectabitur: doloanns* Weber

35:20 *precatio: deprecatio* S-C

35:21 *consolabitur: conrogabitur* Weber

35:22 *longinquabit: elongabit* S-C

<35:22 *slack* KJV: *long* D-R>

36:2 *ut: et* Weber; *tu et: tu ut* Weber

36:5 *agnovimus: cognovimus* S-C

36:9 *Extolle: tolle* S-C

36:13 *et cognoscant: ut cognoscant* S-C; *ut: et* S-C

<36:13 *that they may* S-C: *and let them* D-R; *and* S-C: *that they* D-R>

<36:14 *raised up to be* D-R/C: *made equal to* D-R>

36:17 *his qui: quia* Weber; *praedicationes: precationes* Weber

36:19 *viam: via* Weber; *inhabitant: habitant* S-C

<36:19 *all* D-R/C: omitted in D-R>

<36:20 *yet* KJV: *and* D-R>

36:21 *contingunt: contingit* Weber

<36:21 *palate tasteth* KJV: *iawes taist* D-R>

<36:23 *yet* KJV: *and* D-R>

36:23 *filiae: filia* S-C

<36:24 *a man desireth nothing more* D-R/C: *increaseth the desire aboue al mans concupiscence* D-R>

36:25 *est et: et* Weber; *et misericordiae: misericordiae* Weber; *secundum: contra* Weber

<36:25 *If she have a tongue that can cure and likewise mitigate and shew* D-R/C: *If there be a tongue of curing, there is also of mitigating and of mercie* D-R; *like other men* KJV: *according to the sonnes of men* D-R>

36:26 *mulierem bonam: mulierem* Weber; *secundum: contra* Weber

36:27 *gemescit: ingemescit* S-C

36:28 *Quis: cui* Weber; *ei qui: qui* Weber

<36:28 *will* KJV: *doth* D-R; *the night taketh him* KJV: *it waxeth darke* D-R>

<37:1 *am his friend* KJV: *haue ioyned freindshipe* D-R>

37:3 *malitia et dolositate: malitiam et dolositatem* Weber

<37:3 *thy malice and deceitfulness* D-R/C: *malice, and the deceitfulnes thereof* D-R>

37:4 *oblectationibus: oblectatione* Weber

37:6 *opibus: operibus* Weber

37:7 *eo qui tibi insidiatur: socero tuo* Weber; *eo qui insidiatur* *D-R

<37:9 *And* KJV: omitted in D-R>

37:12 *traiecticio: traiectione* S-C

<37:12–13 *nor* [all seven times] KJV: omitted in D-R>

37:13 *agri: agrario* S-C

<37:14 *nor* [both times] KJV: omitted in D-R>

37:15 *Sed cum: cum* Weber

37:16 *et qui cum titubaveris: quicumque titubaverit* Weber; *condolebit: non condolebit* Weber

37:17 *Et cor: Cor* S-C; *statue tecum: statue* Weber

<37:19 *But* D-R/C: *And* D-R; *above* KJV: *in* D-R>

<37:20 *In* D-R/C: *Before* D-R>

37:20 *omnia opera: omnem operam* Weber

37:21 *cor, ex quo: cor* Weber; *lingua. Est vir astutus multorum eruditor et animae suae inutilis est: lingua* Weber

<37:21 *manner of things* KJV: *partes* D-R; *yet* KJV: omitted in D-R>

37:23 *in omni: omni* Weber

37:24 *non est: non est enim* Weber

37:27 *benedictionibus: benedictione* Weber

37:33 *aviditas: aplestia* Weber; *choleram: cholera* Weber

37:34 *aplestiam: crapulam* S-C

<38:1 *thou hast of him* D-R/C: omitted in D-R>

38:2 *est enim: est* Weber; *dationem: donationem* S-C

38:6 *virtus: virtutis* Weber; *hominibus: homini* Weber

38:7 *mitigabit: mitigavit* Weber; *faciet pigmenta: facit pigmentum* Weber; *sanitatis: suavitatis* Weber

<38:7 *of these* S (in italics in D-R/C): omitted in D-R>

38:9 *non: ne* S-C; *despicias te ipsum: despicias* Weber; *ora: ora ad* Weber

<38:11 *then* D-R/C: omitted in D-R>

38:12 *quoniam: quia* S-C

<38:13 *must* D-R/C: *maist* D-R>

<38:14 *prosper what they give for* KJV: *direct their* D-R>

38:15 *incidet: incidat* Weber

38:16 *contege: contine* Weber

38:17 *delaturam autem: delaturam* Weber

<38:7 *fear of* D-R/C (in italics): omitted in D-R; *then* KJV: omitted in D-R; *in* D-R/C: *for* D-R>

38:18 omitted in Weber

<38:18 *for him* D-R/C: omitted in D-R; *fear of* D-R/C: omitted in D-R>

38:19 *cooperit: cooperiet* Weber; *flectit: flectet* Weber

38:21 *Non: Ne* S-C

38:25 *Sapientia scribae: sapientiam scribe* Weber

<38:25 *cometh* KJV: omitted in D-R>

38:26 verse begins before *qui* S-C, Weber; *qui gloriatur: non gloriatur* Weber; *agit: agitat* S-C; *narratio: enarratio* S-C

<38:26 *whole* D-R/C: omitted in D-R>

<38:28 *by* D-R/C: omitted in D-R>

38:28 *perficiet: perficit* Weber

38:30 *innovat: innovabit* Weber; *vasi: vasis* S-C; *oculus: oculi* Weber

<38:30 *is always in his ears* KJV (*euer* for *always*): *reneweth his eare* D-R; *he maketh* KJV: omitted in D-R>

<38:31 *to* KJV: *wil* D-R>

38:31 *perfectionem: consummatione* Weber

38:32 *in numero: innumera* Weber

<38:32 *maketh all his work by* D-R/C: *al his working is in* D-R>

<38:34 *to* S?: *wil* D-R>

<38:39 *state* KJV: *creature* D-R>

39:1 *sapiens et in prophetis: et in prophetiis* Weber

39:5 *alienarum: alienigenarum* S-C; *temptabit: temptavit* Weber

<39:6 *resort* KJV: *watch* D-R>

39:10 *Et ipse: ipse* Weber

39:14 *enuntiabit: nuntiabit* Weber

39:15 *inmanserit: permanserit* S-C; *plus quam mille: mille* Weber

39:17 *rivos: rivum* Weber

39:19 *et date*: *date* Weber

39:20 *et in*: *in* Weber; *cinyris*: *citharis* S-C

39:28 *Et quomodo*: *quomodo* Weber

39:29 *in siccitatem et*: *et* Weber

<39:31 *principal things* KJV: *beginning of the thing* D-R>

39:31 *sal, lac*: *lac* Weber

<39:33 *lay on grievous* KJV (*sore* for *grievous*): *haue confirmed their* D-R>

39:34 *placabunt*: *confundent* Weber

39:38 *confirmatus sum*: *confirmatus* Weber; *scripta*: *in scripta* Weber

<39:38 *on these things* KJV: omitted in D-R>

<39:41 *Now therefore* KJV: *And now* D-R>

40:3 *a residente*: *residentes* Weber

40:5 *cubile*: *cubili* S-C

<40:6 *and* D-R/C: *is* D-R; *is his* KJV: *in* D-R>

<40:8 *Such things happen to* KJV (*Such things happen* bracketed): *With* D-R>

<40:9 *and* KJV: omitted in D-R>

40:11 *revertentur*: *convertentur* Weber

40:13 *personabunt*: *manebunt* Weber

<40:14 *but* D-R/C: *so* D-R>

<40:16 *weed growing* KJV: *grennes* D-R>

40:16 *ante omnem*: *ante omne* S-C

40:17 *saeculo*: *saeculum* S-C

<40:18 *content with what he hath* KJV: *sufficient for himself* D-R>

40:19 *Filii et*: *fili* Weber

<40:20 *but* KJV: *and* D-R>

<40:21 *but* KJV: *and* D-R>

<40:22 *but* KJV: *and* D-R>

40:22 *haec virides sationes*: *hoc viride sationis* Weber

<40:23 *but* KJV: *and* D-R>

<40:24 *but* KJV: *and* D-R>

40:25 *est constitutio pedum*: *constituet pedem* Weber

<40:25 *make the feet stand sure, but* KJV: *are the establishing of the feete: and* D-R>

<40:26 *but* KJV: *and* D-R>

<40:32 *Begging* KJV: *Pouertie* D-R; *but* KJV: *and* D-R>

41:4 *patientiam*: *sapientiam* Weber

41:6 *tibi in*: *in* Weber; *beneplacita*: *beneplacito* S-C

<41:7 *among the dead* D-R/C: *in hel* D-R>

41:15 *pretiosi et magni*: *magni pretiosi* Weber

41:16 *aevo*: *aevum* S-C

41:17 *invisus*: *occultus* Weber

41:20 *reverentiam*: *inreverentiam* Weber

41:21 *a patre et a matre*: *matrem et patrem* Weber; *a potente*: *potente* Weber

41:22 *et a*: *et* Weber

41:23 *et* [before *a*]: omitted in Weber; *a loco* Λ^{L}Θ^{H}w [Quentin's sigla]: *de loco* S C, Weber

<41:23 *in regard to* S-C: *before* D-R>

<41:24 *with thy elbow over* KJV (*vpon* for *over*): *on* D-R>

41:26 *et ab*: *ab* Weber

<41:28 *Be ashamed* D-R/C (in italics): omitted in D-R>

42:1 *de revelatione*: *nec revela* *D-R

<42:1 *so* D-R/C: *&* D-R>

42:4 *de adquisitione*: *et de adquisitione* Weber

<42:4 *or* KJV: *and* D-R>

42:5 *corruptione*: *correptione* Weber; *et servo*: *servo* Weber

<42:6 *Sure keeping* KJV: *a seale* D-R>

<42:7 *deliver all things in number and weight* KJV: *what soeuer thou shalt deliuer, number, and weigh it* D-R; *or* KJV: *and* D-R>

<42:8 *Be not ashamed to inform* KJV: *Of the discipline of* D-R>

42:8 *vivorum*: *virorum* Weber

42:9 *patris*: *patri* Weber; *aufert*: *auferet* Weber; *adulta*: *adultera* Weber

<42:9 *The father waketh for the daughter when no man knoweth* KJV: *A daughter is the secret watch of the father* D-R; *lest she pass away the flower of her age and when she is married lest she should be hateful* KJV: *lest perhaps in her youth she become past age, & abiding with an husband she become odious* D-R>

<42:10 *lest* [first time] KJV: *lest at anie time* D-R; *and having a husband lest she should misbehave herself* KJV: *lest perhaps abyding with her husband she transgresse* D-R>

42:11 *detractatione*: *detractione* S-C; *obiectione*: *abiectione* Weber

<42:11 *and a byword* KJV: *because of detraction* D-R; *multitude* KJV: *multitude of the people* D-R>

42:14 *est enim*: *est* Weber

<42:14 *bringing shame and* KJV: *shaming vnto* D-R>

42:17 *stabiliri*: *stabilire* S-C [according to apparatus of Quentin, Weber, but not according to 1959 S-C]

<42:19 *signs of the world* KJV: *signe of age* D-R>

<42:20 *can hide* D-R/C: *hideth* D-R>

<42:21 *and to him nothing may be added* KJV: *neither is there added* D-R>

<42:22 *can he be* KJV: omitted in D-R>

42:23 *scintilla quae*: *scintillam quam* Weber

<42:23 *what we can know is but as a spark* D-R/C: *which is as it were a sparke to consider* D-R>

42:24 *vivunt*: *vivent* Weber

43:1 *eius est*: *est* Weber

43:3 *exurit terram, et*: *exuret terram* Weber

<43:3 *his burning heat* KJV: *in the presence of the heate thereof* D-R>

<43:6 *the world* KJV: *age* D-R>

43:8 *mirabiliter*: *admirabiliter* Weber

43:9 *resplendens gloriose*: *resplendens* Weber

43:10 *gloria*: *gloriosa* Weber

43:11 *deficient*: *exardescent* Weber

<43:11 *never* KJV: *not* D-R>

43:12 *eum qui*: *qui* Weber

<43:14 *maketh the snow to fall apace* KJV: *hastened snow* D-R>

43:18 *verberabit*: *exprobravit* Weber

<43:18 *so doth* KJV (in italics in D-R/C): omitted in D-R; *whirlwind* KJV: *gathering together of wind* D-R>

43:19 *Et sicut*: *sicut* Weber

<43:19 *upon the earth* D-R/C: *downe to sitte* D-R>

43:20 *candoris*: *coloris* Weber

43:21 *Gelum*: *Gelu* S-C

43:22 *flavit, et gelavit*: *flabit / et gelabit* Weber

<43:22 *bloweth* KJV: *blewe* D-R; *is congealed* KLV: *frose* D-R>

43:23 *Et devorabit*: *devorabit* Weber; *viridem sicut ignem*: *viride sicut igne* S-C

<43:23 *all that* D-R/C: *that which* D-R; *with* S-C: omitted in D-R>

43:24 *festinationem*: *festinatione* S-C; *et ros*: *ros* Weber

43:25 *siluit ventus, et cogitatione sua placavit abyssum, et plantavit in illa*

Dominus insulas: silebit ventus / et plantavit illum Dominus Iesus
Weber

43:26 navigant mare enarrent pericula: navigat mare enarrat periculum
Weber; nostris: non Weber

<43:27 monstrous creatures D-R/C: creature D-R; whales KJV: mightie beastes
D-R>

43:29 in verbis: verbis Weber

<43:29 all KJV: in al D-R>

43:31 vehementer, et mirabilis potentia ipsius: vehementer Weber

43:32 Glorificantes Dominum quantumcumque quantumcumque Weber,
supervalebit: supervalebit enim S-C

<43:32 Glorify KJV?: Glorifying D-R; for S-C: omitted in D-R>

<43:34 put forth all your strength, and KJV: be ye replenished with strength
D-R; can never go far enough KJV: shal not comprehend D-R>

43:34 comprehendetis: habebitis Weber

43:35 videbit: vidit Weber

<43:36 from us D-R/C: omitted in D-R>

43:36 horum: his S-C

44:1 Laudemus: laus patrum / Laudemus Weber

<44:1 now KJV: omitted in D-R>

<44:3 Such as have borne rule KJV: Ruling D-R>

44:3 prophetis dignitatem: dignitate Weber

44:4 populis: populi Weber

<44:4 instructing KJV?: to D-R; in D-R/C: omitted in D-R>

<44:5 such as KJV: omitted in D-R>

44:5 peritia: pueritia Weber; scripturarum: in scriptura Weber

<44:9 who KJV: they D-R>

44:9 qui non: non Weber

44:11 Cum: et cum Weber; permanent: perseverat Weber

44:12 sancta nepotes: nepotum Weber

44:13 manet: manent S-C

44:14 vivit in generationem et generationem: vivet in generationes et generationes Weber

44:15 et laudem: laudem Weber

44:16 paradisum: paradiso Weber

44:22 gloriam: semen Weber

44:23 *hereditare: hereditari* Weber

44:25 *Dominus et: et* Weber

44:26 *tribubus: tribus* Weber

44:27 *illi: illis* Weber

45:1 *Deo: a Deo* Weber

<45:3 commandments D-R/C: commandment D-R>

45:4 *de: ex* S-C

45:5 *enim eum: eum* Weber

45:6 *et legem: legem* Weber; *testamentum suum: testamentum* Weber

45:9 *zonam* Sangerm. 15 [Sabatier's siglum]: *zona gloriae* S-C, *zonam gloriae* Weber; *et induit: induit* Weber

<45:9 glorious S-C: omitted in D-R; majestic attire D-R/C: furniture of power D-R>

45:10 *umeralem: umerale* S-C

45:11 *successu: incessu* S-C

<45:11 there might be a sound and a noise made that might be KJV: to geue a sound . . . to make sound D-R>

45:12 *Stola sancta: stolam sanctam* S-C

<45:12 He gave him D-R/C: omitted in D-R>

<45:13 and set KJV: in the closure D-R>

45:14 *coronam auream supra: corona aurea super* S-C; *expressam: expressa* S-C; *et gloria: gloria* Weber; *opus: et opus* Weber; *et desideria: desideria* Weber

<45:14 wherein was engraved Holiness, an ornament KJV: grauen with a seale of holines, and the glorie D-R; delightful to the eyes for its beauty D-R/C: the adorned desires of the eies D-R>

45:20 *ab: eum ab* Weber; *offerre: adferre* Weber; *placare pro: placere* Weber

45:21 *Et dedit: dedit* Weber

<45:22 And D-R/C: Because D-R>

45:23 *iracundiae: iracundia* S-C

45:25 *fructuum: frugum* S-C

45:26 *nam et: nam* Weber

45:27 *gentes non: gentes* Weber

<45:27 among D-R/C: omitted in D-R>

45:28 *Finees: et Finees* Weber; *in imitando: imitando* S-C; *eum: tantum* Weber

<45:29 he stood up in the shameful fall D-R/C: to stand in the reuerence D-R>

45:29 *Deo pro Israhel: de Israhel* Weber

45:30 *ad illum: illi* S-C; *et semini eius sacerdotii: in sacerdotium sui* Weber

46:3 *civitates: civitatem* Weber

46:8 *Deum: Dominum* Weber; *potentis: potentes* Weber

46:9 *hostem et: hostem* Weber; *sedare* Sabatier's translation of Septuagint: *perfringere* S-C, Weber

<46:11 *also to Caleb* KJV: *to Caleb himself* D-R>

46:11 *ad: in* S-C

46:12 *quod: quia* S-C

<46:13 *Then* D-R/C· *And* D-R; *by* KJV: *by their* D R>

46:15 *permaneat: permanet* Weber

46:16 *Domino, Deo: Domino* Weber

46:17 *Deus: Dominus* Weber

46:19 *Dominum Omnipotentem: Deum potentem* Weber; *agni: viri* Weber

<46:19 *the name of* D-R/C: omitted in D-R>

46:20 *e: de* S-C

46:21 *conteruit: contrivit* S-C

<46:22 *in* D-R/C: *and* D-R; *protested* KJV: *gaue testimonie* D-R; *or* D-R/C: *and* D-R; *any thing else* D-R: literally would be omitted; *any man* KJV: *al flesh* D-R>

47:1 *haec: hoc* Weber

47:2 *separatus: separatus est* Weber

<47:2 *chosen* KJV (in italics in D-R/C): omitted in D-R>

47:6 *nam: ubi* Weber; *Omnipotentem: potentem* Weber; *dexteram: dextera* S-C; *cornum: cornu* S-C

47:7 *in decem: in* Weber

47:8 *conteruit* [both times]: *contrivit* S-C; *cornum: cornu* S-C

<47:11 *voices* KJV: *sound* D-R>

<47:12 *solemn* KJV: omitted in D-R>

47:13 *Dominus: Christus* Weber; *cornum: cornu* S-C; *regni: regum* Weber

47:15 *es: est* Weber; *tua: sua* Weber

47:16 *es: est* Weber

47:17 *divulgatum est: distulisti* Weber

47:18 *sunt: sunt te* Weber

<47:18 *thee for thy* KJV: *the* D-R>

<47:21 *thyself* D-R/C: *thy thighes* D-R; *by thy body thou wast brought under subjection* KJV: *thou hast had power on thy bodie* D-R>

47:22 *profanasti*: *profugasti* Weber

<47:23 *rebellious* KJV: *stubburne* D-R>

47:24 *derelinquet*: *relinquit* Weber; *corrumpet*: *corrumpit* Weber

<47:25 *Wherefore* KJV: *But* D-R>

47:27 *reliquit*: *dereliquit* S-C

47:28 *inminutum a*: *mutum* Weber

<47:31 *put an end to all their* D-R/C: *rid them from al* D-R>

48:1 *facula*: *fax* Weber

48:2 *irritantes*: *imitantes* Weber

48:3 *continuit*: *exaltavit* Weber; *de caelo*: *a se* Weber; *ter*: *terrae* Weber

48:4 *sic gloriari*: *gloriari* Weber

48:8 *unguis*: *ungues* Weber

48:10 *scriptus es in iudiciis temporum lenire*: *inscriptus es indiciis temporum / et lenis* Weber

48:13 *quidem*: *qui* Weber

<48:14 *No word could* KJV: *Neither did any word* D-R>

48:15 *operatus est*: *opera ipsius* Weber

48:16 *populus*: *populum* Weber; *eiecti*: *deiecti* Weber

48:22 *expandentes manus suas*: *patentes manus* Weber

48:24 *Subiecit*: *deiecit* S-C; *conteruit*: *contrivit* S-C; *Domini*: *Dei* Weber

48:27 *consolatus*: *obsecratus* Weber

49:1 *conpositionem*: *conpositione* Weber; *facti*: *facta* S-C

49:3 *paenitentiam*: *paenitentia* Weber

49:4 *et in*: *in* Weber

49:6 *Altissimi*: *Potentis* Weber

<49:7 *So* D-R/C: *For* D-R>

49:7 *alienae*: *alienigenae* S-C

<49:8 *according to the prediction* KJV: *in the hand* D-R>

<49:10 *was shewn* KJV: *he shewed* D-R>

49:11 *imbri*: *imbri et* Weber

<49:11 *under the figure of rain and of doing* KJV (without *of doing*; *the figure of* bracketed): *in rayne, to doe* D-R>

49:12 *conroboraverunt*: *rogaverunt* Weber

49:13 *manu*: *manu in Israhel* Weber

49:14 *Sic et Iesus, filium*: *et Iesum* Weber; *gloria sempiterna*: *gloriam sempiternam* S-C

49:17 *neque ut Ioseph, qui: et Ioseph* Weber

50:1 *corroboravit templum: corroboravit* Weber

50:2 *et excelsi parietes: excelsa parietis* Weber

50:3 *emanaverunt: remanaverunt* Weber

50:4 *perditione: pernicie* Weber

50:5 *amplificavit: amplificatus est* Weber

<50:8 *and* KJV: omitted in D-R; *bright clouds* KJV: *cloudes of glorie* D-R>

50:8 *effulgens: refulgens* S-C; *inter nebulas: in nebulam* Weber; *veris: vernis* S-C; *et quasi lilia: quasi lilia* Weber

50:11 *cyprossus: gyrus* Weber, *tollens. extollens* S-C; *in consummationem: consummatione* Weber

50:12 *altarii: altaris* S-C

50:13 *Circa: et circa* S-C; *et quasi* grel [Quentin's sigla]: *quasi* S-C, Weber

<50:13 *he himself* KJV: *himself also* D-R; *And* S-C: omitted in D-R>

50:14 *palmae: in palma* Weber

<50:14 *and as* KJV: *as* D-R; *they* KJV: *so . . . they* D-R>

50:15 *consummationem: consummatione* S-C

50:17 *Effudit in fundamento: et fudit in fundamenta* Weber; *altarii: altaris* S-C

50:18 *sonaverunt: sonuerunt* S-C

50:19 *Deum suum: suum* Weber

50:20 *suavitatis: suavitate* Weber

50:24 *Deum: Dominum* Weber

50:26 *liberet nos: sanet vos* Weber

50:29 *scripsit: scripsi* Weber

50:30 *et qui* Sabatier's translation of Septuagint: *qui* S-C, Weber

51:2 *Confitebor: confiteor* S-C

51:4 *praeparatis: paratis* Weber

51:5 *tribulationum: tribulationis* Weber

51:7 *a verbo: verbo* Weber; *a lingua iniusta: lingua iniusta* Weber

51:8 *Laudabit: laudavit* Weber

51:9 *inferno: infero* Weber

51:10 *hominum: meum* Weber

51:12 *eruis: erues* Weber; *te, Domine: te* Weber

51:15 *illud: illum* Weber; *et exaudita: exaudita* Weber

51:16 *Et liberasti: liberasti* Weber

51:17 *nomen: nomini* S-C

51:18 *essem: sum* Weber; *oberrarem: oberrem* Weber

51:19 *templum: tempus* Weber; *et floriet* S [Weber's siglum]: *et effloruit* S-C, *defloriet* Weber

<51:19 *flourished* S-C: *shal flourish* D-R>

51:22 *et multum: multum* Weber

51:23 *Danti: dans* Weber

51:24 *confundar: confundor* Weber

51:26 *insipientiam: insapientia* Weber

51:28 *ipsa: ipsis* Weber

51:30 *mihi: enim mihi* Weber

<51:32 *are ye slow* D-R/C: *slacke ye yet* D-R>

51:34 *iugo: sub iugo* Weber

51:35 *quoniam: quia* S-C; *modicum: modice* Weber

52 omitted in S-C and D-R. Weber's text follows: *1 Et declinavit Salomon genua in conspectu totius ecclesiae Israhel / et aperuit manus suas ad caelum et dixit / 2 Domine Deus Israhel non est tibi similis Deus in caelo sursum / neque in terra deorsum / 3 qui custodis testamentum tuum et misericordiam pueris tuis / euntibus in conspectu tuo in toto corde / 4 servans puero tuo David quae locutus es illi / et locutus es in ore tuo et in manu tua supplesti quasi dies iste / 5 et nunc Domine Deus Israhel custodi puero tuo David quae locutus es illi dicens / non deerit tibi vir a facie mea sedens in throno Israhel / 6 verum si custodierint filii tui manum suam / ut in praeceptis meis ambulent sicut ambulaverunt in conspectu meo / 7 et nunc Domine Deus Israhel creditum est verbum quod locutus es puero tuo David / 8 quoniam si vere habitabit Deus cum hominibus in terra / 9 si caelum caeli non sufficit verum domus quam aedificavi / 10 et respicias ad orationem pueri tui / et precationem Domine ut exaudias placationem orationis / quam puer tuus orat coram te / 11 ut sint oculi tui super domum hanc die et nocte / in locum quem dixisti invocari nomen tuum / et exaudias orationem quam puer tuus orat in hunc locum / 12 et exaudias precationem pueri tui et populi tui Israhel / si oraverint in loco isto / 13 et exaudias in loco habitationis de caelo / et exaudias et propitius sis si peccaverit vir iuxta te*

Alternate Spellings

In general, the translators of the Douay-Rheims edition of the Bible preserved the transliterations of Hebrew names (and words based on those names) found throughout the textual tradition of the Sixto-Clementine edition of the Vulgate Bible. While these transliterations do reflect the Latin sources for the English presented in this edition, they do not represent what is currently thought to be the likely pronunciation of the Hebrew words or, in some books, words from other ancient languages: for example, the name we see in the New Revised Standard Version (NRSV) as "Ahuzzath" (Gen 26:26) was transliterated by the authors and revisers of the Latin text as "Ochozath." This sort of transliteration renders a few well-known characters harder to recognize, such as Noah, or "Noe" in the Latin tradition. Furthermore, there are frequent inconsistencies in the Douay-Rheims translation as to the spellings of names.

Another quirk of the Douay-Rheims and Vulgate Bibles is that they often identify locations by the names they were understood to have had at the time of the Vulgate's composition rather than the names found in Hebrew scripture. For example, "Mesopotamia of Syria" (Gen 28:2) represents a place referred to in the NRSV as "Paddan-aram."

In presenting the Latin text and the Douay-Rheims transla-

tion, the transliterations in the English have been updated for the sake of accuracy and ease of reference. The Latin has been preserved to reflect its own textual tradition in accordance with the principles stated in the Introduction. However, when names given are not simply a matter of representing vowel and consonant sounds, the Douay-Rheims translation has been left intact so that it remains a genuine translation of the facing text.

There are moments in the Bible where the anachronistic place-names are of significance: at the end of Balaam's last prophetic blessing of Israel, he declares, "They shall come in galleys from Italy; they shall overcome the Assyrians and shall waste the Hebrews, and at the last they themselves also shall perish" (Nm 24:24). The Hebrew word rendered as "Italy" is transliterated in the NRSV as "Kittim," and though the meaning is obscure, it is almost certainly not Italy, for reasons outlined by Milgrom (1990), ad loc. Nevertheless, it is fascinating and important to realize that in the Western European tradition from the fourth century CE until the twentieth century, many read, wrote, and learned that Italians would "waste the Hebrews." Because of this and other instances in which the place-names, however unrepresentative of the Hebrew tradition they may be, are important in terms of what readers of these versions of the Bible may have believed, the Vulgate words have been retained.

Below is list of the names in the English translation of this volume. The names are followed by an alternate spelling (or, in some cases, an alternate word) if there is one. An entry presented in italic text signifies a word retained from the Douay-Rheims translation; all other words are the spellings given by

the NRSV. An entry in roman text with no alternative spelling means that the spellings are identical in the two editions; one in italic text with no alternative spelling means that the name is in the Douay-Rheims translation but no parallel was found in the NRSV. In a few cases, words have been based on the spellings of the NRSV and the form in the Douay-Rheims text. For example, the Douay-Rheims text reads "the Sichemites" (Gen 33:18), where the NRSV has "Shechem." To illustrate the translation of the Douay-Rheims while providing an up-to-date transliteration of the Hebrew word, "the Shechemites" has been printed; similarly, in cases where Jerome translated parts of a Hebrew place-name into Latin where the NRSV left the whole name in Hebrew (such as the "temple of Phogor," as opposed to "Beth-peor" at Dt 3:29), the transliterated part of the name has been updated in this edition, but the Latin and English translations have not been changed, yielding "temple of Peor."

Aaron	*Arabia [Sheba]*
Abiram [Abiron]	*Arabians [of Sheba]*
Abraham	Arcturus
Absalom	Asaph
Adam	Assyrian
Ahimelech	Assyrians
Ahimelech [Achimelech]	
Amalek [Amalec]	*Baalpeor [Baal of Peor]*
Amana	Babylon
Aminadab	Barachel
Ammon	Bashan [Basan]
Amorites [Amorrhites]	Bathsheba [Bethsabee]

Behemoth
Benjamin
Bether
Bildad [Baldad]
Buzite

Caleb
Canaan [Chanaan]
Canaanite [Chanaanite]
Canaanites [Chanaanites]
Carmel
Chaldeans
Christ [anointed]
Cocytus
Cush [Chusi]

Damascus
Dathan
daughter of the multitude [Bath-
   rabbim]
David
Day Star
Doeg

Ecclesiastes [the Teacher]
Edom
Edom, children of [Edomites]
Edom, men of [Edomites]
Edomite
Egypt

Egyptian
Egyptians
Eleazar
Elihu [Eliu]
Elijah [Elias]
Eliphaz
Elisha [Eliseus]
En-dor [Endor]
En-gedi [Engaddi]
Enoch
Enoch [Henoch]
Ephraim
Ephraim, sons of
   [Ephraimites]
Ephrathah [Ephrata]
Ethan
Ethan [ever-flowing streams]
Ethiopia
Ethiopians
Euergetes [Evergetes]
Euphrates
Evening Star
Ezekiel [Ezechiel]
Ezrahite

Gath [Geth]
Gatherer [Agur]
Gebal
Gentiles
Gihon [Gehon]

Gilead [Galaad]

Goliath

Haggai [Aggeus]

Hagrites [Agarens]

Ham [Cham]

Heman [Eman]

Hermon

Hermoniim [Hermon]

Heshbon [Hesebon]

Hezekiah [Ezechias]

Horeb

Hyades

India

Isaac

Isaiah [Isaias]

Ishmaelites [Ishmahelites]

Israel

Israelites

Jabin

Jacob

Jeduthun [Idithun]

Jemimah [Dies]

Jemini, son of [Benjaminite]

Jephunneh [Jephone]

Jeremiah [Jeremias]

Jericho

Jeroboam

Jerusalem

Jeshua [Jesus]

Jesse

Jesus

Joab

Job

Jonadab

Jordan

Joseph

Joshua [Jesus]

Joshua [Josue]

Josiah [Josias]

Jozadak [Josedec]

Jozadak [Josedech]

Judah [Juda]

Judas

Judea

Judea [Judah]

Kadesh [Cades]

Kedar [Cedar]

Keren-happuch [Cornustibii]

Keziah [Cassia]

Kishon [Cisson]

Kishon, brook of [Wadi Kishon]

Korah [Core]

Korah, sons of [Korahites]

Lebanon [Libanus]

Lemuel [Lamuel]

Levi

Leviathan

little hill, the [Mount Mizar]

Lot

Maccabees [Machabees]

Mahalath [Maeleth]

Mahalath [Maheleth]

Manasseh [Manasses]

Melchizedek [Melchisedech]

Mercury

Midian [Madian]

Moab

Moses

Naamathite

Naphtali [Nephthali]

Nathan

Nave [Nun]

Nebat [Nabat]

Nehemiah [Nehemias]

Noah [Noe]

Og

Onias

Oreb

Orion

Pentapolis [the Five Cities]

Pharaoh [Pharao]

Philistines

Phinehas [Phinees]

Pishon [Phison]

Pleiades

Ptolemy

Rabsaces

Rabshakeh [Rabsaces]

Rahab

Ram

Red Sea

Rehoboam [Roboam]

Sabeans

Samuel

Satan

Saul

Seba [Saba]

Seir

Senir [Sanir]

Sennacherib

Seth

Sheba [Saba]

Shechem [Sichem]

Shem [Sem]

Shiloh [Silo]

Shuhite [Suhite]

Shulammitess [Shulammite]

Sihon [Sehon]

Simon

Sinai

Sinai [Sina]
Sirach
Sisera [Sisara]
Solomon

Tabor [Thabor]
Tanis [Zoan]
Tarshish [Tharsis]
Tema [Thema]
Temanite [Themanite]
Tigris
Tyre
Tyrians [people of Tyre]

Uz [Hus]

*Waters of Contradiction [Waters
of Meribah]
wood, fields of the [fields of
Jaar]*

Zalmon [Selmon]
Zalmunna [Salmana]
Zebah [Zebee]
Zebulun [Zabulon]
Zechariah [Zacharias]
Zeeb [Zeb]
Zerubbabel [Zorobabel]
Zion [Sion]
Ziph, men of [Ziphites]
Zophar [Sophar]

*Vale of Tabernacles [Vale of Suc-
coth]
Vomiter [Jakeh]*

Bibliography

Carleton, J. G. *The Part of Rheims in the Making of the English Bible*. Oxford: Clarendon, 1902.

Cartmell, J. "English Spiritual Writers: x. Richard Challoner." *Clergy Review* n.s. 44, no. 10 (October 1959): 577–587.

A Catholic. "A new Version of the Four Gospels, with Notes, Critical and Explanatory." *Dublin Review* 2, no. 2 (April 1837): 475–492.

Biblia Sacra: Vulgatae Editionis Sixti V Pont. Max. iussu recognita et Clementis VIII auctoritate edita. Vatican City: Marietti, 1959.

Challoner, R. "The Touchstone of the New Religion: or, Sixty Assertions of Protestants, try'd by their own Rule of Scripture alone, and condemned by clear and express Texts of their own Bible." London, n.p.: 1735.

———. ed. *The Holy Bible translated from the Latin Vulgat: Diligently compared With the Hebrew, Greek, and other Editions in divers Languages. And first published by The English College at Doway, Anno 1609. Newly revised, and corrected, according to the Clementine Edition of the Scriptures with Annotations for clearing up the principal Difficulties of Holy Writ.* 4 vols. Dublin(?): 1752.

———., ed. *The Holy Bible, translated from the Latin Vulgate, Diligently compared with the Hebrew, Greek, and other editions in divers languages. The Old Testament, First published by the English College at Douay, A.D. 1609 and The New Testament, First published by the English College at Rheims, A.D. 1582. With annotations, references, and an historical and chronological index. The whole revised and diligently compared with the Latin Vulgate Published with the approbation of His Eminence James Cardinal Gibbons Archbishop of Baltimore.* Baltimore: John Murphy, 1899.

———., ed. *The New Testament of Our LORD and SAVIOUR JESUS*

CHRIST. Translated out of the Latin Vulgat; diligently compared with the original Greek: and first published by the English *College at* Rhemes, *Anno 1582. Newly revised and corrected according to the* Clementin *Edition of the Scriptures. With Annotations, for Clearing up modern Controversies in Religion; and other Difficulties of Holy Writ.* 2 vols. Dublin(?): 1752.

Cotton, H. *Rhemes and Doway: An Attempt to shew what has been done by Roman Catholics for the Diffusion of the Holy Scriptures in English.* Oxford: University Press, 1855.

de Hamel, C. *The Book: A History of the Bible.* London: Phaidon, 2001.

Dodd, C. [H. Tootell]. *The Church History of England, From The Year 1500, to The Year 1688. Chiefly with regard to Catholicks.* 8 vols. Brussels [London], 1737–1742.

Duffy, E., ed. *Challoner and His Church: A Catholic Bishop in Georgian England.* London: Darton, Longman & Todd, 1981.

English College of Doway. *The Holie Bible Faithfully Translated into English, out of the Authentical Latin. Diligently conferred with the Hebrew, Greeke, and other Editions in diuers languages. With Arguments of the Bookes, and Chapters: Annotations. Tables: and other helpes, for better understanding of the text: for discoueirie of corruptions in some late translations: and for clearing Controuersies in Religion.* 2 vols. Doway: Lavrence Kellam, at the signe of the holie Lambe, 1609–1610.

English College of Rhemes. *The Nevv Testament of Iesvs Christ, Translated Faithfully into English, out of the authentical Latin, according to the best corrected copies of the same, diligently conferred vvithe the Greeke and other editions in diuers languages: Vvith Argvments of bookes and chapters, Annotations, and other necessarie helpes, for the better vnderstanding of the text, and specially for the discouerie of the Corrvptions of diuers late translations, and for cleering the Controuersies in religion, of these daies.* Rhemes: Iohn Fogny, 1582.

Frede, H. J. *Kirchenschriftsteller: Verzeichnis und Sigel.* Freiburg: Herder, 1995.

Gilley, S. "Challoner as Controvertionalist." In E. Duffy, ed., *Challoner and His Church: A Catholic Bishop in Georgian England.* London: Darton, Longman & Todd, 1981, pp. 90–111.

Greenslade, S. L., ed. *The Cambridge History of the Bible: The West, from the Reformation to the Present Day.* Rev. ed. Cambridge: Cambridge University Press, 1975.

BIBLIOGRAPHY

Gryson, R. *Altlateinische Handschriften: Manuscrits Vieux Latins.* Freiburg: Herder, 1999.

The Holy Bible, Conteyning the Old Testament, and the New: Newly Translated out of the Originall tongues: & with the former Translations diligently compared and reuised: by his Maiesties speciall Comandement Appointed to be read in Churches. London: Robert Barker, Printer to the Kings most Excellent Maiestie, 1611; rpr. Thomas Nelson, 1990.

Kaske, R. E. *Medieval Chirstian Literary Imagery: A Guide to Interpretation.* Toronto: University of Toronto Press, ca. 1988.

Knox, T. F. Introduction. In *The First and Second Diaries of the English College, Douay, and an Appendix of Unpublished Documents, Edited by Fathers of the Congregation of the London Oratory, with an Historical Introduction.* Records of the English Catholics under the Penal Laws. Chiefly from the Archives of the See of Westinster 1. London: David Nutt, 1878.

Metzger, B. M., and R. E. Murphy. *The New Oxford Annotated Bible: New Revised Standard Version.* New York: Oxford University Press, 1991.

Milgrom, J., comm. *The JPS Torah Commentary: Numbers.* Philadelphia: The Jewish Publication Society.

Pope, H., and S. Bullough. *English Versions of the Bible.* St. Louis: Herder, 1952.

Quentin, H. *Biblia sacra: iuxta Latinam Vulgatam versionem.* Typis Polyglottis Vaticanis, 1926–[1995].

——. *Mémoire sur l'établissement du texte de la Vulgate.* Collectanea Biblica Latina 6, 1922.

Rahlfs, A., ed., and R. Hanhart, rev. *Septuaginta: Id est Vetus Testamentum graece iuxta LXX interpretes, Editio altera.* Stuttgart: Deutsche Bibelgesellschaft, 2006.

Sabatier, P. *Bibliorum Sacrorum Latinae versiones antiquae, seu Vetus Italica, et Ceterae quaecunque in Codicibus Mss. & antiquorum libris reperiri poterunt: Quae cum Vulgata Latina, & cum Textu Graeco comparantur. Accedunt Praefationes, Observationes, ac Notae, Indexque novus ad Vulgatam è regione editam, idemque locupletissimus.* 3 vols. Rheims: Apud Reginaldum Florentain, Regis Typographicum & Bibliopolam, sub signo Bibliorum aureorum, 1743–1749.

Weber, R., ed. *Biblia Sacra Vulgata.* 5th ed. Stuttgart: Deutsche Bibelgesellschaft, 2007.